GLOBAL ECONOMIC HIS

GLOBAL ECONOMIC HISTORY

Second Edition

Edited by Tirthankar Roy and Giorgio Riello

BLOOMSBURY ACADEMIC
LONDON • NEW YORK • OXFORD • NEW DELHI • SYDNEY

BLOOMSBURY ACADEMIC
Bloomsbury Publishing Plc
50 Bedford Square, London, WC1B 3DP, UK
1385 Broadway, New York, NY 10018, USA
29 Earlsfort Terrace, Dublin 2, Ireland

BLOOMSBURY, BLOOMSBURY ACADEMIC and the Diana logo are
trademarks of Bloomsbury Publishing Plc

First published in Great Britain 2019
Reprinted 2019, 2020 (twice)
This edition first published 2024

Cover design by Grace Ridge
Cover image © DuKai photographer / Getty Images

A catalogue record for this book is available from the British Library.

A catalog record for this book is available from the Library of Congress.

ISBN: HB: 978-1-3502-9007-5
         PB: 978-1-3502-9008-2
         ePDF: 978-1-3502-9010-5
         eBook: 978-1-3502-9009-9

Typeset by Integra Software Services Pvt. Ltd.
Printed and bound in Great Britain

To find out more about our authors and books visit www.bloomsbury.com
and sign up for our newsletters.

This book is dedicated to Patrick O'Brien without whom the field of global economic history would not exist.

CONTENTS

Contents

FIGURES

Figures

TABLES

CONTRIBUTORS

Gareth Austin is Emeritus Professor of Economic History at Cambridge University.

Maxine Berg is Emerita Professor in the History Department of the University of Warwick.

Regina Lee Blaszczyk is Professor of Business History & Leadership and Chair in the History of Business and Society at the University of Leeds.

Trevor Burnard is Director of the Wilberforce Institute for the Study of Slavery and Emancipation at the University of Hull.

Youssef Cassis is Emeritus Professor of Economic History at the European University Institute in Florence.

Karel Davids is Emeritus Professor of Economic and Social History at the Vrije Universiteit Amsterdam.

Leigh Gardner is Professor in Economic History at the London School of Economics.

Jack A. Goldstone is Virginia E. and John T. Hazel, Jr. Professor of Public Policy at George Mason University.

Regina Grafe is Professor of Economic History at Cambridge University.

Bernd-Stefan Grewe is Professor für Didaktik der Geschichte at the University of Tübingen.

Bishnupriya Gupta is Professor of Economics at the University of Warwick.

Karolina Hutková is a Postdoctotal Fellow in Economics at the University of Oxford.

Alejandra Irigoin is Associate Professor in Economic History at the London School of Economics.

J. Thomas Lindblad is retired from his position as Professor at Leiden University.

Andrew B. Liu is Associate Professor in the Department of History at Villanova University.

Debin Ma is Professor of Economic History at the University of Oxford.

John McNeill is Professor of History at Georgetown University.

Patrick O'Brien is Professor of Global Economic History at the London School of Economics.

Prasannan Parthasarathi is Professor of History at Boston College.

Laura Panza is Associate Professor in Economics at the University of Melbourne.

Kenneth Pomeranz is Professor of History at the University of Chicago.

Maarten Prak is Emeritus Professor of Social and Economic History at the University of Utrecht.

Giorgio Riello is Professor of Early Modern Global History at the European University Institute, Florence and Professor of Global History and Culture at the University of Warwick.

Tirthankar Roy is Professor of Economic History at the London School of Economics.

Alessandro Stanziani is Professor of Global History at the École des hautes études en sciences sociales (EHESS) in Paris.

Kaoru Sugihara is Professor of Economic History at the Center for Southeast Asian Studies, Kyoto University.

Peer Vries is Honorary Fellow at the International Institute of Social History in Amsterdam and was previously Professor of Global Economic History at the University of Vienna.

PREFACE

Why does a global perspective matter in the study of economic history? Which are the problems addressed by a new field called Global Economic History? Which are its debates and methodologies? As this book shows, there is a variety of answers to these questions. Because there are a range of answers, instead of imposing our own definition of the field, we (the editors) collected a set of illustrations on why a global perspective matters to economic history.

This book is timely as the field of economic history has seen major developments in the past two decades. Since 2001, the 'divergence debate' first and the scholarship on the history of capitalism in more recent years led to path-breaking new research on Asia, Africa and the Americas, and pushed the boundaries of comparative economic history well beyond the borders of Europe and much further back from the nineteenth century. It also fostered the adoption of new methodologies such as the use of reciprocal comparison and the engagement with new interpretive works on comparative politics and society. We see the positive effects of more detailed research on key questions on regions and localities where we once knew little, though the negative effects of a new fragmentation and retreat to internalist disputes are now equally evident.

We invited twenty-two contributions exploring specific aspects of the question: why a global perspective matters. Originally published in 2018, the second edition of this book includes several new chapters dealing with the history of capitalism, the history of empires and the role of the North American and the Middle Eastern economies in the past two centuries. All other chapters have been revised and updated. The chapters included in this volume are thus an attempt to contextualize the economic history of the world by providing entries and insights into large and small debates. We do not aim for completeness of information, or treatment, or chronologies. But we hope that by breaking up the big question into manageable parts, the book will show why global interconnections and comparisons matter to economic history, and why they matter so much that economic history and global history need serious and continuous dialogue. Let us call that dialogue global economic history.

For students of global economic history, the chapters will show why certain economic concepts, problems and keywords make a difference; why historians and economists debate them; and why they may disagree about them. Ultimately this book should help to make sense of the shape of today's economic world by studying its past transformations, mutations, crises and not infrequent disasters.

We are grateful for the financial support provided by the London School of Economics, the University of Warwick and the European University Institute. Our thanks also to the anonymous referees who provided much-needed advice at different stages of this project and to Helen Clifford and Amber Burbidge who helped us with the editing and indexing of the two editions of this book. Professors Kent Deng (London School of Economics), Pat Hudson (Cardiff University) and Masayuki Tanimoto (Tokyo University) acted as commentators at the workshop held at the London School of Economics in 2016 when several of the papers here included were originally discussed. Their comments have been particularly valuable in shaping the editors' introductions to the first and second editions.

The Leverhulme-funded Global Economic History Network (GEHN), active between 2003 and 2007 and coordinated by Patrick O'Brien, was instrumental in shaping the discipline of global economic history by focusing on issues of divergence and the global integration of markets through commodity exchange. This book draws on these pioneering discussions carried out by groups of scholars gathered together at the London School of Economics and the University of Warwick. It also acknowledges the contribution of scholars in other continents, most especially in Japan, India, China and the United States.

Tirthankar Roy and Giorgio Riello
February 2024

GLOBAL ECONOMIC CHANGE IN HISTORY: AN INTRODUCTION

Giorgio Riello and Tirthankar Roy

Economic History and Its Global Turn

Economic history utilizes historical and quantitative methods to study economic change over long chronologies. Trajectories of economic change vary across space, because of local conditions such as the quality of natural resources, local institutions and a number of other factors including labour markets, and the availability of labour, capital and technologies. Economic change is shaped also by patterns of interaction that occur between localities, nations and wider world regions. Global economic history operates in these realms of variations and interactions between world regions sometimes adopting the world as a unit of analysis.

From the nineteenth century, when Western Europe industrialized, inequality between nations started rising rapidly, and world trade also grew at an unprecedented speed. Intellectuals, economists, social reformers and philosophers became interested in understanding economic change and its history at a global level.[1] One might say that Karl Marx and Max Weber were both global economic historians in this sense. Despite their legacies, however, economic history emerged as a discipline in the first half of the twentieth century and evolved over the following fifty years with a more national than international orientation. In publications of economic historians, the most common mode of analysis was that undertaken at the level of the nation state. Key narratives such as that of industrialization remained centred on national frameworks of analysis: this was the case of the British industrial revolution and the idea of the subsequent industrialization of other nations in continental Europe and beyond.

From the 1980s at least, if not earlier, the so-called world systems school and environmental history proposed a credible case for changing the unit of analysis from the nation to the world. Varieties of Marxist historiography continued to produce books that were global in scope. The movement that later became known as new institutional economic history started as a reinterpretation of economic change in Europe, but its arguments had obvious implications for the rest of the world. Imperial history was, by its nature, global in scope. These were neither exceptional, nor outside the mainstream. However, their impact on the shape of the subject of economic history was, until the 1990s, limited to the 'schools' that they propagated. By and large, these works were more at home on Europe and America than the rest of the world.[2]

Since about 2000, history has witnessed an emphatic global turn, in the wake of the recent phase of globalization and rapid spread of connections between parts of the world.[3] Economic history too began to be transformed by a somewhat distinct set of factors. The availability of cross-country historical income data, the popularity of institutionalism in top economics departments of North America, and new developments in the theory of growth, rekindled interest in an old and half-forgotten question, why do some countries grow rich and others remain poor? In the 2000s, historians criticized institutionalism. The exchange that followed became known as the 'divergence debate'. In the following quarter of a century, the divergence debate formed the stem of the economic history field. The economic emergence of countries like China or India – long regarded as textbook examples of 'why nations stay poor' – questioned Eurocentric world history.

Inequality was key both to the divergence debate and new narratives of global capitalism that emerged in the 2010s.[4] Yet, they captured only one part of the global turn within economic history. There was also a renewed sensitivity to time, especially long chronologies stretching back over millennia. New modes of enquiry emerged. One example is 'historical economics', which tests causal models of economic growth with long-range datasets. Connections across oceans, geographies and frontiers began to be investigated with an interest in economic change. There was a return of the 'grand narrative', which postmodernism had briefly expelled from history. Social and cultural historians reassessed the relevance of economic change to their own fields of study.

In the backdrop of what one might call the 'rediscovery of the world' by economic historians, we may be closer than ever before to a definition of global economic history as a field. This book is an attempt to contribute to that programme, and to think about global economic history as a field.

Global Economic History: Debates and Questions

This book divides up the subject of global economic history into three types of enquiries. The three-part structure of the book reflects the three types of stories that global economic history often tells. Part 1 of the book entitled 'Divergence and Capitalism in Global History' considers the economic trajectories of different world areas and reflects on recent debates about 'wealth and poverty' in relation to economic divergence, inequality and capitalism. Part 2 entitled 'The Emergence of a World Economy' explores the ways in which global economic connectivity changed, especially in the nineteenth and twentieth century, and reflects on the integration and emergence of a world economy. Part 3 on 'Regional Perspectives on Global Economic Change' considers a set of macro-regions and reflects comparatively on simultaneous processes of change in various economies. These chapters also show that the study of the integration between a regional economy and the world economy can offer a useful perspective on the region itself; in other words, global history can be a method to study regions. The three-part structure was adopted because the discussions and debates in global economic history form overlapping but distinct clusters; the three parts try to retain that distinction while the book as a whole represents a shared agenda between these.

Let us follow these themes a little further. The 'Great Divergence' as conceptualized by Kenneth Pomeranz in a book with the eponymous title is a natural starting point for an enterprise of this kind.[5] Divergences in experiences of economic growth and development have led to new investigations as to why the world became richer and why certain parts of the world industrialized first. This well-known debate also encompasses a discussion of the origins of world inequality. Explaining why the world became more unequal in modern times requires comparisons of regions regarding their endowments and attributes, an enterprise that has attracted a great deal of fresh work in the last twenty years, drawn economists and historians together into conversations, and supplied a strong motive for studying global history.[6]

The question of the origins of global inequality (inequality between nations) and its connection with the origins of modern economic growth and of capitalism has been around for a long time, but recent scholarship has made it truly worldwide in reach. Whilst there is no agreement as to the causes and chronologies of divergence, debate has developed to consider a series of old and new topics ranging from institutions to the role of science and technology and the impact of transnational consumption in a comparative global perspective. It has made economic history less insular and more concerned to address the origin and emergence of inequality. The latter topic has generated a great deal of debate not just in relation to global inequality between nations – especially across the classic divides between developed, developing and the underdeveloped world – but also within nations as exemplified by recent literature.[7] The New History of Capitalism has added a further dimension to the history of global inequality claiming it to be one of the motors of modern capitalism through slavery, exploitation and violence.[8] Recent scholarship has also considered whether inequality is ineluctable and has opened up a conversation between inequality, growth (and de-growth) and the connection between economic change and environmental protection.[9]

The second part of the book considers at least two other reasons why global economic history matters. The making of the world economy is a process that has been studied by economic historians through a variety of topics and lenses that include the slave trade and the transformation of human societies, population growth and migration, the adoption of fossil fuels and the consequent change of natural emissions, commodity exchange, knowledge exchange and cross-border investments, and the role of states and world empires, just to cite a few. In such processes, interconnectedness is important. Yet far too often such processes are reduced to a time-flat concept of globalization. Cross-border connections (positive or negative as they might be) are growing rapidly in the present but they need to be understood by using the tools of history: why they grow, when, and what they mean.[10] Beyond connectivity, many of the chapters in this second part of the book focus on integrative processes, led directly or indirectly by the prospect of material gain, and discuss the conditions in which historically such processes can take place.

The study of connections and integration relate to two defining features of what Chris Bayly called 'the birth of the modern world': economic globalization and transcontinental empires.[11] Connections also include possibilities of sharing knowledge and information between sets of people who were not in the same network; 'weak ties' that are sometimes created as externalities of economic exchange like trade, and of course, migration of capital and labour.[12] Yet, connectivity cannot fully explain the functioning of a global economy. Economic historians have to address also 'integration', referring to the process by which regions are drawn into pre-existing networks of economic exchanges. For example, the way the Slave Coast of West Africa was integrated in the Atlantic trade of the seventeenth and eighteenth centuries, or how the textile-producing areas of India were integrated in a similar set of worldwide exchanges that shaped the future of these regions and the future shape of the world economy at the same time.

Connections can be real, or inferred, for example, through the simultaneous emergence of similar institutions in locations that are not necessarily connected in an obvious way.[13] As considered in the final part of this book, the causal link between these processes, which we can call parallel developments, remains open to interpretation.[14] From the seventeenth to the nineteenth century, most manual labour took place under bondage and other legal restrictions imposed on the labourers. These restraints began to weaken, to be replaced by a different set of laws, and were also resisted more easily from the end of the nineteenth century. Was this change – which one contributor in the book calls 'the great transformation of labour' – an outcome of ideology, politics or markets, or a strange set of interrelated but worldwide processes that we do not yet understand?[15]

The final part of this book, dedicated to regional perspectives, acknowledges that world regions have their own distinctive features, nation states play a powerful role on the economies that they manage, and sources needed for historical research are typically produced by states. In short, a global perspective must be consistent with region- and nation-bound histories. If the first two broad themes considered in this book – the comparative history of growth and connectedness – place the 'world' at the centre of the discourse with regions forming building blocks in arguments about economic change in the whole world, there is a counterpart theme, where the 'local' or the regional forms the centre, and the world economy acts as a building block in, for example, arguments about why India, China or West Africa evolved in the way they did. Global history should not ignore differing perspectives, especially those deriving from 'area studies' such as the Americas, Africa, East, South and Southeast Asia and, perhaps more surprisingly, Europe. Nor should global history submerge the distinctness of regions that derives from geography, culture or forms of governance. And the third set of chapters in this book pursues a region-focused agenda.

The different approaches in this volume all use the term 'world economy' and refer to 'global approaches'.[16] Yet, they do so for different reasons and in different ways. At the same time, historians of all kinds use these terms with increasing frequency. Why? In the next section, we consider how the global turn in economic history came into being, and what was distinctive about it from earlier versions of global economic history.

World Economy: The History of a Concept

A search for the term 'world economy' in Google Books turns up a surprisingly large number of books with 'world economy' in their titles, many published in the last twenty years. Apparently, half of them deal with history. These books do not use the term in similar contexts or for similar purposes. The significance of world economy in historical scholarship has tended to shift. These shifts may give global economic history the image of a literature without a centre.

Historians who have studied societies that have access to the seaboard have long been aware of the significance of cross-border economic exchanges in shaping the course of history. The sea as a distinct economic geography, one that helps long-distance transactions and gives these a certain shape, is a concept akin to the world economy, and perhaps the most profound and convincing way in which interconnections on a big scale have been considered by historians. Fernand Braudel's classic *The Mediterranean and the Mediterranean World in the Age of Philip II* (original French ed. 1949), started a new historiography by placing the sea at the centre of a chronological narrative, thus looking at history through the lens of comparisons, connections and diffusion.[17] Braudel inspired a generation of European historians who globalized the programme. Starting from the premise that the growth of European overseas trade in the sixteenth century was a landmark in world history, they explored intercontinental trade, long-distance merchant networks, and 'the rise of merchant empires'.[18] In the 1970s and the 1980s, K. N. Chaudhuri, Kenneth McPherson, Ashin Das Gupta, Om Prakash, Sinnapah Arasaratnam and Anthony Reid, to name only a few of the leading contributors, pursued the same agenda from the perspective of regions bordering the Indian Ocean.[19] Since the 1990s, the Atlantic has also been placed within a similar 'global' perspective, particularly in relation to merchant networks and communities.[20]

These works on the Indian Ocean contained a message that would have surprised the economist looking at nation states in these regions as of 1970. Before the advent of European colonialism in the region, and before the nationalistic and protectionist regimes that followed colonial rule came into being, the Asian economies were integrated. Their seaboard societies formed parts of a larger network. So much so that Africa can be said to have formed a part of India, India a part of Africa, Southeast Asia and China and so on. Similar conclusions can be reached about Latin or North America or Africa in terms of commodity trade and the slave trade. Recognizing the deep interactions suggested a way of understanding the history of any country that differed from what students usually learned from textbooks based on national accounting and national datasets. In this 'alternative history', cross-cultural transactions – more than nation states – were the driving force of history.

The idea that connected geographical spaces could be arranged in a hierarchy became popular in the 1970s, through the influential work of Immanuel Wallerstein. World economy, or the capitalist world economy, became a *world system* in Wallerstein's work. European overseas trade was a pivotal force because it allowed for European hegemony to be established over world trade and politics. The world systems school that followed

Wallerstein's early work joined the idea of connections with the economic concepts of division of labour, surplus appropriation and redistribution of gains from trade, to suggest why Europe gained substantially from the sixteenth century world system and came to dominate the world.[21]

The world systems approach has been criticized for being Eurocentric. A particularly influential revision was a work that retained the idea of a system, but rejected hierarchies. Janet Abu-Lughod's *Before European Hegemony* (1990) showed that, around 1300, something like a world system existed across Eurasia, Europe was a 'peripheral' player, but no other part dominated it either.[22] The book expanded the notion of a 'world system', made Europe's rise a problem to be explained, but did not question Wallerstein's concept of European hegemony in later centuries. K. N. Chaudhuri's similarly titled *Asia before Europe* (1990) can be read as a critique of European hegemony as well.[23] In 1998, Andre Gunder Frank's *ReOrient* made a passionate attack on the concept of European hegemony, suggesting that the world economy was dominated by China for much longer than we think, an idea that resonated well with China's domination of world trade in the early twenty-first century.[24] In the 2000s, further revisions of the concept of world systems were offered, significantly, differentiating world system history from the theory of the 'modern' world system.[25]

The scholarship inspired by the world systems school established a link between interconnectedness and inequality. The world economy became a tool to explain world inequality. On that point, world systems borrowed from other contemporary strands in global Marxist thinking, such as the dependency school or the idea of unequal exchange in trade, a debt that Wallerstein acknowledged. Whereas Karl Marx believed that European expansion and colonialism would shake up stagnant Asiatic societies, Marxist theorists of the 1970s attributed the genesis of stagnation and underdevelopment in what used to be called "the Third World" to those same dynamics.[26] Colonizers created these conditions by imposing free trade, which destroyed the handicrafts and forced the colonies to become mineral and agricultural goods exporters, and by manipulating terms of exchange, especially in labour markets, through the use of political power.[27]

World systems and global Marxism shared several common features. The building blocks in both were the international division of labour and the transfer of surpluses through the system mostly from the periphery to the metropole. The significance of specialization and the meaning of surplus are subject to dispute, but the combined emphasis on market exchange on a world scale popularized the ideas that capitalism has become global since the 1600s, and that capitalism was formed from a series of interconnected market exchanges, an altogether more flexible and easy definition of capitalism than the orthodox Marxist one based on patterns of ownership of assets. Global history should be able to tell us why goods acquired more value as they moved from market to market. And by doing so, we should know not only how capitalism worked in practice but also why it became global, even if that story does not say anything about the origin of growth and inequality.[28]

The notion that modern economic growth and inequality developed from the global interconnectedness that had emerged at least since the seventeenth century, faced a strong challenge from institutional economic history in the 1980s. Douglass North and others argued that the modern West discovered secure property rights and contractual law in the seventeenth and eighteenth centuries, thanks to attributes and processes that were uniquely European.[29] If such was the origin of modern economic growth, one would need to explain the origin of world inequality by showing that the non-West had remained trapped in an economic world that was unsafe and unpredictable. Early institutional economic history implicitly assumed that this was the case, and thereby overlooked huge diversity within the non-Western experience. Nor did early institutional economic history offer interconnectedness a definite role in the explanatory framework. In the 2000s, extensions of the framework tested the idea that European expansion created different types of states and rules of law in the non-European world, because either the motivation to govern differed, or the tools of governance did.[30] Institutional economic history, in this way, rehabilitated interconnectedness. But it did so via state formation, rather than via trade, exchange or capitalism.

In the 2000s two more influential ideas were proposed, again linking growth, inequality and interconnectedness. One of these was Kenneth Pomeranz's proposition that European expansion changed the course of human history by giving Europeans access to plentiful land and minerals.[31] Pomeranz said little about technologies, trade or colonialism as such, but the proposition did suggest that settler colonies in the New World were better off because they were more resource-rich than many Old World societies.[32] The fact that the settlers appropriated these resources by means of labour servitude and land grab institutions does, however, give a very different spin on the intrinsic superiority of European institutions.

Pomeranz's book gave the flood of publications on global history to occur since 2000 a collective name, the 'divergence debate'. Some of these works were statistical, and measured when and to what extent regions forged ahead or fell behind.[33] Some were comparative. Others were done in the narrative history mode, and focused on regions.[34] Some deconstructed Europe and distinguished between 'great' and 'little' divergences.[35] Others re-established the importance of trade in the economic emergence of Western Europe.[36]

While the divergence debate stimulated conversations on comparisons between regions, it did not necessarily induce a rethinking of the regional units being compared. Other writings in the 2000s revised the concept of regions by showing how geographically diverse regions contained several trajectories of change within them, partly mediated by the presence of what Lieberman calls 'exposed zones' within them.[37] This argument has implications for what can be or should be compared in a debate on inequality.

A further idea has re-established the importance of trade both for the early modern and the post-1800 periods. The work by Flynn and Giráldez, and Von Glahn argued for the creation of a world economy in the seventeenth century emanating from the discovery and trade by Europeans of vast reserves of silver in the Americas.[38] Although this does not change the structure or chronologies for Wallersteinian interpretations, it provides for a renewed emphasis on trade, in particular trade in those Asian commodities exchanged for silver. Thus the so-called silverization of the Chinese economy (as a 'silver sink') lubricated world trade in Southeast Asian spices and manufactured commodities such as Chinese silks and porcelain, Indian cottons and later on tea from China and India and other produce such as sugar, coffee and cocoa.[39] Jan de Vries has concluded that, whilst both the Indian and Atlantic Oceans were key to the reshaping and growth of European economies, it was the Atlantic trade (of slaves, cotton and goods manufactured in Europe) that was quantitatively more important for the creation of a world economy.[40]

Notwithstanding the now substantial literature on world trade in the early modern period, suggesting both the creation of an integrated world economy and of a process of 'globalization' through trade, supporters of 'hard globalization' argue that a world economy characterized by both commodity and factor–price convergence emerged only in the nineteenth century.[41] Kevin O'Rourke and Jeffery Williamson in *Globalization and History: The Evolution of a Nineteenth-Century Atlantic Economy* (2001) showed that increasing trade led to specialization and factor–price convergence on both sides of the Atlantic in the late 1800s.[42] Trade was not only an engine of economic growth but also aided transmission of growth until a 'backlash' began to form in the interwar period. In a follow-up work, *Trade and Poverty* (2011), Williamson extended the framework, controversially, to explain why the Third World did not experience convergence in the same way, mainly because it suffered de-industrialization as a result of overconcentration upon the export of primary products.[43]

A new literature has emerged on the institutions that enabled global trade and economic globalization, most especially in the early modern period. The European East India companies are not a new subject of research; yet in the past two decades their role in fostering economic change has been recast. Traditionally interpreted as precursors to the modern corporation, their role in early modern connectivity has been extended from trade to politics. The paradigm of the company-state – according to which companies assumed state-like functions in Asia – has enabled comparative and cross-disciplinary studies most especially at the intersection between economic history and the history of international relations.[44] This scholarship is part of a more critical assessment of politics within economic change and a recasting of the role of the state in the economy.[45]

Global interconnectedness, as said before, mattered in itself, as a feature of modern capitalism, as a factor that shaped regional histories, and as a process that progressively added value to capital, labour and goods, or destroyed values that they commanded in earlier centuries. One did not have to bat for a theory of the Great Divergence to study the world economy. Several new publications were written from this perspective, usually studying a commodity, a time or a region, and in each case contributing to the narrative of globalization and the emergence of global capitalism.[46] At the minimum, this was a Wallersteinian programme, minus the baggage of surplus extraction and appropriation. Some of these works, however, went further and made use of globalization to rethink the rise of the West. Several chapters in the two-volume *Cambridge History of Capitalism* shared the same aim, to explain global capitalism. But contributors were free to smuggle in afterthoughts about the Great Divergence.[47]

A large part of the pre-2000 scholarship discussed in this section interacted with economic history occasionally; the dialogue has become more serious and systematic since then. Their overlap deserves a closer look.

The Tools of Global Economic History

A field should be defined by the questions that it seeks to answer. From before the divergence debate took off, historians have reflected on the methodology of global history. In an influential article published in 1997, Sanjay Subrahmanyam suggested ways to think about connectedness in early modern history.[48] In a now classic statement published in 2006 in the first issue of the *Journal of Global History*, Patrick O'Brien wrote an overview of the field and asked why a craft such as history, that in antiquity frequently engaged with the world, had lost interest in the global since the nineteenth century, and why the global was now making a return. O'Brien contrasted two ways of doing global history, comparisons and connections, and predicted that the rationale of the field in the future would depend on the global historians' ability to construct 'new cosmopolitan meta-narratives' that challenged the 'teleological chronicles designed to reinforce people's very own set of values enshrined in canonical Christian, Muslim, Hindu, Confucian and other sacred texts'.[49]

Varied methodologies have been adopted by the different social sciences in their approach to global (economic) history. Much work has been done on connections, establishing in particular what we might mean by connections and connectivity. But whilst economists and economic historians preferred to concentrate on integration (possibly an outcome of connections), cultural historians explored concepts such as entanglements, *histoire croisée*, connected history, and hybridity among the many.[50] Many historians took O'Brien's call for challenging 'teleological chronicles' seriously, though many shied away from adopting metanarratives (even if cosmopolitan in nature). Global history in the past decade has definitively moved towards more 'micro' approaches. This is the case of global microhistories that raise the issue of agency, of perspective and the relationship between the global and the local.[51] At the same time, however, global history has experienced a continuing success of 'macro' approaches, though these have been less interested than in the past in large-scale metanarrative and more concerned with long-term analysis of change. This is the case of' 'Big' and 'Deep' histories stretching back to the pre-historical period if not the Big Bang.[52] They provide sweeping narratives that pull together comparisons, connections and 'holistic' views of history. They also connect history to the sciences including biology, ecology and psychology.[53]

Global economic history is, among the different types of global history today, the one that has followed O'Brien's view most closely. Whether macro or micro, global economic history has created sustained debate and discussion around major themes and problems, some of which are of long-standing importance for the discipline of economic history. Many of these debates are referred to in contributions in this book. We wish here to highlight three of them as paradigmatic of how the discipline of global economic history has evolved over the past two decades: first, that of technological change and its relationship with industrialization; second, large-scale projects on inputs, outputs, prices and wages that have addressed debates such as industrialization and divergence; and finally, an emerging concern about the 'age of Anthropocene' as an attempt to bridge economic and environmental histories.

The industrial revolution and more widely the process of industrialization in Europe and elsewhere remains a key topic in economic history.[54] Several chapters in this book comment on the ways in which the debate about the origin of modern economic growth, of industry and a drastic transformation of economies worldwide has been reshaped by the divergence debate. Although science technology and knowledge did not play an important role in Pomeranz's original formulation, the work of several economic historians, most prominently Joel Mokyr, has provided new ideas about the role played by technology in economic history.[55] The literature is now vast, but one might say that it has attempted to bridge the gap between historians of science and technology on the one hand and economic historians on the other. The focus on useful and reliable knowledge, for instance, has allowed researchers to consider the ways in which both knowledge and information – and their transfer in time and space – were key to both product and process innovation. Whilst old narratives conceived of Europe (and often the much smaller area of England) as the cradle of world invention, economic historians consider now the ways in which technologies, techniques, scientific principles and information were translated, reshaped and used across continents. This might be the case of new techniques and technologies for the production on cotton textiles, lacquer or porcelain from Asia to Europe, or technologies for silk processing from Europe to Asia.[56]

Technological innovation is at the centre of one set of explanations concerning the capital-intensive path undertaken by the European (and British in particular) economies in the eighteenth century. Based on a large-scale project comparing silver wages across Eurasia from ancient times to the nineteenth century, Robert Allen explains the recourse to mechanical devices in eighteenth-century British manufacturing as a response to high wages. This controversial explanation is based on a large collective quantitative undertaking measuring not just wages in different cities in Europe and Asia but also prices and estimates of GDP.[57] Inspired by Maddison's estimates and relying on comparative methodologies, this project (or better to say series of projects) is in line with Big Data analysis.[58] This project extends analyses that until recently were confined to individual nations. This labour-intensive exercise of data mining, collection and interpretation has produced an important knowledge base that is conscious of its biases, gaps and limitations. It provides economic history with a 'global' dataset that, as always, needs to be interpreted with care if we wish to make use of it in debates over economic divergence and differentials in living standards or simply in comparative work across cultures. The projects on inputs, outputs, wages and prices takes GDP as a key measure and economic growth as the metre through which to evaluate economies over time and space. This approach has faced some criticism, on measurement as well as conceptual grounds.[59]

The Anthropocene suggests emissions. A deeper form of human agency can be seen in land use. Cropland and pastures increased from 8 to 50 million square kilometres between 1750 and 2000 (5.4 to 34.7 per cent of land surface).[60] The numbers suggest a staggering extent of deforestation, contributing to carbon emissions. By changing surface reflectivity, it changed the path of the tropical monsoons. These processes matter to the global historian in several ways, for example, immigration where surplus land is available, or outmigration of population exposed to droughts.

These three examples show how global economic history has been in recent years in a 'revisionist' mood. The enlargement of the chronological and especially the geographic spectrum has led to questioning the very foundations of the discipline. Whilst new debates emerge and others evolve into larger and more ambitious enterprises, the toolkit and methodologies of economic history cannot remain unaltered.[61] Furthering that programme requires taking stock of the cosmopolitan narratives the field has produced in the last twenty years. This anthology takes a step in that direction. Others have done it before us. The distinctive feature of this project is its accent on joining economic history with everything that we know now matters to economic history, from politics, to resources, to culture.[62]

The Structure of This Book

This volume gathers together historians and economists who have, in their careers, tried to think big on one of the three dimensions of global economic history – comparisons, connections and the interaction between the local and the global. The editors gave the contributors an open agenda. The contributors were free to define the questions and the debates that mattered. In that sense, the project is contributor-oriented, subject to the constraint that the chapters do deal with any one of these dimensions. The editors did not think that the field was ready yet for a volume structured around a single big theme or question.

This people-oriented approach left some obvious gaps in the volume. While we can claim to have involved a good cross-section of historians who have made major contributions to global economic history, the list is by no means comprehensive. Further, we did not feel ready to commission chapters on some important themes, where there were shortages of the right people to write. Gender, business history and North America represent some of the potential gaps. These arose because the literature on these subjects/ regions and conversations with colleagues did not suggest an easy way to integrate the theme with a 'global' as well as an 'economic' dimension. These are important themes that are to be found across the book (gender being an important dimension in the discussion of labour and institutions; North America in chapters on silver and slavery, and elsewhere in the book; and business history within trade and finance).

Eight chapters in the first part of this book are dedicated to the re-examination of the divergence debate. Parthasarathi and Pomeranz present an overview of their positions on divergence and extend the original Sino-European comparison to include also South Asia and underline the ways in which the divergence debate has influenced both Chinese and Indian scholarship. Jack Goldstone continues this critical analysis of divergence by concentrating on the part played by the gathering and interpretation of data and the implication that this has on the chronologies of economic development of Europe and Asia.

Patrick O'Brien and Karel Davids consider respectively useful and reliable knowledge, and technology, as two of the key factors explaining differing trajectories of global economic change. Responding to a premise of the divergence debate that the world displayed more similarities than differences before the nineteenth century, O'Brien suggests that global historians should engage with a proposition that Europeanists put forward, that a distinct 'regime for the accumulation of useful and reliable knowledge' had emerged in early modern Europe as a result of an interdependent evolution of natural philosophy and institutions of learning. 'Over the long run,' the thesis goes, 'direct connections between Europe's tradition in natural philosophy which matured into science [and] technological innovation remains unmistakable'. Davids, on the other hand, cautions against the tendency to emphasize sharp breaks or 'divergences' in technological change, and shows how innovations could build on local practices by arguing that big differences could emerge from small variations.

As the debate over divergence matured, new contexts and topics have been added to the discussion. The role of institutions and institutional change in sustaining modern or productivity-driven economic growth is well known to economic historians. The conception of modern economic growth, however, has changed recently, from a sharp break that occurred some time in the nineteenth century, to a gradual and piecemeal transition that began much earlier, and suffered many reversals before strengthening in the nineteenth century. Can the historiography of institutions adapt to this perspective? Regina Grafe and Maarten Prak offer a narrative on institutional change compatible with 'the slow transition from early modern to modern intensive growth'. They consider changes in family systems, collectives and the state, and offer a measured conclusion that cautions against drawing causal link between institutions and growth, and between institutional change and European exceptionalism. Trevor Burnard asks what the role of plantation economies was in the Great Divergence, a topic that has received less attention than expected by historians. Maxine Berg, moving away from traditional concerns over production and the economy, connects divergence and global history to the history of consumption and debates over the standards of living. And finally Andrew Liu brings us back to the Divergence debate and considers the ways in which in recent years it has informed a new discussion on the so-called New History of Capitalism.

The second part of this book explores the emergence of a world economy by concentrating on different aspects of what we might call economic globalization. In a joint chapter, the editors of this book charter the importance of trade in structuring global connections over the long period, showing its changing scale especially in the nineteenth and twentieth century. If trade is often acknowledged as central to the connectedness and integration of the world economy, John McNeill alerts us that due attention should be given also to the environment. Adopting a multidisciplinary perspective, McNeill argues that the creation of a world economy coincided with a new relationship between humans and natural environment, what today is called the 'age of Anthropocene'.

Alessandro Stanziani continues this analysis by concentrating on labour and the mobility of labour as one of the key factors in the creation of global markets and the structuring of a world economy. He challenges established classifications that oppose free versus coerced labour. This line of enquiry is further developed by Kaoru Sugihara in a chapter dedicated to varieties of industrialization. Considering different Asian regions, Sugihara challenges the European industrial paradigm as the template for global economic growth. Leigh Gardner considers instead economic change in the light of empire and colonialism. The final two chapters by Bernd-Stefan Grewe and Youssef Cassis consider respectively the role of commodities and finance in structuring global markets. Global commodity chains and global value chains, Grewe argues, provide unique methodological perspectives to the study of the world economy and challenge established notions of core and peripheries. A similar approach is adopted by Cassis who shows the importance of global cities in the shaping of financial transactions worldwide since the mid-nineteenth century.

The eight chapters in the third and final part of this book shift our perspective from global connectedness to the contribution of specific world areas. They collectively raise the issue of how beneficial the 'lateral thinking' provided by a 'placed' perspective is to global economic history. They also challenge the idea of a 'natural' unit of analysis by showing how discretionary labels such as Africa, North and South America, East Asia, South Asia and even Europe are, and how they subsume a variety of experiences and trajectories of economic change. Gareth Austin considers Sub-Saharan Africa and engages with colonial and post-colonial theories of economic development. This is an approach also embraced by Laura Panza in a chapter dedicated to the economy of the Middle East. Alejandra Irigoin's contribution observes how global economic history has concentrated on Eurasia at the expense of the role played by the Americas, especially in the production and trade of enormous quantities of silver that 'oiled' the world economy in the early modern period. Moving to the modern period, Reggie Blaszczyk provides an analysis of the rise of the North American economy by focusing on business history methodologies. Debin Ma shows instead how a shared culture characterized the economic trajectory of a diverse region defined as East Asia but observes also how modernization and industrialization were accompanied by conflict and warfare.

The acknowledgment of differentiation is also central to a chapter by Peer Vries on the European economy in the past five centuries. Far from constituting a monolithic model of economic development for the rest of the world to follow, Vries presents a continent characterized by deep-rooted economic inequality that has survived to the present. Bishnupriya Gupta and Tirthankar Roy address instead the topic of decline of the South Asian economy especially after 1800. They argue that its loss of status as an exporter of industrial goods should be seen in connection with the development of textile technologies in Europe, thus arguing for an entangled approach to economic history. Finally, a chapter by J. Thomas Lindblad on the economy of Southeast Asia argues that we should appreciate both continuities and discontinuities when evaluating the economic trajectory of a world area and its constituting nation states and areas.

Together these chapters aim to be more thought-provoking than informative. They attempt to charter some of the debates that Global Economic History had developed in the past two decades. This field of enquiry is still novel, ambiguous in its contours and methodologies and uncertain in its findings. Whilst chartering the uncertain terrain of Global Economic History, it is our hope that this collection of chapters might provide inspiration for the field's future direction.

Whom Is This Book For?

Whom is this book for? The book is intended to serve different groups of users. To students doing an economic history course, the book shows why global connections matter. To students doing a global history course, the book shows why economic change matters. Global history is being rethought in the wake of the recent surge in world trade, migration and capital flows; reintegration of emerging economies like China and India in the world economy; and intellectual debates such as that surrounding the economic divergence between Asia and Europe. Historians looking for a statement of how the historiography of economic change has moved since 2000 will hopefully find much useful material in this book. Similarly, anyone with an interest in the economic globalization the world is witnessing now, and would want to know more about how it all began and where the globalizing impulse came from, may find the book worth reading.

Finally, there is an explicit desire in this book to be forward-looking, and ask the question, what next for global history? Economists would say that the divergence debate is running into diminishing return. A new article or book demonstrating what Pomeranz called 'surprising similarities' between a part of Europe and a part of Asia with a new combination of regions, is unlikely to receive enthusiastic endorsement from referees. But the debate has changed the methods and assumptions economic historians use when discussing globalization in the long run. There is far more attention now in comparative economic history on the early modern period, on non-European geographies and topics, and on rethinking Europe in relation to the experience of the rest of the world. Those who believe that the world economy has changed decisively are also likely to believe that deep changes began before industrialization, in the seventeenth and eighteenth centuries, when processes like colonization, the expansion of trade, the expansion of states, warfare and the 'modern' framing of laws, substantially altered in scale, scope and nature. The reader of the book will find here a set of chapters that reflect these methodological shifts. More than that, the scholar who wants to research economic change in global history will discover here many new frontiers to explore.

One of these frontiers – history of capitalism – attracts a great deal of attention in schools of history, especially in North America. Economic historians forty years ago fought over the definition of 'capitalism'. In the present times, definitional debates are rare, and the power of 'capital' to connect the world is in focus.[63] The new history of capitalism and the old history has a common interest in slavery, or turning of people into objects of trade. Slavery figures in this book too, as one of the trades that shaped the modern world economy. But its importance is relative to where we look. If we shift from North America to South Asia, global textile trade might appear to be a bigger deal in the history of capitalism than slavery. This book will appeal to those who acknowledge, like the collective cited above does, the power of capitalism to bridge distances, forge links and drive global change. Where this power comes from could have different answers when we approach the question from different parts of the globe. This book is an attempt to bring these perspectives together.

Notes

1. D. Speich (2011), 'The use of global abstractions: National income accounting in the period of imperial decline', *Journal of Global History*, 6 (1), 7–28; Q. Slobodian (2015), 'How to see the world economy: Statistics, maps, and Schumpeter's camera in the first age of globalization', *Journal of Global History*, 10 (2), 307–22.

2. Giovanni Arrighi and Beverly J. Silver (1999), *Chaos and Governance in the Modern World System*. Minneapolis, MN: University of Minnesota Press; Andre G. Frank (1998), *ReOrient*. Berkeley, CA: University of California Press; Terence K. Hopkins, Immanuel Wallerstein, Reşat Kasaba, William G. Martin and Peter. D Phillip (1987), 'Incorporation into the world-economy: How the world-system expands', *Review*, 10 (5–6), 761–902; Jason W. Moore (2003), '"The modern world-system" as environmental history? Ecology and the rise of capitalism', *Theory and Society*, 32 (3), 307–77.

3. M. Berg (ed.) (2013), *Writing the History of the Global: Challenges for the Twenty-First Century*. Oxford: Oxford University Press; M. Middell (ed.) (2019), *The Practice of Global History: European Perspectives*. London: Bloomsbury.

4. For a summary of the literature see P. Robinson Rössner (2018), 'Great Divergence: Addressing lobal inequalities', in M. Middell (ed.), *The Routledge Handbook of Transregional Studies*. London: Routledge, 235–42.

5. Kenneth Pomeranz (2000), *The Great Divergence: China, Europe and the Making of the Modern World Economy*. Princeton, NJ: Princeton University Press.

6. The literature on divergence is now vast. See the chapter by Pomeranz and Parthasarathi in this volume as well as Parthasarathi's critique of Pomeranz's work. P. Parthasarathi (2002), 'Review article: The Great Divergence', *Past & Present*, 176, 275–93. For an introduction to the debate see the special issue of *Historically Speaking*, 12 (4) published in 2011 and dedicated to the divergence debate as well as two short textbooks: R. B. Marks (2002), *The Origins of the Modern World: A Global and Ecological Narrative*. New York: Rowman & Littlefield Publishers; and J. Goldstone (2008), *Why Europe? The Rise of the West in World History, 1500–1850*. Boston, MA: McGraw Hill Higher Education; P. Parthasarathi (2011), *Why Europe Grew Rich and Asia Did Not: Global Economic Divergence, 1600–1850*. Cambridge: Cambridge University Press; and J. W. Daly (2014), *Historians Debate the Rise of the West*. London: Routledge; ibid. (2019), *How Europe Made the Modern World: Creating the Great Divergence*. London: Bloomsbury.

7. T. Piketty (2014), *Capital in the Twenty-First Century*. Cambridge, MA: Belknap Press; ibid. (2020), *Capital and Ideology*. Cambridge, MA: The Belknap Press; ibid. (2022),

A Brief History of Equality. Cambridge, MA: The Belknap Press. For a recent analysis of how Piketty's book has challenged the discipline of economic history, see P. Hudson and K. Tribe (eds) (2016), *The Contradictions of Capital in the Twenty-First Century: The Piketty Opportunity*. London: Agenda Publishing. There is now a vast literature on inequality though not yet fully global in scale or approach. See in particular: A. Atkinson (2015), *Inequality: What Can Be Done?*. Cambridge MA: Harvard University Press; A. Deaton (2015), *The Great Escape: Health, Wealth, and the Origins of Inequality*, Princeton, NJ: Princeton University Press; and B. Milanovic (2016), *Global Inequality: A New Approach for the Age of Globalisation*. Cambridge, MA: The Belknap Press of Harvard University Press; W. Scheidel (2017), *The Great Leveler: Violence and the History of Inequality from the Stone Age to the Twenty-First Century*. Princeton, NJ: Princeton University Press. For a short overview see F. Bourguignon (2015), *The Globalization of Inequality* Princeton, NJ: Princeton University Press; K. Pistor (2019), *The Code of Capital: How the Law Creates Wealth and Inequality*. Princeton NJ: Princeton University Press; M. Savage (2021), *The Return of Inequality: Social Change and the Weight of the Past*. Cambridge, MA: Harvard University Press, 2021.

8. On the relationship between capitalism, inequality and the Great Divergence, see the chapter by Andrew Liu in this volume.

9. Eli Cook (2020), 'Naturalizing inequality: The problem of economic fatalism in the age of Piketty', *Capitalism: A Journal of History and Economics*, 1 (1), 338–78; B. Milanovic (18 November 2017), 'The illusion of "degrowth" in a poor and unequal world': globalinequality. https://glineq.blogspot.com/2017/11/the-illusion-of-degrowth-in-poor-and.html; Jason Hickel (27 October 2020), 'Degrowth: A response to Branko Milanovic': https://www.jasonhickel.org/blog/2017/11/19/why-branko-milanovic-is-wrong-about-de-growth/.

10. For an excellent analysis of the early modern global economy see P. de Zwart and J. L. van Zanden (2018), *The Origins of Globalization: World Trade in the Making of the Global Economy, 1500–1800*. Cambridge: Cambridge University Press.

11. C. A. Bayly (2004), *The Birth of the Modern World, 1780–1914*, Oxford: Blackwell. See also S. Subrahmanyam (1997), 'Connected histories: Notes towards a reconfiguration of early modern Eurasia', *Modern Asian Studies*, 31 (3), 735–62; ibid. (2004), *Explorations in Connected History: From the Tagus to the Ganges*. Delhi: Oxford University Press; ibid. (2004), *Explorations in Connected History: Mughals and Franks*. Delhi: Oxford University Press.

12. On migration, a good book to begin with is P. Manning with T. Trimmer (2013), *Migration in World History*, 2nd edn. New York: Routledge. On 'weak ties', see M. Granovetter (1983), 'The strength of weak ties: A network theory revisited', *Sociological Theory*, 1 (6), 201–33.

13. See for instance the concept of the 'age of revolutions': D. Armitage and S. Subrahmanyam (2010), 'Introduction: The age of revolutions, c.1760–1840. Global causation, connection, and comparison', in D. Armitage and S. Subrahmanyam (eds), *The Age of Revolutions in Global Context, c.1760–1840*. Basingstoke: Palgrave Macmillan, xii–xxxii.

14. V. Lieberman (2003), *Strange Parallels: Southeast Asia in Global Context, c.800–1830*, vol. 1: *Integration on the Mainland*. Cambridge: Cambridge University Press; ibid. (2009), *Strange Parallels: Southeast Asia in Global Context, c.800–1830*, vol. 2: *Mainland Mirrors: Europe, Japan, China, South Asia, and the Islands*. Cambridge: Cambridge University Press.

15. J. Lucassen (ed.) (2008), *Global Labour History: A State of the Art*. Bern and Oxford: Peter Lang. See also L. Lucassen (2016), 'Working together: New directions in global labour history', *Journal of Global History*, 11 (1), 66–87.

16. While there is a distinction between 'world history' (concentrating on large world areas and civilizations) and 'global history' (preferring instead the analysis of connections), we find this distinction not particularly useful when applied to economic history. See B. Mazlish (1998), 'Comparing global history to world history', *Journal of Interdisciplinary History*, 28 (3), 385–95.

17. F. Braudel (1996), *The Mediterranean and the Mediterranean World in the Age of Philip II*, 2nd edn. Berkeley, CA: University of California Press.

18. N. Steensgaard (1973), *Carracks, Caravans and Companies: The Structural Crisis in the European–Asian Trade in the Early 17th Century*. Copenhagen: Studentlitteratur; and J. D. Tracy (ed.) (1990), *The Rise of Merchant Empires: Long-Distance Trade in the Early Modern World*. New York: Cambridge University Press.

19. For an overview of the literature see P. Parthasarathi and G. Riello (2014), 'The Indian Ocean in the long eighteenth century', *Eighteenth-Century Studies*, 48 (1), 1–19. See also P. Beaujard (2005), 'The Indian Ocean in Eurasian and African world-systems before the sixteenth century', *Journal of World History*, 16 (4), 411–65; M. Pearson (2007), *The Indian Ocean*. London and New York: Routledge; F. Gipouloux (2011), *The Asian Mediterranean: Port Cities and Trading Networks in China, Japan and Southeast Asia, 13th–21st Century*. Cheltenham: Edward Elgar; R. Mukherjee (2013), 'The Indian Ocean: Historians writing history', *Asian Review of World Histories*, 1 (2), 295–307.

20. See for instance F. Trivellato (2012), *The Familiarity of Strangers: The Sephardic Diaspora, Livorno, and Cross-cultural Trade in the Early Modern Period*. New Haven, CT: Yale University Press. See also A. Games (2006), 'Atlantic history: Definitions, challenges, and opportunities', *American Historical Review*, 111 (3), 741–57; E. H. Gould (2007), 'Entangled histories, entangled worlds: The English-speaking Atlantic as a Spanish periphery', *American Historical Review*, 112 (3), 764–86; C. Vidal (2012), 'Pour un histoire globale du monde atlantique au des histoires connectées dans et au-delà du monde atlantique', *Annales: Histoire, Sciences Sociales*, 67 (2), 391–413.

21. I. Wallerstein (1974–2011), *The Modern World-System*, vols 1–4, Berkeley, CA: University of California Press.

22. J. Lippman Abu-Lughod (1991), *Before European Hegemony: The World System A.D. 1250–1350*. New York: Oxford University Press.

23. K. N. Chaudhuri (1990), *Asia before Europe: Economy and Civilisation of the Indian Ocean from the Rise of Islam to 1750*. Cambridge: Cambridge University Press.

24. A. Gunder Frank (1998), *ReOrient: Global Economy in the Asian Age*. Berkeley, CA: University of California Press.

25. Robert A. Denemark and Barry K. Gills (2012), 'World-system history: Challenging Eurocentric knowledge', in Salvatore J. Barbones and Christopher Chase-Dunn (eds), *Routledge Handbook of World-Systems Analysis*. London and New York: Routledge, 163–71.

26. B. K. Gills and W. R. Thompson (eds) (2006), *Globalization and Global History*. New York: Routledge.

27. A. K. Bagchi (1982), *The Political Economy of Underdevelopment*. Cambridge: Cambridge University Press; J. Goody (2004), *Capitalism and Modernity: The Great Debate*, Cambridge: Polity.

28. On the recent interest in the history of capitalism, see L. Neal and J. G. Williamson (2014), *The Cambridge History of Capitalism*, 2 vols. Cambridge: Cambridge University Pres; J. Kocka (2016), *Capitalism: A Short History*. Princeton, NJ and Oxford: Princeton University Press; V. Ogle (2017), 'Archipelago capitalism: Tax havens, offshore

money, and the state, 1950s–1970s', *American Historical Review*, 122 (5), 1431–58; M. O'Sullivan (2018), 'The intelligent woman's guide to capitalism', *Enterprise and Society*, 19 (4), 751–802; S. Beckert and C. Desan (2018), *American Capitalism: New Histories*. New York: Columbia University Press; A. B. Liu (2019), 'Production, circulation, and accumulation: The historiographies of capitalism in China and South Asia', *Journal of Asian Studies*, 78 (4), 767–88; A. D. Edwards, P. Hill and J. Neves-Sarriegui (2020), 'Capitalism in global history', *Past & Present*, 249, 1–32; F. Trivellato (2020), 'Renaissance Florence and the origins of capitalism: A business history perspective', *Business History Review*, 94 (1), 229–51; K. Yazdani and D. M. Menon (eds) (2020), *Capitalisms: Towards a Global History*. New Delhi: Oxford University Press; E. Rothschild (2021), 'Where is capital?', *Capitalism: A Journal of History and Economics* 2 (2), 291–371; R. Bin Wong (2021), 'Modern capitalism's multiple pasts and its possible future: The rise of China, climate change, and economic transformation', *Capitalism: A Journal of History and Economics*, 2 (2), 257–90.

29. D. C. North (1981), *Structure and Change in Economic History*. New York: Norton; and D. C. North and R. P. Thomas (1973), *The Rise of the Western World: A New Economic History*. New York: Cambridge University Press.

30. D. Acemoglu, S. Johnson and J. A. Robinson (2001), 'The colonial origins of comparative development: An empirical investigation', *American Economic Review*, 91 (5), 1369–401; K. L. Sokoloff and S. L. Engerman (2000), 'Institutions, factor endowments, and paths of development in the New World', *Journal of Economic Perspectives*, 14 (3), 7–32; D. Acemoglu and J. A. Robinson (2012), *Why Nations Fail: The Origins of Power, Prosperity and Poverty*. New York: Currency.

31. Pomeranz (2000), *The Great Divergence*.

32. See Parthasarathi, 'Review article: The Great Divergence'; P. H. H. Vries (2001), 'Are coal and colonies really crucial? Kenneth Pomeranz and the Great Divergence', *Journal of World History*, 12 (2), 408–46.

33. See for instance S. Broadberry and B. Gupta (2009), 'Lancashire, India and shifting competitive advantage in cotton textiles, 1700–1850: The neglected role of factor prices', *Economic History Review*, 62 (2), 279–305.

34. J.-L. Rosenthal and R. Bin Wong (2011), *Before and Beyond Divergence: The Politics of Economic Change in China and Europe*. Cambridge, MA: Harvard University Press; P. Parthasarathi (2011), *Why Europe Grew Rich and Asia Did Not: Global Economic Divergence, 1600–1850*. Cambridge: Cambridge University Press; P. Vries, *Escaping Poverty: The Origins of Modern Economic Growth*. Vienna: V&R Unipress; ibid. (2015), *State, Economy and the Great Divergence*. London: Bloomsbury; R. Studer (2015), *The Great Divergence Reconsidered: Europe, India, and the Rise to Global Economic Power*. Cambridge: Cambridge University Press; K. Yazdani (2017), *India, Modernity and the Great Divergence: Mysore and Gujarat (17th to 19th century)*. Leiden and Boston, MA: Brill.

35. J. L. van Zanden (2009), *The Long Road to the Industrial Revolution: The European Economy in a Global Perspective, 1000–1800*. Leiden: Brill; K. Davids (2012), *Religion, Technology, and the Great and Little Divergences: China and Europe Compared, c. 700–1800*. Leiden: Brill.

36. J. E. Inikori (2002), *Africans and the Industrial Revolution in England: A Study in International Trade and Economic Development*. Cambridge: Cambridge University Press.

37. Lieberman (2009), *Strange Parallels*, vol. 2; for a similar project on South Asia, see T. Roy (2012), *India in the World Economy: From Antiquity to the Present*. Cambridge: Cambridge University Press.

38. D. O. Flynn and A. Giráldez (eds) (1997), *Metals and Monies in an Emerging Global Economy*. Aldershot: Ashgate; D. O. Flynn, A. Giráldez and R. von Glahn (eds) (2003), *Global Connections and Monetary History, 1470–1800*. Aldershot: Ashgate.

39. M. Berg (2004), 'In pursuit of luxury: Global history and British consumer goods in the eighteenth century', *Past & Present*, 182, 85–142.

40. J. de Vries (2010), 'The limits of globalisation in the early modern world', *Economic History Review*, 63 (1), 710–33.

41. This position is criticized by P. de Zwart (2016), 'Globalization in the early modern era: New evidence from the Dutch-Asiatic trade, *c.*1600–1800', *Journal of Economic History*, 76 (2), 520–58 who shows price convergence for some key commodities traded by the Dutch East India Company from Asia to Europe in the course of the eighteenth century.

42. K. H. O'Rourke and J. G. Williamson (2001), *Globalization and History: The Evolution of a Nineteenth-Century Atlantic Economy*. Cambridge, MA: MIT Press.

43. J. G. Williamson (2011), *Trade and Poverty: When the Third World Fell Behind*. Cambridge, MA: MIT Press.

44. P. J. Stern (2012), *The Company-State: Corporate Sovereignty and the Early Modern Foundations of the British Empire in India*. New York: Oxford University Press. See also W. A. Pettigrew and D. Veevers (2019), *The Corporation as a Protagonist in Global History, c.1550–1750*. Leiden and Boston, MA: Brill; and D. Veevers (2020), *The Origins of the British Empire in Asia, 1600–1750*. Cambridge: Cambridge University Press; A. Phillips and J. C. Sharman (2020), *Outsourcing Empire: How Company-States Made the Modern World*. Princeton, NJ: Princeton University Press; A. Clulow and T. Mostert (eds) (2018), *The Dutch and English East India Companies: Diplomacy, Trade and Violence in Early Modern Asia*. Amsterdam: Amsterdam University Press; R. Harris (2020), *Going the Distance: Eurasian Trade and the Rise of the Business Corporation, 1400–1700*. Princeton, NJ: Princeton University Press; P. C. Emmer and J. L. L. Gommans (2021), *The Dutch Overseas Empire 1600–1800*. Cambridge: Cambridge University Press.

45. M. Mazzucato (2013), *The Entrepreneurial State: Debunking Public vs. Private Sector Myths*. London: Anthem Press.

46. G. Riello and T. Roy (eds) (2009), *How India Clothed the World: The World of South Asian Textiles, 1500–1850*, Leiden: Brill; Roy, *India in the World Economy*; G. Riello (2013), *Cotton: The Fabric that Made the Modern World*. Cambridge: Cambridge University Press; J. Osterhammel (2014), *The Transformation of the World: A Global History of the Nineteenth Century*. Princeton, NJ: Princeton University Press; S. Beckert (2014), *Empire of Cotton: A Global History*. New York: Knopf; M. Berg et al. (eds) (2015), *Goods from the East, 1600–1800: Trading Eurasia*. Basingstoke: Palgrave; A. Gerritsen (2020), *The City of Blue and White: Chinese Porcelain and the Early Modern World*. Cambridge: Cambridge University Press. On Atlantic commerce, see R. Findlay and K. H. O'Rourke (2007), *Power and Plenty: Trade, War, and the World Economy in the Second Millennium*. Princeton, NJ: Princeton University Press.

47. S. Broadberry and K. O'Rourke (eds) (2010), *The Cambridge Economic History of Modern Europe*. Cambridge: Cambridge University Press.

48. Subrahmanyam, 'Connected histories'.

49. P. K. O'Brien (2006), 'Historical traditions and modern imperatives for the restoration of global history', *Journal of Global History*, 1 (1), 3–39.

50. C. Dean and D. Leibsohn (2003), 'Hybridity and its discontents: Considering visual culture in colonial Spanish America', *Colonial Latin American Review*, 12 (1), 5–35. Gould,

'Entangled histories, entangled worlds'; C. Douki and P. Minard (2007), special issue on 'Histoire globale, histoires connectées', *Revue d'Histoire Moderne et Contemporaine*, 54 (4 bis).

51. F. Trivellato (2011), 'Is there a future for Italian microhistory in the age of global history?', *California Italian Studies*, 2 (1), 1–24; S. D. Aslanian, J. E. Chaplin, A. McGrath and K. Mann (2013), 'AHR conversation. How size matters: The question of scale in history', *American Historical Review*, 118 (5), 1431–72; J.-P. A. Ghobrial (ed.) (2019), Special issue on 'Global History and Microhistory', *Past & Present*, 242, suppl. 14; R. Bertrand and G. Calafat (2019), issue on 'Micro-analyse et histoire globale', *Annales*, 73 (1).

52. D. Christian (2005), *Maps of Time: An Introduction to Big History*. Berkeley, CA: University of California Press; C. Stokes Brown (2007), *Big History: From the Big Bang to the Present*. New York: New Press; A. Shryock and D. L. Smail (2012), *Deep History: The Architecture of Past & Present*. Berkeley, CA: University of California Press.

53. On the methodological approaches to global history see M. Berg (2013), *Writing the History of the Global: Challenges for the Twenty-First Century*. Oxford: Oxford University Press and British Academy; S. Conrad (2016), *What Is Global History?*. Princeton, NJ: Princeton University Press.

54. See, for instance, K. Bruland, A. Gerritsen, P. Hudson and G. Riello (eds) (2020), *Reinventing the Economic History of Industrialisation*. Montreal: McGill-Queen's University Press.

55. J. Mokyr (1990), *The Lever of Riches: Technological Creativity and Economic Progress*. Oxford: Oxford University Press; J. Mokyr (2002), *The Gifts of Athena: Historical Origins of the Knowledge Economy*. Princeton, NJ: Princeton University Press; J. Mokyr (2017), *A Culture of Growth: The Origins of the Modern Economy*. Princeton, NJ: Princeton University Press.

56. Berg, 'In pursuit of luxury'; G. Riello (2010), 'Asian knowledge and the development of calico printing in Europe in the seventeenth and eighteenth centuries', *Journal of Global History*, 5 (1), 1–28; K. Hutková (2017), 'Transfer of European technologies and their adaptations: The case of the Bengal silk industry in the late-eighteenth century', *Business History*, 59 (7), 1111–35.

57. See for instance: R. C. Allen (2001), 'The great divergence in European wages and prices from the middle ages to the First World War', *Explorations in Economic History*, 38, 411–47; R. C. Allen, J.-P. Bassino, D. Ma, C. Moll-Murata and J. L. van Zanden (2011), 'Wages, prices, and living standards in China, Japan, and Europe, 1738–1925', *Economic History Review*, 64 (supplement S1), 8–38; R. C. Allen (2015), 'The high wage economy and the industrial revolution: A restatement', *Economic History Review*, 68 (1), 1–22; S. Broadberry (2021), 'Historical national accounting and dating the Great Divergence', *Journal of Global History*, 16 (2), 286–93 and other articles in the same issue by Jack Goldstone, Jan Luiten van Zanden and Jutta Bolt, and Paolo Malanima.

58. Datafiles of Historical Prices and Wages: http://www.iisg.nl/hpw/data.php (accessed 15 April 2017). J. Bolt and J. L. van Zanden (2014), 'The Maddison Project: Collaborative research on historical national accounts', *Economic History Review*, 67 (3), 627–51.

59. P. K. O'Brien, and K. Deng (2015), 'Locating a chronology for the great divergence: A critical survey of published data deployed for the measurement of nominal wages for Ming and Qing China', *Economic History Working Paper Series*, 213 (The London School of Economics and Political Science); ibid. (2016), 'Establishing statistical foundations of a chronology for the great divergence: A survey and critique of the primary sources for the construction of relative wage levels for the construction of relative wage levels for Ming–Qing China', *Economic History Review*, 69 (4), 1057–82. On the concept and historical usage of GDP

see D. Coyle (2015), *GDP: A Brief but Affectionate History*. Princeton, NJ: Princeton University Press.

60. K. Klein Goldewijk, A. Beusen, G. van Drecht and M. de Vos (2011), 'The HYDE 3.1 Spatially Explicit Database of Human-Induced Global Land-Use Change over the Past 12,000 Years', *Global Ecology and Biogeography* 20, 73–86.

61. Boldizzoni and Hudson, 'Introduction'.

62. J. Baten (2016), *A History of the Global Economy: 1500 to the Present*. Cambridge: Cambridge University Press.

63. Sven Beckert et al. (2014), 'Interchange: The history of capitalism', *Journal of American History*, 101 (2), 503–36.

PART I
DIVERGENCE AND CAPITALISM IN GLOBAL HISTORY

CHAPTER 1
THE GREAT DIVERGENCE DEBATE
Prasannan Parthasarathi and Kenneth Pomeranz

The question why parts of Europe surged ahead economically from the eighteenth century while much of Asia, Africa and even the Americas (with the exception of the United States), lagged behind has been debated for more than a century. Great thinkers of the nineteenth and twentieth centuries, ranging from Karl Marx to Max Weber, have addressed this large and important issue, as have a number of leading historians in our own times, including Eric Jones, Douglass North and David Landes. The 'Great Divergence' as it has come to be known is, therefore, a very old question, but the contours of the present debate were shaped by the publication of Kenneth Pomeranz's book of that title in 2000. While Pomeranz's book focused on China – and more precisely on the Yangzi Delta – it ranged into Japan, India and Southeast Asia, but the entry of India into the debate more fully would await the publication of Prasannan Parthasarathi's *Why Europe Grew Rich and Asia Did Not* in 2011.

The predilections of the two authors and the different perspectives that China and India bring to the problem have meant that the explanations for divergence differ in the two books. While Pomeranz has a far greater environmental history focus, Parthasarathi devotes more time to questions of technology and the state. Nevertheless, both works devote considerable attention to the economic conditions and institutions in the run-up to divergence. All of the above have been subject to great debate. In the last twenty years one can distinguish several overlapping strands of contention and not surprisingly the debate has focused far more on China than on India. In part, this is due to the earlier publication of the Pomeranz work and the long dominance of China–Europe comparisons. Such a debate is also not surprising, given the greater number of historians of China than India in the United States and Europe, which has kept the discussion alive and thriving. There has also been more interest in the question of divergence in China and Japan than in India. While economic history is currently a flourishing field in East Asia, in South Asia it has gone into sharp decline since its heyday in the 1960s and 1970s.

This chapter will focus on comparisons between the advanced regions of Europe, China and India, which have been the areas upon which much of the literature on the question has concentrated. It takes up four sets of issues. The first has to do with methodological questions connected to how we explain divergence. The chapter contrasts the structural approach that characterized an older and conventional approach to the problem with a conjunctural approach that has been introduced in the writings of

Pomeranz and Parthasarathi. The structural approach rests upon enduring differences between Europe and Asia, which have been challenged in recent writings. Several important contemporary writings explain divergence as a consequence of conjunctures, which led to different paths of economic development in different parts of the world.

The recent arguments for comparability between the advanced regions of Europe, China and India in the period before divergence at the end of the eighteenth century bring us to the second set of issues considered in this chapter. The Pomeranz and Parthasarathi claims for broad similarity have inspired debates and challenges to their position. The chapter reviews these debates, as well as the closely related question of the timing of divergence, and concludes that there is still striking disagreement on both these issues as well as on issues related to institutions and scientific knowledge and the role that these played in divergence. This brings the chapter to the third set of issues, which has to do with the problem of how to settle upon the 'truth' in economic history. The writing of history is an interpretive act, and it relies upon the reading of complex and fragmentary evidence. Theoretical biases and questions of value shape how one analyses the evidence. In such a situation is it possible to settle upon an explanation of divergence which receives wide assent? Finally, this chapter considers the ways in which a global and comparative debate, such as that on divergence, has been received and has influenced scholarship in India and China.

Structure versus Conjuncture

The classic writings of Karl Marx and Max Weber argued that the exceptional path of European economic development emerged from exceptional European conditions. Europe, in other words, was fundamentally different in some way from the advanced regions of China and India, and it was this difference that gave Europeans an economic edge and put the continent on a different trajectory. Such explanations are often called 'structural' in that they argue for deep social, political, economic or cultural differences.

For Marx this difference was capitalism. Europe gave rise to a new economic order which rested on private property and wage labour, which was dynamic, innovative and ever changing. Capitalism began in the countryside, where it transformed the agrarian order, but it soon spread to the world of manufacturing and its restlessness and dynamism produced the Industrial Revolution in the eighteenth century. However, capitalism as a new mode of production had longer origins, which means that the process of divergence began long before the eighteenth century, a point that the chapter will return to. By contrast, China and India remained static and unchanging, trapped in an Asiatic mode of production. As Marx wrote of India: 'Indian society has no history at all, at least no known history. What we call its history, is but the history of successive intruders who founded their empires on the passive basis of that unresisting and unchanging society.'[1]

While Max Weber took a more cultural tack to understanding capitalism, he shared with Marx an approach which emphasized deep-seated differences between Europe, in particular its Protestant areas, and China and India. For Weber, the critical development in Europe was the affinity between the tenets of Protestantism and a spirit of capitalism, which transformed the approach to economic activity, making it more systematic, calculating and rational. These changes laid the foundation for the economic transformation of Western Europe from the eighteenth century, but in Weber's view predated that era. Weber argued that the affinity between religious thinking, economic rationality and a transformative impulse found in Europe had no counterpart in China or India. Therefore, it was Europe which led the way to a new economic order.[2]

Twentieth-century historians approached the problem of divergence in much the same way as Marx and Weber as they sought to identify what made Europe different from even the economically advanced and thriving regions of Asia. Douglass North and Robert Paul Thomas assert the superiority of the political and economic institutions that emerged in Western Europe during the seventeenth century. For Eric Jones, Europe possessed exceptional environmental conditions and a competitive state system which was not found in Asia. David Landes attributed Europe's success to an advantageous culture. And Joel Mokyr has pinpointed the scientific culture of Europe as exceptional and critical to its economic path.[3]

Parthasarathi and Pomeranz, on the other hand, built on arguments for rough comparability and similarities between the advanced regions of Europe, China and India and they argued that there is little evidence for European exceptionalism. In their view, divergence was the product of conjunctures between needs and opportunities.[4]

Pomeranz's book emphasized ecological relief, which was provided by coal and overseas trade. Pomeranz argued that Britain and the Yangzi Delta – the most advanced regions in Europe and China, respectively – both faced pressures on the land, which provided the food, fuel and fibre that were needed for survival. Britain was able to overcome its land constraint by substituting wood with coal and by importing foodstuffs and raw cotton from the Americas. In effect, Britain vastly expanded its land area. The Yangzi Delta, by contrast, did not have such ecological windfalls. While China as a whole had plentiful deposits of coal, these were difficult to access because they were located in Northwest China, at some distance from the Yangzi region, which was in the south. The external trade of the Yangzi Delta did not provide the same ecological benefits. (Pomeranz recognizes that a stream of new machines cannot be explained simply by the availability of energy to fuel them, and he has no quarrel with scholars who emphasize the contributions of European science as long as they do not claim that this is a complete explanation.)

For Parthasarathi, ecological relief in the form of coal is certainly part of the explanation and is especially critical for understanding the process of industrial development from the 1820s during the 'the railway age', to use the language of an earlier generation – although he notes that the advanced regions of India did not face the ecological pressure of shortages of wood which were found in Britain and the Lower Yangzi. Parthasarathi argues that ecological relief must itself be placed in a larger political and economic context in which state policies were important in shaping the coal revolution as well as technological change more broadly. His approach to science questions its centrality for European economic change in the late eighteenth and early nineteenth centuries.

He also challenges the differentiation of science along geographical boundaries and views it as a global enterprise, arguing that, in early modern scientific endeavours, India was an important contributor and participant. (Pomeranz also points to non-European contributions to some emerging sciences, such as forestry, but emphasizes this point less than Parthasarathi.)

For Parthasarathi, ecological relief marks a later stage in the onset of divergence and becomes of central importance in the nineteenth century. In the late eighteenth century, however, a dramatic reshaping of global trade in manufactures began to take shape as Britain displaced India as the chief supplier of cotton textiles to the consumers of the world. The key to this shift was technical and organizational innovations, which, Parthasarathi argues, emerged as a response to the competitive pressures placed on Britain, as well as other regions, from Indian cotton manufacturers, combined with state policies of protection. The textile producers of India and China were not subject to these pressures and thus did not face any need to innovate, which pressed upon Western Europe (as well as other parts of the world such as the Ottoman Empire).

As can be seen from these very brief summaries, both *The Great Divergence* and *Why Europe Grew Rich and Asia Did Not* built upon long-standing lines of thinking in British economic history. Pomeranz, for instance, stands on the shoulders of E. A. Wrigley, while Parthasarathi's point of departure includes classic works such as *The Cotton Trade and Industrial Lancashire* by A. P. Wadsworth and Julia de Lacy Mann. However, both scholars take these lines and develop them in new ways as a consequence of the global and comparative frameworks which they develop.[5]

How Much Divergence, and When?

The conjunctural approaches of Pomeranz and Parthasarathi rest on arguments on the comparability of living standards, as indicated by various measures (each of them imperfect on its own), well into the eighteenth century. The divergence between Europe and Asia, or more accurately, the advanced regions in those two continents, was in their view a recent phenomenon, dating back to the late eighteenth or early nineteenth century. This position has been hotly contested, and there have been lively debates on the timing and location of divergence as measured by living standards, wages and so on. These discussions are critically important, but can quickly lead one into a thicket of fine details. Although this is not the place to wade into those details, some sense of the broad contours of the disagreements is essential.

China

One of Pomeranz's key claims, and confirmed by others, is the strength of the agricultural order in the Lower Yangzi. Robert Allen's reconstructions suggest that, as late as 1820, productivity per labour day in Yangzi Delta farming was 90 per cent of England's and that annual net income for a Delta tenant family (including a wife who made cloth part time, as was quite common) was slightly higher than for a similar English household. Another study puts labour productivity in Yangzi Delta farming c.1800 as equivalent to that of Holland, which was 94 per cent of English levels.[6] Meanwhile, land productivity was far higher in the Delta than anywhere in the world except parts of Japan and was roughly nine times that of England. Thus, the Delta's total factor productivity was also extremely high and much higher than in various European countries that did industrialize in the nineteenth century. Agricultural labour productivity in Germany, for instance, was about 50 per cent of English levels, and its land productivity was also lower.[7] These and other points challenge 'agrarian fundamentalism', which argues that readiness for industrialization must be a direct function of agricultural efficiency as this makes it possible to free labour and capital for other uses and keeps food prices, and thus wages, low.[8] Agrarian fundamentalism has also been challenged from the Indian perspective, which we will turn to shortly.

A different version of agrarian fundamentalism had also long held sway in Chinese historiography. *The Great Divergence* has generally been well received in China, but there have also been criticisms, many of which have come from scholars convinced that peasant production (as opposed to large farms largely worked by wage labour) cannot have yielded either the surpluses above subsistence or the flexibility necessary to begin sustained per capita growth. This position had long been a given of mainland Chinese historiography, but it cannot be reconciled with labour and total factor productivity figures like those cited earlier, or the impressive twentieth-century economic performances of Japan, Taiwan and, more recently, Eastern China – all places featuring small-scale farming by families with strong ownership or usufruct rights.

The Great Divergence's larger claim that living standards and per capita incomes were comparable between Europe and China, and between England and the Yangzi Delta has required some revision. Originally, Pomeranz suggested that this was probably still true in 1800, and almost certainly around 1750. The 1750 claim remains plausible, though disputed; the former less so. A 2014 paper by Stephen Broadberry, Hanhui Guan and David Daokui Li suggests a divergence in per capita GDP at a date closer to 1700 than 1750. However, this may be a sign that the range of disagreement is narrowing, since Guan and Li had previously claimed that a huge gap already existed in the fifteenth century.[9] Still more recently, Patrick O'Brien and Kent Deng have questioned the feasibility of any GDP or wage comparisons and argued for a focus on consumption, beginning with grain; even here, numbers vary, but they suggest comparability between the Lower Yangzi and England at least until 1750, and maybe beyond.[10] More recently, a group of 2021 articles by scholars who mostly remain committed to GDP calculations showed divergence occurring no earlier than the eighteenth century (and later for much of continental Europe). Taken collectively, these articles seem to suggest that divergence occurred mostly because China's economy faltered in the late eighteenth century, not because any part of Europe – even England – was firmly launched on *sustained* per capita growth before 1800.[11]

India

The debate on standards of living in India is more spatially scattered and at an earlier stage than that on China, for which there are more contributions and which are centred regionally on the Yangzi. The debate may be said to have been launched in 1998 with the publication of Parthasarathi's 'Rethinking wages and competitiveness', which has been challenged by several economic historians but most forcefully in several writings by Broadberry and Gupta.[12]

Broadberry and Gupta have summarized their position in a paper published in 2006. They argue that silver wages were substantially lower in India than in England in the seventeenth and eighteenth centuries, which is a point that Parthasarathi made in 1998 and which he argued was the reason for the competitiveness of Indian cotton cloth exports. While Parthasarathi argued that grain wages (a rough measure of the real wage) were comparable in the mid-eighteenth century, Broadberry and Gupta conclude that while they were roughly comparable in the seventeenth century – the Indian figure ranged between 80 and 95 per cent of the English – in the eighteenth century there was a sharp decline and the Indian grain wage was only 33–40 per cent of the English.[13]

This final conclusion has found support from a 2020 article on North India by Pim De Zwart and Jan Lucassen.[14]

Broadberry and Gupta's findings for the eighteenth century have been disputed by not only Parthasarathi but also Sashi Sivramkrishna. The latter has drawn upon the voluminous material contained in Francis Buchanan's account of a journey through South India, mainly Mysore, in the early nineteenth century and has showed a rough comparability of real wages based on a broader basket of consumption goods. Parthasarathi has questioned Broadberry and Gupta's conclusions as they exclude well-known estimates for earnings of outcaste labourers in agriculture, which would have represented a wage floor in South India, and derive earnings for skilled weavers that fall in the same range as those of these degraded labourers.[15]

There are other problems with the Broadberry and Gupta figures: there is no allowance for non-monetary perquisites, which Parthasarathi included in his original calculations; we have no information on how many days per week labourers worked in England and India and the extent of unemployment and underemployment (impressionistic evidence suggests that these labour market conditions favoured workers in India, where there were widespread labour shortages before the nineteenth century). Finally, Broadberry and Gupta do not provide any explanation for their findings, especially given what we know about structures of contracts and the bargaining power of labourers in the two places, which again favoured labourers in India.

Obviously the jury is still out on the question of the comparability of wages and standards of living in India and Europe. However, it is unlikely that quantitative evidence alone will be sufficient to resolve this issue, and broader conditions of work and the position of labourers in the political and economic orders must also be considered. In his original contribution, Parthasarathi brought a broad perspective to the problem, but his critics have tended to be narrowly quantitative. To continue this discussion requires a deep immersion in regional economies and deep familiarity with local conditions and prices. Broadberry and Gupta range widely over the Indian subcontinent as a whole and mix together prices from diverse areas, which can be seen in their most recent summing up of the debate. Finally, the low-estimate earnings that Broadberry and Gupta provide for the eighteenth century raise the question of how labourers survived in that period. We know from other sources such as anthropometric data that South Indian workers, for instance, shrank in size over the course of the nineteenth century. The second half of the nineteenth century was also an extraordinary period of famine in several regions of India. Why did these things not happen in the eighteenth century?[16]

Discussion

Even if we accept the most pessimistic estimates, which suggest that rough parity in standards of living had vanished by 1750 (in the case of China) or as early as 1700 (for India), this represents a major revision of previously dominant views. Angus Maddison's widely cited per capita GNP estimates, for instance, suggested that both China and India fell behind Europe centuries earlier,[17] and many other scholars claimed that a fundamental divergence had occurred by 1500, year 1000, or even earlier.[18] Fixing a precise date is probably not crucial or even possible. Nevertheless, some rough dating is needed because that will determine the universe of plausible explanations for divergence. For, if there was rough parity between the advanced regions of Eurasia in 1700, then some traditional favourite explanations would be eliminated. For instance, if the cause of divergence was, as David Landes claims, a difference between freedom and despotism that went back to ancient Greece, and gave Europeans a much greater propensity to innovate, it would be very hard to explain why East and South Asia remained so close to Europe more than 2,000 years after Pericles.[19]

Even if economic divergence came later than we once thought, a significant gap appears to have emerged by 1800 between the advanced regions of Europe and China, and perhaps between those of Europe and India as well. Certainly, the gap grew rapidly thereafter. This was largely because the productivity of non-agricultural workers exceeded that of farmers by a much greater margin in Europe and England than in China and Japan, and the number of non-farmers was growing at both ends of Eurasia.[20] Again, this suggests that explanations are best sought outside agriculture, and without relying on black-and-white contrasts between entire societies. This still leaves us far from consensus, but it narrows the range of possibilities considerably.

Divergence seems to have come earlier to unskilled wages, both urban and rural, than to living standards. Though the data are poor, especially on the Chinese side, they indicate that by the mid-eighteenth century – when other indicators still suggest close comparability between Jiangnan and advanced regions of Europe – Delta wages had already fallen far behind, resembling those of Milan or even Warsaw more than those of London.[21]

At first these two points seem irreconcilable; but a gap in real wages can be quite consistent with comparable living standards. Wage labourers were probably under 10 per cent of rural adults even in the highly commercialized Lower Yangzi, where one might expect widespread landlessness. By contrast, nearly half of the working population in England and Holland in c.1700 probably relied on wage earning.[22] Because most tenants in the Delta had strong usufruct rights, they earned much more than unskilled labourers – almost three times as much, according to the best estimates Pomeranz can put together (smallholders would have netted almost five times what a labourer earned).[23] Thus, a comparison of unskilled real wages is a comparison of the bottom of the income scale in Jiangnan with something close to the middle in northwest Europe, reconciling significant wage differences with comparable average living standards.

The Role of Institutions

Since politics as well as markets structured global trade flows, institutions are also of importance. And institutions, of course, also figure in other explanations of East–West divergence. Indeed, the variety of institutional differences that have been invoked by one scholar or another can seem endless: domestic political arrangements; property rights; contract enforcement; fiscal and financial systems; institutions for encouraging, suppressing, and/or protecting inventions; organizations for trading and building empires overseas; and so on. These debates have been a good deal broader than those about the extent and timing of divergence, and participants have often talked past each other – not only because they have been working on many different subtopics but also because it has not always been clear how to move from describing differences to assessing their significance. We here highlight a few points that have become relatively well accepted.

Although East Asian property rights and contract enforcement differed from those taking shape in northwest Europe, Pomeranz argues that they were adequate for the efficient product markets that Smithian growth requires (i.e. growth based on the expansion of the market and the extension of the division of labour).[24] When it comes to factor markets, the previous discussion of agriculture makes it hard to deny the effectiveness of Chinese (and Japanese) systems for allocating access to land. The evidence on capital markets is more mixed. It appears that capital in Japan and China was more expensive than in Europe, but the higher costs did not inhibit typical eighteenth-century kinds of economic activity such as handicraft production, commerce (including long-distance trade), agricultural improvement, or even early factories. East Asian manufacturing techniques tended to be less capital intensive than those in Europe, but not necessarily less efficient.[25] And very recent work – admittedly based on nineteenth- and early twentieth-century sources – suggests that Chinese credit markets may have been far more sophisticated and self-integrated than we had previously recognized.[26]

The biggest differences related to capital markets were in the area of public finance. European states clearly had much more effective systems for raising immediately available funds by pledging future revenues. However, it is not clear that this mattered much to the overall economic growth in early modern times, due to three crucial conditions:

a) The overwhelming majority of European government spending was for warfare, and so was not very constructive in the short run, although long-run linkages were important.

b) China, and especially Japan, faced much lower and more episodic military costs; these could generally be met by temporary exactions which were not large or frequent enough to discourage wealth accumulation.

c) The technologies available did not require either very large-scale fixed investment that took many years to fully repay initial costs (as, for instance, railroads would in the nineteenth century) or really major public investments in physical and human capital (e.g. universal schooling), some of which also took a number of years to begin yielding a return.

In the nineteenth century, all of these conditions changed. Moreover, Europe after 1800 reaped large *delayed* rewards from the overseas colonization it had carried out earlier: an activity that had required large amounts of patient capital, and was tied in various ways to military/fiscal issues. But the relevant institutions here were not simply matters of 'secure property' or 'competitive markets': they represented a much messier, and often far from liberal, set of arrangements. Perhaps the most important point here, which seems to be fairly well established, is about discontinuity. Institutions that were functional (or dysfunctional) for an economy with one set of constraints and possibilities could be much less (or more) facilitative of growth under the very different conditions of a later period.

The Role of Science

One of the most contentious areas in the divergence debate continues to be the contribution of science. Three positions may be identified in the literature. The first argues that science was not relevant, at least in the early stages of industrialization, and that it was artisanal knowledge that was important. Allen and Pomeranz are representative of this perspective.[27] The second argues that by the eighteenth century – if not even earlier – European science was critical and that what Europeans brought to the enterprise of production was in global terms a unique approach to knowledge and its application. Margaret Jacob, Joel Mokyr and Patrick O'Brien may be seen as exemplars of this position.[28] A final position may be seen as a hybrid of the two aforementioned positions and is articulated by Parthasarathi. On the one hand, it argues that the application of knowledge to production was found outside Europe, in this case early modern India; that in important respects early modern science must be seen as transcending national or continental frames and emerged from contact; and finally, this approach agrees with Allen that, in the early stages of industrialization, artisanal knowledge was more important than scientific and that the creation of knowledge of the natural world often followed technical breakthroughs.[29]

The role that European science and knowledge systems played in divergence will continue to be debated for some time. However, it is striking that economic historians address these issues in radically different ways compared with historians of science. First, historians of science have moved away from an old emphasis on the laboratory or bench top as the main site of scientific activity to include field sciences such as botany, in which there was widespread cooperation across the world. With this shift in approach, historians of science have uncovered the contributions that scientific-minded individuals outside Europe made to the development of modern science. The label 'global science' would be a more accurate description of many things that have been labelled as 'European science'. Second, historians of science have found it very difficult to connect scientific knowledge and technological change at the micro level and therefore have moved away from making blanket statements about the connection between the two. There are many instances well into the nineteenth century of major technological advances emerging in the workshop and the science that lay behind the new technology was understood only afterwards. The steam engine is the quintessential example. The scientific principles, what we know as thermodynamics, were fully worked out long after the steam engine had been put to work for many decades. Finally, the growing evidence of scientific interest in seventeenth- and eighteenth-century South Asia and political and economic interest in knowledge production for its usefulness mean that arguments for the exceptional nature of European science have to be rethought. In sum, the differing approaches of economic historians and historians of science will need to be reconciled if the debate is to advance.[30]

Telling What's Right

Both *The Great Divergence* and *Why Europe Grew Rich and Asia Did Not* drew upon generations of scholarship on the British Industrial Revolution and the industrialization of Europe more broadly. The Industrial Revolution is one of the most intensely debated events in the discipline of history. Its only rival may be the French Revolution, the other event which, along with the Industrial Revolution, gave rise to the modern world in Eric Hobsbawm's famous and enduring formulation of dual revolutions.[31]

The Great Divergence builds upon classic writings on coal and British industrialization. The energy approach may be traced back to the nineteenth century with works such as the *Coal Question* by William Stanley Jevons. In the 1930s, John Nef published a major two-volume study of the rise of the British coal industry. The most important recent exponent of the energy approach is Tony Wrigley, who, in 1988, brought coal back to the centre of the story of Britain's exceptional path of economic development. Pomeranz also draws upon the work of Eric Jones, who introduced the concept of 'ghost acres' in his classic study of divergence, *The European Miracle*, and in a more indirect way on Eric Williams's study of Caribbean slavery and English growth.

Why Europe Grew Rich and Asia Did Not picks up on other significant strands of writing on the British Industrial Revolution. The book's focus on cotton has a long lineage and may be traced back to nineteenth-century works such as Edward Baines's *History of the Cotton Manufacture in Great Britain*. In the twentieth century, cotton was central to numerous classic accounts – from that of Paul Mantoux's *The Industrial Revolution in the Eighteenth Century* to David Landes's *Unbound Prometheus* and Eric Hobsbawm's *Industry and Empire*. It was Hobsbawm who declared that 'whoever says industrial revolution says cotton'.[32] *Why Europe Grew Rich and Asia Did Not*'s periodization of British industrialization into stages, cotton followed by coal, is faithful to that offered by John Clapham.

As the overview of the debate on divergence has indicated, the lines of debate and disagreement are many. These revolve around the relative 'levels' of economic development in the advanced areas of Europe and Asia, the nature of the industrialization process, the contribution of institutions, and the contribution of science and knowledge to that process. How are we to judge between competing explanations and settle upon which one is right or true?

In the case of several of these issues, adjudicating between different positions rests on the interpretation of qualitative data.[33] The contribution of institutions to the process of economic development or the level of scientific knowledge is not amenable to quantification; thus, to some extent, the judgement of these factors is subjective and 'in the eye of the beholder'. The interpretation of these sorts of factors is made more difficult by the lack of research on them in the Asian context, and thus places limits on our historical knowledge. The historical scholarship is far thinner on science in the seventeenth and eighteenth centuries for India than for Europe, for example.

A focus on factors that can be quantified is not a solution to this dilemma. If only such factors, such as wages, incomes, and prices, are part of the analysis, important dimensions of social, cultural, economic and political life, which play a significant role in economic development, could be excluded. Quantification does not eliminate the interpretive and subjective elements that are present in the case of qualitative evidence. Making sense of quantitative evidence is no less 'in the eye of the beholder'.

The creation of quantitative data rests upon hundreds, if not thousands, of judgements, each of which can introduce error into the final figures. This is the case today when economists construct national income and other figures of economic performance. However, these difficulties are compounded when dealing with historical data and are made worse the further back we go. Eric Hobsbawm, who was not averse to quantification but recognized the difficulties, put it well more than fifty years ago when he pointed to the complexities of calculating money wages for even British workers in the nineteenth century: 'We know next to nothing of what people actually earned. How much overtime or short time did they work? How often were they unemployed and for how long? Who knows?'[34] Converting these money wages into real wages introduces further pitfalls and is no easy task even in contemporary times. Hobsbawm writes: 'We know from modern experience how full of pitfalls cost-of-living indices can be even in our own time, when considerable efforts are made to collect statistics specially for their compilation.'[35]

Kent Deng and Patrick O'Brien have pointed to a number of these same issues in a critical review of the wage and price data that are available for China. They urge scholars to 'remain sceptical towards all published comparisons of wage levels and trends for the Chinese and by extension other Asian empires'.[36] While their careful analysis focuses on the sources for a quantitative economic history of China, they conclude that the same limitations apply to those for India and the Middle East.

Even if we were able to assemble quantitative information that was able to accurately represent economic reality, that data would still have to be interpreted, which is neither simple nor straightforward. Stephen Marglin, in his classic comparison of economic paradigms, writes that it is difficult to conclude on the basis of empirical tests whether neoclassical or non-neoclassical frameworks better describe the workings of the economy because even sophisticated statistical analysis yields results that are consistent with both theoretical approaches.[37] Marglin draws this conclusion from the analysis of savings in the US economy, and the difficulty is that the results of even sophisticated statistical analysis are consistent with a number of approaches to why individuals and firms save.

What is one to do? Marglin argues:

We must either back off from purely empirical means of distinguishing between theories, or despair of sorting out the competing claims. Consistent positivists should prefer agnosticism. The rest of us will prefer to look more closely at the premises of the theories … to examine the extent to which these theories correspond to a plausible conception of the world. In short, if we are to choose between theories of saving at this stage of our knowledge, it must be on the basis of their inherent plausibility.[38]

Applying Marglin's recommendation to the divergence debate, a plausible explanation must take into account *all* the available evidence, both quantitative and qualitative. At a minimum, such an explanation must acknowledge three important facts about China, India and the global economy in the period between 1600 and 1900. First, for 200 years, the advanced regions of China and India maintained what might be thought of as export surpluses.[39] These regions shipped large quantities of manufactured goods throughout the world, cotton textiles in the case of India and porcelains and silk cloth (as well as an agricultural product, tea) in the case of China, in exchange for silver, and in the Indian case, to a lesser extent gold. These exports suggest that these regions possessed sophisticated economies and commercial systems, which were able to maintain a competitive hegemony for a period of centuries. Second, the military encounters between Europeans and Asians were more or less evenly matched till the early nineteenth century, which indicates that technological capability was comparable and that technological development in places like India was not stagnant.[40] Finally, it is widely acknowledged that the economies of the advanced regions of India and China regressed in the nineteenth century. This regression suggests some degree of prosperity in the eighteenth century from which the economies of these areas fell back.

The Divergence Debate in China and India

In the English-speaking-and-reading world, the divergence debate has been dominated by scholars based in the United States and Western Europe. However, a surprising degree of discussion of the question has been taking place in East Asia. South Asia, by contrast, has witnessed very limited interest in the issue, perhaps because of the decline in economic history in what had been major global centres of research in economic history, such as the Delhi School of Economics.

Driven by scholars in China and some Western Sinologists, two pre-existing debates in Chinese historiography have been connected to that on divergence. One debate was about whether the late imperial Chinese economy had contained within it 'sprouts of capitalism', and if so, what had prevented them from blossoming. The second debate ensued as it became clear that the absence of a thorough capitalist transformation in China could not be fully explained by external forces such as the Manchu conquest in the seventeenth century or Western imperialism in the nineteenth as some scholars had suggested, and therefore, had to have explanations rooted in Chinese society.[41] This discussion centred on to what extent rural China in particular could have experienced any sustained per capita growth within the late imperial social system, and what the relationship might be between the limited (or according to some, non-existent) extent of per capita growth and the undoubted growth in population during the late imperial period. Both these debates thus take us back to 'agrarian fundamentalism', but in two rather different guises: one essentially Marxist, the other Malthusian.

The Marxist debate has analogues in Indian history, particularly Mughal, where in the 1960s the 'potentialities of capitalist development' in Mughal India were explored, most extensively by Irfan Habib. Since then, South Asian history has moved away from the applicability of these types of totalizing frameworks that have been derived from the European historical experience, which marked a larger retreat from Marxism. An important moment in this shift was the debate in the *Journal of Peasant Studies* in the early 1980s on the applicability of feudalism to medieval India, which was initiated by Harbans Mukhia. Parthasarathi developed Mukhia's insights to query the utility of the category of capitalism for the study of early modern India in a volume of essays in honour of Mukhia.[42]

In Chinese economic history, one of the central debates in the People's Republic of China – which, not coincidentally, often focused on the *advanced* Yangzi Delta – concerned the so-called 'sprouts of capitalism': whether or not one could find in the sixteenth to eighteenth centuries an emerging Chinese capitalism that was then aborted by the Qing conquest of 1644 (or for some scholars, by the Opium War of 1839–42). The emphasis in this debate was firmly on identifying China's dominant 'mode of production' in a Marxist sense, and development was charted above all based on evidence that wage labour was becoming increasingly prevalent (with a subsidiary effort to track growing markets for land and capital), rather than by looking for changes in per capita income, productivity or technology.[43] While many scholars were, by the late

1980s, increasingly unsatisfied with this focus, it was not clear what might replace it in Chinese historiography.

More than anyone else, Li Bozhong began to push Chinese economic history towards an emphasis on output, rather than labour relations. He also argued for a long period of slow but generally steady per capita growth based on market-driven organizational and technical change, beginning perhaps as early as the eighth century, but becoming particularly strong between the mid-sixteenth and mid-nineteenth centuries.[44] Some important senior scholars once associated with the 'sprouts' debate, such as Wu Chengming, endorsed Li's approach, though most have not been willing to go as far as he did; the scholars who were impressed by Li's work have been generally receptive to *The Great Divergence*.

The Sinologists who have been most sceptical about *The Great Divergence*, both in China and in the United States, have been those who have combined some influences from the 'sprouts of capitalism' literature with a strong emphasis on the negative consequences of late imperial population growth. Probably the most notable has been the Chinese–American historian Philip Huang (Huang Zongzhi); while based for many years at the University of California, Los Angeles (UCLA), Huang has also been active in scholarly circles in China. Huang reaffirmed the argument of his UCLA colleague Robert Brenner that only capitalist farms based on wage labour (and ruthlessly minimizing costs by driving 'excess' workers off the land) could generate rising labour productivity, capital accumulation and sustained growth. Much of Brenner's work has been devoted to insisting that these essential dynamics emerged only in England, and to explaining why.[45]

In an influential 1990 book, Huang took China, including the Yangzi Delta, to represent an even more extreme case of the qualitative stagnation that Brenner attributes to continental Europe. As he sees it, most Chinese peasants held on to their land (much like in France, but unlike in Britain). As population grew and plot sizes shrank, they had to maximize per acre yields; this is what enabled them to pay such high rents that landlords had no incentive to replace them with wage labourers. These high yields were achieved by working extraordinary numbers of labour days per acre, and by putting even more days into labour-intensive handicrafts; this labour intensification continued even at the cost of reducing peasants' earnings per labour day to extraordinarily low levels. Households working this hard could sustain large families, but only at bare subsistence levels, and at the cost of further increasing pressure on the land in the next generation. This locked in a process of numerical growth that was the antithesis of true development, and which Huang calls 'involution'.[46]

This is not the place to rehearse all the details of the debate that followed.[47] Suffice it to say that Pomeranz's views have largely prevailed, in part because the debate uncovered a basic error in Huang's work: in estimating the earnings per labour day for Yangzi Delta weavers, he misplaced a decimal point, throwing his calculations of gross earnings off by a factor of 10 (and of net earnings by even more).

Unsurprisingly, it is the sections of *The Great Divergence* that deal with China (as opposed to Europe or other places) that have excited the most interest in China. Most of that discussion has treated the book as part of a larger 'California school', which has become the topic of a number of articles. The members of this 'California school' vary with the person defining it – which is hardly surprising since it has never had a firm institutional identity or a complete consensus on the issues – but R. Bin Wong, James Lee and his collaborators, Li Bozhong, Robert Marks, Richard Von Glahn, Jack Goldstone and Pomeranz are usually included.

Chinese responses to this 'school' have naturally been varied, but it is fair to say that it has stimulated increased interest in comparative history within China. Moreover, this has been comparative history which, unlike the 'sprouts' and 'involution' literatures, goes beyond comparing China to a 'typical' (i.e. stylized European capitalist) path. In fact, one common feature of 'California school' comparisons has been an insistence that neither society should be treated as defining a norm from which the other society is a deviation.[48] It has helped stimulate new approaches to the Qing era, in which the state is (for better or worse) a less overwhelming presence, and the motors of social change are to be found elsewhere in society. Increased interest has been paid to long-run, slowly developing trends in Chinese society – perhaps going all the way back to the Song dynasty – that continue up into the twentieth century. Such a view, quite forcefully expressed in a conference volume called *The Song-Yuan-Ming Transition*,[49] seems to be replacing older stories in which 'revolutionary' changes in Song and late Ming were followed by equally sharp reversals, frustrating what both Marxism and Western modernization theory thought 'should' have happened next, and defining Chinese history in terms of those alleged blockages.

Conclusion

As this chapter has shown, the debate on divergence is remarkably broad, touching upon not only prices and incomes, the traditional bread and butter of economic historians, but also ranging far and wide to include science, rationality, the environment, politics and the state. While the debate has raised difficult empirical questions, it has also brought to the fore equally challenging problems of method. Its sheer scope and complexity make the question an enduring one not only for historians but also for a range of social scientists from sociologists to economists and political scientists. It will continue to remain a central problem for decades to come.

Notes

1. K. Marx (1978 [1853]), 'The future results of British Rule in India', in R. C. Tucker (ed.), *The Marx-Engels Reader*. New York: Norton, 659.

2. M. Weber (1930), *The Protestant Ethic and the Spirit of Capitalism*, trans. Talcott Parsons. New York: Scribner; M. Weber (1951), *The Religion of China*, trans. H. H. Gerth. New York: Free Press; M. Weber (1958), *The Religion of India*, trans. H. H. Gerth and D. Martindale. New York: Free Press.

3. D. C. North and R. P. Thomas (1973), *The Rise of the Western World: A New Economic History*. Cambridge: Cambridge University Press; E. L. Jones (1981), *The European Miracle: Environments, Economies, and Geopolitics in the History of Europe and Asia*. Cambridge: Cambridge University Press; D. Landes (1998), *The Wealth and Poverty of Nations*. New York: W. W. Norton; J. Mokyr (2002), *The Gifts of Athena: Historical Origins of the Knowledge Economy*. Princeton, NJ: Princeton University Press.

4. K. Pomeranz (2002), *The Great Divergence: China, Europe, and the Making of the Modern World Economy*. Princeton, NJ: Princeton University Press; P. Parthasarathi (2012), *Why Europe Grew Rich and Asia Did Not: Global Economic Divergence, 1600–1850*. Cambridge: Cambridge University Press.

5. E. A. Wrigley (1988), *Continuity, Chance and Change: The Character of the Industrial Revolution in England*. Cambridge: Cambridge University Press; A. P. Wadsworth and J. de Lacy Mann (1931), *The Cotton Trade and Industrial Lancashire*. Manchester: Manchester University Press.

6. B. Li and J. L. van Zanden (2012), 'Before the Great Divergence? Comparing the Yangzi Delta and the Netherlands at the beginning of the nineteenth century', *Journal of Economic History*, 72 (4), 956–89.

7. R. C. Allen (2000), 'Economic structure and agricultural productivity in Europe, 1300–1800', *European Review of Economic History*, 4 (1), 20.

8. See for instance R. Brenner (1985), 'Agrarian class structure and economic development', and 'The agrarian roots of European capitalism', in T. H. Aston and C. H. Philpin (eds), *The Brenner Debate*. Cambridge: Cambridge University Press, 10–63, and 213–327; M. Overton (1996), *Agricultural Revolution in England: The Transformation of the Agrarian Economy 1500–1800*. Cambridge: Cambridge University Press. For the term 'agrarian fundamentalism' see R. C. Allen (1992), *Enclosure and the Yeoman: The Agricultural Development of the South Midlands*. New York: Oxford University Press, 2–3.

9. S. Broadberry, H. Guan and D. Li (2014), 'China, Europe, and the Great Divergence: A study in historical national accounting, 980–1850', http://eh.net/eha/wp-content/uploads/2014/05/Broadberry.pdf. Guan and Li had previously argued that China was far behind by the fifteenth century, if not earlier, and had fallen even further behind over the succeeding centuries. See H. Guan and D. Li (2010), 'Mingdai GDP ji jiegou shitan' [A study of GDP and its structure in China's Ming dynasty], *Zhongguo jingji jikan*, 9 (3), 787–829, http://en.cnki.com.cn/Article_en/CJFDTotal-JJXU201003003.htm.

10. P. K. O'Brien and K. Deng (2016), 'Nutritional standards of living in England and the Yangtze Delta (Jiangnan), circa. 1644 – circa 1820: Clarifying data for reciprocalcomparisons', *Journal of World History*, 26 (2), 233–67; P. K. O'Brien and K. Deng (2017), 'How well did the facts travel to support protracted debate on the history of the Great Divergence between Western Europe and Imperial China?' February 2017, available at New Economics Papers, http://econpapers.repec.org/paper/pramprapa/77276.htm; K. Pomeranz (2017), 'The data we have vs. the data we want: A comment on the date of the Divergence Debate', Pt. I and Pt II, New Economics Papers (8 June 2017), https://nephist.wordpress.com/2017/06/06/the-data-we-have-vs-the-data-we-need-a-comment-on-the-state-of-the-divergence-debate-part-ii/ (Part 1, immediately below).

11. J. Goldstone (2021), 'Dating the Great Divergence', with comments by Stephen Broadberry, Paolo Malanima, Jan Luiten Van Zanden and Jutta Bolt, and a response by Goldstone, *Journal of Global History*, 16 (2), 266–314. For a discussion of these articles, plus several others that take similar approaches but discuss other parts of Europe, see Pomeranz's preface to the 2021 edition of *The Great Divergence*, Princeton, NJ: Princeton University Press.

12. P. Parthasarathi (1998), 'Rethinking wages and competitiveness in the eighteenth century: Britain and South India', *Past & Present*, 98, 79–109.

13. S. Broadberry and B. Gupta (2006), 'The early modern Great Divergence: wages, prices and economic development in Europe and Asia, 1500–1800', *Economic History Review*, 59 (1), 2–31.

14. P. de Zwart and J. Lucassen (2020), 'Poverty or prosperity in North India? New evidence on real wages, 1590s to 1870s', *Economic History Review*, 73 (3), 644–67. See also J. Lucassen and R. Seshan (eds) (2022), *Wage Earners in India, 1500–1900: Regional Approaches to an International Context*. New Delhi: Sage.

15. S. Sivaramakrishna (2009), 'Ascertaining living standards in erstwhile Mysore, Southern India, from Francis Buchanan's *Journey* of 1800–01: An empirical contribution to the Great Divergence debate', *Journal of the Economic and Social History of the Orient*, 52 (3), 695–733; Parthasarathi, *Why Europe Grew Rich and Asia Did Not*, 37–46.

16. L. Brennan, J. McDonald and R. Shlomowitz (1994), 'Trends in the economic well-being of South Indians under British rule: The anthropometric evidence', *Explorations in Economic History*, 31 (2), 225–60; M. Davis (2002), *Late Victorian Holocausts: El Niño Famines and the Making of the Third World*. London: Verso.

17. A. Maddison (2001), *The World Economy: A Millennial Perspective*. Paris: OECD, 42, suggesting that Western Europe overtook China in *c*.1300.

18. See D. Lal (1998), *Unintended Consequences: The Impact of Factor Endowments, Culture, and Politics on Long-Run Economic Performance*. Cambridge, MA: MIT Press; London: Eyre Methuen; E. Jones (1987), *The European Miracle*, 2nd edn. Cambridge: Cambridge University Press; I. Wallerstein (1976), *The Modern World-System*, vol. 1. New York: Academic Press.

19. Landes, *The Wealth and Poverty*, 33–5, 59, and *passim*.

20. See Li and van Zanden, 'Before the Great Divergence'.

21. R. C. Allen, J. P. Bassino, D. Ma, C. Moll-Murata and J. L. Van Zanden (2011), 'Wages, prices and living standards in China 1738–1925: In comparison with Europe, Japan, and India', *Economic History Review*, 64 (1), 8–38. This article's estimates of agricultural wages in China are, as the authors note, actually very close to Pomeranz's. R. C. Allen (2009), 'Agricultural productivity and rural incomes in England and the Yangzi Delta, *ca*.1620–1820', *Economic History Review*, 62 (3), 544, suggests that Lower Yangzi wages were about the same as English ones in the mid-seventeenth century, and Delta peasants were far more prosperous than English farm labourers at that time. Ibid., 546. And see R. C. Allen (2004), 'Mr. Lockyer meets the index number problem: The standard of living in Canton and London in 1704', available at http://www.iisg.nl/hpw/papers/allen.pdf, for a different (smaller) dataset, suggesting comparable wages in Canton and London in 1704.

22. C. Tilly (1984), 'Demographic origins of the European proletariat', in D. Levine (ed.), *Proletarianization and Family History*. Orlando, FL: Academic Press, 1–85 uses a looser definition, and gets even higher figures: see esp. 36.

23. Calculations in K. Pomeranz (2006), 'Standards of living in rural and urban China: Preliminary estimates for the mid-eighteenth and early twentieth centuries'. Paper for Panel 77, World Economic History Congress, Helsinki.

24. On market integration in China and Europe, see W. Keller and C. Shiue (2007), 'Markets in China and Europe on the eve of the Industrial Revolution', *American Economic Review*, 97 (4), 1189–216.

25. See esp. J. L. Rosenthal and R. B. Wong (2011), *Before and Beyond Divergence: The Politics of Economic Change in China and Europe*. Cambridge, MA: Harvard University Press. See also Pomeranz, *The Great Divergence*, 180–2, on why interest rates per se may not be the best indicators of whether credit markets were obstructing development.

26. See especially M. Lowenstein (2021), 'Financial markets in Late Imperial China, 1820–1911', PhD dissertation, University of Chicago.

27. R. C. Allen (2009), *The British Industrial Revolution in Global Perspective*. Cambridge: Cambridge University Press; Pomeranz, *The Great Divergence*.

28. M. Jacob (2014), *The First Knowledge Economy: Human Capital and the European Economy, 1750–1850*. Cambridge: Cambridge University Press; Mokyr, *Gifts of Athena*; and Patrick O'Brien's chapter in this volume.

29. Parthasarathi, *Why Europe Grew Rich and Asia Did Not*, ch. 7.

30. H. J. Cook (2007), *Matters of Exchange: Commerce, Medicine, and Science in the Dutch Golden Age*. New Haven, CT: Yale University Press; K. Raj (2007), *Relocating Modern Science: Circulation and the Construction of Scientific Knowledge in South Asia and Europe*. Delhi: Permanent Black.

31. E. J. Hobsbawm (1962), *The Age of Revolutions: Europe, 1789–1848*. London: Weidenfield & Nicolson.

32. E. J. Hobsbawm (1969), *Industry and Empire*. London: Penguin, 56.

33. See the chapter by Jack A. Goldstone in this volume.

34. E. J. Hobsbawm (1964), *Labouring Men: Studies in the History of Labour*. London: Weidenfield & Nicolson, 107.

35. Hobsbawm, *Labouring Men*.

36. K. Deng and P. K. O'Brien (2016), 'Establishing statistical foundations of a chronology for the great divergence: A survey and critique of the primary sources for the construction of relative wage levels for Ming–Qing China', *Economic History Review*, 69 (4), 1075. Also see K. Deng and P. K. O'Brien (2016), 'China's GDP per capita from the Han Dynasty to communist times', *World Economics*, 17 (2), 79–123; and Deng and O'Brien (2017), 'How well did the facts travel?'

37. S. A. Marglin (1984), *Growth, Distribution, and Prices*. Cambridge, MA: Harvard University Press, ch. 18.

38. Marglin, *Growth, Distribution, and Prices*, 430.

39. But on the dangers of treating precious metals as equivalent to modern money, as an 'export surplus' reading does, see D. O. Flynn (1995), 'Arbitrage, China, and world trade in the early modern period', *Journal of the Economic and Social History of the Orient*, 38 (4), 429–48; and D. O. Flynn and A. Giráldez (1997), 'Introduction', in D. O. Flynn and A. Giráldez (eds), *Metals and Monies in an Emerging World Economy*. Aldershot: Variorum, xv–xl.

40. It might be objected here that since the battles were fought in Asia, leaving Europeans with very long supply lines, this is a risky inference. But for an argument that the decisive advantage of East India Company forces in India was not technological, see K. Roy (2011), 'The hybrid military establishment of the East India Company in South Asia, 1750–1849', *Journal of Global History*, 6 (2), 195–218.

41. It is worth noting that the earlier preference for externally driven explanations of Chinese 'failure' was convenient both for mainland scholars committed to the universality of a rigid Marxist set of stages of society and for nationalists wishing to emphasize the damage done to China by imperialism.

42. T. J. Byres and H. Mukhia (eds) (1985), *Feudalism and Non-European Societies*. London: Frank Cass; P. Parthasarathi (2008), 'Was there capitalism in early-modern Indian history?' in R. Datta (ed.), *Rethinking a Millennium: Perspectives on Indian History from the Eighth to the Eighteenth Century: Essays for Harbans Mukhia*. New Delhi: Aakar Publications, 342–60.

43. W. Chengming (1985), *Zhongguo zibenzhuyi yu guonei shichang* [Chinese capitalism and the national market]. Beijing: Zhongguo shehui kexue chubanshe; and X. Dixin and W. Chengming (1985), *Zhongguo zibenzhuyi de mengya* [The sprouts of capitalism in China]. Beijing: Zhongguo shehui kexue chubanshe, are the most important compendia of this work.

44. B. Li (1998), *Agricultural Development in Jiangnan, 1620–1850*. New York: St. Martin's Press; B. Li (2000), *Jiangnan de zaoqi gongyehua* [Proto-industrialization in Jiangnan]. Beijing: Shehui kexue wenxian chubanshe; B. Li (2003), *Fazhan yu zhiyue: Ming Qing Jiangnan shengchanli yanjiu* [Development and constraint: Research on productive capacity in Ming-Qing Jiangnan]. Taibei: Lianjing; B. Li (2005), 'Farm labour productivity in Jiangnan', in R. C. Allen, T. Bengtsson and M. Dribe (eds), *Living Standards in the Past: New Perspectives on Well-Being in Asia and Europe*. Oxford: Oxford University Press, 55–76; B. Li (2010), *Zhongguo de zaoqi jindai jingji: Huating-Louxian diqu GDP yanjiu* [China's early modern economy: Research in the GDP of the Huating-Louxian region]. Beijing: Zhonghua shuju.

45. R. Brenner (1985), 'Agrarian class structure and economic development', and 'The agrarian roots of European capitalism'; R. Brenner and C. Isett (2002), 'England's divergence from the Yangzi Delta: Property relations, microeconomics, and patterns of development', *Journal of Asian Studies*, 61 (2), 609–62. Pomeranz's complete answer to Brenner is not yet published (it is supposed to appear in a long-delayed volume based on a debate held at UCLA) but some comments are included in K. Pomeranz (2009), *La Force de L'Empire: Révolution industrielle et écologie, ou pourquoi l'angleterre a fait mieux que la Chine*, ed. with an introduction by Philippe Minard. Alfortville: Éditions ère, coll. 'Chercheurs d'ère', 77–110.

46. P. Huang (1990), *The Peasant Family and Rural Development in the Lower Yangzi Region, 1350–1988*. Stanford, CA: Stanford University Press.

47. P. Huang (2002), 'Development or involution in eighteenth century Britain and China? A review of Kenneth Pomeranz's *The Great Divergence: China, Europe and the Making of the Modern World Economy*', *Journal of Asian Studies*, 61 (2), 501–38; P. Huang (2002), 'Fazhan haishi neijuan? Shiba shiji Yingguo yu Zhongguo – Ping Peng Mulan 'Da fenliu: Ouzhou, Zhongguo ji xinadai shijie jingji de fazhan', *Lishi yanjiu*, 149–76; P. Huang (2003), 'Further thoughts on eighteenth-century Britain and China: Rejoinder to Pomeranz's response to my critique', *Journal of Asian Studies*, 62 (1), 157–67; K. Pomeranz (2002), 'Beyond the East–West binary: Resituating development paths in the eighteenth century world', *Journal of Asian Studies*, 61 (2), 539–90; K. Pomeranz (2003), 'Facts are stubborn things: A response to Philip Huang', *Journal of Asian Studies*, 62 (1), 167–81; K. Pomeranz (2003), 'Shijie jingji shi zhong de jinshi Jiangnan: bijiao yu zonghe guancha' [Early modern Jiangnan in global economic history: Comparative and integrative perspectives], *Lishi yanjiu*, 284, 3–48. See also essays by R. B. Wong (2003), 'Integrating China into world history', *Journal of Asian Studies*, posted at www.aasianst.org/catalog/wong.pdf; J. A. Goldstone (2003), 'Europe vs. Asia: Missing data and misconceptions', *Science and Society*, 67 (2), 184–94; J. Lee, C. Campbell and F. Wang (2002), 'Positive check or Chinese checks?' *Journal of Asian Studies*, 61 (2), 591–607; S. Cao and Y. Chen (2002), 'Maerasi lilun he Qingdai yilaide de Zhongguo renkou: ping Meiguo xuezhe jinnianlai de xiangguan yanjiu' [Malthusian theory and Chinese population from the Qing dynasty onwards: A critique of recent American scholarship], *Lishi yanjiu*, 275, 41–54; and A. Wolf (2001), 'Is there evidence of birth control in late Imperial China?', *Population and Development Review* 27 (1), 133–54, among others.

48. R. B. Wong (1997), *China Transformed: Historical Change and the Limits of European Experience*. Ithaca, NY: Cornell University Press; Pomeranz (2000), *The Great Divergence*.

49. P. Smith and R. von Glahn (eds) (2003), *The Song-Yuan-Ming Transition in Chinese History*. Cambridge, MA: Harvard University Press.

CHAPTER 2
DATA AND DATING THE GREAT DIVERGENCE
Jack A. Goldstone

The Problem of the Great Divergence

Since the classic works of Karl Marx and Max Weber, a distinction has been drawn between dynamic European economies, which in an early modern period experienced the onset of modern economic growth, and Asian societies, particularly China, which were considered to have remained economically stagnant until they were overwhelmed by Western influences in the nineteenth century.[1] In this view, since at least 1500 (some scholars place the date earlier, in the Italian Renaissance or even medieval times), an accumulation of capital and productive technologies began in Europe that had no equal outside the continent.[2] By 1800, Europe's industrialization was enabled and propelled by prior economic advances that had already long supported more consumption, more innovation, more consistent income growth and more production per head than in any other major world economy.

This process was not synchronous across Europe; various countries took the lead at different times. Yet scholars see this as a *single process*. Italy made its contribution in the Renaissance; then the Netherlands made their contribution in the sixteenth and seventeenth centuries; England made its contribution in the eighteenth and early nineteenth centuries, then Germany in the late nineteenth and early twentieth centuries. Cumulatively they put Europe on a steady path of rising income between 1500 and 1900.

Twenty years ago, a small group of scholars, based mainly in California, argued that this view, which had prevailed among researchers for over a hundred years, was profoundly mistaken.[3] What has been defined as the 'California School' has drawn on new scholarship in China's economic and social history[4] as well as that on Japan, India and the Ottoman Empire, to argue that despite differences in culture and politics, the economic and technological conditions in Europe were not greatly superior to those previously achieved in the leading Asian empires until the early nineteenth century. The Great Divergence that was apparent by the middle of the nineteenth century, with Europe enjoying clearly superior military and economic technology, and rapid and sustained growth in both population and income per capita, was thus a far more recent phenomenon, starting not much before 1800, or about 300 years later than was previously thought.

Members of the California School did not agree on what caused the Great Divergence. Pomeranz fell back on the established idea of capital accumulation, arguing that Europe's access to convenient coal and to land reserves in overseas colonies provided a key advantage. Andre Gunder Frank argued that Europe surged ahead of China only because of the temporary failure of China's political institutions in the late Qing. Bin Wong and Jack Goldstone put more emphasis on Europe's scientific and engineering advances that began to accumulate over the course of the eighteenth century. Since then, others have argued that labour/capital ratios, or physical geography, better political organization, or still other factors were responsible, on various time scales.[5]

Unfortunately, despite the importance of this dispute to understanding the major patterns of world history for the last millennium, the arguments on both sides were made with data that were, admittedly, fragmentary. Ideally, it would have been desirable to have annual or at least decadal data on GDP and GDP per capita to assess the rates and levels of economic growth in various regions and societies since at least 1500. But, of course, GDP as a concept and measure was only invented in the twentieth century. Scholars have thus had to make do with proxies for living standards, including wills and testaments, tax assessments, estimates of farm income, scattered wage contracts, and estimates of consumption of agricultural and manufactured goods. Estimates of output based on trade data, tax rolls, diaries, gazetteers and handbooks, and census data (where available) have also been used.

To get at levels of economic development, one also has to determine economic output per capita. This requires data on population, which is severely limited before modern censuses. Some pre-modern censuses were compiled, but these are only available at long intervals, sometimes centuries, during which wars and plagues may have greatly altered the population. Such censuses usually focused on households, not individuals, and households varied in size and composition across regions and times. Parish records in Catholic and Anglican countries provide excellent local data, as do lineage records in Asia, with identification of specific individuals by birth, marriage, death and households. But such information is painstaking and difficult to collect and aggregate.[6]

Things get even more complex when we compare different world regions: what geographical or social unit should be the basis for estimation? Is it fair to compare income levels in Holland, which was the richest, most urban, and most internationally supplied portion of the still-small country of the Netherlands – which was in turn the richest and most urbanized country in Northern Europe for several centuries – with the much larger and more diverse countries of England and Wales, or France, much less China? Pomeranz tried to compare what he called the 'most advanced' regions of Europe and China, but even here, how to proceed? Should one take the Yangzi delta in the seventeenth and eighteenth centuries, as he did, which is still a diverse region of 25 million in population, and compare it with regions such as England (6 million) or the Netherlands (2 million) or even Holland (800,000)? Also when should one make the comparison? Each region had its own economic cycles of prosperity and decay, and comparing one region during a boom with another during a slump could give a very misleading picture of longer-term conditions.

The Challenge of New Data

Given the enormous difficulties discussed above, the creation of a comprehensive set of national accounts for Britain and Holland from 1500 to 1800 that are unprecedented in their comprehensiveness and detail is a true achievement.[7] Such datasets survey agriculture, including grain and livestock and other crops; output in manufacturing, including the production of textiles, ceramics, leather goods, mining and metals, soap, beer, books and so on; and services, analysing trade and transport, finance, housing, and government spending. They attempt to track output in each of these sectors year by year over several centuries, in some cases going all the way back to the early Middle Ages.

These estimates open up new possibilities for evaluating several of the arguments over the Great Divergence. One can scrutinize the national accounts for Britain and Holland to seek internal patterns: by what dates do they seem to have achieved a self-sustaining pattern of growth in income per head? We can compare these data with more fragmentary but still useful estimates of output per capita in other times and places to ask: by what dates do they seem to have achieved a level of income per capita that goes beyond levels previously achieved in pre-modern times? Finally, this income data can be checked against other sources and estimates for consistency, such as data on physical heights or competing estimates of consumption.

As far as the compilers of the new data are concerned, some feel they have now firmly dated the origins of the Great Divergence, and that their data strongly support the classical view that it began centuries before 1800. They argue that the data show early and sustained growth in GDP per capita in northwest Europe, starting from the late Middle Ages. This is a return to the views of scholars such as Fernand Braudel, Immanuel Wallerstein and Carlo Cipolla, who saw a commercial revolution starting in the thirteenth and fourteenth centuries in Europe with great fairs and growing cities, and trade then expanding through the age of exploration and colonial empires from the sixteenth through the nineteenth centuries.[8] All this created a distinctive growth path in Europe long before the Industrial Revolution. For example, De Pleijt and van Zanden state that the Industrial Revolution was 'a continuation of trends going back to the late Middle Ages'.[9] Rather than seeing the process as uniform across Europe, these compilers of the new GDP data argue that this process began with a 'Little Divergence' in which first the Netherlands and then Britain launched on the path to higher income per head while other parts of Europe fell behind; at the same time, the great empires of Asia were falling into stagnation or decline from now distant medieval peaks of productivity, leaving only northwest Europe poised to develop further into industrial nations. However, other scholars, such as Broadberry and his collaborators, do grant that the Great Divergence arose much later, around 1700, though they identify this mainly as the date from which China's economy badly falters rather than the date from which northwest Europe surges forward.[10]

This chapter focuses on identifying the date at which economic growth becomes distinctly *modern*. By *modern* economic growth, I mean the ability to sustain *both* significant increases in population *and* increases in income per capita over many decades. This does happen first in Europe, specifically in Great Britain. I argue that the new GDP studies, on closer scrutiny, show that there was a sharp break in the pattern of economic growth only *after* 1750, and that there is no evidence of an exceptional pattern of sustained or rapid growth in GDP per capita in Europe before that.

This chapter proceeds as follows. First, I show that while Holland had a very impressive efflorescence of growth in real income during its sixteenth-century Golden Age, it thereafter returned to a centuries-long stagnation. Next, I demonstrate that before 1750 England did not experience both population growth and significant growth in income per capita. Finally, I compare the levels of income per capita found in Holland and Britain with data on GDP per capita from other times and places. They show that the economic achievements of Holland and Britain before 1800 are notable but not unprecedented. When industrialization arose in Europe, it therefore came without any steady advances in income per capita, or attainment of exceptional pre-industrial incomes, during earlier periods.

Dutch Economic Growth, 1510–1800: Efflorescence or Modern Growth?

In 2002, I introduced the concept of 'efflorescences' in economic history to counter the notion that all nations' economic history was binary – that there was only Malthusian stagnation or modern steady increases in income.[11] I argued that while most pre-modern economies were usually bound by Malthusian constraints, unable to sustain any growth in income per capita if population was growing, there were exceptions to the rule scattered throughout history.

At various times, even pre-modern societies made breakthroughs in productivity through improvements in agricultural tools and practices (in the use of animals, crops, and crop rotations); through improvements in energy and water transport (windmills, watermills, exploiting peat or coal, new designs for boats and canals); the importation or creation of new production techniques and products (e.g. for paper, silk, ceramics, metals, glass or textiles); or advances in organization and finance (e.g. more extensive and systematic accounting, banking, credit, insurance and monetary instruments). The added value of these advances encouraged higher levels of urbanization and of trade. More extensive trade, both within the society and without, led to further gains from exploiting comparative advantage, which often involved taking market share from other regions. Such a burst of creativity could augment population increase, leading to a rapid rise in both population and income per capita, thus breaking the Malthusian bounds through 'Schumpeterian' or innovation-led growth. In such periods – often deemed 'Golden Ages' – even pre-modern societies start to look more 'modern', as surging productivity, gains in the service sector and investments in libraries and education, and high levels of cultural production and consumption created a richer and more diversified economy and lifestyles. Whether in Song China (remarkable for its production of iron), or the Caliphate of Baghdad (famed for its libraries as well as its science), Renaissance Italy (renowned for its art), or Golden Age Holland (bustling with trade and manufacturing), such episodes set standards for sophistication that often stood for centuries.

Yet unlike in modern economic growth, where we have seen centuries of steady increases in output per capita, such episodes usually lasted only a few decades. Once the gains of the initial productivity breakthroughs had been absorbed and exhausted, there were no further such 'Schumpeterian' gains. At that point, population growth would again push against the new resource boundary. At best, slowing population growth and much more moderate gains in total output could sustain the prior levels of GDP per capita; but there would be no further marked gains in GDP per capita in succeeding centuries. At worst, a new period of war or revolution, or competition from other societies experiencing a surge of productivity and taking market share away, or simply continued population increase, could lead to a decline in GDP per capita. One might still see income per capita rise in subsequent periods if there is a subsequent decline in population that is greater than the decline in output, or if output grew modestly while population remained constant or depressed. However, total GDP per capita would still remain within the bounds of pre-modern efflorescence peaks, and the vigorous sustained growth in both GDP/cap and population that is characteristic of modern economic growth does not reappear. Rather, after the efflorescence has peaked, a new Malthusian equilibrium pattern takes over.

Jan Luiten van Zanden and Bas van Leeuwen have painstakingly reconstructed a set of national accounts for Holland going back to the late Middle Ages. I will here focus on their data for the period of 1510–1807. This is the period that encompasses Holland's 'Golden Age', and is a period in which many observers, including van Zanden and van Leeuwen, as well as Jan de Vries and Ad Van den Woude, have claimed to find evidence for the emergence of 'modern' economic growth.[12]

Holland in its Golden Age has many features of a modern economy, including a low fraction of GDP in agriculture; a high level of artistic and educational output and consumption; and a high level of government and economic organization. But some of this is inherent in the selection of the province of Holland in isolation as the unit of analysis. Holland, anchored by Amsterdam and its other coastal cities, was an exceptionally urbanized area: its 337,000 residents were far more dependent on services and trade than any regions with ten to twenty times that population could be – indeed far more so than even other parts of the United Provinces, of which it was the largest and richest. As early as 1510, 49 per cent of Holland's GDP came from services, with 29 per cent from crafts and manufacturing and only 22 per cent from agriculture and fisheries. Many of those services derived from Holland's role in the international economy, where it was a depot for trade between the Baltic and the North Sea and the Atlantic, and provided financial and warehousing services to merchants from throughout Europe. The economy of Holland would be more like the economy of today's Greater London, or for that matter the cities of Rome, Florence or Constantinople in their heydays, for apt comparison. It was thus unlike the economy of any other pre-modern European economy, where typically half or more of the population was engaged in agriculture.

The chronological developments for Holland are shown in Figure 2.1. The left scale shows real GDP in constant 1800 prices in Dutch guilders; the right scale shows real GDP per capita in the same measure.[13] GDP started to rise strongly from the 1540s to the 1560s, faltering slightly in the next decade when the Dutch war for independence with Spain began. However, after the 1570s there was rapid and unbroken growth up to the 1640s, when total GDP was four times larger than in the early sixteenth century.

The trajectory of this growth shows a clear 'efflorescence' pattern. From the 1540s to the 1570s there was a sudden, one-time shift in the composition of GDP, as more efficient services and new energy, transport and manufacturing processes took hold. In the 1540s, the sectoral distribution of Holland's GDP was still virtually identical to that in 1510, with 48.4 per cent in services, 30.3 per cent in crafts and manufacturing, and 21.3 per cent in agriculture. But by the 1560s, as new techniques spread, there was a dramatic shift, with services leaping to 64.7 per cent of output, while crafts and manufacturing dropped to 21.7 per cent and agriculture to a mere 13.6 per cent. Over the next century, this pattern would be preserved, so that by 1640, services still contributed 62.5 per cent of output, crafts and manufacturing 26.9 per cent, and agriculture 10.6 per cent. Most of Holland's growth in output during this Golden Age was thus in services, and specifically in trade, whose real value increased fivefold to sixfold. Still, these trade gains reflected widespread gains in the economy as every sector grew in absolute terms.

After 1640, however, the picture changed. For over a century after the 1640s, until the 1750s, real GDP was never more than 2 per cent above the 1640s peak. And the sectoral structure of the economy remained unchanged: in the 1750s, services still contributed 59.4 per cent of GDP, crafts and manufacturing 30.1 per cent, and agriculture 10.5 per cent. Indeed, this pattern remains unchanged all the way up to the 1790s.

There was a slight spurt of new growth in the late eighteenth century, with GDP in the 1760s, 1770s and 1790s up by about 10 per cent from the 1640–1750 level; but this too faltered and by 1800–07 GDP was back to within 5 per cent of the then 160-year-old

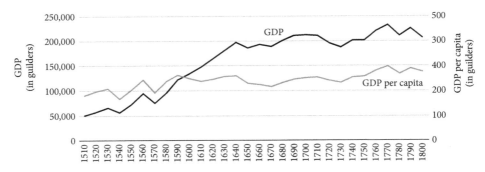

Figure 2.1 GDP and GDP per capita in Holland, 1510–1800 (decade averages in constant 1800 prices).

Source: Decadal averages calculated by the author from the annual data provided in Jan Luiten van Zanden and Bas van Leeuwen, 'Reconstruction: National Accounts of Holland', at: http://www.cgeh.nl/reconstruction-national-accounts-holland-1500-1800-0.

peak. According to this new data, real GDP grew by 300 per cent from 1540 to 1640, but by no more than 5 per cent for the next 150 years. That certainly represented, as Simon Schama has written, an 'embarrassment of riches' in the seventeenth century.[14] However, this efflorescence was followed by no further changes in the size or structure of the economy for 150 years after the 1640s.

Further evidence for this conclusion comes from looking at changes in GDP per capita over this period. From 1540 to 1590 GDP per capita grew strongly, gaining roughly 56 per cent in these five decades. This was accompanied by vigorous population growth, increasing 37 per cent from 337,000 in the 1540s to 462,000 in the 1590s. After these five wondrous decades, however, gains in per capita income disappeared. GDP grew strongly for another half-century, but in those years population growth more than kept pace, so that GDP per capita dipped after the 1590s, inched up to that level again in the 1640s, but then fell for the next century, so that not until the 1760s did GDP per capita again reach its level of the 1590s, more than 150 years earlier.

Even more striking is that the rise in GDP per capita in the last few decades of the eighteenth century is hardly accompanied by evidence of vigour in the economy; rather it looks more like a slight Malthusian positive wave. For the GDP per capita level in 1800–07, which was still only 4.5 per cent higher than that of the 1590s, rose mainly because Holland's population declined. Shortly after the 1640s peak in GDP, population also hit a peak in the 1670s, at 876,000. By the 1750s, population had declined by almost 100,000 to 783,000, and then fell yet another 34,000 by the years 1800–07.

All of this can be observed in Table 2.1. The annual GDP growth rates from the 1540s to the 1640s stand out; they are wholly atypical for the period as a whole. GDP growth steadily declined thereafter, virtually disappearing after the 1640s. Even more striking, GDP per capita shows tremendous growth in the five decades from the 1540s to the 1590s, but that is all. After the 1590s, growth in per capita income turned negative for over a century, and even the return of growth in GDP per capita in the eighteenth century was almost risible, reaching 0.08 per cent per year only because the decline in Holland's population over the eighteenth century (−0.11 per cent per annum) was greater than the decline in real GDP (−0.03 per cent per annum).

In sum, the Netherlands illustrate a classic pre-modern economic 'efflorescence': several decades of truly remarkable growth in GDP, GDP per capita and population, followed by a return in the succeeding two centuries to virtually zero growth. Indeed, for all these quantities, their level in the first decade of the nineteenth century is indistinguishable from their level in the 1640s, as is the sectoral composition of the economy. In my view, these facts not only make the late sixteenth-century Dutch Golden Age even more impressive but also indisputably distinguish it from being the onset of true modern economic growth. However, several economic historians have argued that, although growth faltered in the Netherlands, from the seventeenth century onwards it took off in England. They argue that we should see the joint trajectories of England and the Netherlands as comprising a 'Little Divergence' from the rest of Europe that carried this world region into new frontiers of economic performance.

British Growth, 1270–1800

There is no dispute that, after 1800, Great Britain was launched upon a remarkable period of economic growth. Fuelled by vast gains in productivity in agriculture, transport, and especially in textiles, mining and metallurgy, Britain had so transformed itself by 1850 as to be the wonder of the world. Its railways moved people and freight at previously unimaginable speeds, its steam-powered and iron-clad warships subdued the mightiest empires in the world, and its factories allowed this small island to replace the centuries-old leadership of the vast Indian and Chinese empires and become the world's leading exporter of cotton goods.

What is still a matter of great debate, however, is how far in this direction Britain's economy had moved prior to 1800. Was Britain, already by 1700 or earlier, embarked on a path of economic growth that showed a clear break with past Malthusian patterns? Or was such growth only evident after the onset of industrialization, in the late eighteenth or even only the early nineteenth century?

Table 2.2 shows recent data for growth in real GDP per capita in half-century periods from the 1270s through the 1860s, along with data on population growth. If we exclude two periods – the late fourteenth century and the late seventeenth century – then the average annual growth rate in real GDP per capita for all other periods from the 1270s to the 1700s, a period of over 400 years, was essentially zero. By contrast, in the two growth periods, we see very rapid gains in income per capita, of 0.57 per cent and 0.72 per cent per year. These stand out as periods of remarkable pre-modern growth, greater in fact than the growth rates in GDP per capita observed from 1800 to 1830. The new GDP data thus show that all the growth in English GDP per capita between the Middle Ages and the eighteenth century was due to growth in these two periods.

The late fourteenth century of course was the era of the Black Death, and income gains were largely derived from population decline. But it should not be thought that these gains were automatic. Many other areas, including Egypt, China and Eastern Europe, suffered equally devastating losses in population. Yet they did not sustain their gains in real GDP per capita as England did. In England, the demographic decline was accompanied by major changes in the organization of the economy. In the fifteenth and sixteenth centuries, serfdom was largely abolished, a flourishing export trade in wool was developed, and the country's legal and judicial system continued to evolve. By contrast, in Eastern Europe, peasant labour was enserfed after the Black Death, while in Egypt vast areas fell out of cultivation and in China the plague helped usher in the collapse of the Mongol Yuan Empire.

Nonetheless, in Britain for the first 250 years after the Black Death, slow growth in total GDP just barely kept pace with slow growth in population.[15] If we were to stop the clock in 1650, it would be obvious that England had not yet embarked on anything like modern economic growth. From 1400 to 1650, England floated on a Malthusian equilibrium, with population and GDP both slowly recovering, and two-and-a-half centuries with no gains at all in income per capita. There were also no major shifts in the

Table 2.1 Growth in Holland, 1510s–1800s: GDP, population and GDP per capita

	GDP (1510s = 100)	GDP Growth since prior date (% p.a.)	Population (1510s = 100)	Population Growth since prior date (% p.a.)	GDP per capita (1510s = 100)	GDP per capita Growth since prior date (% p.a.)
1510s	100		100		100	
1540s	111.1	0.35	121.4	0.64	91.4	−0.30
1590s	241	1.56	166.4	0.63	144.7	0.92
1640s	389	0.96	271.4	0.98	143.3	−0.02
1700s	418.5	0.12	301.6	0.18	138.8	−0.05
1800s	407.9	−0.03	269.9	−0.11	151.2	0.08

Source: Decadal averages calculated by the author from the annual data provided in Jan Luiten van Zanden and Bas van Leeuwen, 'Reconstruction: National Accounts of Holland', at: http://www.cgeh.nl/reconstruction-national-accounts-holland-1500-1800-0.

Table 2.2 Growth rates for population and real GDP per capita in England and Great Britain (% per annum)

	Population	Real GDP per capita
England		
1270s–1300s	0.23	−0.02
1300s–1340s	−0.06	0.07
1340s–1400s	−1.32	0.57
1400s–1450s	−0.14	−0.07
1450s–1500s	0.29	0.11
1500s–1550s	0.66	−0.16
1550s–1600s	0.64	0.18
1600s–1650s	0.45	−0.05
1650s–1700	−0.06	0.72
Great Britain		
1700s–1750s	0.31	0.18
1750s–1800s	0.82	0.39
1800s–1830s	1.43	0.41
1830s–1860s	1.17	1.15

Source: Stephen Broadberry, Bruce Campbell, Alexander Klein, Mark Overton and Bas van Leeuwen (2015), *British Economic Growth, 1270–1870*. Cambridge: Cambridge University Press, Appendix 5.3.

structure of the economy: agriculture's share in real GDP was 45.5 per cent in 1381, 39.7 per cent in 1522, and 41.1 per cent in 1600.[16]

After 1650, however, there are clearly signs of change. From 1650 to 1700 income per capita grew more strongly than ever before, although this was accompanied by a slight population decline. From 1700 onwards, Britain was able to combine growth in both population and GDP per capita. Yet growth in both population and income per head were still very weak from the 1700s to the 1750s. Only after 1750 do we see stronger growth in both population and income per head, with the growth rate of GDP per capita moving well above pre-modern levels.

Determining precisely when England's modern economic growth began thus depends greatly on how we view events from 1650 to 1800. When in this period do we clearly see a break from past patterns of pre-modern, Malthusian growth? When does income per capita break free from both population constraints and pre-modern rates of economic growth?

Let us first focus on the half-century from 1650 to 1700 – what happened in these decades? The answer is that a significant structural transformation in the economy coincided with a period of slight population decline, to produce a huge surge in income per capita. The structural transformation was threefold. First, in manufacturing there was a leap in the export production of textiles, driven by the 'new draperies', a blend of wool and other fibres that was lighter than the 'old draperies' of heavy wool. The new draperies were wildly popular, and allowed England to seize market share from Holland and other European wool producers. This success propelled a large number of workers into spinning for merchants.[17] Second, there was the importation of Dutch agricultural techniques into England, leading to shifts in crop rotations, and the use of fodder crops (clover and turnips) that allowed light-soil regions to greatly increase their productivity for wheat, allowing heavy-soil regions to specialize more in livestock raising.[18] And finally, religious shifts in this period were favourable to Britain. Despite the turmoil of the Puritan Revolution, Restoration, and the Glorious Revolution, Britain in the late seventeenth century remained a region open to Protestants. Britain thus attracted Protestant refugees from the continent, especially from France, who brought capital and skills with them, providing a positive shock for production and trade.

Nonetheless, it is clear that these changes were not transformative. Changes in agriculture, for instance, were minimal and real output in agriculture in these decades rose only 0.2 per cent per year. Industrial output rose rapidly, by 1.01 per cent per year in this period, as did output in services, at 0.71 per cent per year. The slow growth in agricultural output compared to industry in this period means that industry's fraction of the economy rose and agriculture's fell – but this did not yet reflect a fundamental change in the economy. According to Broadberry and his co-authors' analysis of labour shares, the male workforce in agriculture in 1688 was still 46 per cent, and remained 43 per cent as late as 1759. While this was a significant reduction from the 67 per cent level that had prevailed in the fourteenth to sixteenth centuries, it did not yet presage the modern increases in productivity that would follow.[19]

Even in the period 1700 to 1750, we do not see anything in the GDP figures that looks like modern economic performance. In this half-century population growth was also quite slow, only half the rate of the entire sixteenth century, and only equal to the rate of population growth in the late fifteenth century. Surely with such modest population growth a modern economy should have been able to produce significant gains in income per head. Yet in fact the momentum of the late seventeenth century petered out, and growth in income per head was no different from that in earlier centuries. Indeed, the growth in income per head in 1700–50, of 0.18 per cent per year, was identical to the growth rate for the period from the 1270s to 1700.

Perhaps most striking is that Broadberry and his co-authors find no continuation of the strong growth in industrial productivity and output that sparked the per capita income growth from 1650 to 1700. Instead, where industrial output per capita in Britain had risen by 73 per cent from 1650 to 1700, such gains came to an abrupt end by 1700, as in the next half-century it rose only 9 per cent, or just one-eighth as much.[20] This was a much lower rate of growth in industrial output per person than England had seen even in the late sixteenth century, to say nothing of the late seventeenth. In short, there was nothing distinctive about the rate of growth in either British GDP per capita or industrial output per head in the first half of the eighteenth century. Macroeconomic performance in this period, with slow population growth and minimal (0.18 per cent) growth in GDP per capita, is simply typical of what was observed since the Middle Ages.

Our analysis of Broadberry et al.'s data is reinforced by additional long-term studies of the British economy. Crafts and Mills undertook a partition of British trends in GDP per capita into long-term trends during the period from 1270 to 1920. They found a near zero-growth trend for over three centuries prior to 1660, then a sharp upward growth trend to 1707. This was followed by much slower growth in GDP per capita until the early 1800s – with most of the growth in this period arising after 1750 – and then a second acceleration of growth after 1820. Broadberry and de Pleijt examined capital accumulation over a similar period; they found that capital per head stagnated from 1700 to 1780, only increasing rapidly after 1820. And while there is good reason to be sceptical of real-wage data for pre-modern societies, the best data show that while days worked rose strongly from 1690 to 1700, they then declined considerably from 1690 to 1750, suggesting a slow-down in economic activity. This coincided with family earnings slowing from 1710 to 1715, after growing strongly in the preceding half-century.[21] In sum, the available data indicate that while Britain experienced a marked increase in income per capita from 1650 to 1700, while population growth was absent, these gains clearly slowed or stopped once population growth returned to modest levels after 1700, showing a still-strong Malthusian response. It was only after 1750 that income per head again started rising at the same time as population, and only after 1800 do both show strong and consistent growth.

Comparing Divergence across Cases

One could argue that even if the rate of growth in Holland and Britain was neither sustained nor historically exceptional prior to 1750, it was the level of output per capita achieved that was unusual, and so marked a 'Divergence' from prior global patterns. If the Netherlands, or Britain, were precocious in achieving levels of GDP per capita that went significantly beyond the attainments of other pre-modern societies, it could be that achievement which set the stage for their later breakthroughs to modern growth. Drawing on data assembled by Broadberry and others, I argue that this is not the case.

What is remarkable in fact is how rigid the ceiling appears to be on pre-modern peak levels of GDP per capita. Table 2.3 shows estimates of the highest levels of GDP per capita found for a variety of societies, along with the dates at which those levels were achieved, at any time up to 1800.[22] These were generally associated with 'efflorescences' that marked peaks of high culture and economic achievement, along with technical advances that boosted output and trade. They include Song China in the eleventh century, medieval Spain, Renaissance northern Italy, the Netherlands at the dawn of the nineteenth century (we only have data for Holland earlier, which for reasons noted above is not an apt unit of comparison with much larger countries), and Britain in the mid-eighteenth and beginning of the nineteenth centuries.

It is astonishing that with the exception of medieval Spain, which was low, and Great Britain in 1800, which is exceptionally high, the figures are almost all within 10–15 per cent of each other. Even compared to Song China, almost 800 years earlier, the Netherlands in 1800 had a GDP per capita only 15 per cent higher; and they were only 4 per cent richer than the level northern Italy had achieved 350 years earlier. Great Britain in 1750 was not yet evidently any better off than any prior successful pre-modern country – GDP per capita was only 13 per cent higher than Song China and only 1 per cent higher than Renaissance Italy. If we exclude the bottom two lines – that is, look at the world's leading economies from 1020 to 1750 (or 1800 for the Netherlands) – the message is one of remarkable uniformity: none of the European countries at any time achieves any meaningful advantage in GDP per capita over any other's peak achievement, nor over the peak achievement of China. At least as regards peak GDP per capita, as late as 1750 there is no divergence of any kind, anywhere.

In sum, if one confines one's view to the years before 1800, there is nothing in either the pattern of growth or the level attained in GDP per capita anywhere in northwest Europe that is at all indicative of a break with prevailing pre-modern patterns. This is not to deny that crucial things were happening, such as the flurry of inventions in Europe, the advance of parliamentary governments, the rise of learning, the conquest of the seas, the advance of religious pluralism, or dozens of other factors that contributed to subsequent economic achievements. It is only to say that one cannot find, in the available GDP data, evidence of sustained, rapid growth in GDP per capita nor advances to unusual pre-modern levels at any time before the nineteenth century. Both the Netherlands and Britain did have episodes of impressive growth in GDP per capita; but these merely raised them to levels seen earlier by other very successful countries. Once they reached those heights, they were marooned there – the Netherlands had no further growth in GDP per capita from the 1590s to 1790s, and Britain had no return to the growth rates in GDP per capita seen in 1650–1700 until at least 1750 and perhaps not until after 1800.

Table 2.3 Peak GDP per capita in various societies in history in Geary-Khamis International 1990 dollars

Country (Year)	Peak GDP per capita	Ratio: compared to Song China/ to Renaissance Italy
China (1020)	1,518	1.00/0.90
Spain (1348)	1,030	0.68/0.61
Northern Italy (1450)	1,688	1.11/1.00
The Netherlands (1800)	1,752	1.15/1.04
Great Britain (1750)	1,710	1.13/1.01
Great Britain (1800–	2,080	1.37/1.23

Source: Stephen Broadberry, Bruce Campbell, Alexander Klein, Mark Overton, and Bas van Leeuwen (2015), *British Economic Growth, 1270–1870*. Cambridge: Cambridge University Press, Table 10.02.

It is true that other nations suffered a considerable decline in GDP per capita over the centuries since their peak, leaving the Netherlands and Britain in a relatively stronger position as the nineteenth century opened. History makes clear, however, that such an advantage is no automatic guarantee of further progress. Song China and Renaissance Italy in their day held commanding leads in GDP per capita over their neighbours, and did so at a level of income per capita not significantly different (evidently within 10 per cent in real terms) from that of Britain and the Netherlands, without subsequently progressing to take GDP per capita to further heights. For that matter, the Netherlands' great riches relative to other nations achieved in the late sixteenth century appear to have done nothing to boost its GDP per capita in the succeeding two centuries. Relative advantage is nice to have, but it in no way guarantees a better future.

Conclusion

This chapter has said nothing about the ultimate causes of the 'Great Divergence'. That debate remains open and is considered in other chapters in this book. Still, in order to explain something, it is important to know exactly what is to be explained. The new data make it indisputable that the onset of a distinctive and new pattern of economic growth was a relatively late phenomenon, only evident in the GDP per capita data from 1750 onwards. Whatever caused the Great Divergence to arise *c.*1750, it was not a centuries-long prior record of exceptional growth rates or levels of GDP per capita in northwest Europe.

This new analysis of the data of Broadberry and co-authors makes it clear why even expert observers of the British economy in the eighteenth century, such as Adam Smith, could not see signs of any economic divergence. There was simply no evidence of any departure from pre-modern growth patterns before 1750.

Explanations for the 'Great Divergence' that claim to find its roots in late medieval or early modern growth patterns are thus mistaken. Certainly there were episodes of prior growth, but such episodes lasted only a few decades and then stalled, and only led the Netherlands and Britain to catch up with levels of GDP per capita attained many centuries earlier in northern Italy and Song China. To understand the onset of distinctively modern economic growth – with sustained increases in both population and real income at high rates leading to levels of income not seen in prior eras – we need to develop explanations for a relatively late and sudden transition to a new mode of economic growth that appeared only after 1750.

Notes

1. Ho-fung Hung (2003), 'Orientalist knowledge and social theories: China and the European conceptions of East–West differences from 1600 to 1900', *Sociological Theory*, 21 (3), 254–79. Adam Smith offered the same view: 'China has been long one of the richest, that is, one of

the most fertile, best cultivated, most industrious, and most populous countries in world. It seems, however, to have been long stationary'. A. Smith (1776), *An Inquiry into the Nature and Causes of the Wealth of Nations*, Feedbooks, http://en.wikisource.org, 48.

2. See, for instance, P. Hoffman (2015), *Why Did Europe Conquer the World?* Princeton, NJ: Princeton University Press; G. Clark (2007), *A Farewell to Alms: A Brief Economic History of the World*. Princeton, NJ: Princeton University Press; T. Huff (2003), *The Rise of Early Modern Science: Islam, China and the West*. Cambridge: Cambridge University Press; I. Wallerstein (2011), *The Modern World System*. Berkeley, CA: University of California Press; D. N. McCloskey (2016), *Bourgeois Equality: How Idea, not Capital or Institutions, Enriched the World*. Chicago, IL: University of Chicago Press; J. Mokyr (2016), *The Culture of Growth: The Origins of the Modern Economy*. Princeton, NJ: Princeton University Press; S. R. Epstein (2000), *Freedom and Growth: The Rise of States and Markets in Europe, 1300–1750*. London: Routledge.

3. Pomeranz, *The Great Divergence*; Bin Wong, *China Transformed*; Frank, *ReOrient*; Bozhong, *Agricultural Development in Jiangnan*; R. Marks (2006), *Tigers, Rice, Silk and Silt*. New York: Academic Press; J. A. Goldstone (1991), *Revolution and Rebellion in the Early Modern World*. Berkeley, CA: University of California Press; ibid. (1998), 'The problem of the "Early Modern" world', *Journal of the Economic and Social History of the Orient*, 41 (3), 249–84; ibid. (2000), 'The rise of the West – or not? A revision to socio-economic history', *Sociological Theory*, 18 (2), 157–94; D. O. Flynn and A. Giráldez (2010), *China and the Birth of Globalization in the Sixteenth Century*. Farnham: Ashgate; Parthasarathi, *Why Europe Grew Rich and Asia Did Not*; P. Vries (2003), *Via Peking Back to Manchester: Britain, the Industrial Revolution and China*. Leiden: Leiden University.

4. Among the most important were W. Skinner (1977), *The City in Late Imperial China*. Stanford, CA: Stanford University Press; W. Rowe (1992), *Hankow: Commerce and Society in a Chinese City, 1796–1889*. Stanford, CA: Stanford University Press; J. Z. Lee and W. Feng (2001), *One Quarter of Humanity: Malthusian Mythology and Chinese Realities*. Cambridge, MA: Harvard University Press; P. Perdue (2005), *China Marches West: The Qing Conquest of Central Eurasia*. Cambridge, MA: Belknap Press; T. Brook (1998), *The Confusions of Pleasure: Commerce and Culture in Ming China*. Berkeley, CA: University of California Press; S. Naquin and E. S. Rawski (1987), *Chinese Society in the Eighteenth Century*. New Haven, CT: Yale University Press.

5. On labour/capital ratios, see Allen, *The British Industrial Revolution*; J.-L. Rosenthal and R. Bin Wong (2011), *Before and Beyond Divergence: The Politics of Economic Change in China and Europe*. On physical geography, see I. Morris (2010), *Why the West Rules – For Now*. New York: Farrar, Straus and Giroux; J. Diamond (1999), *Guns, Germs and Steel*. New York: W. W. Norton. On political organization, see P. Vries (2013), *Escape from Poverty: The Origins of Modern Economic Growth*. Vienna: University of Vienna Press.

6. The classic demonstration of how population data can be extracted from parish records is E. A. Wrigley and R. S. Schofield (1989), *The Population History of England and Wales 1541–1871*. Cambridge: Cambridge University Press. Additional research using data from local registers in Europe and lineage and other records in China can be found in Allen, Bengtsson and Dribe (eds), *Living Standards in the Past*; T. Bengtsson, C. Campbell and J. Z. Lee (eds) (2009), *Life under Pressure: Mortality and Living Standards in Europe and Asia, 1700–1900*. Cambridge, MA: MIT Press; and N. O. Tsuya, W. Feng, G. Alter, J. Z. Lee et al. (eds) (2010), *Prudence and Pressure: Reproduction and Human Agency in Europe and Asia, 1700–1900*. Cambridge, MA: MIT Press.

7. The British data have been published in S. N. Broadberry, B. M. S. Campbell, A. Klein, M. Overton and B. van Leeuwen (2015), *British Economic Growth, 1270–1870*.

Cambridge: Cambridge University Press. Kindle Edition. The Dutch data have been published online by the Centre for Global Economic History by J. L. van Zanden and B. van Leeuwen as the 'Reconstruction National Accounts of Holland', http://www.cgeh.nl/reconstruction-national-accounts-holland-1500-1800-0.

8. F. Braudel (1973), *Capitalism and Material Life 1400–1800*. New York: Harper Collins; I. Wallerstein (1974), *The Modern World System I: Capitalist Agriculture and the Origins of the European World Economy in the Sixteenth Century*. New York: Academic Press; C. M. Cipolla (1976), *Before the Industrial Revolution: European Society and Economy, 1000–1700*. New York: W. W. Norton.

9. A. M. de Pleijt and J. L. van Zanden (2016), 'Accounting for the "Little Divergence": What drove economic growth in pre-industrial Europe 1300–1800', *European Review of Economic History*, 20, 387–409.

10. S. Broadberry, H. Guan and D. Li (2018), 'China, Europe and the Great Divergence: A study in historical national accounting', *Journal of Economic History*, 78 (3), 955–1000; ibid. (2021), 'China, Europe and the Great Divergence: A restatement', *Journal of Economic History*, 81 (3), 958–74.

11. J. A. Goldstone (2002), 'Efflorescences and economic growth in world history: Rethinking the "Rise of the West" and the Industrial Revolution', *Journal of World History*, 13 (2), 323–89.

12. De Pleijt and van Zanden, 'Accounting for the "Little Divergence"'; J. de Vries and A. Van der Woude (1997), *The First Modern Economy: Success, Failure and Perseverance of the Dutch Economy*, 1500–1815. Cambridge: Cambridge University Press.

13. The decadal averages shown in Figure 2.1, and the period growth rates in Table 2.1 below, are calculated by the author from the annual data provided in 'Reconstruction National Accounts of Holland', at: http://www.cgeh.nl/reconstruction-national-accounts-holland-1500-1800-0.

14. S. Schama (1988), *The Embarrassment of Riches*. Berkeley, CA: University of California Press.

15. Population and GDP data from Broadberry et al., Table 5.06.

16. Broadberry et al., Table 5.01.

17. C. Muldrew (2012), '"Th'ancient Distaff" and "Whirling Spindle": Measuring the contribution of spinning to household earnings and the national economy in England, 1550–1770', *Economic History Review*, 65 (2), 498–536. It also helped that England won a series of naval wars with Holland in this half-century, greatly expanding British access to international trade.

18. J. A. Goldstone (1988), 'Regional ecology and agrarian development in early modern England and France', *Politics and Society*, 16 (2–3), 287–334; R. C. Allen (1999), 'Tracking the agricultural revolution in England', *Economic History Review*, 52 (2), 209–35.

19. Productivity data from Broadberry et al., Table 5.07; male labour in agriculture from Broadberry et al., Table 9.08.

20. Computed from Broadberry et al., Table Appendix 5.3.

21. N. Crafts and T. C. Mills (2017), 'Six centuries of British economic growth: A time-series perspective', *European Review of Economic History*, 21, 141–58; S. Broadberry and A. M. de Pleijt (2021), 'Capital and economic growth in Britain, 127–1870: Preliminary findings', Oxford Economic and Social History Working Papers No. 186, University of Oxford Department of Economics; J. Humphries and J. Weisdorf (2019), 'Unreal wages? Real income and economic growth in England, 1260–1850', *The Economic Journal*, 129, 2867–87; S. Horrell, J. Humphries and J. Weisdorf (2022), 'Beyond the male breadwinner: Life-cycle

living standards of intact and disrupted English working families, 1260–1850', *Economic History Review*, 75, 530–60.

22. The collection of macro-data on national GDP and GDP per capita, and its reduction to comparable real levels through Geary-Khamis constant dollars or other metrics, has been roundly criticized on the basis of difficulties in making meaningful comparisons in terms of highly varied local currencies and the diverse regional economies in any large state, e.g. K. Deng and P. O'Brien (2017), 'Why Maddison was wrong', *World Economics Journal*, 18 (2), 21–41. Yet this project is seen by many others as valuable and worth perfecting, e.g. J. Bolt and J. L. van Zanden (2014), 'The Maddison Project', *Economic History Review*, 76 (3), 627–51.

CHAPTER 3
USEFUL AND RELIABLE KNOWLEDGE IN EUROPE AND CHINA
Patrick O'Brien

Metanarratives celebrating the economic rise of the West have been challenged in recent times by two theses proposed by the California and World Systems Schools of historical sociology.[1] The first insists that economic divergence between Europe and Asia became apparent much later than previous generations of historians have suggested. It reconfigures the economic history of the pre-modern era into a world of 'surprising resemblances' to use Kenneth Pomeranz's now famous expression.[2] It also rejects assertions that Europe alone possessed the cultures and institutions for modern economic growth.[3] The second thesis explains more than three centuries of divergence between East and West with reference to Europe's favourable location and natural endowments. These, combined with high and persistent levels of investment in warfare, colonization, and mercantilist policies (by way of coercion and unequal exchange), enabled Europeans to garner most of the gains from trade from the fifteenth to the nineteenth century.[4]

As observed by Jack Goldstone in this book, critiques among European and American historians have concentrated upon the statistical evidence deemed to demonstrate that divergence could be located earlier in time.[5] The divergence debate cannot be conducted only with reference to macroeconomic statistics. This chapter considers and compares regimes (clusters of connected elites and institutions) engaged with the discovery, development, diffusion and application of innovations based upon 'useful and reliable knowledge' in China and Europe. It is deemed that such innovations augmented the productivity of labour employed by households, farms and firms.[6]

Global histories of science and technology suggest that some European cultures became permeated by a cosmography that was conducive to the accumulation of useful and reliable knowledge. Gradually, the embrace of new knowledge by educated and wealthy elites embodied a cultural and a more directly applicable potential for advances in total factor productivities that allowed Western populations to escape from age-old Malthusian threats into modern economic growth before the populations of Asia.[7] This view was supported by a programme of historical research led by Joseph Needham, expanded by Mark Elvin, analysed in a series of conference papers by the Achievement Project in the 1990s, synthesized in three books by Joel Mokyr, and became an accepted theme among scholars engaged in the divergence debate.[8] Assuming that the established consensus which suggests that the locus of scientific discovery and technological innovation shifted from Asia to Europe by, if not sometime before, the end of the fifteenth century, this chapter provides an outline comparing Europe's own trajectory towards the formation and consolidation of a regime for the sustained generation of useful and reliable knowledge with China.

I wish to address the hypothesis posed by Weber, and developed by Butterfield, Needham and later followers, who suggested that the innovations introduced into early modern European agriculture and industry were connected to changes in conceptions of the natural world held by Europe's educated, wealthy and political elites. Cultural change led these elites to support networks of proto-scientists, inventors and artisans and to establish institutions that might conceivably generate and adapt knowledge with potential to generate private profit, support the geopolitical power of states, and secure the health, security and material welfare of European societies.[9] The thesis that a switch in mentality shaped by science came on stream in the seventeenth and eighteenth centuries became the subject of a debate between two great Sinologist historians of science that is ongoing.[10]

Stimulated by debates on the Great Divergence, challenges to this view have been mounted on two fronts. The first repeats familiar arguments from traditional controversies between science and religion, namely that beliefs espoused and enforced by Christian churches were at best neutral and at worst repressive towards investigations into the natural world.[11] The second and more recent wave of literature from histories of science maintains that knowledge discovered, developed and utilized for purposes of production was 'socially constructed'.[12] This literature points out that science originated from several parts of the world and that its connections to the beliefs promoted by European elites were, at best, of tenuous significance for technological change.[13]

Recent histories of science are more inclined to accept that monotheistic Christendom evolved into a culture that *ceteris paribus* embodied elements recognized as significant for the promotion of a functional cosmography for the comprehension of nature.[14] Before the Reformation, European Christianity had consolidated its role as a hegemonic quasi-autonomous, hierarchically organized religion that over time had suppressed all but one system of beliefs about nature and the operations of the natural world in favour of its own revealed truths for which its clergy held a monopoly of interpretation. Nevertheless, as it evolved over the centuries into a supranational organization, the hierarchy of the Roman Church recognized that faith in truths as revealed in the New Testament, the Bible and other canonical references would not be sufficient for competition with monotheistic Islam, to combat heresies or to retain its ideological influence over royal power. Thus, the papacy and bishops found it expedient to establish, patronize and control institutions based upon Greek and Roman models for the higher education of clerical and secular elites that included classical modes of conducting 'rational' arguments in law, medicine, natural philosophy and even theology.[15]

Under strictly regulated conditions, proto-universities spread across the cities of medieval Europe and established faculties and curricula for compulsory introductory courses in natural philosophy based upon texts by Aristotle, Plato, Ptolemy, Galen, Hippocrates and other pagan authors. These included a corpus of classical speculations about the operations of the celestial, terrestrial and biological spheres of what the church resolutely insisted was a divinely created and ordered natural world.[16]

In recent years, scholars working on the medieval origins of modern science have rehabilitated this long tradition of classical and post-classical endeavours to comprehend the natural world.[17] They have researched how far and how deeply European levels of cosmographical comprehension had developed, before they were displaced by Copernicus' seminal work on astronomy in 1543. Thereafter, the introduction of innovative paradigms for an accelerated accumulation of more useful and reliable knowledge marked the onset of what many historians continue to recognize as the 'Scientific Revolution'.[18]

That plateau in knowledge formation depended upon the diffusion of printed books, which formed the basis for conversations, correspondence, associations, and debate among Europe's growing numbers of natural philosophers and theologians dissatisfied with, or sceptical of, revealed spiritual truths.[19] Scholars belonging to what has been called the 'Republics of Letters' became interested in the workings of God's natural world and in the possibilities for its control and manipulation.[20] They widened agendas for discussion and education to comprehend a range of natural phenomena including the age, size, shape, geography and limits of planet earth; movements of the sun, moon and stars; seas and their tides; climates; earthquakes; minerals; chemical substances; soils; plants; animals; fish; and human bodies. They engaged in debates concerned with mathematical and rational methods for the study of medicine, law and even theology, which coexisted in a hegemonic but uneasy relationship with natural philosophy.

That tension became more fraught during the Renaissance when another cycle of humanist scholarship recovered a series of classical texts, which opened up a wider range of discourse about the nature and operations of God's universe.[21] Thus a wave of classical scholarship not only questioned Aristotelian natural philosophy as expurgated and beatified by the church, but came dangerously close to challenging the logical and evidential basis of revealed truths about the world contained in the Scriptures and other sacrosanct texts propounded by theologians in the service of the Roman Church.[22] Thereafter, irreversible and fundamental changes in a cosmography embodied in the cultures of European elites, in line with developments cautiously anticipated and outlined by a minority of precursors during the Middle Ages, became clear and powerful.[23]

The period also witnessed the European 'discovery' of a new continent, the division of Christendom into Catholic and Protestant countries and communities, horrendous wars of religion, and the consolidation of regular transcontinental commerce. This eventful conjuncture has also been contentiously, but plausibly, configured by historians of Europe to mark a new regime for the accumulation of useful and reliable knowledge that actively promoted and supported sustained economic growth.[24] Its development was neither revolutionary in pace nor linear in trend. Its historically validated connections to an ongoing but gradual process of innovation were for many decades confined to a limited range of technologies that in time became useful and reliable for navigation by sea, the surveying of space, the derivation of energy from water, atmospheric pressure and steam power, drainage, the accuracy of artillery, the bleaching of textiles, and the like.[25]

Debate over their nature and economic significance has been protracted and remains unresolved. Nevertheless, the contention of this chapter is that the significance of this famous conjuncture for narratives concerned with the economic divergence between Asia and Europe resides essentially in an unmeasurable but unmistakable impetus towards the formation of confident conceptions among Europe's educated and wealthy elites that the natural world was in the process of becoming more intelligible and manipulable for material gain and human health than their ancestors living in Roman and feudal times had ever imagined.[26] Unfortunately, that impetus in the conceptions and perceptions of Western elites cannot be validated because historical evidence for its emergence consists essentially of books written by famous names in the histories of science, technology and cosmography, which have been subsequently selected as contributions to the development of a plethora of specialized disciplines which were part of the natural sciences.[27] Attempts to validate this hypothesis statistically have produced some positive but inconclusive results in the form of a dramatic rise in the numbers and discernible decline in the prices of printed books published between 1450 and 1750 in Western Europe, following the invention and diffusion of the printing press.[28]

The flow of published knowledge representing a reformed cosmography was almost certainly rising rapidly during a period when the number of students attending universities and taking a compulsory course or two in natural philosophy was also increasing faster than populations at large.[29] Nevertheless, the case for an increasing flow of knowledge about the operations of a natural world remains almost impossible to demonstrate. Thus, an argument for cultural shifts in the cosmographical beliefs of an increasing proportion of educated Europeans can only be made on a priori and probabilistic grounds and with reference to the beliefs that their counterparts held about the natural world and prospects for its control before, say, 1450 or in other parts of the world in early modern times.[30]

One tenet remained hegemonic: it was dangerous to challenge Christianity's foundational belief that the universe had been created by God; that operations of its celestial, terrestrial and biological spheres were divinely ordained and regulated; and that mankind's primary purpose was to live but a short interlude on earth according to moral principles enunciated in sacred Christian texts as interpreted by God's one and only true Roman Catholic Church. Its hierarchy had, moreover, ordained that if men wished to understand the operations of a divine natural world, they should first seek guidance from the Scriptures. Alternatively, they could consult a rather restricted range of licensed classical authorities: first and foremost, Aristotle on anything, but particularly on logical ways of comprehending the universe, Ptolemy on the heavens and solar system, Galen on the human body, Hippocrates on medicine, Pliny on plants and animals, Euclid on mathematics and so on.[31]

Centuries passed before Europe's traditional belief system became 'secularized' by a scientific cosmography. Before the age of Enlightenment, elite culture changed slowly. Progress could certainly have been assisted by appealing to the authority of a wider number of classical authors other than Aristotle – particularly to Plato, Archimedes, Lucretius and Epicurus.[32] Paradoxically, the worldly and politicized hierarchy of the

Catholic Church advised by Jesuit intellectuals acted from time to time as a buffer against fundamentalist attacks on the diffusion of knowledge that endangered 'truths' about nature as revealed in Christianity's sacred texts.[33]

By 1750 – in contrast to their ancestors – most educated Europeans supported what had matured into a tradition of state and private investment in voyages of 'discovery' and intra-continental exploration. Most believed that the skies and heavens could be mapped and that their own planet earth, displaced from the centre of an infinite universe, rotated daily on its axis and circled the sun along with all other planets. Within an infinitely expanded universe, they recognized their own insignificance.[34] Man and his common sense were no longer the measure of all things. His sensory perceptions and understandings of nature were recognized as limited, but had and would predictably continue to be successfully extended by instruments in the service of speculations, hypotheses, and controlled experiments designed and monitored by 'networks of experts' with credentials and codes of conduct maturing into scientific disciplines.[35]

These men had not only produced maps of the world and its seas and oceans with more mathematically precise coordinates for purposes of trade and navigation but also were mapping the skies for the same utilitarian purposes. After decades of inconclusive investigations into the powers of flowing water and the pressures and weight of air, they had also discovered new sources of energy with potential to be developed, harnessed and diffused for production.[36] In the course of a protracted intellectual conflict between 'ancients and moderns' marked by 'battles of the books', the traditional classical authorities such as Aristotle, including Ptolemy, Galen and Hippocrates, had been effectively degraded by the systematic exposure of their errors, by geographical discoveries, by solar observations, and by the elevation of mathematical logic and experimental methods into hallmarks for new and more productive ways of accumulating reliable and useful knowledge about the natural world.[37]

For economic development, clear and direct links between Europe's reconfigured and extended investigations in natural philosophy and breakthroughs in technologies for agronomy, mechanical engineering and bodily health have proved difficult to document.[38] Moreover, in recent years, historians of science have argued that many acclaimed natural philosophers including Galileo, Hooke, Boyle, Beekmans, Huygens and Newton continued to engage seriously with the claims to knowledge by alchemists and astrologers involved with rather unsystematic and unexplained manipulations of materials and natural sources of energy sold to gullible customers and powerful patrons.[39] In any case, the 'experiments' of alchemists and observations of astrologers contributed to debates about scientific ways of knowing and understanding how the natural world really worked.[40]

Natural Philosophy and the Transition to Science in the West

Over the long run, direct connections between Europe's tradition in natural philosophy, which matured into science allied to technological innovations, remain unmistakable.[41] Global economic history's concerns have, however, been latterly with the economic divergence between Europe and Asia. In the absence of bodies of secondary literatures comparable in volume, scope and sophistication to recent historical analyses of European science, religions and cosmography, it may be premature to agree with Joseph Needham's insights and conclusions published two generations ago. As a Christian Marxist of unsurpassed erudition in global histories of science and technology, Needham also remained deeply aware of the significance of the fortuitous but ultimately fortunate religious and classical antecedents and foundations for Europe's peculiar but promotional cosmology for the accumulation of useful and reliable knowledge.[42]

Furthermore, global historians need to be reminded that Butterfield saw Europe's 'scientific, agrarian and industrial revolutions as forming such a system of complex and interrelated changes that in the lack of a microscopic examination, we have to heap them altogether as aspects of a general movement'.[43] Herbert Butterfield's view could never develop into the kind of history that could appeal to economists. To be elevated into a key chapter for narratives of divergence, it could only be tested for plausibility by way of reciprocal comparisons with the cosmographies and regimes for the production, development and diffusion of useful and reliable knowledge operating within Islamic empires, China and India in pre-modern times.

Of course, to paraphrase Ben Elman, Asian intellectuals continued to be engaged in endeavours that understood the natural world on their own terms and in their own ways.[44] Nevertheless, the question of how effective their engagement became for the discovery, development and diffusion of technological, institutional and biological innovations is the issue. The 'cultural' dispositions towards innovation displayed by the political, economic and intellectual elites managing early modern Asian societies continue to be represented as embedded in traditions of belief and thought that appear to be indifferent and sometimes even hostile to systematic investigations into nature and technology.[45]

Unfortunately, only a limited literature is currently available for the construction of a comprehensive academic survey of the beliefs of elites and institutions in South, West and Central Asia.[46] At present, the only prospect for an intellectual engagement in reciprocal comparisons with the evolution of Asian beliefs and institutions that is comparable to and coterminous with the conjuncture in the culture of Western Europe can be read in histories of imperial China.[47]

Thanks to the Needham programme for the history of science and civilization in China, relevant secondary literature that could be plausibly taken to represent East Asian thoughts and beliefs has become extensive, diverse and sophisticated enough to enable a brief but tentative survey of relevant literatures published in English.[48] A number of scholars still accept Needham's view that developments in the formation of useful and reliable knowledge faltered sometime after if not before 1500.[49] Thereafter Chinese contributions can be plausibly discussed not as stasis but rather as a history of relative retardation. No consensus exists, however, as to when and why a climacteric emerged and persisted during the Ming and Qing dynasties.

Constructivist and cultural narratives have pointed to several theoretically and potentially salient contrasts with the economies of Western Europe.[50] For example, and in order of significance, the share of the empire's population located in towns and cities regarded as hospitable locations for the formation of the human capital and institutions required to engage with scientific and technological innovation declined from a 20 per cent level under the Song dynasty (960–1279 CE) to well below the ratios estimated for the advanced economies of Europe by 1700.[51] Furthermore, a high proportion of the empire's stock and flows of men (with the education, skills, talents and motivation required for the discovery, development and diffusion of useful and reliable knowledge) invested time and family money on acquiring the credentials and qualifications prescribed by the Chinese state for entry into and advancement within a bureaucracy recruited on merits as displayed in a competitive and empire-wide examination.

The curricula for this admirably meritocratic system, which persisted dynasty after dynasty, exercised a dominant influence on the mission, form and content of all types of education undertaken by Chinese males beyond levels of basic literacy. Secondary education was, moreover, regulated by and for the state to serve two other purposes essential for the governance of an extensive and complex empire. The first was to endow its mandarinate of officials with the prestige and authority derived from their status as a meritocracy, implementing the decrees and orders of an emperor whose power to rule over the heterogeneous populations and territories of a vast empire was widely proclaimed as a mandate from heaven.[52]

The second purpose of imperial China's tightly regulated system of secondary education was to clarify, disseminate and debate how a set of interrelated moral principles enshrined in ancient texts for the governance of an extensive, complex and agrarian empire could be internalized into personal and social behaviour. China's ancient philosophical texts (as Jesuit missionaries to the empire appreciated) can be plausibly represented as analogous to the canonical texts of Christendom. Over centuries that predated the birth of Christ by way of commentaries, critiques, adaptations and the selective absorption of elements from rival systems of belief including Buddhism, Daoism and Monism, the theology cum ideology of Ming and Qing China became consolidated into a code for righteous behaviour framed by the writings of Confucius, which is conventionally referred by intellectual historians as Neo-Confucianism.[53]

Neo-Confucian texts dominated the syllabus for the imperial examination system and curricula for the education of China's elites. These texts were studied, memorized and analysed using philological methods by the best and brightest young minds in China, and they instilled a quasi-spiritual reverence for ancient classical authorities including Mencius and Laozi and particularly Confucius.[54] This ancient and quasi-sanctified 'wisdom' can be understood as providing an education in moral and political philosophy that inculcated the virtues embodied in the cultivation of personal enlightenment through humanistic and didactic forms of scholarship and, above all, through respect for and compliance with hierarchy reposed in patriarchy, within families, and politically in dynasties of emperors mandated from heaven and served by officials exercising paternal and moral rule over the peoples of an agrarian empire.[55]

From a Euro-centred perspective, the content of Chinese education, the forms of teaching adopted by institutions for secondary education, and the absence of a tradition of disputation among masters and their pupils, as well as its enlightened but overwhelming concerns with personal behaviour, social stability and political order seem to be less hospitable and encouraging towards the study of investigations of the natural world than was apparently the case for the cosmography evolving in medieval and early modern Europe.[56] Nevertheless, it would be entirely erroneous to conclude that knowledge that was useful and reliable for the comprehension, control and manipulation of the celestial, terrestrial and biological spheres of that world had not accumulated at a more impressive rate in the Chinese Empire than in Western Europe before 1500 or that it lapsed into stasis thereafter.[57]

Apart possibly from theories of probability, all approaches to investigations into the natural world operating in Europe between the sixteenth and the eighteenth centuries were also at least present in China.[58] Furthermore, only a minority of the empire's educated elite obtained posts in the bureaucracy and even those privileged scholar officials found it necessary to acquire some practical knowledge of agronomy, meteorology, hydrology, pharmacology and medicine. Growing numbers of men (literati) educated in Neo-Confucian philosophy and statecraft became experts and wrote treatises, manuals and entries for encyclopaedia, on the properties, uses and purposes of 'things' such as birds, coinage, copper, drugs, dyestuffs, lacquerware, porcelain, salt, sugar and textiles. They consorted with craftsmen in order to publish specialized and presumably useful knowledge of many 'things' (gewu) as well as speculations about the 'concrete forces' embodied in sound, light and magnetism.[59]

In China, however, the pursuit of this type of knowledge was neither rewarded with prizes from the state nor protected for purposes of individual material gain by patents for monopoly. Above all, this knowledge was not regarded as anything like as prestigious as classical forms of learning that contributed to harmonious family life, to stability for the social order, and to the benign governance of a huge pre-modern empire.[60] By late Ming times, some scholars began to question the hegemony and utility of classical learning and sought, with limited success, to redefine the social and cultural status of more practical and material forms of knowledge including knowledge imported into China, as artefacts and industrial technologies as well as the new mathematics, astronomical methods and observations communicated by Jesuit missionaries and European merchants.[61] All proposals for reform were predictably resisted by scholar officials concerned to protect their own status and cultural capital. Under the Qing dynasty, reformers could be persecuted but generally they failed to convince the political establishments of either the more open Ming regime or the alien Manchu dynasty (who conquered the empire between 1636 and 1683) to modify let alone overturn Neo-Confucian ways of thinking about an interconnected and harmonious cosmic and moral order that included the heavens and all things on earth including man and his organic relations with nature. After all, the development and dissemination of that cosmology had for millennia served efficiently as an ideology for the maintenance of centralized rule by a long succession of dynasties.[62]

There may have been, as some revisionist historians have recently claimed, lost moments and promising opportunities for reform to the ways that China's talented and educated elites conceived of ways to explore and interrogate the natural world under late Ming emperors.[63] Greater attention and respect might have been paid to Western knowledge that only became accessible to China's literati through the less than objective conduits of Jesuit missionaries educated in Western natural philosophy and resident at court, as well as self-interested European merchants trading through Canton.[64] Perhaps the takeover of the empire by an alien dynasty anxious to secure legitimacy by suppressing departures from classical Han Chinese traditions as misplaced, degenerate and potentially destabilizing can be plausibly represented post hoc as an obstacle to the relocation and reconfiguration of ways of investigating the natural world in new and potentially more productive ways?[65]

Conclusion: China and Europe

Technological advances had appeared in China within the framework of a cosmography that remained virtually intact until the fall of the empire in 1911. The Chinese had certainly discovered and accumulated a great deal of useful and reliable knowledge and observations about the natural world long before Europeans embarked upon a more sustained and innovatory quest to comprehend its operations largely for purposes of material gain and geopolitical power, and which complemented a religious conviction that investigations into nature revealed God's creation to mankind.

For centuries Chinese intellectuals promoted the accumulation of knowledge within parameters of a different cosmology that seems to have been far more flexible and less intolerant towards notions of discovery than Christendom with its theology of revealed truths, conveyed and interpreted by hierarchal religions.[66] Yet, that epistemology provided almost no support for a separable intellectual role with its own autonomous institutional base that embodied social prestige for systematic and sustained interrogations of nature. Investigations (*gewu*) into 'things' of immediate practical and political concern continued to take place in a piecemeal manner. In a recent book, a distinguished Sinologist suggested that these genres in the Ming and Qing era could be represented as 'a scattered landscape of individual reactions, rather than a unified or linear narrative of knowledge in the making'.[67] The study of many things not only occupied a small space and place below the study of texts in Confucian philosophy but also struggled for credibility and attention by presenting evidence, findings and recommendations in a traditional Confucian style and manner.

For the discovery, development and diffusion of useful and reliable knowledge, those elements included not merely the social and political status accorded to Chinese intellectuals who allocated time and resources to 'evidential research' into the natural phenomena but also the conceptual frameworks, vocabularies and mindsets they brought to the task. 'Things' were studied less for their potential utility and more for their qualities, authenticity, and provenance within a system of thought that remained deferential towards the dominant tendency in Confucian and other classical authorities to conceive of man as part of nature and of nature as one harmonious organic whole in which all things were somehow conducted through the prisms of such philosophical notions as *qi* and *li* and *ying* and *yang* and to be correlated and connected.[68]

Needham recognized that 'the Chinese, wise before their time, had worked out an organic theory of the universe which included nature and man, church and state and all things past, present and to come', and added that the Chinese 'had no confidence that the code of nature could be read'.[69] Poignantly he added that unlike their European counterparts, the Chinese lacked 'confidence that the code of Nature laws could be unveiled and read because there was no assurance that a divine being ever more rational than ourselves had ever formulated a code capable of being read'. Needham's scholarship, insights and questions cannot be evaded.[70] Along with most Western scientists and the educated and wealthy elites of his times, England's great eighteenth-century chemist and theologian, Joseph Priestley, would have agreed with Needham. 'If', Priestley wrote, 'there were no laws of nature ... there could be no exercise for the wisdom for the understanding of intelligent beings and no man could lay a scheme with a prospect of accomplishing it.[71] And as Iliffe has demonstrated, Newton also 'believed that natural philosophy was largely a religious entreprise'.[72]

Notes

1. J. Daly (2015), *Historians Debate the Rise of the West*. London: Routledge.
2. K. Pomeranz (2000), *The Great Divergence: China, Europe and the Making of the Modern World Economy*. Princeton, NJ: Princeton University Press.
3. R. B. Wong (1997), *China Transformed: Historical Change and the Limits of European Experience*. Ithaca, NY: Cornell University Press.
4. I. Wallerstein (1974, 1980, 1989, 2011), *The Modern Word System*. New York: Academic Press; A. Gunder Frank (1998), *ReOrient: Global Economy in the Asian Age*. Berkeley, CA: University of California Press.
5. A. Maddison (2007), *Chinese Economic Performance in the Long Run, 960–2030*. Paris: OECD Publications; S. B. Broadberry and S. Hindle (eds) (2011), 'Asia in the Great Divergence', *Economic History Review*, 64 (Special Issue).
6. J. Mokyr (2002), *The Gifts of Athena*. Princeton, NJ: Princeton University Press.
7. J. Mokyr (2017), *A Culture of Growth: The Origins of the Modern Economy*. Princeton, NJ: Princeton University Press.
8. J. Needham (1969), *The Great Titration: Science and Society in East and West*. Toronto: Toronto University Press; M. Elvin (1973), *The Pattern of the Chinese Past*. Stanford, CA: Stanford University Press; P. Gouk (1995), *The Achievement Project 1990–1995* (www. alanmacfarlane.com); Pomeranz, *The Great Divergence*; M. Elvin (2010), 'Overview and introduction', in H. U. Vogel and G. Dux (eds), *Concepts of Nature: A Chinese-European Cross-Cultural Perspective*. Leiden: Brill, 1–55.
9. Vogel and Dux, *Concepts of Nature*.
10. Needham, *The Great Titration*; J. T. Fraser (ed.) (1986), *Time, Science and Society in China and the West*. Amherst, MA: Massachusetts University Press; N. Sivin (1995), *Science in Ancient China and Medicine, Philosophy and Religion in Ancient China. Researches and*

Reflections. Aldershot: Variorum and Ashgate; D. Wootton (2015), *The Invention of Science*. London: Penguin.

11. E. Grant (2004), *Science and Religion from Aristotle to Copernicus, 400 BC–AD 1550*. Baltimore: MD: Johns Hopkins University Press.

12. J. Golinski (1998), *Making Natural Knowledge: Constructivism and the History of Science*. Cambridge: Cambridge University Press.

13. M. Biagioli (ed.) (1998), *The Science Studies Reader*. London: Routledge; and M. Osler (ed.) (2000), *Rethinking the Scientific Revolution*. Cambridge: Cambridge University Press.

14. J. Hannam (2009), *God's Philosophers: How the Medieval World Laid the Foundations for Modern Science*. London: Icon Books.

15. D. C. Lindberg (ed.) (2007), *The Beginnings of Western Science: The European Scientific Tradition in Philosophical, Religious and Institutional Context 600 BC–AD 1450*. Chicago, IL: Chicago University Press.

16. V. L. Bullough (ed.) (2004), *Universities, Medicine and Science in the Medieval West*. Aldershot: Ashgate.

17. Lindberg, *The Beginnings of Western Science*.

18. E. Grant (2007), *A History of Natural Philosophy: From the Ancient World to the Nineteenth Century*. Cambridge: Cambridge University Press.

19. P. Rossi (1970), *Philosophy, Technology and the Arts in the Early Modern Era*. New York: Harper & Row.

20. P. Rossi (2001), *The Birth of Modern Science*. Oxford: Blackwell; and J. V. Field and F. A. S. L. James (1993), *Renaissance and Revolution: Humanists, Scholars, Craftsmen and Natural Philosophers in Early Modern Europe*. Cambridge: Cambridge University Press.

21. P. Long (2001), *Openness, Secrecy Authorship, Technical Arts and the Culture of Knowledge from Antiquity to Renaissance*. Baltimore, MD: Johns Hopkins University Press.

22. T. Rabb (2006), *The Last Days of the Renaissance and the March to Modernity*. New York: Basic Books.

23. S. Gaukroger (2006), *The Emergence of Scientific Culture and the Shaping of Modernity. 1210–1685*. Oxford: Oxford University Press.

24. P. Dear (2006), *The Intelligibility of Nature: How Science Makes Sense of the World*. Chicago, IL: Chicago University Press.

25. Mokyr, *The Gifts of Athena*.

26. Dear, *The Intelligibility of Nature*.

27. J. F. Cohen (1994), *The Scientific Revolution: A Historiographical Inquiry*. Chicago, IL: Chicago University Press.

28. J. L. van Zanden and M. Prak (eds) (2013), *Technology, Skills and the Premodern Economy*. Leiden: Brill.

29. De Ridder-Symoens (ed.) (1996), *A History of the University in Early Modern Europe, 1500–1800*. Cambridge: Cambridge University Press.

30. S. Gaukroger (2010), *Science and the Shaping of Modernity, 1660–1760*. Oxford: Oxford University Press; and Wootton, *The Invention of Science*.

31. J. Bona (1995), *The Word of God and the Language of Man: Interpreting Nature in Early Modern Science*. Madison, WI: University of Wisconsin Press.

32. M. A. Gillespie (2008), *The Theological Origins of Modernity*. Chicago, IL: University of Chicago Press.

33. T. Worcester (2008), *Cambridge Companion to the Jesuits*. Cambridge: Cambridge University Press; and M. Feingold (2002), *Jesuit Science and the Republic of Letters*. Cambridge, MA: MIT Press.

34. Wootton, *The Invention of Science*; and Gaukroger, *Science and the Shaping of Modernity*.

35. G. E. R. Lloyd (2009), *Disciplines in the Making*. Oxford: Oxford University Press; and D. Headrick (2000), *When Information Comes of Age*. Oxford: Oxford University Press.

36. I. Inkster and K. Deng (eds) (2004), *History of Technology*, vol. 25 (Special Issue). London: Institute of Historical Research.

37. J. M. Levine (1991), *The Battle of the Books: History and Literature in the Augustan Age*. Ithaca, NY: Cornell University Press; and P. Smith and B. Schmidt (eds) (2007), *Making Knowledge in Early Modern Europe: Practices, Objects and Texts, 1400–1800*. Chicago, IL: Chicago University Press.

38. This excludes a significant and well-documented history of experiments concerned with the properties of atmospheric pressure, with magnetism, with acids, human anatomy, and navigation.

39. P. Smith (1994), *The Business of Alchemy: Science and Culture in the Holy Roman Empire*. Princeton, NJ: Princeton University Press.

40. W. R. Newman and A. Grafton (2001), *Secrets of Nature: Astrology and Alchemy in Early Modern Europe*. Cambridge, MA: MIT Press.

41. D. Noble (1997), *The Religion of Technology: The Divinity of Man and the Spirit of Invention*. London: Penguin.

42. P. K. O'Brien (2009), 'The Needham question updated: A historiographical survey and elaboration', *History of Technology*, 29, 7–28.

43. H. Butterfield (1949), *The Origins of Modern Science, 1300–1800*. London: Bell, 36–8.

44. B. Elman (2005), *On Their Own Terms: Science in China, 1550–1900*. Cambridge, MA: Harvard University Press.

45. Sivin, *Science in Ancient China*.

46. J. E. McClellan and H. Dorn (1999), *Science and Technology in World History*. Baltimore, MD: Johns Hopkins University Press.

47. C. A. Ronan (1983), *The Illustrated History of the World's Science*. Cambridge: Cambridge University Press.

48. R. Temple (1998), *The Genius of China*. London: Prism Books.

49. D. Bodde (1991), *Chinese Thought, Society and Science*. Honolulu: Hawai'i University Press.

50. J. Lin (1995), 'The Needham puzzle: Why the Industrial Revolution did not originate in China', *Economic Development and Cultural Change*, 43 (2), 269–92.

51. R. von Glahn (2016), *The Economic History of China: From Antiquity to the Nineteenth Century*. Cambridge: Cambridge University Press; and J.-L. Rosenthal and R. Bin Wong (2011), *Before and Beyond Divergence: The Politics of Economic Change in China and Europe*, Cambridge, MA: Harvard University Press.

52. B. Elman (2000), *A Cultural History of Civil Examinations in Late Imperial China*. Berkeley, CA: California University Press.

53. W. T. de Bary (1981), *Neo Confucian Orthodoxy and the Learning of Mind and Heart*. New York: Columbia University Press.

54. B. Elman (1984), *From Philosophy to Philology*. Cambridge: Cambridge University Press.

55. L. M. Jensen (1997), *Confucianism: Chinese Tradition and Universal Civilization*. Durham, NC: Duke University Press; and Y. Xinzhong (2002), *An Introduction to Confucianism*. Cambridge: Cambridge University Press.

56. G. E. R. Lloyd and N. Sivin (2002), *The Way and the Word: Science and Medicine in Early China and Greece*. New Haven, CT: Yale University Press.

57. Sivin, *Science in Ancient China*; and Elman, *A Cultural History of Civil Examinations*.

58. M. Elvin (2004), *The Retreat of the Elephants: An Environmental History of China*. New Haven, CT: Yale University Press.

59. P. S. Ropp (1990), *Heritage of China: Contemporary Perspectives on Chinese Civilization*. Berkeley, CA: University of California Press; and B. Elman and A. Woodside (eds) (1994), *Education and Society in Late Imperial China, 1600–1900*. Berkeley, CA: University of California Press.

60. J. B. Henderson (1991), *Scripture, Canon and Commentary*. Princeton, NJ: Princeton University Press.

61. T. Brook (2010), *The Troubled Empire: China in the Yuan and Ming Dynasties*. Cambridge, MA: Harvard University Press.

62. J. B. Henderson (1984), *The Development and Decline of Chinese Cosmology*. New York: Columbia University Press.

63. H. Zurndorfer (2002), 'Old and new visions of Ming society and culture', *Toung Pao*, 87, 151–69.

64. C. Jami, P. Engelfreit and G. Blue (eds) (2001), *Statecraft and Intellectual Renewal in Late Ming China*. Leiden: Brill.

65. R. J. Smith (1994), *China's Cultural Heritage: The Qing Dynasty, 1644–1912*. Boulder, CO: Westview Press.

66. Vogel and Dux, *Concepts of Nature*.

67. D. Schäfer (2011), *The Crafting of 10,000 Things: Knowledge and Technology in Seventeenth-Century China*. Chicago, IL: Chicago University Press, 19.

68. J. Needham (ed.) (1956), *Science and Civilization in China*, vol. 1. Cambridge: Cambridge University Press, 543–82; J. Needham (ed.) (1961), *Science and Civilization in China*, vol. 2. Cambridge: Cambridge University Press, 1–43; and Y. S. Kim (2010), 'Confucian scholars and technical knowledge in traditional China', *East Asian Science: International Journal*, 4, 207–28.

69. Needham, *The Great Titration*, 120; see also Mokyr, *A Culture of Growth*.

70. Needham, *The Great Titration*, 120.

71. J. T. Rutt (ed.) (1817), *The Theological and Miscellaneous Works of Joseph Priestley*. London: George Smallfield.

72. R. Iliffe (2017), *Priest of Nature: The Religious Worlds of Isaac Newton*. Oxford: Oxford University Press.

CHAPTER 4
TOOLKITS, CREATIVITY AND DIVERGENCES: TECHNOLOGY IN GLOBAL HISTORY
Karel Davids

Economic historians agree that technological change after 1800 has been much more rapid and pervasive than in earlier centuries, and since the late nineteenth century, the United States has been the frontrunner in this development. As Robert Gordon claimed, if productivity growth in the United States is now slowing down and the potential for further revolutionary innovations is limited, this could mean that the pace of technological change globally will diminish once the fruits of catching up with the United States have been reaped.[1] But will it? The nature and timing of future innovations remain notoriously hard to predict, even though examples of successful forecasting exist.[2] There is no compelling reason why technological leadership should rest with the United States forever. Historians surely cannot offer a safe guide to the future. What historians, and especially global historians, *can* do is analyse and explain underlying patterns and contexts of long-term technological change. Looking at connections and making comparisons between different parts of the world, global historians can propose answers to big questions such as: To what extent do different societies share the same bodies of knowledge? When, where and why do innovations take place? When and why do divergences in technological development occur, and why does technological leadership shift from one place to another?

These are the questions that figure prominently in the debate on the Great Divergence. Answers, however, vary wildly. At one extreme are David Landes and Joseph Needham. Landes claimed that from the Middle Ages onwards, Europe saw a continuous flow of inventions and accumulation of technical knowledge, which eventually (also aided by other factors) culminated in the Industrial Revolution in Britain.[3] Joseph Needham, by contrast, insisted that China was far ahead of the West in many areas of technological achievement up to at least 1500.[4] At the other extreme are those who play down differences in technological development between Eurasian societies before the nineteenth century and reject the idea that Europe had any advantage over China, India or the Middle East. In their view, differences in technology between these societies were far outweighed by broad similarities. Eurasian societies in this period by and large supposedly shared the same 'toolkits' of technical knowledge – to borrow a term coined by prehistorians and archaeologists.[5]

Andre Gunder Frank denied that there was such a thing as 'European technology' at all, let alone 'European technological superiority', before 1800. The 'very substantial' diffusion of technology and worldwide division of labour implied that technological development was a 'world economic process' rather than a regional or national one. Frank insisted that even the technological advances of the Industrial Revolution, whose importance he acknowledged, should not be seen as purely European achievements.[6] John Hobson and Jack Goody likewise lambasted the idea of a European lead in technological development before the Industrial Revolution.[7] Edmund Burke III argued that the Islamic world, borrowing innovations from a variety of sources, between about 650 CE and 1700 CE played a central role in the formation of standardized 'toolkits' of knowledge on subjects such as water management, writing, information processing and mathematics, which Europeans later turned to good account. These 'technological complexes', as he prefers to call them, include both specific technologies and 'the culture knowledge' that made this technology possible.[8] More generally, Jared Diamond postulated that for all societies much or most new technology is not invented locally but is instead borrowed from other societies. According to Diamond, diffusion is key to technological development. For the rest, 'technology tends to catalyse itself '.[9] This is a long way from Robert Gordon's techno-pessimism.

Other scholars hold a position somewhere between these extremes. Comparing science and technology in India and Europe in the seventeenth and eighteenth centuries, Prasannan Parthasarathi concluded that 'Europe indeed showed a "scientific and technological verve"' but that the key Revolution did not reside in 'any purported cultural, economic or social exceptionalism' but in 'the specific challenges the Europeans faced'. The technological breakthrough in Britain resulted from a combination of external competitive pressures, ecological shortfalls and a mercantile state.[10] Kenneth Pomeranz acknowledged that 'a surge in European technological inventiveness certainly [was] a necessary condition of the Industrial revolution', but stressed the crucial role of 'coal and colonies' in removing the constraints for sustained growth of per capita income.[11] Peer Vries, by contrast, argued that coal and colonies could only become relevant factors in the divergence between Europe and China because Western Europe, in contrast with China, had experienced 'a long process of continuing and self- sustaining invention and innovation' and by the eighteenth century had established a 'wide-ranging lead'. The West was leading especially in fields 'that had most potential for increasing productivity', and this lead was not a matter of accident but the outcome of a long-term development.[12] Joel Mokyr, too, emphasized that the divide between the East and the West essentially sprang from prior differences in technology. More specifically, Mokyr related this development to the Scientific Revolution in the seventeenth century, which contributed to the rise of a new and unique environment for the creation of useful forms of knowledge, which he called the 'Industrial Enlightenment'. Useful knowledge was 'knowledge of natural phenomena and regularities that had the potential to affect technology'. As a follow-up, Paola Bertucci argued that the role of artisanal knowledge in the development of key 'Enlightenment' notions such as 'useful knowledge' should not be ignored.[13]

Yet another perspective has been suggested by Jack Goldstone. On the one hand, he underscored the similarities between all societies in world history that experienced a period of economic, political and cultural 'efflorescence' (such as Song China,

Northwestern Europe in the high Middle Ages, Golden Age Holland or high Qing China). On the other hand, he pointed to the unique emergence of 'engine science' – a reliance on engines for understanding the world – and its spread into popular culture in eighteenth-century England, which eventually led to the Industrial Revolution. Thus, there was perhaps something special about the development in this part of Europe after all.[14]

This chapter will discuss the three big questions introduced earlier, and the different answers to these, in relation to the debate on the Great Divergence. The first section examines the matter of toolkits. To what extent did different societies in the past share the same bodies of knowledge? Was much or most new technology indeed borrowed from other societies, and if so, how? The second section concerns the issue of technological creativity. How did new technical knowledge come into being and how can its creation be explained? The third section, finally, addresses the question of divergences. When and why did divergences in technological development occur, and why did technological leadership shift from one place to another? If there was a shared body of knowledge between Eurasian societies, why did Europe, and in particular Britain, eventually move into the forefront of technological development?

Toolkits and Travelling Knowledge

Although scholars have used the notion of a common human 'toolkit' of technology, implicitly or explicitly, for quite some time, it is actually not firmly established whether such a toolkit has existed at all. Andre Gunder Frank's confident assertion that technological development was a world economic process and that there was no 'European' technology at all is not substantiated by evidence. Similarly, Jared Diamond does not offer evidence for his far-reaching claim that 'much or most new technology' is borrowed from other societies instead of being invented locally. Edmund Burke III does indeed provide support for his thesis that major technological complexes in the lands of Islam partly rested on innovations that had been developed in various regions in 'Afroeurasia' and subsequently underwent a process of standardization, but he is much more sparing with offering proof that the Islamic world then served as a vital source of knowledge for other parts of the world concerning, for example, water management and the development of universities. Whether there really has been a toolkit on which all societies could draw still remains a moot point.

The notion of 'toolkit' actually conflates several modes and layers of technological development that analytically can be kept apart. It presents an oversimplified answer to questions that in reality are quite complex: the issue of the relation between mobility and rootedness of knowledge and the issue of the relation between diffusion of knowledge and multiple independent inventions or improvements. 'Toolkit' suggests that technical knowledge was transmitted across societies and cultures rather than being developed or discovered locally. Yet, demonstrating that a certain item or process existed at the same time in different places, or that it existed earlier in one region than another, does not imply that there was some underlying common reservoir of knowledge or that knowledge actually travelled. The fact that dikes can be found both in China and in the Low Countries does not necessarily mean that the Chinese borrowed knowledge on dike-building from the North Sea area or vice versa. Coexistence does not imply common origin, nor does precedence entail causation. On the other hand, connections *can* have existed and diffusion *can* have taken place.

Technology could in fact be borrowed or shared in a variety of ways. First of all, it could remain more or less stable in space, yet move between different societies and cultures. The debate on the 'Watson thesis' shows that both phenomena could well go together in historical reality. Andrew Watson claimed that agriculture in the Mediterranean and West Asia was transformed between about 700 CE and 1100 CE under the impact of the rise and expansion of Islam. Once the entire region between Spain and Afghanistan had been unified under Muslim rule, Watson propounded, many 'new' crops and farming techniques were diffused in this area, which mostly 'originated' and had been 'domesticated' in the Indian subcontinent or lands farther to the East. Among these 'new' crops were sorghum, rice, hard wheat, sugar cane, cotton, lemons, limes, bananas, spinach, mango, watermelons and coconut palms. The diffusion of these plants and the techniques that facilitated their cultivation (especially improvements in irrigation) led to a rise in agricultural productivity, which made possible a growth of trade, an increase in specialization and a rise in urbanization in the Islamic world.[15]

Historians of technology and specialists on the history of the Mediterranean and West Asia have criticized Watson's thesis at many points, arguing notably that Watson got his chronology of innovation seriously wrong. Evidence showed that several crops on his list were already present in the Mediterranean and Western Asia before the rise of Islam and that irrigation and other techniques had been more advanced than Watson acknowledged. Peregrine Horden and Nicholas Purcell insisted that 'innovation of the utmost importance (was) going on continuously' in antiquity. Michael Decker, too, took issue with the idea of 'rapid and deep changes in Muslim agricultural practices'. In his view, 'Islamic farming structures were built atop earlier Roman and Persian landscapes; these were usurped rather than swept away.'[16] Although, as Paolo Squatriti remarked,[17] such critiques do not invalidate the thesis – because Watson stressed diffusion rather than introduction or invention – they nevertheless make an important point about technological development. Change was multi-layered; innovations were embedded in pre-existing local practices and structures.

Once we view technological development in a given region in a long-term perspective, labels turn out to be crude at best. The fact that an innovation emerged or thrived in a place and time when a particular culture in this region reigned supreme (e.g. during the Roman Empire or the Abbasid Caliphate) does not necessarily mean that this innovation can be labelled as a product of that culture. 'Roman' technology was partly based on technical knowledge developed in the Mediterranean and West Asia under Hellenistic regimes and 'Islamic' technology partly rested on technical knowledge developed in the same region during the Roman, Byzantine and Sassanid empires.[18] Michael Lewis's case study on the development of windmills between about 800 CE and 1200 CE suggests that key innovations such as the introduction of the horizontal mill, the vertical mill and the tower mill first appeared on the Iranian plateau and in the Aegean due to successive combinations of ideas of Greeks, Persians, Byzantines and Seljuk Turks.[19]

A second way in which technology could be borrowed or shared was by the movement of culture groups from one place to another. David Anthony showed that speakers of proto-Indo-European dialects brought revolutionary innovations such as horseback riding and the use of wheeled vehicles and chariots from the Eurasian steppes to the lower Danube Valley, Iran and the Indian subcontinent from the fourth millennium BCE. These very innovations in transportation also opened up the steppes as 'a corridor of communication' between China, India, Iran and the West.[20]

Finally, technology could also move from one place or culture to another via the travelling of people and the circulation of storage devices such as manuscripts, drawings, prints, books and artefacts. According to Watson, travelling people were essential agents for the diffusion of knowledge about new crops in the lands of Islam. Apart from envoys acting on the authority of rulers, 'thousands of mostly unknown individuals from many levels of society', including soldiers, pilgrims and traders, must have been instrumental in the movements of plants 'over shorter or longer distances'.[21] Sweet potatoes (and the knowledge of how to grow and to store them) reached China from Central America by way of the Philippines, thanks to Spanish seafarers crossing the Pacific and a Chinese merchant visiting Manila in the 1590s.[22] The 'Silk Road', which connected China and Transoxiana from the second century BCE, functioned as a passageway for refugees, missionaries, craftsmen, traders and other groups of travellers, who – among other things – transmitted technologies from one side of Eurasia to another. While the art of glass making moved to China from the West, the techniques of weaving silk and making paper travelled from China in the opposite direction. Paper making was probably introduced in Transoxiana by Buddhist monks by the end of the seventh century.[23] The wide availability of paper and the invention of printing, which followed in the eighth century, further helped to enhance the mobility of knowledge, even apart from the physical movement of people. The growth in the production of books, whether copied by hand or printed with woodblocks or movable type, meant that technical knowledge could be stored and circulated on a much larger scale than ever before.[24]

Movements of knowledge between places and cultures were not a neutral process. Circulation of knowledge involved both translation and transformation. Moreover, as Harold Cook and Sven Dupré observed, 'the parties involved, whether speakers or listeners' were changed in the process of translation as well.[25] The massive Graeco-Arabic translation movement under the early Abbasid Caliphate, for example, according to Dimitri Gutas did not only generate 'an Arabic scientific literature with a technical vocabulary for its concepts' but also preserved many non-literary Greek texts in Arabic translation and 'contributed, through the demand it created for secular Greek works, to their preservation … in Greek' by accelerating their transcription in manuscript copies.[26] Knowledge in transit was thus not a ready set of tools packed in a box. Knowledge changed in the very process of movement.

Technological Creativity

How did new technical knowledge come about? Does technology tend to catalyse itself, as Jared Diamond argues? Arguably technological advances often 'depend upon previous mastery of simpler problems' and 'new technologies and materials make it possible to generate still other new technologies'.[27] But this process is far from automatic. Technological development can take unexpected turns. In many areas in Europe during the early Middle Ages, for example, sophisticated water systems from Roman times were neglected or abandoned. Aqueducts fell into disrepair. Fired brick (and concrete) was not used in building north of the Alps for a long time.[28] In North Africa, the Middle East and Iran, wheeled vehicles were abandoned in favour of the camel as a means of transport for over a thousand years.[29] The extensive use of paper and the proliferation of books in the lands of Islam were not followed by an early adoption of the printing press.[30] Watermills were well known in the Mediterranean and West Asia from Roman times onwards, but it was only in medieval and early modern Europe that water power was harnessed for a wide variety of industrial purposes on a massive scale.[31]

The rate and direction of technological change thus vary considerably in time and space. How can it be explained? A common type of argument holds that factor prices determine when and where inventions are adopted. The lack of more mechanization in the Roman Empire, for example, has been ascribed to the abundance of cheap labour, notably slave labour, relative to other factors of production. Scarcity of labour relative to the abundance of land has been adduced as a crucial stimulus to mechanization in the antebellum era in the United States. High wages relative to cheap energy have been proposed as the single most important factor in explaining why the Industrial Revolution happened in Britain in the eighteenth century.[32]

This approach is illuminating up to a point. Private entrepreneurs doubtless take relative prices of production factors into account when making decisions about whether or not to adopt a particular technique. But the explanatory power of this sort of argument is limited. For one thing, it is not evident that other types of actors who had an impact on technological change in the past, such as governments, princes, religious organizations and community associations, likewise based their decision making on information about relative factor prices. The fact that until 1719 Muslims in the Ottoman Empire were not allowed to operate a printing press had more to do with the high esteem for the handwritten word in the Islamic world and with the economic and political power of thousands of copyists in Istanbul than with the relative prices of production factors.[33] Secondly, even if decisions about the adoption of inventions partly depended on information on factor prices, this does not mean that the direction of inventive activities themselves was determined by these particular conditions. Christine MacLeod has shown that, contrary to expectations, most applicants for patents in eighteenth-century England did *not* state the saving of labour as the goal of their invention but the saving of capital or the improvement of the quality of products.[34] Thirdly, and most fundamentally, factor prices do not explain where knowledge embodied in technology actually came from. How was knowledge supplied? How were inventions generated? What made the creation of new techniques possible? Relative factor prices, in short, can be proximate causes for the adoption of technologies, but they do not regulate the process of creation of knowledge itself and they are certainly not the ultimate cause of technological creativity.

Like the diffusion of knowledge, the creation of knowledge could occur in a multiplicity of ways. One of them was the creation of what are called 'inventions'. The term 'invention' suggests that the production of new knowledge is a discrete, distinct event, a kind of happening which can be exactly pinpointed in place and time. This is, historically speaking, quite a recent idea. It arose in Italian cities during the high Middle Ages as part of an increasing tendency to consider knowledge as a type of 'property'. These growing proprietary attitudes manifested themselves on the one hand in formal or informal arrangements to limit specific knowledge to practitioners of a particular craft or trade, and on the other hand in institutional provisions to protect property rights on knowledge in the form of patents for invention. While, from the thirteenth century onwards, patents for invention of new techniques of mechanical devices were granted on an ad hoc basis, the practice became enshrined in law in many parts of Europe at the end of the fifteenth century. The first law that guaranteed a right to the ownership and commercial exploitation of a new invention was enacted by the Senate of the Republic of Venice in 1474.[35] The chief criterion for granting a patent in this Venetian statute and subsequent regulations by other governments in early modern Europe was not the originality of an invention as such, but its novelty to a particular locality. Apart from providing a reward for the labours of private inventors, patents were equally used as an instrument by cities and states to attract 'new' knowledge from elsewhere to give a boost to their own economies.[36] After the idea of an invention as something 'new', which could be clearly identified, had taken hold in Renaissance Europe, literati began to produce catalogues of inventions or discoveries that had not been known in the ancient world. The most famous one is no doubt the set of three 'inventions' that 'changed the face and state of the world', mentioned in Francis Bacon's *Novum Organum* in 1620: gunpowder, the compass and the printing press.[37] Following Bacon's example, data on the frequency and significance of inventions in the historiography of technology long remained a yardstick for comparing the technological creativity of societies.[38]

The number of patents for invention granted in European countries increased by leaps and bounds from the sixteenth century onwards. The level of patenting reached in Venice was exceeded in the Dutch Republic after 1590, which was in its turn surpassed by Britain in the eighteenth century. Britain during the nineteenth century ceded place to the United States, which saw the ratio of patents relative to its total population truly explode after the Civil War.[39] Figures on patenting can to some extent be taken as an indicator of technological creativity. However, even after the institution of patenting came into existence, inventive activities continued to take place outside patent systems as well. Prizes, premiums, contracts, tax exemptions and other sorts of privileges or rewards granted by public authorities or private organizations could in early modern Europe fulfil similar functions for individual inventors as patents.[40] Even in the United States, the patent system was not always the only institution that promoted or protected inventive activities. Robert Gordon observed that patenting in the United States actually declined during part of the twentieth century, when inventive activities came to a large extent to be concentrated in research laboratories of large corporations.[41]

Technological creativity, however, could manifest itself in other ways than through the development or discovery of a distinct new thing or process, which could qualify for a patent for invention or for some other kind of reward. 'Macro-inventions', that is 'inventions in which a radical new idea, without clear precedent, emerges more or less ab nihilo' (as Joel Mokyr defines them), have been quite rare. One of the few inventions that comes close to this ideal type is the steam engine. Throughout much of human history, technological advance, on the contrary, largely proceeded through 'micro-inventions', 'small, incremental steps that improved, adapted, and streamlined existing techniques already in use' (again as defined by Mokyr), or what Eric Jones has called 'technological drift'.[42] Trial and error, random mutations, learning by doing, or learning by using all could help to make this slow change possible.[43] Although such mundane, gradual improvements, adaptations, or refinements often have not been identified as distinct 'inventions' – let alone patented – they nevertheless have made a contribution to the growth of productivity and were sometimes instrumental in realizing major breakthroughs. The successful ventures of European seafarers across the Atlantic and into the Indian Ocean in the 1490s, for example, owed much to slow improvements in shipbuilding and navigation during the Middle Ages, as well as to the continuous, painstaking accumulation of knowledge about wind patterns in the northern and southern Atlantic.[44]

However, variations in the rate and direction of technological change must be related to more factors than mere steady, ordinary technological drift or movements of knowledge between places or cultures. These factors in themselves after all cannot explain why creativity *differed*. Historians have sought additional underlying causes of technological creativity in contextual variables such as competition between states, warfare population growth, environmental challenges, cultural climates and institutional arrangements. On closer inspection, however, many of these factors turn out not to have as much explanatory power as suggested. Sometimes they appear to stimulate innovation, sometimes they appear to inhibit it, and sometimes they do not seem to have much effect on technological creativity at all. Warfare, for example, can work out both ways. Ecological pressures and/or population growth do not invariably lead to technological breakthroughs.[45] Some values and attitudes, such as respect for manual labour, may have provided a more favourable climate for technological creativity than others, such as a submissive attitude to authority, but it is doubtful whether the presence of such cultural characteristics in itself has been a necessary or sufficient condition for innovation.

Still, cultural factors may have affected technology in an indirect way, namely by influencing the development of institutions, which facilitated technological creativity. Apart from arrangements specifically rewarding inventive activities, such as patents, prizes or privileges, these technology-friendly institutions also include institutions supporting the dissemination, certification and creation of knowledge more broadly such as craft guilds, schools, academies, libraries and research laboratories. David Mowery and Nathan Rosenberg even termed the emergence of a R&D system in the United States in the twentieth century as the 'institutionalization of innovation'.[46] At the present state of inquiry, this institutional perspective, with a focus on infrastructures of knowledge, offers the most promising strategy for understanding variations in technological creativity. It may also help explain divergences in technological development between different parts of the world which emerged over time.

Divergences

In the nineteenth century, global divergences in technological development became patently obvious. While technological change generally was faster and more comprehensive than before, Europe and the United States were clearly ahead of other regions in the world. Technological advantage translated into an edge in productivity as well as into political and military ascendancy. Western imperialism made great strides, thanks to the use of advanced technologies. Innovations such as steamships, telegraphs, rifles and quinine after 1840 became effective 'tools of empire', as Daniel Headrick called them, and connections between technology and imperialism persisted long into the twentieth century.[47] But when and why did these divergences in technological development come about?

The debate on this issue has mostly concentrated on comparisons between Europe and Asia – in particular China and India – and to a lesser extent on comparisons between regions within Europe between about 700 CE and 1800 CE. Taking the 'Great Divergence' in technology first, we should consider the matter from two sides. On the one hand, there is no convincing evidence that either Europe, China or India had achieved technological 'superiority' over any other world area by the end of the eighteenth century. Extravagant claims for the supremacy of Europe or China such as those put forward by David Landes or Joseph Needham are not solidly grounded in facts. All the different types of machines and mechanical devices described in Needham's *Science and Civilisation in China*, for example, can equally be found in late medieval and early modern Europe while energy and the use of energy sources before the middle of the eighteenth century did not greatly differ.[48] Like Europe, Qing China still saw gradual technological change, especially in the agricultural sector. A 'relative technological standstill', as Mark Elvin surmised, did not occur.[49] As for India, Prasannan Parthasarathi has made a plausible case for the thesis that the knowledge and skills of eighteenth-century artisans on the subcontinent were not inferior to those of European craftsmen in industries such as textile making, shipbuilding, arms manufacture and iron smelting.[50] In 1800, the level of technology that was actually used in Europe, China or India did not yet substantially differ.

On the other hand, we should be careful to be fixated on similarities alone. If there were no differences between these regions of Eurasia before 1800 at all, where did the disparity in the nineteenth century come from? How can the technological lead of European countries and the United States after 1800 be explained? Parthasarathi sought the answer in 'the specific challenges' Europeans faced. In his view, the threat of being outcompeted by Indian textiles on global markets and the increasing scarcity of traditional sources of energy acted as triggers for 'revolutionary technological breakthroughs' in Britain, which laid the foundation for the Industrial Revolution. Maxine Berg in the same vein argued that imports of luxury goods from Asia 'activated' product innovation and invention in Britain.[51] But this kind of explanatory reasoning begs the question why Britain in particular, or Europe more generally, was able to meet these challenges by developing a radical new response. Failures to meet challenges are after all not uncommon in history. Industrial revolutions on the contrary rarely happen. What made this unprecedented leap forward in technological capability possible?

On closer inspection, differences in technological development between various regions of Eurasia already existed before the end of the eighteenth century. Even though the general level and rate of technological change in China and Europe did not vary greatly before 1800, there were differences in the nature of technological development, the formation of human capital, the circulation of technical knowledge, and processes of technological creativity. The potential of specific innovations was not always realized as fully in China as in Europe. Clocks, cannon, the magnetic compass and printing by movable type are cases in point. In addition, technological change in early modern Europe had a wider scope: it took place not only in the agricultural sector and in urban industries but also in various other branches of economic activity, such as the shipping industry. Formation of human capital through specialist, technical education in China developed not as far as in European countries. Schools with a vocational emphasis, for example, remained a relatively rare phenomenon. Moreover, although the output of printed books, including technical writings, in late Ming and Qing China strongly grew, the extent of circulation of these materials did not increase accordingly; libraries were often only accessible to the selected few. As for processes of creation, Chinese technicians, unlike European artisans, did not use drawings to 'think on paper'.[52]

India and Europe were not similar in every respect either. Parthasarathi argues that modes of transmission for 'useful' knowledge present in early modern Europe, such as 'schools, universities, lecture halls, associations', were not entirely absent in India, but he admits that evidence about their actual importance is hard to discover. Infrastructures of knowledge in India cannot be demonstrated to have been the same as in Europe. Furthermore, while patronage of states may have been 'critical' for the diffusion of knowledge in India, especially through the establishment of libraries and the sponsorship of translations, Europe saw, besides states, also other actors and institutions such as cities, trading companies and religious organizations playing an important role in the circulation of technical knowledge. Europe probably surpassed India with regard to the circulation of printed books and periodicals.[53] This may have been a relevant factor in the emerging divergence as well. Although much technical knowledge in the past did not find its way into print, this does not mean that all forms of knowledge could circulate at the same rate and advance through learning by doing or learning by using. Not all knowledge can be subsumed in a broad, hybrid category called 'the mindful hand'.[54] Distinctions between 'tacit' and 'explicit' knowledge or between 'manual abilities' and 'inquiry into nature' *do* matter. 'Prescriptive knowledge' (knowledge 'how') and 'propositional knowledge' (knowledge 'what'), as Mokyr terms them, *can* be distinguished.[55] And the latter type of knowledge in Europe increasingly circulated in storage devices such as printed texts, which made a significant contribution to technological advance. Prescriptive knowledge alone would not have made it possible for European seamen to sail regularly from Europe to India or China, and back, nor have enabled European inventors to design the steam engine, the railway, the telegraph and the internal combustion engine.

Divergences between Europe and Asia thus began to arise long before the end of the eighteenth century. Some of the foundations for the spurt in technology capability in Europe after 1800 were put in place as early as the late Middle Ages. But technological change was not equally spread over Europe. Divergences within Europe emerged as well. Some regions advanced earlier and developed more rapidly than others. Technological leadership in Europe first rested with Northern Italy, south Germany and the Southern Netherlands, then shifted to the Dutch Republic and eventually moved to England. 'Technological leadership' meant that a given country, region, town or cluster of towns played an initiating role in the development of new technologies in a wide variety of fields for a lengthy period of time.[56]

Life cycles of technological leaders before 1800 showed a more or less fixed pattern. Before starting on a prolonged technological advance, a future leading region, town or cluster of towns first developed into the hub of a widespread trading network. The scope of the technological advance was at first usually rather narrow, but once the domination over an extended trade network had been firmly established, it broadened in many ways. No centre of leadership started from scratch. Each new centre partly built on the achievements of its precursors, while expanding and transforming the body of knowledge in the process. South Germany borrowed from Northern Italy, Flanders and Brabant borrowed from Italy and South Germany, the Dutch Republic borrowed from all three, and Britain in its turn borrowed from the Dutch and its predecessors. Movements of knowledge and skills via the travelling of people and the circulation of storage devices such as books, manuscripts, drawings and artefacts thus contributed to the accumulation of know-how from one centre of leadership to another.[57] Although a technological leader often did not succeed in retaining a competitive edge in all those areas where it achieved its initial supremacy, it still could for a while compensate for the loss of the original strongholds by building new ones. Frontrunners explored new routes of technological advance. While initial achievements of technological leaders usually consisted more in improvements in physical productivity than in gains in quality, the order was often reversed later on. Eventually, however, substitutions of old sectors of growth by new ones became ever rarer. Leadership moved to a place that showed a higher rate of innovation.[58]

At the end of the seventeenth century, foreign observers considered the Dutch Republic as a model of technological creativity. A Swedish traveller called Holland in the 1690s an 'officina machinarum'. In his travelogue *The Grand Tour* of 1749, Irish writer Thomas Nugent stated that 'there (was) no nation where the people apply themselves with more diligence to all manners of mechanical arts, than the inhabitants of the United Provinces'.[59] In the course of the eighteenth century, however, England achieved a still higher rate of technological innovation than the Netherlands by realizing a combination of 'prescriptive knowledge' and 'propositional knowledge' which the Dutch did not achieve. As Goldstone and Mokyr observed, English society and culture offered a uniquely congenial environment for the emergence of 'engine science' or, more broadly, the creation of 'useful knowledge' in the sense of knowledge of natural phenomena and regularities that had the potential to affect technology. This 'Industrial Enlightenment' was a powerful factor in the making of the Industrial Revolution. The technological leadership of the United States, which became manifest from the late nineteenth century onwards, in its turn built on the foundation laid by these revolutionary breakthroughs in industry in Britain.[60]

Conclusion

Technological change took place more or less continuously throughout history, though at different rates and with different consequences. Sometimes advances occurred with leaps and bounds, and often they were barely noticeable at all. Over time, divergences emerged between technological developments in different parts of the world. This chapter argues that these variations between times and places should neither be magnified nor smoothed over. Neither point of view is very helpful for understanding technological change and its role in global history.

This chapter proposes a more analytical, comparative perspective instead. It suggests the adoption of a differentiated view of the circulation of knowledge and of its relation with local inventions and improvements, rather than to utilize the notion of a common human toolkit of technology. It suggests that we look beyond relative factor prices to explain the rate and direction of technological change and that we examine more closely the varied ways in which new technical knowledge actually could come about and the congenial institutional settings in which creativity could flourish. Finally, the chapter argues that similarities in the level and rate of technological change at a certain point in time may well go together with slowly emerging differences in development, which can eventually build up into major disparities. The Great Divergence in technology between China and India on the one hand and Europe and the United States on the other, which became patently clear in the nineteenth century, had its origins in initially minor differences which began to appear many centuries before.

Notes

1.   R. J. Gordon (2016), *The Rise and Fall of American Economic Growth: The U.S. Standard of Living since the Civil War*. Princeton, NJ: Princeton University Press, 1–8.

2.   Cf. J. Mokyr (2013), 'Is technological progress a thing of the past?', http://voxeu.org/article/technological-progress-thing-past; and Gordon, *Rise and Fall*, 590–2.

3.   D. Landes (1998), *The Wealth and Poverty of Nations*. New York: W. W. Norton, 44–54, 187–93.

4. J. Needham (1965), *Science and Civilisation in China*, vol. 4: *Physics and Physical Technology*: Part 2 *Mechanical Engineering*. Cambridge: Cambridge University Press; J. Needham, W. Ling and D. K. de Solla Price (1960), *Heavenly Clockwork: The Great Astronomical Clock of Medieval China*. Cambridge: Cambridge University Press.

5. E. Burke III (2009), 'Islam at the center: Technological complexes and the roots of modernity', *Journal of World History*, 20 (2), 166.

6. A. Gunder Frank (1998), *ReOrient: Global Economy in the Asian Age*. Berkeley, CA: University of California Press, 186, 204 and 285.

7. J. Hobson (2004), *The Eastern Origins of Western Civilization*. Cambridge: Cambridge University Press, 50–61, 190–214; J. Goody (2004), *Capitalism and Modernity: The Great Debate*. Cambridge: Cambridge University Press, 19–20, 25–7.

8. Burke, 'Islam at the center', 167–8.

9. J. Diamond (1997), *Guns, Germs and Steel: A Short History of Everybody for the Last 13,000 Years*. London: W. W. Norton, 254, 258–9.

10. P. Parthasarathi (2002), 'Review Article: The Great Divergence', *Past & Present*, 176, 282; Ibid. (2011), *Why Europe Grew Rich and Asia Did Not: Global Economic Divergence, 1600–1850*. Cambridge: Cambridge University Press, 222 and 263.

11. K. Pomeranz (2000), *The Great Divergence: Europe, China, and the Making of the Modern World Economy*. Princeton, NJ: Princeton University Press, 68.

12. P. Vries (2001), 'Are coal and colonies really crucial? Kenneth Pomeranz and the Great Divergence', *Journal of World History*, 12 (2), 437; ibid. (2013), *Escaping Poverty: The Origins of Modern Economic Growth*. Vienna and Göttingen: Vienna University Press and Vandenhoeck & Ruprecht, 307–11.

13. J. Mokyr (1990), *The Lever of Riches: Technological Creativity and Economic Progress*. Oxford: Oxford University Press, 81; ibid. (2002), *The Gifts of Athena: Historical Origins of the Knowledge Economy*. Princeton, NJ: Princeton University Press, 4–21, 34–42; ibid. (2017), *A Culture of Growth: The Origins of the Modern Economy*. Princeton, NJ: Princeton University Press, 274; P. Bertucci (2017), *Artisanal Enlightenment: Science and the Mechanical Arts in Old Regime France*. New Haven, CT and London: Yale University Press, 7.

14. J. Goldstone (2002), 'Efflorescences and economic growth in world history: Rethinking the "rise of the West" and the Industrial Revolution', *Journal of World History*, 13 (2) 323–89; ibid. (2008), *Why Europe? The Rise of the West in World History, 1500–1800*. New York: McGraw Hill Education, ch. 8.

15. A. M. Watson (1974), 'The Arab agricultural revolution and its diffusion', *Journal of Economic History*, 34 (1), 8–35; ibid. (1983), *Agricultural Innovation in the Early Islamic World: The Diffusion of Crops and Farming Techniques, 700–1100*. Cambridge: Cambridge University Press, 2–3, 5, 77–8.

16. P. Horden and N. Purcell (2000), *The Corrupting Sea: A Study of Mediterranean History*. Oxford: Wiley, 257–63, esp. 262; M. Decker (2009), 'Plants and progress: Rethinking the Islamic agricultural revolution', *Journal of World History*, 20 (2), 187–206.

17. P. Squatriti (2014), 'Of seeds, seasons, and seas: Andrew Watson's medieval agrarian revolution forty years later', *Journal of Economic History*, 74 (4), 1210–15.

18. K. D. White (1984), *Greek and Roman Technology*. London: Thames & Hudson; A. Y. al-Hassan and D. R. Hill (1986), *Islamic Technology: An Illustrated History*. Cambridge: Cambridge University Press.

19. M. J. T. Lewis (1993), 'The Greeks and the early windmill', *History of Technology*, 15, 141–89; Horden and Purcell, *Corrupting Sea*, 257.

20. D. W. Anthony (2007), *The Horse, the Wheel and Language: How Bronze-Age Riders from the Eurasian Steppes Shaped the Modern World*. Princeton, NJ: Princeton University Press, 457–63.

21. Watson, *Agricultural Innovation*, 88–94, esp. 90.

22. C. C. Mann (2011), *1493: How Europe's Discovery of the Americas Revolutionized Trade, Ecology and Life on Earth*. London: Granta, 168–9.

23. V. Hansen, (2012), *The Silk Road: A New History*. Oxford: Oxford University Press, 137–9, 238–9; J. M. Bloom (2001), *Paper before Print: The History and Impact of Paper in the Islamic World*. New Haven, CT: Yale University Press, 43.

24. Cf. Hansen, *Silk Road*, 138; Bloom, *Paper*, 110–23; E. Eisenstein (1979), *The Printing Press as an Agent of Change: Communications and Cultural Transformations in Early-Modern Europe*. Cambridge: Cambridge University Press.

25. K. Raj (2007), *Relocating Modern Science: Circulation and the Construction of Knowledge in South Asia and Europe, 1650–1900*. Basingstoke: Palgrave Macmillan, 20–1; H. J. Cook and S. Dupré (2012), 'Introduction', in H. J. Cook and S. Dupré (eds), *Translating Knowledge in the Early Modern Low Countries*. Zurich and Berlin: LIT Verlag, 10.

26. D. Gutas (1998), *Greek Thought, Arabic Culture: The Graeco-Arabic Translation Movement in Baghdad and Early 'Abbāsid Society (2nd–4th/8th–10th Centuries)*. London: Routledge, 192.

27. Diamond, *Guns, Germs and Steel*, 258–9.

28. A. Wilson (2002), 'Machines, power and the ancient economy', *Journal of Roman Studies*, 92, 32; R. Magnusson (2001), *Water Technology in the Middle Ages: Cities, Monasteries, and Water Works after the Roman Empire*. Baltimore, MD: Johns Hopkins University Press, 4; S. Aiyar, C-J. Dalgaard and O. Moav (2008), 'Technological progress and regress in pre-industrial times', *Journal of Economic Growth*, 13 (2), 127–8.

29. R. W. Bulliet (1975), *The Camel and the Wheel*. Cambridge, MA: Harvard University Press, 30.

30. Bloom, *Paper*, 110–16, 220–4.

31. Ö. Wikander (2000), 'The water-mill' and 'Industrial applications of water-power', in Ö. Wikander (ed.), *Handbook of Ancient Water Technology*. Leiden: Brill, 371–400 and 401–10; White, *Greek and Roman Technology*, 56; al-Hassan and Hill, *Islamic Technology*, 52–4; T. S. Reynolds (2003), *Stronger than a Hundred Men: A History of the Vertical Water Wheel*. Baltimore, MD: Johns Hopkins University Press.

32. White, *Greek and Roman Technology*, 56; Mokyr, *Lever of Riches*, 165, 103–95; J. J. Habakkuk (1962), *American and British Technology in the Nineteenth Century*. Cambridge: Cambridge University Press; Allen, *The British Industrial Revolution*, 2, 142.

33. Bloom, *Paper*, 222.

34. C. MacLeod (1988), *Inventing the Industrial Revolution: The English Patent System, 1660–1800*. Cambridge: Cambridge University Press, 158–81, esp. 159–60; Mokyr, *Lever of Riches*, 165–6.

35. P. O. Long (2001), *Openness, Secrecy, Authorship: Technical Arts and the Culture of Knowledge from Antiquity to the Renaissance*. Baltimore, MD: Johns Hopkins University Press, 89, 93–6; L. Molà (2000), *The Silk Industry of Renaissance Venice*. Baltimore, MD: Johns Hopkins University Press, 186–9.

36. M. Belfanti (2004), 'Guilds, patents, and the circulation of technical knowledge: Northern Italy during the Early Modern Age', *Technology and Culture*, 45 (3), 569–89; MacLeod, *Inventing*, 11.

37. Eisenstein, *Printing Press*, 20–1; M. Popplow (1998), *Neu, Nützlich und Erfindungsreich. Die Idealisierung von Technik in der frühen Neuzeit*. Münster: Waxmann; J. Spedding, R. L. Ellis and D. D. Heath (eds) (1857), *The Works of Francis Bacon*, vol. 1: *Novum Organum*. London: n.a., Aphorism CXXIX.

38. For a recent example, see Vries, *Escaping Poverty*, 305–11.

39. K. Davids (1993), 'Technological change and the economic expansion of the Dutch Republic', in K. Davids and L. Noordegraaf (eds), *The Dutch Economy in the Golden Age: Nine Studies*. Amsterdam, 95–6; MacLeod, *Inventing*, 146, 150; Gordon, *Rise and Fall*, 570–1.

40. MacLeod, *Inventing*, 97–114; L. Hilaire-Pérez (1994), 'Inventions et inventeurs en France et en Angleterre au XVIIIe siècle', 4 vols. Paris: doctoral thesis; K. Davids (2008), *The Rise and Decline of Dutch Technological Leadership: Technology, Economy and Culture in the Netherlands, 1350–1800*. Boston, MA and Leiden: Brill, 410–16, 481–2; P. Moser (2012), 'Innovation without patents: Evidence from world's fairs', *The Journal of Law and Economics*, 55 (1), 43–74.

41. B. Zorina Khan (2015), 'Inventing prizes: A historical perspective on innovation awards and technology policy', *Business History Review*, 89 (4), 631–60; Gordon, *Rise and Fall*, 571–2; David C. Mowery (1998), *Paths of Innovation: Technological Change in 20th-Century America*. Cambridge: Cambridge University Press, 11–46.

42. Mokyr, *Lever of Riches*, 12–13; E. Jones (2003), *The European Miracle: Environments, Economies and Geopolitics in the History of Europe and Asia*. Cambridge: Cambridge University Press, 45–69.

43. K. G. Persson (1988), *Pre-industrial Growth: Social Organization and Technological Progress in Europe*. New York: Blackwell, 7–12; G. N. von Tunzelmann (1995), *Technology and Industrial Progress: The Foundations of Economic Growth*. Cheltenham: Edward Elgar Publishing, 7–9, 117–19 and 399; Mokyr, *Lever of Riches*, 13.

44. F. Fernández-Armesto (2000), *Civilizations*. London: Macmillan, 488–500.

45. Jones, *European Miracle*, 45; Mokyr, *Lever of Riches*, 159–92; Diamond, *Guns, Germs and Steel*, 249–51; Landes, *Wealth and Poverty*, 45–59; D. R. Headrick (2010), *Power over Peoples: Technology, Environments, and Western Imperialism, 1400 to the Present*. Princeton, NJ: Princeton University Press, 4; L. White Jr (1978) 'Cultural climates and technological advance in the Middle ages', in L. White Jr (ed.), *Medieval Religion and Technology: Collected Essays*. Berkeley, CA: University of California Press, 217–53; D. Acemoglu and J. A. Robinson (2012), *Why Nations Fail: The Origins of Power, Prosperity and Poverty*. London: Profile, 76–9.

46. Mowery and Rosenberg, *Paths of Innovation*, 11–46.

47. Headrick, *Power over Peoples*, 5–6; Headrick (1981), *The Tools of Empire: Technology and European Imperialism in the Nineteenth Century*. New York: Oxford University Press; Mokyr, *Lever of Riches*, 81–148; A. Grübler (1998), *Technology and Global Change*. Cambridge: Cambridge University Press, 117–26.

48. Needham, *Science and Civilisation in China*, vol. 4, part 2, table 56; P. Malanima (2006), 'Energy crisis and growth 1650–1850: The European deviation in a comparative perspective', *Journal of Global History*, 1 (1), 101–12; K. Davids (2013), *Religion, Technology and the Great and Little Divergences: China and Europe Compared, c.700–1800*. Boston, MA and Leiden: Brill 5–8.

49. Cf. M. Elvin (1973), *The Pattern of the Chinese Past*. London: Eyre Methuen, 301, 312–15.

50. Parthasarathi, *Why Europe Grew Rich*, 210–13, 217–19.

51. Ibid., 221–2; M. Berg (2004), 'In pursuit of luxury: Global origins of British consumer goods in the eighteenth century', *Past & Present*, 87, 91, 97, 99, 126 and 182. Cf. also B. Hahn (2020), *Technology in the Industrial Revolution*. Cambridge: Cambridge University Press.

52. Davids, *Religion*, 9, 13–14, 162, 188–9, 227 and 229; P. J. Golas (2001), 'Technological illustration in China: A post-Needham perspective', in A. Arrault and C. Jami (eds), *Science and Technology in China: A Post-Needham Perspective*. Belgium: Turnhout Brepols, 43–58.

53. On India, Parthasarathi, *Why Europe Grew Rich*, 214–16, 313 footnote 98; on Europe, see Davids, *Religion*, chs 2, 3 and 4.

54. L. Roberts and S. Schaffer (2007), 'Preface', in L. Roberts, S. Schaffer and P. Dear (eds), *The Mindful Hand: Inquiry and Invention from the Late Renaissance to Early Industrialization*. Amsterdam: Koninklijke Nederlandse Akademie van Wetenschappenpp, xv, xix, xxiv.

55. Mokyr, *Gifts of Athena*, 4–17; Parthasarathi, *Why Europe Grew Rich*, 219–21. See also Patrick O'Brien's chapter in this volume.

56. E. Ames and N. Rosenberg (1963), 'Changing technological leadership and industrial growth', *Economic Journal*, 73, 13–31; D. S. L. Cardwell (1972), *Turning Points in Western Technology*. New York: Watson Publishing International, 190, 206; Mokyr, *Lever of Riches*, 207; Davids, *Rise and Decline*, 2–7.

57. K. Davids (1995), 'Shifts of technological leadership in early modern Europe', in K. Davids and J. Lucassen (eds), *A Miracle Mirrored: The Dutch Republic in European Perspective*. Cambridge: Cambridge University Press, 339–41; ibid., *Rise and Decline*, chs 4 and 5.

58. Davids, 'Shifts', 342.

59. Thomas Nugent (1749), *The Grand Tour*, vol. 1. London, 32. See also Davids, *Rise and Decline*, 48.

60. R. R. Nelson and G. Wright (1992), 'The rise and fall of American technological leadership: The postwar era in historical perspective', *Journal of Economic Literature*, 30 (4), 1931–64; G. Wright (2007) 'Historical foundations of American technology', https://web.stanford.edu/~write/papers/Historical%20FoundationsR.pdf.

CHAPTER 5
FAMILIES, FIRMS AND POLITIES: INSTITUTIONS, PRE-MODERN ECONOMIC GROWTH AND THE GREAT DIVERGENCE*
Regina Grafe and Maarten Prak

Institutions are usually defined as 'the humanly devised constraints that shape human interaction'. They include not only formal rules and organizations but also informal norms and customs.[1] Since the 1980s, a whole field of studies, New Institutional Economics, has turned them into a core element in the debate about development, economic and otherwise. In its briefest form, the argument is that 'poor' institutions drive up the so-called transaction costs associated with doing business. Economic growth slows when information is hard to find, traders cheat, cartels corner the market, the police want a cut and the courts do not function.[2] That begs the question we ask in this chapter: what role, if any, did public and private institutions play in economic growth across the globe in the centuries leading up to the Industrial Revolution, and do such institutions explain at least some of the divergences that eventually emerged between different countries and world regions?

Initially, institutional economics focused mostly on the insecurity of individuals' property rights. Whenever those were threatened, transaction costs rose, and economic growth was stymied. In this story, rulers and elites mostly featured as revenue-maximizing predators of private property.[3] More recently, North, Wallis and Weingast have recognized that states as organizations were also needed to check uncontrolled violence. Rulers not only created rents by interfering with open markets to line their own pockets but also used rents as a means of co-opting an elite that served as a check on violence. For North and his co-authors, only the emergence of democratic constraints on political elites in a small number of 'Open Access' societies during the nineteenth century eventually unleashed the productive forces of industrialization.[4]

It is beyond doubt that institutions mattered, but tracing their impact is a challenge. Institutions come in many shapes. This chapter covers rules as well as organizations, both formal and informal, including practices and beliefs.[5] At the same time, their impact on economic efficiency depends not only on the form they take but also on the varying mixtures of allocation mechanisms in the economy which were available to historical actors. Markets were and are a very important allocation mechanism. But they are not the only one. As Polanyi argued, non-market exchanges (reciprocity), and redistribution also serve as coordination tools that can produce economic efficiency or inefficiency, and social equality or inequality.[6] Part of the complexity of understanding institutions is that the three allocation mechanisms played varying roles at distinct levels, which we identify as the family, the firm and the polity.

To complicate matters further, choices on one level mattered for those at the others.[7] For example, Greif has argued that family structures tended to impose a logic of collective behaviour in Asia and the Middle East, but favoured individualistic behaviour in Western Europe. That turned out to be good for family firms in the former, but placed them in the very long run at an economic disadvantage vis-à-vis the latter.[8] The interactions between institutional and organizational arrangements regarding families, firms or entire states also imply that the effects of the same institution can be positive (efficient) in one context and negative (inefficient) in another. Institutions come in interrelated sets, which are 'co-evolutionary'.[9]

In this chapter, we will use the comparative method to identify institutional environments that seem to coincide with positive economic outcomes in the short, medium and long term. We start from the smallest scale of organization, kinship, and move on to the next, institutions that governed production and trade, such as firms, trading diasporas, guilds and mercantile companies. Finally, we turn to political governance proper.

The Family and Economic Development

One influential way in which families as an institution have been connected with economic development is through their choices of how to allocate their labour inputs and the products of their labour. Families are a fertile space to understand better the coexistence of market engagement, reciprocity and redistribution across productive and reproductive labour. The theory of the 'family economy' held that peasant households tried to minimize their contacts with markets and sustained a situation of economic self-sufficiency, by combining the labour inputs from all family members and redistributing returns within the household. Historians of gender portrayed the family economy as an environment of relative equality between the sexes. With the arrival of capitalism and its labour markets, women were relegated to the poorly paid jobs, and as a result also lost much of their clout within the household, where the male 'breadwinner' used his higher wages to obtain all sorts of privileges.

In the 1970s, the theory of the family economy was extended to the world of 'proto-industry'. European peasant households in regions of poor soils incorporated work for putting-out merchants in their annual schedule in an attempt to save their smallholdings. More recent research on proto-industrial regions and on farming families has undermined the idea of the household as a closed unit of production, and the idea of a 'family economy' stage, preceding capitalism, has therefore been by and large abandoned.[10] Nonetheless, historians have remained sensitive to the household as a place where economic decisions on consumption, production and reproduction were actively being taken.[11]

A second close connection between families and economic development is through reproduction. Pre-modern societies balanced population and economic capacity through Malthusian checks, that is, reproductive constraints that reduced, or epidemics that wiped out excess population. The theory of the European Marriage Pattern (EMP) argues that, with the help of late marriage and a high degree of celibacy, Europeans were able to actively limit the number of children. While in other regions of the world population growth outstripped economic resources, Europeans managed to free those resources for investments in education and innovation. It was argued that this EMP emerged in the late Middle Ages, especially in northwest Europe, through a fortuitous confluence of Catholic doctrine sponsoring juveniles' agency in the choice of a partner, inheritance practices that favoured the establishment of separate households (neo-locality) and a strong demand for wage labour after the Black Death.[12] The implication suggested that European demographic patterns were more growth-friendly.

Yet, the picture of a pre-modern world mired in Malthusian constraints has been equally questioned from the Asian perspective. China's spectacular population growth during the Ming and Qing eras was achieved without a substantial decline in living standards. In Asia generally, where the age of marriage was lower than in Europe, the regulation of fertility worked partially through infanticide. Because it was applied sex-specifically, the percentage of male bachelors in the Chinese population around 1800 was on a par with England and Scandinavian countries. Chinese females, moreover, had lower fertility within marriage than Europeans, suggesting a capacity to proactively regulate family size.[13] Overall, pre-modern societies in both Europe and Asia are now understood to have been more capable of demographic self-regulation than neo-Malthusian theories assumed.

A third approach to the connection between family and economy has been through 'family systems'. Some scholars argue that Middle Eastern and Asian social structures favoured a collective mindset, compared to European incipient individualism, an idea that harks back to Max Weber's attempts to similarly frame the distinct trajectories of Europe and Asia. The argument is that the structure of economic organization was shaped by whether responsibility for wrongdoing was collective (i.e. an entire family can be punished for wrongdoing) or individual. Societies organized around collective responsibility would find the size of business organization capped. This was because organizations could rely on internal monitoring mechanisms, which were the very strength of such societies. But such internal mechanisms became less effective as the size of the organization increased. By contrast, systems shaped by more individualist social structures, where organizations could not rely on strong internal monitoring, would have increased the demand for a 'third-party enforcer', an independent political body that enforced rules and punished infractions. In Europe, where family-, lineage- or clan-based monitoring was deficient, organizations were keener to see the town or princely authorities control misbehaviour. But this, paradoxically, had the unintended consequence of increasing the optimum size of the organization, and with it the market.[14] Critics of this view argue that it misrepresents the notion of family or lineage across Eurasia. In China, lineage was, to some extent, a fiction created by adoption. In eighteenth-century Beijing, adoption rates varied between 6 and 10 per cent. And Japan may have actually benefited from its traditional family structure, with three-generation households and emphasis on lineage. Stable family relationships led to lifelong learning and employment that created eventually the conditions for Japan's steep growth trajectory.[15] Family systems were, in other words, flexible, and their economic outcomes not predetermined.

At the same time, new data sets and daring attempts to classify societies according to family systems have produced some intriguing results for the post-1800 period. The first and most significant is that the connection between family and economy runs to an important extent through the channel of female agency. In so far as family systems support the education and labour participation of women, the economy will benefit; when female agency is constrained, the economy tends to suffer. Yet, the size of the effect clearly depends on the interactions with other institutional levels. Cultural restrictions for Chinese women to work outside the household might have been less important since a large share of the population had access to their own land and were thus less involved in waged labour anyway, according to Pomeranz.[16]

In the modern world, positive correlations can be established not only between family systems and economic growth directly but also between late marriage, educational attainment and female voting rights, which in turn also have a positive effect on economic development. For the pre-modern period, the evidence for northwest Europe suggests an economic stimulus emanating from the institution of the family, but for other regions we still lack the evidence to fully understand its economic impact during the pre- modern era.[17] Still, the argument could be made that at this lowest level of institutional structures, belief systems and religious and social norms were of particular importance because they determined gender relations and reproductive behaviour, both of which have been shown to be subject to particular persistence. In turn, they created limits (or not) to productive organization within and outside the household.

Firms, Guilds and Chartered Companies

At the meso level, three distinct types of organizations have dominated the debates about efficient institutions: firms, guilds and similar types of collective organizations, and finally chartered and joint-stock companies. All of them faced the main challenges of any economic enterprise of the early modern period: insecurity (the known unknowns) and uncertainty (the unknown unknowns). The unpredictability of the business environment started at the very basic level of bookkeeping: merchants and entrepreneurs used methods to record their transactions that made it practically impossible to keep track of the sources of profit and loss. Epidemics, fires, shipwrecks, piracy and other natural and human infringements of production and exchange likewise posed external risks. To combat these problems, entrepreneurs would try to shield their activities through collaboration and collusion.[18] Practices that restricted the access of outsiders to markets and protected insiders were ubiquitous. Sometimes such institutional arrangements produced both private and social gains, but at other times the private gains were a social loss.

The early modern firm was an organization of production and trade set up around the family and kin as one way to deal with business risks. By pooling human and physical capital, handling the redistribution of returns partially as a non-market transaction, and guaranteeing succession in business, it introduced elements of stability. At the same time, family firms were also subject to limitations in size. The selection of the most skilled workers and succession in the firm were prone to mere chance. Traditionally, scholars have argued that the transition to legally backed organizational forms of business from Italian medieval family firms, via joint-stock trading companies, to the modern corporation was an important element in economic growth. Companies could increase in size, guarantee inter-temporal persistence and raise larger amounts of capital. The path towards the modern company in Europe was juxtaposed to a supposed continued reliance of businesses centred on kin or religious institutions in Asia and the Middle East as one part of the story of economic divergence.

There are several problems with this attractive but oversimplified story. At the European end of the story, chartered and joint-stock companies were central to the modernization argument. As handmaidens of a 'world economy', the Dutch East India Company (Vereenigde Oostindische Compagnie – VOC) and the English East India Company (EIC) were the first to be financed by shares traded on the stock market. Yet, more recent research has shown that the VOC created its first shares more or less by mistake and used the instrument hardly at all after the company's start-up phase. Moreover, very few other companies were financed through shares. Profits moved from an early high on a downward trend, and by the mid-eighteenth century, the VOC traded at a loss. The EIC was subject to the same trend.[19] That is not to say that the companies were not economically important. The VOC alone was responsible for 13 per cent of the Dutch Republic's foreign trade, and its trading volume was larger than all the imports from the Baltic ports into Holland combined. Yet, commercial expansion beyond Europe had arguably as much to do with aggressive state policies as with the particular organizational form of the companies themselves. As Fernand Braudel had already observed, chartered companies, with their state backing and strong-arm tactics, were ill-fitted to act as role models of 'free enterprise'.[20]

At the Asian and Middle Eastern ends, the story of the path towards the modern firm is also more complicated than was once thought. There is strong evidence that in China the concept of lineage as the basis of business organization and credit networks remained central. It is also likely that the co-evolution of norms and institutions might well have reinforced those initial conditions that favoured clan-based business structures.[21] However, Chinese lineages worked very differently from European families: lineage-based businesses were not organized in a strict genealogical sense; they could rewrite the past if that was useful in the present and for the future. Not surprisingly, evidence of Chinese business practices has been uncovered that looks remarkably akin to those in the West.[22]

A separate argument holds that Middle Eastern development was at a disadvantage vis-à-vis European business because Islamic family and business law made it harder to guarantee the inter-temporal persistence of businesses. At the same time, alternative institutions that were used to pool capital, especially religious foundations known as *waqf*, were allegedly too inflexible to substitute for what some see as the quintessential European credit institution, the bank.[23] Yet, that argument, too, has been criticized. Too little research exists right now for us to understand the application of Islamic law as related to business practices. Moreover, in parts of Europe and its overseas empires, notably the Hispanic world, much of the credit market was organized in the form of religious institutions, too, which seems to have sustained commercial expansion and economic development at relatively low costs (i.e. interest rates) well into the eighteenth century.[24]

Just as important as individual firms were organizations that looked after shared interests of trades in most pre-modern societies. Professional associations are still common today and by no means a hallmark of the 'traditional' economy. What distinguished pre-modern trade organizations, guilds and trading nations was the routinely imposed requirement for everyone in the same trade to become a member. This requirement was usually backed up by legislation that established a 'monopoly' position for the members of the guild as a group. It is important, though, to stress that they would continue to compete with one another inside the association. This set them apart from joint-stock companies such as the VOC or EIC, which held a proper monopoly in the sense understood by modern economists.[25]

Craft guilds in turn should be distinguished from commercial organizations. In Europe, merchant guilds emerged before craft guilds, to reduce the risks related to commitment and enforcement in long-distance trade. They were still active in the sixteenth century. But at least in the more advanced centres of trade, they were gradually losing ground by 1600 as market institutions became sufficiently solid to support transactions without the guild framework as an enforcement mechanism. Locally, shopkeepers' guilds remained active, but with low entrance barriers and, as a result, broad membership.[26]

Chinese guilds usually recruited their members on the basis of shared geographical backgrounds. As these often also determined the line of trade, economic and regional identities tended to overlap. Most Chinese guilds emerged out of temple organizations and shared their premises with religious buildings. They regulated weights and measures, set prices (usually in conjunction with the local authorities), maintained codes of professional conduct, and lobbied local government to promote the interests of their members. There is, however, no hint of an exclusive access to particular trades for members of a specific guild. Membership was available to anyone who fit the membership profile, that is, originated from the region or was active in the occupation covered by the guild.[27]

Craft and merchant guilds were also common phenomena in Ottoman towns and cities. Ottoman guilds set quality controls and prices for both raw materials and final products. Guilds regularly made their wishes known by petitioning the authorities, and their proposals were usually accepted and absorbed into the body of regulations. Guilds were numerous, as well as popular in the sense that they organized a very substantial part of urban populations in the Ottoman Empire.[28]

European craft guilds took on a number of distinct roles. Economically, they sometimes coordinated the purchase of raw materials and the branding of products. More commonly, they provided training through apprenticeship schemes and tests of acquired skills in the form of master examinations. Some guilds, especially in export trades, branded goods by attaching a seal of approval after the product had been examined by guild officials. Guilds might also provide recourse for dissatisfied customers. Socially, some guilds assisted members in need through mutual support schemes. Guilds could double as civic militias, and guilds everywhere lobbied local authorities, seeking support for their trade.[29]

Strong claims have been made for and against the economic benefits of guilds, especially in the European historiography. Against the guilds, Adam Smith famously argued in *The Wealth of Nations* (1776) that they were a 'conspiracy against the public'. Modern critics of the guilds argue that they used their 'monopoly' rights to exclude newcomers, minorities and women and to create rents for established masters and their offspring. The question is how widespread this was. In one area, the debate has been settled in favour of the pessimists: with some notable exceptions, women were excluded from the corporate world.[30]

The optimists have nonetheless raised a number of counter-arguments. One is that guilds were the pre-modern equivalent of the firm; they improved the monitoring of the workforce without the costly logistic of a centralized factory floor. A second is that centres of economic growth, like Antwerp, Amsterdam and London, also had a strong guild presence.[31] A third and perhaps the most relevant claim is that guilds helped organize the training of the workforce or, in other words, the creation and transmission of human capital through skills education.

In its strongest form, this argument claims that apprenticeship contracts, enforced by guilds, helped to iron out the mismatch between masters' investment in training during the early stages of the process and the temptation for apprentices to move elsewhere once they had gone through those early stages to claim a higher wage. New research has demonstrated that the relationship between master and apprentice was much more fluid than this model assumes. Guilds did not oversee the apprenticeship process, but merely registered its progress. Their role in the training process may therefore have been more limited to the registration of an apprenticeship, and as appeal boards for contracts that broke down.[32]

Perhaps most importantly, research on the geographical background of guild membership has clearly demonstrated that many masters, very often a majority, originated from another town than the one in which they were working. This implies a choice of business location. The same applied to merchants. In the late fifteenth century, many migrated from Bruges to Antwerp. When the Dutch Revolt broke out in the second half of the sixteenth century, a second wave of migration took Antwerp merchants first to London, Hamburg and Cologne, and ultimately to Amsterdam. In the same vein, Jewish merchants from Iberia who wanted to settle in Holland negotiated with various local governments about the conditions these could offer them. All of this points to the fact that European towns were competing to establish comparative advantages. Institutionally, such advantages consisted of a bundle of arrangements. Like the guilds themselves, they served multiple purposes at the same time. Inter-urban competition also supported the diffusion of innovations.[33]

All these arguments are much more difficult to verify outside the European contexts, where guild documents have not been preserved as abundantly as in European archives. In India and Japan, there were no formal guilds; it has been argued that Indian castes were their functional equivalents, while Japan had brotherhoods that brought together businessmen in the same trades. Guilds were introduced in the New World by European colonizers, but in differentiated ways. In the Spanish colonies, they were numerous and often admitted people of all ethnic backgrounds and sometimes even enslaved craftsmen. In their North American colonies, British authorities were reluctant to create special interest organizations for industrial producers, which might become a source of protectionism against imports from the metropolis. As far as we know, the regulation of apprenticeship had no equivalent in China or the Middle East.[34] We have no way to test numbers against economic performance.

Nevertheless, certain organizational structures seem to have been almost ubiquitous across cultures and geographies. Such is the case of the clustering of certain crafts people in urban settings. Whether these were imposed by urban institutions on the crafts, or emerged out of the self-organization of the crafts, or responded to a location around a religious shrine, clearly they were an early response to the benefits of external economies of scale, and of agglomeration economies. Examples are the famous porcelain makers of Jingdezhen and the production of cotton in parts of Bengal.[35] The same might be true for the role of the polity in creating enterprises. Several European countries – France and Austria stand out – created state manufactures.[36]

What can we make of this? There certainly were distinctions in the way business was organized across the globe in the pre-modern world. With the wisdom of hindsight, certain institutional forms can be identified that would eventually emerge as being very significant. The importance of shareholding companies in the long run is uncontested, but their precursors were probably more important as the extended military arm of European states than as capital-raising business enterprises or revolutionary management solutions. Producer and trader associations raise similar concerns: why was urban economic development associated with their presence for centuries? And why did their disappearance not create more growth in all places where this happened? Finally, why did China not reap benefits from being less constrained by 'monopolistic' guild structures?

States and Empires

This takes us to the third level of our analysis, the polity. Early modern political formations were characterized by diversity, not only globally but also within larger continental spaces. City states, territorial states and empires coexisted across Asia, Africa and Europe. Only in the Americas, transatlantic empires prevailed. Such overseas empires existed, however, side by side with land-based empires, like Mughal India or Safavid Persia. Polities also differed strongly in how they were constituted socially, economically and politically. The question to ask is whether we can observe clear correlations between particular sets of political institutions and societies' potential for long-term economic growth.

Political structures, generally quite loosely described as 'states', have long been central to arguments about the economic benefits of parliamentary versus so-called absolutist regimes in early modern Europe. The underlying problem is that societies face a contradiction: without enforcement of a set of rules that govern political and economic life, the survival and property of individuals are permanently at risk, damaging their willingness to engage with the market. An independent third-party enforcer is therefore needed to protect subjects/citizens from random violence, and to enforce contracts where necessary. But a political regime strong enough to protect is also strong enough to blackmail and act as predator.[37] So how could the institutions of governance be designed in such a way that power holders would refrain from predating and extortion and thus from raising transaction costs in society?

The answer given by much of the literature was that rulers needed to be constrained by formal rules and parliamentary institutional arrangements that created sufficient checks, such as those in place in England after the Glorious Revolution of 1688. Economic historians have pointed out that the transition from pre-modern to modern intensive growth was initially less about an acceleration of growth rates than about economies no longer going into reverse gear. 'Growth without a reverse gear' was only thought to be possible once political regimes relied on representation within a formal (though not necessarily written) constitution. A related line of research has claimed that particular legal systems were more suited to guaranteeing subjects/ citizens property rights, also singling out anglophone legal origins as particularly growth-friendly.[38]

This returns us to the problem that any polity tasked first to guarantee external defence and second to provide a third-party enforcer service also needs to be financed. The legal capacity of the state depends on the coercive power to defend the state's public property rights to taxation, that is, its fiscal capacity.[39] But all early modern polities were states 'under construction'. Their administrative capabilities were severely constrained by rudimentary administrative systems, limited information and high costs of administering sometimes far-flung territories. Estimates of the share of GDP that polities could hope to appropriate as tax income, a proxy for state capacity that is often called the state quota, are notoriously hard to come by. Today it ranges in OECD countries from 30 to over 50 per cent. In the sixteenth century, the revenues in terms of share of GDP per capita of the Ottoman Empire and most European polities are estimated at 2 to 5 per cent. By the later eighteenth century, Ottoman revenues still hovered around 6 per cent of GDP and that of China might have been somewhere between 4 and 8 per cent.[40] But in Britain, it had in the meantime reached 12–15 per cent, with other Western European states somewhere between this and Asian or Ottoman levels.[41] Was the divergence in fiscal capacity at the heart of growth divergence?

Several hypotheses have been advanced that link institutional forms of state formation to the likelihood of a more capable state emerging. Underpinning many of them is the idea that there was an optimum size of the state, or more precisely a particular combination of size, degree of centralization and administrative efficiency. City states did not suffer from the information costs that larger polities faced and might well have benefited from an easier alignment between citizens' interests and the fiscal exigencies of the polity. But in competitive state systems, especially in Eurasia, the internal success of city states might over time be cut off by the external threat from larger neighbours. Also, local elites that had guaranteed the financial survival of many of the most successful city states for centuries sometimes turned into conservative and exclusionary ruling oligarchies. Princes were not as aligned with commercial interests as urban burghers, but they did quite often explicitly seek to foster economic development. Territorial states, princely or republican, had an advantage when it came to raising the revenue to withstand inter-polity competition. But in order to turn the advantage of more taxpayers into more revenues, they needed to achieve a certain degree of centralization that afforded the state a greater ability to appropriate and redistribute resources.[42]

If city states were considered too small, empires in general, but in particular land-based empires, were considered too large and as lacking the resources necessary to develop state capacity. While early institutionalists blamed excessive centralization for their poor growth performance, now imperial decentralization is stressed as an obstacle for growth. In the Ottoman Empire, an increasing share of fiscal resources remained in the regions, where it attracted a large number of intermediaries that ate into the receipts of the central state. Similarly, China's very large size delayed the organization of effective tax systems when compared to early modern Japan. In the Spanish Americas, too, only a very small share of the fiscal resources ever made it to the supposed centre of the empire; most continued to circulate on the western side of the Atlantic.[43]

Caution, however, seems warranted in accepting too close an association between the share of the product appropriated by the polity and state capacity. At very low levels of fiscal capacity, polities clearly struggled to develop legal capacity. In Africa, underpopulation in large parts of the continent probably resulted in a high land–labour ratio, which in turn limited the ability of polities to tax. Low population density was initially driven by a combination of sleeping sickness limiting the availability of draught animals and few fertile lands. Where land was abundant, peasants could move on if taxed. That left rulers with a choice of either very coercive means of extraction of rents from labour or taxes that were imposed on major trade routes, which could not be avoided by merchants for reasons of climate and geography, as for example in the trans-Saharan trade. This delivered at least four blows to prospects for growth. Labour markets were pushed into forced labour, because slavery and forced labour were forms of population tax. Trade, which already suffered from high costs caused by environmental conditions, was burdened even more, and the consolidation of efficient and effective political power was held back. Low levels of state capacity might have pushed economies off their growth path repeatedly. Finally, fiscally weak polities were also very exposed to external threats to their survival as independent polities that manifested themselves in the nineteenth-century 'scramble for Africa' on the part of European states.[44]

Most Eurasian polities and the American territories attached to them, however, had during the early modern period lean but reasonably stable administrative structures that could tax land and population, as well as trade and consumption. The assumption that empires were too large to achieve efficient degrees of fiscal capacity can also be challenged. Most of the large land-based and overseas empires were by 1800 not the 'dead men walking' that early institutionalists had described them as. They had successfully guaranteed their survival as political units, and a new historiography now sees significant indications of economic dynamism in many of them as late as the eighteenth century.[45]

More important, a focus on the gross revenue as a means to assess state capacity is in danger of confusing two fundamental state functions: that of third-party enforcer and that of coordinating the articulation of the economy domestically and in the growing international economy. The function of third-party enforcer could be achieved by one of two means. A state that was centralized and therefore could exert coercion at relatively low cost could also rely on such coercion to raise the necessary fiscal means. However, high degrees of coercion provoked resistance because they undermined the legitimacy of the state. In such a polity, fiscal capacity and legal capacity could only be aligned through formal constraints that guaranteed some restraint in discretionary coercion and a use of the state's means that met the approval of the represented elites. Historically, the mechanisms to achieve such balance probably emerged by chance. Royal power in England was stronger and the realm more centralized than any other European polity early on. Thus, English medieval monarchs could force the nobility to attend parliamentary sessions while their continental neighbours had trouble calling up the nobility for duty. But centuries later, the English Parliament managed to turn its forced meetings into a representative institution in large part because nobles *had* to attend.[46]

A second and more common model, however, was that of the poorly integrated polities. This was the case of most empires, constituted as composite or polycentric states. Coercion was expensive under such circumstances. Polycentric states were also less characterized by the centre–periphery dynamics of nineteenth-century colonialism. Instead they featured a governance regime that allowed for the retention of resources at various locations and sub-centres; co-optation was likely more efficient than coercion in these cases because it supported the state's legitimacy. Here, decentralization, rather than a sign of state weakness, was actually promoting the efficient use of resources that bought off opposition and reduced the cost of coercive practices, while still offering strong legal capacity.[47] Local and regional agency converted large parts of local elites into stakeholders of the polity. It generated quasi-voluntary compliance, as some have argued for the Spanish Americas, and hence reduced inefficiencies in fiscal systems compared to states that had to apply more force.[48] Likewise, in the notoriously de-centralized Dutch Republic, the urban heritage may have helped to create trust and cooperation between citizens and their rulers. The state could thus collect high taxes efficiently and provide useful public goods. Quasi-voluntary compliance increased efficiency by reducing coercion costs and left more revenue to be spent on other purposes.[49]

Still, polycentric forms of political institution building might have engendered collateral damage in terms of economic growth. Powerful territorial and/or urban elites in larger polities often created non-market obstacles to the movement of goods, capital and people in defence of local power. They did not hinder market development because of their tendency to disrespect private property rights. Instead, their political and social aspirations led to smaller and shallower markets, which in turn meant that allocative efficiencies were removed only very slowly.[50] Domestic markets remained poorly integrated. Perhaps the engagement in the creation of state manufactures with strong polycentric features, from China to the Austrian Habsburg Monarchy, was a response to a perceived need to substitute for market forces in the deepening of the market.

Polycentric rule also made it impossible for rulers to develop cohesive external commercial policies at a time when the share of international trade in economic development was strongly increasing. Mercantilist policies of the kinds that Britain or France developed in the eighteenth century presupposed a relatively high degree of political integration. The transfer of sovereign power to the English East India Company and the creation of a company-state were possible because sovereignty could be understood as hybrid on the Indian subcontinent. But it was also an expression of a powerful domestic centralized ruler, with real military might and increasingly ill at ease with such hybridity.[51] Where mercantilist policies were used to control market access, as in British competition in the textile sector with India, such policies were able to significantly change the growth path of both economies, upwards in the former case, downwards in the latter. Polycentric states, by contrast, lacked the ability to create functioning mercantilist systems. Giving priority to one territorial interest over another would have entailed very high coercive costs. The Dutch case was an interesting intermediate example that combined strong polycentric structures in the Netherlands with mercantilist policies in its colonies.[52]

This then brings us back to the co-evolution of institutions. Perhaps the debate about states and empires has been wrong-footed from the very beginning. In a very nineteenth-century manner, historians have assumed that states (and empires) are the proper level of analysis to capture the effect of governance structures. However, given the constraints states faced, more attention should probably be paid to the way they connected to other levels of society. The role of towns and their citizens particularly merit our attention.[53] After all, towns acted as hubs in commercial networks and were also the locus of industrial activity. Increasing levels of urbanization always indicated rising economic prosperity, even if specialists in European and Japanese proto-industry insist that non-agricultural production in the country might well have been an alternative source of growth.[54] Urban elites' personal interest in trade and industry and the efficiencies emerging from an overlapping of economic and political elites remain good candidates as growth-fostering institutions.[55]

Nevertheless we should be careful not to impose too simple a causality. Europe's economically most vital regions developed mechanisms to translate urban interests into state policies: the city state in Renaissance Italy, federalism in the Dutch Republic and parliamentary rule in post-1688 England. At the same time, not all European areas with very strong urban traditions were able to turn this heritage into faster economic development. One notable example is Spain, where strong urban political rights (together with territorial rights) acted as effective constraints of political power – but failed to promote market development. Urban interests sometimes needed to be overridden to let the market grow. In China, it has been argued, cities and towns were not so much suppressed, as left in the cold: poorly regulated, poorly funded and far removed from state supervision, they were an easy prey for opportunistic officials and corrupt practices.[56]

The co-evolution of political and economic institutions at various levels of social organization produced an almost infinite number of variations. In a world of poor transport and high information costs, that is, one in which using the market could be costly, urban spaces were relatively privileged because here the market could function more easily. Where higher-level political institutions left those urban markets at the mercy of greedy lords or officials, their development was hindered just as much as where higher-level political institutions left urban elites entirely in charge, allowing them to restrict market size and depth. The role of states in coordinating the market has probably been underestimated, but it was rarely independent of governance at the urban level or at that of the many historical territories or provinces that had been joined up in larger units.

Conclusion

The notion of a static early modern world, proclaimed by Emmanuel Le Roy Ladurie in 1974, has since been comprehensively overturned.[57] However, we still only partially understand the forces that determined the tension between stasis and change. The slow transition from early modern extensive growth to modern intensive growth was mostly about economies stopping to go into reverse gear. The data, however imperfect, suggest that this was achieved in pockets of Europe earlier than elsewhere. Any explanation for that exceptional surging ahead cannot overlook the Industrial Revolution. However, a growing consensus suggests that some European economies were going through fundamental changes well before 1800, while the impact of modern industry took quite a while to materialize after 1800. If we accept that industrialization was part of a larger process of transformation that took several centuries, can we then argue that institutional change was the driving force that took the reverse gear out of the engine?

At the most basic level, family systems clearly mattered because they decided over production and reproduction, market participation and reciprocity. But for our period it has so far proved difficult to produce convincing evidence that particular family systems were associated with more or less growth, even if gender relations and inheritance systems remained important. The analytical problem might in part be the co-evolution of institutional forms: a particular form of lineage or family evolves in combination with organizational forms of production, say the craft workshop or the agricultural unit of the extended family, and is regulated and sanctioned by urban, religious or state regulation. For the historian, it is difficult to identify which part of that set of institutions helped or hindered growth. Looking at each of them in isolation might in fact be unpromising to start with from a methodological standpoint.

Historians have traditionally paid much attention to the intermediate organizational level. The current state of research highlights the role of guilds, that is, merchants' and producers' associations, as significant, but guilds' ubiquity at the same time reduces their value as an explanation for divergence between civilizations. Business innovations from Italian family firms to joint-stock companies have been seen as being at the heart of European divergence. We are not convinced. As new research emerges on business practices and legal structures underpinning credit and goods markets in Asia and the Middle East, perceived dramatic divergences seem smaller. As for joint-stock companies, much of their impact before the late eighteenth century was limited to overseas trade. On balance, we would argue that the large diversity in institutional solutions to commercial challenges and the development of crafts, and the competition between them, might have been more important. Here we do see a link with the more or less autonomous towns and a range of states in Europe that offered such diversity.

Finally, we see the role of the state as that of a coordinator of economy and society. Property rights were a part of that remit, but the Dutch Revolt or the Glorious Revolution were concerned with legitimacy as much as anything else. Given the constraints of distance and limited means of communication, coordination was expensive as well as difficult to achieve effectively in large territorial units. The most successful states tended to be small to medium-sized, even in the European context; the Industrial Revolution itself was a regional, rather than a national, phenomenon. The more successful polities also had institutional mechanisms that enabled the articulation of local concerns at state level. The presence of multiple states, moreover, offered a mixed menu of institutional combinations as well as various routes for 'exit', and therefore 'voice', to economic interest groups, and an escape route for those who had fallen foul of a particular elite or ruler.[58] We do not believe that Europe had many superior institutions. But it might have benefited from more institutional diversity that developed in, and benefited from, the co-evolution at various levels of articulation.

There is thus not one single institutional factor that explains the 'Great Divergence'. Insofar as institutions contributed to diverging trajectories of growth and stagnation, we have tried to demonstrate that it was not 'Europe' versus the 'rest'. Both categories are too heterogeneous. The exceptional pockets in Europe were institutionally distinct because of their small family units, strong urban institutions and small state units. There are indications that, precisely as a result of these features, those same regions managed to create organizations that embraced more people and covered larger distances. Theoretically, there could have been other sets of co-evolved norms, organizations and institutions that might have eventually led to the same path; historical examples of such alternative trajectories are, however, not available.

Notes

*   Thanks are due to the Social & Economic History Group at Utrecht University and to the helpful suggestions of the audience at the authors' workshop for this volume at the London School of Economics in May 2016.

1. D. C. North (1990), *Institutions, Institutional Change and Economic Performance.* Cambridge: Cambridge University Press.

2. D. C. North (1992), *Transaction Costs, Institutions, and Economic Performance.* San Francisco, CA: International Center for Economic Growth.

3. D. C. North and B. R. Weingast (1989), 'Constitutions and commitment: The evolution of institutions governing public choice in seventeenth-century England', *Journal of Economic History*, 49 (4), 803–32; North, *Institutions*; R. B. Ekelund and R. D. Tollison (1999), *Politicized Economies, Monarchy, Monopoly, and Mercantilism.* Enskede: TPB.

4. D. C. North, J. J. Wallis and B. R. Weingast (2009), *Violence and Social Orders: A Conceptual Framework for Interpreting Recorded Human History.* Cambridge and New York: Cambridge University Press.

5. T. Kuran (2009), 'Explaining the trajectories of civilizations: The systemic approach', *Journal of Economic Behaviour and Organizations*, 71 (3), 593–605.

6. K. Polanyi (2001), *The Great Transformation: The Political and Economic Origins of Our Times.* Boston, MA: Beacon Press.

7. A. Greif (2005), 'Commitment, coercion, and markets: The nature and dynamics of institutions supporting exchange', in C. Menard and M. M. Shirley (eds), *Handbook of New Institutional Economics.* Dordrecht: Springer, 727–86.

8. O. Williamson (2000), 'The new institutional economics: Taking stock, looking ahead', *Journal of Economic Literature*, 38 (3), 595–613; A. Greif (1994), 'Cultural beliefs and the organization of society: A historical and theoretical reflection on collectivist and individualist societies', *Journal of Political Economy*, 102 (5), 912–50.

9. E. Ostrom (2005), *Understanding Institutional Diversity.* Princeton, NJ: Princeton University Press.

10. L. Tilly (1977), *Women, Work, and Family.* New York: Holt, Rinehart & Winston; P. Kriedte, H. Medick and J. Schlumbohm (1981), *Industrialization before Industrialization: Rural Industry in the Genesis of Capitalism* [orig. ed. in German 1978]. Cambridge: Cambridge University Press; A. Knotter (2000), 'Problems of the "family economy": Peasant economy, domestic production and labour markets in pre-industrial households', in M. Prak (ed.), *Early Modern Capitalism: Economic and Social Change in Europe, 1400–1800.* London: Routledge, 135–60.

11. J. de Vries (2013), 'The industrious revolutions in East and West', in G. Austin and K. Sugihara (eds), *Labour-Intensive Industrialization in Global History.* London and New York: Routledge, 65–84; ibid. (2008), *The Industrious Revolution: Consumer Behavior and the Household Economy, 1650 to the Present.* Cambridge and New York: Cambridge University Press.

12. J. Hajnal (1965), 'European marriage patterns in perspective', in D. Glass and D. V. Eversley (eds), *Essays in Historical Demography.* London: Arnold, 101–43, J. L. van Zanden, T. De Moor and S. Carmichael (2019), *Capital Women: The European Marriage Pattern: Female Empowerment and Economic Development in Western Europe 1300–1800.* Oxford: Oxford

University Press; N. Voigtländer and H.-J. Voth (2013), 'How the West "invented" fertility restriction', *American Economic Review*, 103 (6), 2227–64; T. Dennison and S. Ogilvie (2014), 'Does the European marriage pattern explain economic growth?', *Journal of Economic History*, 74 (3), 651–93.

13. J. Lee and W. Feng (1999), 'Malthusian models and Chinese realities: The Chinese demographic system 1700-2000', *Population and Development Review*, 25 (1), 33–65.

14. A. Greif (1994), 'On the political foundations of the late medieval commercial revolution: Genoa during the twelfth and thirteenth centuries', *Journal of Economic History*, 54 (2), 271–87.

15. D. Faure (1996), 'The lineage as business company: Patronage versus law in the development of Chinese business', in R. A. Brown (ed.), *Chinese Business Enterprise: Critical Perspectives on Business and Management*. London: Routledge, 82–106; Lee and Feng, 'Malthusian models'; O. Saito (2010), 'The stem family and labour markets: Reflections on households and firms in Japan's economic development', unpublished conference paper presented in Utrecht.

16. K. Pomeranz (2013), 'Labour-intensive industrialization in the rural Yangzi Delta: Late imperial patterns and their modern fates', in G. Austin and K. Sugihara (eds), *Labour-Intensive Industrialization*, 122–43; ibid. (2005), 'Women's work and the economics of respectability', in B. Goodman and W. Larson (eds), *Gender in Motion*. Lanham, MD: Rowman & Littlefield, 239–63.

17. S. Dilli (2017), 'The deep causes of economic development: Family systems and female agency', in J. L. van Zanden, A. Rijpma and J. Kok (eds), *Agency, Gender, and Economic Development in the World Economy, 1850–2000: Testing the Sen Hypothesis*. London: Routledge, 138–61; R. Maseland (2021), 'Contingent determinants', *Journal of Development Economics*, 151, 102654.

18. D. W. Allen (2012), *The Institutional Revolution: Measurement and the Economic Emergence of the Modern World*. Chicago, IL and London: University of Chicago Press; P. Gervais (2014), 'Early modern merchant strategies and the historicization of market practices', *Economic Sociology – The European Electronic Newsletter*, 15, 19–29.

19. G. Dari-Mattiacci, O. Gelderblom, J. Jonker and E. C. Perotti (2017), 'The emergence of the corporate form', *Journal of Law, Economics, and Organization*, 33 (2), 193–236; L. Petram (2014), *The World's First Stock Exchange*. New York: Columbia Business School Publishing; J. de Vries (2003), 'Connecting Europe and Asia: A quantitative analysis of the Cape-route trade, 1497–1795', in D. O. Flynn, A. Giráldez and R. von Glahn (eds), *Global Connections and Monetary History, 1470–1800*. Aldershot: Ashgate, 35–106; J. de Vries and A. van der Woude (1997), *The First Modern Economy: Success, Failure, and Perseverance of the Dutch Economy, 1500–1815*. Cambridge: Cambridge University Press; see also R. Harris (2020), *Going the Distance: Eurasian Trade and the Rise of the Business Corporation, 1400–1700*. Princeton, NJ: Princeton University Press.

20. P. K. O'Brien (2013), 'The formation of states and transitions to modern economies: England, Europe, and Asia compared', in L. Neal, and J. G. Williamson (eds), *The Cambridge History of Capitalism*, vol. 1: *The Rise of Capitalism: From Ancient Origins to 1848*. Cambridge: Cambridge University Press, 357–402; S. Beckert (2014), *Empire of Cotton: A Global History*. New York: Alfred A. Knopf; F. Braudel (1984), *Civilization and Capitalism, 15th–18th Century*. London: Collins, vol. 2, ch. 4.

21. A. Greif and G. Tabellini (2017), 'The clan and the corporation: Sustaining cooperation in China and Europe', *Journal of Comparative Economics*, 45 (1), 1–35.

22. T. W. Guinnane, R. Harris, N. Lamoreaux et al. (2007), 'Putting the corporation in its place', *Enterprise & Society*, 8 (4), 687–729; M. Zelin (2009), 'The firm in early modern China',

Journal of Economic Behavior and Organizations, 71 (3), 623–37; K. Pomeranz (1997), '"Traditional" Chinese business forms revisited: Family, firm and financing in the history of the Yutang Company of Jining', *Late Imperial China*, 18 (1), 1–38; Gelderblom, de Jong and Jonker, 'The formative years'.

23. T. Kuran (2010), *The Long Divergence: How Islamic Law Held Back the Middle East*. Princeton, NJ: Princeton University Press.

24. C. Milhaud (2015), 'Priests or bankers? The ecclesiastical credit in modern Spain', *Working Paper HAL Archives Ouvertes*, https://hal-pse.archives-ouvertes.fr/hal-01180682; A. Lavrín (1966), 'The role of nunneries in the economy of New Spain in the eighteenth century', *Hispanic American Historical Review*, 46 (4), 371–93; R. Grafe (2012), *Distant Tyranny: Markets, Power and Backwardness in Spain 1650–1800*. Princeton, NJ: Princeton University Press.

25. F. van Waarden (1992), 'Emergence and development of business interest associations: An example from the Netherlands', *Organization Studies*, 13 (4), 521–62; G. Richardson (2001), 'A tale of two theories: Monopolies and craft guilds in medieval England and modern imagination', *Journal of the History of Economic Thought*, 23 (2), 217–42.

26. O. Gelderblom and R. Grafe (2010), 'The rise, persistence and decline of merchant guilds: Re-thinking the comparative study of commercial institutions in pre-modern Europe', *Journal of Interdisciplinary History*, 40 (4), 477–511; O. Gelderblom (2013), *Cities of Commerce: The Institutional Foundations of International Trade in the Low Countries, 1250 – 1650*. Princeton, NJ: Princeton University Press; S. Ogilvie (2011), *Institutions and European Trade: Merchant Guilds, 1000–1800*. Cambridge and New York: Cambridge University Press.

27. C. Moll-Murata (2018), *State and Crafts in the Qing Dynasty (1644–1911)*. Amsterdam: Amsterdam University Press; R. Belsky (2005), *Localities at the Center: Native Place, Space, and Power in Late Imperial Beijing*. Cambridge, MA: Harvard University Asia Center, distributed by Harvard University Press; W. T. Rowe (1984), *Hankow: Commerce and Society in a Chinese City, 1796–1889*. Stanford, CA: Stanford University Press; L. Tan (2013), 'Market-supporting institutions, gild organisations, and the Industrial Revolution: A comparative view', *Australian Economic History Review*, 53 (3), 221–46.

28. S. Faroqhi (2009), *Artisans of Empire: Crafts and Craftspeople under the Ottomans*. London, New York: I.B. Tauris; E. Yi (2004), *Guild Dynamics in Seventeenth-Century Istanbul: Fluidity and Leverage*. Leiden and Boston, MA: Brill; A. Raymond (1973), *Artisans et Commerçants au Caire au XVIIIe Siècle*. Damascus: Institut Français d'Etudes Arabes de Damas.

29. The literature on early modern European craft guilds is huge, and growing, but see A. Guenzi, P. Massa and F. Piola Caselli (eds) (1998), *Guilds, Markets, and Work Regulations in Italy, 16th–19th Centuries*. Aldershot: Ashgate; M. Prak, C. Lis, J. Lucassen et al. (eds) (2006), *Craft Guilds in the Early Modern Low Countries: Work, Power and Representation*. Aldershot: Ashgate; A. Kluge (2007), *Die Zünfte*, Stuttgart: Steiner; S. R. Epstein and M. Prak (eds) (2008), *Guilds, Innovation, and the European Economy, 1400–1800*. Cambridge: Cambridge University Press; J. Lucassen, T. De Moor and J. L. van Zanden (eds) (2008), *The Return of the Guilds*. Cambridge: Cambridge University Press; S. Ogilvie (2019), *The European Guilds: An Economic Analysis*. Princeton, NJ: Princeton University Press.

30. See S. R. Epstein (2008), 'Craft guilds in the pre-modern economy: A discussion', *Economic History Review*, 61 (1), 155–74 versus S. C. Ogilvie (2008), 'Rehabilitating the guilds: A reply', *Economic History Review*, 61 (1), 175–82. Also C. H. Crowston (2008), 'Women, gender and guilds in early modern Europe: An overview of recent literature', in Lucassen, De Moor and van Zanden, *The Return of the Guilds*, 19–44.

31. U. Pfister (2008), 'Craft guilds, the theory of the firm, and early modern proto-industry', in Epstein and Prak, *Guilds, Innovation and the European Economy*, 25–51; G. S. de Krey

(1985), *A Fractured Society: The Politics of London in the First Age of Party 1688–1715*. Oxford and New York: Oxford University Press, ch. 10.

32. S. R. Epstein (1998), 'Craft guilds, apprenticeship, and technological change in preindustrial Europe', *Journal of Economic History*, 58 (3), 684–715; D. de la Croix, M. Doepke and J. Mokyr (2018), 'Clans, guilds, and markets: Apprenticeship institutions and growth', *Quarterly Journal of Economics* 133 (1), 1–70; M. Prak and P. H. Wallis (eds) (2020), *Apprenticeship in Early Modern Europe*. Cambridge: Cambridge University Press.

33. M. Prak, C. Crowston, B. De Munck, C. Kissane, C. Minns, R. Schalk and P. Wallis (2021), 'Access to the trade: Monopoly and mobility in European craft guilds in the seventeenth and eighteenth centuries', *Journal of Social History*, 54 (2), 421–52; Gelderblom, *Cities of Commerce* ; R. G. Fuks-Mansfeld (1989), *De Sefardim in Amsterdam tot 1795: Aspecten van de Ontwikkeling van een Joodse Minderheid in een Hollandse Stad*. Hilversum: Verloren; Gelderblom and Grafe, 'The rise, persistence and decline of merchant guilds'; R. Grafe (2014), 'Polycentric states: The Spanish reigns and the "failures" of mercantilism', in P. Stern and C. Wennerlind (eds), *Mercantilism Reimagined: Political Economy in Early Modern Britain and Its Empire*. Oxford: Oxford University Press, 241–62.

34. T. Roy (2008), 'The guild in modern South Asia', in J. Lucassen, T. De Moor, and J. L. van Zanden, *The Return of the Guilds*, 95–120; and M. L. Nagata (2008), 'Brotherhoods and stock societies: Guilds in pre-modern Japan', in ibid., 121–42; L. L. Johnson (1986), 'Artisans', in L. S. Hoberman and S. Socolow (eds), *Cities and Society in Colonial Latin America*. Albuquerque, NM: University of New Mexico Press, 227–50; C. I. Archer (1977), *The Army in Bourbon Mexico, 1760–1810*. Albuquerque, NM: University of New Mexico Press; C. S. Olton (1975), *Artisans for Independence: Philadelphia Mechanics and the American Revolution*. Syracuse, NY: Syracuse University Press.

35. G. Riello and T. Roy (eds) (2009), *How India Clothed the World: The World of South Asian Textiles, 1500–1850*. Leiden: Brill; C. Moll-Murata (2013), 'Guilds and apprenticeship in China and Europe: The case of the Jingdezhen and European ceramics industries', in M. Prak and J. L. van Zanden (eds), *Technology, Skills and the Pre-modern Economy in the East and the West: Essays Dedicated to the Memory of S.R. Epstein*. Leiden: Brill, 225–58; A. Gerritsen (2020), *The City of White and Blue: Chinese Porcelain and the Early Modern World*. Cambridge: Cambridge University Press, ch. 9.

36. P. Deyon and P. Guignet (1980), 'The royal manufactures and economic progress in France before the Industrial Revolution', *Journal of European Economic History*, 9 (3), 611–32.

37. North and Thomas, *The Rise of the Western World*; M. Levi (1988), *Of Rule and Revenue*. Berkeley, CA: University of California Press.

38. North and Weingast, 'Constitutions and commitment'; R. La Porta, F. Lopez-de-Silanes and A. Shleifer (2008), 'The economic consequences of legal origin', *Journal of Economic Literature*, 46 (2), 285–332.

39. Epstein, *Freedom and Growth*; T. Besley and T. Persson (2009), 'The origins of state capacity: Property rights, taxation, and politics', *American Economic Review*, 99 (4), 1218–44. See also M. Olson (2000), *Power and Prosperity: Outgrowing Communist and Capitalist Dictatorships*. New York: Basic Books.

40. K. K. Karaman and S. Pamuk (2010), 'Ottoman state finances in European perspective, 1500–1914', *Journal of Economic History*, 70 (3), 608–9; P. H. H. Vries (2015), *State, Economy and the Great Divergence: Great Britain and China, 1680s–1850s*. London: Bloomsbury.

41. N. Palma and J. Reis (2019), 'From convergence to divergence: Portuguese economic growth, 1500–1850', *Journal of Economic History*, 79 (2), 477–506.

42. A. Alesina and E. Spolaore (2003), *The Size of Nations*. Cambridge, MA: MIT Press; J. L. van Zanden and M. Prak (2006), 'Towards an economic interpretation of citizenship: The Dutch Republic between medieval communes and modern nation-state', *European Review of Economic History*, 10 (2), 111–45; S. R. Epstein (2006), 'The rise of the West', in J. A. Hall and R. Schroeder (eds), *An Anatomy of Power: The Social Theory of Michael Mann*. Cambridge: Cambridge University Press, 233–62; H. Spruyt (1994), *The Sovereign State and Its Competitors: An Analysis of Systems Change*. Princeton, NJ: Princeton University Press; Epstein, *Freedom and Growth*; D. Stasavage (2011), *States of Credit: Size, Power, and the Development of European Polities*. Princeton, NJ and Oxford: Princeton University Press. For a quantitative test of the hypothesis see M. Dincecco (2011), *Political Transformations and Public Finances: Europe, 1650–1913*. Cambridge and New York: Cambridge University Press.

43. Karaman and Pamuk, 'Ottoman state finances'; C. Moriguchi and T. H. Sng (2014), 'Asia's little divergence: State capacity in China and Japan before 1850', *Journal of Economic Growth*, 19 (4), 439–70; R. Grafe and A. Irigoin (2012), 'A stakeholder empire: The political economy of Spanish imperial rule in America', *Economic History Review*, 65 (2), 609–51.

44. J. I. Herbst (2000), *States and Power in Africa: Comparative Lessons in Authority and Control*. Princeton, NJ: Princeton University Press; G. Austin (2010), 'African economic development and colonial legacies', *International Development Policy*, 1 (1), 11–32.

45. K. Pomeranz (2000), *The Great Divergence: China, Europe and the Making of the Modern World Economy*. Princeton, NJ: Princeton University Press; R. B. Wong (1997), *China Transformed: Historical Change and the Limits of European Experience*. Ithaca, NY: Cornell University Press; P. Parthasarathi (2011), *Why Europe Grew Rich and Asia Did Not: Global Economic Divergence, 1600–1850*. Cambridge: Cambridge University Press.

46. D. A. Boucoyannis (2015), 'No taxation of elites, no representation: State capacity and the origins of representation', *Politics and Society*, 43 (3), 303–32.

47. P. Cardim, T. Herzog, J. J. Ruiz Ibáñez et al. (2012), *Polycentric Monarchies: How Did Early Modern Spain and Portugal Achieve and Maintain a Global Hegemony?*. Eastbourne and Portland, OR: Sussex Academic Press; Karaman and Pamuk, 'Ottoman state finances'; R. Grafe and A. Irigoin (2013), 'Negotiating power: Fiscal constraints and financial development in early modern Spain and the Spanish Empire', in D. Coffman (ed.), *Questioning Credible Commitment: Perspectives on the Rise of Financial Capitalism*. Cambridge: Cambridge University Press and Winton Centre for Financial History, 188–227.

48. Grafe and Irigoin, 'A stakeholder empire'.

49. M. Prak and J. L. van Zanden (2022), *Pioneers of Capitalism: The Netherlands 1000–1800*. Princeton, NJ: Princeton University Press; Levi, *Of Rule and Revenue*.

50. Grafe, *Distant Tyranny*.

51. P. J. Stern (2011), *The Company-State: Corporate Sovereignty and the Early Modern Foundations of the British Empire in India*. New York: Oxford University Press.

52. O'Brien, 'The formation of states'; Parthasarathi, *Why Europe Grew Rich and Asia Did Not*.

53. See for instance, P. Clark (ed.) (2013), *The Oxford Handbook of Cities in World History*. Oxford: Oxford University Press, 3, 221, 231, 386, 421, 452 and 584.

54. de Vries, 'The industrious revolutions in East and West'.

55. J. B. De Long, and A. Shleifer (1993), 'Princes or merchants: European city growth before the Industrial Revolution', *Journal of Law and Economics*, 36 (2), 695–6; J. L. van Zanden, E. Buringh and M. Bosker (2012), 'The rise and decline of European parliaments 1188–1789', *Economic History Review*, 65 (3), 835–61.

56. M. Prak (2018), *Citizens without Nations: Urban Citizenship in Europe and the World, 1000–1789.* Cambridge: Cambridge University Press; L. Brandt, D. Ma and T. G. Rawski (2014), 'From divergence to convergence: Re-evaluating the history behind China's economic boom', *Journal of Economic Literature*, 52 (1), 61–80.

57. E. Le Roy Ladurie (1974), 'L'histoire immobile', *Annales: E.S.C.*, 29, 673–92.

58. S. Pollard (1981), *Peaceful Conquest: The Industrialization of Europe, 1760–1970.* Oxford and New York: Oxford University Press; also M. Prak (1994), 'Regions in early modern Europe'; and S. Pollard (1994), 'Regional and interregional economic development in Europe in the eighteenth and nineteenth centuries', *Debates and Controversies: Proceedings Eleventh International Economic Congress (A-sessions).* Milan: Bocconi University, 17–55 and 57–92 respectively; and J. de Vries (2001), 'Economic growth before and after the Industrial Revolution: A modest proposal', in Prak, *Early Modern Capitalism*, 177–94; A. O. Hirschman (1970), *Exit, Voice, and Loyalty: Responses to Decline in Firms, Organizations, and States.* Cambridge, MA: Harvard University Press; J. D. Tracy (ed.) (1991), *The Political Economy of Merchant Empires.* Cambridge: Cambridge University Press; Mokyr, *A Culture of Growth*.

CHAPTER 6
PLANTATIONS AND THE GREAT DIVERGENCE
Trevor Burnard

Few institutions define world history in the early modern period more than the plantation complex. It has been argued that the plantations in America provided one of two crucial ingredients (along with the presence of large coal deposits allowing for cheap energy) propelling Britain and then Europe to the economic superiority of Europe over China by 1800. Kenneth Pomeranz suggests that 'the extraordinary ecological bounty of the new world' lifted previous limits to the supply of land. Plantations added millions of 'ghost acres' to Britain's supply of agricultural land, providing food for a growing population and freeing up resources for other activities.[1] The plantation system is thus vital for determining the extent to which wealth coming from the Americas in the seventeenth century and, especially, in the eighteenth century can be seen as crucial in the foundations of 'the Great Divergence'. Significantly, the important role that is often attached to plantations in accounts of 'the Great Divergence' suggests an importance for plantations that is sometimes absent in the literature, where the plantation system seems only to have added to the immiseration of humans generally and to the underdevelopment of Africa specifically.[2] In this chapter, I examine the role of plantations in fostering 'the Great Divergence', paying particular attention to Britain which, as a major imperial actor in the plantation societies of the Americas and the first industrial nation, is especially crucial to arguments connecting the plantations of the Americas to eighteenth-century industrial development.

That the Americas would be crucial to Europe in overtaking China as the driver of the global economy by 1800 would have seemed surprising before the maturation of the plantation system in the eighteenth century. By 1650, the settlement of the Americas was mostly a failure. There were some successes. Spain and Portugal had placed themselves firmly into Central and South America, with the Spanish developing silver mines in Potosí in upper Peru that provided a torrent of bullion to the home country, albeit with decidedly mixed results for economic development.[3] The Portuguese had established the first plantation complex in the Americas, producing sugar for export to Europe from the 1550s, though this innovative use of American land had less positive results for Portugal than might have been expected.[4] Some new foodstuffs, like maize, tobacco and potatoes, had made their way from the Americas to the rest of the world, as did exotic drugs like tobacco, leading to transformations of parts of the world economy.[5]

The overall effect of the Columbian encounter, however, was mostly catastrophic, especially for the native inhabitants of the Americas. Much of the Americas reverted to wilderness, possibly taking some carbon out of the atmosphere and perhaps contributing to the Little Ice Age of the seventeenth century.[6] Population decline was good news for forests, which grew bigger and taller in the Americas than they had done for millennia. For European settlers, these gigantic forests looked as if they were ancient but in fact they were very new. These huge trees when chopped down provided the nutrients for extensive agricultural cultivation, notably in north-eastern Brazil from the 1550s and in the smaller islands of the eastern Caribbean, settled by the British and the French, in the second quarter of the seventeenth century. Once cleared, however, especially in places like Barbados where there was no indigenous population to hamper European colonization efforts, the rich soils of deforested land proved perfect places for the establishment of farms for the production of tropical crops – in the Americas, these included tobacco, cotton, rice, indigo, coffee, and above all sugar.[7]

Key to these developments was the Caribbean, especially in the seventeenth and eighteenth centuries. Sidney Mintz argued that the dynamic vitality of plantations in the Caribbean meant that the Caribbean was 'Europe's first economic bridgehead outside itself ... Europe's first overseas colonies [that was] one of the truly great arenas for the interpenetration of African, European, American, Asian and other traditions.[8] The Caribbean was a vital site in the creation of the modern Western world. It was a highly diverse and hybrid place, not just of people but of animals, plants and microbes. A 'creole ecology' emerged from the constant arrival, dispersal and mingling of new plants and animals. This ecology, Stuart Schwarz et al. insist, 'drew on indigenous wisdom, traditional European ideas about weather and astrology, limited reference to classical authorities, but mostly on maritime and local experience.[9] The environmental history of the Caribbean is still in its infancy but current studies point to the ecological distinctiveness of the plantation. Sugar plantations were revolutionary enterprises in part because of the demands they placed on resources but also because they were proto-industrial enterprises relying on processing equipment and an unparalleled reliance on indoor labour, well before that became common during the Industrial Revolution. Increasingly, historians see the plantation in environmental terms, as highly focused centres of energy transfer, a series of interconnected energy flows rather than merely a collection of shared human experiences. They were devastating enterprises, both for humans and the environment, and were dependent on the work of enslaved Africans and hard-working livestock. In this way, sugar plantations were part of industrial change similar to other central commodities in the Industrial Revolution, such as coal. What might be seen as a consequence of the Industrial Revolution – consumers enjoying new inputs of global goods, while being indifferent to how those goods were made – is actually an older and fundamentally agroecological phenomenon based on the precocious development of Atlantic farms.[10]

In English America, these farms were called 'plantations'. The rise of plantation agriculture after 1650 and the nearly coincidental beginnings of the financial and then industrial revolutions in seventeenth- and eighteenth-century England and later Britain is the focus of fierce historiographical attention with less attention paid to similar connections in other European empires. Nevertheless, despite the concentration in this chapter on developments in Britain, if slavery and the slave trade created capitalism and made a major contribution to the Industrial Revolution, then the place where industrialization should also have occurred was France. The French Caribbean, especially the powerhouse of Saint-Domingue, expanded far more rapidly than the British Caribbean after 1714 and particularly after 1763. By 1776, the French Caribbean produced 43 per cent more crops by value than was the case for the British Caribbean. [11]

But it was in Britain where the connections between the plantation system and the 'Great Divergence' have been most explored. The term 'plantation' was derived from English settlement in Ireland in the late sixteenth century, initially denoting an overseas colony.[12] By the middle of the seventeenth century, the term had assumed its meaning of a large agricultural enterprise in a tropical region, managed for profit, which produced an export crop for sale in Europe and elsewhere and which had a labour force that was hierarchically stratified. That labour force could be local or imported. Nevertheless, the contingencies of history – which meant that the most important early manifestations of the plantation complex were in the Americas and in places where indigenous labour was unavailable for exploitation – led to the management and ownership of plantations being in the hands of Europeans while the mixed-sex labour force was African or of African descent.

The make-up of the labour force meant that for the majority of the period in which plantations were most important for world economic growth, the plantation complex was intimately linked to another global phenomenon: the forced migration through the Atlantic slave trade of 11 million enslaved persons, mostly from West and Central-West Africa. In the early modern period, that enslaved population tended (except in the American South from the mid-eighteenth century) not to be self-sustaining, as heavy mortality rates necessitated the continual replacement of workers through the slave trade. The plantation was also an inherently colonial form of economic organization, with control over the complex lying in the metropolitan centres of Britain, the Netherlands, France, Portugal, Spain and Denmark until the nineteenth century. Most important of all, plantations, as they existed from the mid-seventeenth century in British and French America, were large-scale agricultural enterprises requiring anything from fifty to several hundred workers. All facets of production were done within the physical boundaries of the plantation, making these farms capitalist in economic orientation, even if (especially in sixteenth-century Brazil) they retained some elements of feudalism.[13]

Plantations and Economic Growth

The development of plantation agriculture was crucial for the success of colonization in the Americas.[14] As Barbara Solow notes, 'It was slavery that made the empty lands of the western hemisphere valuable producers of commodities and valuable markets for Europe and North America. What moved in the Atlantic in these centuries was predominantly slaves, the output of slaves, the inputs of slave societies, and the goods and services purchased with the earnings on slave products.'[15] What planters in Barbados did in the

1650s was to create a form of labour organization that produced large enough quantities of sugar to bring wealth sufficient for substantial reinvestment. The organization of labour involved ganged labour, with its lockstep discipline and its liberal use of the whip that forced slaves to work as hard as possible. Having gained effective forms of coercion over recalcitrant, demoralized and traumatized African enslaved people, slave forces increased dramatically in size, reaching well over a hundred slaves per plantation in the West Indies and over fifty per plantation in the American South. These large integrated plantations had significant economies of scale over other agricultural enterprises. Most importantly, planters worked slaves very hard. Slaves on sugar plantations in Jamaica worked on average 3,288 hours per year in the later eighteenth century, which pushed them to the outer edge of work hours in the pre-industrial world.[16] Significantly, these hours included more backbreaking work than was normal for European or African peasants. It was not just the hours that were worked that accounted for the remarkable growth of productivity on plantations; it was the manner of the work that was performed. Planters were relentless in their demands on enslaved people. They worked women as hard as, if not harder than, men (most women worked in the field while some men were trained as tradesmen), and set children to work very young. Planters approached slave welfare with great indifference. A project comparing 12,000 skeletons from various countries since 1000 BCE placed eighteenth-century South Carolina field hands in rice planting near the bottom of all historical populations, in the same range as pre-Columbian populations facing extinction or demographic disaster.[17] Not surprisingly, the victims of such punishing work regimes hated doing what they were forced to do. A slave rebel in seventeenth-century Barbados declared that 'the Devel is in the Englishman; that he makes everything work, he makes the Negro work, the Horse work, the wood work, the water work and the winde work'.[18]

Over time, these methods work became refined. Planters paid great attention to enhancing the value of their human capital, using scientific methods of accounting and modern management methods to make sure that enslaved people were placed in jobs that enhanced their rising capital value. In places like Jamaica, such assiduous attention to the developing science of modern management led to remarkable advances in productivity.[19] Barry Higman estimates that per capita output increased from roughly £8 to £29 4s. by 1800. He concludes that in the second half of the eighteenth century, Jamaica 'performed strongly not only by comparison with other plantation economies but also relative to emerging industrial nations'.[20] It achieved these strong productivity gains mostly through the application of basic concepts of what today we call modern management in the division of labour and specialization of tasks within a large labour force, all deployed in a disciplined and coordinated way. By contrast, the gains in agricultural productivity obtained in late eighteenth-century English agriculture lay in increasing the quantity of work done rather than by improving productivity in any real sense, as can be seen in a dramatic increase in the days worked by the average person from 258 in 1760 to 333 in 1800.[21]

A plantation was in important respects therefore a precursor of the modern factory, based on its scale of capital investment in land, machines and people, and in regard to its output, technology, processing functions and large labour force. The success of the late eighteenth-century plantation system as an example of modern management encouraged planters and merchants to keep investing in plantations well after the emancipation of slavery (which occurred between 1834 and 1888 in various slave-holding countries). Indeed, around 1900, the plantation sector followed a wave of new colonization efforts to become important in a range of new locations, notably in different areas of Asia. Its advantages over other forms of agricultural organization lay in its rational and scientifically based form of cultivation and in the ability of plantation owners, normally by this stage resident in Europe with operatives working on their behalf in colonial areas, to extract maximum labour from a generally uneducated and often imported workforce. By 1900, plantations had strong industrial components, notably in the production of rubber in Malaya and Cochin China (Vietnam) where plantations were especially like factories. The main move was towards free enterprise capitalism and away from forced labour. But the state became ever more important, especially in places like Java in Indonesia, where the Dutch government declared all land to be the property of the state. Thus, government control over agrarian development was exercised through control over space, territory and property rather than through direct control over people's bodies.[22]

Pomeranz's 'Great Divergence' argument makes sense in the nineteenth century when cotton production in the United States meant that, due to the elasticity of raw material supplied from America, the cotton industry could develop at a uniquely rapid rate without substantial real price increases for raw cotton fibres. Even then, if cotton had not existed, one can imagine industrialization happening, albeit probably more slowly and in different forms, perhaps based on woollen textiles sourced from Australia (which had the advantage of being a British possession) or linen from Russia.[23] For the seventeenth and eighteenth centuries, Pomeranz's 'ecological bounty' is less convincing, given that most of the commodities produced by plantations were subtropical groceries and semi-luxuries. Their impact on economic growth was likely to be indirect, rather than direct, creating a demand for commodities that needed to be purchased for cash, thus encouraging specialization in household economies.[24]

We concentrate too much on production rather than consumption when looking at what the plantations provided to Europe. Each of the crops produced could be sold only through an exploitation of demand that had previously not existed: people had to learn how to smoke tobacco, to use sugar in puddings, and to replace woollen clothing with more fashionable cotton clothing. Demand was thus very important. Take sugar, for example. It moved in a century from being an elite commodity to being a product that ordinary people could afford.[25] These new plantation products fed into the rise of capitalist farming and into changes in consumer demand. These changes led people to want to do new things in a society with steadily growing productivity in agriculture, permitting a shift in the structure of demand for necessities, comforts and even luxuries. It was during the early modern period, for example, that Europeans first acquired a sweet tooth and the nicotine habit, closely tied to new ways of marketing desires for such products.[26]

The Plantations and the Fiscal–Military State

Plantation agriculture, of course, was important for several European countries besides England/Britain. Before England had established a viable plantation system in Barbados in the mid-seventeenth century, the Portuguese had developed a highly productive plantation system – partly capitalist and partly feudal in nature – that revolved around small farmers growing cane on rented land before taking canes to be harvested in mills owned by *senhores de engenhos*.[27] Yet Portugal was too small, too poor and too economically underdeveloped to be able to use the considerable plantation wealth it acquired from Brazil and from the Atlantic slave trade with Angola to enhance its own economy. Indeed, during the ministry of the most important eighteenth-century Portuguese statesman, the Marquis of Pombal (1750–77), a strict adherent to classical mercantilism, Portuguese efforts in Atlantic commerce were mainly directed towards stimulating and diversifying Brazil's plantation economy with little effort put into using plantation money to enhance the metropolitan Portuguese economy.[28]

The Dutch were better placed in Europe than the Portuguese to benefit from their involvement in the development of plantations because of the advanced nature of their commercial economy in the early seventeenth century and their aggressive expansion in the 1620s and 1630s into imperial conquest in Africa, Asia and the Americas. But when the Portuguese retook Brazil in 1654, combined with the end of the seventeenth-century Dutch 'Golden Age', the ability of the Dutch to prosper from their involvement in plantation agriculture was severely dented. The 'Dutch moment' in the Atlantic passed quickly.[29] The Dutch, however, remained important as a nation devoted to plantation agriculture in Southeast Asia, especially in Java, which was the most important plantation sector in nineteenth- and twentieth-century Asia.[30]

In regard to Britain, it is interesting to speculate on the coincidental timing of the start of the large integrated plantation system in Barbados and upon significant changes in the economic history of England.[31] What happened in Barbados in the middle of the War of the Three Kingdoms in the 1650s came at a propitious time in English history. Meticulous research into English and British economic growth over the long durée suggests that sustained positive economic growth only began from this period. Recent estimates show that between 1650 and 1760, GDP in England/Britain grew at 0.61 per cent per annum, increasing to 0.83 per cent per annum from 1780 to 1800 before attaining modern growth rates in the nineteenth century of over 1.6 per cent per annum. Due to rapid population growth in the eighteenth century, growth in GDP per capita was less impressive after 1690, being just 0.23 per cent per annum between 1700 and 1780, before returning nearly to rates of per capita GDP growth attained between 1650 and 1690.[32]

Correlation is not causation but it is worth investigating what role the new-found wealth of the plantation colonies played in stimulating a permanent rise in English wealth.[33] Gregory King estimated that by 1688 England's overseas trade accounted for about 20 per cent of national income.[34] Nuala Zahedieh argues in a detailed exploration of the growth of colonial trade that England's increasing stake in the Atlantic shaped the long build-up of economic change that culminated in the Industrial Revolution. The trade in plantation-produced goods expanded wealth, relieved Malthusian pressures and encouraged investment in new skills, useful knowledge and adaptive efficiency. As she states,

> Endogenous responses to the market opportunities created by imperial expansion stimulated adaptive innovations on several main fronts: the accumulation and improvement of manufacturing capacity in the capital and beyond; the extension and enhancement of transport networks to create an increasingly integrated and commercialized national economy; and a major investment in the mathematical and mechanical skills which raised England to technological leadership in Europe.[35]

Zahedieh's study of the copper industry is a specific example of how colonial trade facilitated improvements in England's technological capabilities in the late seventeenth century. She shows that colonial demand for fairly mundane copper vessels helped foster inventive mentalities, uniting interest in natural knowledge with craft skills, providing the means whereby a once-moribund industry was able to attract the human and financial investment necessary for applying major technological breakthroughs in industries like smelting and mining.[36]

The development of the large integrated plantation in Barbados also coincided with the beginning of the fiscal–military state in England – an institutional evolution that distinguished England from every other state in Europe. Patrick O'Brien connects the rise of the fiscal state with conflict in the English Civil War in the mid-seventeenth century. He insists that Britain came to be a high-taxing, fiscally powerful state because wealthy elites were so devastated by the destruction of the Civil War that they were willing to make a government fiscally powerful in order that this government would pass legislation that secured individual property rights. Thus, England was able to develop a fiscal state in which revenue from taxation was much higher than anywhere else in Europe. As O'Brien notes, it was fortunate that this domestic reconstruction of the state occurred 'when England's domestic economy began to generate the kind of accelerated commercialization, colonization, urban concentration and proto-industrialization that facilitated the collection of duties on domestic production and imports'.[37]

Plantation profits played a crucial role in making the fiscal–military state a success. Pat Hudson notes that the fiscal–military state gave a great stimulus to growth and innovation, with plantation produce, which was liable to consumption taxes, very important in redistributing wealth from taxpayers and government creditors to merchants and manufacturers, especially in emerging industrial regions like Lancashire. Although export dependence at the national level was never more than 35 per cent before the American Revolution, some firms and industrial sectors in Lancashire depended upon exports for 70 to 80 per cent of their markets, with much capital finding its way across the Atlantic or to Africa as a result of the slave trade and the plantation economy. She emphasizes how plantation trade had strong multiplier effects, stimulating process, product and financial innovations, and generating institutional provisions that affected wide areas of the economy. In short, the effect of the plantation goods coming into Britain from the late seventeenth century led to hothouse conditions conducive to technological and organizational innovations, in response to accelerating demand for exotic crops.[38]

Imperial Benefits

The argument about whether American plantations were valuable to Britain is handicapped by a methodological problem that obscures the true relationship of the American colonies to Britain. Colonies of settlement, which all the American colonies were before the American Revolution, were not like colonies of exploitation, like India, attached to Britain lightly and by ties of economic interest only. By contrast, the American colonies were, as British Americans insisted, an intrinsic part of Britain, full of proud British subjects who considered themselves just as British as any resident of England, Wales or Scotland and more British than Roman Catholic residents of Ireland. That Britons and Americans were fundamentally the same, tied together by ties of mutual affection and shared inheritances, was a central point in Benjamin Franklin's 'Observations on the Increase of Mankind' (1751), a pioneering essay in the developing field of political economy. Franklin predicted that in a few generations white settlers in British North America would eventually outnumber the number of people in the metropolis, to the mutual benefit, he thought, of both areas, adding to the great glory of the empire. He crowed that rapid population increase in North America meant that there 'in another Century, the greatest Number of *Englishmen* will be on this Side of the Water. What an Accession of Power to the *British* Empire by Sea as well as Land! What Increase of Trade and Navigation! What Numbers of Ships and Seamen!' These new Britons would be firm defenders of the empire, as 'there is not a single native of our country who is not firmly attached to our King by principle and affection'. Britain had to do nothing to maintain that affection. There was no danger, he thought, of America 'uniting against their own nation, which protects and encourages them, with which they have so many connections and ties of blood, interest and affection and which 'tis well known they all love more than they love one another'. Indeed, Franklin continued, 'I will venture to say, an union among them for such a purpose is not merely improbable, it is impossible'.[39]

Some Britons also recognized that the colonies could not be divided from Britain just because they happened to be overseas possessions. For Joshua Gee, writing in 1720, British growth and prosperity was inseparable from its connection to the colonies. 'If we take a view of our own Kingdom,' he wrote, 'we shall find our Trade and Riches came but very slowly till our Plantations began to be settled, and as they throve, our Trade and Riches increased, our Lands rose in value, and our Manufactures increased also.'[40] Malachy Postlethwayt extended the theme:

> Since we have established colonies and plantations our condition … has altered for the better, almost to a degree above credibility. Our manufactures are prodigiously

increased, chiefly by the demand for them in the plantations, where they at least take off one and a half and supply us with many valuable commodities for re-exportation, which is as great an emolument to the mother kingdom as to the plantations themselves.[41]

C. Knick Harley insists that while the Atlantic economy made a central contribution to the causes of the Industrial Revolution, the route through which this contribution came was through trade to the non-plantation colonies of British North America. These colonies wanted industrial goods from Britain and financed them by developing the burgeoning provision trade to the West Indies.[42]

The greatest benefit that British North America and the West Indies brought to Britain, however, was not the sugar, tobacco, rice and cotton that they sent to metropolitan Britain, nor was it even their importance as a market for British manufactures and a potential reservoir of manpower for any war Britain wanted to embark upon against European rivals. The most important benefit was their overall wealth and the opportunities that such wealth afforded for British migrants. That wealth was extraordinary as early as 1700 and exceptional by 1774. Free white people in the Thirteen Colonies that later became the United States of America had higher levels of income and, more importantly, much higher standards of living in 1700 than their fellow countrymen in England. Their wealth increased by 1774, although the differential between income levels in Britain and the Thirteen Colonies diminished due to remarkable population growth in America that increased dependency ratios and kept the increase in colonial incomes lower than otherwise.[43]

British movement to the Americas was part of an expansion of the physical space of Britain analogous to how England absorbed Wales in the fourteenth century and to how England joined together with Scotland in the eighteenth century. Consequently, Pomeranz's contention that the colonies provided 'ghost acres' for Britain that allowed it to overcome Malthusian constraints is misplaced. By 'ghost acres', Pomeranz means lands that were not part of the landmass of Britain and thus were additional acres that could be added to British agricultural potential. The problem was that such acres were not 'ghost acres' unless one takes the reductionist belief that only acres in the British Isles counted as part of British possessions and that acres in the British Americas were somehow not owned by the British. Neither Britons nor Americans or West Indians made such a fundamental distinction between 'local' and 'foreign' acres: all belonged to an expansionary British state. These American acres devoted to plantation agriculture were 'real' acres that formed part of the physical and economic expansion of a Greater Britain.[44] They were no more 'ghost acres' than were acres devoted to sheep in Sussex or grain in East Anglia. Moreover, these 'ghost acres' were farmed by real Britons. All acres were part of a growing territorial empire.

The wealth that the plantation sector produced for Britons who lived in these regions was remarkable. British American prosperity helps explain its settled political state before the American Revolution and makes clear why many Britons were willing to risk very high mortality, especially in the areas of greatest wealth, like the Carolina

Lowcountry and the British West Indies, for the chance to make a decent competency or even a large fortune. Estimations of the total physical wealth of British America compared to that of Britain on the eve of the American Revolution make clear just how much money had been accumulated in plantation America within a century of the large integrated plantation system being established in Barbados. Britain had total physical wealth of £314 million around 1774, of which 87 per cent was in England and Wales and 13 per cent in Scotland. The wealth of British America was over half of this sum, at £162 million, with plantation America accounting for £104 million, or 64.4 per cent of British American wealth or 21.9 per cent of the wealth of Britain and its American colonies combined (excluding Ireland, for which GDP figures are unavailable, but which had probably a GDP of £50 million and per capita GDP of about £12, assuming a population of 4 million).

To put this in perspective, plantation America was almost three times as economically valuable to Britain as was Scotland and twice as valuable as Ireland. Of course, a large proportion of the wealth of plantation America – perhaps £28 million if we value the 800,000 slaves in the colonies as worth £35 each – was in the form of human capital, which did not exist in Britain. If we exclude this form of capital from our analysis, then plantation America had total physical wealth of £76 million, or more than twice the wealth of Scotland. Almost all the benefits of this wealth accrued to white settlers. British Americans had in general over twice the wealth of people in England or Wales and 3.5 times the wealth of Scots. But real wealth was concentrated among free whites in the plantation colonies, especially in the West Indies. Average per capita white wealth in plantation America was £201 if wealth tied up in slaves is counted and £147 if enslaved people are excluded. In the West Indies, average per capita white wealth was £1,144 if wealth in slaves is included and £826 if the value of enslaved people is excluded. Whatever else can be said about the economic value of the plantations, it is clear that they afforded in the eighteenth century a degree of wealth for white people that made them appreciably richer than any group of white people in Greater Britain.[45]

One way of appreciating the wealth of white West Indians is to note that if the wealth of the 45,401 whites in the British West Indies in 1774 was added to the 6,572,104 residents of England and Wales, average per capita white wealth, excluding wealth in the form of slaves, would have increased by £5.81. If the wealth of the 519,301 white inhabitants of the plantation regions of British America in 1774, excluding wealth in slavery, is added to those of England and Wales, then average white per capita wealth would have increased by £8.46. If slaves are included, then average white per capita wealth would have increased by £11.62. By contrast, much lower wealth in Scotland and especially Ireland substantially reduced average per capita white wealth in the British archipelago. If Scottish and Irish wealth was added to that of England and Wales, then average per capita white wealth drops to £30 – a fall of £12.3. Moreover, the wealth of these plantation regions was advancing at a much greater rate than was wealth in Britain. Whereas the GDP of England and Wales increased by a healthy 426 per cent between 1700 and 1774, total physical wealth grew by an astounding 1,100 per cent in Jamaica in the same years.[46]

The Plantations and Industrialization

Our discussion still leaves the question moot about the extent what happened in the colonies contributed to economic growth in other sectors of the British economy, notably in industrial sectors. Most attention has been paid to crops sent from the British plantations to Britain in the eighteenth century. There is little doubt that the amount of such crops sent to Britain was considerable and was the most dynamic part of eighteenth-century overseas trade from the colonies to Britain. Sugar was supplemented and then surpassed by American-grown cotton. Cotton imports were spectacular in size and crucial to the development of the quintessential industry in the Industrial Revolution. Between 1750 and 1810, European cotton consumption increased between sixfold and eightfold.[47] The size of the imports was so large that South Carolina senator, James Henry Hammond, famously declared on the floor of the Senate in 1858 that 'no power on earth dares to make war upon it. COTTON IS KING'. Without southern cotton, he thundered, 'England would topple headlong and carry the whole civilized world with her, save the South'. It was one of the more famously mistaken statements in American history, as Great Britain had no intention of ever supporting the Confederacy against the Union, given how much it had staked its international reputation upon its commitment to anti-slavery.[48]

There have been some recent attempts to prove that Hammond was right. Historians heavily influenced by Wallerstein world-systems theory have argued that slave-produced cotton was responsible for British and north-eastern industrialization.[49] Their polemical intentions are different from Hammond (they argue that slavery was key to the invention of capitalism because they want to associate capitalism with illiberalism) but their arguments are similar. And, like Hammond, they overstate the case for cotton in the development of the British and then the global economy. American cotton arrived on the scene – becoming only important after the invention of the cotton gin in 1793 and dominant only from the 1820s – too late to determine the beginnings of industrialization.[50]

By 1700, England's transoceanic trade was not overwhelmingly large but in its dynamic growth it was essential for new industries, like copper, and for sustaining industries, like shipbuilding, vital for British defence. Moreover, it was central in encouraging the financial innovations vital to the commercial 'revolution'. Many of the advances were hindered by vested interests diverting capital and enterprise into rent-seeking activities but what the British state realized from around 1700 was that the success of the American plantations showed that mercantilism worked. As Nuala Zahedieh concludes, the highly performing plantation trade not only outperformed other sectors but also stimulated 'adaptive innovations which took the country to a new plateau of possibilities from which Industrial Revolution was not only possible but increasingly likely'.[51] Between the Glorious Revolution of 1688 and the end of the Seven Years War in 1763, the British state supported planters wholeheartedly. It had reason to do so, as John Gee and Malachy Postlethwayt recognized. The plantations brought great profits, benefited significant economic agents like London and Bristol merchants, and provided desirable consumer goods that added to the happiness of its inhabitants. The plantations were rewarded for their contributions to the greater welfare of Britain by favourable imperial legislation, by support for an increasingly efficient and effective slave trade, and by tacit acceptance of colonial demands that slaves should be thought of as property, not as humans.[52]

Opinion later turned against the planter class, and the system of economic exploitation that sustained them. Here Eric Williams was also right. But, contrary to what Williams believed, the decline of the influence of the planter class was not due to notions that plantations were economically ineffective and could be discarded as soon as industrial capitalism took over. Plantations were efficient means of organizing labour to gain profits and were as capitalist an enterprise as any factory, even if work was organized differently. Fogel and Engerman's controversial *Time on the Cross* (1974) showed conclusively how slavery and capitalism could work together and that nineteenth-century views of plantation agriculture as being inherently backward and thus just a way station between feudalism and industrial capitalism were incorrect.[53]

Plantations did more than just provide 'ghost acres' that provided Britain with an ecological release from Malthusian constraints. They gave the owners and managers of plantations, if never workers, high incomes and notable social prestige. But their economic success was accompanied by pernicious social, and usually racial, consequences in a colonial context that became increasingly disturbing to metropolitan observers. Eventually, the plantation became a place in the European imagination that was so ideologically suspect that its economic benefits needed to be denied. But if ideologically suspect, it was never anything but economically successful.

Conclusion

Plantations were a principal means whereby Europeans could exploit the Americas, through the agency of West Africans. There is no doubt that plantations brought great wealth to their owners, enormous misery to enslaved people, and considerable economic and geopolitical benefits to European imperial nations with American possessions, including France, the Netherlands and Britain. Some historians, following in the footsteps of Eric Williams, have argued for an even greater impact of the plantation system – as the impetus towards Britain's precocious late eighteenth-century industrialization. Such arguments are overstated. We do not need to have the plantations be responsible for British industrialization in order to accept their enormous role in advancing British wealth and power (as also in France, where little emphasis has been customarily put on the role of plantations in fostering French industrialization). Britain's transoceanic trade contributed significantly to various areas of trade and helped cement financial innovations that secured Britain's eighteenth-century commercial revolution. It is in these areas that profits from the plantations were most important. It helps explain Britain's wholehearted support of planters and the plantation system before the Seven Years War brought into public discourse less positive assessments of the effects of the plantation economy upon the British sense of morality about their overseas empires.

Notes

1. K. Pomeranz (2000), *The Great Divergence: China, Europe and the Making of the Modern World Economy*. Princeton, NJ: Princeton University Press, 275–7. This method of 'ghost acres' was pioneered in E. L. Jones (2003), *The European Miracle: Environments, Economies and Geopolitics in the History of Europe and Asia*, 3rd edn. Cambridge: Cambridge University, ch. 1.

2. D. Eltis (2000), *The Rise of African Slavery in the Americas*. Cambridge: Cambridge University Press; and W. Rodney (1972), *How Europe Underdeveloped Africa*. London: Bogle L'Ouverture Books.

3. B. Yun-Casalilla (1996), 'The American empire and the Spanish economy: An institutional and regional perspective', *Revista de Historia Económica*, 16 (1), 123–56.

4. S. B. Schwartz (1985), *Sugar Plantations in the Formation of Brazilian Society, Bahia, 1550–1835*. Cambridge: Cambridge University Press.

5. N. D. Cook (2015), 'The Columbian exchange', in J. H. Bentley et al. (eds), *The Cambridge World History*, vol. 6: *The Construction of a Global World, 1400–1800 CE*. Part 2 *Patterns of Change*. Cambridge: Cambridge University Press, 103–35. See also the chapters by J. R. McNeill and Alejandra Irigoin in this volume.

6. G. Parker (2013), *Global Crisis: War, Climate Change and Catastrophe in the Seventeenth Century*. New Haven, CT: Yale University Press.

7. D. Watts (1987), *The West Indies: Patterns of Development, Culture and Environmental Change since 1492*. Cambridge: Cambridge University Press.

8. S. W. Mintz (1974), *Caribbean Transformations*. Baltimore, MD: Johns Hopkins University Press, 33.

9. P. Morgan, J. R. McNeill, S. Schwartz and M. Mulcahy (2022), *Sea and Land: An Environmental History of the Caribbean*. New York: Oxford University Press, 194.

10. N. Oatsvall and V. Scribner (2018), '"The devil was in the Englishman that he makes everything work": Implementing the concept of "work" to re-evaluate sugar production and consumption in the early modern British Atlantic world', *Agricultural History*, 92 (4), 461–90.

11. D. Eltis and S. W. Engerman (2000), 'The importance of slavery and the slave trade to industrializing Britain', *Journal of Economic History*, 60 (1), 130–31; T. Burnard and J. Garrigus (2016), *The Plantation Machine: Atlantic Capitalism in French Saint-Domingue and British Jamaica*. Philadelphia, PA: University of Pennsylvania Press.

12. N. Canny (1998), 'The origins of empire: An introduction', in N. Canny (ed.), *The Oxford History of the British Empire*, vol. 1: *The Origins of Empire*. Oxford: Oxford University Press, 8.

13. P. D. Curtin (1990), *The Rise and Fall of the Plantation Complex: Essays in Atlantic History*. Cambridge: Cambridge University Press, 11–13. See also K. Morgan (2016), *A Brief History of Transatlantic Slavery*. London: I.B. Tauris.

14. T. Burnard (2015), 'Plantation societies', in J. H. Bentley et al. (eds), *Cambridge World History*, vol. 6, part 1. Cambridge: Cambridge University Press, 263–82.

15. B. Solow (1991), 'Slavery and colonisation', in B. Solow (ed.), *Slavery and the Rise of the Atlantic System*. Cambridge: Cambridge University Press, 21–42.

16. J. Roberts (2013), *Slavery and the Enlightenment in the British Atlantic, 1750–1807*. New York: Cambridge University Press, 86.

17. T. A. Rathbun and R. H. Steckel (2002), 'The health of slaves and free blacks in the East', in R. H. Steckel and J. C. Rose (eds), *The Backbone of History: Health and Nutrition in the Western Hemisphere*. Cambridge: Cambridge University Press, 208–25.

18. Anon. (1676), *Great Newes from the Barbadoes*. London: L. Curtis, 6–7.

19. C. Rosenthal (2016), 'Slavery's scientific management: Accounting for mastery', in S. Beckert and S. Rothman (eds), *Slavery's Capitalism: A New History of American Economic Development*. Philadelphia, PA: University of Pennsylvania Press, 62–82.

20. B. W. Higman (2005), *Plantation Jamaica 1750–1850: Capital and Control in a Colonial Economy*. Kingston: University of the West Indies Press, 2–3, 8–9.

21. G. Clark (1987), 'Productivity growth without technical change in European agriculture before 1850', *Journal of Economic History*, 47 (2), 419–32; H.-J. Voth (2001), 'The longest years: New estimates of labor input in England, 1760–1830', *Journal of Economic History*, 61 (4), 1065–82.

22. J. Breman (1989), *Taming the Coolie Beast: Plantation Society and the Colonial Order in Southeast Asia*. Delhi and New York: Oxford University Press; Breman (2015), *Mobilizing Labour for the Coffee Market: Profits from an Unfree Work Regime in Colonial Java*. Amsterdam: Amsterdam University Press.

23. G. Riello (2013), *Cotton: The Fabric that Made the Modern World*. Cambridge: Cambridge University Press, 240–6.

24. J. de Vries (2008), *The Industrious Revolution: China, Europe and the Making of the Modern World Economy*. New York: Cambridge University Press. See also the chapter by Maxine Berg in this volume.

25. S. Mintz (1985), *Sweetness and Power: The Place of Sugar in Modern History*. New York: Penguin.

26. E. A. Wrigley (2008), *Continuity, Chance and Change: The Character of the Industrial Revolution in England*. Cambridge: Cambridge University Press; C. Shammas (2000), 'The revolutionary impact of European demand for tropical goods', in J. J. McCusker and K. Morgan (eds), *The Early Modern Atlantic Economy*. Cambridge: Cambridge University Press, 163–85.

27. S. B. Schwartz (2004), *Tropical Babylons: Sugar and the Making of the Atlantic World, 1450–1680*. Chapel Hill, NC: University of North Carolina Press.

28. K. Maxwell (1995), *Pombal: Paradox of the Enlightenment*. Cambridge: Cambridge University Press, 119–28, 134–48.

29. W. W. Klooster (2016), *The Dutch Moment: War, Trade, and Settlement in the Seventeenth-Century Atlantic World*. Ithaca, NY: Cornell University Press.

30. A. Reid (1988–93), *Southeast Asia in the Age of Commerce*, 2 vols. New Haven, CT: Yale University Press. See Thomas Lindblad's chapter in this volume.

31. R. R. Menard (2006), *Sweet Negotiations: Sugar, Slavery, and Plantation Agriculture in Early Barbados*. Charlottesville, VA: University of Virginia Press; and S. D. Newman (2013), *Free and Bound Labor in the British Atlantic World: Black and White Workers and the Development of Plantation Slavery*. Philadelphia, PA: University of Pennsylvania Press, 54–9.

32. S. Broadberry et al. (2015), *British Economic Growth, 1270–1870*. Cambridge: Cambridge University Press.

33. D. Acemoglu, S. Johnson and J. Robinson (2005), 'The rise of Europe: Atlantic trade, institutional change, and economic growth', *American Economic Review*, 95 (2), 546–79.

34. P. Laslett (ed.) (1973), *The Earliest Classics: Graunt and King*. Farnborough: Gregg, 207.

35. N. Zahedieh (2010), *The Capital and the Colonies: London and the Atlantic Economy, 1660–1700*. Cambridge: Cambridge University Press, 4, 7, 285. But see P. K. O'Brien (1982), 'European economic development: The contribution of the periphery', *Economic History Review*, 35 (1), 1–18.

36. N. Zahedieh (2013), 'Colonies, copper, and the market for inventive activity in England and Wales, 1680–1730', *Economic History Review*, 66 (3), 805–25.

37. P. K. O'Brien (2011), 'The nature and historical evolution of an exceptional fiscal state', *Economic History Review*, 64 (2), 435–36.

38. P. Hudson (2014), 'Slavery, the slave trade and economic growth: A contribution to the debate', in C. Hall, N. Draper and K. McClelland (eds), *Emancipation and the Making of the British Imperial World*. Manchester: Manchester University Press, 36–59. See also J. E. Inikori (2002), *Africans and the Industrial Revolution in England: A Study in International Trade and Economic Development*. Cambridge: Cambridge University Press; and P. Hudson and M. Berg (2023), *Slavery, Capitalism and the Industrial Revolution*. Cambridge: Polity Press.

39. B. Franklin (1959), 'Observations on the increase of mankind', in L. W. Labaree et al. (eds), *The Papers of Benjamin Franklin*. New Haven, CT: Yale University Press, vol. 4, 225–34.

40. J. Gee (1720), *A Letter to a Member of Parliament, Concerning the Naval-Stores Bill*. London: n.a., 18.

41. M. Postlethwayt (ed.) (1764), *Universal Dictionary of Trade and Commerce*, 2 vols, 4th edn. London: H. Woodthall, vol. 1: entry under 'Colonies'.

42. C. K. Harley (2015), 'Slavery, the British Atlantic Economy, and the Industrial Revolution', in A. B. Leonard et al. (eds), *The Caribbean and the Atlantic World Economy*. Basingstoke: Palgrave Macmillan, 182.

43. P. Lindert and J. Williamson (2016), *Unequal Gains: American Growth and Inequality since 1700*. Princeton, NJ: Princeton University Press, chs 2–3.

44. R. R. Davies (2000), *The First English Empire: Power and Identities in the British Isles, 1093–1343*. Oxford: Oxford University Press; D. Armitage (1999), 'Greater Britain: A useful category of historical analysis?', *American Historical Review*, 104 (2), 427–45.

45. T. Burnard (2015), *Planters, Merchants and Slaves: Plantation Societies in British America, 1650–1820*. Chicago, IL: University of Chicago Press, 9–10. For Scotland's GDP as 13.1 per cent of Britain's, see Maddison, *The World Economy*, 247. He also suggests that Ireland's GDP in 1774 was between 16 and 20 per cent of England Wales, suggesting GDP of around £50 million or £12 per capita. Thus, the average white West Indian, including slave wealth, was over 100 times as rich as the average Irish person. Dependency ratios in the various regions, of course, were very different, with the West Indies having very few children or old people.

46. Burnard, *Planters, Merchants, and Slaves*, 167; Broadberry et al., *British Economic Growth*.

47. P. Bairoch (1993), *Economic and World History: Myths and Paradoxes*. Hemel Hempstead: Harvester Wheatsheaf, 158.

48. S. Drescher (2002), *The Mighty Experiment: Free Labor versus Slavery in British Emancipation*. New York: Oxford University Press, 202–3, 231–7.

49. See in particular, S. Beckert (2014), *Empire of Cotton: A New History of Global Capitalism*. New York: Alfred A. Knopf, 29–82.

50. Harley, 'Slavery, the British Atlantic economy, and the Industrial Revolution', 182.

51. Zahedieh, *Capital and Colonies*, 292.

52. L. S. Walsh (2010), *Motives of Honor, Pleasure & Profit: Plantation Management in the Colonial Chesapeake, 1607–1763*. Chapel Hill, NC: University of North Carolina Press.

53. R. W. Fogel and S. W. Engerman (1974), *Time on the Cross: The Economics of American Negro Slavery*. Boston, MA: Little, Brown; New York: Norton.

CHAPTER 7
CONSUMPTION AND GLOBAL HISTORY IN THE EARLY MODERN PERIOD
Maxine Berg

Introduction

There is a large recent historiography on consumption and social and cultural history, yet there is much less on consumption and economic history. Recent textbooks of British economic history have no chapters on consumption. Instead, there is a traditional place for chapters on wages and the standard of living.[1] And yet consumption is a key factor in economic policy formation, for it is currently the source of much British tax revenue. During the eighteenth century, too, a key source of much government revenue was excise taxes and customs duties – that is, taxes on consumer goods. Political debate over these taxes fuelled radical reform movements and contributed to the American Revolution.[2]

Consumption, especially of luxury goods, was the key factor in debates on economic improvement during the Enlightenment; indeed, discourse around consumption stimulated the emergence of political economy as an intellectual subject area. Today, consumer economic theory and other social science theory raise many fascinating subjects, and in recent years have moved towards behavioural psychology.[3] And yet economic historians, apart from a few exceptions, have been reluctant to engage in an analysis of consumption in economic change.

Economists from Jevons to Marshall introduced analysis of consumption in terms of marginal utility.[4] But mainstream economists showed little interest, even at the end of the nineteenth century and the early twentieth century, in the wider aspects of consumption. It was those of heterodox views who took it up: Veblen, Ruskin and Hobson. Heterodox voices converged between the end of the nineteenth century and the First World War to analyse, deconstruct and criticize a period of rapid growth of new wealth and luxury expenditure in Europe and America. Luxury goods, excess consumption and collecting were manifestations of Europe's and America's new super-rich bourgeois classes. Banking and industrial families built palatial residences to be filled with all manner of globally sourced luxury goods, and they collected antique objects, pictures and other art objects. There was a whole fin-de-siècle debate on the decline of capitalism, moral corruption and social division. Sombart, Simmel and Veblen all published their critical texts on hedonism during this period.[5]

There was some interest in consumption among economists in the 1960s and 1970s, but the subject remained on the margins of mainstream economics. While product development was advancing rapidly in this period, economists focused on productivity change. There was much discussion of consumer choice, but this was conceived as a choice between price and quantity; tastes, products and qualities were assumed by most economists to be fixed. Two critical voices from within mainstream microeconomic theory, Kelvin Lancaster and Duncan Ironmonger, pointed out in the 1960s that consumers selected not just a consumer good, but among the many characteristics and qualities contained by such a good, but few took up the analysis of tastes that this implied.[6]

A few years later, Tibor Scitovsky argued the case for the importance of novelty to consumer choice. Habituation in meeting demands needed to be punctuated by novelty and uncertainty; thus he highlighted novelty, variety, complexity and surprise, which aroused the senses and stimulated pleasure.[7] In recent years, Marina Bianchi used these ideas to develop her concept of the 'active consumer': one who is not a passive price taker, but who actively engages to form tastes, responds to new goods, and combines these in diverse ways to make an identity. This active consumer might well base her choices on sensual satisfaction over everyday convenience and even necessity.[8]

The use by these economists of 'hedonic indices' and the psychological theories that underpin them also stimulated the economic historian Avner Offer to use such theories to explain twentieth-century consumer trends. He argues that many economists assume that individuals can rank their different wants consistently, that they want as much as they can get, and that they act on their own preferences. But this is not frequently the case. Wants become less compelling the more they are satisfied; and many people shift their preferences sequentially to more psychologically pressing ones. We live in states of anticipation and consummation, seeking the serial fulfilment of our transient desires.[9] True prosperity in Offer's view is a good balance between short-term arousal and long-term security; the challenge is not to maximize consumption, but to pace it back to a level of optimal satisfaction.[10]

These issues of the factors lying behind consumption – the choices, the stimuli and the complexities of satisfaction – are central to explaining a history of consumption in the early modern world. What difference has global history made to the history of consumption? What part has consumption played in the factors considered in global economic history?

The Great Divergence and Consumption

In his work dedicated to the concept of the Great Divergence, Kenneth Pomeranz compared consumption and luxury consumption across Europe, China, Japan and India to argue that these were not significant factors explaining differences between the great regions of the pre-modern world. As he mainly adopted a comparative methodology, he offered little analysis of the global connections in commodity trade as a factor behind the Great Divergence.

Pomeranz's findings suggested that sugar consumption in China in 1750 was higher than in continental Europe, even as late as 1800; but at some point after this, China's per capita consumption of sugar declined, while Europe's grew rapidly, especially after 1840.[11] China's tea consumption was also much higher than Europe's at 11 ounces per person as compared to Europe's 2 ounces per person in the 1780s.[12] Pomeranz also compared the consumption of textiles and clothing in both regions to argue that Chinese textile consumption compared quite well against that of Europe in the mid- to late eighteenth century.

There was, furthermore, evidence of a moral debate on excess consumption among the popular classes and peasants in the Lower Yangtze region of China and in eighteenth-century Japan. And there was evidence of fashion in clothing and some consumer durables in Ming China and Muromachi and Tokugawa Japan, though not in India or Southeast Asia.[13] Pomeranz found less change in the use of houses and their contents and the generations they contained in Asia than in Europe. But there was nevertheless a market for high-quality purchased goods even in villages in China's remote macro-regions. There were likewise many consumer products in late Tokagawa and early Meiji era villages.[14]

Pomeranz reinforced his support for the case for high standards of living in eighteenth-century China and East Asia more generally. He found higher consumption there of tea and silk than in Europe, widespread consumption of tobacco, and per capita cloth consumption on par with Germany. Expenditure on ritual was high, and though meat and dairy consumption in China was lower than that in Europe, comparable levels of protein intake could be found in these two world regions.[15]

What differed was the role of trade and imports. The Chinese consumed their own domestically produced sugar, tobacco and tea. These products – so crucial to Europe's changing consumer habits – in China produced only a low profit margin trade among small merchants, no significant revenues for the state, and thus no powerful lobbies to encourage their increased consumption. Europe, by contrast, grew all its sugar, tobacco and coffee in overseas colonies, and bought tea from China in exchange for silver from the Americas. Europe drew its cotton from colonies or ex-colonies, while China grew much of its own.[16] The regional connections of commodities were thus missing from the divergence debate. As Jan de Vries pointed out, trade was toppled in this new historiography from the central role ascribed to it by Andre Gunder Frank.[17] Instead, Pomeranz focused on the trade that did not emerge in Ming/Qing China. There was no extensive specialization and interregional trade, and the Chinese trading diaspora in Southeast Asia did not give rise to a large trade in tropical goods to the Chinese metropole.

Both Pomeranz and Parthasarathi argued that China and India did not cultivate long-distance trade links because they had no need of them. The need for silver in both places did, however, lead to production of goods for export sufficient to secure an influx of silver from Europe capable of 'oiling the wheels of the Chinese economy' and acting as the 'motor' of the Indian subcontinent.[18] The point made by Pomeranz for China and Parthasarathi for South Asia was that Asia and Europe had at least similar levels of consumption of goods such as sugar, tobacco, tea and textiles. However, the part played by traded goods in consumption was much higher in Europe, and it escalated in the eighteenth century.

What part, then, did traded consumer goods play in Europe? Jan de Vries compared the levels of East India Company trade between Asia and Europe on the one hand and Atlantic trade on the other. His data showed that Atlantic trade grew more than twice as fast as the Asia–Europe trade, and contributed twice the value to European GDP, and yet the indirect effect of the Asia–Europe trade was disruptive and highly significant in shifting consumer cultures.[19]

Standard explanations for the appeal of Asian commodities in early modern Europe are that they were exotic, unique or superior, and cheap. But more important than their appeal was the information flows they brought in their wake. Merchants brought new knowledge about goods, and participated in developing innovative ways of incorporating these into European lifestyles with new uses and new products.[20] The East India companies were effective in gathering, processing and analysing large amounts of information about access to goods and ways of developing markets for them. In Europe, most of these imported Eastern goods were sold in the company auctions, but distributing these goods out to wider European markets and re-exporting them beyond Europe were left to private trade. The variety of these goods and gradations of quality brought a new signifier to taste and product development in Europe. Such goods drew more households into the market. In de Vries's words, 'information and industriousness were highly correlated'.[21]

Pomeranz recognized the impact of new goods on shifting social behaviours. He acknowledged Adam Smith's fine analysis of the role of exotic baubles that appealed to the senses in motivating elites to acquire objects in lieu of retainers. Exotic goods, Pomeranz wrote, also stimulated societies with strict sumptuary laws because such goods were previously unknown and thus not yet assigned or forbidden to any specific group. Goods with remote origins were more easily mystified, and acquired greater 'value' than local or known goods with similar uses.[22] Pomeranz accepted Jan de Vries's case for an 'industrious revolution', that is, that the demand for newly available goods helped to create new worker and consumer behaviours, but he did not provide any analysis for what difference this might have made for diverging paths of economic development.

Part of the reason for this lies in the view held by China's historians that external trade was less important for Chinese industry than it was for that of Western economies. As we have seen, sugar and cotton were internally produced in China. Europeans, facing supply constraints and high transactions costs in acquiring these goods externally, were stimulated to seek substitutes in other parts of the world that they controlled as colonies or through their own process and product innovation. Europeans learned to produce to Asian standards, varieties and qualities.

The key external commodity which stimulated the economies of China and India was silver, but even this was not, in Pomeranz's view, transformative. Since the publication of *The Great Divergence*, there has been much research on various aspects of consumption in many parts of the world, China among these. Zheng Yangwen's work, for instance, investigates the taste for European goods in early modern China. Goods from fragrances and clocks to foodstuffs and architecture were 'indigenized' and contributed to commercial specialization. There may be parallels in the transformation of the Chinese economy and society by foreign goods to the European experience, but they did not entail the connections that de Vries drew between the 'industrious revolution' and the Industrial Revolution.[23]

Much of the more recent research on the history of consumption in other parts of Asia is focused on the nineteenth and twentieth centuries, and addresses social and cultural history.[24] Similarly, research on the Mughal and princely courts of India reveals rapid changes in fashion, taste and styles, but these remained confined to the court environment and did not penetrate into urban communities.[25] Bayly depicted this consumer culture as a collecting culture, and a part of what he termed 'archaic globalization'. Rulers amassed goods from distant lands, and there was also a tributary flow of consumption; the nawabs and other rulers controlled flows of goods and services for the rest. The courts also sought unique or highly specialist goods. Whereas modern complexity demands the uniformity of Levis and trainers, the archaic simplicity of everyday life demanded that 'great men prized difference in goods … In one sense archaic lords … were collectors, rather than consumers.'[26]

While imported goods, fashion and extensive product and quality differentiation were significant to consumption in India, they did not reach out to wider urban society, nor embed themselves in the everyday life of large groups of the population. While they existed, they were not the stuff of the kind of 'industrious revolution' of Northern Europe.[27]

Historiography: Is There an Economic History of Consumption?

To what extent do we have an economic history of consumption for the early modern world, or even parts of the early modern world apart from Europe? When we look to Europe, that historiography is focused on Jan de Vries's 'industrious revolution'.[28] What debate we have in the historiography generated in the wake of the 'Great Divergence' is not one over consumption, but one over wages and standards of living. Again, this is a debate over comparisons and not connections. It does not tell us about consumer goods, or incentives to produce or to buy these; it does not tell us about the impact of some parts of the world on others, for example, the impact of the Columbian Exchange of foods, plants and diseases, nor of colonial groceries or the impact of a global trade in resources and materials, nor of that in manufactured goods.

What can we glean from that debate on wages and standards of living? Carole Shammas asks 'When and why did consumption of material goods become the measure of the "standard of living"?'[29] Up to the years immediately following the Second World War, the standard of living was conceived in purely material terms – that is, the goods and services at one's disposal. Thus GDP per capita became the yardstick, but as we know, these indices did not show inequality or investment in human capital. Now most indices of well-being skip over household budgets and real wages, and turn instead to life expectancy, health status and heights, as well as other indices of well-being such as education.[30]

Shammas summarized a widely accepted position on European living standards to date: prior estimates of early nineteenth-century income growth were revised downwards, and pre-industrial standards were revised upwards. New products were brought into Western Europe; diets became more varied, cotton fabric entered the clothing market and textile prices dropped. Brick and stone replaced wood and clay in many cities, glass windows became widespread and interior furnishings improved. This was not due to lower grain prices, but to higher real incomes, lower costs of durables and semi-durables, or better use of household labour.[31]

Among economic historians of the early modern period, there has been intense debate over levels of wages and living standards; most of this centred on explaining industrialization and divergence. Was there a great divergence in 'wages and prices'? What does this add to an older debate on wages and the standard of living led by Hobsbawm in the 1960s? The purpose of the debate in the 1960s and after, and in more recent configurations in studies of working-class budgets led by Horrell and Humphries, was to discover the impact of industrialization on the poor.[32] The purpose for the current wage divergence debate is different. That purpose for one leading contender, Robert Allen, is to discover high wages in Britain compared with the rest of the world, and thence to argue that this wage premium could explain her prescient and rapid pace of technological change and subsequent industrialization.[33]

These debates over wages do not, however, take us much further into the history of consumption beyond that of basic foodstuffs. Allen's work remains a good example. He refers to an Indian diet of rice, millets and pulses; in some areas, fish provided the only source of animal protein. He writes of the poverty of 'scanty clothing and barefoot', of mud huts with thatched roofs, of few furnishings beyond bamboo mats, and of cooking done in earthen pots. His sources are Raychaudhuri and Habib from 1982.[34] He finds similar dearth in China, based on an account of Charles Lockyer, an early eighteenth-century merchant traveller. It seems obvious to him that northwest Europe with its white bread, meat, dairy products and beer had the highest standard of living. But is this so clear? The new histories of food and its preparation need to be linked to the wage baskets used by economic historians, as do the data we now have on the consumption of luxuries and novelties: tropical foodstuffs such as tea, sugar, coffee and chocolate and imported Asian manufactures – cotton, silk, porcelain and British and European imitations. Economic historians now need to look more deeply into the consumption of specific types of goods – those associated with inequality and those that shifted behaviours.

Inequality

Recent research on inequality focuses on the macroeconomic picture of the distribution of income and wealth. Thomas Piketty's *Capital in the Twenty-First Century* (2015) compares rising inequality in the period from the 1970s with the growth in inequality in the later eighteenth and early nineteenth centuries. Piketty compares the wealthy elites inheriting patrimonial wealth with the growth of elites from the eighteenth century whose wealth was increasingly based on interest earned on private holdings of government debt. Rentiers living off increasingly lucrative investment earnings contrasted with the labouring poor whose relative wages did not rise in any degree until after the mid-nineteenth century. Furthermore, property incomes rose from the mid- eighteenth century in Europe, and increased inequality. Technical change during the late eighteenth and in most of the nineteenth century in Western Europe and in the United States reinforced this inequality, as capital was substituted for labour in many manufacturing processes. Factories employed less skilled labour; processes were simplified and products standardized for mass production in factories.

What impact did these trends to rising inequality as well as changes in technology mean for consumption? Once again the research we have is about wages without precise assumptions over what goods comprised the wage basket. Comparisons of wages and standards of living have focused on the working classes consuming ordinary commodities, and budget studies are mainly based on foodstuffs. But as we know, the rich and the poor consume different things. Philip Hoffman has argued that economic historians have been over-reliant on the price series of staple products, especially food, standardized older products, internationally traded goods, and physical goods, and they underuse luxury goods, labour-intensive goods, new products, non-traded products, retail products, and services.[35]

Luxury goods in the eighteenth century became cheaper relative to staple foods, but their impact is as hard to quantify as that for introducing new goods and services into today's cost-of-living indices. Fashion and luxury goods changed constantly, frustrating the search for consistent time series. Hoffman looked at price changes over a whole series of standardized commodities, and found the biggest advances of prices in fuel, rent and cinnamon, and the greatest reductions of prices in textiles, sugar, silver, paper, beer and unskilled labour. He found rising food prices and falling wages of unskilled labour. Many of those luxury products falling in price made use of factors that were getting cheaper across the seventeenth and eighteenth centuries: clothing and textiles, paper, chocolate, pewter and sealing wax became cheaper along with the labour that went into them.[36] Adjusting the cost-of-living index with clothing, light, fuel and beverages shows standards of living declined a little less in the period than previously estimated. But we also need to look further to class-specific cost of living indices.

Lower prices of luxury and staple goods brought real income gains for the wealthier and for richer regions. Hoffman also charted the temporal cycles in this inequality. Between 1500 and 1650, the top income groups experienced a 20 per cent reduction in their cost of living. But between 1650 and 1750, there was a reversal, with the common people gaining. This swing reversed again in the second half of the eighteenth century, with wealthier groups gaining from the impact on prices of luxury goods of greater trade and new technologies. It was not until the last half of the nineteenth century that inequality moved again in favour of the lower classes.[37] In the period 1500–1650, the wealthier benefited most from cheaper new luxury goods as well as old luxuries such as domestic servants, and higher land rents added to their wealth. The poor faced scarcer food and higher costs of housing and land. In England, a second inegalitarian trend took place between 1740 and 1795–1815.

Hoffman poses that these trends favouring the wealthier classes in early modern northwest Europe might help to explain the Great Divergence. The gains to the early phases of industrialization might well have contributed to changing behaviours associated with the 'industrious revolution'.

These trends in inequality within Britain need also to be set alongside wider global inequalities arising from Europe's new consumer goods, both colonial groceries and the resource inputs to material goods. The greatest inequality arose in the production of the wider-world luxury goods imported especially into Europe and North America. Europe's highly fashionable consumption of Chinese porcelain between the sixteenth and the eighteenth centuries relied on recruitment of huge numbers of poorly paid unskilled labourers from great distances away to the kilns and factories of China's Jingdezhen.[38] The plantation system was developed for the mass production of sugar, tobacco, coffee and tea in Brazil and the Caribbean, in the southern colonies of North America, and in India.[39] Along with this production of luxury foodstuffs was cultivation of resource inputs to material goods; cotton, indigo, mahogany among them. Enslaved peoples and indentured labour did the work.

Europe's taste for the exotic in food, drink, fabrics and furnishings brought 11 million enslaved workers to the New World, their numbers rising by about 2 per cent per annum between 1525 and 1790, and accelerating after 1650. Europe's imports of commodities from the New World also rose at this level, a level twice what it imported from Asia. Sugar made up most of these imports at this stage, and sugar imports by the 1770s were four times the level of total Asian exports to Europe.[40] Sugar consumption and slave production rose together. Sugar production in the Western hemisphere was 54,000 tons in 1700; this figure doubled by 1740, and tripled by 1776.[41] Sugar imports into England and Wales in one year, 1774, reached a value of £2,634,000, and by c.1770 estimated annual profits of £1,700,000 accrued from the cultivation of sugar throughout the British Caribbean.[42] Sugar rose to become the top-ranked commodity import into Britain by the early 1770s, and it continued among the top three imports even after the mid-nineteenth century.[43] After the abolition of slavery in the British territories, slave imports continued from Spanish and Portuguese territories, and the plantation system was redeveloped, drawing on new global supplies of impoverished unfree contract and indentured labour from Asia. The Victorian tea taste was now fed by tea plantations and indentured labour in India, and mass consumer Victorian cotton was cultivated with enslaved then bonded, sharecropping and indentured labour in the southern states of America, India, Brazil and Egypt.[44]

The Problems with Budgets, Probates, Orphans and Thieves

Accounting for inequality addresses some of the problems we have with diametrically opposed, but equally widely accepted positions on standards of living even within Europe.

But much speculation, new sources and different data sets remain at odds. Horrell and Humphries investigated 1,350 household accounts and budgets of the labouring poor in Britain over the period 1790–1850 to draw a pessimist case on trends in family incomes over the later eighteenth and early nineteenth centuries.[45] Their results, though resting on data from the end of the eighteenth century, also led them to give little credence to ideas of an 'industrious revolution' or a 'consumer revolution' reaching below the levels of the middling classes.[46] Horrell's recent summing up reinforces earlier positions. 'Studies of the standard of living in the classic Industrial Revolution have failed to find evidence of increases in material welfare reflected in the consumption patterns of the mass of the population between 1790 and 1850.'[47] She argued that most studies based on probate inventories might support a hypothesis of rising consumption, but only for the middling classes; they anyway showed only a very gradual spread in the ownership of innovative goods across England.[48]

Wider European probate inventories, however, indicated greater ownership of new goods, both imported and British and European; these inventories were gathered from many parts of Britain and Northern Europe. They were gathered from those of the middling classes, but also included many from the labouring classes.[49] These demonstrate possession of new and imitative consumer goods, and evidence of new eating practices, with the use of ceramics, glass and cutlery replacing pewter and wooden platters. Jan de Vries put the social history of new consumer practices in Europe together with probate accounts gathered for England and some other parts of Europe, especially for the Netherlands, to underpin his concept of the 'industrious revolution'.[50] This has been the one serious analysis of an economics of consumption for the early modern period that was not about prices and wages, but about changing tastes and household behaviour. De Vries drew on Gary Becker's analysis of household allocation of time to argue for a shift in household labour priorities from home- produced goods and services to market production. More within the household in early modern Europe sold their labour, and bought some of those goods they had formerly made themselves. They also worked longer and harder in order to satisfy a new taste and demand for goods imported into the locality or region, imitations of these, or entirely new goods. De Vries called this more intensive labour across the household an 'industrious revolution'. Decisions about consumption could be seen, therefore, as intra-household decisions on time use and expenditure, with wider effects on labour supply and intensity. Though wages were falling in the second half of the eighteenth century, probate inventories and other evidence of material possessions indicated that ownership of material objects was increasing. De Vries thus provided an explanation for this paradox, and one that engaged directly with an economic history of consumption. His case has been challenged by those who argue that labour intensification was driven by necessity rather than by consumer aspiration.[51]

Research on other North European data sets have, however, endorsed his position. Orphans' accounts from the Netherlands indicated wide use of tea and of tea and coffee wares and ownership of a range of cheaper and more expensive textiles in Amsterdam and other Dutch cities.[52] Textile identifying markers from the London Foundling Hospital – thousands of swatches of mothers' clothing that were attached to records of the infants they left in the orphanage – indicated widespread ownership of printed cottons and mixed cotton and linen fabrics, fabrics that imitated more expensive imports from India, but were made in small Lancashire mills.[53] Toll records in Hamburg also indicate the rapid uptake of colonial goods, and especially coffee in Germany and Northern Europe.[54]

It was not only orphans who revealed the hidden material lives of the poor but also thieves. Beverly Lemire and John Styles drew on the records of stolen goods in the Old Bailey to show the wide use in London of cotton textiles and of fashionable items and accessories.[55] More recent research developing these records into datasets shows a much greater impact of fashion aspiration and the desire for variety and differentiation, fashion and taste among common people than once recognized.[56] Cotton stockings were popular items of theft from poor households as were napkins and table linen from marginally better-off households.[57]

Where Is the Economic History of Consumption?

We appear to have reached a stalemate on the economic history of consumption in the early modern period. Most of the research has been on northwest Europe. It is still focused on wages and standards of living, with a great divide between those making the case for higher wages and/or more food and material possessions, and those arguing for stasis or immiseration. Wage baskets are estimated mainly on basic foodstuffs. Can an approach through large data sets take us in new directions? What analysis and questions lie behind the data sets? What was consumed, who consumed it, how and why did they consume it?

We could, instead, move down to a micro scale in order to connect an economics of consumption with the significant research on the social and cultural history of consumption. We can then engage with issues over choice and new products, encountering and integrating not only strange goods, desire and stimulus-seeking in the Scitovsky model, but also social interaction and awareness. We can investigate why and when taste mattered, the choice of qualities over quantities, and the role of fashion.

Foodstuffs are one example. Grains, as we have seen, need to be converted to flour for consumption. Food, furthermore, needs to be prepared and cooked. Even within early industrial Britain, there were great differences in cooking practices related to the availability of coal. The labouring poor in Yorkshire cooked their meals and heated their homes. Those in the South of England, though there were fewer women working in arable areas, faced much greater fuel constraints; they cooked much less and bought their bread.[58] Different food baskets also connected to different work regimes. Coffee consumption spread quickly in the proto-industrial regions of Germany. Textile workers consumed less grain and protein-rich foods than agricultural labourers. Coffee could be prepared quickly, it increased concentration in long hours of repetitive tasks, and it suppressed hunger. Merchants organizing the textile trade also dealt in coffee, and often paid their outworkers in coffee.[59]

The case of coffee takes us to that of sugar. Its slow entry into European diets from the sixteenth century escalated sharply in the eighteenth century. British per capita sugar consumption rose from 7 lb per person in 1700 to over 24 lb per person in 1790.[60] Of course this was distributed very differently across different classes and regions. The elites consumed great quantities, and had access even in remote areas to several different varieties of fine white sugars; the poor consumed small amounts of mainly treacle, molasses and muscovado sugar. It was used as a wage payment in the customs houses and made up part of the rations of workhouses.[61] A modest northern rural tenant family consumed 50 lb of sugar and 20 lb of treacle a year in the 1760s.[62] Sugar was not only a luxury sweetener, but widely used as a preservative and in brewing, baking and alcoholic beverages. As early as 1700 sugar was a common additive to hot beverages, and in Britain especially in tea. Along with other colonial groceries, tobacco, coffee and tea, it comprised *c.*10 per cent of household budgets.[63] The significant and rapidly rising part played by sugar consumption in budgets and diets does not feature in the economic historians' data sets of real wages, and rarely rates a mention in estimates of nutrition.[64]

Consuming new colonial foodstuffs also drove a new material culture, and taste extended from the senses to aesthetics. Rituals of social connection embedded sweetened tea and pastries consumed in the material culture of the tea equipage, not only porcelain cups and saucers imported from China, but mahogany sugar boxes and tea tables, and silver bowls, sugar tongs and silver tea pots. These in turn drove British product innovation in Staffordshire earthenware, Sheffield plate and Chippendale furnishings.[65] Tastes and fashions for differentiated and exotic goods brought a wider range of qualities and types to domestically produced goods and imports, especially from Asia. Data sets drawn from the Old Bailey records show that consumers substituted towards more expensive cotton stockings and counterpanes and away from worsted and linen. This was not about emulation, but about respectability, politeness and differentiation. They sought greater variety and higher quality.[66] Exotic goods such as Asian imports in Jan de Vries's analysis changed tastes, and created new markets and products. Asian imports, especially textiles and porcelain, stimulated a commercialization of societies in retailing, and drew households into the market.[67]

Lynn Hunt's *Writing History in the Global Era* (2014) links a cultural history of society and the self in late seventeenth- and eighteenth-century Europe to how exotic goods were experienced and chosen. Internal European factors interacted with wider global connections. Europeans developed a culture in which exotic goods made sense. Larger numbers, especially in specific places with higher discretionary incomes, wanted more choice. A desiring, stimulus-seeking attitude developed in tandem with social awareness: different varieties and individual choices among these demarcated new social groups. Tastes changed as experiences of the self changed.[68]

We can thus understand the varieties of goods carried in East India Company cargoes and constantly sought in East India Company orders. This was no random collection of goods, but one constantly responding to large-scale buyers at the autumn and spring company auctions, and these were closely affected in turn by the choices of all the small retailers and peddlers they sold on to. French colourways dictated Swedish silk imports from China; East India Company orders went out with letters criticizing the colours of earlier cargoes, and demanding dynamic, responsive and intuitive designs and patterns. Dutch and English East India companies and private European and Indian merchants competed vigorously for the finest figured Jamdani muslins.[69]

The Case of Textiles

A global history of the consumption of cotton textiles provides an opportunity to address some of these issues. As in the case of consumer durables in the early modern period, most of the research has focused on Europe, but there is now more on the Americas, Africa, South Asia and East Asia. In all of these regions, fashion, sumptuary codes, tribute and gifts provided incentives to consume a commodity that was newly traded between some large areas of the globe, and then newly manufactured in Europe and the Americas. Cotton is also the subject of two recent large-scale global histories.[70]

What are the key markers of this textile consumption across the early modern world? The entry of cotton into European ways of dress was slower than we once thought. Merchants in the sixteenth and seventeenth centuries needed to 'educate' their potential market, and cotton only became truly popular from the mid-eighteenth century. Colour fastness, novelty and new distribution channels were all important to their uptake. The Dutch consumed the new fabrics right down the social ladder by the early eighteenth century; at least a quarter of households in the Amsterdam inventories had them. By the later eighteenth century, there were many substitutes, and cottons were widely used in the dress of wage earners in Paris and in Castile.[71]

Well before Europe's encounter with Indian cottons, Gujarati traders tapped into a lively demand in East Africa. The Portuguese traded cotton from Gujarat, Sindh and Cambay for slaves that were then sold on at a very high profit in Brazil, Mexico and the Caribbean. By the late seventeenth century, the Gold Coast imported 20,000 metres of European and Asian cloth a year, and between 1690 and 1800, cloth made up 68 per cent of all commodities exported from England to Africa; 40 per cent of this was from India.[72] Sumptuary codes on colour and high demand for geometric patterns and stripes in vibrant colours shaped the trade. From an early period, Indian cottons were a highly desirable luxury good in many parts of Africa.[73]

Gujarati cottons exported to East-Central and Southeast Africa responded to highly specific and changeable tastes. They were used as a currency, and were important in social, cultural and political life in both coastal and interior areas. Cloth bestowed moral and social qualities; it marked high and low status, was a significant diplomatic gift, and marked political and cultural ceremony. Taste and fashion dictated these markets.[74]

The Latin American market was divided into higher-quality imported goods and cheaper local products. Indian cottons came to Mexico via the Pacific Manila–Acapulco route or via European imports, and were preferred in bright colours and floral patterns. Cottons entered rapidly into the wardrobes of the colonists of French and British North

America and the Caribbean; consumers sought a 'more refined and expensive product'. By the last decade of the eighteenth century, one-quarter of London's cotton imports went on to Africa, and high proportions were also re-exported to the Americas. In Riello's words, 'cotton became a global commodity'.[75]

Historians are now exploring the motivations of cotton's consumption in these different regions of the world. A commodity that connected India to Europe, East Asia, Africa and the Americas also conveyed very different meanings to its consumers. Plebeian families distinguished between 'best' and working clothes; they owned changes of clothing and duplicates, and dressed up for church and popular festivities. They focused their consumer expectations on clothes; clothes were a sign of self-respect. They chose and they benefited from new kinds of fashionable clothing made from cotton.[76]

There were also highly diverse markets for many medium-quality as well as fine-quality materials. India's cottons changed over time; they appealed to different social status and aesthetic preference. Their markets also revealed fashionability, and finishing in dyeing, printing and embroidery appealed to consumers across India and outside.[77]

Conclusion

An economic history of consumption has eluded many economic historians. Many have continued instead to create larger data sets and to compare like with unlike on levels of wages and standards of living. In the space left by Pomeranz in the Great Divergence debate, they have debated whether wages were different between regions of the world and whether this factor drove other economic stimulants such as technological change. But all those factors explored by social and cultural historians behind changing consumer behaviour from status and social structure to gifts, diplomacy and display, and on to fashion, sensibility and identity have remained beyond the purview of most economic historians. The window opened to such investigation by Jan de Vries's concept of 'industriousness' has still provided little illumination into key consumer practices. Global economic history in fact turned attention away from such investigation. The dearth of economic analysis into these many motivations behind consumer behaviour underpins an economic history which continues to avoid the history of consumption in favour of the history of wages.

A global economic history must include global connections as well as global comparisons. The impact of exotic goods and of encounters between merchants from different parts of the world helped to transform the contents of the probate inventories, toll registers, thefts, foundling hospital identifiers, and indeed food baskets. Individual, micro and local studies are now revealing these in research such as that recounted here on cotton textiles. Different products and distinctive qualities and different preparations and presentations affected food baskets as much as domestic interiors and dress.[78] There is much for global economic historians to discover at the micro level that will move us beyond the now very dated questions and materials still informing the big data sets of wages and prices.

Notes

1. M. J. Daunton (1995), *Progress and Poverty: An Economic and Social History of Britain 1700–1850*. Oxford: Oxford University Press; J. Mokyr (2009), *The Enlightened Economy: An Economic History of Britain 1700–1850*. New Haven, CT: Yale University Press; R. C. Allen (2009), *The British Industrial Revolution in Global Perspective*. Cambridge: Cambridge University Press. Though the most recent edition of the *Cambridge Economic History of Britain* does have a chapter on consumption, a closer look reveals that this too is mainly about wages and the standard of living.

2. See J. Brewer (1990), *The Sinews of Power: War, Money and the English State 1688–1783*. Cambridge, MA: Harvard University Press; T. Breen (2004), *The Marketplace of Revolution: How Consumer Politics Shaped American Independence*. Oxford: Oxford University Press.

3. L. Hunt (2014), *Writing History in the Global Era*. New York: W. W. Norton.

4. D. Winch (2009), *Wealth and Life: Essays on the Intellectual History of Political Economy in Britain, 1848–1914*. Cambridge: Cambridge University Press, 149–76 and 332–66; F. Trentmann (2016), *Empire of Things: How We Became a World of Consumers, from the Fifteenth Century to the Twenty-First*. London: Allen Lane, 151–3.

5. W. Sombart (1967 [1913]), *Luxury and Capitalism*. Ann Arbor, MI: University of Michigan Press; T. Veblen (1899 [1912]), *The Theory of the Leisure Class*. New York: Macmillan. Mandeville's *The Fable of the Bees*, first published early in the eighteenth century, reappeared at this time in a new American edition published by Kaye, and it was at the same time translated into German.

6. K. Lancaster (1971), *Consumer Demand: A New Approach*. New York and London: Columbia University Press; D. Ironmonger (1972), *New Commodities and Consumer Behaviour*. Cambridge: Cambridge University Press.

7. T. Scitovsky (1977), *The Joyless Economy: The Psychology of Human Satisfaction*. Oxford: Oxford University Press.

8. M. Bianchi (ed.) (1998), *The Active Consumer: Novelty and Surprise in Consumer Choice*. London: Routledge.

9. A. Offer (2012), 'Consumption and well-being', in F. Trentmann, *The Oxford Handbook of the History of Consumption*. Oxford: Oxford University Press, 653–72.

10. Offer, 'Consumption and well-being', 666.

11. K. Pomeranz (2000), *The Great Divergence: China, Europe and the Making of the Modern World Economy*. Princeton, NJ: Princeton University Press, 122.

12. Pomeranz, *The Great Divergence*, 117.

13. Ibid., 131.

14. Ibid., 144–6.

15. K. Pomeranz (2005), 'Standards of living in eighteenth-century China: Regional differences, temporal trends and incomplete evidence', in R. C. Allen, T. Bengtsson and M. Dribe (eds), *Living Standards in the Past: New Perspectives on Well-being in Asia and Europe*. Oxford: Oxford University Press, 7–10, and 21–4.

16. Pomeranz, *The Great Divergence*, 122–5.

17. J. de Vries (2015), 'Understanding Eurasian trade in the era of the trading companies', in M. Berg et al. (eds), *Goods from the East, 1600–1800: Trading Eurasia*. Basingstoke: Palgrave, 1–39, esp. 10–11; P. Parthasarathi (2011), *Why Europe Grew Rich and Asia Did Not: Global Economic Divergence, 1600-1850*. Cambridge: Cambridge University Press.

18. de Vries, 'Understanding Eurasian trade', 11, 23–4.

19. J. de Vries (2010), 'The limits of globalisation in the early modern world', *Economic History Review*, 63 (1), 710–33.

20. de Vries, 'Understanding Eurasian trade', 15–16, 34–6.

21. Ibid., 17.

22. K. Pomeranz (2012), 'Commerce', in U. Rublack (ed.), *A Concise Companion to History*. Oxford: Oxford University Press, 111.

23. See Zheng Yangwen (2012), *China on the Sea: How the Maritime World Shaped Modern China*. Leiden: Brill. See R. Bin Wong (2016), 'The early modern foundations of the modern world: Recent works on patterns of economic and political change', *Journal of Global History*, 11 (2), 135–46; Also see J. de Vries (2008), *The Industrious Revolution: Consumer Behavior and the Household Economy, 1650 to the Present*. Cambridge: Cambridge University Press.

24. See for example, D. Haynes, A. McGowan, T. Roy and H. Yanagisawa (eds) (2010), *Towards a History of Consumption in South Asia*. New Delhi: Oxford University Press.

25. J. Gommans (2015), 'For the home and the body: Dutch and Indian ways of early modern consumption', in Berg et al. (eds), *Goods from the East*, 331–49.

26. C. A. Bayly (2002), '"Archaic" and "Modern" globalization in the Asian and African arena c. 1750–1850', in A. G. Hopkins (ed.), *Globalization in World History*. London: Pimlico, 52.

27. de Vries, *The Industrious Revolution*.

28. Ibid.

29. C. Shammas (2012), 'Standard of living, consumption, and political economy over the past 500 years', in Trentmann (ed.), *The Oxford Handbook of the History of Consumption*, 212.

30. Shammas, 'Standard of living', 219. Also see A. Offer (2012), 'Consumption and well-being', 653–71.

31. Shammas, 'Standard of living', 212.

32. See J. Humphries (2004), 'Household economy', in R. Floud and P. Johnson (eds), *The Cambridge Economic History of Modern Britain*, vol. 1. Cambridge: Cambridge University Press, 238–67; S. Horrell and J. Humphries (1992), 'Old questions, new data, and alternative perspectives: Families' living standards during the Industrial Revolution', *Journal of Economic History*, 52 (4), 849–80.

33. See Allen, *The British Industrial Revolution*, 106–31 and 135–55; ibid. (2001), 'The Great Divergence in European wages and prices from the Middle Ages to the First World War', *Explorations in Economic History*, 38 (4), 411–47; R. C. Allen, J.-P. Bassino, D. Ma, C. Moll-Murata and J. L. van Zanden (2011), 'Wages, prices and living standards in China, 1738–1925: In comparison with Europe, Japan, and India', *Economic History Review*, 64 (Supplement 1), 8–38; See J. Humphries (2013), 'The lure of aggregates and the pitfalls of the patriarchal perspective: A critique of the high wage economy interpretation of the Industrial Revolution', *Economic History Review*, 66 (3), 693–714. Allen also refined his data to include the wages of women and children. R. C. Allen (2015), 'The high-wage economy and the Industrial Revolution: A restatement', *Economic History Review*, 68 (1), 1–22.

34. Allen, *The British Industrial Revolution*, 32.

35. T. Piketty (2015), *Capital in the Twenty-First Century*. Cambridge, MA: Belknap Press; P. Hoffman (2005), 'Sketching the rise of real inequality in early modern Europe', in Allen et al. (eds), *Standards of Living in the Past*, 24.

36. Hoffman, 'Sketching the rise of real inequality', 25–9.

37. Ibid., 51.

38. A. Gerritsen (2020), *The City of Blue and White*. Cambridge: Cambridge University Press, 176–83.

39. M. Harvey (2019), 'Slavery, indenture and the development of British industrial capitalism', *History Workshop Journal*, 88, 66–88.

40. J. de Vries (2010), 'The limits of globalization in the early modern world', *Economic History Review*, 63 (3), 718–19.

41. B. L. Solow (1987), 'Capitalism and slavery in the exceedingly long run', in B. L. Solow and S. Engerman (eds), *British Capitalism and Caribbean Slavery: The Legacy of Eric Williams*. Cambridge: Cambridge University Press, 70–2; K. Morgan (1993), *Bristol & the Atlantic Trade in the Eighteenth Century*. Cambridge: Cambridge University Press, 184–5.

42. J. R. Ward (1978), 'The profitability of sugar planting in the British West Indies, 1650–1834', *Economic History Review*, 31 (2), 197–213.

43. N. Zahedieh (2014), 'Overseas trade and empire', in R. Floud, J. Humphries and P. Johnson (eds), *The Cambridge Economic History of Modern Britain*, vol. 1: *1700–1870*. Cambridge: Cambridge University Press, Table 14.4.

44. M. Ellis, R. Coulton and M. Mauger (2015), *Empire of Tea: The Asian Leaf that Conquered the World*. London: Reakton Books, 240–44; G. Riello (2013), *Cotton: The Fabric that Made the Modern World*. Cambridge: Cambridge University Press, 187–210; S. Beckert (2014), *Empire of Cotton: A Global History*. New York: Alfred A. Knopf, 274–311.

45. Horrell and Humphries (1992), 'Old questions, new data', 849–80.

46. S. Horrell (1996), 'Home demand and British industrialization', *Journal of Economic History*, 56 (3), 561–604.

47. S. Horrell (2014), 'Consumption, 1700–1870', in R. Floud, J. Humphries and P. Johnson (eds), *The Cambridge Economic History of Modern Britain*, 3rd edn, vol. 1. Cambridge: Cambridge University Press, 239.

48. Horrell (2014), 'Consumption, 1700–1870', 241. Horell's findings rely on a data set compiled by C. Muldrew in his (2011), *Food, Energy, and the Creation of Industriousness: Work and Material Culture in Agrarian England, 1550–1780*. Cambridge: Cambridge University Press. See the fundamental critique to this dataset in C. Shammas (2012), 'Review of food, energy, and the creation of industriousness: Work and material culture in agrarian England, 1550–1780', *Journal of Modern History*, 84 (4), 951–3.

49. See the table of probate inventories for early modern England in Horrell, 'Consumption', 240.

50. de Vries, *The Industrious Revolution*.

51. See Trentmann's critique of de Vries in Trentmann, *Empire of Things*, 75; P. Vries (2016), 'What we do and do not know about the Great Divergence in 2016', unpublished paper, 20.

52. Anne McCants argued there had to be a widespread consumer demand for these commodities so that they were incorporated into budgets and daily routines in sufficient amounts to alter overall standards of living. See A. McCants (2007), 'Exotic goods, popular consumption and the standard of living: Thinking about globalization in the early modern world', *Journal of World History*, 18 (4), 433–62; ibid. (2008), 'Poor consumers as global consumers: The diffusion of tea and coffee drinking in the eighteenth century', *Economic History Review*, 61 (Supplement 1), 172–200; ibid. (2013), 'Porcelain for the poor: The material culture of tea and coffee consumption in eighteenth-century Amsterdam', in P. Findlen (ed.), *Early Modern Things: Objects and Their Histories 1500–1800*. London: Routledge, 316–41; ibid. (2015), 'Becoming consumers: Asiatic goods in migrant and native-

born middling households in eighteenth-century Amsterdam', in Berg et al. (eds), *Goods from the East*, 197–215.

53. J. Styles (2006), *The Dress of the People: Everyday Fashion in Eighteenth-Century England*. New Haven, CT: Yale University Press; J. Styles (2010), *Threads of Feeling: The London Foundling Museum's Textile Tokens 1740–1770*. London: The Foundling Museum.

54. C. Fertig and U. Pfister (2016), '"Coffee, mind and body": Global material culture and the eighteenth-century Hamburg import trade', in A. Gerritsen and G. Riello (eds), *The Global Lives of Things*. London and New York: Routledge, 227.

55. See B. Lemire (1991), *Fashion's Favourite: The Cotton Trade and the Consumer in Britain, 1660–1800*. Oxford: Oxford University Press; Styles, *Dress of the People*.

56. J. Humphries, S. Horrell and K. Sneath (2015), 'Consumption conundrums unravelled', *Economic History Review*, 68 (3), 841 and 855.

57. Humphries, Horrell and Sneath, 'Consumption conundrums', 847 and 853.

58. D. Zyllerberg (2015), 'Fuel prices, regional diets and cooking habits in the Industrial Revolution, 1750–1830', *Past & Present*, 229, 91–122.

59. Fertig and Pfister, 'Coffee, mind and body', 229.

60. C. Shammas (1993), 'Changes in English and Anglo-American consumption from 1550 to 1800', in J. Brewer and R. Porter (eds), *Consumption and the World of Goods*. London: Routledge, 117–205.

61. W. Ashworth (2003), *Customs and Excise: Trade, Production and Consumption in England 1649–1845*. Oxford: Oxford University Press, 157; J. Stobart (2013), *Sugar & Spice: Grocers and Groceries in Provincial England 1650–1830*. Oxford: Oxford University Press, 221.

62. L. Weatherill (ed.) (1990), *Richard Latham's Account Book*. Oxford: Oxford University Press, xxiv.

63. C. Shammas (1984), 'The eighteenth-century diet and economic change', *Explorations in Economic History*, 21 (3), 257.

64. See Muldrew, *Food, Energy and the Creation of Industriousness*, 135–40. He includes a little sugar and treacle in his constructed budgets for the eighteenth century, but gives no discussion to these. There is likewise little specific mention of sugar in broader discussions of caloric intake and nutrition in D. Meredith and D. Oxley (2014), 'Food and fodder: Feeding England, 1700–1900', *Past & Present*, 222, 163–214; E. Griffin (2018), 'Diets, hunger and living standards during the British Industrial Revolution', *Past & Present*, 239, 71–111.

65. H. Clifford (1999), 'Concepts of invention, identity and imitation in the London and provincial metal-working trades, 1750–1800', *Journal of Design History*, 12, 241–56; H. Clifford (1999), 'A commerce with things: The value of precious metalwork in early modern England', in M. Berg and H. Clifford (eds), *Consumers and Luxury: Consumer Culture in Europe, 1650–1850*. Manchester and New York: Manchester University Press, 147–68; M. Berg (2005), *Luxury and Pleasure in Eighteenth-Century Britain*. Oxford: Oxford University Press, 162–7.

66. Humphries, Horrell and Sneath, 'Consumption conundrums', 853–4.

67. de Vries, 'Understanding Eurasian trade', 14 and 22.

68. Hunt, *Writing History in the Global Era*, 114–41.

69. See essays by Prakash (2015) and Berg (2015) in Berg et al. (eds), *Goods from the East*, 119–38, and 183–96. Also see H. Hodacs (2015), *Silk and Tea in the North*. Palgrave: Basingstoke.

70. Giorgio Riello combined extensive research on museum collections of printed cotton textiles with archival research to argue for the existence of a globalized economy based in the wider world trade in printed cotton textiles from India throughout the early modern period. This trade stimulated industrialization in Europe, and especially Britain, as Europeans sought to build an industry to match the fine material attributes of these cottons at low consumer prices. Riello, *Cotton*. Sven Beckert's book provided another history of raw cotton and cotton manufacture, but mainly in Europe and America in the modern period. Beckert, *Empire of Cotton*.

71. Riello, *Cotton*, 114–5.

72. Ibid., 137–8.

73. Trentmann, *Empire of Things*, 124.

74. P. Machado (2009), 'Gujarat, Africa and the Western Indian Ocean', in G. Riello and P. Parthasarathi (eds), *The Spinning World: A Global History of Cotton Textiles, 1200–185*. Oxford: Oxford University Press, 161–79; Machado (2009), 'Cloths of a new fashion: Indian Ocean networks of exchange and cloth zones of contact in Africa and India in the eighteenth and nineteenth centuries', in G. Riello and T. Roy (eds) (2009), *How India Clothed the World*, 53–84. Also see Trentmann, *Empire of Things*, 124–5, and 129.

75. Riello, *Cotton*, 147–8.

76. Styles, *The Dress of the People*, 241–3, 263, 307–14, 323–6; R. DuPlessis (2009), 'Cotton consumption in the North Atlantic', in Riello and Parthasarathi (eds), *The Spinning World*, 231–4. See the developing uses of cotton by gender and race in Spanish America and the Caribbean as discussed by M. Vicente (2009), 'Cottons in Colonial Spanish America', in Riello and Parthasarathi (eds), *The Spinning World*, 260. See also Rebecca Earle (2003), 'Luxury, clothing and race in Colonial Spanish America', in M. Berg and E. Eger (eds), *Luxury in the Eighteenth Century: Debates, Desires and Delectable Goods*. Basingstoke: Palgrave, 219–27.

77. P. Parthasarathi and G. Riello (2012), 'From India to the world: Cotton and fashionability', in Trentmann, *The Oxford Handbook of the History of Consumption*, 148–50.

78. On foodstuffs, see Jan de Vries's research on bread in the Dutch Republic. J. de Vries (2009), 'The political economy of bread in the Dutch Republic', in O. Gelderston (ed.), *The Political Economy of the Dutch Republic*. Aldershot: Ashgate, 85–114.

CHAPTER 8
FROM THE GREAT DIVERGENCE TO NEW HISTORIES OF CAPITALISM
Andrew B. Liu

Introduction

The initial major works on what came to be called the 'Great Divergence' debate at the turn of the century emphasized commercial and environmental similarities and linkages across Eurasia in the early modern world. They came at a moment when the end of the Cold War and the rise of East Asia inspired both optimistic predictions of globalization but also dire warnings about the shared prospects of ecological disintegration.[1] The novelty of 'divergence' scholarship was geographic but also disciplinary. Observers had long noted the decline of mainstream economic history since the 1970s – in the United States, the field had migrated largely to economics departments – simultaneous with the rise to dominance of cultural and intellectual history.[2] Kenneth Pomeranz's major work represented a reintroduction of sorts of the tools of global economic analysis into mainstream historical debates.[3] For many, although *The Great Divergence* ostensibly veered from the trends of cultural history, it also shared sensibilities with contemporaneous post-colonial criticism and its challenge to a narrow, Eurocentric Marxist interpretation of world history.[4]

Soon after, and in another corner of the US academy, a new generation responded to the same set of real-life conditions by rediscovering the study of material economic life for themselves. In the past decade, the term 'New History of Capitalism' (NHC) has gained wide prominence inside and beyond academia, inspiring special issues, book series, faculty positions, graduate fields, and research centres.[5] It is a broad category whose contours can only be sketched heuristically. On the one hand, it is widely acknowledged that there have always been historians who took capitalism as their analytical object, both prior to and throughout the putative cultural turn.[6] On the other, a new generation in the 2000s coalesced around a self-conscious desire to reverse declining historiographical interest in economic life.[7] The earliest and most recognizable collection of NHC scholars can be traced to an ongoing Harvard University workshop on the 'Political Economy of Modern Capitalism' jointly organized by Sven Beckert and Christine Desan from 2005 until the late 2010s. As they explained, initial interest emerged from the same globalized context that inspired the 'divergence' scholarship. Rather than optimism, however, it was the recurrent upheavals of the new millennium, from the dotcom bubble of 2000 to the debt crises of Latin America and Africa, that pushed them to historicize a system that was beginning to fray at the edges – culminating, of course, with the meltdown of 2008.[8] For wider audiences, the new history of capitalism first entered mainstream consciousness with a 2013 *New York Times* article cataloguing major publications within the field. 'The events of 2008 and their long aftermath', it noted, 'have given urgency to the scholarly realization that it really is the economy, stupid'.[9]

Many NHC scholars explicitly cite their debt to the 'divergence' scholarship and its global scale. But from the beginning, many acknowledged that the new interest in capitalism and its history remained 'provincial'. Too often, the 'history of capitalism', Peter Hudson noted, had simply meant the 'history of U.S. capitalism'.[10] The tension, thus, is that NHC's origins stemmed from a regional network of scholars concerned with the study of one part of the world – as do, naturally, almost all intellectual movements – yet 'capitalism' itself is by nature a category demanding transnational frames of analysis and research. In the intervening years, new works have begun to emerge pushing the NHC idea into new directions. The broad resonance of NHC is testament to both the fertility of the 'capitalism' concept and the desire by supporters to keep definitions open ended and receptive to different approaches.

In the following pages, I begin by sketching out the major overarching themes of the subfield's first generation, roughly from the late 2000s to early 2010s. Next, I highlight two particular lines of argument connecting the NHC and 'divergence' literatures, one explicit and one implicit. First, the new histories of slavery have endorsed a global approach to analysing economic change, adopting Pomeranz's transatlantic framing of nineteenth-century English divergence in order to draw out the significance of US cotton. Second, they also share a critique of the orthodox view that free wage labour is the linchpin to capitalist development, instead spotlighting enslaved and indentured workers in the United States to complement the 'divergence' literature's focus on family farms and domestic handicrafts. In these sections, I concentrate on a cluster of works focused on slavery and cotton in particular, for they have received the most attention as the fulcrum of the NHC literature; more importantly, they also share the greatest overlap with the concerns of the 'divergence' debate. Finally, I conclude by assessing recent criticisms of the NHC literature, focused on whether it has been able to realize the category's ambitious promise, and by examining new scholarship that pushes the study of capitalism into wider fields.

The Major Contours of the History of Capitalism

The earliest NHC works spanned a variety of topics in US history, including the early history of money, counterfeiting, and financial speculation; efforts at corporate risk management through insurance, futures, and industrial trusts; the rise of Walmart and the service economy; the proliferation of consumer credit; popular investment in public stock markets; diverse forms of manual labour in early America; and, the topic receiving the most attention, histories of enslaved labour and the cotton economy of the US south.[11]

Synthesizing these along with several historiographical essays that established the field's contours, I see a handful of key uniting themes.[12]

First is the mobilization of empirical history against naturalistic economic theory. The latter includes both neoclassical models of profit-maximizing individuals as well as orthodox Marxist teleologies from unfree to free labour. Ultimately, many NHC works can be glossed as critical expositions of the 'extra-economic' power concealed in free-market ideology, both political and physical coercion, reflecting heightened real-world scrutiny of neoliberal globalization. If mainstream theories presumed that private, individual activity naturally gave rise to homogeneous market behaviour, then NHC works have foregrounded the historical role of the state in the creation of markets. Beckert's *Empire of Cotton*, for instance, argues that the global economy grew polarized in the nineteenth century according to which states were strong enough to forge advantageous markets for capital (Euro-America) and which were not (Egypt, Brazil, India, China). And Stephen Mihm's *A Nation of Counterfeiters* concludes that free-market dynamics in the postbellum period relied, paradoxically, upon the federal government abolishing the patchwork, local monetary system in favour of a national currency.[13]

Second, within the endeavour of history pitched against economics, NHC scholars stressed a mixture of different genres of historical writing, drawing together subfields that traditionally ask distinct questions about economic life: labour and social history, concerned with working-class formation; business history, which spotlights the careers of individual capitalist firms; and economic history, with its central macroeconomic question of what drives national growth.[14] Under the banner of 'capitalism', these authors have given themselves the latitude to move between genres, ranging from Seth Rockman's social history of putatively unskilled labour in Baltimore to Julia Ott's intellectual history of a corporate-backed 'shareholder democracy' ideal, each contributing to Louis Hyman's call for 'history from below, all the way to the top'.[15] Jeffrey Sklansky argues that historians of capitalism were beginning to reintegrate the fields of social and intellectual history, a move enabled by embracing the category 'commodification', which shared a long tradition of combining analyses of both objective social relationships organized around money with subjective histories of seeing, valuing and classifying the world anew.[16]

Third, and related to the emphasis on interdisciplinarity, is NHC's refusal to define capitalism in advance and instead allow the object to arise organically from empirical case studies. Beckert and Desan recall that in their seminar, they considered it 'an advantage, not a defect' to avoid overarching definitions. They instead entertained a diversity of foci, including the relation between wage labour and capital; the predominance of market relations; acquisitiveness and profit-seeking; racial and gender hierarchies; and the role of credit and finance.[17] Throughout the field's development, many have objected to the lack of terminological clarity.[18] Others have offered their own attempts to pin down the concept's fundamental meaning.[19] No single interpretation has prevailed, but each attempt can perhaps be seen as validation for Beckert and Desan's insistence that ambiguity is a positive motor for debate.

Fourth, and finally, has been an attempt to expand the parameters of 'capitalism' outward, temporally and geographically, from its association with urban industrialization. Historians have pushed back the starting date of capitalism to the eighteenth century, which has meant a reinterpretation of the British colonies, the American Revolution, and the slavery economy of the US south.[20] They have also sought to locate capitalism in rural and international settings, linking US history with that of the Americas, Europe, Asia and Africa. It is on this point that NHC scholars have most explicitly credited the influence of 'divergence' scholarship and Pomeranz's work in particular.[21]

Transnational Stories of Capitalist Development

In their major works on Eurasian 'divergence', Pomeranz and later Prasannan Parthasarathi stressed that the conventional story of English exceptionalism, grounded in simplistic oppositions between Europe and Asia, no longer withstood scrutiny from new globally oriented research. Pomeranz challenged the myth that Europeans held exceptionally high levels of capital stock in the early modern world, arguing that Asian societies presented comparable levels of livestock, transport capital and agricultural output. The same held true for Europe's purportedly exceptional rates of life expectancy, caloric intake, demographic patterns, and technological and scientific know-how.[22] Similarly, Parthasarathi challenged the Eurocentric biases colouring analyses of South Asia, arguing Mughal India was comparable to Europe in terms of political decentralization, economic mobility, market integration, labour reallocation, protection of property rights, and fertility rates.[23]

Making sense of industrializing England's unquestioned economic superiority, then, required looking beyond national and regional units in isolation. By the end of the eighteenth century, Pomeranz wrote, both England and the Yangzi Delta had exhausted their supplies of labour and land and were headed toward a proto-industrial 'cul de sac'. Europe was unique in finding recourse in, first, greater deployment of coal as a source of energy, but also, more significantly, the land and labour resources of the New World.[24] There, enslaved Africans produced farm exports such as sugar and cotton, in addition to raw materials such as timber, while also absorbing industrial imports, chiefly cotton goods, from north-west Europe. Sugar and cotton were far more efficient sources of calories and clothing than local British alternatives: sugar was four times as efficient as potatoes and cotton about nine times as wool. Adding together the amount of land needed to produce sugar, cotton and timber exports, Pomeranz concluded that Britain would have needed an additional 25 to 30 million extra acres to equal the Americas, what he called 'ghost acres' – sobering to consider when the entirety of Britain's arable landed only added up to 17 million![25]

The New World aspect of Pomeranz's argument has been the most concrete foothold enabling scholars to link new histories of US capitalism with 'divergence' scholarship. Citing Pomeranz, works by Edward Baptist, Johnson and Beckert, in particular, have argued that southern cotton was fundamental to England's industrialization and divergence from the rest of the world, entailing a new era of world–historical capitalist development. Notably, two versions of the 'New World' argument can be located in Pomeranz. Though he ultimately concludes with an ecological explanation, he earlier weighs the famous '(Eric) Williams thesis', originating from the Trinidadian statesman's 1944 *Capitalism and Slavery* and its claim that Caribbean slavery financially enabled British industrialization. Profits from the Atlantic triangle trade, he documented, including slave-trading, privacy, mining and cash-crop production, found their way into the principal of Liverpool banks, Welsh ironworks, London insurance houses, and countless mines and cotton mills.[26] Pomeranz agreed with the overall net gains of the slave trade but concluded they ultimately were not decisive in England's divergence from China, certainly less consequential than the New World's ghost acres.[27] Pomeranz thus drew a heuristic distinction between the financial value of New World industries versus the natural, ecological value of its land and labour.

But in borrowing from Pomeranz, NHC scholars have liberally mixed the two types of explanations together, a source of criticism from economic historians. In his work, Beckert underscores the significance of cotton as 'the world's most important manufacturing industry' by emphasizing how England's textile industry could not have taken off without the 'ghost acres' of the Americas.[28] Similarly, Edward Baptist focuses on the role of the cotton industry to break out of the mid-eighteenth-century Malthusian traps bedevilling Eurasian, American and African economies. New industrial inventions in England, he stresses, 'would have been short-circuited if embryo industries had run out of cotton fiber', and the development of Mississippi Valley cotton 'enabled the United States to seize control of the world export market for cotton' and allowed Britain to 'escap[e] the old Malthusian trap with the help of the New World's ghost acres'.[29] Still, for these authors, the New World's greatest boon was the economic and financial gains of slavery, a variation on the Williams thesis that substitutes eighteenth-century sugar with nineteenth-century cotton.

Such emphasis comes out in Beckert's main anecdote illustrating the origins of English industrialization, namely, the story of Samuel Greg, a Manchester entrepreneur whose starting capital originated from family fortunes in West Indies sugar and the trade in enslaved Africans. 'Industrial capitalism', Beckert argues, 'was the offspring of war capitalism', his description of previous centuries of enslavement, land expropriation and imperial expansion.[30] Baptist goes further, attempting to tally the total value of cotton-based profits and cotton-related businesses in the US economy, including transportation costs, durable goods sold to plantations, and financial and insurance products. Extending the logic of the Williams thesis, he claims that a million-plus enslaved workers in the US South accounted for about one-half of the US's total economic value, which meant the 'northern economy's industrial sector was built on the backs of enslaved people'.[31]

Economic historians have objected strongly to many of these claims. On the specific question of slavery's role in industrialization, Alan Olmstead and Paul Rhode see the chronological importance of US cotton, taking off in the 1790s, as too late to explain British development. They further push back on Baptist's methods in estimating the overall significance of cotton and slavery to the US economy, pointing out instances of double counting that would ultimately give total figures exceeding 100 per cent of the nation's GDP.[32] Such controversies seem to undercut the more extravagant attempts to bring the Williams thesis to the US context by attributing overall US economic growth to slavery. Still, what is historiographically noteworthy is the conscious choice by historians of US capitalism to employ the 'divergence' scholarship's transatlantic scale of analysis.

Transcending the Wage Labour Ideal-type

The second line of argument linking 'divergence' and NHC scholarship is a shared rejection of the centrality of free wage labour as the linchpin of capitalist development. In fact, the proletarian ideal-type has been under scrutiny for decades at least, since Immanuel Wallerstein and Jairus Banaji's pioneering interventions in the 1970s and with new forays in 'global labour history' since the 1990s.[33] Though wage labour-centred interpretations are often associated with the Marxist tradition, they were quite universal in the nineteenth century, appearing in the works of Weberians and Ricardians alike, coincident with the rapid spread of industrialization.[34] Still, among social historians, the name most frequently associated with the claim is Marxist historian Robert Brenner, whose 1970s essays on the topic have inspired heated debate since.[35]

In a representative essay from 1977, Brenner followed Marx's phrase 'doubly-free labor' to argue that truly capitalist labour meant workers were 'freed' both from their masters and lords and also from owning any property themselves. This meant capitalism's history, modelled on Marx's origin story of 'primitive accumulation' in England, excluded two broad categories of people around the world: first, slaves, serfs and indentured workers, and, second, peasants or households that could provide for their own subsistence through agriculture and domestic work. For Brenner, the market pressures of 'capitalism' could only continually revolutionize techniques when producers depend entirely upon the market for survival. Although villagers in Asia or slave plantations in the Caribbean clearly made export-oriented goods, the world market did not have the leverage to push them toward new industrial technologies or productivity gains, dooming them to underdevelopment.

Within English-language Chinese historiography, such arguments were expressed in the classic works of Mark Elvin and Philip Huang, the latter of whom was Brenner's colleague and ambassador for his model in the field. Both authors, Pomeranz argued, relied upon a one-sided comparison between a revolutionary industrial England versus an unchanging Chinese society, which, absent proletarianization, was stuck in a trap of declining returns from labour inputs, described in the literature as a high-level equilibrium trap (Elvin) or involutionary spiral (Huang). For Pomeranz, Elvin's argument relied upon vast wage differences between England and China that have since been disproven, and his model for how high English wages spurred innovation was riddled with logical inconsistencies. Further, Brenner and Huang's absolute division between proletarian versus property-owning labour has been undermined by new research on the 'industrious revolutions' spanning early modern Eurasia, led by Jan de Vries and Kaoru Sugihara. Rather than commercial retreat, households across China, Japan and Europe increasingly allocated family labour in order to sell and buy on the marketplace, spurring the sort of pre-industrial productivity gains from specialization described in Adam Smith.[36] As Pomeranz and Parthasarathi write in this volume, this new approach de-emphasizes a static fixation on wage-labour relations in favour of a dynamic analysis of flows of inputs and outputs.[37]

Likewise, the new histories of slavery confront the exclusion of unfree labour from capitalism's history. Johnson frequently links Brenner's argument with a longer tradition in US history separating slavery from capitalism, especially the works of Eugene Genovese and Elizabeth Fox-Genovese.[38] Johnson, too, criticizes static categorizations of class, which are undermined by dynamic portrayals of the 'eighteenth- and nineteenth-century Atlantic' and its 'flows of people, money, and goods, its nested temporalities set by interlocking (though clearly distinct) labour regimes, cyclical rhythms of cultivation and foreign exchange, and shared standards of calculability and measurement'.[39]

Johnson's point is that the enslaved African worker, though mismatched with the proletarian ideal-type, nevertheless laboured to produce commodities that earned profits for the global capitalist class. However, this is a concession already accounted for in Brenner's model. The latter called such commodity production merely 'commercial', organized around extensive economic growth (or absolute surplus-value), which fell short of capitalism's defining trait, intensive growth (relative surplus-value), characterized by rising efficiency. The question of slavery's productivity has been addressed most directly in the works of Baptist and Caitlin Rosenthal. In his reconstruction on the slave-labour system, Baptist outlines a collection of techniques for monitoring and forcing up the productivity of enslaved workers he called the 'pushing system'. Overseers used a system of escalating daily quotas for its workers, backed it with physical 'torture', and extracted productivity increases that were epoch-defining. He cites Olmstead and Rhode's research that argued that from 1800 to 1860, the productivity of enslaved cotton pluckers rose by 400 per cent, underscoring the link between planter violence and capitalism. Again, however, the two economists have strongly objected to Baptist's analysis of their figures. They question whether the 'pushing system' could really be discovered in archival materials but also, more significantly, the causal link between physical torture – which they do not deny – and the gains in productivity, which they conclude could be isolated and traced to the spread of new cotton varieties.[40]

Such objections to the pushing system are substantive, but Olmstead and Rhode's own data can also be interpreted to confirm the broader point that cotton planters were capitalists who consciously strove to raise productivity over the lifetime of the antebellum economy, as James Oakes observes.[41] Rosenthal's *Accounting for Slavery* offers a compromise. For her, the rise in output resulted from a combination of both extractive violence and new cotton breeds, with the latter, crucially, dependent on the former to realize the gains of biological improvement. The combination of different strategies points towards an underlying calculative rationality shared across the planter class, which kept detailed records on daily cotton picking, shifting projections and targets, and experiments in crop rotations and labour allocation. Regardless of the specific mechanism, Rosenthal demonstrates an overarching 'relentless drive' to raise productivity, thereby refuting traditional claims of slavery's pre-capitalist character, whether the Weberian rationality and 'bourgeois spirit of accumulation' the Genoveses claimed were missing in the South or the lack of response to competitive pressures in Brenner's account of slave societies.[42] Such arguments parallel the 'divergence' literature's own claim that rural and domestic labour across early modern Eurasia, despite the absence of industrialization and full proletarianization, exhibited their own patterns of 'industrious' productivity gains.

Critical Assessments from Global Economic History

Together, 'divergence' and NHC scholarship present a picture of recognizably modern economic change that de-emphasizes urban industrialization in favour of the geographically expansive movement of goods, money and people. Notably, 'divergence' scholars tend to use the term 'capitalism' only sparingly, with its Eurocentric baggage. To the extent they refer to the concept, they heuristically rely upon the vision offered by Braudel, a world of luxury commerce and large, overseas trading firms.[43] Similarly, NHC scholars have championed the historical significance of pre-industrial labour relations tied to distant networks of merchant and finance capital, categories reformulated by Beckert as 'war capitalism'.[44] One of the hallmarks of NHC scholarship has been the 'privileging of motion'.[45]

Labour concerns have certainly not disappeared, but NHC works have, in line with rethinking the place of slavery, shifted emphasis away from the traditional, binary categories of free and unfree, 'enslavement' and 'proletarianization', toward the umbrella term of labour 'commodification'.[46] Seth Rockman's *Scraping By* stands out as the most sophisticated empirical engagement with the complex questions raised by a capacious notion of commodification. Surveying industries all across early Baltimore – from shipbuilding to child rearing to street scraping – he observed that employers at the time 'constantly adjusted their workforces, shifting between and combining laborers who were enslaved, indentured, and unfree; black and white; male and female; young and old, native born and immigrant'.[47] Such practical 'interchangeability' across Baltimore's workers, pitted against one another on an early capitalist labour market, suggests the need for a more theoretically robust, unified conception of labour under capitalism beyond the binaries of freedom, race and sex.

However, others such as Sklansky express concern that the 'commodification' concept may also signal a waning interest in class relations and production, instead reducing human labour to human capital, that is, to just another asset in the realms of commerce and finance.[48] Alongside debates over slavery's productivity, NHC scholars have paid equal attention to the financialization of enslaved workers, with human property rendered into fungible 'fictitious capital' and exchanged among the Barings and Rothschilds of the ostensibly free North Atlantic.[49] Indeed, slavery and finance stand out as the two major analytical foci of new histories of capitalism. What they share in common are forms of profit that contravene triumphalist stories of industrial innovation from the twentieth-century golden age of US capitalism.

I have elsewhere speculated that the 'divergence' scholarship's interventions emerged from the eclipse of nationally organized, Fordist–Keynesian economies in the post-war period by a new international division of labour featuring more informal, smaller-scale arrangements in Asia.[50] Among NHC scholars, the neoliberal era has also spurred a re-evaluation of US capitalism as far less 'noble' and 'clean' than the imagery touted by its ideologues.[51] In an essay for the *New York Times*'s '1619 Project', Matthew Desmond foregrounds the simultaneous physical violence and abstract financialization of slavery as symbols of American 'low-road capitalism'. If slave-based production embodied the dirty, obscene essence of labour's exploitation by capital, then finance represented its sanitation, cut up and parcelled out across a global, impersonal system of counting figures. The politics of NHC scholarship imply, then, that a direct connection can be drawn between slavery and contemporary predatory lending, crisis-prone financial fads, and the prison–industrial complex.[52]

NHC works have been praised for their timely relevance and moral conscience, but global historians have often found their accounts of the nineteenth-century economy too unsystematic. Among the most controversial positions is some version of the statement that slavery was 'central' to – or 'decisive', 'constitutive of', 'integral', 'essential', 'powered', 'shaped', 'crucial', 'the epitome of', or 'necessary' and 'indispensable' for – the development of US capitalism.[53] There is also the similar claim that capitalism 'depended on' or was forged 'on the backs of' the slave-driven cotton economy, as well as formulations suggesting the inseparability of capitalism from slavery, such as Johnson's 'slavery racial capitalism'.[54] The exact contours of what these claims mean remain unclear. There is no denying that slave-based cotton production generated tremendous volumes of wealth that contributed to overall national growth and also that the system was brutally extractive, revealing the outer limits of capitalist exploitation. But the relative magnitude of such claims appears different when placed within a broader comparative context – a charge, notably, that 'divergence' scholars also once made against the national histories of England, China and India.

What economic historians have disputed is the suggestion that slavery was a net positive for the US, and world, economies, given the coexistence of free-labour alternatives by the nineteenth century. Historians Trevor Burnard and Giorgio Riello and economist Gavin Wright have each argued that, certainly, slavery *did have* an indispensable function in capitalism's early history, when a global market for commercialized agriculture had not yet fully developed. The relevant period, however, was not the antebellum south but the pre-1800s West Indian sugar industries of the Williams thesis.[55] After 1815, Wright argues, the preservation of southern slavery was antithetical to development for three reasons: it created artificial labour inelasticity; it stymied investment into infrastructure; and it undermined specialized commercial interdependence.[56] 'The best evidence that slavery was not essential for cotton supply', Wright notes, 'is what happened after slavery's demise'. Within a few years of emancipation, industrial textile manufacture recovered by sourcing raw cotton from Asia, the Middle East, and Latin America, undermining arguments for slavery's economic indispensability, both by contemporaneous defenders of slavery and from recent historiography. Rather than softening the immorality of slavery, Wright argues, this cold economic assessment only magnifies the tragedy of the system as cruel, unnecessary and senseless.[57]

Such comparative economic claims could be brushed off as what Johnson calls 'ahistorical ideal types', a kind of reasoning that obsesses over 'what *should* have happened' or how 'capitalism *might* have developed' at the expense of a materialist history of 'actually existing' slavery.[58] Really, though – and I believe this is crucial – two very different questions are being posed, each intellectually valid. For most NHC scholars, their point of departure and object of analysis is the study of American slavery itself – how it has been represented in the past; how do we understand it today; and whether it could be classified as modern and capitalist? New works have successfully overturned an older consensus that slavery was exempt from market dynamics, arguments replete with contemporary implications. But the limitation of such questions is that they can often wind up framing capitalism in binary terms – is it or not? – flattening different trajectories of uneven yet interconnected accumulation. Ultimately, the question of how to interpret slavery is different from asking how to understand capitalism itself: what are its fundamental dynamics, how can it be historically disaggregated, and where can we locate the place of slavery along its terrain, side by side with free labour and industry?[59] Many NHC scholars appear indifferent to such epochal questions. The 'what is capitalism' debate, after all, is one that many of its authors proudly evade.

Similar observations can be made about the category 'racial capitalism', originating with Cedric Robinson's *Black Marxism* (1983) and taking on new life in Johnson's work and other recent scholarship. Steven Hahn has objected that if slavery and capitalism are inseparable, then it must be admitted that unfree labour forms could be found across countless other early societies as well – European, African, Asian – few of which could be mistaken for being developmental in any modern sense. What, then, are we left with that could account for the historically specific dynamics of our own economic system, for what makes capitalism *capitalism*?[60] This is the question that preoccupied generations of economic historiography – whatever one thinks about the specific hypotheses – whether organized around energy usage, free labour, free markets or the global scale of trade. Naturally it also drove the 'divergence' debates. None of this is to suggest slavery was unimportant historically. But to frame it as exhaustive of, or co-extensive with, capitalism makes it more difficult to distinguish the latter from its antecedents and alternatives – to see capitalism's 'strangeness', as Sewell has put it.[61]

Put another way, we can readily agree that *slavery was capitalist* but also push the inquiry further and specify how it can be related back to capitalism as a totality, a question that unavoidably takes on geographic dimensions. For, although NHC scholars have admirably widened the scale of analysis beyond national borders, critics have highlighted indications of a residual methodological nationalism. For Burnard and Riello, to portray southern slavery as 'indispensable' to, and 'inseparable' from, cotton's industrial development is to myopically ignore cotton's global scale at the time. Such claims betray how the earliest NHC works were 'heavily America-centric', they write, 'more intended to make the practice of US history international than one that is truly global'.[62]

New Directions for Globalizing the History of Capitalism

In the years since the first wave of NHC scholarship, scholars studying diverse world regions have sought to redeploy the category in their respective fields. Conferences, seminars and new research centres dedicated to a more *globalized* history of capitalism have been hosted in New York University, the European University Institute, the University of Chicago, Fordham University, Oxford University, and SOAS, University of London. In print, two of the most useful resources have been *Capitalism: A Journal of History and Economics*, launched in 2019, and an annotated bibliography by Rockman and Brown University graduate students from spring 2021, providing an invaluable, deftly curated snapshot of the field.[63]

First, within the US field, several NHC scholars have set their sights on larger-scale synoptic works, such as Beckert and Levy's new histories of global and US capitalism, respectively.[64] Newer first-author books have pushed the nineteenth-century story of growth to postwar apex and decline, examining post-industrial histories of urban inequality, including Gabriel Winant's study of Pittsburgh's steel and healthcare workers, Paige Glotzer's story of Baltimore segregation, and Destin Jenkins's analysis of San Francisco's municipal bond market.[65] The latter two place their work squarely within the tradition of 'racial capitalism', while Zachary Sell has pushed the same category into global directions, linking the nineteenth-century Anglo-US slave trade with imperial expansion, colonial violence and Asian indentured labour.[66]

Another notable cluster consists of new works seeking to historicize the late twentieth-century global economic order, summed up for many as 'neoliberalism'. Standouts include Quinn Slobodian's research on European ordoliberalism; Vanessa Ogle and Patrick Neveling on the creation of exceptional spaces for tax-free banking and manufacture; and Amy Offner's study of US experts promoting austerity and privatization in development-era Colombia.[67] These works share the common theme of Euro-Americans 'experimenting' with extreme, free-market ideas in the colonial periphery before re-importing them in the 1970s. They also seek to push the start date of neoliberalism to long before the 1970s, with the wartime transition from empire to nation as a major milestone.[68]

The study of capitalism has also been taken up by younger scholars in area studies. Among South Asia historians, Tariq Ali has tried to do for Bengal jute what Beckert did for cotton; Matthew Shutzer has linked the story of Indian energy to global regimes of finance; and Meghna Chaudhuri is writing a history of how the Indian peasant became an object of global financial investment.[69] Works in East Asia include Timothy Yang's business history of Japanese pharmaceuticals and also my own work on the tea trades of China and India.[70] And two works by Fahad Bishara and Johan Mathew shed light on the economic life of the Indian Ocean, focused on the relationship between law, legality, and the marketplace.[71]

Two world regions that have been strongly receptive to the study of capitalism are Africa and the Middle East. Works by Aaron Jakes on Egypt, Kristen Alff on the Levant, and Alden Young on Sudan have confronted the question of capitalism and economic restructuring in their local forms.[72] This elective affinity may be linked to the centrality of imperialism and energy in the region's history, especially manifest in an ongoing debate over the creation of the category 'national economy' in the mid-twentieth century, inspired by the work of Middle East scholar Timothy Mitchell.[73] Notably, the 'economy' debate among Middle East scholars gained momentum in the 2000s, coincident with the NHC turn in US history, originating out of an earlier moment when the region's wars and occupations drew international attention, and likewise amplified by the post-2008 outrage over so-called economic expertise. In their attempts to historicize 'the economy', these scholars share with NHC a commitment to denaturalize the categories of economics and to bring the tools of cultural and intellectual history to political economy. As Jakes has warned, however, an overly idealist approach to 'the economy' can ignore how those ideas corresponded to a deeper social history of capitalism in action – 'a whole constellation of social practices' – that made the category legible to actors in the first place.[74]

The 'economy' debate points to larger questions surrounding the evolution of the NHC field. Its proponents originally championed its novelty, weaving a story from economic to cultural back to economic history. But Nan Enstad has called this a distorted 'jeremiad', reinforcing the false distinction between culture and economics.[75] If, as Enstad avers, cultural historians were in fact concerned with capitalism all along, then so too do many new NHC scholars largely rely upon the tools of cultural and political history, found in intellectual genealogies revolving around slavery, finance, neoliberalism and economic growth. There are many salutary benefits to this approach, especially placing greater critical scrutiny on archives and materials from the elite classes. But the risk is that scholars will wind up stuck at the same 'abstract and general level' of ideas as their objects of inquiry, Adam Tooze has warned. This would obscure the 'actual workings of the system', that is, the elementary 'processes of accumulation, production, and distribution' that could illuminate the real-world consequences of such ideas concretely.[76] In my view, what is most valuable in the nascent field are those works that marry intellectual and theoretical conceptualization of capitalism with the kind of material–economic analysis found, for instance, in the 'divergence' debates and the richest contributions from the first NHC works.

Writing a methodologically versatile, theoretically precise and sincerely global history of capitalism is, of course, something of an impossible dream. 'One would need to be a god to write a truly adequate history of capitalism', Sewell observes.[77] But recent directions in scholarship are encouraging. They provide a foundation of new materials, reinvigorated debates, and, above all, an enthusiasm for the study of economic life palpably absent when I entered graduate school nearly two decades ago. It is possible that the NHC designation will hereafter spin off in multiple directions, losing coherence as a field. Such a fate would stem from a generational desire to push the limits of the earliest NHC scholarship, largely US-centred; but it would also attest to the latters' success in generating a site of fertile debate and interaction with, and between, those of us studying the 'rest' of the world.

Notes

1. See Kenneth Pomeranz and Prasannan Parthasarathi's chapter in this volume.
2. W. H. Sewell (2010), 'A strange career: The historical study of economic life', *History and Theory*, 49 (4), 146–66; J. Adelman and J. Levy (2014), 'The fall and rise of economic history', *The Chronicle of Higher Education*, December 2014, https://www.chronicle.com/article/the-fall-and-rise-of-economic-history
3. K. Pomeranz (2000), *The Great Divergence: China, Europe, and the Making of the Modern World Economy*. Princeton, NJ: Princeton University Press.
4. See, for instance, W. Johnson (2013), *River of Dark Dreams: Slavery and Empire in the Cotton Kingdom*. Cambridge, MA: Belknap Press of Harvard University Press, 481 n20.
5. S. Rockman (2014), 'What makes the history of capitalism newsworthy?', *Journal of the Early Republic*, 34 (3), 439–40; S. Beckert and C. Desan (2018), 'Introduction', in S. Beckert and C. Desan (eds), *American Capitalism: New Histories*, New York: Columbia University Press, 1–2.
6. (2014) 'Interchange: The history of capitalism', *Journal of American History*, 101 (2), 504.
7. Sewell, 'Strange career'.
8. S. Rockman, O. Ahmad, M. Chen et al. (2021), 'History of capitalism bibliography', Brown University Library: https://doi.org/10.26300/z7sp-2v963; Beckert and Desan, 'Introduction', 2–4; 'Interchange', 506.
9. J. Schuessler (2013), 'In history departments, it's up with capitalism', *The New York Times*, 6 April 2013.
10. 'Interchange', 535.
11. S. Mihm (2007), *A Nation of Counterfeiters: Capitalists, Con men, and the Making of the United States*. Cambridge, MA: Harvard University Press; J. Levy (2012), *Freaks of Fortune: The Emerging World of Capitalism and Risk in America*. Cambridge, MA: Harvard University Press; B. Moreton (2009), *To Serve God and Wal-Mart: The Making of Christian Free Enterprise*. Cambridge, MA: Harvard University Press; L. Hyman (2011), *Debtor Nation: The History of America in Red Ink*. Princeton, NJ: Princeton University Press; J. C. Ott (2011), *When Wall Street Met Main Street: The Quest for an Investors' Democracy*. Cambridge, MA: Harvard University Press; S. Rockman (2009), *Scraping By: Wage Labor, Slavery, and Survival in Early Baltimore*. Baltimore, MD: Johns Hopkins University Press; E. E. Baptist (2014), *The Half Has Never Been Told: Slavery and the Making of American Capitalism*. New York: Basic Books; S. Beckert (2014), *Empire of Cotton: A Global History*. New York: Alfred A. Knopf; Johnson, *River of Dark Dreams*; C. Rosenthal (2018), *Accounting for Slavery: Masters and Management*. Cambridge, MA: Harvard University Press.
12. S. Beckert (2011), 'History of American capitalism', in E. Foner and L. McGirr (eds), *American Capitalism Now*. Philadelphia, PA: Temple University Press, 314–35; Rockman, 'What makes'; J. Sklansky (2012), 'The elusive sovereign: New intellectual and social histories of capitalism', *Modern Intellectual History*, 9 (1), 233; (2014) 'Interchange: The history of

capitalism', *Journal of American History*, 101 (2), 504–48; J. Sklansky (2014), 'Labor, money, and the financial turn in the history of capitalism', *Labor*, 11 (1), 23–46; S. Beckert and S. Rockman (2016), 'Introduction', *Slavery's Capitalism: A New History of American Economic Development*. Philadelphia, PA: University of Pennsylvania Press, 1–27; Beckert and Desan, 'Introduction'.

13. Beckert, *Empire of Cotton*, ch. 6; Mihm, *Counterfeiters*, 361–2.

14. Sewell, 'Strange career', 149.

15. Quoted in J. Schuessler (2013), 'In History Departments, It's Up with Capitalism', *The New York Times*, 16 April.

16. Sklansky, 'Elusive sovereign', 239–46.

17. Rockman, 'What makes', 442–3; Beckert and Desan, 'Introduction', 4–5.

18. 'Interchange', 516–29.

19. J. Levy (2017), 'Capital as process and the history of capitalism', *Business History Review*, 91 (3), 483–510; C. Rosenthal (2020), 'Capitalism when labor was capital: Slavery, power, and price in antebellum America', *Capitalism: A Journal of History and Economics*, 1 (2), 296–337; J. J. Clegg (2015), 'Capitalism and slavery', *Critical Historical Studies*, 2 (2), 281–304.

20. Rockman, 'What makes'.

21. For instance, Beckert and Desan, 'Introduction', 31 n51; Johnson, *River*, 481 n20.

22. Pomeranz, *The Great Divergence*, ch. 1.

23. P. Parthasarathi (2011), *Why Europe Grew Rich and Asia Did Not: Global Economic Divergence, 1600–1850*. Cambridge: Cambridge University Press, ch. 3.

24. Pomeranz, *Great Divergence*, chs 5 and 6.

25. Pomeranz, *Great Divergence*, 274–6.

26. Eric Williams (1966 [1944]), *Capitalism & Slavery*. New York: Capricorn Books, ch. 5.

27. Pomeranz, *Great Divergence*, 186–8.

28. Beckert, *Empire of Cotton*, xii–xv.

29. Baptist, *The Half*, 82–3, and 126–8, 315. See also Beckert and Rockman, 'Introduction', 8–9.

30. Beckert, *Empire of Cotton*, 61.

31. Baptist, *The Half*, 320–1.

32. A. L. Olmstead and P. W. Rhode (2018), 'Cotton, slavery, and the new history of capitalism', *Explorations in Economic History*, 67 (3), 12–14.

33. I. Wallerstein (1983), *Historical Capitalism*. New York: Verso; J. Banaji (1977/2011), 'Modes of production in a materialist conception of history', in *Theory as History: Essays on Modes of Production and Exploitation*, Chicago, IL: Haymarket Books, 45–102. See also R. Steinfeld (2001), *Coercion, Contract, and Free Labor in the Nineteenth Century*. Cambridge: Cambridge University Press.

34. S. Amin and M. van der Linden (1997), 'Introduction', in S. Amin and M. van der Linden (eds), *'Peripheral' Labour?: Studies in the History of Partial Proletarianization*. Cambridge: Cambridge University Press, 1–8.

35. T. H. Aston and C. H. E. Philpin (eds) (1985), *The Brenner Debate: Agrarian Class Structure and Economic Development in Pre-industrial Europe*. Cambridge: Cambridge University Press; R. Brenner (1977), 'The origins of capitalist development: A critique of neo-Smithian Marxism', *New Left Review*, 1 (104), 25–92.

36. Pomeranz, *Great Divergence*, 49–53, 91–106.

37. Pomeranz and Parthasarathi in their chapter in this book make a point analogous to Banaji's argument about distinguishing forms of exploitation from a conception of modes of production that operate at a deeper level of analysis. Banaji, 'Modes of production', 50–61.

38. Johnson, *River*, 252–4; Johnson, 'Veil', 303.

39. Johnson, 'Veil', 304–5.

40. Olmstead and Rhode, 'Cotton, slavery', 8–12.

41. J. Oakes (2016), 'Capitalism and slavery and the Civil War', *International Labor and Working-Class History*, 89, 205–6.

42. Rosenthal, *Accounting*, 103; E. D. Genovese (1989), *The Political Economy of Slavery: Studies in the Economy and Society of the Slave South*. Middletown, NY: Wesleyan University Press, 16–17.

43. Pomeranz, *Great Divergence*, 166; R. B. Wong (1997), *China Transformed: Historical Change and the Limits of European Experience*. Ithaca, NY: Cornell University Press, 50–1.

44. Beckert, *Empire of Cotton*, xv–xvi; see Johnson, *River*, 11. Beckert's revival of the concept mirrors other recent works that have found merchant capitalism a newly relevant category for analysis; N. Lichtenstein (2012), 'The return of merchant capitalism', *International Labor and Working-Class History*, 81, 8–27; J. Banaji (2020), *A Brief History of Commercial Capitalism*. Chicago, IL: Haymarket Books.

45. 'Interchange', 522.

46. Johnson, 'Veil', 299–300; Sklansky, 'Sovereign', 234; Rockman, 'What makes', 450–2; Beckert and Rockman, 'Introduction', 9; Rosenthal, *Accounting*, 209 n4.

47. Rockman, *Scraping By*, 8. See also Rockman, 'What makes', 449–52.

48. Sklansky, 'Sovereign', 237–8; Sklansky, 'Labor, money', 34.

49. Johnson, *River*, ch. 9.

50. A. B. Liu (2019), 'Production, circulation, and accumulation: The historiographies of capitalism in China and South Asia', *Journal of Asian Studies*, 78 (4), 779–80. See also G. Arrighi (2007), *Adam Smith in Beijing: Lineages of the Twenty-First Century*. New York: Verso, ch. 1.

51. Beckert, *Empire of Cotton*, xviii.

52. M. Desmond (2019), 'American capitalism is brutal. You can trace that to the plantation', *The New York Times*, 14 August 2019.

53. For 'central' see Hyman, 'Interchange', 515; Rockman, 'What makes', 445; Beckert and Rockman, 'Introduction', 10; for 'decisive', see Beckert and Rockman, 'Introduction', 3; for 'constitutive', Beckert and Rockman, 'Introduction', 10; for 'integral', Rockman, 'What Makes', 444; for 'essential', Beckert, *Empire of* Cotton, 91; for 'crucial', Baptist, *The Half*, xxi; for 'necessary', Baptist, *The Half*, 414.

54. For 'depended', see Johnson, *River*, 7; Beckert, *Empire of Cotton*, 119; Baptist, *The Half*, 311–22; for 'slavery racial capitalism', Johnson, *River*, 10–14.

55. G. Wright (2020), 'Slavery and Anglo-American capitalism revisited', *Economic History Review*, 73 (2), 358–66; T. Burnard and G. Riello (2020), 'Slavery and the new history of capitalism', *Journal of Global History*, 15 (2), 234–8.

56. Wright, 'Revisited', 367–72.

57. Wright, 'Revisited', 372; Burnard and Riello, 'Slavery', 238–40. See also Olmstead and Rhode, 'Cotton, slavery', 3–7. Here, I am referencing Wright's sentiments from an earlier draft: 'The Industrial Revolution and slave-grown cotton were undeniably linked, but this connection

was no means historically inevitable or necessary. As will be argued here, that is the true tragedy of American slavery'.

58. Johnson, *River*, 254, 10.

59. See Oakes, 'Civil War', 216–18. The exception here is Beckert's careful distinction between 'war' and 'industrial capitalism'. Nevertheless, Oakes and Wright both contend that Beckert's distinctions were in contradiction to his broader generalizations.

60. S. Hahn (2021), 'The arch of injustice', *Public Books*, 16 February 2021,

    https://www.publicbooks.org/the-arch-of-injustice

61. W. H. Sewell Jr (2008), 'The temporalities of capitalism', *Socio-Economic Review*, 6 (3), 533.

62. Burnard and Riello, 'Slavery', 226, 234, 239–40.

63. Rockman et al., 'Bibliography'.

64. J. Levy (2021), *Ages of American Capitalism: A History of the United States*. New York: Random House; and S. Beckert (forthcoming), *Capitalism: A Global History*. New York: Penguin.

65. G. Winant (2021), *The Next Shift: The Fall of Industry and the Rise of Health Care in Rust Belt America*. Cambridge, MA: Harvard University Press; P. Glotzer (2020), *How the Suburbs Were Segregated: Developers and the Business of Exclusionary Housing, 1890–1960*. New York: Columbia University Press; D. Jenkins (2021), *The Bonds of Inequality: Debt and the Making of the American City*. Chicago, IL: University of Chicago Press.

66. Z. Sell (2021), *Trouble of the World: Slavery and Empire in the Age of Capital*. Chapel Hill, NC: University of North Carolina Press.

67. Q. Slobodian (2018), *Globalists: The End of Empire and the Birth of Neoliberalism*. Cambridge, MA: Harvard University Press; V. Ogle (2017), 'Archipelago capitalism: Tax havens, offshore money, and the state, 1950s–1970s', *American Historical Review*, 122 (5), 1431–58; A. C. Offner (2019), *Sorting out the Mixed Economy: The Rise and Fall of Welfare and Developmental States in the Americas*. Princeton, NJ: Princeton University Press; P. Neveling (2017), 'The global spread of export processing zones and the 1970s as a decade of consolidation', in K. Andresen and S. Müller (eds), *Changes in Social Regulation: State, Economy, and Social Protagonists since the 1970s*. Oxford: Berghahn Books, 23–40.

68. J. Martin (2022), *The Meddlers: Sovereignty, Empire, and the Birth of Global Economic Governance*. Cambridge, MA: Harvard University Press; C. Thornton (2021), *Revolution in Development: Mexico and the Governance of the Global Economy*. Oakland, CA: University of California Press.

69. T. O. Ali (2018), *A Local History of Global Capital: Jute and Peasant Life in the Bengal Delta*. Princeton, NJ: Princeton University Press; M. Chaudhuri (2020), 'Lives of value: Land, labor, and agrarian finance in South Asia, 1830–1950', PhD Dissertation, New York University; M. Shutzer (2023), 'Oil, money and decolonization in South Asia', *Past & Present*, 258, 212–45.

70. T. M. Yang (2021), *A Medicated Empire: The Pharmaceutical Industry and Modern Japan*. Ithaca, NY: Cornell University Press; A. B. Liu (2020), *Tea War: A History of Capitalism in China and India*. New Haven, CT: Yale University Press.

71. J. Mathew (2016), *Margins of the Market: Trafficking and Capitalism across the Arabian Sea*. Oakland, CA: University of California Press; F. A. Bishara (2017), *A Sea of Debt: Law and Economic Life in the Western Indian Ocean, 1780–1950*. Cambridge: Cambridge University Press.

72. A. Young (2018), *Transforming Sudan: Decolonization, Economic Development, and State Formation*. Cambridge: Cambridge University Press; K. Alff (2020), 'Landed property, capital accumulation, and polymorphous capitalism: Egypt and the Levant', in J. Beinin, B. Haddad and S. Seikaly (eds), *A Critical Political Economy of the Middle East and North Africa*. Stanford, CA: Stanford University Press, 25–45; A. Jakes (2020), *Egypt's Occupation: Colonial Economism and the Crises of Capitalism*. Stanford, CA: Stanford University Press.

73. T. Mitchell (1998), 'Fixing the economy', *Cultural Studies*, 12 (1), 82–101. See also V. Bivar (2022), 'Historicizing economic growth: An overview of recent works', *Historical Journal*, 65 (5), 1470–89.

74. Jakes, *Egypt's Occupation*, 17–18.

75. N. Enstad (2019), 'The "sonorous summons" of the new history of capitalism, or, what are we talking about when we talk about economy?', *Modern American History*, 2 (1), 83–95.

76. A. Tooze (2018), 'Neoliberalism's world order', *Dissent Magazine*, Summer, https://www.dissentmagazine.org/article/neoliberalism-world-order-review-quinn-slobodian-globalists.

77. Sewell, 'Temporalities of capitalism', 535.

PART II
THE EMERGENCE OF A WORLD ECONOMY

CHAPTER 9
TRADE AND THE EMERGENCE OF A WORLD
ECONOMY, 1500–2000

Tirthankar Roy and Giorgio Riello

The relationship between trade and the emergence of a world economy has been the subject of several differing ideas and conceptualizations over the past two generations. Economic historians have chartered the intensification of long-distance – and especially transcontinental – trade over the course of the early modern period (*c*.1500–1800) and since the nineteenth century, but there is little consensus on the chronology and reasons for major shifts in this long period. The relative size of trade fluxes is a subject of debate especially for the pre-modern period as is a general definition of what the making of a global market might entail. Economic historians have provided rather different chronologies of the making of a global economic system of exchange. The same can be said of the relationship between trade and economic growth, a topic of disagreement especially for the period of the Industrial Revolution.

This chapter starts by charting the scale and movements of world trade over the five centuries from the start of European direct trade with Asia and the Americas to the late twentieth century. It introduces the historiography explaining these movements. It considers the complex relationship between trade, politics and economic development. It concludes with a short overview of the points in the debates and controversies.

The Shape and Scale of Global Trade

Historians have argued that trade can be taken as one of the indicators of the level of globalization. The exchange of goods – and more recently of an increasing amount of services – across national borders is taken to be a measure of not only economic but also social and cultural interconnection. Since 1500, world trade has mostly grown at rates far higher than those of world GDP, suggesting that national economies have become increasingly connected to each other through the exchange of raw materials, foodstuffs and manufactured commodities (Table 9.1).

With a growth rate of just under 1 per cent a year in the pre-1820 period, world trade grew at three times the rate of world GDP. In 1820, the size of world trade might have been five times larger than in 1500. Yet, this growth was modest compared to the following two centuries. It is estimated that world trade increased from $700 million (in 1970 US$) in 1700 to $38 billion in 1913.[1] On the eve of the First World War, world trade was between twenty-five and thirty-three times larger than a century earlier.[2]

Table 9.1 Growth of world trade and GDP, 1500–2003 (annual average compound growth rates in percentage)

	World trade	World GDP	Ratio trade to GDP
1500–1820	0.96	0.32	3.0
1820–1870	4.18	0.94	4.4
1870–1913	3.40	2.12	1.6
1913–1950	0.90	1.82	0.5
1950–1973	7.88	4.90	1.6
1973–2003	5.38	3.17	1.7
1820–2003	3.97	2.25	1.8

Source: A. Maddison (2007), *Contours of the World Economy: Essays in Macro-Economic History*. Oxford: Oxford University Press, Table 2.6.

With a growth rate of over 4 per cent in the period 1820–80, there was a ninefold increase in world trade with a period of very high growth between 1840 and 1873 and slightly more contained growth over the following forty years. This was the period of liberalization of the European economies and the heyday of imperial projects on the part of European nation states.

The First World War was a moment of disruption in world trade and foreign direct investment, and it was followed by a period of slow growth. Autarchic regimes, monetary and financial instability, economic stagnation and a weakening of empires meant in some cases an absolute reduction in world trade. It was only in the post-1945 period that trade began to grow again, indeed at a pace unmatched even during the so-called first age of globalization of the second half of the nineteenth century. Already by the early 1950s, the size of world trade had returned to 1913 levels, though it took until the mid-1970s for the level of trade as a share of world output to be back to 1913 levels.[3] At the same time, the pursuit of protectionist industrial policies in the developing world after 1950 reduced the importance of foreign trade for some of these economies (such as those of India or China), which had been highly open before 1950. The forty years between 1980 and 2020 were a period of further liberalization of commodity and financial markets and the 'multilateralization of trade'. Both world GDP and world trade grew at very high rates. The Covid-19 pandemic caused a significant decline in world trade in 2020–21 (–6 per cent for goods and –20 per cent for services), and a fourfold increase in the cost of shipping. However, by 2022 when this chapter was written, world trade had already returned to 2019 pre-pandemic levels.[4]

This overall picture needs, however, to be disaggregated in order to consider the contribution of specific countries. In 1913, the merchandise export of Britain was worth an estimated $39.35 billion (in 1990 US$), the largest in the world and just ahead of Germany, and roughly double the size of US export. Britain, the United States and Germany – the three largest industrial economies at the time – accounted for possibly

Table 9.2 Value of Export of selected countries, 1820–1992 (1913 = 100)

	1820	1870	1913	1929	1950	1973	2003	Great Britain = 100 in 1913	United States = 100 in 1929	Germany = 100 in 2003
Great Britain	3	31	100	81	100	240	816	100	105	41
Germany	4	18	100	92	35	508	2055	97	115	100
France	4	31	100	147	149	922	3578	29	55	51
Italy	7	39	100	161	126			12		
Russia	–		100					-		
United States	1	13	100	158	225	909	4176	49	100	102
Japan	–	3	100	258	210	5647	23922	4	14	51
China		33	100	149	151	278	10811	11	21	58
India		37	100	87	58	102	908	24	27	11
World	3	24	100		128	797		-	-	-

Size of the export (1913 = 100)

Source: A. Maddison (2007), *Monitoring the World Economy, 1820-1992* (Paris, OECD Development Centre, 1995); Id, *Contours of the World Economy: Essays in Macro-Economic History*. Oxford: Oxford University Press, 170.

two-thirds of all trade in the world (Table 9.2). The preponderance of industrial economies has remained a feature of world trade throughout the twentieth century. In 2003, the export of Great Britain was eight times larger than it had been ninety years earlier, a modest performance compared to Germany (twenty times larger), France (thirty-five times) and the United States (forty-two times). Trade grew exponentially for China (108 times larger in 2013 compared to 1914) and Japan (239 times), but enormous increases for Asian countries hide the fact of the relatively small size of their trade in 1913. At the beginning of the twenty-first century, the major Western industrial nations – the United States and Germany in particular – still controlled a large part of world trade.

The Beginning of a Global Economy: The Early Modern Period

The shape of global trade in the twentieth century could not be more different from its contours just four centuries earlier. In 1500, China and India accounted for more than half of the world manufacturing output and were the engines of global trade. Silk, porcelain, iron and copperware from China were exchanged for silver, cotton, spices and foodstuff. Palm oil, nuts and precious metals from Africa and the Middle East found their way to India in exchange for cotton textiles. Yet historians have disputed as to whether this was in any sense a global system of exchange. Janet Abu-Lughod put forward the idea that, already in 1250–1350, a system of global exchange existed but was neither coordinated by any specific world area nor unified into one system. She proposed instead a model based on a series of overlapping spheres of trade that included long-established routes such as the silk routes across Central Asia, the China Sea, the Indian Ocean and the Mediterranean.[5] The work of David Christian on the silk routes showed how trade was based on a system of 'repeated transaction' with numerous disruptions caused by warfare and political instability.[6] Technology was one of the limiting factors for intercontinental trade as direct trade between the two extremes of Eurasia was all but impossible. Traders operated instead on specific segments of this Eurasian system and were organized in 'nations' or trading communities that negotiated the protection of local governments.[7]

The sixteenth and seventeenth centuries saw a restructuring of this system, though historians dispute the scale and consequences of such change. It has been suggested that the direct trade between Europe and Asia via the Cape first by the Portuguese Carreira da Índia from 1500 onwards and a century later by the Dutch, English and other European companies inaugurated a new period in world trade. This was a trade that was direct for Europe and did not have to rely on a series of intermediaries; it was in the hands of Europeans and was structured through large-scale organizations, the East India companies, that have been seen as the precursors of modern corporations.[8]

However, the idea that Europe's direct trade with Asia and the Americas inaugurated a new era for the early modern world economy has been debated. Critics point to the fact that such a trade might have been rather modest. Extra-European markets were small and the profitability of both colonial trade and slavery remained low.[9] In the three centuries between 1500 and 1800, just over 10,600 vessels travelled from Europe to Asia, two-thirds of which in the eighteenth century.[10] At an estimated 700 tons per vessel, the total trade between Asia and Europe was in the region of 7.5 million tons, roughly fifteen present-day container ships. By contrast, coastal, short-distance, and port-to-port trade remained far more important than long-distance trade in this period. The majority of trade was carried out within the borders of specific regions. While India is often hailed as key to Britain's early modern intercontinental trade, estimates of the subcontinent's trade and GDP reveal that long-distance trade was small.[11]

Intercontinental trade was not just small but also slow as it took the best of two years for a European ship to go to China and return to Europe. It was also expensive: although profit margins were high, recent research has underlined the cost of an 'armed trade' that relied on violence and coercion as well as a sophisticated system of diplomatic relations. This was also a trade with profound social costs, as shown by de Vries's estimates of the high number of people who left Europe in the service of the East India companies. In the case of a small nation such as Portugal, this constituted in all probability a large drain of its human capital.[12]

Yet, quantities might not be the entire story. Dennis O. Flynn and Arturo Giráldez argue that Europeans brought together separate areas of trade into one unified system. From the 1560s onwards, vast reserves of silver mined in Latin America 'oiled' this newly integrated system of exchange and allowed it to expand in size. Because of the high value of silver in China and more generally in Asia, bullion could be used as a means of payment for a variety of Asian commodities that found their way to European and Atlantic markets.[13]

Silver was monetized and the Portuguese and Spaniards first, and later other European nations, expanded trade by integrating the American and Asian economies. The connection between the American, African and Asian economies was furthered by the setting up of plantations in the Americas cultivating a variety of tropical commodities such as sugar, coffee, cocoa and later raw materials such as cotton through the use of enslaved labour.[14] The incorporation of the Atlantic coincided with – and was fostered by – the expansion of the slave trade by the hands of European traders. It is estimated that in the period 1525–1790, up to 10 million people were enslaved in Africa and transported to the Americas. Two-thirds of such slaves were transported in the eighteenth century, the period of maximum expansion of the production of tropical colonial goods.[15]

The system of intercontinental trade changed substantially over the course of the early modern period and especially in the eighteenth century. Three main changes should be underlined. First, while in the sixteenth century spices and what we might call 'traditional luxuries' had been central to global trade, by the seventeenth and eighteenth centuries their role was taken over by cheaper cotton textiles as well as tropical goods such as tea, coffee and sugar. Tropical commodities and luxury goods were items that were, at least initially, not available or not produced within the borders of Europe and North America.

Second, over time Europe started becoming a direct competitor in the production of Asian commodities. Unlike Portugal and Spain – the key trading players of the sixteenth century – England, France and the Netherlands possessed export-oriented industries such as the English woollens, French silks and the Dutch lighter new draperies.[16] Over time, they started manufacturing imitations of Indian cotton textiles, Chinese porcelain and Japanese lacquerware for domestic and export markets.[17] High tariffs and total bans were part of the mercantilist policies embraced by several, though not all, European states. The ban of import and wearing of Indian cotton and silk textiles in most European nations between 1689 and the 1770s tends to be seen, if debatably, as an example of mercantilist policies aimed at fostering local production and re-export, and extended to include colonial policies against export of manufactured commodities towards the mother country. In the case of Britain, long-distance trade had to be carried out on English ships and colonial commodities had to be sent to England before being re-exported. Duties on tobacco, tea, sugar and spirits accounted for a quarter of government revenue in Britain in the late eighteenth century.[18] In the 1820s, British tariffs still averaged between 45 and 55 per cent.[19]

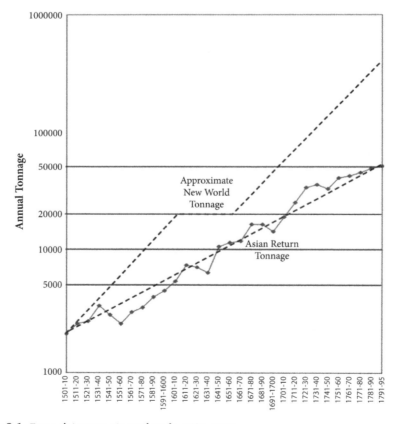

Figure 9.1 Europe's intercontinental trade, 1501–1795.

Source: J. de Vries (2010), 'The limits of globalisation in the early modern world', *Economic History Review*, 63 (1), 720.

Over time, the Atlantic economy came to have a larger weight for Europe than the eastbound Asian trade, even though the scale of Asian and tropical trade with Europe increased substantially (Figure 9.1).[20]

Industrialization and Reconfiguration of World Trade

Historians agree that the nineteenth century saw a dramatic change in both the nature and scale of global trade. The rise of the industrial West created a demand there for raw materials and produced a surplus of finished commodities that needed to find markets all over the world. If at the beginning of the seventeenth century British imports were equally divided into manufactured commodities, foodstuffs and raw materials, a century later industrial Britain had become a net exporter of manufactured commodities with less than 10 per cent of its imports in the form of manufactured goods. By 1800, Britain relied on the import of foodstuffs (45 per cent of all imports) and of a range of raw materials necessary as industrial inputs (46.5 per cent of all imports).[21] Britons in the mid-Victorian period spent one out of every four pounds sterling on foreign goods, mostly food and primary materials.[22]

As we saw earlier, the ratio of trade to GDP (growth rates) grew from a level as low as 1 per cent in the 1820s to ten times as much on the eve of the First World War, indicating a pronounced opening up of economies, especially those in Europe and North America (Table 9.3).[23] Besides industrialization, the transcontinental railways, transoceanic steamships with compound steam engines, and undersea telegraph cables contributed to the process. The opening of new maritime routes such as the Suez Canal in 1869 and the completion of the Union Pacific Railroad the same year allowed for cheaper and more reliable means of transport. Improvements in navigation technology and the introduction of steam decreased the cost of ocean freight by 80 per cent over the course of the nineteenth century.[24] The general peace in Europe and the balance of power in the century between 1815 and 1914 allowed for the establishment of specific imperial spheres of influence by European nations in Asia and Africa. The infrastructure of empire in turn facilitated the migration of people and the mobility of capital through foreign direct investment. Between 1870 and 1914, the stock of capital invested outside the place of origin increased from $9 billion to $44 billion.[25]

How 'free' was trade? There is a consensus that the general liberalism inaugurated with the repeal of the Corn Laws in Britain in 1846 started a new age of free trade. The Cobden-Chevalier treaty of 1860 in which Britain removed all tariffs on the import of French goods (with the exception of wine and brandy) included a 'most-favoured-nation clause' that allowed further treaties to be signed with other industrialized countries in Europe. Bairoch, however, insists that liberalism was more a 'myth' than a reality in nineteenth-century Europe as most economies did not readily embrace free trade. Even considering the relative relaxation of duties and other protectionist measures in the period 1860–80, Bairoch and Kozul-Wright conclude that in 1913 the developed world could be 'best described as islands of liberalism, surrounded by a sea of protectionism'.[26] The financial crisis of 1873 gave voice to those who had been arguing for protection.

Three features characterized the new world trade system of the nineteenth century. The first one is the creation of markets for standardized commodities such as cotton, wool, coal, wheat, maize and iron. Unlike the commodity exchange of the pre-modern period, this was a trade in bulk commodities. These were also no longer non-competing goods as they had been in the early modern period but competed directly with producers in different continents.[27] Chris Bayly, for instance, conceptualizes this as a shift from what he calls an 'archaic system' of exchange based on the trade of luxury items to one that can be defined as 'modern' based instead on capitalist expansion and global imperialism.[28] The interlinking of world commodity trade came to be strongly associated with international specialization of labour and, as we will see, to economic development more widely. The second element of this new system was the preponderance of Europe and Britain in particular. In 1910, 60 per cent of the tonnage passing through the Suez Canal was British. Western shipping dominated world trade.[29] The same could be said of direct foreign investment. At an estimated £4 billion, British overseas investment accounted for 43 per cent of the world total in 1913. France accounted for a further 20 per cent and Germany 13 per cent.[30] Finally, this system was based on a differentiation between industrial and primary produce economies. In 1913, primary products accounted for nearly two-thirds of all world trade, with food accounting for 27 per cent of all trade, agricultural raw materials 23 per cent, and minerals 14 per cent. While Western Europe and North America were importers of raw materials, they exported manufactured products to Africa, Latin America, Asia and Oceania.[31]

Table 9.3 World merchandise export as percentage of GDP, 1820–1998

1820	1.0 **
1850	5.1*
1870	4.6 **
1880	9.8*
1913	11.9 (7.9**)
1929	9.0**
1950	7.1 (5.5**)
1973	11.7 (10.5**)
1985	14.5*
1993	17.1**
1998	17.2*

Source:
*P. Krugman (1995), 'Growing World Trade: Causes and Consequences', *Brookings Papers on Economic Activity*, 1, 331;
** A. Maddison (2001), *The World Economy: A Millennial Perspective*. Paris: OECD.

Historians have argued that it was not just the logic of trade or its size that distinguished the nineteenth from previous centuries. O'Rourke and Williamson make a claim that a true globalization, in the sense of closer market integration driven by a sharp fall in trade and transportation cost, began only from the 1820s, whereas trade connections grew between 1500 and 1820, driven by demand and supply stimulations.[32] They take what de Vries calls a definition of 'hard globalization' and posit that the integration of markets to form an international commodity system could only happen when prices of basic commodities across the world started to converge as they did in the nineteenth century.[33] For instance, the cotton price spread between Bombay and Liverpool decreased from 57 to 20 per cent in the forty years between 1873 and 1913.[34] Other historians prefer instead a definition of so-called soft globalization based on the idea of a continuative and sustained exchange of goods across different world areas as a key identifier of a global market.[35] In defence of soft globalization, the process induced some of the key societal changes without which hard globalization would have been impossible, including financial innovation, the joint-stock company, codification of commercial law, mass demand for Asian tea or textiles, and the incentive to substitute imports and develop better ships (more on this point later). In short, the distinction between the weak eighteenth-century and the strong nineteenth-century globalization may be an artificial one.

Trade and Economic Growth

The analysis of the nineteenth century brings to the fore the relationship between economic development (especially industrialization) and intercontinental trade. This topic has been at the centre of attention for economic historians for decades and has seen opposing opinions. A traditional approach going back to W. W. Rostow, and before him, historians of the Commercial Revolution, argued that trade was key to capital accumulation. More recently, academic scholarship has considered a wider spectrum of socio-economic returns with C. A. Bayly arguing that merchant capitalists reaped the benefits of new global patterns of trade well before industrialization took place.[36] In the 1960s, Phyllis Deane, John Habakkuk and Ralph Davis gave great attention to trade, but by the 1970s and 1980s, Joel Mokyr, Deirdre McCloskey, and Nick Crafts dismissed the existence of a strong connection between trade and economic growth, arguing that it was technological change rather than trade or capital accumulation that was the main driver of industrialization.[37] The Industrial Revolution became mostly an endogenous affair. In fact, they observed that Britain's terms of trade should have increased during the Industrial Revolution although in practice they fell due to cost-reducing technological innovation. They observed that trade reallocates resources to its existing optimum but does not shift that optimum itself.[38]

A more extreme position relies instead on counterfactual methodologies. Clark, O'Rourke and Taylor show that as late as the 1850s the absence of trade with the New World would have had little impact on Britain's growth, as substitutes for the cotton, sugar, corn and timber imported from the New World could be found in Asia and Eastern Europe. However, they also agree that after 1850 the British economy became highly dependent on foreign trade, especially considering that its key sector, cotton textile manufacturing, sold 60 per cent of its production in foreign markets.[39] There is now the acknowledgement that trade in British industrial goods increased substantially during the period of the Industrial Revolution but that was due to falling prices. The overall outcome was that the value of exported goods increased at a much slower pace than the volume of traded goods.[40] O'Brien and Engerman, though sceptical of the overall importance of overseas markets for British economic growth, underline the increasing employment opportunities in export-oriented industries.[41] Furthermore, the expansion of commerce that preceded industrialization allowed the flourishing of legal, financial and commercial institutions that underpinned the subsequent phase of industrialization and sustained growth.[42] Trade in the Atlantic strengthened the power of merchants and secured property rights.[43] Kenneth Pomeranz's ecological narrative shows through counterfactual scenarios that the imports of food and raw materials from the Americas were key to the lifting of environmental limits to growth in Europe and in Britain more specifically.[44]

A second debate on the relationship between trade and economic growth relates to the relationship between the richer industrial and the poorer economies worldwide. The nineteenth century saw a 'great specialization' of the world between the Western world (North) engaged mainly in the production and trade of industrial goods and a so-called Third World (South) specialized instead in the production of raw materials and foodstuffs.[45] This is not a perfect differentiation as both Eastern Europe and the United States produced and traded extensively in raw materials and other industrial inputs. However, historians agree that in the nineteenth century trade facilitated the economic convergence between richer and poorer economies, thanks to the export growth in raw materials by non-industrialized countries.[46] Terms of trade swung in favour of non-industrial economies as the price of primary products increased over the course of the nineteenth century, while the price of manufactured commodities fell dramatically.[47]

A more cautious position is proposed by Patrick O'Brien who argues that if food and raw materials were a major import into Europe, the same could not be said of energy and minerals whose import from the other hemisphere remained negligible. Even for the case of raw materials such as cotton, oil seed, jute, hemp, dyestuffs and wood, Europe's reliance on Asia, Africa and Latin America decreased over the course of the nineteenth century as the supplies of these primary products from North America and Australia expanded. In 1913, Asia, Africa and Latin America contributed less than 20 per cent of global trade, with Africa's contribution being as little as 3.7 per cent. In 1913, Europe received hardly any manufactured goods from beyond its borders, and only 20 per cent of all goods and services consumed by Europeans came from the Third World (Table 9.4).[48] Bairoch argues that we should, however, distinguish between the United Kingdom and the rest of the Western world. Britain was responsible for a large share of the trade between South and North while other 'North' economies traded more extensively between each other in both manufactured and primary products.[49]

Table 9.4 Regional distribution of world trade in 1913 (in percentage)

	World trade	World primary products exports (in %)	World manufactured exports (in %)
United Kingdom	62	6.2	26.9
Rest of Europe		39.9	50.3
North America	13.2	17.2	11.1
Asia	11.1	14.7	6.2
Africa	3.7	22.0	
Rest of the world	10		5.5

Sources: N. Crafts (2004), 'Globalisation and economic growth: a historical perspective', *World Economy*, 27 (1), 52; K. O'Rourke (2003), 'Long-distance trade between 1750 and 1914', in Mokyr ed., *The Oxford Encyclopedia of Economic History*. Oxford: Oxford University Press, 368; R. Cameron (3rd ed. 1997), *A Concise Economic History of the World*. Oxford: Oxford University Press, 304.

Over the twentieth century, one can observe a widening of the gap between rich and poor countries in per capita income.[50] O'Brien argues that trade did not benefit the Third World as it did not bring diversification of investment and most of the production of raw materials remained firmly in the hands of European entrepreneurs.[51] The shift in global trade in the twentieth century from primary products (64 per cent of all trade in 1913) to the trade in manufactured commodities (79 per cent of all trade in 1992) has exacerbated the isolation of Africa and parts of Asia in the post-colonial period.[52] Over the twentieth century, the North-to-North trade remained as high as 60 per cent of world trade, while South-to-South just 10 per cent. Only a third of all world trade took place between North and South.

A part of this divergence had occurred before 1950, when colonialism shaped the North–South economic exchanges, which brings us to the issue of politics.

Trade and Politics, 1500–1950

Growth of world trade between 1500 and 1930 is intimately connected with the growth of states, especially European colonial states. Why was trade and state power so closely interconnected? Did colonialism influence distribution of the gains from trade? Did politics create new patterns of international economic inequality? These three questions have been central to a number of debates on the implications of the modern world economy. Why was trade and power interdependent? The question can be approached from two ends – that of politics and that of business organization.

In the pre-industrial era, mercantilism created a reason for states to intervene in foreign trade. The European merchants needed licences and contracts to negotiate with indigenous merchants and rulers. The slave trade by its nature involved coercion as a business strategy. The slave trade in Africa was indigenous, extensive and politically controlled before it turned into a source of supply of workers in the New World. European involvement in the African slave trade changed not only its volume but also its quality, with the introduction of a new kind of racialized chattel slavery proverbially ruthless in its instrumental brutality and unrelenting in its demand for work from these slaves, who were literally worked to death on a routine basis on British, Dutch, Portuguese and French plantations. Such brutal and dehumanizing regimens did not exist in Africa before the arrival of Europeans. The depopulation of West Africa also had a long-term negative legacy. The trade also left a political legacy in the form of states that were readier to do opportunistic deals with the world market than to invest in the local economy and in the population living on it.[53]

European intrusion in the Indian Ocean around 1500 entailed the systematic use of gunships by the Portuguese and the subsequent attempts by them to tax trade. In the seventeenth and eighteenth centuries, naval power shifted from the Portuguese to the Dutch, the English and the French. While these groups ordinarily relied on diplomacy and negotiation, they could in theory receive military and naval support from the sponsor states, which made them a different type of merchant group from what the region had seen before.[54] The merchant companies enjoying state monopoly can be seen as extensions of mercantilist states of Europe. Institutionally, the Dutch and the British attempts to use a more efficient and sparing use of power would suggest a successful strategy to internalize the heavy cost of protecting their monopoly from European rivals, private traders and indigenous groups. As Findlay and O'Rourke show, in the eighteenth century, European expansion gave the English complete mastery over the slave trade, and gave the English, the Dutch and the French territorial control in Asia and Africa.[55]

In India, the seeds of an empire were sown in the move by the British East India Company (and on a more limited scale by its rivals) to acquire sites on the coast for the creation of fortified ports. Thanks to these ports, as the Mughal Empire collapsed in the mid-eighteenth century and contests for power intensified in India, the British and the French companies found themselves well placed to join these contests and conduct proxy war between themselves. In this way, trading rivalry, combined with turmoil in India and Europe, shaped the emergence of modern imperialism. In Indonesia, the Dutch, who moved to consolidate their control on the world spice trade, saw it as a way to extend their territorial power. The consolidation of Dutch maritime power forged new links between the ports of East and Southeast Asia, even as it 'decisively decoupled historical trajectories in the archipelago from those in mainland [Southeast Asia]'.[56]

The propensity of the East India companies to engage in local politics raises the question: what kind of firms these were? Like all corporate firms, in the British East India Company too, there were 'principals' (shareholders) and 'agents' (employees stationed in trading ports). But unlike in modern firms, these two sets of actors were not located in close proximity to one another, nor were they able to communicate frequently or effectively. The limited ability of the principals to monitor the agents suggests two lessons on the nature of these firms. First, agents were given more freedom than would be allowed in a modern firm. They were more than salaried servants, and were given incentives to trade on the side, and their behaviour was monitored by an incentive–punishment mechanism. Studies on contract enforcement in the East India Company and the Hudson's Bay Company find that the incentive–punishment mechanism worked more or less effectively from the angle of the principals.[57]

Secondly, the agents' interest could differ systematically from that of the firm, partly because they were traders on the side and partly because they were exposed to certain types of political risks and opportunities that the principals did not face. Ordinarily, the divergence of interest was not a serious matter to the firm, but in the late eighteenth century, the divergence widened because the risks and opportunities involved in taking part in local politics changed. Adam Smith's famous criticism of the British East India Company in *The Wealth of Nations* (1776), in one view, needs to be seen in the context of this particular agency problem and its late eighteenth-century manifestation.[58]

Subsequent to the formation of states, in India by the British East India Company and in Indonesia by the Dutch East India Company (VOC), economic policies in both retained a focus on trade. The influence of merchants and bankers behind British imperial policy has been explored in a well-known scholarship. The famous, if controversial, thesis of P. J. Cain and A. G. Hopkins that the support for the expansion of the British Empire formed of a coalition between landlords and capitalists is the most cited example.[59] Imperial history has also long reminded us of the deep connections that had developed between British manufacturing and services and European trading firms overseas. For example, the managing agency companies operating in India in the nineteenth century formed formal or informal partnerships with British counterparts that organized marketing and re-export businesses, and sometimes supplied finance and skilled manpower.

The British Empire functioned as if it wished to maintain open borders to trade in goods and services. Was this policy beneficial for the colonies? A recent empirical exercise shows that belonging to an empire roughly doubled trade relative to those countries that were not part of an empire. The use of a common language, the establishment of currency unions, 'the monetization of recently acquired colonies, and the establishment of preferential trade agreements and customs unions help to account for the observed increase in trade associated with empire'.[60] The finding needs to be qualified with the statement that within the British Empire, a greater share of the increased trade occurred in trade between Britain and the settler colonies of the New World.[61] But even for the non-settler colonies, the trade growth was unprecedented, not only in scale but also in a whole range of new relationships that it forged. For example, the opium trade linked China with India, while Dutch trading operations in East and Southeast Asia likewise integrated Japan and Burma in the Eurasian trade.

Was growth of trade under colonial conditions beneficial for the colonizer and the colonized peoples? For the colonizer, trade growth led to accumulation of wealth, integrated markets and induced specialization and productivity gains. On the other hand, there is a view that the captive market of the imperial domain made the colonizer, Britain being the eminent example, less innovative than it would be otherwise. The belief feeds into an explanation of British decline in the twentieth-century world economy.[62] Of course, the strength of the belief should depend on how 'captive' or 'soft' imperial markets really were, and in turn, what we mean by these terms. One investigation concludes that it is difficult to presume that businesses could take colonial markets for granted simply because they were colonial markets.[63]

Was trade growth beneficial to the colonized people? In answer to the question, four points need to be considered. First, there was sometimes an element of pure 'extraction' using state power and institutional manipulation by the settlers or the state. But such distortions were more the exceptions than the norm.

Secondly, trade growth caused 'de-industrialization' in the colonies. The trade boom after industrialization began was driven by a large fall in the prices of manufactured goods produced in Western Europe, and a rise in the demand for primary commodities available in the tropics. So large was the rise in demand and so large the technological leap that they jointly led to a long-term increase in the terms of trade, that is, in the price of tropical exports as a ratio of the price of its imports. The tropics experienced a better utilization of idle land and mining capacity, and could buy manufactured goods in increasing quantity and increasingly better quality over time for an unchanging bundle of primary products. On the other hand, most colonies were deprived of the spillover benefits of industrialization (innovation, increasing returns to scale), experienced a decline of their own artisan manufactures, and experienced 'Dutch disease' or shift of resources away from other sectors towards exportable goods and more exposure of the export economies to commodity price fluctuations.[64] De-industrialization did occur in many primary-product-exporting economies, but not in all. In East Asia, terms of trade *fell* in the long run. In South Asia, the rise happened earlier and to a much smaller extent than in Southeast Asia, Latin America, the Middle East and the European periphery. India did not de-industrialize as much as the other regions did, and experienced a significant growth of cotton textile mill industry.[65] The emergence of a factory textile industry shows that while trade growth might have hurt the artisans, it led to accumulation of capital by merchants, who invested money in modern factory industry. [66]

Third, despite growth of trade, specialization in a small basket of commodities for export exposed the colonies to cyclical fluctuations. In the mid-twentieth century, these risks were a ground for trade pessimism. Individual country studies, however, show that global terms of trade boom in favour of primary commodity exporters on the whole benefited the exporting countries until the early twentieth century, even when the process increased inequality between the exporting sector and the rest of the economy.[67]

Fourth, trade growth and factor market integration were connected processes in the colonial territories. For example, British India relied heavily on net import of skilled services and capital to run public administration, to finance and then run the railways, to maintain the army and to create and manage private businesses. To fund its deficit on the services account, the regime needed a trade surplus. Indian nationalists called the deficit a 'drain' of potential saving and investment. This interpretation remains controversial, but the interdependence of the growth of trade and services was a feature of many colonial relationships. The East India companies left a legacy on trade in services worldwide.

The emergence of a secondary market in VOC shares, for example, helped establish Amsterdam as the world's leading financial centre.[68] The close interdependence between trade and investment that had developed during the first globalization is illustrated with railroad construction in India and Argentina in the late nineteenth century. With the development of a market in London for Argentine debt, foreign money then found other avenues, such as infrastructure. Analysis of the Baring crisis in the 1890s finds that trade also acted as a channel of transmission of the crisis.[69]

Migration, of course, was one of these factor market effects. Before 1800, long-distance migration flows were not always driven by market forces. New works on the early history of empires written by cultural historians shed light on movements driven by free migration, slavery, the military labour market, forced migration, exile and penal colonies, and of course settlement on new land frontiers.[70] By contrast, the sugar and cotton plantations in the Americas integrated world trade and migration closely. The largest flows of the post-1800 migration were driven by economic concerns, though not always connected with international trade.[71] After the transatlantic telegraph started working (c.1858), it was possible for European workers in Africa and the Americas to remit money home.[72] To some extent at least, trade, by encouraging migration, stimulated factor income flows. Studies on the New World export economies suggest a link between export of goods, investment boom, migration of labour in new fields where investment took place, government expansion by borrowing abroad, migration of labour and export of capital, though the interpretation of the causal chain between these variables remains open.[73]

What can we conclude from this discussion on the effects of trade upon the colonized world? The generalization that trade-induced poverty is hard to sustain. A cautious generalization could be that port cities gained from trade in commodities and services irrespective of where they were located. Philip Curtin's work on trade diaspora made global historians familiar with the idea that a string of cosmopolitan coastal settlements played a pivotal role in trade before modern transportation and communication technologies forged a closer link between the ports and their hinterland. Abu-Lughod's phrase 'archipelago of ports' has a similar connotation.[74] Strikingly, maritime trade and port cities retained this role in organizing world trade long after the advent of industrialization. Bayly shows in *The Birth of the Modern World* that most of the world's cities in the nineteenth century were trading cities rather than industrial ones.[75] Located in very different world regions, they collectively represented a convergence in institutions, living standards, political and cultural discourses, and bourgeois interest.

The convergence, wrought by the connections that trade created, in many cases included a late industrialization element. In this way, Bombay, Calcutta, Shanghai, Singapore and São Paulo formed part of a convergent club of cities that also included New York and Liverpool. This is not to dispute that on an international scale inequality increased, but the roots of that inequality need to be searched in production conditions and resource endowments, rather than trading conditions.

Conclusion

This chapter considers some of the main ways trade shaped a new world economy. Specialization, market integration, growth of companies, expansion in financial services, industrialization, and migration of labour and capital were some of the ways trade could have such an effect. The institutional effects, on commercial law or evolution of the company, for example, did not just follow from market integration but also from the particular legacies of early modern trade, such as the presence of the East India companies in those parts of Asia and Africa where family firms ruled the world of trade.

Economic historians will continue to explore whether international economic inequality, the distance between rich and poor countries, also increased because of trade. While that debate remains unfinished, it is necessary to point out that whether in a richer country or in a poorer one, the cities engaged in international trade were often distinct from the rest of the country as the ones with more firms, more services and more capitalists committed to keep the system going. Equally, there were cities and regions that were 'left out' of the capital accumulation process that trade encouraged.

Liberal regimes of the nineteenth century were strongly connected to colonial power. Liberalism as an ideal did not live easily with lack of liberty and political choices in a wide area of the globe, but since the wealthy communities in these areas developed a stake in openness and globalization, support for an independence movement was initially limited. The situation changed in the interwar period. The First World War disrupted trade completely, and empowered the wealthy indigenous businesses in the colonies. The Great Depression induced indigenous capitalists to look inward and towards the home market. Some of them were now more willing to fund the independence movement. By the mid-twentieth century, the world economy that had started taking shape from the trade between Europe and the tropical regions from the 1600s had more or less ended.

Notes

1. P. D. Curtin (1984), *Cross Cultural Trade in World History*. Cambridge: Cambridge University Press, 251.

2. R. Cameron (1997), *A Concise Economic History of the World*, 3rd edn. Oxford: Oxford University Press, 296; V. Zamagni (2015), *Perché l'Europa ha cambiato il mondo: una storia economica*. Bologna: Il Mulino, 145.

3. M. D. Bordo (2002), 'Globalization in historical perspective', *Business Economics*, January, 22.

4. 'How has Covid affected global trade?', Bank of England, 23 July 2021, https://www.bankofengland.co.uk/bank-overground/2021/how-has-covid-affected-global-trade.

5. J. Abu-Lughod (1993), 'The world system of the 13th century', in M. Adas (ed.), *Islamic & European Expansion: The Forging of a Global Order*. Philadelphia, PA: Temple University

Press, 75–103; ibid. (1991), *Before European Hegemony: The World System A.D. 1250–1350*. New York: Oxford University Press.

6. D. Christian (2000), 'Silk roads or steppe roads? The silk roads in world history', *Journal of World History*, 11 (1), 1–26.

7. J. de Vries (2003), 'Long-distance trade between 1500 and 1750', in J. Mokyr (ed.), *The Oxford Encyclopedia of Economic History*. Oxford: Oxford University Press, 361.

8. R. Harris (2020), *Going the Distance: Eurasian Trade and the Rise of the Business Corporation 1400–1700*. Princeton, NJ: Princeton University Press.

9. R. C. Allen (2009), *The British Industrial Revolution in Global Perspective*. Cambridge: Cambridge University Press, 107.

10. J. de Vries (2003), 'Connecting Europe and Asia: A quantitative analysis of the Cape route trade, 1497–1795', in D. O. Flynn, A. Giráldez and R. von Glahn (eds), *Global Connections and Monetary History, 1470–1800*. Aldershot: Ashgate, 35–106.

11. The debate concerns whether the axis of world trade was located in Europe or Asia, especially China. For different positions and arguments in this debate, see A. Gunder Frank (1998), *ReOrient: Global Economy in the Asian Age*. Berkeley, CA: University of California Press, esp. ch. 2; P. Vries (2015), *State, Economy and the Great Divergence: Great Britain and China, 1680s–1850s*. London: Bloomsbury, 348–9.

12. de Vries, 'Connecting Europe and Asia'.

13. D. O. Flynn and A. Giráldez (1996), 'China and the Manila Galleons', in D. O. Flynn (ed.), *World Silver and Monetary History in the 16th and 17th Centuries*. Aldershot: Variorum; ibid. (1997) (eds), *Metals and Monies in an Emerging Global Economy*; ibid. (2002), 'Cycles of silver: Global economic unity through the mid-eighteenth century', *Journal of World History* 13 (1), 1–16.

14. See the chapters by Trevor Burnard and by Alejandra Irigoin in this volume.

15. For a general account of the Atlantic slave trade, see H. S. Klein (2010), *The Atlantic Slave Trade*, 2nd edn. Cambridge: Cambridge University Press. On the transition from slave trade to other types of trade in one large exporting region, see R. Law (2009), 'Introduction', in R. Law (ed.), *From Slave Trade to 'Legitimate' Commerce: The Commercial Transition in Nineteenth-Century West Africa*. Cambridge: Cambridge University Press, 1–31.

16. G. Riello (2022), 'Cotton textiles and the Industrial Revolution in a global context', *Past & Present*, 255, 87–139.

17. M. Berg (2004), 'In pursuit of luxury: Global history and British consumer goods in the eighteenth century', *Past & Present*, 182, 85–142.

18. J. Brewer (1989), *The Sinews of Power: War, Money and the English State, 1688–1783*. London: Unwin; C. Knick Harkey (2004), 'Trade: Discovery, mercantilism and technology', in R. Floud and P. Johnson (eds), *The Cambridge Economic History of Modern Britain*. Cambridge: Cambridge University Press, 188. On the role of duties, see W. Ashworth (2003), *Customs and Excise: Trade, Production and Consumption in England, 1640–1845*. Oxford: Oxford University Press; and W. Ashworth (2017), *The Industrial Revolution: The State, Knowledge and Global Trade*. London: Bloomsbury.

19. Vries, *State, Economy and the Great Divergence*, 339–41.

20. de Vries, 'Long-distance trade', 364. See also ibid. (2010), 'The limits of globalisation in the early modern world.' See also M. Berg, 'Consumption in eighteenth- and early nineteenth-century Britain', in Floud and Johnson (eds), *Cambridge Economic History*, 366–7;

Broadberry et al., *British Economic Growth*, 287; C. Knick Harley (2004), 'Trade: Discovery, mercantilism and technology', in R. Floud and P. Johnson (eds), *The Cambridge Economic History of Modern Britain*. Cambridge: Cambridge University Press, 176; K. Pomeranz (2000), *The Great Divergence: China, Europe and the Making of the Modern World Economy*. Princeton, NJ: Princeton University Press, esp. ch. 2.

21. Berg, 'Consumption', 365.

22. Harley, 'Trade', 191.

23. P. K. O'Brien (1997), 'Intercontinental trade and the development of the Third Word since the Industrial Revolution', *Journal of Word History*, 8 (1), 77.

24. Curtin, *Cross Cultural Trade*, 252. This is a factor recently underlined by Luigi Pascali who, however, argues that the adoption of steam shipping in particular helped market integration but that the process benefited a small number of Western countries. L. Pascali (2014), 'The wind of change: Maritime technology, trade and economic development', *Warwick Economics Research Papers Series* (TWERPS), no. 1049.

25. O'Brien, 'Intercontinental trade', 80 and 84.

26. Bairoch and R. Kozul-Wright (1996), 'Globalization myths: Some historical reflections on integration, industrialization and growth in the world economy', *UNCTAD Working Paper*, 113, 5. See also Bairoch (1993), *Economics and World History: Myths and Paradoxes*. New York: Harvester, 16–29.

27. The concept of 'non-competing' good is somewhat misleading as practically all goods are substitutable. In this case, we mean the production and trade of identical goods.

28. C. A. Bayly (2004), *The Birth of the Modern World*. London: Blackwells, 44–5. See also ibid. Bayly (2002), '"Archaic" and "modern" globalization in the Eurasian and African arena, *c.*1750–1850', in A. G. Hopkins (ed.), *Globalization in World History*. London: Pimlico, 47–73.

29. Curtin, *Cross Cultural Trade*, 252.

30. Cameron, *A Concise Economic History*, 308–9 and 311.

31. K. O'Rourke (2003), 'Long-distance trade between 1750 and 1914', in Mokyr (ed.), *The Oxford Encyclopedia of Economic History*, 367.

32. K. O'Rourke and J. G. Williamson (2002), 'After Columbus: Explaining Europe's overseas trade boom, 1500–1800', *Journal of Economic History*, 62 (2), 417–56; and ibid. (2002), 'When did globalisation begin?', *Journal of Economic History*, 62 (1), 23–50. See also ibid. (2000), *Globalization and History*, esp. chs 3–6.

33. This has been recently challenged by P. de Zwart (2016), *Globalization and the Colonial Origins of the Great Divergence*. Leiden: Brill.

34. O'Rourke and Williamson, 'After Columbus'.

35. On soft and hard globalization, see de Vries, 'The limits of globalisation'.

36. Bayly, *The Birth of the Modern World*, 52.

37. J. Mokyr (1977), 'Demand vs. supply in the Industrial Revolution', *Journal of Economic History*, 37 (4), 981–1008; D. N. McCloskey (1981), *Enterprise and Trade in Victorian Britain: Essays in Historical Economics*. London: Allen & Unwin, 139–54; D. N. McCloskey and R. Thomas (1981), 'Overseas trade and empire, 1700–1820', in R. Floud and D. N. McCloskey (eds), *The Economic History of Britain, 1700–Present*, vol. 1. Cambridge: Cambridge University Press, 87–102; N. F. R. Crafts (1985), *British Economic Growth during the Industrial Revolution*. Oxford: Clarendon.

38. P. Vries (2013), *Escaping Poverty: The Origins of Modern Economic Growth*. Vienna and Göttingen: Vienna University Press and Vandenhoeck & Ruprecht, 283.

39. G. Clark, K. O'Rourke and A. N. Taylor (2008), 'Made in America? The New World, the Old, and the Industrial Revolution', *American Economic Review*, 98 (2), 523 and 527. See also ibid. (2014), 'The growing dependence of Britain on trade during the Industrial Revolution', *Scandinavian Economic History Review*, 62 (2), 126.

40. Harley, 'Trade', 199. One of the critiques against the approach that minimize the contribution of trade to economic growth is that it is based on static approaches that do not take into consideration both capital accumulation and technological change. K. O'Rourke, L. Prados de la Escosura and G. Daudin (2010), 'Trade and empire', in S. Broadberry and K. O'Rourke (eds), *The Cambridge Economic History of Modern Europe*. Cambridge: Cambridge University Press, 110.

41. P. K. O'Brien and S. L. Engerman (1991), 'Exports and the growth of the British economy from the Glorious Revolution to the peace of Amiens', in B. R. Solow (ed.), *Slavery and the Rise of the Atlantic System*. Cambridge: Cambridge University Press, 177–209. See P. K. O'Brien (1982), 'European economic development'; and S. L. Engerman (1972), 'The slave trade and British capital formation in the eighteenth century: A comment on the Williams thesis', *Business History Review*, 46 (4), 430–43.

42. Harley, 'Trade', 190.

43. O'Rourke, Prados de la Escosura and Daudin, 'Trade and empire', 112.

44. Pomeranz, *Great Divergence*.

45. Vries, *Escaping Poverty*, 272.

46. Bairoch and Kozul-Wright, 'Globalization myths', 5.

47. Vries, *Escaping Poverty*, 272.

48. O'Brien, 'Intercontinental trade', 88–9.

49. Bairoch and Kozul-Wright, 'Globalization myths', 9.

50. N. Crafts (2004), 'Globalisation and economic growth: A historical perspective', *World Economy*, 27 (1), 50.

51. O'Brien, 'Intercontinental trade', 95.

52. J. Foreman-Peck (2003), 'Long-distance trade since 1914', in Mokyr (ed.), *The Oxford Encyclopedia of Economic History*, 374–5.

53. Discussed in M. Vaughan (2006), 'Africa and the birth of the modern world', *Transactions of the Royal Historical Society*, Sixth Series, 16, 143–62.

54. On the Dutch case, see J. I. Israel (1989), *Dutch Primacy in World Trade, 1585–1740*. Oxford: Clarendon Press.

55. R. Findlay and K. H. O'Rourke (2007), *Power and Plenty: Trade, War, and the World Economy in the Second Millennium*. Princeton, NJ and Oxford: Princeton University Press.

56. V. Lieberman (2008), 'Protected rimlands and exposed zones: Reconfiguring premodern Eurasia', *Comparative Studies in Society and History*, 50 (3), 692–723, cit. 720.

57. S. Hejeebu (2005), 'Contract enforcement in the English East India Company', *Journal of Economic History*, 6 (2), 496–523; A. M. Carlos and S. Nicholas (1990), 'Agency problems in early chartered companies: The case of the Hudson's Bay Company', *Journal of Economic History*, 50 (4), 853–75.

58. G. M. Anderson and R. D. Tollison (1982), 'Adam Smith's analysis of joint-stock companies', *Journal of Political Economy*, 90 (6), 1237–56. P. J. Cain and A. G. Hopkins (1987), 'Gentlemanly capitalism and British expansion overseas II: New imperialism, 1850–1945', *Economic History Review*, 40 (1), 1–26.

59. For a criticism of the view, see R. Hyam (2010), *Understanding the British Empire*. New York: Cambridge University Press.

60. K. J. Mitchener and M. Weidenmier (2008), 'Trade and empire', *Economic Journal*, 118 (533), 1805–34.

61. G. B. Magee (2007), 'The importance of being British? Imperial factors and the growth of British imports, 1870–1960', *Journal of Interdisciplinary History*, 37 (3), 341–69.

62. On British declinism in general, essays compiled in J.-Dormois and M. Dintenfass (eds) (1999), *British Industrial Decline*. London: Routledge, are useful.

63. A. Thompson and G. Magee (2003), 'A soft touch? British industry, empire markets, and the self-governing dominions, *c.*1870–1914', *Economic History Review*, 56 (3), 689–717. See also, ibid. (2010), *Empire and Globalisation: Networks of People, Goods and Capital in the British World, c. 1850–1914*. Cambridge: Cambridge University Press.

64. The Dutch disease syndrome, which occurs when a specific tradeable draws resources away, can frustrate prospects of industrialization and diversification of economic activity. Angus Deaton applies the concept to post-war African development, the principle of it could apply to some tropical colonial regions as well. A. Deaton (1999), 'Commodity prices and growth in Africa', *Journal of Economic Perspectives*, 13 (3), 23–40.

65. J. G. Williamson (2011), *Trade and Poverty: When the Third World Fell Behind*. Cambridge MA and London: The MIT Press. See also Tirthankar Roy (1999), *Traditional Industry in the Economy of Colonial India*. Cambridge: Cambridge University Press.

66. T. Roy (2020), *The Crafts and Capitalism: Handloom Weaving Industry in Colonial India*. New Delhi and London: Routledge.

67. N. H. Leff (1973), 'Tropical trade and development in the nineteenth century: The Brazilian experience', *Journal of Political Economy*, 81 (3), 678–96.

68. O. Gelderblom and J. Jonker (2004), 'Completing a financial revolution: The finance of the Dutch East India trade and the rise of the Amsterdam capital market, 1595–1612', *Journal of Economic History*, 64 (3), 641–72.

69. K. J. Mitchener and M. D. Weidenmier (2008), 'The Baring crisis and the great Latin American meltdown of the 1890s', *Journal of Economic History*, 68 (2), 462–500.

70. For example, K. Ward (2009), *Networks of Empire: Forced Migration in the Dutch East India Company*. New York: Cambridge University Press.

71. Sunil S. Amrith (2011), *Migration and Diaspora in Modern Asia*. New York: Cambridge University Press.

72. G. B. Magee and A. S. Thompson (2006), 'The global and local: Explaining migrant remittance flows in the English-speaking world, 1880–1914', *Journal of Economic History*, 66 (1), 177–202.

73. H. W. Richardson (1972), 'British emigration and overseas investment, 1870–1914', *Economic History Review*, 25 (1), 99–113; Leff, 'Tropical trade and development'.

74. Abu-Lughod, 'The world system in the thirteenth century'.

75. Bayly, *The Birth of the Modern World*.

CHAPTER 10
THE ENVIRONMENT AND THE WORLD ECONOMY SINCE 1500
John McNeill

The world economy and the global environment form the warp and weft of the fabric of history. Always and everywhere, the global environment has affected the world economy. Always and everywhere, the world economy has affected the global environment. Economy and environment have been tightly bound together, and have evolved together, often slowly but sometimes in leaps and bounds. This chapter will focus more on the leaps than on the pauses between them.

As a rule, the environment has shaped the economy by defining the limits of the possible. Climate, soils, vegetation, animals, diseases, waters and winds (and a few other components of the environment) have always shaped what human communities could produce, at what costs, and in what amounts. The environment never fully determined what or how much people might produce. Culture, choice, contingency and social circumstance (and a few other components of social systems) always played a role too. But environments did determine the limits of the possible. People might have chosen to raise camels in Iceland or build ships in the Sahara, but productivity would have been low due to environmental constraints.

As another rule, economic activity always altered the environment. Often those alterations were direct, as in the case of hunting or farming. Sometimes they were less direct, as in the case of trade. Trade, say of wine for wool, inspired one set of production decisions over all others, and thus shaped the regional environments where wine and wool were produced. In the contemporary world, some economic activities have only negligible environmental impacts – devising training plans for amateur triathletes, for example. Others have outsized impacts, magnified by powerful technologies unknown in prior times – squeezing oil out of Alberta's tar sands, for example. By and large, pre-modern economies were tied more visibly to the natural environment than modern ones. Modern economies, by and large, have had larger, less local and less consistent environmental consequences than did pre-modern ones.

This chapter takes up a small but consequential subset of the range of possible subjects involving the global environment and the world economy since 1500. First, the intercontinental exchanges of plants, animals and microbes following the discovery of oceanic sailing routes in the late fifteenth century. Second, the environmental implications of the creation and expansion of plantation economies, mainly in the American tropics after 1640. Third, the global environmental implications of industrialization. And fourth, the concept of the Anthropocene.

Global Economic History

Biological Exchanges, 1492–1800

Some fifty years ago, Alfred Crosby assembled the scattered stories of the transfers of crops, weeds, animals and microbes across the Atlantic between the Americas and (mainly) Europe into the concept of the Columbian Exchange. The concept deserves amplification, because, in his day, Crosby could not do full justice to the involvement of Africa and Asia in intercontinental biotic exchanges.[1] Moreover, lesser exchanges developed across the Pacific in the wake of Magellan (c.1480–1521), important especially for the Philippines and sometimes described as the Magellan Exchange.[2] Some scholars consider the post-Columbian epoch of biological exchange so fundamental as to merit its own term in the style of earth history's epochs: the Homogenocene.[3]

After 1450, mariners, most of them Atlantic Europeans, linked almost every nook and cranny of the humanly habitable earth into a biologically interactive web, beginning with the continental littorals. The world's seas no longer served to isolate different biogeographical regions. The world acquired more permeable biological borders, as plants, animals and microbes migrated wherever ecological conditions permitted their spread, although how soon and how thoroughly they did so normally depended on human factors such as transport technologies and skills, and patterns of trade, production and politics.[4]

Columbus inaugurated regular exchanges across the Atlantic in 1492. The most conspicuous result was that Amerindians acquired a host of devastating diseases hitherto unfamiliar to them. Those diseases included smallpox, measles, mumps, whooping cough and influenza, all acute viral infections which had already become widespread in the sprawling interactive zone of Eurasia and northern Africa. From Japan to Senegambia, these infections were usually endemic, childhood diseases (sometimes called 'crowd diseases' because they require large, interacting populations to stay in circulation). They contributed to high rates of infant mortality, but most adults were survivors, and either resistant or fully immune to most or all of these infections. In addition to the crowd diseases, the Columbian Exchange brought some lethal vector-borne African diseases to the Americas, such as yellow fever and falciparum malaria. In the Americas, all these were new diseases, so no Amerindians carried any acquired resistance. Thus these infections ravaged the American hemisphere between 1500 and 1650. Together with widespread violence, expropriation, slaving and famine – all of which likely intensified thanks to European colonial expansion in the Americas – these diseases lowered populations by 60 to 95 per cent in one of the two largest demographic disasters in world history, the other being the Black Death in the mid-fourteenth century.[5]

The sharp reduction in population in the Americas, over the period 1492–1650, carried both environmental and economic consequences on multiple scales. Within the Americas, it opened the way for the creation of new 'wilderness'. With far less farming, hunting and fire, wild plants and animal species recolonized formerly humanized landscapes. On the global scale, resurgent vegetation in the Americas took some carbon out of the atmosphere, weakening the greenhouse effect slightly. That may have added a chill to the Little Ice Age, a cooler interval in climate history, ca.1250–1850, when global average temperature dipped by about 1 degree Celsius below long-term averages.[6] In economic terms, the population catastrophe checked global GDP growth by shrinking the economy of the Americas for a century or two. It also paved the way for the formation of a plantation complex, as will be discussed below.

The Amerindians had little in the way of lethal infectious disease to export to Africa and Eurasia. When the first migrants arrived in North America some 15,000 years ago (or more), they passed through north-eastern Siberia and Alaska during an Ice Age. Brutal cold is not conducive to the survival of most pathogens.[7] Beyond that filtering effect, the first Americans had left Siberia when no animals but dogs had been domesticated, so that the human infections derived from viruses of cattle, camels, and pigs (e.g. smallpox, measles and influenza) had not yet emerged. Once arrived in the Americas, Amerindians did not domesticate any herd animals other than alpacas and llamas, which seem, by chance, not to have hosted pathogens that evolved into agents of human disease. For these reasons, as regards pathogens, the Columbian Exchange was extremely unequal: the Americas received a lot and gave only a little.[8]

The same was true of domesticated animals. The Americas had few domesticated animals, and those few (e.g. turkeys, llamas and alpacas) did not travel well. By contrast, Eurasian and African species flourished when transported to the Americas. Cattle, goats, sheep, pigs, donkeys and horses were the most important animal immigrants to the Americas. They provided Amerindians with new sources of animal protein, hides and wool. Horses and oxen offered an important source of traction, making ploughing feasible in the Americas for the first time, and improving transportation possibilities through wheeled vehicles and, together with donkeys (and mules) greater variety of pack animals. That extended the potential of commerce and specialization, inviting Smithian growth wherever human populations recovered.

Horses in North America upset the economic and political order. The Amerindians of the North American prairies acquired horses from Spanish Mexico in the seventeenth century, and some of them quickly mastered the equestrian arts. On horseback, they became far more adept as bison hunters, solving any subsistence problems as long as the bison lasted. Moreover, those with horses easily inflicted military defeat on those without, so by the mid-nineteenth century, peoples such as the Sioux and Comanche had built considerable 'empires' on the basis of mounted warfare.[9]

Equestrian Amerindians also used their military prowess to create sizable slave trades to New Spain (Mexico). Spanish imperial legislation from 1542 had banned the enslavement of Amerindians, but did not forbid the purchase of people already enslaved. This law had the unintended effect of outsourcing the business of capture of people for the Mexican market to the horse nomads of North America, who from 1680 until 1870 or so seized women and children from communities that lacked the military power to protect them. Thus the Columbian Exchange in animals affected the Americas in political as well as economic respects.

The Columbian Exchange was more even-handed in its economic impacts when it came to crops. The Eurasian staples of wheat, rye, barley and rice met welcoming niches in the Americas. Sometimes those niches had to be created through human (and animal) labour, as for example with rice. Some of the new crops could survive in cold and dry landscapes where indigenous crops fared poorly. Aside from grains, the Americas also acquired citrus fruits, bananas, grapes and figs from Eurasia, and millets, sorghum, yams, okra and watermelon from Africa. So the new food crops extended the possibilities of American agriculture and allowed a more varied diet. But they did not constitute a vast improvement, because the Americas already had maize and potatoes and plenty of fruits and vegetables.

Drug crops changed the Americas at least as profoundly as the new food crops. Sugar, both a mild drug and a food, became the mainstay of a plantation economy based on African slave labour. Coffee, originally from Ethiopia and Arabia, also became a plantation crop in the eighteenth century. Without these imported crops, the plantation complex of the Americas would have been much smaller (see later in this chapter and Trevor Burnard's chapter in this volume).

Maize and potatoes, together with cassava, tomatoes, cacao, peanuts, sweet potato, pumpkins, squashes, pineapples and tobacco formed the core contribution of the Americas to global agriculture. Some of these crops had revolutionary consequences in Africa and Eurasia. Potatoes, for example, nicely suited soil and climate conditions across Northern Europe from Ireland to Russia. In Europe, potatoes contributed to a surge of population growth in the eighteenth and nineteenth centuries, which helped supply the manpower for both overseas empires and the Industrial Revolution.[10] Potatoes stored well, especially in cold climates, and they provide excellent nutrition. In their native Andes, where production and storage had been raised to a high art, potatoes had helped fuel the expansion of the Inca Empire in the fifteenth century. A few centuries later they played a broadly similar role in Northern Europe.[11]

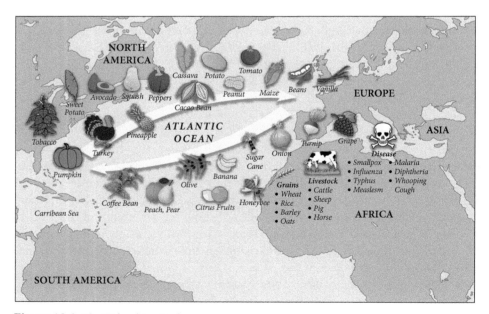

Figure 10.1 The Columbian Exchange.

Maize, another American crop, had a more diffuse impact than the potato. It did well in conditions as varied as those of Southern Europe, China and large swathes of Africa. Maize allowed new lands to be brought under cultivation, because it prospered where grains and tubers would not. It undergirded population growth and famine resistance in China and Southern Europe, but nowhere was it more influential than in Africa. In the two centuries after 1550, maize became a staple in Atlantic Africa, from Angola to Senegambia, and in parts of eastern Africa as well. Different varieties suited the several different rainfall regimes in Africa, and improved chances of surviving drought.

In addition, maize stores much better than millets, sorghums or tubers. It thus allowed chiefs and kings to enhance their power by centralizing the storage and distribution of food. In the West African forest zone, maize encouraged the formation of larger states. The Asante kingdom embarked on a programme of expansion after the 1670s, spearheaded by armies which carried dried maize with them on distant campaigns. Maize also served well as a portable food for merchant caravans, which contributed to commercialization in Atlantic Africa, including the slave trade. The slave trade could more easily reach far inland if merchants, and their human property, had an easily portable food supply. Storehouses of maize also made it more practical to imprison large numbers of slaves in the infamous barracoons of the West African coast. By the late eighteenth century, maize-fed caravans also extended the domain of slave-raiding in East Africa. Just as sugar and coffee heightened the demand in the Americas for slave imports, so too maize within Africa increased the practicality of slave exports.[12]

Cassava, also known as manioc, was the Americas' other great contribution to African agriculture. A native of Brazil, cassava is admirably suited to drought and poor soils and resistant to many crop pests. Like maize it provided a portable food that underlay state formation and expansion in West Africa and Angola. Cassava, like potatoes, need not be harvested at a particular season but may be left in the ground for weeks or more. So it is an ideal crop for people who might need to run away for their own safety – for example, people routinely subject to slave-raiding. In this respect it served as a counterpoint to maize: it helped peasantries to flee and survive slave-raids, while maize helped slavers to conduct and extend their business.[13] Together, maize and cassava gave Africa a much larger stock of portable and storable food, making the continent more like the rice lands of Asia and grain lands of western Eurasia, more likely to sustain long-distance trade and larger state structures. Africanists do not adopt this nomenclature, but they might well speak of pre-Columbian and post-Columbian African history.

The Columbian Exchange was the largest, fastest and most important intercontinental biological transfer in world history, but it was not the only one. A modest trans-Pacific exchange resulted from Magellan's voyages (1519–22), at first affecting chiefly the Philippines. It intensified in the wake of Captain Cook's meanderings throughout the world's largest ocean in the late eighteenth century. The Pacific Islands, rather than the ocean's rim, felt the greatest effects. As in the Americas (or in Australia after 1788), the most striking result was sharp depopulation in the wake of repeated epidemics.

Many American food crops became important in East Asia, such as sweet potatoes, maize and peanuts in south China, but they probably arrived not across the Pacific in the wake of Magellan, but across the Atlantic and the Indian Oceans via Portuguese and Dutch traders.[14]

Taken together, the whirlwind of intercontinental biological exchange in the centuries between 1500 and 1800 brought astounding changes around the world. It led to demographic catastrophes in lands unfamiliar with the crowd diseases. It improved the quantity and reliability of food supplies almost everywhere. In cases where horses were new, it reshuffled political relations by providing a new basis for warfare.

All these early modern exchanges carried historical consequences. European imperialism, in the Americas, Australia and New Zealand, simultaneously promoted and was promoted by the spread of Eurasian and African animals, plants and diseases. Europeans brought a biota that unconsciously worked as a team to favour the spread of European settlers, European power and Eurasian species, and thereby helped to create what Alfred Crosby called neo-Europes – including Australia, New Zealand, most of North America, southern Brazil, Uruguay and Argentina.[15]

Beyond the neo-Europes, something of a neo-Africa emerged in the Americas. More than 10 million Africans arrived in the Americas in slave ships between 1550 and 1860. Slave ships also brought West African rice, which became not only the foundation of the coastal economy in South Carolina and Georgia in the eighteenth century, but important in Surinam as well. Other African crops came too: okra, sesame and (although not in slave ships) coffee. All this combined to create a world where indigenous culture, including foodstuffs, was partially absorbed into a neo-African matrix. In this it resembled the neo-Europes. But at the same time neo-Africa was profoundly different from the neo-Europes: until the Haitian Revolution (1791–1804), nowhere in the Americas outside maroon communities were Africans and people of African descent politically, economically or socially dominant, whereas Europeans and their descendants soon dominated all the neo-Europes.

As the Columbian Exchange indicates, sailing ships brought the continents together as never before. But they did not prove hospitable conveyances to every form of life. They filtered out a few species that could not survive a long journey. The age of steam, and then of air travel, broke down remaining barriers to biological exchange, accelerating the dispersal of old and new migratory species alike. Although its greatest impacts came in the sixteenth and seventeenth centuries, in a sense the Columbian Exchange never ended. American raccoons, grey squirrels and muskrats for example colonized parts of Europe in the nineteenth and twentieth centuries. Nor did the Magellan Exchange come to an end. If anything, it sped up in the nineteenth and twentieth centuries, not least because of deliberate introductions of species such as the kiwi fruit (from China to New Zealand to Chile and California, and Southern Europe) and eucalyptus trees (from Australia to almost everywhere). But the economically (and demographically) transformative impacts of biological globalization came mainly between 1500 and 1800.

The Plantation Regime in the Americas, 1550–1850

The plantation system of the Americas, transplanted from Mediterranean and Atlantic islands in the early sixteenth century, occupied a huge zone of Atlantic America, from north-eastern Brazil to Chesapeake Bay, in which the slave plantation was the primary mode of production. The ecological significance of the plantation system had several aspects.

The first point is the simplest one, one which historians and geographers have been making for thirty years now, which is that every plantation, whether of tobacco, cotton, rice, sugar or coffee, typically required the clearing of forests to make room for crops. Beginning in the 1550s, a surge of deforestation swept over the coastlands of north-eastern Brazil and then from the 1620s the smaller islands of the eastern Caribbean. The surge reached the larger Caribbean islands by the 1690s and climaxed in Cuba in the nineteenth century. The same process was under way on a very considerable scale in the American South, c.1690–1860, where tobacco and cotton plantations likewise required the clearing of forests.[16]

One entirely inadvertent consequence of this land cover change in the Caribbean was improved breeding and survival conditions for two kinds of mosquitoes, the vectors of malaria and yellow fever. With respect to *Anopheles* mosquitoes, the vectors of malaria, deforestation in those Caribbean islands with mountains and hills increased run-off, floods, siltation and deposition in the lowlands, which in turn created more marshland, swamps and wetlands around the coasts of the islands. Montserrat and Martinique, just to give two examples, became the perfect breeding grounds for *Anopheles* mosquitoes, which thrive in swampy terrain.

The *Aedes aegypti* mosquito, the vector for yellow fever, is particularly connected to the sugar plantation, rather than to plantations in general. *A. aegypti* is a rather peculiar mosquito; it has a strong preference for laying eggs in artificial water containers, for example, buckets, pots and wells. It is therefore effectively a domesticated mosquito which thrives on its association with human beings – it almost never lays eggs in puddles, ponds or ditches, as most mosquitoes do. This is the reason for its link to sugar plantations, because every sugar plantation had a great number of pots but they were in use only during the initial sugar refining phase. A large plantation might have had ten thousand or more pots, which for most of the year sat unused, some broken, many collecting rainwater, thereby providing the ideal conditions for *A. aegypti* to reproduce.

Plantations fed as well as bred mosquitoes. All mosquitoes like sweet liquids, which provide them with much of their energy, and female mosquitoes also require blood meals in order to make eggs. Individual mosquitoes can survive on cane juice. So a sugar plantation was a veritable smorgasbord for *A. aegypti* – all of the sweet liquid they could possibly want was within reach, as were the blood meals needed for their reproduction, due to the accessibility of human and livestock populations. The conditions for the survival and expansion of *A. aegypti* mosquito populations were rapidly improved by the installation of plantations, specifically sugar cane plantations, in the Caribbean and Brazil.[17]

The plantation system also had far-reaching consequences as far as soils were concerned. In the wake of the Columbian Exchange, the indigenous populations of the Americas – not just Atlantic America, but across continental North and South America – declined by 60 per cent to 95 per cent in most areas. This human calamity permitted forest growth and regrowth. In almost all cases, the indigenous populations of the Americas had regularly used forests and forest soils, which entailed widespread forest burning, either for agricultural clearance or else to favour the proliferation of the grazing animals which they hunted. Following the population decline, forests in the Americas grew bigger and taller than they had been for a very long time.

Big trees held mother lodes of soil nutrients. Visitors to the Atlantic American coastal regions mistook what they saw for ancient, primeval forests, but in fact the forests were usually only a century or two old, even when they included towering specimens such as the American chestnut (*Castanea dentata*) or the Venezuelan giant *Gyranthera caribensis* (one of which attained 17 metres in circumference and 63 metres in height). The tissues of these trees contained cornucopian concentrations of potential soil nutrients. In effect, the trees had been drawing up nutrients from the soil and subsoil for 100 or 200 years, largely from depths which crop roots simply could not reach. They were the functional equivalent of the water towers which are such a familiar sight in North America, pumping up ground water from the depths and storing it for later distribution.

The success of plantation agriculture in some measure depended upon the nutrients locked in these mammoth and majestic trees. Felling and burning tall forests, the chief occupation of most male slaves early in the life of every plantation, unlocked stores of nitrogen, phosphorus, potassium and a dozen other nutrients. Char and ash, mixed into topsoil, ensured the prospering of tobacco, cotton and sugar for several years. Soon, however, the nutrient bonus was gone, carried off across the sea in tobacco leaf or raw cotton – or carried to the sea via soil erosion. Planters had to move their operations at certain intervals – after twenty, then ten or even five years – as the key nutrients that limit plant growth became ever scarcer. Evidence of this enforced mobility can be found on a small scale on individual plantations, in the way in which landowners deforested and burned over new patches of land within their holdings and planted tobacco, cotton or sugar in them. It can also be seen on a large scale, in the migration of the centre of the plantation economy from the small islands of the eastern Caribbean to the bigger islands of the western Caribbean, including Jamaica, Hispaniola and Cuba. The same pattern prevailed in the American South, where the cotton plantation regime migrated from the eastern seaboard of Georgia, the Carolinas and the Chesapeake westward into Alabama, Mississippi, Louisiana and East Texas.[18] Similarly, tobacco planters moved from the Chesapeake area to the piedmont region of North Carolina, and even further west into Kentucky and Tennessee. Plantations were a form of shifting agriculture on a macro scale. In many environments, soils quickly became too poor to ensure profitability once the subsidy of nutrients in forest ash wore thin. Plantation agriculture as practised in the Atlantic Americas was decidedly unsustainable due its demands on soils. By the time of the abolition of slavery in the Americas (1791–1888), the prospects for continued profitability of plantation agriculture in Atlantic America were growing poor, as the one-off gift from the post-Columbian nutrient towers had vanished.

The plantation economy of the Americas, one of the characteristic business innovations of the early modern centuries, exemplifies the connections between ecology and economy. Its existence rested on the ecological reshuffling of the Columbian Exchange. The important plantation crops all came from Eurasia or Africa. Plantation labour came mainly from Africa. The plantation economy's efflorescence over two centuries (c.1650–1850) led to sharp ecological changes in Atlantic America, notably deforestation, the entrenchment of mosquito-borne diseases, and the drawdown of soil nutrients. In short, the plantation economy of the Americas was born of unique and fragile ecological circumstances and its prosperity undermined those circumstances. It was a model unsustainable economy.

The Industrial Revolution as Global Ecological Change

Conventional conceptions of the Industrial Revolution consider it an English event with profound social and economic ramifications. That it was. But it was also a global event with profound ecological ramifications. From Spain to South Africa, from Argentina to Australia, lands and ecologies far from Lancashire or Tyneside took part in the Industrial Revolution.

The vast and ever-growing use of fossil fuels during the first century or so of industrialization began a permanent revolution in global environmental history. Cheap and abundant energy has probably done more to shape the human–environment relationship than anything else in the past two centuries.[19] Coal mining, oil and gas drilling, energy transport and fossil fuel combustion help explain much of the ecological tumult since about 1850, especially in the realms of air, water and soil pollution. But the environmental meaning of cheap and abundant energy extends well beyond the obvious to include countless 'ecological teleconnections', some of them of considerable magnitude on local and regional scales.

The phrase 'ecological teleconnections' refers to linkages that involve places far apart and carry significant environmental consequences.[20] An example, alluded to above, is the replacement of (mainly) forest land in Alabama, Mississippi, Louisiana and East Texas by cotton plantations from 1825 to 1860, driven (mainly) by the mounting demand for raw cotton in Britain. The plantation system, slavery included, colonized the warm and humid lowlands from Georgia to Texas. Tens of thousands of farmers and slaves migrated into these lands from further east. Upon settling down, their first object was to clear the existing vegetation. They slashed and burned their way through millions of hectares, and then planted maize and cotton. They arranged both crops in rows for convenience in planting and harvesting, inadvertently maximizing the susceptibility of their soils to erosion in the downpours characteristic of the humid South. One northern traveller passing through cotton country in the early 1830s noted the rapid erosion of topsoil: 'Every plough furrow becomes the bed of a rivulet after heavy rains – these uniting are increased into torrents before which the impalpable soil dissolves like ice under a summer's sun.'[21] A survey of the cotton South at the end of the nineteenth century found 'a miserable panorama of … rain-gullied fields … dirt, poverty, disease, drudgery, and monotony that stretches for a thousand miles across the cotton belt'.[22] The Industrial Revolution's demand for long-staple cotton had transformed the landscape of the American South: an ecological teleconnection.

By 1840, growing demand for cotton had begun to inspire environmental transformations elsewhere besides the American South. These transformations accelerated suddenly when the American Civil War (1861–5) and the Union blockade of the Confederacy cut North American cotton exports to a trickle. Efforts to ramp up cotton production took place in Central Asia, Tahiti, India, Anatolia and Egypt among other lands. In Egypt, cotton's growth season did not fit the natural rhythm of the Nile flood (unlike wheat, the staple crop for forty-five centuries along the Nile). So Egyptian rulers, beginning with Muhammad Ali (r. 1805–49), undertook to impound some of the flood in order to release it when cotton in the delta needed water, and to shield the crop from potential damage from unseasonable high water. Thus mechanized cotton mills in Britain inaugurated the large-scale re-plumbing of Egypt that culminated in the Aswan High Dam in the 1970s.[23]

Cotton was not the only cloth whose manufacture led to conspicuous landscape change; silk did as well. In Lebanon, for example, peasant families boiled silk cocoons to disentangle the threads. The process required fuelwood, which in the early nineteenth century was still available on the slopes of Mount Lebanon. When the power looms of Lyon, Milan and other silk-manufacturing centres geared up in the 1840s, silk cloth became cheap enough for middle-class consumers, no longer merely the raiment of the elites. Lebanese mountain families began a bonanza of silk cultivation that lasted several decades, putting mounting pressure on the fuelwood supply of Mount Lebanon. The near eradication of the famous cedars of Lebanon is often laid at the door of the Ottoman Turks and the Hejaz railway built at the end of the nineteenth century. However, the odds are that the greater part of that spurt of deforestation resulted from the efforts of rural Lebanese to take advantage of the strong market for raw silk that mechanization and cheap energy in France and Italy created: another ecological teleconnection.[24]

Cloth was only part of the story. Gutta-percha was another. The world's telegraph system took shape from the late 1840s. Outdoor wiring required insulation against the elements, a job for which tarred cotton was used at first. But engineers – notably Werner von Siemens – soon found that gutta-percha served admirably as wire insulation, suitable even for duty on the seafloor where other materials, such as rubber, suffered from salt corrosion. The first undersea cable insulated with gutta-percha made its debut at Folkestone (UK) in 1849. Between 1859 and 1900, special purpose-built ships laid about 200,000 miles of undersea telegraph cable, all of it insulated with gutta-percha.

Gutta-percha is a resinous gum found only in about eight species of trees, especially one called *Isonandra*, all of which grow exclusively in Southeast Asia. Extraction of the latex involved Dayak, Chinese or Malay men finding and felling suitable trees, and collecting their latex in bowls. Once dried, that latex would be gathered in the ports of Southeast Asia. Raw gutta-percha was shipped from Singapore, Saigon or Batavia to London's East End or smaller centres of gutta-percha works, where it was heated, cleaned (of mud, etc.), cooled and applied to copper cables destined for decades of service as telegraph wire at the bottom of the sea.

A big *Isonandra* tree might yield a little more than a kilogram of gutta-percha; a typical one yielded about 300 grams. A transatlantic cable required about 250 tonnes of gutta-percha. The 200,000 miles of undersea cable in place by 1900 needed about 27,000 tonnes, or about 80 to 100 million trees' worth of gutta-percha. In 1898–9, when two trans-Pacific cables were laid, 15–20 million trees were cut to supply the needed gutta-percha. Several observers noted the unsustainable character of gutta-percha exploitation. But cutting proceeded apace, to the point where the wild tree neared extinction in the accessible landscapes of Southeast Asia. Efforts at plantations of *Isonandra* and other gutta-percha trees began, unfruitfully, in the 1880s. By 1900, however, fairly successful plantations existed. Eventually, wireless telegraphy and radio (1920s) would reduce the demand for undersea cables and gutta-percha, making moot the ecological sustainability or unsustainability of gutta-percha exploitation. But in the meantime, between 1860 and 1900, an ecological teleconnection inaugurated by the desire to send information via electrons through copper wire had brought a rain forest species to the brink of extinction and made a significant dent in the forest cover of Southeast Asia.[25]

It is possible to tell other stories of ecological teleconnections created by the Industrial Revolution and cheap energy. I will quickly sketch some, beginning with two about leather. The slaughter of 20–40 million bison on the great plains of North America between 1865 and 1881 is the largest and fastest anthropogenic reduction in wildlife biomass in history. It had several motives, but prominent among them was the demand for bison hide as leather belting in the textile mills of New England (and to a small extent in Britain). Bison leather helped to make cotton cloth. As a result, by 1882, the US bison herd amounted to about 1,000 animals, a close brush with extinction.

Tanning leather made it more flexible, suitable for fine shoes, belts, purses and so forth. Until the invention of chemical substitutes, tanning required tannin. Suitable tannins came from a number of plants, but after 1867 among the best came from trees in South America colloquially called quebracho (*Schinopsis lorentzii*). Their heartwood, if chipped and boiled, yielded an exquisite tannin. Found in northern Argentina, southern Bolivia and Paraguay, quebracho provided tannin to British, German and American tanneries at the end of the nineteenth century, until the tree became too rare to reward the effort. As bison leather helped to make cotton cloth, quebracho trees helped to make consumer leather.[26]

Copper, tin, lead and iron were core ingredients of the Industrial Revolution. Some of these ores lay underground not far from industrial zones, for example, Cornish tin. But most came from faraway places such as Chile, Montana, Malaya, Andalusia or Australia. As metallurgical industries went from strength to strength in the nineteenth and early twentieth centuries, miners hacked out more and more ore, most of which required fuel-intensive smelting or processing. Everywhere this brought a cascade of environmental consequences – more ecological teleconnections. The province of Almería, in southern Spain, provides a fine example. It was the most active lead-mining zone in the world, 1830–60, and its best customer was Britain. But lack of fuel for on-site smelting hampered the business. Bare mountains eroded quickly, filling rivers with enough silt to change the Spanish coastline.[27]

Machines of all sorts required lubricants to work properly and enduringly. Before petroleum derivatives became practical, several sorts of vegetable oils served as lubricants, not least palm oil. Palm oil came at first from the Niger Delta but in the early twentieth century became a plantation crop throughout West Africa and Southeast Asia. Peanut oil, mainly from Senegambia, also lubricated the Industrial Revolution. Whale oil was another important lubricant in the nineteenth century, as well as an illuminant. The quest for whale oil lay behind a determined assault on the right and sperm whales worldwide, led by Anglo-American whalers. Ecological teleconnections extended to the seven seas as well as to every inhabited continent.[28]

The first century of the Industrial Revolution helped to inspire changes in vegetation all around the world. Charcoal stratigraphical analysis shows that global biomass burning declined for seventeen centuries before 1750. It then spiked until 1870 or so, before again declining for several decades.[29] This spike probably represents frontier agricultural expansion in Russia, north China, North and South America and elsewhere, places where pioneers torched vegetation in order to plant food crops – abetted in their pioneer pursuits by the waning of the Little Ice Age after about 1820. But it also represents the work of people firing woodlands in order to try to make a living providing fibres such as wool and cotton for the mills of Lancashire and New England, and the work of others cutting and burning forests for rubber or palm oil plantations. The ecological teleconnections of the Industrial Revolution helped to shape the vegetation cover of every inhabited continent.

Britain, of course, was only the first nation to experience industrialization and to scour the world for industrial ingredients. Parallel processes appeared almost simultaneously in Northwestern Europe, eastern North America, and later in Japan and Russia. All these industrial revolutions needed fibres, ores and lubricants. Some of these ingredients came from close by. But many, perhaps most, as in the case of Britain, came from afar (even if in the case of Russia, materials came from within the Russian Empire). These later industrial revolutions also provoked ecological teleconnections, contributing to the environmental tumult of modern times.

The pell-mell industrialization of China since 1980, the fastest and largest-scale such process in world history, has crafted its own environmentally consequential teleconnections, from the iron mines of Western Australia to the soybean plantations in Goias (Brazil), to the copper belt of Zambia. This latest incarnation of the general phenomenon of ecological teleconnections, like its predecessors, is predicated on fossil fuel energy, without which China would remain the poor peasant country it was in 1950.[30]

The Anthropocene

Since 1750, global population has grown about tenfold, energy use has increased roughly a hundredfold, and the size of the world economy, if we can trust the figures assembled by Brad Delong or Angus Maddison, increased by well more than a hundredfold.[31] The scale of these changes is so great, and their consequences so profound, that it may be time to reconceptualize the material relationships between economy and environment, between humankind and planet earth, and between modern history and deep history.

The term 'Anthropocene' now increasingly serves as a shorthand way to recognize the great power that humankind now exerts – clumsily – over some of the earth's basic biogeochemical systems, over life on earth, and upon the face of the earth itself. Several chemical compounds and elements, including water, nitrogen, phosphorus, sulphur and carbon, are constantly moving around our planet, cycling among living things, the earth's rock and sediments, the oceans and the atmosphere – these are the major biogeochemical cycles. They did this planetary cycling before humans existed and they will likely do so after humans no longer exist. But for a few thousand years (just how many is a subject of debate), humans have affected those cycles. And in the last few decades, human actions have radically altered some of them (on this, there is no debate). The crux of the original Anthropocene concept is that the earth had entered upon a new interval in its history in which human actions have overshadowed the quiet persistence of microbes and the endless orbital wobbles and eccentricities, and therefore defined a new interval of geological time. That new interval follows the Holocene epoch, which began 11,700 years ago.

Meanwhile, in addition to monkeying with biogeochemical cycles, humankind has also inaugurated what appears to be the sixth mass extinction in the 4-billion-year history of life on earth. This we achieve mainly by converting habitats, in which millions of species have learned to live over millions of years, into fields and pastures that help feed us.[32] And humankind has been clawing, scratching and scraping rock and soil to such an extent that we are now, by some measures, the most active geological agent on our planet, outstripping the earth-moving work of glaciers and rivers. We have even created new 'rocks' that will survive for millions of years in the earth's crust, including half a trillion tonnes – and more each year – of concrete.[33]

To put the matter differently, in recent decades, human action has nudged the earth into a state it has never been in during the Holocene. Greenhouse gas concentrations, the acidity of the oceans and the proportion of biomass put to human use are all now outside the previous ranges of variation in the Holocene. The nitrogen and sulphur cycles are notably different from any prior incarnations at any time in the history of the earth. Global average temperatures and the share of the earth's surface covered by ice will, in all probability, soon be outside the Holocene envelope as well. It is recognition of this torrent of anthropogenic environmental change that has inspired some geoscientists to claim that the Holocene is over, to recommend formally adding the Anthropocene to the official roster of epochs and eras in earth's history. Just when the Anthropocene began (presuming it exists) is up in the air. The most common view is that the Anthropocene commenced only with the advent of sustained fossil fuel use and is only as old as coal-fired industrialization. Coal use on a global scale remained negligible until a transient process of industrialization took place in north China. Under the Song dynasty (960–1279), coal became an important fuel in a steel-and-iron complex that flourished for a century or more after 1020. Greenland's ice cap contains the wind-blown sulphurous residue of Song-era smelting. After the Song's metallurgical boom withered, coal slipped into obscurity as regards economic and environmental history. It returned to the edge of the stage when it became a routine heating fuel in London in the sixteenth century. But the real departure came with increasingly effective steam engines, developed over the course of the eighteenth and nineteenth centuries. Steam engines could convert the chemical energy of coal first into heat energy and then – this was the revolutionary part – into kinetic energy, useful for making things and going places. As a result of the new uses for coal, British coal consumption more than doubled from 1750 to 1800, and then quintupled from 1800 to 1850 and peaked in 1913.[34]

In the Anthropocene debates, coal is important mainly because when it burns it releases carbon dioxide to the atmosphere. By virtue of its abundance, carbon dioxide is the most important, although not the most powerful, of the greenhouse gases. It helps regulate the temperature of the earth's surface and lower atmosphere – where we live – and the oceans too. For the last 800,000 years – until very recently when fossil fuels entered the picture – carbon dioxide accounted for between 175 and 285 parts per million (ppm) of the atmosphere. At the very end of the eighteenth century, that proportion, as recorded in air bubbles trapped in polar ice, began to climb slowly. That appears as the beginning of the secular trend that continues to this day, and has brought those concentrations from about 260–280 ppm, their range for the last 11,000 years, to a little more than 420 ppm today. This is the quickest rise in the past 800,000 years. It is probably the fastest in the entire history of the atmosphere.

An alternative view that is gaining adherence holds that the better choice is a later Anthropocene, beginning about 1950. The subsequent decades brought tremendous surges in fossil fuel energy use, population growth, urbanization, tropical deforestation, carbon dioxide emissions, sulphur dioxide emissions, stratospheric ozone depletion, freshwater use, dam-building, irrigation, river regulation, wetlands drainage, aquifer depletion, fertilizer use, toxic chemical releases, species extinctions, fish landings, ocean acidification and much else besides.[35]

There is, perhaps, a way to reconcile the arguments for an eighteenth-century Anthropocene and a mid-twentieth-century one. It rests upon the concept of the Great Acceleration. In effect, the Anthropocene has stages. It may have roots reaching back to, and even before, 1800, but the scale, scope and pace of anthropogenic environmental change all grew enormously from the mid-twentieth century. To offer just a few examples, primary energy use has quintupled since 1950, the number of large dams (15 metres high or taller) has sextupled, the methane concentration in the atmosphere has nearly doubled, the quantity of nitrogen flowing into coastal waters has quintupled, and marine fish harvests sextupled (and then fell off a bit after the 1990s). That hectic post-1945 period is the Great Acceleration, and, depending on one's view, lies within a longer

Anthropocene or is coincident with the Anthropocene.[36] Ultimately, the distinction between an Anthropocene originating in the late eighteenth century and including within it the Great Acceleration and an Anthropocene beginning in the mid-twentieth century is a small one, a matter of definition of terms, although fiercely fought over at the moment.[37]

Confining ourselves to planet earth may prove too narrow a view of the Anthropocene. Since 1957, earthlings have launched a few thousand rockets into nearby precincts in space. The rockets have left landing pads on Mars, Venus and the moon. Humans have put thousands of satellites into orbit. Millions of pieces of 'space junk' now career around the earth's general neighbourhood, ranging in size from paint flakes to rocket boosters. Two cameras, a glove, a toothbrush and countless bits of metal, mainly aluminium, are zooming above earth in low orbit, and will do so at least for centuries to come. In all, about 9,000 tonnes of space junk are in earth's orbit, equivalent to a fleet of 4,500 cars parked overhead. In any case, the Space Age on our planet is also an age of anthropogenic environmental change in our solar system, and the Anthropocene concept might deservedly apply beyond the earth itself.[38]

Conclusion

The four tales I have narrated about biological exchange, American plantations, industrialization, and the Anthropocene will suffice to sustain the case that the bond between the world economy and global ecology is always present, yet never constant. The two have co-evolved, inciting one another to change shape or direction, to mutate or to grow. They always did and always will. But in the period since 1500, the bond has somehow changed. The situation is a bit like two children across from one another on a merry-go-round: if they step closer to each other, they make the merry-go-round spin faster. The scale and speed of environmental change has accelerated, and so has the pace of economic change. Both now proceed at rates unimaginable before 1500.

Whether such a pace can continue is uncertain and one of the great questions of our time. Perhaps, metaphorically speaking, the merry-go-round will spin out of control and we shall fly off. Perhaps we can carefully step further from the axis of rotation and slow to a safer speed, one we can sustain indefinitely without danger. Perhaps, somehow, we can loosen the bond between global ecology and the world economy, redesign the merry-go-round, so as to be able to enjoy the comforts of economic growth without the perils (or with reduced perils) of ecological convulsion. As usual, only time will tell.

Notes

1. A. Crosby (1972), *The Columbian Exchange*. Westport, CT: Greenwood Press; J. Carney and R. Rosomoff (2011), *In the Shadow of Slavery: Africa's Botanical Legacy in the Atlantic World*. Berkeley, CA: University of California Press.

2. Roughly 15–20 per cent of plant species in the Philippines today are of American origin. J. R. McNeill (1994), 'Of rats and men: A synoptic environmental history of the Island Pacific', *Journal of World History* 5 (2), 299–349.

3. M. Samways (1999), 'Translocating fauna to foreign lands: Here comes the Homogenocene', *Journal of Insect Conservation*, 3 (2), 65–6.

4. For details, see J. R. McNeill (2012), 'Biological exchange in global environmental history', in J. R. McNeill and E. S. Mauldin (eds), *A Companion to Global Environmental History*. Oxford: Wiley-Blackwell, 433–52.

5. M. Livi-Bacci (2008), *Conquest: The Destruction of the American Indios*. Cambridge and Malden: Polity. Other important overviews include S. A. Alchon (2003), *A Pest in the Land: New World Epidemics in a Global Perspective*. Albuquerque, NM: University of New Mexico Press; N. D. Cook (1998), *Born to Die: Disease and New World Conquest, 1492–1650*. New York: Cambridge University Press; ibid. (2010), *La Catástrofe Demográfica Andina: Perú 1520–1620*. Lima: Pontificia Universidad Católica del Perú.

6. This idea remains controversial. See Alberto Boretti (2020), 'The European colonization of the Americas as an explanation for the Little Ice Age', *Journal of Archaeological Science*, 29, https://doi.org/10.1016/j.jasrep.2019.102132; A. Koch, C. Brierley, M. M. Maslin and S. L. Lewis (2019), 'Earth system impacts of the European arrival and the Great Dying in the Americas after 1492', *Quaternary Science Reviews*, 207, 13–36, https://doi.org/10.1016; R. Dull, R. J. Nevle, W. I. Woods, D. K. Bird, S. Avnery and W. M. Denevan (2010), 'The Columbian encounter and the Little Ice Age: Abrupt land use change, fire, and greenhouse forcing', *Annals of the Association of American Geographers*, 100 (4), 755–71; S. Lewis and M. A. Maslin (2015), 'Defining the Anthropocene', *Nature*, 519, 171–80.

7. A. Drake and M. Oxenham (2013), 'Disease, climate, and the peopling of the Americas', *Historical Biology*, 25 (5), 565–97, are sceptical of the role of cold in shaping the slender disease burden of the pre-Columbian Americas.

8. The likeliest candidate for a significant disease of American origins is syphilis, but expert opinion remains divided. The debate as regards North America is presented in M. L. Powell and D. C. Cook (eds) (2005), *The Myth of Syphilis*. Gainesville, FL: University of Florida Press. See also K. Harper et al. (2011), 'The origin and antiquity of syphilis revisited: An appraisal of Old-World pre-Columbian evidence of treponemal infection', *American Journal of Physical Anthropology*, 146 (Supplement 53), 99–133; Karen Giffin et al. (2020), 'A treponemal genome from an historic plague victim supports a recent emergence of yaws and its presence in 15th-century Europe', *Nature: Scientific Reports*, https://doi.org/10.1038/s41598-020-66012-x.

9. P. Hämäläinen (2008), *The Comanche Empire*. New Haven, CT: Yale University Press. Whether or not the word 'empire' applies to these political formations is up for debate.

10. N. Nunn and N. Qian (2011), 'The potato's contribution to population and urbanization: Evidence from a historical experiment', *Quarterly Journal of Economics*, 126 (2), 593–650. The authors say potatoes accounted for 25 per cent of Europe's population growth, 1700–1900.

11. The potato's impact on Northern Europe's food supply required another biological migrant: clover. Clover, although not from the Americas, was essential to the impact of the Columbian Exchange in Europe. Clover hosts microorganisms that fix nitrogen from the air in the soil, putting it where plant roots can absorb it. Potatoes are especially nitrogen-hungry, and cannot yield well consistently without nitrogen supplements to the soil. Although as yet unsung by historians, clover can claim an impact on European history as great as that of the potato. T. Kjaergaard (2003), 'A plant that changed the world: The rise and fall of clover, 1000–2000', *Landscape Research*, 28 (1), 41–9.

12. On maize in Africa, see J. McCann (2005), *Maize and Grace: Africa's Encounter with a New World Crop, 1500–2000*. Cambridge, MA: Harvard University Press. On East Africa's slave trade: A. Sheriff (1987), *Slaves, Spices and Ivory in Zanzibar: Integration of an East African Commercial Empire into the World Economy, 1770–1873*. Athens, OH: Ohio University Press.

13. J. Miller (1988), *Way of Death: Merchant Capitalism and the Angolan Slave Trade, 1730–1830*. Madison, WI: University of Wisconsin Press, 19, 103, 193.

14. On the 'Magellan Exchange', see J. R. McNeill (1998), 'Islands in the Rim: Ecology and history in and around the Pacific, 1521–1996', in D. O. Flynn, L. Frost and A. J. H. Latham (eds), *Pacific Centuries: Pacific and Pacific Rim History since the Sixteenth Century*. London: Routledge, 70–84.

15. A. Crosby (1986), *Ecological Imperialism: The Biological Expansion of Europe, 900–1900*. New York: Cambridge University Press.

16. W. Dean (1994), *With Broadax and Firebrand: The Destruction of the Brazilian Atlantic Forest*. Berkeley, CA: University of California Press; D. Watts (1987), *The West Indies*. Cambridge: Cambridge University Press; R. Funes (2008), *From Rainforest to Canefield in Cuba: An Environmental History since 1492*. Chapel Hill, NC: University of North Carolina Press.

17. J. R. McNeill (2010), *Mosquito Empires*. New York: Cambridge University Press.

18. A. Rothman (2007), *Slave Country: American Expansion and the Origins of the Deep South*. Cambridge, MA: Harvard University Press.

19. On energy and the Industrial Revolution in England, see E. A. Wrigley (2010), *Energy and the English Industrial Revolution*. Cambridge: Cambridge University Press; R-P. Sieferle (2001), *The Subterranean Forest*. Winwick: White Horse Press.

20. 'Teleconnection' is a recognized term in the atmospheric sciences and climatology, used to describe linked events thousands of miles apart.

21. J. J. Ingraham (1835), *The South-west, by a Yankee*. New York: Harper, 86, quoted in W. Johnson (2013), *River of Dark Dreams: Slavery and Empire in the Cotton Kingdom*. Cambridge, MA: Harvard University Press, 155.

22. C. Johnson, E. Embree and W. W. Alexander (1935), *The Collapse of Cotton Tenancy: Summary of Field Studies and Statistical Surveys, 1933–1935*. Chapel Hill, NC: University of North Carolina Press, 14.

23. J. Waterbury (1979), *Hydropolitics of the Nile Valley*. Syracuse, NY: Syracuse University Press.

24. G. Pitts (2016), *Fallow Fields: Famine and the Making of Lebanon (1914–1952)*, PhD dissertation, Georgetown University, ch. 2; Giovanni Federico (1994), *Il filo d'oro: l'industria della seta dalla Restaurazione alla Grande Crisi*. Venice: Marsilio. The energy for the silk industry often came from water power.

25. J. Tully (2009), 'A Victorian ecological disaster: Imperialism, the telegraph, and gutta-percha', *Journal of World History*, 20 (4), 559–79; L. Potter (2005), 'Community and environment in colonial Borneo: Economic value, forest conversions and concern for conservation, 1870–1940', in R. Wadley (ed.), *Histories of the Borneo Environment: Economic, Political and Social Dimensions of Change and Community*. Leiden: Verhandelingen van Het Koninklijk Instituut voor Taal, Landen Volken-kunde, 116. The 1911 *Encyclopedia Britannica* entry on gutta-percha explains some of the refining processes, https://en.wikisource.org/wiki/1911_Encyclop%C3%A6dia_Britannica/Gutta_Percha.

26. A. G. Zarrilli (2008), 'El oro rojo: la industria del tanino en Argentina (1890–1950)', *Silva Lusitana*, 16 (2), 239–59.

27. For the case of lead in southern Spain, see A. Sánchez Picón (1983), *La Minería del Levante Almeriense, 1838–1930*. Almería: Cajal. See also J. R. McNeill and G. Vrtis (eds) (2017), *Mining North America: An Environmental History*. Berkeley, CA: University of California Press.

28. S. M. Martin (1988), *Palm Oil and Protest: An Economic History of the Ngwa Region, South-Eastern Nigeria*. Cambridge: Cambridge University Press, ch. 1; Jonathan Robins (2021), *Oil Palm: A Global History*. Chapel Hill, NC: University of North Carolina Press; J. N. Tønnessen and A. O. Johnsen (1982), *The History of Modern Whaling*. Berkeley, CA: University of California Press.

29. J. R. Marlon et al. (2008), 'Climate and human influences on global biomass burning over the past two millennia', *Nature Geoscience*, 1 (10), 697–702.

30. For a journalistic discussion of the Chinese case, see E. C. Economy and M. Levi (2014), *By All Means Necessary: How China's Resource Quest Is Changing the World*. New York: Oxford University Press.

31. J. B. Delong (2008), 'Estimates of world GDP', http://delong.typepad.com/print/20061012_ LRWGDP.pdf; Maddison's figures: The Maddison Project: https://www.rug.nl/ggdc/ historicaldevelopment/maddison/releases/maddison-project-database-2020. Delong estimates the world economy increased in size 320-fold between 1750 and 2008. Maddison's estimates do not take 1750 as a data point, but by inference it appears his estimate would be higher still.

32. By 'learned' I mean became adapted over many generations via evolution by natural selection. Only a very few species 'learn' anything in the human sense. For the ongoing extinction spasm, see Robert Cowie, Philippe Bouchet and Benoit Fonataine (2022), 'The Sixth Mass Extinction: Fact, fiction or speculation?' *Biological Reviews*, https://doi.org/10.1111/brv.12816; E. Kolbert (2014), *The Sixth Extinction: An Unnatural History*. New York: Macmillan; G. Ceballos et al. (2015), 'Accelerated modern human-induced species losses: Entering the sixth mass extinction', *Science Advances*, 1 (5), e1400253, https://doi.org/10.1126/sciadv.1400253.

33. See, for instance, Julia Adeney Thomas, Mark Williams and Jan Zalaciewicz (2020), *The Anthropocene: An Interdisciplinary Approach*. London: Polity; J. Syvitski et al. (2020), 'Extraordinary human energy consumption and resultant geological impacts beginning around 1950 CE initiated the proposed Anthropocene epoch', *Nature Communications: Earth & Environment*, 1, 1–13, https://doi.org/10.1038/s43247-020-00029-y; B. H. Wilkinson (2015), 'Humans as geologic agents: A deep-time perspective', *Geology*, 33 (3), 161–4.

34. Data on the quantitative history of coal in Britain are scattered throughout volumes 2 and 3 of (1983–87), *The History of the British Coal Industry*. Oxford: Oxford University Press, written by M. Flinn and R. Church, respectively.

35. A detailed argument to this effect appears in J. R. McNeill and P. Engelke (2016), *The Great Acceleration*. Cambridge, MA: Harvard University Press. See also Syvitski et al. (2020). 'Extraordinary Human Energy Consumption'.

36. This term, intended to echo the title of Karl Polanyi's 1944 book, *The Great Transformation*, which took a holistic view about the origins of modernity, made its debut in this sense at a workshop in Dahlem, a Berlin suburb, in 2005. The proceedings of that workshop can be found at R. Costanza, L. Graumlich and W. Steffen (eds) (2007), *Sustainability or Collapse: An Integrated History and Future of People on Earth*. Cambridge, MA: MIT Press; for an explicit presentation of stages of the Anthropocene, see W. Steffen, P. Crutzen and J. R. McNeill (2007), 'The Anthropocene: Are humans now overwhelming the great forces of Nature?', *Ambio*, 36 (8), 614–21.

37. The debates may be followed in journals such as *The Anthropocene Review, Anthropocene Science, Elementa: Science of the Anthropocene*, and *Anthropocene*.

38. A. Gorman (2014), 'The Anthropocene in the solar system', *Journal of Contemporary Archaeology*, 1 (1), 87–91.

CHAPTER 11
LABOUR REGIMES AND LABOUR MOBILITY FROM THE SEVENTEENTH TO THE NINETEENTH CENTURY
Alessandro Stanziani

Why Coercion?

Many economists and economic historians follow Domar's model according to which labour coercion is likely to develop when labour is scarce compared to land. This model was based largely on Russian and medieval European serfdom, but it has since been used to describe several other contexts, not only in Russia, Africa and Asia but also in Britain and the United States as well. Such models are interesting not so much for what they explain but for what they fail to explain.[1] Thus, Domar's model suggests that slavery and serfdom were established when labour was scarce; in contrast, Habakkuk, Postan, North and Thomas stressed that in Western Europe, scarcity of labour accounts not for the strength but for the decline of serfdom and resulting capital intensification. In the first case, labour scarcity led to coercion, in the second, it led to increased wages and hence to capital intensification.[2] However, empirical evidence for this thesis is scanty.

Similarly diverging views and limited empirical confirmation of Domar's model emerge with regard to the colonial worlds. The cases of Australia and Canada testify to the fact that the colonization of new territories did not necessarily entail massive imports of slaves as in the United States.[3] In Russia itself, the scarcity of labour was never mentioned in sources contemporary with the emergence of serfdom,[4] while the abolition of slavery in the British Atlantic colonies had little to do with demographic trends. As Seymour Drescher puts it, there was no fundamental change in demographic patterns in the tropical world beyond Europe in the watershed period of 1760–90.[5] Wrigley and Schofield show that Britain established its overseas slave system during the very decades when the net emigration rate reached a three-century peak (1641–61); in contrast, British abolitionism took off exactly when the net emigration rate sank to a tercentennial low (1771–91).[6]

Yet, it was not just a matter of supply and demand of labour between masters and labouring people. In the period here considered, contract enforcement was a substitute for higher wages: masters used it as long as they could, in order to secure labour.[7] This was possible because of two further conditions: first, society considered labour as a service and an obligation vis-à-vis the head of the family, the village, the master, the town and/or the state; second, labouring people had few political, civil and legal rights compared to those of their masters.[8] In the European context, unequal political rights and the exclusion of labouring people from the benefit of the Glorious Revolution in Britain and its colonies, of the Revolution in France and its colonies as well, allowed masters to limit wage increase, despite the lack of labour. Moreover, in both areas, free labour, even where a contract existed, was considered the property of the employer and a resource for the whole community to which the individual belonged.[9] Labour was part of the broader public order. In the following pages I will discuss the relationship between labour, contract and public order in Britain, then France, and then the colonial world. Why these areas?

In this context, the French case is of interest not because it was the land of Colbertism and opposed to liberal England, but because its labour norms in the nineteenth century were actually quite well suited both to a capitalist economy and to the heritage of the Old Regime. Highlighting the case of France and comparing it with England leads us to question the differences between liberalism and regulationism – or between free labour and guilds within the capitalist world – and from there to narrow the distance separating free labour from varieties of bondage. Contrary to widespread preconceptions, common law in England was in fact accompanied by a considerable degree of regulation and state intervention, and labour remained subject to punitive constraints until the end of the nineteenth century.

While British and French norms and perceptions translated into various forms of bondage in the Atlantic and the Indian Ocean region (thereby helping perpetuate slavery well after its official abolition), slavery nevertheless existed prior to any European intervention. The adopted solution did not result solely from British and French influences, but from the interaction between those influences and local traditions.

These comparisons on the national and imperial levels are valid only as a rough approximation. No doubt, legal rules (civil, tax and customs laws) refer to the national and imperial dimension of these phenomena; yet those rules were only one component of economic action, along with symbolic, cultural and political aspects. Hence we cannot ignore the importance of local components and the great differences between the dynamics of different regions. Several institutions coexisted on the local level, and even when a process of national unification took place, institutional pluralism continued. Institutional pluralism was more widespread on the level of empires, where legal pluralism was an important instrument of economic and political action.[10]

Labour, Contracts and Public Order in Britain

The idea that capitalism and in particular the British Industrial Revolution was made possible thanks to institutions that facilitated free contracts and (according to some) a proletarianized peasantry is supported by a long tradition. It dates back at least to the nineteenth century and classical economists such as Smith and Marx, continuing with Tawney and Polanyi and in most works of historical sociology and economic history in the twentieth century. Even the world system approach, while stressing the existence of mixed forms of labour and exploitation on the periphery and quasi-periphery, has always assumed that free wage labour typified the 'core'.[11] However, in recent decades, several pieces of research have contested the impact of enclosures and the existence of a truly free labour market in industrializing Britain.[12]

Until at least the mid-nineteenth century, the term 'free labour' did not mean what we are now accustomed to it meaning.[13] It included indenture, debt bondage and several other forms of unfree labour.[14] Conversely, the official abolition of slavery did not see the disappearance of forced labour, but rather the emergence of new forms.[15] Thus, from the sixteenth to the nineteenth centuries, laws on runaway slaves and indentured servants were adopted not only in the colonial Americas but also in Great Britain, where runaway workers, journeymen and the like were subject to quite similar laws under the Master and Servant Acts and the Statute of Artificers and Apprentices of 1562. Apprenticeship, advances in wages and raw materials, and simple master–servant relations justified such provisions. Since the mid-seventeenth century, the Poor Laws related relief directly to workhouses. Any person lacking employment or permanent residence was no longer considered simply a 'poor' person, but became a 'vagrant', and as such was subject to criminal prosecution. Anti-vagrancy laws did not decline but became stricter in the nineteenth century, particularly after the adoption of the New Poor Law in 1834. Between 1834 and the mid-1870s, there were about 10,000 prosecutions for vagrancy.[16]

In this context, the workhouse system was far from marginal: it has been estimated that in periods of crisis during the eighteenth and nineteenth centuries, about 6.5 per cent of the British population was in a workhouse at any given time.[17] Many have seen a strong influence of Bentham in the New Poor Law of 1834. The commission in charge of the New Poor Law insisted that workhouse labour would be applied for discipline rather than for profit.[18] Thus the years following the adoption of the new rules saw an increasing number of paupers committed to workhouses for offences: the number of committals rose from 940 in 1837 to 2,596 in 1842, while over 10,500 committals for breach of workhouse discipline were recorded during the same period.[19]

Yet paupers and inmates increasingly resisted the Poor Laws and the workhouse principle, resorting to petitions, sabotage and, in particular among women, self-mutilation. If one adds the massive protests against the Poor Laws in the 1830s, one would have a complex picture in which different central government orientations faced equally various local elites' attitudes and popular protests.[20]

Indeed, the history of workhouses has been one-sidedly linked to that of prisons, while the link with 'normal' labour has been ignored. This link was strong not only for the forms of discipline and rights but also for the way wages and assistance were related. The Statute of Labourers (1350–1) was enacted two years after the Ordinance of Labourers had been put in place and was followed by a set of laws gathered under the umbrella of the Master and Servant Acts, which multiplied in the sixteenth century and accompanied the Statute of Artificers and Apprentices (1562). During the term of service, the labour of servants was legally reserved for their masters. Even at the expiration of the term of service, servants were not allowed to leave their masters unless they had given 'one quarter's warning' of their intention to leave.[21] Workers could be imprisoned until they were willing to return to their employers to complete their agreed-upon service. Any untimely breach of contract on the part of the servant was subject to prosecution. In fact, in early modern Britain, resident servants were like wives and children: all were members of the household and all were the legal dependents of its head.[22] All of them were supposed to be under his authority, the family head benefiting from a higher legal status and more legal entitlements and rights than his dependents and family. Both marriage and labour contracts were actually status contracts: they gave rise to a different legal status for wives and servants on the one hand, and for masters and husbands on the other.

In general, labour was seen as akin to domestic service, with the employer purchasing the worker's time.[23] It is important to stress the chronology of these rules: the measures of the Master and Servant Acts grew stricter starting in the 1720s, when penalties against servants who broke their contracts were reinforced. Between 1720 and 1792, ten acts of Parliament imposed or increased the term of imprisonment for leaving work or for misbehaviour. Almost all these acts were a new departure: the Master and Servant Acts not only attempted to provide for social and political stability but required tighter control of workers by their masters while guaranteeing 'fair' competition among masters (i.e. they should not try to entice away other masters' working people). Specific groups promoted these changes: tailors, shoemakers, leatherworkers, mariners and lace makers. Monetary or raw material investments made by the employer were used to further justify such sanctions against wage earners who left their jobs.[24]

This trend had its basis in the huge expansion of the putting-out system in the eighteenth century, which added to the mounting need for agrarian labour.[25] Competition between sectors and the intense seasonality of labour strongly buttressed these new labour laws.[26] The idea that high wages were necessary to encourage technological creativity, as expressed by Habakkuk and many others, is based on the assumption that technological progress was primarily a choice between equivalent alternatives and that these choices depended on relative prices.[27] However, there is no persuasive evidence that technological progress emerged as labour-saving in the eighteenth century and the first half of the nineteenth century. Agricultural innovations in particular tended to be labour-using rather than labour-saving: the new techniques of husbandry demanded more labour, not less.[28] Recent analyses come to the same conclusion: labour and labour intensity were the main source of agricultural growth before 1850, with human and physical capital playing a secondary role.[29] Long after steam had become the dominant form of power employed in manufacturing, the major sources of energy available to farmers continued to be men, animals, wind and water.[30] Labour-intensive techniques linked to the diffusion of knowledge and attractive markets (with increasing agriculture prices) were dominant between the seventeenth and last quarter of the nineteenth century, when this trend reversed (decreasing agricultural prices and increasing wages).[31]

This trend was not limited to agriculture. The rate of capital intensification in British industry was relatively limited until the mid-nineteenth century.[32] Unlike conventional views on the Industrial Revolution, stressing capital intensification,[33] the most frequently declared goal of innovation was either improving the quality of the product or saving on capital, not labour.[34] By 1850, there were relatively few workers employed in factories. Only a small proportion of the workforce worked in technologically advanced industries such as cotton, iron and steel, and other metalworking: the full impact of steam power in transport and production was yet to be felt.[35] The unmechanized, subcontracted work of the sweating system surely played a greater role in the intensification of work than did mechanization.[36]

De Vries's notion of an 'industrious revolution' explains this trend perfectly: even if the author mostly refers to the period between 1650 and 1750, the main features of this model were still relevant up through the mid-nineteenth century in Britain, long after other areas of Europe and Asia.[37]

This also contributes to explain why, contrary to E. P. Thompson's argument, working hours per day increased significantly during the eighteenth century and the first half of the nineteenth century.[38] Masters often had an incentive to increase the workday during rush periods to get the goods out and then to lay off or reduce hours in the dead season. As the pace of mechanization was slower than painted in the textbooks, the working hours increased, in particular in the textile mills.[39]

Seasonal needs in agriculture were a crucial variable. Seasonal local shortages of manpower were overcome by interregional migration and – only later in the nineteenth century – by a transformation of hand-harvesting techniques and tools.[40] In fact, the labour requirements of harvesting were particularly important since labour output peaked sharply at the harvest. [41] All this helps explain the main features of labour contracts. The labour market did not operate as an 'auction market'.[42] By the eighteenth century, an oral or written contract for workers other than day labourers was presumed to last a year, particularly in husbandry, unless specific terms had been explicitly negotiated. However, the frequency of departures, mostly in connection with the harvest, proved the relatively limited impact of the law on workers' behaviour. Masters therefore looked for other solutions, such as the possibility of workers subleasing looms and tools and finding a substitute. This solution was particularly widespread in textile mills, where family members who received a family wage usually worked small spinning mules.[43]

In general, short-term contracts allowed employers to lay off workers when there was a sudden downturn of trade or if workers became troublesome. A positive trend in business, with little unemployment, made short-term contracts favourable to workers; the reverse was true when unemployment rose. The county and police-district records for the years 1857 to 1875 show that some 10,000 people were prosecuted each year for Master and Servant offences. Overall, 5–8 per cent of servants were prosecuted, but the percentage peaked at 17 in some areas and even 20 in London in specific years. There were no significant differences between the prosecution rate under the Master and Servant Acts in rural areas as opposed to urban counties, or between agricultural, putting-out and manufacturing areas.[44] Instead, the response to changing economic trends and the rate of prosecution was stronger in the countryside than in town, most likely because of the major impact of seasonal labour shortages on agriculture.[45] Given the strong family ties between the town and the countryside, only persistently increasing earnings would have encouraged permanent residence in town. But most masters preferred to use coercion rather than attractive wages to keep the labour force, and they thus ultimately encouraged 'fugitive' workers. In other words, unlike the Harrod-Domar's model, coercion did not increase just because labour was scarce, but because masters could rely upon institutions which allowed them to escape from increasing wages despite a lack of labour. The situation could change only with a new political equilibrium (increasing strength of unions land labour movement) and accelerating technical progress in both agriculture and industry, creating a capital-intensive path of growth. This occurred only after 1850, with the Second Industrial Revolution and the increasing expulsion of the working force from agriculture.

French Servants

In the past, historians have been fond of opposing the persistence of guilds and the corporatist spirit in French labour law to the free market of Anglo-Saxon labour.[46] This contrast is no longer tenable as the regulation of labour in France is no longer viewed as being in opposition to market growth.[47] France, for instance, was the first country to abolish lifelong domestic service as well as criminal penalties in labour disputes.[48] The chronology of these developments requires further explanation.

As late as the eighteenth century, French official texts, estates, guilds and local administrations considered labour to be a service provision.[49] Moreover, French case law made no clear distinction between hiring a person for services and 'hiring' a thing.[50] Although the French Revolution eliminated lifelong domestic service, it retained two forms of contracts from earlier times: hiring for labour (*louage d'ouvrage*) and hiring for services (*louage de service*). While the former brought the status of the wage earner more in line with the independent artisan, the latter represented an important legacy from earlier forms of domestic service. Cottereau has emphasized the importance of hiring for services in nineteenth-century France and its ability to protect wage earners. Such contracts and the overall attitude of *prud'homme* (law courts for labour conflicts) law courts strongly protected workers.[51] This argument, while not incorrect, is restricted to specific sectors such as the textile industry and certain urban milieus. But what about the other sectors, especially agriculture?

A variety of contractual arrangements to limit mobility existed at the time along with general provisions.[52] Thus from the sixteenth to the eighteenth century, agricultural labourers and servants were free to move about and change employers only at certain times of year – that is, according to the critical periods in the agricultural calendar. The seasonal nature of agricultural labour gave rise to a significant amount of regional mobility, which was already considerable in the seventeenth century and remained high until around the end of the nineteenth century.[53]

This mobility, together with the notion of labour as service, is precisely what helps to explain the harsh penalties imposed on labourers and servants. They were not allowed to leave their masters until the end of their contract; otherwise they lost their earnings.

The master, on the other hand, could discharge them at any time.[54] The situation changed during the second half of the century, when the rate of disputes went up and the demand for agricultural wage earners and domestic servants increased due to emigration to the cities.[55]

This had an influence on industrial labour as well; about 25 per cent of labour moved from one sector to another during the summer in the mid-nineteenth century. Industrial employers could either shut down in the summer or increase wages. The adopted choice depended on the branch of the industry and the region.[56] Indeed a national market was still missing in nineteenth-century France (at least until after the 1880s) and peasant workers considered comparatively local wages in agriculture and industry. This explains why in *départments* where industrial wages were high, agricultural wages followed, and vice versa: workers compared and eventually balanced the two wages. For this reason, summer shutdowns were more widespread among firms that paid their workers less than the summer wage for farm labour. This system made of local arrangements and seasonal markets left room for different kinds of farms. Smallholders and even communal fields provided seasonal work for industry and large agricultural units as well. Only between 1860 and 1890 did the earlier practice of combining agricultural and industrial employment largely come to an end. During the summer of 1860, at least 500,000 – and most probably 800,000 – workers quit their jobs. By 1890, this number had fallen to 100,000.[57] Despite important regional and sectoral differences, as a whole, the agrarian crisis and the Second Industrial Revolution attracted more stable workers, who were mostly unskilled, into the towns and the manufactures.

In short, in Western Europe, between the sixteenth and the end of the nineteenth century, labour was submitted to serious legal constraints. This was so for several interrelated reasons including the fact that labour was considered a service to the community and that labour and labour intensification were the main sources of growth. National markets still lagged far behind local and international markets. These rules were hard to enforce but they were more effective at keeping working people in place than limiting their voice and wages.

The major exception to this labour-intensive path and labour rules in the eighteenth and nineteenth centuries was not so much Britain but its northern American colonies, and later the United States. Since Habakkuk's work, the argument has been that scarcity of labour led to free markets, high wages and precocious mechanization.[58] Again, this issue runs against the Harrod-Domar's model and this was so for social and institutional conditions: in the American north, there was no way to use coercion to get more labour. More recently, several authors have developed this argument: factor endowment and in particular the lower land-to-labour ratio in Britain compared to the United States had encouraged its agriculture sector to invest in grain; thus, a more seasonal culture was created, which in turn sustained proto-industry and multiple activity. By contrast, in the United States, scarcity of labour and agricultural diversification reduced pluri- activity and led to a quick concentration of industry.[59] Unlike Britain, increasing labour demand did not lead to coercion but to its opposite. Social and political equilibria more favourable to labour contributed to this outcome. Yet, this does not clarify the relationships between these dynamics in the north of the American colonies on the one hand, and, on the other hand, slavery in the south of the United States, and the persistent importance of the indentured labour in the North itself before, during and after the age of slavery.

Indentured Immigrants versus Slaves

As the definition and practice of bonded labour in the colonies were linked to the definition and practice of wage labour in Europe, the development of labour in the two areas was interconnected. The blurred boundaries between freedom and unfreedom, property in persons and their labour, found new definitions and became closer to our understanding only in the transmutation of the English state into Imperial Britain. The same can be said of France. The British and the French exported specific notions and practices of wage earner: the servant and the indentured labour. This peculiar contract derived from two types of extant contracts: that of the sailor and that of the agrarian labourer.[60]

In the French colonies, the contract of *engagement* or indentured service was developed in the seventeenth century. It was initially intended for white settlers whose transport expenses were advanced by employers or their middlemen in exchange for a commitment to work for several years. The *engagés* were subject to criminal penalties and could be transferred along with their contract to other masters. The contract of *engagement* should not be understood in opposition to these other labour relationships, but as an extension of them in the colonial situation. Indeed, the notaries of Normandy in charge of drafting the first contracts of *engagement* in the seventeenth century explicitly relied on two types of contracts that already existed: the agricultural daily labourer's contract and the sailor's contract. It is no accident that contracts of *engagement* explicitly mention hiring for service: the *engagé* rented his services, that is, the totality of his time, to his master. Terminating a contract was therefore difficult, especially for the *engagé*. Similarly, contracts of *engagement* explicitly invoked apprenticeship contracts: the master had the same requirement to provide for the care of the *engagé* as he did for the apprentice, the same expenses in case of illness, and the same word in the margins: bondage.[61]

Two clauses differentiated the apprenticeship contract from the contract of *engagement*: the act of apprenticeship emphasized training in a trade, whereas in the contract of *engagement*, the *engagé* first owed his labour to his master who, in exchange, was to teach him about colonial farming. It was also the master who gave a lump sum to his *engagé* and not the other way around, as in the case of an apprentice.[62]

In general, the *engagés* were not allowed to marry without authorization from their masters, but an *engagé* had the right to redeem his indenture and could force his master to agree to do so. Differences nevertheless appear between the *engagés* 'with no trade' and those who left as doctors, carpenters and so on. The latter committed themselves for three years instead of five; they received wages but were not subject to the servitude clauses imposed on the others.

In the seventeenth and eighteenth centuries, the contract of *engagement* concerned mainly whites who went not only to the French West Indies and Canada but also to the Indian Ocean region. Between 1660 and 1715 alone, 5,200 *engagés* left for the French West Indies from La Rochelle. This figure is much smaller than the 210,000 indentured Britons who left for North America between 1630 and 1700.[63] Excluding the Caribbean, in the period 1630–1780, the colonies received between 472,000 and 510,000 migrants, 50,000 of whom were convicts and the rest were half indentured and half 'voluntary' migrants.[64] A similar relationship between mother country and colonial labour contracts existed within the British Empire. Just as a master in Great Britain had the right to pursue fugitives, so too in the colonies: indentured servants who fled were subject to criminal penalties.

Two periods can be distinguished: the first, from the seventeenth century to the 1830s, concerned some 300,000 European indentured servants. It coincided with a period when slavery was still legal and European traders engaged in the slave trade. The indentured servants were intended to be engaged in tobacco plantations and, to some degree, in manufacturing. The second phase, in the nineteenth and twentieth centuries, concerned 2 million indentured servants, mostly Chinese and Indians, but also Africans, Japanese and immigrants from the Pacific Islands. They were employed in sugar plantations and in manufacturing. Unlike the indentured servants of the first phase, these new bonded labourers seldom returned to the world of free labour once their period of commitment ended. Their indenture contracts were therefore renewed.[65]

What is the relationship between indenture and slave labour? Menard argues that, in North America, indentured servants and slaves were close substitutes and that planters shifted from servants to slaves not because they preferred slaves but due to changes in the supply and cost of the two forms of labour. Around 1660, the supply of servants began to decline as in England population fell and real wages rose, thus leading to improved opportunities at home.[66] Consequently, after the mid-century, migration to America fell. However, other scholars argue that this shift reflected the planters' preferences for black slaves, whom they considered to be more docile and productive than white servants.[67]

The case of Barbados, where the development of sugar plantations transformed the island in the mid-seventeenth century, shows the relationship between the two forms of labour. With the rise of sugar, monoculture replaced diversified farming, and blacks arrived by the thousands while whites left. The island began to import food and fuel and the great planters rose in wealth and power. Because of its substantial economies of scale and large profits, sugar was most efficiently grown on big plantations that greatly increased demand for labour.[68] This is the ultimate confirmation that the Harrod-Domar's model did not fit with historical realities: at the end of the seventeenth century, therefore, the influx of slaves was not a response to a general lack of labour on the island, but to a specific lack of coerced labour and indentured immigrants in particular. Increasing demand for labour was hard to meet with native Indians and white indentured immigrants and convicts. Native Indians were difficult to control and less productive than either indentured whites or African slaves.

Some significant changes appeared at the end of the seventeenth century when colonial indentured servitude began to be distinguished from other forms of resident service and, above all, from slavery. It was slavery that enabled Virginians to achieve a stable relationship between work and rights: different contracts expressed different statuses (slaves, indentured immigrants) and, starting from this, they enabled different rights to the slave on the one hand, and to the immigrant on the other hand. In the Chesapeake and the Delaware valley, the relationship between British rules and indentured immigration was reaffirmed, though in the eighteenth century it acted as a way to differentiate indentured from slave labour. Decreasing costs of transportation encouraged shipowners to enter the migration market, where labour became a tradeable commodity. William Blackstone concluded that service was temporary property of labour, while *villeinage* and slavery were perpetual conditions.[69] Progressively, indentured labour was confined to minors alone, while adult working men and women refused to accept strong hierarchical power in labour relationships as they considered it a vestige of the British yoke. White indenture declined during the 1820s and came to an end in the following decade. By the late 1830s, penal sanctions for breach of contracts for white adult workers disappeared. It was, however, in this period that indentured contracts became commonplace for 'coloured' immigrants in the Americas as well as in the British and French colonies following the abolition of slavery.

While the legal and contract status of white indentured immigrants improved over time, those of servants (black until the mid-seventeenth century) progressively deteriorated into chattel slavery. This shift was the result of political and economic forces: the excess of labour demand was strong with the expansion of coffee, and then sugar and cotton cultivation in the colonies. The Restoration and then the Glorious Revolution at the end of the seventeenth century were decisive for the change of the legal status of black people in the American colonies.[70] London asserted the rights of the metropolis over its colonies. In this context, Locke, a member of this board, published his *Two Treatises of Government* (1690) in which he defended English liberty and freedom and justified slavery, to his eyes perfectly compatible with liberty.[71]

The shift from indentured labour to slavery was the outcome of a lack of labour in the colonies, aggravated by the labour-intensive path in Europe itself. The rise of the plantation system – labour-intensive and carried out on large-scale estates – bucked this trend. The sugar boom was constrained by a narrow range of technological possibilities. Crude cane-crushing mills, powered by animals, wind or water, remained the basic forms of heavy equipment.[72] On mainland America, tobacco and then cotton plantations also relied on labour-intensive production.[73]

Indentured after Abolition

Debates about abolitions have essentially focused on two interrelated questions: first, whether nineteenth- and early twentieth-century abolitions were a major breakthrough compared to previous centuries (or even millennia) in the history of humankind during which bondage had been the dominant form of labour and human condition; and second, whether they express an action specific to Western bourgeoisie and liberal civilization.

It is true that the number of abolitionist acts and the people concerned throughout the extended nineteenth century (1780–1914) had no equivalent in history: 30 million Russian peasants, half a million slaves in Saint-Domingue in 1790, 4 million slaves in the US in 1860, another million in the Caribbean (at the moment of the abolition of 1832–40), a further million in Brazil in 1885 and 250,000 in the Spanish colonies were freed during this period. Abolitions in Africa at the turn of the nineteenth century have been estimated to involve approximately 7 million people.[74] Yet this argument has been criticized by those who have argued that the abolitionist legal acts take into consideration neither the important rate of manumission and purchase of freedom in Islamic societies, in areas such as Africa, Southeast Asia and the Ottoman Empire,[75] nor the equally important rate of manumission in Russia and Brazil prior to general abolition, nor the legal and social constraints on freed slaves and serfs.

The first British abolitionist campaigns (1770s–1820) combined moral, political, religious and economic arguments. The latter were probably the weakest, not just because slavery was objectively profitable but also because in England itself Adam Smith's arguments did not become widespread until the mid-nineteenth century. Indeed, religious anti-slavery groups were opposed to both materialism and utilitarianism and used this argument to criticize slavery. Abolition of slave trade caused Britain to lose profits not only from this trade but also from the reduced production of sugar in the West Indies in the years following the abolition of the slave trade. After that period, despite the slow recovery of production, on the European markets Britain constantly lost shares of sugar and coffee to the benefit of Spain and Brazil.[76]

In England, many had believed that the abolition of slave trade would lead to the eventual abolition of slavery. This was not the case, as France, Spain and Portugal continued to import slaves. A new anti-slavery society was founded; it shifted its agenda from gradual to immediate abolition of slavery. A period (usually six to seven years, in line with the time frame of individual emancipation and apprenticeship contracts) was imposed, during which the quasi-former slaves were given apprenticeship status.[77] Slaves did not enjoy full legal status inasmuch as they were not yet 'civilized'.[78] Apprentices worked forty-five hours a week for their former owners in exchange for food, clothing, lodging and medical care. Absenteeism or low performance (according to standards set by the planters themselves) led to severe penalties and increased the period and the amount of apprentices' obligations. Physical punishment, which had been suppressed under slavery during the 1820s, was now reintroduced for apprentices. Abuse was thus extremely frequent.[79]

Thus, even though former slave owners had received compensation of £20 million, many planters used the apprenticeship programme as additional compensation, and, to this end, they sought to extract as much unpaid labour as possible. The final social and economic outcome differed from one colony to another according to the availability of land, previous forms of bondage and types of culture, and new forms of labour and their rules (different Masters and Servants acts enacted in each colony), and to systems of credit.[80] In Barbados, the planters monopolized all the land and rented it in part to former slaves, few of whom therefore left their original plantations. In Jamaica, Trinidad and English Guyana, many former slaves had formal access to land, but many of them ended up indebted to their former masters and found themselves back on the plantations.[81] This did not prevent former slaves (when they did not run away) from providing extremely irregular (in their masters' eyes) labour. A fall in sugar output in Jamaica was one of the major expressions of resistance.

The abolition of slavery gave new life to indentured immigration worldwide. In the nineteenth and twentieth centuries, more than 2.5 million people became indentured servants, mostly Chinese and Indian but also African, Japanese and migrants from the Pacific Islands. They were employed in sugar plantations and in manufacturing. Unlike white settlers during the first phase of indentured immigration, during the 1850s and 1860s, many indentured migrants – especially Indians – returned home. A third of all indentured servants in Mauritius, the Caribbean, Surinam and Jamaica and up to 70 per cent of those in Thailand, Malaya and Melanesia returned home. Distance and the cost of transport were the two main variables affecting repatriation, though politics, concrete forms of integration, and death from disease were also important factors. Between the official abolition of slavery in 1834 and 1910, 450,000 indentured servants, mostly from India but also from Madagascar, arrived in Mauritius. Two-thirds of them remained, and as a result, the Indian population grew steadily – from 35 per cent of the island's population in 1846 to 66 per cent in 1871.[82] Numerous observers drew attention to the inhuman living conditions of these immigrants.[83] These figures must also be expanded to include other indentured servants from Southeast Asia and Africa: 30,000 in 1851 and twice that number ten years later.

The real conditions of workers depended on when they arrived, their ethnic origin and which specific estates they worked on. Small plantation owners were more concerned about fugitive, insubordinate and vagrant indentured servants,[84] whereas large plantation owners, who complained of the excessive cost of slave surveillance, often advocated a liberal ideology for the colonial systems. Immigrants often complained of ill treatment, withheld wages and poor food.[85] The number of cases in which indentured servants brought proceedings against their masters – something that rarely happened in the 1850s – rose sharply thereafter. In the 1860s and 1870s, about 10 per cent of all indentured servants sued their masters, in virtually every case for non-payment or insufficient payment of wages, and they won in more than 70 per cent of cases.[86] Such a result was partly due to pressure from England and can hardly indicate that a 'march to equality' was under way. In subsequent decades, the percentage of contracts disputed by coolies declined first to 5 per cent at end of the 1870s and later dropped to a mere 0.3 per cent between 1895 and 1899, with their success rate falling to less than 40 per cent.[87] This can be explained by the fact that, after the results of the 1860s and thanks to a new law on labour contracts adopted in 1867, an increasing number of contracts were oral, making it more difficult for the coolies to produce any proof that would hold up in court. Above all, the coolies' contracts were no longer signed with plantation owners but were drawn up instead with Indian middlemen, which no doubt helped to quash many conflicts.

Retention of coolies increased with the percentage of contract renewals, rising from 40 per cent in 1861 to more than 70 per cent twenty years later.[88]

In Mauritius, 14,000 indentured and domestic servants were prosecuted each year in the 1860s; during the same period in Great Britain, proceedings were brought against 9,700 servants per year for breach of contract and almost always resulted in convictions. By contrast, masters were seldom indicted and even more rarely convicted for breach of contract, ill treatment or non-payment of wages. At the same time, even though the real conditions of indentured servants were not necessarily better than those of the slaves who preceded them, the rights they enjoyed and the fact that their status was not hereditary were essential differences that were to play an increasingly important role in the twentieth century.

The Great Transformation of Labour in the Twentieth Century

Labour contracts (*contrats de travail* in French, *contracts of employment* in English) emerged between the 1890s and the 1920s. These new legal institutions marked a departure from the forms of labour that had sustained the economic growth and societal transformation in Europe between the seventeenth century and mid-nineteenth century.

In England, at the start of the 1870s, most industrial enterprises were still independent family-run firms that employed fewer than a hundred workers. Mass production was slow in evolving and was still limited.[89] By the mid-nineteenth century, a decisive shift occurred towards an industrialized economy in which sustained increases in output per capita served to support a growing population, which, in turn, provided a source of rising demand.[90] From the mid-1880s onwards, large combinations of firms began to emerge, notably in textile manufacturing, coal mining and engineering. Vertical integration, the welfare state, and changing labour institutions went hand in hand. Vertical integration required a stable labour force and large units; the peasant worker, the traditional poor, and Poor Laws hardly fit this process. The removal of criminal sanctions from the individual employment relationship in the 1870s was soon followed by the first legislative interventions of the welfare state.[91] These changes meant that the Poor Law remained in place but dealt only with residual cases that fell outside the range of the statutory social-insurance scheme.[92] Despite advances, seasonal and casual workers were excluded from these provisions as they were designated as independent contractors. Litigation thus occurred over the definition of 'independent', with employers trying to avoid responsibility for the social risks of illness, injury and unemployment.

Along an analogous path, in France, the law of 21 March 1884 legalized trade unions. The notion of the labour contract (*contrat de travail*) first appeared. The term *contrat de travail* was not in widespread use in France before the mid-1880s. However, once the term became established, it was used in turn-of-the-century legislation with respect to industrial accidents (law of 1898), which introduced the employer's objective responsibility in case of accident. This in turn opened the way to social insurances, which were being developed precisely during this period. However, the new labour law widened rather than reduced legal, social and economic inequalities among working people. It excluded large categories, such as small enterprises, craftsmen and peasants.[93] All these groups were marginalized as 'independent' workers.[94]

Migration

Since the 1870s, the declining prices of these items and the joint process of mechanization led to decreasing immigration of indentured Indians, Chinese and Africans in many production areas in the islands in the Antilles and the Indian Ocean regions. Yet migratory fluxes increased in the last quarter of the nineteenth century. In Europe, mechanization and concentration compelled people to migrate, while massive population flows helped create a single global economy for both labour and capital. Thus, between 1840 and 1940, 55–58 million Europeans and 2.5 million Africans and Asians reached the Americas; during this same period, 29 million Indians, 19 million Chinese and 4 million Africans and Europeans moved to Southeast Asia, the Pacific Islands and the Indian Ocean rim. Finally, 46–51 million people from Northeastern Asia and Russia moved (or were compelled to move) to Siberia, Manchuria and Central Asia.[95]

Economic factors were important, but they were not alone in causing this mass migration. Thanks to the transport revolution of steamboats and railroads, global migrations caused a significant shift in the distribution of the world's population. All three aforementioned destinations (Americas, Central Asia and the Indian Ocean) experienced enormous population growth, increasing by factors of 4 to 5.5 from 1850 to 1950. Growth rates in these areas were more than twice that of world population as a whole. By comparison, growth rates in the regions of emigration were lower than world population growth and less than half of those in the regions of immigration. Taken together, the three main destination regions accounted for 10 per cent of the world's population in 1850 and 24 per cent in 1950.[96]

Even if relocation within the same empire was important (in particular, in the Russian and British empires), trans-imperial, intra-continental, regional and local forms of migration were also important – and they clearly show the inadequacy of the Eurocentric paradigm, which consists of explaining migration as an 'expansion of the West'.[97] Indeed, migration was multi-scale and involved almost all areas of the world. Nearly 4 million Indians travelled to Malaysia, over 8 million to Ceylon, over 15 million to Burma and about 1 million to Africa, other parts of Southeast Asia and islands throughout the Indian and Pacific Oceans. Up to 11 million Chinese (most from the southern provinces) travelled from China to the Straits Settlements, although more than a third of these transhipped to the Dutch Indies, Borneo, Burma and places farther west. Nearly 4 million travelled directly from China to Thailand, 2–3 million to French Indochina, more than 1 million to the Dutch Indies (for a total of more than 4 million if transhipments from Singapore are included) and just under 1 million to the Philippines.[98]

At the same time, railroad construction and a relative relaxation of frontiers between Russia and China also led 28–33 million northern Chinese to migrate to Siberia and Manchuria.[99] Migration within each area increased and interacted with long-distance emigration. Migrants from Ireland travelled to England for work; others moved from Eastern and Southern Europe to industrial areas in Northern Europe, especially France and Germany. In Russia, migrants moved into the growing cities and southern agricultural areas. Within India, they moved to tea plantations in the south and northeast, to the mines and textile-producing regions of Bengal, and to newly irrigated lands and urban areas throughout the subcontinent.[100]

Thus it would be reductive to explain twentieth-century migrations as simply an 'expansion of the West' and the triumph of free labour and free emigration over bondage. To be sure, whole sets of laws in defence of 'freedom' were adopted on all continents. 'Free' migration expanded with the increasing restriction of indenture contracts and their final abolition in 1920. In the United States, the Anti-Peonage Act of 1867 extended the prohibition of servitude (voluntary or involuntary) to all states in the Union. The government of India first restricted and then forbade Indian indentured contracts in 1916, while in 1874 an agreement between the Chinese and Portuguese governments stopped the transport of Chinese contract labour from Macao. Chinese authorities investigated the conditions of Chinese migrants in Cuba, Peru and the United States, which led to the suspension of most of these contracts.

At the same time, formal rules for migration were not always supported by real legal rights granted to immigrants once they reached their destination. For example, the conditions of former indentured labourers were extremely different, precisely as they had been for former slaves. The access to landowning that one had on Mauritius and Reunion Island was hardly the rule. Elsewhere, between 1899 and 1938, most of the indentured immigrants served as day labourers in agriculture or in commerce; this was the case with Chinese, Indian and Japanese immigrants in Cuba, British Guyana, Trinidad and Hawaii. Servant contracts or 'independent' commercial activity was much more widespread in Cuba (40 per cent of the immigrants) and Hawaii (48 per cent) than in British Guyana (8 per cent) or Trinidad (24 per cent).[101]

Most importantly, different forms of bondage and debt obligations survived far into the twentieth century. Chinese, Africans, Indians and, to a certain extent, even European emigrants were still subject to disguised forms of indenture contracts and bondage.[102] The same can be said for Africans, who even if officially freed from slavery were still under multiple forms of bondage in both intra-African and African–European relations. Local bondage coexisted with the intercontinental flow of free and less-free people. This was the case for various reasons: labour markets remained highly segmented, unequal skills adding to important institutional constraints. Migration was never really free; laws and reciprocal and multilateral agreements between powers obtruded and thus regulated the flow. The rise of the welfare state and protection of the 'national' working force went hand in hand with the increasing control, if not limitation of immigration and the exclusion of the colonies from the new welfare state.

Conclusion

Unfree labour cannot exist unless political institutions intervene and limit the free market; the institutions regulating labour did not only respond exclusively to efficiency, scarcity (of labour), and profit calculations but also to power and values. Violence, constraints and contract enforcement were not only substitutes for higher wages but also the expression of the belief that labour was a service to the master, the head of the family, the village, the community and, ultimately, the state, and was accompanied by strongly unequal distribution of civil and human rights between labouring people and their masters. This global trend was at the very ground of economic growth through the seventeenth to the mid-nineteenth century, certainly in Eastern Europe and in the Western European colonial world (long after that date) and partially in the West as well. Since the mid-nineteenth century, increasing labour and civic and human rights in the West went along with capital-intensive growth, unions and political shifts more favourable to welfare capitalism. Yet, this turn consciously excluded the colonial world through the decolonization process, but even then, only for a short period, under the post-war reconstruction in Europe. Since the end of the 1970s, restrictions to the welfare state in the West went along once again with increasing restrictions to immigration and immigrants' social rights. Paradoxically, these two trends are increasingly perceived as being in opposition, the defence of national welfare being incompatible with immigration.

Notes

1. E. D. Domar (1970), 'The causes of slavery or serfdom: A hypothesis', *Journal of Economic History*, 30 (1), 18–32; E. D. Domar and M. J. Machina (1984), 'On the profitability of Russian serfdom', *Journal of Economic History*, 44 (4), 919–55. Domar's model was strongly inspired by Nieboer, a Dutch ethnographer in the late nineteenth to early twentieth century. H. Nieboer (1900), *Slavery as an Industrial System: Ethnological Researches*. The Hague: Martinus Nijhoff.

2. H. J. Habakkuk (1958), 'The economic history of modern Britain', *Journal of Economic History*, 18 (4), 486–501; ibid. (1962), *American and British Technology in the Nineteenth Century*. Cambridge: Cambridge University Press; D. North and R. Thomas (1971), 'The rise and fall of the manorial system: A theoretical model', *Journal of Economic History*, 31 (4), 777–803; M. M. Postan (1973), *Cambridge Economic History of Europe: Expanding Europe in the Sixteenth and Seventeenth Centuries*. Cambridge: Cambridge University Press. For a more recent work, see R. C. Allen (2009), *British Industrial Revolution in Global Perspective*. Cambridge: Cambridge University Press.

3. S. Engerman (ed.) (1999), *Terms of Labor: Slavery, Freedom and Free Labor*. Stanford, CA: Stanford University Press; M. Klein (1993), *Breaking the Chains: Slavery, Bondage and Emancipation in Modern Africa and Asia*. Madison, WI: University of Wisconsin Press.

4. A. Stanziani (2014), *Bondage: Labor and Rights in Eurasia from the Sixteenth to the Early Twentieth Centuries*. New York: Berghahn.

5. S. Drescher (1987), *Capitalism and Antislavery: British Mobilization in Comparative Perspective*. New York: Oxford University Press; London: Palgrave, 11.

6. E. A. Wrigley and R. S. Schofield (1981), *The Population History of England: A Reconstruction*. Cambridge: Cambridge University Press, 218–21.

7. M. Huberman (1986), 'Invisible handshakes in Lancashire: Cotton spinning in the first half of the nineteenth century', *Journal of Economic History*, 46 (4), 987–98.

8. Stanziani, *Bondage*.

9. R. Steinfeld (1991), *The Invention of Free Labor: The Employment Relation in English and American Law and Culture, 1350–1870*. Chapel Hill, NC: North Carolina University Press; Stinfeld (2001), *Coercion, Contract, and Free Labor in the Nineteenth Century*. Cambridge: Cambridge University Press; M. Postan (1937), 'The chronology of labour services', *Transactions of the Royal Historical Society*, 20, 169–93; T. Brass and M. van der Linden (eds) (1997), *Free and Unfree Labour: The Debate Continues*. Berne: Peter Lang.

10. L. Benton (2002), *Law and Colonial Culture: Legal Regimes in World History, 1400–1900*. Cambridge: Cambridge University Press.

11. I. Wallerstein (1974), *The Modern World-System: Capitalist Agriculture and the Origins of the European World-Economy in the Sixteenth Century*. New York and London: Atheneum.

12. R. Steinfeld, *Coercion, Contract*; S. Deakin and F. Wilkinson (2005), *The Law of the Labour Market: Industrialization, Employment, and Legal Evolution*. Oxford: Oxford University Press; D. Hay and P. Craven (eds) (2004), *Masters, Servants, and Magistrates in Britain and the Empire, 1562–1955*. Chapel Hill, NC: University of North Carolina Press.

13. Brass and van der Linden, *Free and Unfree Labour*.

14. D. W. Galenson (1981), *White Servitude in Colonial America: An Economic Analysis*. Cambridge: Cambridge University Press; D. Northrup (1995), *Indentured Labor in the Age of Imperialism, 1834–1922*. Cambridge: Cambridge University Press.

15. P. C. Emmer (ed.) (1986), *Colonialism and Migration: Indentured Labour before and after Slavery*. Dordrecht and Boston, MA: Martinus Nijhoff Publishers; Engerman, *Terms of Labor*.

16. S. Naidu and N. Yuchtman (2009), 'How green was my valley? Coercive contract enforcement in nineteenth-century Britain', *NBUR Working Papers*. http://www.econ.ucla.edu/workshops/papers/History/Naidu.pdf?origin=publication_detail/.

17. D. Fraser (2009), *The Evolution of the British Welfare State*, 4th edn. London: Palgrave Macmillan, 67.

18. British Parliamentary Papers (from now on BPP) (1834), *Report from the Commissioners for Inquiring into the Administration and Practical Reform of the Poor Laws, 1834*, XXVIII, appendix A.

19. D. Green (2006), 'Pauper protests: Protests and resistance in early nineteenth-century London workhouses', *Social History*, 31 (2), 141.

20. F. Driver (1993), *Power and Pauperism: The Workhouse System, 1834–1884*. Cambridge: Cambridge University Press.

21. Steinfeld, *Invention of Free Labor*, 32.

22. A. Kussmaul (1981), *Servants in Husbandry in Early Modern England*. Cambridge: Cambridge University Press.

23. Postan, 'The chronology of labour services'.

24. D. C. Woods (1982), 'The operation of the Masters and Servants Act in the Black Country, 1858–1875', *Midland History*, 7, 93–115.

25. R. Rudolph (ed.) (1995), *The European Peasant, Family, and Society: Historical Studies*. Liverpool: Liverpool University Press.

26. Hay and Rogers, *English Society*.

27. Habakkuk, *American and British Technology*. For a critique, see J. Mokyr (1990), *The Lever of Riches: Technological Creativity and Economic Progress*. Oxford: Oxford University Press, 165.

28. C. Timmer (1969), 'The turnip, the New Husbandry, and the English agricultural evolution', *Quarterly Journal of Economics*, 83 (3), 375–95.

29. G. Grantham (1989), 'Agricultural supply during the Industrial Revolution: French evidence and European implications', *Journal of Economic History*, 49 (1), 43–72; G. Federico (2005), *Feeding the World: An Economic History of Agriculture, 1800–2000*. Princeton, NJ: Princeton University Press.

30. P. K. O'Brien (1977), 'Agriculture and the Industrial Revolution', *Economic History Review*, 30 (1), 166–81; Clark, 'Productivity growth without technical change in European agriculture before 1850'.

31. F. M. L. Thompson (1968), 'The second Agricultural Revolution, 1815–1880', *Economic History Review*, 21 (1), 62–77.

32. N. F. R. Crafts (1985), *British Economy during the Industrial Revolution*. Oxford: Clarendon Press; J. H. Williamson (1984), 'Why was British growth so slow during the Industrial Revolution?', *Journal of Economic History*, 44 (3), 687–712; C. K. Harley (1982), 'British industrialization before 1841: Evidence of slower growth during the Industrial Revolution', *Journal of Economic History*, 42 (2), 267–89; P. Deane and W. A. Cole, *British Economic Growth, 1688–1959*. Cambridge: Cambridge University Press; C. Feinstein and S. Pollard (eds) (1988), *Studies in Capital Formation in the United Kingdom, 1750–1920*. Oxford: Clarendon Press.

33. A recent summary of this approach in Allen, *The British Industrial Revolution*.

34. C. MacLeod (1988), *Inventing the Industrial Revolution*. Cambridge: Cambridge University Press.

35. Deakin and Wilkinson, *Law of the Labour Market*, 20.

36. D. Bythell (1978), *The Sweated Trades: Outwork in Nineteenth-Century Britain*. London: Batsford; J. Schmiechen (1982), *Sweated Industries and Sweated Labor: The London Clothing Trades, 1860–1914*. Urbana, IL: University of Illinois Press.

37. J. de Vries (2008), *The Industrious Revolution: Consumer Behavior and the Household Economy, 1650 to the Present*. Cambridge: Cambridge University Press.

38. H.-J. Voth (1998), 'Time and work in eighteenth century London', *Journal of Economic History*, 58 (1), 29–58.

39. E. Hopkins (1982), 'Working hours and conditions during the Industrial Revolution: A re-appraisal', *Economic History Review*, 25 (1), 52–67.

40. E. J. T. Collins (1976), 'Migrant labor in British agriculture in the nineteenth century', *Economic History Review*, 29 (1), 38–59; G. Postel-Vinay (1994), 'The dis-integration of traditional labour markets in France: From agriculture *and* industry to agriculture *or* industry', in G. Grantham and M. MacKinnon (eds), *Labour Market Evolution*. London and New York: Routledge, 64–83.

41. K. D. M. Snell (1981), 'Agricultural seasonal unemployment, the standard of living, and women's work in the South and East, 1690–1860', *Economic History Review*, 34 (3), 407–37.

42. Huberman, 'Invisible handshakes in Lancashire'.

43. M. Huberman (1996), *Escape from the Market: Negotiating Work in Lancashire*. Cambridge: Cambridge University Press.

44. D. Hay (2004), 'England, 1562–1875: The law and its uses', in Hay and Craven, *Masters, Servants, and Magistrates*, 67.

45. Naidu and Yuchtman, 'How green was my valley?'.

46. E. Coornaert (1941), *Les corporations en France*. Paris: Gallimard; E. P. Thompson (1963), *The Making of the English Working Class*. London: Vintage Books; W. Sewell (1983), *Gens de métier et révolution. Le langage du travail de l'Ancien régime à 1848*. Paris: Aubier.

47. M. Sonenscher (1989), *Work and Wages: Natural Law, Politics and the Eighteenth-Century French Trades*. Cambridge: Cambridge University Press; P. Minard (1998), *La fortune du Colbertisme: Etat et industrie dans la France des lumières*. Paris: Fayard.

48. A. Cottereau (2002), 'Droit et bon droit. Un droit des ouvriers instauré, puis évincé par le droit du travail, France, XIXe siècle', *Annales*, 57 (6), 1521–57.

49. J. Domat (1697), *Les Lois Civiles dans leur Ordre Naturel*, reproduced in *Œuvres*. Paris: 1835, vol. 1; and R. Pothier (1861), *Traité du Contrat de Louage*. Paris: Bugnet.

50. Sonenscher, *Work and Wages*, 75.

51. Cottereau, 'Droit et bon droit'.

52. P. Hoffman (1996), *Growth in a Traditional Society: The French Countryside, 1450–1815*. Princeton, NJ: Princeton University Press, 45–6.

53. Postel-Vinay, 'The dis-integration'.

54. (1865), *Recueil des Usages Locaux en Vigueur dans le Département de la Vienne*. Poitiers: Bertrand; A. Pages (1855), *Usages et Règlements locaux, Servant de Complément à la Loi Civile et Topographie Légale du Département de l'Isère*. Grenoble: Baratier frères. See also the 1870 parliamentary enquiry in Archives Nationales de France (henceforth AN) C 1157–61.

55. Cottereau, 'Droit et bon droit'.

56. T. Magnac and G. Postel-Vinay (1977), 'Wage competition between agriculture and industry in mid-nineteenth century France', *Explorations in Economic History*, 34 (1), 1–26.

57. Postel-Vinay, 'The dis-integration'.

58. Habakkuk, *American and British Technology*.

59. K. Sokoloff and D. Dollar (1997), 'Agricultural seasonality and the organization of manufacturing in early industrial economies: The contrast between England and the United States', *Journal of Economic History*, 57 (2), 288–321.

60. U. Chakravarti (1985), 'Of Dasas and Karmakaras: Servile labour in ancient India', in U. Patnaik and M. Dingawaney (eds), *Chains of Servitude: Bondage and Slavery in India*. New York: Oxford University Press, 40–54; Benton, *Law and Colonial Culture*; M. Galanter (1989), *Law and Society in Modern India*. Delhi: Oxford University Press.

61. Bibliothèque Nationale de France, section des manuscrits, 'Nouvelles acquisitions de France', 9328.

62. For treatments of apprenticeship contracts, see Sonencher, *Works and Wages*.

63. Galenson, *White Servitude in Colonial America*.

64. Indentured were 60–5 per cent of all migrants in the seventeenth century and 40–2 per cent in the following century; see C. Tomlins (2010), *Freedom Bound: Law, Labor, and Civic Identity in Colonizing English America, 1580–1865*. Cambridge: Cambridge University Press, 34–5.

65. Northrup, *Indentured Labour*, 156–7, table A.1.

66. R. Menard (1977), 'From servants to slaves: The transformation of the Chesapeake labor system', *Southern Studies*, 16 (4), 366–7.

67. T. W. Allen (1994), *The Invention of the White Race*, 3 vols. New York: Verso; A. S. Parent Jr. (2003), *Foul Means: The Formation of a Slave Society in Virginia*. Chapel Hill, NC: North Carolina University Press.

68. S. Engerman (1993), 'Europeans and the rise and fall of slavery in the Americas: An interpretation', *American Historical Review*, 98 (5), 1399–1423.

69. Sir W. Blackstone (1765–9), *Commentaries on the Laws of England*, Oxford, 4 vols, vol. 2, 16.

70. R. Blackburn (1988), *The Overthrow of Colonial Slavery, 1776–1848*. London: Verso; Tomlins, *Freedom Bound*.

71. D. Armitage (2004), 'John Locke, Carolina, and the two treatises of government', *Political Theory*, 32 (5), 602–27; B. Hinshelwood (2013), 'The Carolinian context of John Locke's theory of slavery', *Political Theory*, 41 (4), 562–90.

72. R. Sheridan (1974), *Sugar and Slavery: An Economic History of the British West Indies, 1623–1775*. Barbados: Canoe Press.

73. Fogel and Engerman (1974), *Time on the Cross*; R. Fogel (1989), *Without Consent or Contract*. New York: Norton.

74. S. Drescher (2009), *Abolitions: A History of Slavery and Antislavery*. Cambridge: Cambridge University Press.

75. J. C. Miller (1999), *Slavery and Slaving in World History: A Bibliography, 1900–1996*. Armonk, NY: M. E. Sharpe; J. Watson (ed.) (1980), *Asian and African Systems of Slavery*. Berkeley, CA and Los Angeles, CA: University of California Press; W. G. Clarence-Smith (ed.) (1989), *The Economics of the Indian Ocean Slave Trade*. London: Frank Cass.

76. D. Eltis (1989), *Economic Growth and the Ending of Transatlantic Slave Trade*. Oxford: Oxford University Press.

77. Drescher, *Capitalism and Antislavery*.

78. BPP (1830–1), *Papers in Explanation of the Condition of the Slave Population, 5 November 1831*, CCXXX, 59–88.

79. J. R. Ward (1988), *British West India Slavery, 1750–1834: The Process of Amelioration*. Oxford: Oxford University Press.

80. M. Turner (2004), 'The British Caribbean, 1823–1838: The transition from slave to free legal status', in Hay and Craven, *Masters, Servants and Magistrates*, 322.

81. T. Holt (1992), *The Problem of Freedom: Race, Labour and Politics in Jamaica and Britain, 1832–1938*. Baltimore, MD and London: Johns Hopkins University Press.

82. R. Allen (1999), *Slaves, Freedmen and Indentured Labourers in Colonial Mauritius*. Cambridge: Cambridge University Press, 16–17. See also A. Toussaint (1974), *Histoire de l'Île Maurice*. Paris: PUF.

83. Colony of Mauritius, Annual Report, 1854; *BPP*, XLII, 2050. See also Jan Breman, *Taming the Coolie Beast*.

84. Mauritius National Archives (MNA), HA 66 (planters' petitions); BPP (1842), XXX (26), 25.

85. BPP (1842), XXX (26).

86. BPP (1875), '*Report of the Royal Commissioners Appointed to Enquire into the Treatment of Immigrants in Mauritius*', XXXIV, paragraph 704 and appendix A and B. Colony of Mauritius, printed documents, *Annual Report of the Protector of Immigrants, 1860–1885*.

87. Ibid.

88. Allen, *Slaves*, 72.

89. Mokyr, *The Level of Riches*, 114.

90. Wrigley, *Continuity, Chance and Change*.

91. Deakin and Wilkinson, *The Law of the Labour Market*, 86–7.

92. G. Bentley (1966), *The Evolution of National Insurance in Great Britain: The Origins of the Welfare State*. London: Joseph; J. Harris (1972), *Unemployment and Politics: A Study in English Social Policy, 1886–1914*. Oxford: Clarendon Press.

93. R. Salais, N. Bavarez and B. Reynaud (1986), *L'invention du chômage*. Paris: PUF.

94. A. Stanziani (2012), *Rules of Exchange: French Capitalism in Comparative Perspective, Eighteenth to Early Twentieth Century*. Cambridge: Cambridge University Press.

95. A. McKeown (2004), 'Global migration, 1846–1940', *Journal of World History*, 15 (2), 155–89; D. Treadgold (1957), *The Great Siberian Migration: Government and Peasant in Resettlement from Emancipation to the First World War*. Princeton, NJ: Princeton University Press, 33–5; T. Gottschang and D. Lary (2000), *Swallows and Settlers: The Great Migration from North China to Manchuria*. Ann Arbor, MI: University of Michigan, Center for Chinese Studies, 171.

96. McKeown, 'Global migration'.

97. O'Rourke and Williamson, *Globalization and History*.

98. K. Singh Sandhu (1969), *Indians in Malaya: Some Aspects of Their Immigration and Settlement (1786–1957)*. Cambridge: Cambridge University Press.

99. R. H. G. Lee (1970), *The Manchurian Frontier in Ch'ing History*. Cambridge, MA: Harvard University Press.

100. A. de Haan (1999), 'Migration on the border of free and unfree labour: Workers in Calcutta's jute industry, 1900–1990', in J. Lucassen and L. Lucassen (eds), *Migration, Migration History, History: Old Paradigms and New Perspectives*. Bern: Peter Lang, 197–222.

101. Northrup, *Indentured Labor*, 150.

102. McKeown, 'Global migration'.

CHAPTER 12
COLONIALISM AND ECONOMIC CHANGE IN ASIA AND AFRICA
Leigh Gardner

Any study of the economic legacies of colonial rule needs to confront the diverse trajectories of countries that experienced it. Nigeria, South Korea, Indonesia and Somalia all achieved independence from their respective colonizers in the years following the end of the Second World War. All had different conditions before colonial rule, different experiences during the colonial period, and have followed different paths since, both economically and politically. Understanding this diversity presents a challenge for the development of any single theory about the ways in which colonialism influenced patterns of economic change both during and after the colonial period.

This chapter examines how colonialism impacted economic development in Africa and Asia. In the middle of the twentieth century, the two regions were comparable in terms of their levels of per capita income, with some analysts at the time predicting a brighter future for Africa than for Asia. However, the decades since independence have seen a striking divergence. Both saw rapid economic growth through the post-war golden age, but from the 1970s until the 1990s many African economies experienced a prolonged period of economic shrinking – often described as the continent's 'lost decades' – while most Asian economies continued to grow. As a result, a wide gap emerged and the narrative shifted decisively in the other direction.

This 'south–south divergence' has solidified in the minds of both scholars and the general public the idea that Africa's relative poverty has persisted over centuries, and made explaining why Africa is (and has always been) the poorest region in the world a favourite topic of research in economics and economic history.[1] The comparison with Asia shows that this became true only after independence. However, this chapter argues that the seeds for the divergence were sewn farther back in history, to the different economic endowments of the two regions and the strategies adopted by colonial powers in governing them.

In order to address such a large question within a single chapter, the chapter will focus on a comparison between India and four former British colonies in Africa (Ghana, Kenya, Nigeria and South Africa). The selection of these cases is not to suggest that India is necessarily representative of colonies in Asia, nor that this set of British colonies reflect the whole of colonial African history. Neither is the case. India was exceptional in many ways during the colonial period and, as numerous scholars have noted, has had a different pattern of post-independence development than other Asian economies, with growth based more on services than industry.[2] In Africa, it is frequently speculated that during the colonial scramble of the late nineteenth century, Britain acquired the 'plums', territories already better developed than its colonial rivals.[3] However, a restricted comparison of British colonies has the virtue of being able to hold constant the policies and preferences of a single colonizer, and focus on how differences in local conditions shaped the ways in which those policies were implemented on the ground. In the British Empire, India often served as a proving ground for policies adapted to the governance of a larger and more diverse range of colonies in the nineteenth century. In particular, colonial officials who became influential in the shaping of British governance in Africa often began their careers in India and drew on that experience in making policies in Africa.[4] Thus a comparison between the two serves as a fruitful way to illustrate the ways in which British colonial policy was extended and adapted, and the legacies of these adaptations for former colonies after independence.

The next section compares and contrasts patterns of long-run growth in the two regions. Section 3 focuses on the types of colonial institutions established at both national and local levels and highlights the ways in which lessons from India were applied in the later colonization of Africa. Sections 4 and 5 examine patterns of investment during the colonial period, including both physical capital such as railways and canals, and also human capital in the form of education. Section 6 concludes by comparing the decolonization experiences of the two regions and reflecting on how this colonial history influenced the contrasting patterns of post-independence development.

Long-run Growth in Asia and Africa

This section compares and contrasts patterns of long-run growth in Asia and Africa before, during and after the colonial period. It shows that the two regions had much in common during the nineteenth and early twentieth centuries. Along with much of the rest of the pre-industrial world, their economies were characterized by periods of growth followed by periods of shrinking, which offset many of the gains accrued during periods of growth, leading to long-run stagnation.[5]

It is only relatively recently that new scholarship has allowed for comparisons of long-run growth in the two regions, and there remain significant disparities in the amount of data available between and within regions. For larger Asian economies like India and China, GDP per capita can be calculated back to the medieval period.[6] For others, data on aggregate economic performance are only available for more recent periods or have yet to be estimated. For most of Africa, data on GDP per capita are available only from the late nineteenth century.[7] South Africa is an exception, with data going back to the eighteenth century.[8]

Figure 12.1 compares the GDP per capita of India and Sub-Saharan Africa. The data show that levels of per capita income were comparable between the two regions during the nineteenth century and the first half of the twentieth. The measure used is 1990 international dollars, the standard metric in studies of historical national accounting. In

1990 the World Bank determined a poverty rate of a dollar a day, and thus in historical national accounting subsistence level is generally estimated to be $400 1990 international dollars, or a dollar a day for most people plus a small elite. The minimum level of GDP per capita for physical survival is estimated to be $300.[9] Levels of GDP per capita may dip below these levels for very brief periods – for example during agricultural crises or conflict – but it is not possible to sustain life below this level for very long.

Both Africa and India had levels of GDP per capita which were above subsistence during the colonial period. In both cases, levels of income were around $500 1990 international dollars at the close of the nineteenth century. In India's case, this represented a decline from early modern levels of income of around $700 at the height of the Mughal Empire. There are numerous debates about why this decline occurred. One explanation focuses on the pattern of structural change. India went from being a leading exporter of manufactures – principally textiles – during the early modern period, to being an agricultural exporter by the nineteenth century. This process of de-industrialization is unlikely to have had a major impact on GDP per capita, however, as in the early modern period industry was a relatively small share of the total economy. Others attribute decline to a stagnation in the productivity of agriculture, the largest sector of the economy which employed the vast majority of the population.[10]

This pattern can be compared to Fourie and van Zanden's estimates of GDP per capita for the Cape Colony going back to the eighteenth century. Their estimates show GDP per capita at a high level of around $2000 at the beginning of the eighteenth century, supporting other evidence that the settler society of the Cape was comparatively affluent

Figure 12.1 GDP per capita in India and Sub-Saharan Africa.
Source: S. N. Broadberry and L. A. Gardner (2022), 'Economic growth in Sub-Saharan Africa, 1885–2008: Evidence from eight countries', *Explorations in Economic History* 83, 101424.

at this early date.[11] However, this level declined to less than $1000 by the middle of the nineteenth century and by the 1880s the Cape Colony was no better off than the commercialized coastal economies of West Africa. Figure 12.2 compares the Cape Colony (South Africa after 1912) with Nigeria, the colonial Gold Coast and Kenya. It shows that South Africa only surged ahead during the interwar period.

Early economic histories of Africa often assumed that, prior to European colonialism, incomes were at subsistence level. In one of the first books on Africa's economic history, published in 1926, Allen McPhee attributed growth in Africa to 'the three Rs,' namely railways, the rule of the British, and 'Ross's medical achievements' (malaria prophylaxis).[12] However, qualitative histories of pre-colonial economies suggest that this assessment is incorrect. African economies participated in the global commercial revolution of the thirteenth century, particularly through the export of gold and, like India, saw the development of significant handicraft textile production.[13] In the absence of sufficient quantitative data, Jerven offers a qualitative narrative speculating about the likely impact of these early periods of growth on per capita incomes.[14]

Levels of GDP per capita above subsistence level did not, however, mean that there was sustained growth in either region. Periods of growth were followed by periods of shrinking which erased any gains achieved, leading to long-run stagnation.[15] This pattern held during the colonial period. For both India and Africa, the First World War saw significant shrinking as the war disrupted trade and caused a sharp increase in the relative price of manufactured goods. India's economy suffered a longer period of shrinking during the Great Depression of the 1930s and the Second World War. In

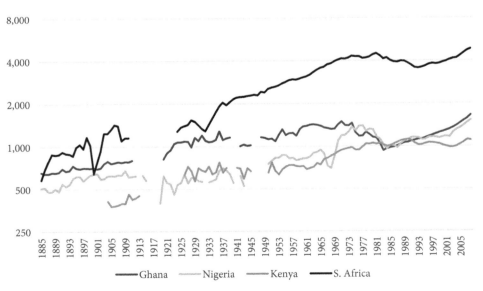

Figure 12.2 GDP per capita in selected African countries.
Source: S. N. Broadberry and L. A. Gardner (2022), 'Economic growth in Sub-Saharan Africa, 1885–2008: Evidence from eight countries', *Explorations in Economic History* 83, 101424.

Africa, the impact of the war was blunted by Africa's importance as a supplier of strategic commodities after the fall of much of Southeast Asia to Japanese imperialism. The interwar period saw the beginning of what is known in African history as the 'second colonial invasion' when Britain and other colonial powers began to invest more heavily in the expansion of commodity production.

GDP per capita captures only one dimension of development, overall output. In the long run, improvements in aggregate output and living standards are generally linked to structural change, or the shift from the production of primary products to manufactured goods and services.[16] The history of structural change is more varied than the history of overall output, though overall it shows more similarities than differences between the two regions. Economies remained largely agricultural through the colonial period and into the first decades of independence. India experienced significant growth in industry, which was given a boost by the introduction of protective tariffs in the 1930s.[17] Similarly, South Africa also made use of the natural protection provided by the trade shock of the First World War followed by tariffs imposed during the 1920s to build its industrial sector. Early industrial leaders in South Africa were often linked to the mining sector, but managed to become competitive in their own right and, as a result, industry became a more important sector than mining during the first half of the twentieth century. In this period South Africa surged ahead of the West African leaders to become the wealthiest economy in the Sub-Saharan region.[18] Kenya also made use of tariffs to encourage the growth of manufacturing.[19]

Despite this, agriculture remained the largest sector in terms of both its share of GDP and employment, even after post-independence governments in both India and Africa made economic diversification a key priority. Table 12.1 shows the share of the labour force in agriculture in 1960 and 1970 for all five countries. Only in South Africa did agriculture employ less than half the labour force, and India's share was second only to Kenya in 1970. Furthermore, government-led programmes to encourage the expansion of industry in the post-independence decades appear to have made little impact apart from in Nigeria and South Africa.

Table 12.1 Share of the labour force in agriculture, 1960 and 1970, in percentage

	1960	1970
India	72	72
Ghana	61	57
Kenya	n.a.	81
Nigeria	78	66
South Africa	49	35

Sources: G. J. de Vries, M. P. Timmer and K. de Vries (2015), 'Structural transformation in Africa: Static gains, dynamic losses', *Journal of Development Studies* 5, 674–88; M. P. Timmer and G. J. de Vries (2007), 'A cross-country database for sectoral employment and productivity in Asia and Latin America, 1950–2005', GGDC Research Memorandum GD-98. Data on Kenya only available from 1969.

Divergent patterns of structural change in terms of the allocation of the labour force thus do not help explain why India surged ahead in the 1980s while Africa entered its 'lost decades'. Studies of African growth during the 1990s attributed the severity of the downturn to policies adopted by post-independence governments.[20] However, subsequent work has begun to investigate how the policies of the colonial period influenced the structural weaknesses which exacerbated the downturn. As Bishnupriya Gupta writes regarding India, 'colonization left a deep imprint that shaped the development of states in the post-colonial decades'.[21] The next sections of the chapter compare the colonial histories of the two regions to investigate the origins of their divergent patterns of development.

Colonial Institutions

Recent literature in the economic histories of both Asia and Africa has accorded colonial institutions an important role in shaping the economic and political development of both regions.[22] Colonial policies, it is argued, promoted – sometimes at gunpoint – the development of extractive industries which created few opportunities for building local capacity that could sustain development. They empowered expatriate enterprise at the expense of indigenous business, and often supported the use of coercive labour policies. This line of argument assumes that European officials had significant freedom to impose whatever institutions suited their economic interests. Others, however, have argued that understaffed and under-resourced colonial administrations had limited capacity to get their way, and were heavily dependent on the cooperation of indigenous institutional structures and intermediaries. The impact of colonialism was not therefore simply a function of European policies but the ways in which those policies depended on and interacted with existing institutions.

In both regions, colonial officials faced similar constraints. Territorial rule was costly – and increasingly unpopular with expanding electorates in European capitals. One early strategy used in India and in Africa was to outsource these costs to private firms willing to bear both cost and risk in return for privileged rights over trade or resources. This method of imperial expansion was used first in the Americas but arguably made its biggest mark in India, with the development of the East India Company (EIC). Territorial expansion was not a central aim of the EIC's original charters, which were issued in the seventeenth century. However, efforts to exert control over production and trade ultimately during the eighteenth century led to the negotiation of agreements with elites in the collapsing Mughal Empire. Through this process, the company shifted from merchant firm to what was, in effect, a colonial state governing extensive territories in South Asia.[23]

This method of territorial expansion had the advantage of shifting costs and risks away from the Imperial treasury, but the disadvantage of creating agency problems which could still impact the metropolitan government.[24] The scale of these risks became evident to the British government with the 1857 rebellion India. What began as a mutiny amongst Indian soldiers in one garrison town soon spread, and ultimately threatened to overthrow British rule in the Subcontinent. As a result, the Company ceded administrative control to the British government, much as later chartered companies would do in Africa.

Unlike the EIC's original charter, the charters granted to companies in Africa were often more explicit about the intention to take over territory, particularly those issued in the late nineteenth century to companies like the Imperial British East Africa Company (IBEC) or the British South Africa Company (BSAC).[25] Perhaps reflecting the fact that their origins were more political than economic, these proved to be less resilient over time. The IBEAC received its charter in 1888, but ceded control over East Africa just five years later. Cecil Rhodes's BSAC – chartered 1889 – lasted longer, owing to its ability to draw on the profits of Rhodes's South African mining operations, but it also ceded administrative control over Northern and Southern Rhodesia (post-independence Zambia and Zimbabwe) by 1924.[26]

Direct administrative control over colonies reduced some of the agency problems created by Company rule, but it did not solve the problem of cost. Efforts to reduce the costs and risks of colonial governance to the British treasury influenced the structure and policies of colonial administrations in profound ways which had lasting impacts after independence. While the precise impact varied between colonies and regions, there were several common methods adopted across the British Empire which will be discussed in this and subsequent sections. These included restricting the number of British administrators, whose salaries were high relative to local tax revenues, and by consequence depending on indigenous institutions and elites to sustain the machinery of colonial rule. It also included limiting the scope of central government activities to those which either maintained security or had a direct revenue return.

Limited numbers of British officials meant that colonial governments in all regions relied on the incorporation of indigenous agents to govern, often referred to as a system of 'indirect rule'. While this phrase has become widely used, it does not have a precise definition. Writing in the early 1940s, Lord Hailey – a former member of the Indian civil service later commissioned to examine the system of colonial governments in Africa – refused to use the phrase because it had 'no claim to precision'.[27] One study by political scientists Adnan Naseemullah and Paul Staniland argues that indirect rule represented not a single form of government but rather a variety of ways of sharing power.[28]

As the debate about definitions suggests, the exact structure of this incorporation varied, in large part due to variation in the structure of indigenous institutions. In India, the flat, fertile Indo-Gangetic Basin supported the rise of centralized states through the easy taxing of both trade and land. By contrast, states in more rugged or arid zones tended to be smaller and less centralized.[29] Similarly, in Africa, most people lived in polities where authority was centred at the village level rather than in centralized states. Larger political units tended to emerge in centres of long-distance trade like the edge of the Sahara or the Swahili Coast, or around natural resources like the gold mines of west and central Africa.[30]

Where more centralized states prevailed, as for example in India's princely states or the Emirates of Northern Nigeria – powers of domestic governance were often left entirely in the hands of indigenous states, which gave up their powers of military intervention and foreign policy making in return for support and confirmation by the colonial government. In other regions where indigenous institutions were either less centralized or less willing to cooperate with colonial governments, the structure and degree of power sharing varied. Outside the princely states, for example, the colonial government in India varied in terms of whether powers of revenue collection were placed in the hands of landlords or whether revenue was collected directly from cultivators. In the Gold Coast, the Asante state resisted overtures by colonial officials, who in turn sought to strengthen rival states. In Kenya and eastern Nigeria, where indigenous institutions were highly decentralized, African village heads were initially employed by the colonial state and given only limited authority. Colonial institutions can thus be characterized as the product of a long series of compromises and accommodations shaped by indigenous institutional structures and the constraints and priorities of colonial governments.[31]

This story applies primary to rural areas, which in both India and Africa were home to the vast majority of the population. Institutional strategies in urban areas – particularly port cities and colonial capitals – were different. In these areas, and also in regions with extensive migration from Europe or other parts of the empire, indigenous institutions were more forcefully displaced by European legal frameworks. Again, this did not mean a wholesale displacement of indigenous institutions – rather, it created an additional source of variation and fragmentation. For example, in areas of European settlement in Kenya and South Africa, land rights were reconfigured on terms of individual ownership, while systems of communal ownership persisted in areas 'reserved' for indigenous habitation. However, the reduced scale of land availability in the reserves prompted endogenous changes in the ways in which land rights were allocated and enforced.

The persistent importance (but varied roles) of indigenous institutions presents a challenge to efforts by economists to disentangle links between colonial institutions and later patterns of development. This question has been an important one in the study of comparative economic performance during the past two decades. The most common way of approaching the question is to divide colonial institutions into approximate categories, based for example on the type of institution or the identity of the colonizer. However, these categories are based on relatively superficial features of colonial regimes, and do not reflect the complexities of power sharing with indigenous institutions. In concrete terms, these complexities meant that important features of economic life in colonial India and Africa – from access to land to the regulation of credit – were governed very differently in different parts of the same country. Economists and economic historians have yet to come to a consensus about how this variation affected economic development over time.

In answer to this, there have been attempts to link the structure of pre-colonial and colonial institutions to present-day spatial inequalities in levels of development. In one well-known, if contested, claim for India, Abidjit Banerjee and Lakshmi Iyer find that the regions where landlords were responsible for collecting tax revenue have lower levels of development in the decades after independence.[32] For Africa, Stelios Michalopoulos and Elias Papaioannou have found, for example, that parts of Africa with more centralized pre-colonial institutions seem to be more developed in the present day.[33] On the basis of this finding, they argue that pre-colonial institutions remained the most important providers of public goods through the colonial period owing to the limited capacity of colonial states. However, the mechanism for this finding remains the subject of debate – using evidence from Uganda, Sanghamitra Bandyopadhyay and Elliott Green argue that the link simply reflects a persistence in local income inequalities rather than the provision of public goods.[34]

Institutions thus reflected and consolidated local inequalities in colonial economies. However, they were not the only source of such inequalities. The next two sections examine two other factors which shaped differences in economic development between and within colonies. The first section focuses on railways, which were a central investment priority for colonial states urgently seeking to build and expand sources of tax revenue. The second section, by contrast, examines investment in education, which offered little immediate revenue return but nevertheless had a lasting impact on the development of former colonies in the two regions.

Colonial Investments: Railways

The urgent fiscal imperatives faced by colonial states expected to pay their own way exerted a powerful influence on their development policies. Their first priority, beyond maintaining stability and avoiding costly conflict, was to increase revenue. In most places, this meant expanding the production of exports, generally primary commodities. The main obstacle to this objective was transport costs, which had previously restricted commodity production to specific areas. As a result, transport infrastructure was a central target of colonial investment in both Asia and Africa. There remain debates about the extent to which these investments improved overall levels of development. However, there is little doubt about the fact that they shaped the economic (and sometimes political) geography of the colonies, both during and after the colonial period. This section focuses particularly on railways, because while colonial investments in transport infrastructure also included things like roads, ports and canals, the railways were a key focus, absorbing the largest share of resources and also generating the most extensive debates about their impact.

Railways came first to India, starting in the middle of the nineteenth century. It was no coincidence that the construction of railways began just a few years after the 1847 Mutiny and the end of Company rule. The newly installed governor of India – James Ramsay, Marquess of Dalhousie was 'committed, in the first place, to unifying British sovereignty both territorially and legally'. In this quest, he was notable for his 'embrace of the new technologies that were transforming the west', which at that point included railways.[35] The first lines were constructed in 1853, and the network continued to expand until the 1930s, becoming one of the largest railway networks in the world.[36] However, investments infrastructure remained unevenly distributed. Latika Chaudhary and Dan Bogart note that 'while the four major ports were well connected to the interior, there were few interior-to-interior connections. Moreover, less developed parts of the country, like the southeast, had few lines even as late as 1930'.[37]

Regional inequalities were even more pronounced in the construction of African railways, which were similarly focused on connecting ports to regions of either economic or political significance. Ralph Austen describes Africa's colonial railway as 'a classic element of what is called a dendritic market system, i.e. a leaflike network emanating from the outlets of international trade to the various regions of the African interior but not linking the latter to one another'.[38] The first railways in Africa were at the southern and northern extremes of the continent. In North Africa, the first railway connected Alexandria to Cairo in 1857, and reached Suez in 1858. In that same year, construction of the Algerian railway began. In 1876 Tunisia built a small railway line. Other parts of North Africa, such as Libya and Morocco, did not begin railway construction until the twentieth century.[39] In the Cape Colony, railway construction began just a few years after India, in 1859, but expansion was slow, and as late as 1870 only one line was in operation covering the 57 miles between Cape Town, Wynberg and Wellington. The railway network expanded rapidly with an influx of British capital following the discovery of gold on the Witwatersrand in 1886. By 1912, the South African rail network was by far the densest in Africa. It even outstripped India in terms of railway density per capita, with 2.19 kms per 1,000 people as compared with 0.18.[40]

In the rest of Sub-Saharan Africa, infrastructure investments were much more limited. West Africa was the next region to see the construction of railways beginning in the 1890s, As noted in section 2, West Africa had been growing in terms of its commercial significance as the producer of agricultural and forest products. However, the construction of railways could not begin until colonial control had been firmly established towards the end of the century. The first railway in Nigeria extended from Lagos on the coast to Ibadan, with construction starting in 1896. In the Gold Coast, the first railway from the port of Sekondi to Tarkwa was begun in 1898 but proceeded slowly due to labour shortages and the upheaval of the Asante wars. The end of the war allowed for the completion of the initial line and an extension to Kumasi, the Asante capital.[41] The final years of the nineteenth century also saw the construction of the Uganda Railway, initially intended to connect the source of the Nile in Uganda to the coast. Work began in 1896 and the railway was completed by 1901.[42]

That railway construction was a key priority of colonial governments is evident, from the share of total expenditure devoted to infrastructure, which remained the largest category of colonial government spending once the initial military costs of colonial conquest had declined.[43] It was also evident from the extensive government intervention required to secure the financing for these large and uncertain projects. There was little interest from private investors in funding railway construction, and as a result, colonial states were required to step in. In India, the government guaranteed returns on railway investments at 5 per cent. Such a guarantee was costly. Early construction costs exceeded estimates by a significant margin, in part because the guarantee might have incentivized the use of higher-cost methods.[44] In Africa, most railways were constructed through loans raised in London by colonial governments.[45]

The impact of railway construction on economic development remains the subject of debate in both Asia and Africa. They had a clear impact on transport costs and, by consequence, trade. Both regions saw a rapid increase in exported produce, following the construction of the railways. Previously, as already noted, long-distance trade had been limited mostly to high-value goods. Railways made it possible to move low value-to-weight goods over longer distances at much lower costs, particularly for regions that lacked easy access to water transport. In West Africa, for example, colonial officials estimated the cost of head porterage to be between 3 and 5 shillings per ton-mile. In contrast, shipping by rail cost an estimated 2 pence per ton-mile.[46] There is significant uncertainty in these numbers: the financial cost of head porterage depended on the extent to which labour could be coerced, while shipping rates on the railways were influenced by a variety of factors. In regions where water transport was accessible, the difference was less. For example, in the Gangetic plains water transport was competitive with railways into the twentieth century.[47]

Uncertainties about precise numbers aside, it is clear that railways could decrease the cost of overland transport significantly. In so doing they often created the conditions for commercialization. Even railways not constructed for commercial reasons had an impact on trade. In Northern Nigeria, for example, railways initially served primarily strategic purposes, facilitating the movement of British troops into the region. However, the reduction of transport costs facilitated export of groundnuts and the development of one of Nigeria's most important export industries of the colonial period.[48] In other cases, the main target of railways had unanticipated impacts. In the Gold Coast, railways constructed for the purposes of accessing the gold mines in Tarkwa swiftly became most important as the means by which the cocoa-growing areas in forest zones could access global markets.[49]

The wider developmental impacts of these shifts remain the subject of debate in both regions. Beyond relatively thin rail networks, transport costs to railway stations remained high, which meant that the extent to which benefits were achieved depended very heavily on proximity. Several studies have shown that investments in railways – and also in other infrastructures like roads – had lasting effects on the human geography of former colonies, providing the foundation for cities and other population settlements.[50] Nairobi, now the main commercial hub of East Africa, began its life as the headquarters of the Uganda Railway before displacing older cities like Mombasa. In India, railways played a key role in the reduction of famine mortality in the twentieth century through the integration of domestic markets for food.[51] However, in other ways, developmental impacts were limited or ambiguous. For several colonial railways, dependence on coerced labour in their construction meant that their short-run impacts on living standards might have been negative. In both Asia and Africa, spillover effects from their construction – which might have otherwise promoted industrial development – were limited owing to the importation of rolling stock and other equipment from Britain.

These limited spillover effects form part of a larger story of the narrow development aims of colonial states. Railways and other infrastructure projects were intended primarily to promote the expansion of trade, and in particular the export of primary commodities.

Broader structural transformations in colonial economies were never part of the aims of colonial governments. As the next section shows, these narrow development aims were reflected in a lack of investment in human capital.

Colonial Investments: Education

The focus of colonial development policies on the rapid expansion of export production meant that in neither of the regions considered did colonial governments invest heavily in the human capital of indigenous populations. Shares of total expenditure on education, healthcare and other services remained low through most of the colonial period, only rising to a limited degree from the interwar period onwards. With such limited contributions from the state, private actors were often important providers of social services, though their presence and activities varied widely within as well as between colonies. This section uses the comparison with Africa to support arguments that differences in investments in human capital can help explain the divergence in economic performance.

In part, the neglect of education (and also healthcare) by colonial governments reflected contemporary norms of political economy which prescribed a limited role for the state outside the provision of defence and internal security. Even in metropolitan states, government intervention did not expand much beyond these narrow confines until the interwar period.[52] Restrictions on the range of public sector activities continued to inform colonial fiscal policies even after they began to lose influence in Britain itself, reinforced by the relative penury of colonial governments and the high costs of other public expenses such as the salaries of European officials or infrastructure construction.

Even by the standards of colonial governments in the early twentieth century, these spent little on education. Comparative data collected by Lance Davis and Robert Huttenback shows that India spent £0.01 per capita per year on human capital, equivalent to 5.9 per cent of its budget in 1910–12. In contrast, the indigenous-ruled Princely States spent £0.04 per capita (or 11 per cent of their total budget) in the same period. The average rate for dependent colonies, which included Kenya, Nigeria and Ghana, was £0.19 per capita or 14.1 per cent. Breaking this down to examine the individual budgets of the African colonies shows they were closer to India's level. Table 12.2 compares Davis and Huttenback's data for India with data for the four African colonies. Only the Cape Colony stands out for a higher level of spending, but this is misleading, as a large share of this expenditure was devoted to providing education to European settlers. In 1909, education spending was allocated as follows: £50,444 within the reserves and a much higher £471,244 outside. The white population in that same year was estimated to be 610,680 while the non-white population was 1,896,820. This meant that the colonial government spent approximately £0.77 per capita on education for the white population, and £0.02 on the non-white population, similar to the spending by the other governments.

What limited funds governments spent on education were devoted mostly to subsidizing schools run not by the state but by a range of private actors. In India, missionaries had been important providers of education in the early nineteenth century, but fell out of favour after a change in education policy issued in 1854. After that, most schools were private, and run by Indians. Some of these received funding from the colonial state (aided schools) while others were unaided but still classified under the official education system. The numbers of indigenous schools began to decline as the official system expanded.[53]

Missionaries remained important in British Africa, where the vast majority of students enrolled in any form of education were enrolled in mission-run schools. Even in 1938, 97 per cent of students in Southern Nigeria were enrolled in mission schools. In Kenya, it was 92 per cent. The Gold Coast had a higher share of students in state schools than most British colonies in Africa, but even there the share in mission schools was 83 per cent.[54] British colonial governments were more enthusiastic about assisting mission schools, which helped expand education provision. In a comparative study of Cameroon, which was divided between Britain and France after the First World War, Yannick Dupraz shows that men growing up on the British side of the border during the interwar period were more likely to have attended school and for longer than on the French side.[55]

However, access to education was not distributed evenly across colonies. After the displacement of missionaries from the Indian education system, responsibility for education was decentralized to district boards. Funding was strongly linked to local tax revenues and the resources available to local government. Districts with higher tax revenues also had higher literacy rates.[56] Mission schools were also not evenly distributed. Colonial governments restricted mission activity in some areas, particularly regions that were predominantly Muslim or ruled in the pre-colonial period by Islamic states.[57] This

Table 12.2 Education spending, 1910–12, in GBP

	Spending per capita	*Share of total spending*
India	0.01	0.06
Cape Colony	0.21	0.06
Ghana (Gold Coast)	0.05	0.03
Kenya	0.04	0.01
Nigeria	0.01	0.02

Sources: L. E. Davis and R. A. Huttenback (1986), *Mammon and the Pursuit of Empire: The Political Economy of British Imperialism, 1860–1912*. Cambridge: Cambridge University Press, 134; E. Frankema (2011), 'Colonial taxation and government spending in British Africa, 1880–1940: Maximizing revenue or minimizing effort?', *Explorations in Economic History*, 48, Table A1; Cape Colony (1910), *Statistical Register of the Province of the Cape of Good Hope for the Year 1909*. Cape Town: Government Printer.

led to substantial inequalities in the availability of formal education in these regions. While indigenous systems of Islamic education continued to exist throughout the colonial period, these could not generally provide the formal qualifications recognized for employment in colonial and post-independence economies.

There is growing evidence that these investments had a lasting impact on the lives and livelihoods of people who had access to colonial education. In India, districts with greater spending on education and higher literacy rates during the colonial period continue to have comparatively higher rates of education well into the post-independence period, though government efforts to expand access to education began to reduce these differences from the 1970s onwards.[58] Similarly, in a study of French West Africa, Elise Huillery finds that districts which had greater colonial-era investments in schools and medical provision continued to have greater access to these services in the post-independence period.[59] Survey data from Benin shows that access to education had lasting impacts not only for the people who received but for their relatives and descendants as well.[60] Several studies of mission locations have argued that places where missions were located had higher levels of economic development decades later.[61]

Colonial policies were not the only factor shaping the distribution of education. Indigenous demand was also an important factor in determining both who would be educated and to what level. In Africa, most mission stations were founded not by Europeans but rather by Africans, in large part to meet local demand for schooling. One critique of the arguments presented above arguing that mission education contributed to later development notes that missions tended to be in localities which already had higher levels of underlying development, making it difficult to establish a causal link between the location of missions and later economic outcomes.[62] Local social and economic factors also had an impact; in India, districts that were more diverse providing less public education but more private education.

The importance of private demand in India led to the disproportionate expansion of secondary schooling over primary. Table 12.3 compares gross enrolment rates in primary and secondary schools across the five countries in 1920. At that stage, secondary school enrolment in India was several times that of the other countries, while primary enrolment was not very different. South Africa had the highest rate of secondary enrolment among the African countries, and a higher rate of tertiary enrolment than India, but as in the case of expenditure this is likely to have been dominated by the European population. Chaudhary notes that international comparisons make India's level of secondary school enrolment even more striking: 'In 1916/17, British India had a larger share of the population enrolled in secondary schools than either France or Japan and it was only marginally below England and Wales'.[63]

The high level of secondary school enrolment reflected the high level of demand from amongst Indian elites. With their focus on investments in infrastructure that would help increase trade – and, by consequence, tax revenue – colonial states invested little in the human capital of the people they governed. Private actors, whether private schools or missionaries, were the key providers of education. Their actions were, in turn, shaped

Table 12.3 Gross enrolment rates in five countries, 1920

	Primary	*Secondary*	*Tertiary*
India	12.4	2.7	0.2
South Africa	30.3	0.6	0.3
Ghana	8.5	0.1	0
Kenya	5.5	0	0
Nigeria	2	–	–

Sources: J.-W. Lee and H. Lee (2016), 'Human capital in the long run', *Journal of Development Economics*, 122, 147–69; E. H. P. Frankema (2012), 'The origins of formal education in sub-Saharan Africa: Was British rule more benign?', *European Review of Economic History*, 16, 335–55.

by patterns of indigenous demand which often consolidated spatial inequalities that had existed previously or were created by investments in infrastructure.

Conclusion: Legacies of Colonial Economic Development in India and Africa

European colonial rule collapsed after the Second World War. India paved the way for others, with independence in 1947 bringing to a rapid end what had been a long process of negotiated devolution of power from London. Decolonization in Africa followed a decade or so later, beginning with Ghana in 1957. Most of British Africa followed by the early 1960s. At this point, as noted in the introduction, India and Africa had similar levels of economic output. Three decades later, India surged ahead. What role did colonialism play in this divergence?

As this chapter has shown, there were numerous common threads running through the colonial experiences of both regions. Economies in both regions were largely agricultural, and vulnerable to global market shifts. Efforts to promote economic diversification in the decades following independence struggled to make permanent changes, a subject that remains in need of more systematic investigation. In both, the limited capacity of colonial governments led to the establishment of a mixed set of institutions which drew both from European policies and indigenous precedents, resulting in substantial variation within as well between colonies in the ways in which important areas of economic life were governed. This variation was exacerbated by uneven investments in both physical infrastructure and education.

These common threads only run so far as explanations. Despite what is now a substantial literature attempting to make broad claims about the legacies of colonial rule for economic development, local variations in colonial policies – and, perhaps more importantly, indigenous responses to them – make such generalizations difficult. Further, the legacy of the colonial period is shaped partly by post-independence contingencies. For example, in a study comparing the productivity of the Indian economy with that of the United Kingdom, Stephen Broadberry and Bishnupriya Gupta argue that the substantial investment in secondary education during the colonial period set the stage for the rapid improvement in productivity in the service sector, claiming that 'the recent dynamic performance of services is not something which suddenly emerged during India's recent phase of overall catching up, but rather has long historical roots'.[64]

In contrast, underinvestment by African economies in human capital has arguably held back productivity, particularly in sectors outside agriculture. While services have expanded as a share of GDP in African economies, particularly since the 1990s, productivity has not yet begun to catch up. In South Africa, the only one of the African economies studied here to achieve similar rates of enrolment in secondary and tertiary education, the unequal distribution of investments made it difficult for businesses in manufacturing and services to recruit sufficient skilled labour.[65]

All of these links remain speculative and deserving of further research. Comparative studies between India and other countries hoping to achieve similar growth through technology-led services suggest that a number of factors beyond the pattern of education led to India's success.[66] However, the comparison between the impact of colonialism in India and a selection of African colonies suggests that any story about economic change during colonialism and its legacies for post-independence economic performance must address the extent to which local factors – including indigenous responses – shaped colonial policies in order to understand diversities in political and economic development after the end of the colonial period.

Notes

1. E. Frankema (2021), 'Why Africa is not that poor', in Alberto Bisin and Giovanni Federico (eds), *Handbook of Historical Economics*. London: Academic Press, 557–84.

2. B. Bosworth and S. M. Collins (2008), 'Accounting for growth: Comparing India and China', *Journal of Economic Perspectives*, 22 (1), 45–66; B. Gupta (2019), 'Falling behind and catching up: India's transition from a global economy', *Economic History Review*, 72 (3), 803–27.

3. J. Burbank and F. Cooper (2010), *Empires in World History: Power and the Politics of Difference*. Princeton, NJ: Princeton University Press.

4. Examples of such officials include Frederick Lugard, who was born in Madras and whose father and uncle served in the British military there; Sir Alan Pim, who spent his career in the Indian Civil Service before going on to chair several commissions on the finances of African colonies; and Lord William Malcolm Hailey, who was governor of several Indian provinces before authoring three influential studies of colonial administration in Africa.

5. S. N. Broadberry (2021), 'Accounting for the Great Divergence: Recent findings from historical national accounting', *Oxford Economic and Social History Working Papers*, 187.

6. S. N. Broadberry, J. Custodiis and B. Gupta (2015), 'India and the Great Divergence: An Anglo-Indian comparison of GDP per capita, 1600–1871', *Explorations in Economic History*,

55, 58–75; S. N. Broadberry, H. Guan and D. D. Li (2018), 'China, Europe and the Great Divergence: A study in historical national accounting', *Journal of Economic History*, 78 (40), 955–1000.

7. L. Prados de la Escosura (2012), 'Output per head in pre-independence Africa: Quantitative conjectures', *Economic History of Developing Regions*, 27, 1–36; S. N. Broadberry and L. A. Gardner (2022), 'Economic growth in Sub-Saharan Africa, 1885–2008: Evidence from eight countries', *Explorations in Economic History*, 83, 101424; M. Jerven (2022), *The Wealth and Poverty of African States: Economic Growth, Living Standards and Taxation since the Late Nineteenth Century*. Cambridge: Cambridge University Press, ch. 3.

8. J. Fourie and J.-L. van Zanden (2013), 'GDP in the Dutch Cape Colony: The national accounts of a slave-based society', *South African Journal of Economics*, 81 (3), 467–90.

9. Prados de la Escosura, 'Output per head'.

10. Gupta, 'Falling behind and catching up'.

11. J. Fourie (2013), 'The remarkable wealth of the Dutch Cape Colony: Measurements from eighteenth-century probate inventories', *Economic History Review*, 66 (2), 419–48; J. Fourie and F. Garmon (2023), 'The settlers' fortunes: Comparing tax censuses in the Cape Colony and early American republic', *Economic History Review*, 76 (2), 525–50.

12. A. McPhee (1926), *The Economic Revolution in British West Africa*. London: Routledge.

13. K. Frederick (2020), *Twilight of an Industry in East Africa: Textile Manufacturing 1830–1940*. Cham: Palgrave Macmillan.

14. M. Jerven (2010), 'African growth recurring: An economic history perspective on African growth episodes, 1690–2010', *Economic History of Developing Regions*, 25 (2), 127–54.

15. S. N. Broadberry and J. Wallis (2017), 'Growing, shrinking and long run economic performance: Historical perspectives on economic development', NBER Working Paper 23343.

16. H. Chenery and M. Syrquin (1975), *Patterns of development, 1950–1970*. Oxford: Oxford University Press.

17. Gupta, 'Falling behind and catching up'.

18. C. H. Feinstein (2005), *An Economic History of South Africa: Conquest, Discrimination, and Development*. Cambridge: Cambridge University Press.

19. R. M. A. van Zwanenberg and A. King (1975), *An Economic History of Kenya and Uganda, 1800–1970*. London: Macmillan.

20. See, for example, P. Collier and J. W. Gunning (1999), 'Why has Africa grown slowly?', *Journal of Economic Perspectives*, 13 (3), 3–22.

21. Gupta, 'Falling behind and catching up', 821.

22. For a review, see L. A. Gardner and T. Roy (2020), *Economic History of Colonialism*. Bristol: Bristol University Press, ch. 1.

23. S. Hejeebu (2015), 'The colonial transition and the decline of the East India Company, c.1746–1784', in L. Chaudhary et al. (eds), *A New Economic History of Colonial India*. London: Routledge, 33–51.

24. Such incidents had been commonplace since the earliest days of colonial expansion. See L. Benton (2009), *A Search for Sovereignty: Law and Geography in European Empires, 1400–1900*. Cambridge: Cambridge University Press.

25. These were called chartered companies because they operated under a royal charter in which they agreed to take on the costs of establishing British rule in East and Southern Africa, respectively, in exchange for privileged rights to the resources and trade of these regions.

26. For more on this process, see K. Ronnbäck and O. Broberg (2022), 'From defensive to transformative business diplomacy: The British South Africa Company in Rhodesia, 1910–1925', *Business History Review*, 96 (4), 777–803.

27. Lord Hailey (1944), *Native Administration and Political Development in British Tropical Africa*. London: HMSO, 13.

28. A. Naseemullah and P. Staniland (2016), 'Indirect rule and varieties of governance', *Governance*, 29 (1), 13–30.

29. T. Roy (2012), *India in the World Economy: From Antiquity to the Present*. Cambridge: Cambridge University Press.

30. R. A. Austen (1987), *African Economic History: Internal Development and External Dependency*. London: James Currey; J. Bolt, L. A. Gardner, J. Kohler, J. Paine and J. A. Robinson (2022), 'African political institutions and the impact of colonialism', NBER Working Paper 30582.

31. J. Bolt and L. A. Gardner (2020), 'How Africans shaped British colonial institutions: Evidence from local taxation', *Journal of Economic History*, 80 (4), 1189–223.

32. A. Banerjee and L. Iyer (2005), 'History, institutions and economic performance: The legacy of colonial land tenure systems in India', *American Economic Review*, 95 (4), 1190–213.

33. S. Michalopoulos and E. Papaioannou (2013), 'Pre-colonial ethnic institutions and contemporary African development', *Econometrica*, 81, 113–42; S. Michalopoulos and E. Papaioannou (2014), 'National institutions and subnational development in Africa', *Quarterly Journal of Economics*, 129 (1), 151–213.

34. S. Bandyopadhyay and E. Green (2016), 'Pre-colonial political centralization and contemporary development in Uganda', *Economic Development and Cultural Change*, 64 (4), 185–205.

35. B. D. Metcalf and T. R. Metcalf (2012), *A Concise History of Modern India*. Cambridge: Cambridge University Press, 95–96.

36. I. D. Derbyshire (2022), *The Iron Raj: Railways' Economic Impact on Uttar Pradesh and Colonial North India (1860–1914)*. Newcastle upon Tyne: Cambridge Scholars Publishing; Roy, *India and the Global Economy*.

37. D. Bogart and L. Chaudhary (2015), 'Railways in colonial India: An economic achievement?', in Chaudhary (ed.), *New Economic History*, 141.

38. Austen, *African Economic History*, 127.

39. C. Issawi (1982), *An Economic History of the Middle East and North Africa*. New York: Columbia University Press, 54–5.

40. A. Herranz-Loncan and J. Fourie (2017), '"For the public benefit"? Railways in the British Cape Colony', *European Review of Economic History*, 22, 75–6.

41. House of Commons (1904), *Papers Relating to the Construction of Railways in Sierra Leone, Lagos, and the Gold Coast*. London: HMSO; R. Jedwab and A. Moradi (2016), 'The permanent effects of transportation revolution in poor countries: Evidence from Africa', *Review of Economics and Statistics*, 98 (2), 268–84.

42. R. Jedwab, E. Kerby and A. Moradi (2015), 'History, path dependence and development: Evidence from colonial railways, settlers and cities in Kenya', *Economic Journal*, 127, 1471.

43. E. Frankema (2011), 'Colonial taxation and government spending in British Africa, 1880–1940: Maximizing revenue or minimizing effort?' *Explorations in Economic History*, 48, 136–49; L. Gardner (2012), *Taxing Colonial Africa: The Political Economy of British Imperialism*. Oxford: Oxford University Press, ch. 3.

44. Bogart and Chaudhary, 'Railways in colonial India'.

45. For more on African railway loans, see L. A. Gardner (2017), 'Colonialism or supersanctions: Sovereignty and debt in West Africa, 1871–1914', *European Review of Economic History*, 21, 236–57.

46. I. Chaves, S. L. Engerman, and J. A. Robinson (2014), 'Reinventing the wheel: The economic benefits of wheeled transportation in early colonial British West Africa', in E. Akyeampong et al. (eds), *Africa's Development in Historical Perspective*, Cambridge: Cambridge University Press, 258.

47. Roy, *India in the World Economy*, 160.

48. J. S. Hogendorn (1978), *Nigerian Groundnut Exports: Origins and Early Development*. Ibadan: Oxford University Press.

49. Jedwab and Moradi, 'The permanent effects of transportation revolution'.

50. Jedwab, Kerby and Moradi, 'History, path dependence and development'; L. Maravall (2019), 'The impact of a "colonizing river": Colonial railways and the indigenous population in French Algeria at the turn of the century', *Economic History of Developing Regions*, 31 (1), 16–47. Road investments had a similar impact. See M. Bertazzini (2022), 'The long-term impact of Italian colonial roads in the Horn of Africa, 1935', *Journal of Economic Geography*, 22, 181–214.

51. R. Burgess and D. Donaldson (2010), 'Can openness mitigate the effects of weather fluctuations? Evidence from India's famine era', *American Economic Review: Papers and Proceedings* 100 (20), 449–53; D. Donaldson (2018), 'Railways and the Raj: The economic impact of transportation infrastructure', *American Economic Review* 108, 899–934.

52. See, for instance, P. H. Lindert (2004), *Growing Public: Social Spending and Economic Growth since the Eighteenth Century*. Cambridge: Cambridge University Press; V. Tanzi and L. Schuknecht (2000), *Public Spending in the 20th Century: A Global Perspective*. Cambridge: Cambridge University Press.

53. L. Chaudhary (2009), 'Determinants of primary schooling in British India', *Journal of Economic History*, 69, 269–303.

54. E. H.P Frankema (2012), 'The origins of formal education in sub-Saharan Africa: Was British rule more benign?', *European Review of Economic History*, 15, 348.

55. Y. Dupraz (2019), 'French and British colonial legacies in education: Evidence from the partition of Cameroon', *Journal of Economic History*, 79 (3), 628–68.

56. L. Chaudhary and M. Garg (2015), 'Does history matter? Colonial education investments in India', *Economic History Review*, 68, 937–61.

57. V. Bauer, M. R. Platas and J. M Weinstein (2022), 'Legacies of Islamic rule in Africa: Colonial responses and contemporary development', *World Development*, 152, 105750.

58. Chaudhary and Garg, 'Does history matter?'.

59. E. Huillery (2009), 'History matters: The long-term impact of colonial public investments in French West Africa', *American Economic Journal: Applied Economics*, 1, 176–215.

60. L. Wantchekon, M. Klasnja and N. Novta (2015), 'Education and human capital externalities: Evidence from colonial Benin', *Quarterly Journal of Economics*, 130 (2), 703–57.

61. See, for instance, N. Nunn (2014), 'Gender and missionary influence in Colonial Africa', in Akyeampong et al. (eds), *Africa's Development in Historical Perspective*, 489–512.

62. R. Jedwab, F. Meier zu Selhausen and A. Moradi (2021), 'Christianization without economic development: Evidence from missions in Ghana', *Journal of Economic Behavior & Organization*, 190, 573–96.

63. Chaudhary, 'Determinants', 281.

64. S. Broadberry and B. Gupta (2020), 'The historical roots of India's service-led development: A sectoral analysis of Anglo-Indian productivity differences, 1870–2000', *Explorations in Economic History*, 47, 270.

65. M. Mariotti (2012), 'Labour markets during apartheid', *Economic History Review*, 65, 1100–22.

66. J. Kleibert and L. Mann (2020), 'Capturing value amidst global restructuring: Economic development and information and technology enabled services in India, the Philippines and Kenya', *European Journal of Economic Research*, 32, 1057–79.

CHAPTER 13

VARIETIES OF INDUSTRIALIZATION: AN ASIAN REGIONAL PERSPECTIVE

Kaoru Sugihara

Discussion on the comparative history of industrialization usually focuses on the changes of technology and institutions, and makes a sharp distinction between the first industrializer, England, and its followers. The latter, including continental Europe, Japan and Asia's emerging states, are often seen as having gone through a 'catch up industrialization' or 'big push industrialization'.[1] Technological and institutional innovations and mobilization of capital, among others, are highlighted as factors accounting for the first industrialization, while explanations for the diffusion of industrialization often focus on the transfer of technology, institutions, and values and norms, and the role of the state in it.

Such an approach leaves out the importance of the mobilization of natural resources and the innovative role played by local and regional forces. The recent literature on Asia's long-term path of economic development has discussed how diverse the region's resource endowments were before industrialization and how it responded to the need for procuring a much wider range and larger quantities of resources in the period of industrialization.[2] The best-known 'initial condition' in monsoon Asia was the presence of a large peasant family economy centred on rice cultivation, which could provide almost 'unlimited' supplies of labour.[3] The most-discussed constraint the region suddenly faced when industrializing was the availability of energy, especially coal, needed to serve modern industry and transport.[4] Another, equally serious constraint, emphasized in the literature, was the shortage of arable land because of population growth. Economic and social historians have discussed the widespread poverty, social inequality, and instability of the last two centuries, often by linking them to the resource shortages, especially that of land. Low agricultural productivity and a low land–labour ratio have been taken to be among the most important indicators of a resource-poor country.[5]

Asia's answer to such constraints was engaging in trade and migration within the region. The growth of intra-Asian trade and migration significantly mitigated local resource constraints, by trading coal and land-derived commodities such as rice and raw cotton and by moving labour. Monsoon Asia is richly endowed with water and biomass, but local endowment conditions vary greatly. It also suffers from the variability of water supply, acute infectious diseases and frequent natural disasters. It is this vast range of diverse environmental circumstances that offered the region opportunities for trade and migration. Yet, the impact of these local and regional resource transfers on industrialization has not been sufficiently recognized.

Asia also had to earn foreign exchange vis-à-vis advanced Western countries if it wanted to import modern machinery and associated sets of knowledge needed for industrial, urban and infrastructural development. Exports of primary products were dependent on international demand as well as on climate variations. The longer the region took to build a competitive export sector, the more important it became to make efficient use of available local resources.

As labour was abundant and land was scarce, and in order to minimize the amount of imports from the West and to exploit local resources, technology and institutions were geared towards labour-intensive and local-resource-dependent industrialization. Japan and other East Asian countries secured comparative advantage in labour-intensive industries when they were relatively free from local resource constraints, especially at the initial stage of industrialization. Where the availability of water was variable and its shortage or precariousness affected the quality of land and the environment, efforts were directed towards the more efficient use and governance of water to secure food and sustain livelihood. On the whole, the economies of India and Southeast Asia under Western domination were integrated into the international economy as exporters of primary products through the development of steamship lines and the construction of railways. While there was a significant development of labour-intensive industries in colonial India, there was also an impressive growth in the network of Asian merchants, and the migration and remittances across colonial boundaries in Southeast Asia.

In none of these countries or regions was technological and institutional innovation directed specifically towards higher labour productivity. Of course raising labour productivity is of crucial importance for any type of industrialization. But labour productivity was usually part of wider concerns about sustaining a large agrarian population and ensuring their welfare, regardless of whether the state was colonial or independent. It was important that not just a small modern sector but the local or regional economy as a whole would find its own path of economic development. Any rush for capital-intensive and resource-intensive technology would have to be financed with borrowing, often involving political costs or international risks. The adaptation of traditional or intermediate technology to serve modern needs was a great advantage, better still if it was accompanied by a fuller use of local resources. For example, where wood was plenty, timber, rather than coal, was used for heating. Charcoal could be made from timber relatively cheaply. Timber was also used instead of iron in the construction of the frame of power looms, thus lowering their cost.

This chapter considers the importance of these path dependencies for Asia's industrialization in regional perspective. The sub-regions discussed are East Asia (though Japan and China are often treated separately), Southeast Asia and India (or South Asia). The task is twofold. First, this chapter identifies Asia's factor endowment conditions and their diversity, to describe how the sub-regions interacted to enhance the possibility of industrialization. I argue that the concurrent growth of local, regional and global trade has been key to shaping the pattern of economic development of each sub-region in the nineteenth and the first half of the twentieth centuries. Second, the chapter traces the process of resource-intensive industrialization on a regional scale for the second half of the twentieth century, and reviews the process of diffusion and its consequences. In the last section, it compares the Asian and European regional paths of industrialization, and suggests that, while Europe initiated the diffusion of industrialization, Asia made it environmentally, technologically and institutionally much more inclusive than the original version. This was achieved by creating the resource nexus and by exploiting, often overexploiting, the extraordinary environmental and cultural diversities of monsoon Asia and beyond.

Initial Conditions in 1820 and After

In 1820, China had 381 million people, or 37 per cent of world population; India had 209 million (20 per cent), while Japan had 31 million (3 per cent), and nine Southeast Asian states had about 38 million (4 per cent). This is obviously a crude estimate, but the difference in the size of the four sub-regions is important for the argument of this chapter. China and India had the capacity to hold a very large population, while their neighbouring sub-regions of Japan and Southeast Asia scarcely matched them but sustained distinct units as the periphery.[6] This is arguably the most important 'initial condition' for Asia's industrialization, in that the region was potentially able to both absorb the largest pool of labour on earth and connect it to the outside world.

In explaining post-war economic development up to c.1980, Harry Oshima stressed the common socio-environmental characteristics of monsoon Asia, stretching from East and Southeast Asia to South Asia, in terms of seasonal rainfall patterns induced by monsoon winds and the centrality of the large river delta for the growth of rice farming and dense population. His formulation focuses on the sequence of intensive rice farming, population growth, availability of cheap labour, and labour-intensive industrialization leading to economic growth.[7] This sequence implicitly assumed several topics, which have been more explicitly taken up by other scholars, mainly with reference to East Asia. The development of intensive farming under land scarcity implied successful labour absorption.[8] It also implied the intensive use of water and manure required for commercial crop production.[9] Population growth also required the maintenance of social order.[10] Proto-industrialization and commercialization of agriculture meant the growth of intra-regional trade through merchant networks.[11] Finally, labour-intensive industrialization implied the capacity to engage in intercontinental trade, to exchange primary products at an initial stage and increasingly to export labour-intensive manufactured goods in return for fossil fuels, other resources and capital-intensive goods.[12] In other words, monsoon Asia's feeding capacity came as much from the development of the ability to acquire resources as from the basic water and air circulation regime. Each country or sub-region responded to this challenge with varying difficulties and policy support, and eventually incorporated resource-intensive industrialization into its development path.

251

Second, maritime Asia, represented by present Southeast Asia but stretching from the coasts of the Indian Ocean to the western side of the Asia-Pacific region, was able to organize two very large sets of regional trading networks, involving local, regional and global trade. In the early modern period, they were a China-trading network east of the Strait of Malacca and an Indian Ocean trade from the west of the strait to the western Indian Ocean. Together with the Atlantic trade, which was oriented more towards intercontinental trade, they comprised the three major regional networks in the world in the seventeenth and eighteenth centuries. Arab traders were extremely important in connecting Asia with Europe. Moreover, the English and Dutch East India companies conducted world trade on the basis of the two Asian trading networks locally conducted by Asian traders. Nevertheless, many would agree that the two Asian trading networks had a degree of cultural cohesiveness and diversity within it at the same time. The East Asian networks were governed by the tendency to regulate intercontinental trade, and when by the end of the seventeenth century pirate activities were curtailed, the East Asian seas became peaceful. In addition to, and partly in replacement of, tributary trade relations, China developed a more equal regime of managed trade (the Hushi system), and both Japanese and Chinese governments recognized the utility of bilateral trade relationships. In other words, Asian traders had the capacity and the environment to conduct local and regional trade comparable to European traders, though not to engage in intercontinental trade. This is the second 'initial condition' which other non-European regions did not have on a comparable scale around 1820.

It should be noted that maritime states based on port cities and surrounding rural areas grew along the coasts of the Indian Ocean, including maritime Southeast Asia. Here the key organizing agents were port cities (or port city states) and networks of merchants.[13] Even in mainland Southeast Asia, the agrarian population was not necessarily the mainstay.[14] Products derived from sea, land and forest were all involved in the exchange economy. If the state was relatively urban or commercially oriented, it could shift its fiscal base from one commodity to another, or from one economic activity to another, relatively easily. This flexibility was one important strength for securing resources and livelihoods. The first serious economic contacts with Europe often began via these states.

Setting up Industrialization in Monsoon Asia

Let me recapture the relative importance of the four sub-regions in terms of regional GDP. In 1820, China's share in Asia's GDP (sum of the four sub-regions) was 59 per cent and South Asia 29 per cent, while Japan, South Korea, Taiwan and Hong Kong (using later territorial categories for the sake of comparison) comprised 7 per cent and Southeast Asia 5 per cent.[15] By 1950, China's share had declined to 28 per cent, while that of Japan and others rose to 21 per cent, Southeast Asia to 17 per cent, and South Asia to 33 per cent (Figure 13.1). Thus the four sub-regions became much more equal in terms of economic weight, though not concerning the size of the population. Within China and India, economic progress mainly came from the coastal regions. The weight of Asia's contribution to the world GDP shifted from the two agrarian empires in China and India to maritime monsoon Asia.

Key to this transformation was location. The economies of maritime monsoon Asia absorbed Western technology and institutions on the one hand, and mobilized local and regional resources on the other, through the development of transport networks, trade and migration. Two paths emerged as a result. In Meiji Japan, and a little later in coastal China, commercial ports in or near major cities such as Yokohama, Kobe and Shanghai connected imported and local resources to help modern cities and industries grow. It was important that the emerging area had both the will to industrialize (thus committed to import technology and build an infrastructure to absorb it) and the social capacity to mobilize local resources, natural and human (including the ability to import or recruit them from other places). At the same time, in India and Southeast Asia, commercial ports, built by Western colonial powers, also connected imported and local resources to develop economies on port cities, but driven by the exports of primary products. They included Bombay, Madras, Calcutta, Singapore and Jakarta. Hong Kong acted as a colonial port serving both China and Southeast Asia.

The two paths were interrelated and were not necessarily geographically separate. For example, the first modern industry in Asia emerged in Bombay in the middle of the nineteenth century, and soon met competition from Japan. Both China and Japan

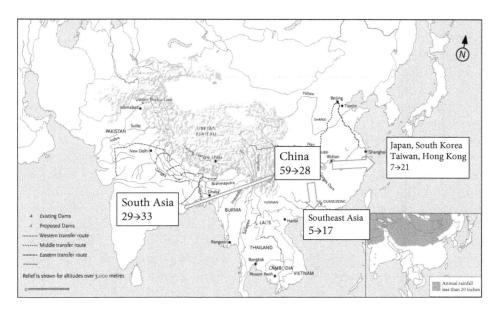

Figure 13.1 Change in the regional share in Asia's GDP, 1820–1950.

Notes and Sources: Figures are from A. Maddison (2011), 'Statistics on World Population, GDP and Per Capita GDP, 1–2008 AD': http://www.ggdc.net/Maddison/. Map is adapted from K. Pomeranz (2009), 'The Great Himalayan watershed: Agrarian crisis, mega-dams and the environment', *New Left Review*, 58, 5–39.

exported tea and raw silk in large quantities to earn foreign exchange. Commercial ports in Korea and Taiwan were developed by Japanese colonial authorities, to connect their primary exports to Japan. But there was also a divergence within maritime parts of modern Asia. South and Southeast Asia tended towards the path of primary produce economies, while East Asia tended towards industrialization.

Japan's labour-intensive industrialization was both dependent on the growth of maritime economies and one of its major drivers. In the early stages of industrialization, Japan exported rice and coal, but soon became an importer of these commodities as well as raw cotton and sugar. It competed with India in the cotton yarn market of central China during the 1890s. By the early twentieth century, Japan imported raw cotton from India, rice and sugar from Southeast Asia, Korea and Taiwan, and soybeans and their derivates from Manchuria; in exchange, it exported labour-intensive manufactured goods such as cotton yarn, cotton cloth and sundries to other parts of Asia. The environmental implication of this division of labour was a mitigation of local resource constraints, which enabled Japan to expand its industrial base, and most especially its cotton textile industry. In this respect the basic logic was similar to England's discovery of 'ghost acreages' in North America during the period of the Industrial Revolution.[16]

In the interwar period China went through import-substitution industrialization, which pressed Japanese manufacturers to find more processed or higher-value-added products for export. Under the regime of selective protectionism, Japanese manufacturers also increased the exports of textile machinery to China, which started regional industrialization. This was an original 'flying geese', which has become a basic mechanism of progressively including higher value-added commodities and commodities made with the more advanced technology in intra-regional trade. Figure 13.2 shows that Japan adopted a policy of selective protectionism, setting up tariff barriers only against imports directly competing with the domestic industry. It encouraged import substitution but pursued the benefit of free trade, and as a result its overall tariff rate remained relatively low, while China and India raised tariff rates, partly for revenue purposes but also to more comprehensively protect domestic industries. Japan's dependence upon import of raw materials was much greater than that of the other two countries.

Countries involved in intra-Asian trade included a number of European colonies in South and Southeast Asia, as well as countries of East and Southeast Asia under unequal treaties and the treaty port system. Under this system of 'forced free trade', Japanese merchants brought a wide range of cotton manufacture (cloth and apparel) and sundries (matches, soap, toothpaste and tooth brushes, traditional medicine, umbrellas, bicycles, and noodle-making machines) to Asian peoples, and they interacted with Indian, Chinese and other Asian merchant networks. It was these networks, together with the Japanese trade associations (and government efforts to help them to compete with Asian networks), that facilitated the export of labour-intensive manufactured goods. With a time lag and political disturbances, labour-intensive industrialization spread to China and eventually to other parts of Asia.

This was also a crucial moment for modern (initially mostly colonial) states in Southeast Asia. In the late nineteenth to the first half of the twentieth century, most of the region was put under Western colonial rule, but it continued to interact with other Asian countries, as the region traditionally had done. In fact it developed new trade links with Japan, China and India, roughly at the same speed as it did with the West. With the improvement of transport and information networks under Western impact, the fusion between the two former agrarian empires (of China and India) and Southeast Asia resulted in a massive (mostly temporary) migration of Indians and Chinese to Southeast Asia.

Furthermore, across Asia, there emerged a shared demand for modern consumption goods among ordinary peoples (from rice, dried fish, spices and a range of non-timber forest products to Japanese manufactured goods mentioned above). The traditional commodity complex shared in the region (rice, sugar, tea, silk and cotton) remained important, and a modern Asian consumer culture emerged. A complex set of commodity chains were created: while the growth of the market for intermediate goods (e.g. cotton yarn of low counts) meant a degree of 'culture-neutralization' of the Asian international

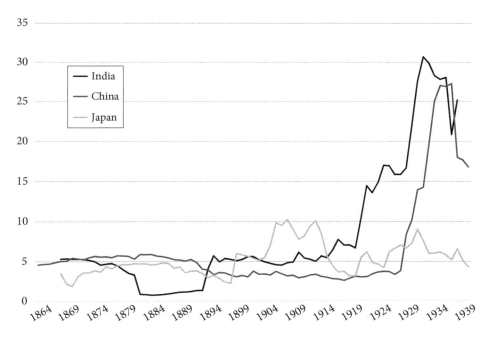

Figure 13.2 Import tariff rates in India, China and Japan, 1868–1938.

Notes and Sources: India: K. Sugihara (2002), 'Indo Kindaishi ni okeru Enkakuchi Boeki to Chiiki Koueki, 1868–1938-nen [The long-distance trade and regional trade in modern Indian history, 1868–1938]', *Toyo Bunka*, 82, 30–1; China: Liang-lin Hsiao (1974), *China's Foreign trade Statistics, 1864–1949*. Cambridge, MA: Harvard University Press, 22–4, 132–3; Japan: Okurasho Shuzeikyoku [Japanese Ministry of Finance Government Bureau of Taxation] (1948), *Dai-15-kai Kokkai Kanzei Sankosho* [Reference material on customs tariff for the 15th Parliament], Tokyo: Okurasho. Rates refer to total import revenue divided by total value of imports. The Japanese data exclude colonial imports after 1919.

market, these goods in turn served for a diverse range of final demand (e.g. traditional – kimono – clothing and apparel to its modernized versions). Meanwhile, unbleached cotton cloth was brought to the hinterland (and also other parts of the developing world including East Africa) by Asian merchants and enhanced the scope of regional integration. This in turn made it easier to transfer labour-intensive technology and managerial know-how to culturally diverse areas, and underpinned regionally driven industrialization in the post-Second-World-War period.

Thus, although many parts of Asia, especially India, were affected by the influx of English cotton cloth in the nineteenth century, and traditional textile industries declined to a certain extent, Asia was not just de-industrialized. It reorganized itself into a new form of industrialization. In this period two different routes of the diffusion of industrialization emerged: the capital-intensive route originating in the West and the labour-intensive one originating in East Asia. The latter was too small to be recognized by global economic historians in terms of the size of value added at this stage, but it was already an important source of employment. It also tended to be less resource-intensive than the former. Therefore, what actually emerged in the period from the nineteenth century to the 1930s was a three-tier international division of labour: capital-intensive manufactured goods, labour-intensive manufactured goods, and primary products, and an increasingly uneven global resource allocation in favour of Europe and regions of recent European settlement. It also developed an international division of labour within Asia, in which Japan, China, India and Southeast Asia were hierarchically placed in the order of industrialization. The growth of intra-Asian trade was faster than that of world trade or Asia's trade with the West between 1880 and 1938. In one estimate, the share of intra-Asian trade in Asia's export trade was 41 per cent in 1928. By 1938 it was 49 per cent.[17] By contrast, it has been observed that regional integration through local and regional merchant networks appears to have been less marked in most parts of Africa, the Middle East and Latin America where the local economies were integrated into the metropolis-led international economy as satellites.[18] However, even in Asia, the productivity of proto-industries with traditional technology, modern labour-intensive factories and commercial agriculture built on the low land–labour ratio remained low. The standard of living rose very slowly.[19]

Finally, both intra-Asian trade and labour-intensive industrialization were severely disrupted by Japanese imperialism and territorial expansion. From 1931 to 1936, Japan grew faster than most Western countries and proceeded with heavy industrialization. This partly came from the 'import-substitution industrialization', in the sense that competitive pressure from the West was eased, largely as a result of the Great Depression. Under the collapse of world trade, the rise of protectionism and the demise of the international gold standard, an East Asian monetary order with a tendency to devalue against key currencies worked in favour of regional industrialization.[20] The intra-yen bloc trade now included a significant proportion of machinery trade. But it was also a move towards autarky, anticipating post-war India and China, in that most new industries were linked to the research and development efforts of Japan's military industries. If the direction of industrial development was driven by political and military interests (and in Japan's case without a full understanding of global military and resource balances), there was no guarantee, or even a prospect, that the country was adopting a sensible import-substitution strategy based on factor endowment considerations. To some extent, therefore, the ecologically uneven exchange between Europe and colonial Asia was extended to a similar resource transfer between Japan and other parts of Asia, not least Japan's own colonies.

Looking at the period from 1820 to 1950 as a whole, the intra-regional trading sphere of Asia showed a common tendency to expand by commercializing its agriculture and reorganizing its traditional industries, and by linking modern manufacturing to this expansion, which resulted in the evolution of the system comprising a division of labour between agriculture and industry within the region. The difference between the structure of consumption in Asia and the West was another important factor that made it possible for Asia to industrialize. Sustained by demand within the region, the traditional textile industries managed, to some extent, to develop their hand-weaving industry with the use of machine-reeled yarns and to form modern mass consumption markets somewhat different from those in the West, and thereby coped with the 'Western impact' while maintaining employment at certain levels. Such a labour-intensive path of economic development was well suited to Asia's factor endowments, and comparative advantages were established in India, China and Japan. Although formed under many difficulties that were caused by the imposition of the free trade regime and domestic political disorders, this constituted the core part of Asia's development path, and served as the pillar for the expansion of its trade. Perhaps one of the most significant contributions from the growth of world trade, as viewed from a broader perspective that takes intra-regional transactions into due consideration, may be the fact that it triggered this type of response to the 'Western impact' and thereby helped to revitalize the region's employment absorption mechanism, which had at one time been seriously damaged.

Post-war Diffusion of Industrialization

After the emergence, development and abrupt collapse of the Yen bloc in the 1930s and the first half of the 1940s, intra-Asian trade recovered fast among a smaller number of countries. The post-war reforms under the US-led allied occupation changed the character of Japanese political, economic and social organizations into a more democratic one. By 1950, India, China, many Southeast Asian countries and North Korea withdrew from the regime of free trade, while the countries along the western Pacific Rim (Japan, South Korea, Taiwan, Hong Kong and Malaya-Singapore among others) were integrated into the US-led world economy.

The post-war diffusion of industrialization, beginning in Japan and spreading to other Asian countries, followed the same interactive path between intra-regional trade and industrialization as in the pre-war years, first among a small number of countries under the regime of free trade and the technological transfer from the West, and gradually embracing others. This is the case of the 'Asian textile complex' in the 1970s, in which Japan produced rayon yarn, Taiwan wove rayon cloth, and Hong Kong made the cloth into apparel and exported the apparel to the United States.[21] New intermediate goods included cheap plastics, man-made fibres, machine parts and eventually IC chips. Again, we do not see such a dynamic relationship between regions in Africa, the Middle East or Latin America in this period. South Africa and Brazil proceeded with industrialization without any accompanying regional integration. It is only in East Asia that economic nationalism has embraced regional integration.

Import-substitution industrialization, strictly interpreted, was based on the building of a full industrial structure equivalent to that in developed countries, by imposing very high tariffs against imports of industrial goods from the West. This strategy seemed politically viable in many countries, including India and China, though it turned out to be relatively short-lived. In India, by the Third Five-Year Plan period, it became clear that the benefits of heavy industrialization, modelled largely on the Soviet experience, did not 'trickle down', resulting in the growth of 'disguised unemployment' in rural areas and the urban 'informal sector'. In communist China during the Mao period, human development indicators improved faster than in India, but the country struggled to develop competitive heavy industries (also influenced by the Soviet experience) in the absence of technological transfer from more developed countries, especially from the West.

By contrast, some East and Southeast Asian countries – such as Japan; the newly industrializing economies (NIEs) of South Korea, Taiwan, Hong Kong and Singapore; and the ASEAN-4 consisting of Thailand, Malaysia, Indonesia and the Philippines – pursued an export-oriented path to industrialization. They experienced relatively high rates of growth, by taking advantage of the gains from trade more than India and China.[22] Figure 13.3 shows a further shift in the economic weight from China to Japan and NIEs between 1950 and 1980.

We record some evidence of the regional dimension of industrial upgrading. In post-war Japan, rapid technological transfer from the West led to the development of machinery industries (transport, electrical, heavy and machine tool) along the lines of the extension of labour-intensive industries. Between 1972 and 1985, 'new' industries, driven by microelectronics technology such as computer and communication industries, grew faster in Asia than in the United States and Western Europe, although the technology originated mainly from the United States. These industries did not necessarily require industrial concentration and the kind of infrastructure which heavy industries needed such as ports and transport to carry heavy material. Nor did they need the supply of a very large amount of capital. As long as competitive labour, access to information, and commercial and financial networks were available, they would move to any location where the best combination of factor endowments and policy packages was on offer.[23] Thus semiconductor and consumer electronics factories that were established across the emerging economies became part of the 'global supply chains', and contributed to the emergence of a large, semi-skilled to skilled labour force.

ILO studies in labour-intensive industries and human resource development extensively discussed the 'matching' between the nature of new demand for skills on the one hand, and education and formal training on the other.[24] They were conscious of the transferability of the experiences of Japan and NIEs to Southeast Asia. Not many attempts were successful, nor were they comprehensively pursued by the government; however by the 1980s, the direction of thinking was clearly towards the development of human capital, or in manufacturing, that of a workforce of good quality. This was linked to a shift towards a more balanced allocation of educational expenditure between primary, secondary and tertiary sectors.[25] The overall result was a simultaneous rise of per capita GDP and the Human Development Index.

ASEAN-4 countries started a developmental policy under authoritarian regimes around 1965. They gradually turned to the export-oriented strategy, and proceeded to industrialization in the 1980s. This can be seen in the radical change in their commodity composition of trade. In spite of a criticism of 'shallowness' of industrialization, and limited scale of institutional reforms, such as land reform, industrialization occurred with varying degrees of success.[26] Indeed, it became a mainstay of Asia's economic policy. From a regional perspective, Southeast Asia mainly acted as an importer of East Asia's manufactured goods and capital, but was also a committed industrializer.

Under 'open regionalism', which helped the formation of ASEAN and underpinned the emergence of APEC (Asia-Pacific Economic Cooperation), the region would not

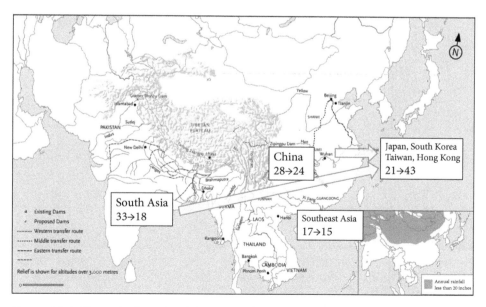

Figure 13.3 Change in the regional share in Asia's GDP, 1950–80.
Sources: As per Figure 13.1.

discriminate against countries outside its boundaries. The underlying ideology is different from both the hegemonic regime of free trade (as in Britain and the United States) and the continental European regime of free trade through treaty networks.[27] Historically, the region was used to low tariff levels and exposure to the international economy, especially in the late nineteenth and early twentieth centuries under the regime of 'forced free trade'. It was natural for these Asian countries to engage in trade between neighbouring countries with similar economic structures, to compete for similar markets, seek complementarity in trade, and exploit regional sources of growth. China and India joined the network of trade and economic growth after policy changes in 1979 and in 1991, respectively.

In the early post-war period, the share of the United States (and other Western countries) in Asia's trade was large, and its influence in industrial development was dominant. However, the US share rapidly declined, and was replaced by the growth of regionally driven trade. In 1965, Asia's share in world exports was 11 per cent, but this share increased to 27 per cent in 2000, and to 35 per cent in 2015. More important, the share of intra-Asian trade in Asia's exports increased from 32 per cent in 1965 to 49 per cent in 2000, and to 54 per cent in 2015 (Figure 13.4).

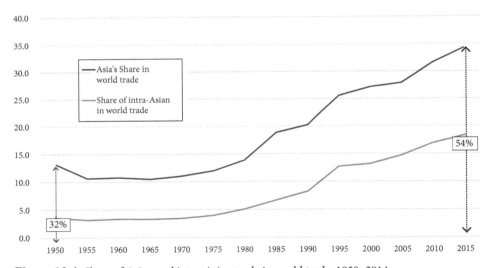

Figure 13.4 Share of Asian and intra-Asian trade in world trade, 1950–2014.
Notes and Sources: Calculated from export figures or equivalent from K. Takanaka (2000), *Higashi-ajia Choki Keizai Tokei 9: Gaikoku Boeki to Keizai Hatten* [Long-term economic statistics of East Asia, vol. 9, Foreign Trade and Economic Development], Tokyo: Keiso Shobo, 500–17 for 1950–99; and IMF, *Direction of Trade Statistics Yearbook* for 2000–15. Taiwanese figures from 2000 are based on the Republic of China (Taiwan) Ministry of Finance, *Trade Statistics*, and *National Statistics, External Trade*. Asia's exports refers to exports from sixteen Asian countries (Japan, four NIEs, six ASEAN countries, China and four South Asian countries) to all Asian countries. Intra-Asian trade refers to trade between the sixteen countries in export values and the value of their imports from the smaller Asian countries (adjusted by FOB-CIF conversion). Percentage in box shows the share of intra-Asian trade in Asia's exports.

Development of Resource-intensive Industrialization

To some extent rapid industrial upgrading in Japan along the lines of labour-intensive industrialization was complementary to the more capital- and resource-intensive industries, especially in the United States. But it also resulted in the upgrading and expansion of capital- and resource-intensive industries within Asia. Imports of fossil fuels, including oil and liquefied natural gas, and other raw materials became essential for this purpose.

In the 1950s there was a debate over how Japan's resources should be secured, especially as to whether its energy demand should depend on domestic coal or on imported oil. High economic growth and rapidly rising demand favoured the latter option. There was also a coordinated attempt by the Ministry of International Trade and Industry to spread the energy-saving methods of production in steel and electrical machinery industries. In the second half of the 1950s, serious attempts were made to develop a 'seafront industrial complex' (*rinkai kogyo chitai*) consisting of an oil refinery, and a petrochemical and electricity generation plant, among other industries. There was an accumulation of know-how prior to this period, including the idea of establishing the 'industrial port' as distinct from the 'commercial port'. International circumstances also strongly favoured this strategy. A sudden expansion of oil production in the Middle East was not being met by a matching increase of demand in Europe, and majors were looking for their customers. This gave Japanese companies the opportunity to negotiate with Western firms on technology transfer on good terms.[28]

Pursuit of the seafront complex involved a number of industrial and infrastructural developments. Against the background of low prices of resources and energy, Japanese shipbuilding companies and shipping lines attempted to utilize the latest technology of large oil tankers and other specialist bulk vessels (e.g. for iron ore) to the full. Equally important was a rapid introduction of container cargoes for other commodities, which standardized shipments across international ports and helped coordinate the transfer of goods between different means of transport in industrial ports. The seafront complex was constructed with dredging and reclamation, on deep harbours which could take large vessels. Railway lines and roads were built to ensure access. The establishment of the industrial site required pursuit of economies of scale on the one hand, and political and public approval on the other. In the 1960s the Japanese political will was strong enough to push the 'Pacific industrial belt' development at a speed inconceivable in the established industrial districts in the West.

Resource-intensive industries were typically located not in the central parts of major cities such as Tokyo and Osaka, but in neighbouring areas. For example, Tokyo retained employment-absorbing labour-intensive (by then mostly skill-intensive) industries within the central wards, while the bay areas of Yokohama became home to a resource-intensive cluster. After the second half of the 1960s, environmental protection movements began to spread, and the municipal government gave voice to the citizens before the central government did. Such politico-social dynamics were partly responsible for the diffusion of the industrial complex to the more distant and less politically sensitive or powerful areas, without necessarily mitigating the potential environmental damage.[29]

Unlike the 'global supply chain' – which in this context essentially consists of a network of factories (plus perhaps headquarters) scattered in various parts of Asia – the key feature here is what might be called the 'resource nexus': the creation of a spatial cluster designed for combining specific sets of resources. In particular, local and domestic resources were to be efficiently combined with imported resources. As industrialization proceeded, the resource nexus began to reorganize the entire spatial allocation of human and natural resources in the country. It encouraged the growth of cities, which provided resource-intensive industries with labour and the market (e.g. for electricity). A large proportion of the population moved to the cities, while a large part of rural areas became 'urban' at the same time. A new relationship between the city and the countryside was formed with the premise that industries would have access to global resources to lead economic growth.

Other East Asian countries also adopted the seafront industrial complex strategy. In South Korea initial conditions for heavy and chemical industries were low, because most of the colonial legacy was located in the North. In 1973, the developmental state declared the programme for 'heavy and chemical industrialization'. A series of seafront complexes were subsequently established in the far south. They were distinctly separate from the traditional light-industry zones. The new nexuses included shipbuilding, automobile, steel and military-related machinery industries. In addition to the steel industry, which grew out of domestic demand and joined this development, petrochemical and shipbuilding industries were especially successful in exports. Meanwhile, in Seoul and its neighbouring regions and some other clusters, labour-intensive industries were transformed into 'new' industries driven by the microelectronics revolution.[30]

In Taiwan, where traditionally fragmented small and medium-sized businesses were scattered across the island, the government-led strategy for heavy and chemical industrialization lasted for a relatively short period, from the late 1960s to the early 1970s. Even so, steel, petrochemical and shipbuilding industries were established, and they played a supporting role in the growth of labour-intensive and high-technology industries.[31]

In China, the initial phase after the policy reform of 1979 was characterized by a slow and difficult process of transition. Many heavy industries were located inland for political and strategic reasons and because of the idea that they should be developed close to where coal and other resources were found. Experts had to be persuaded that imports of resources were essential for further industrialization. The Pearl River Delta, on the strength of the rich historical tradition of Hong Kong as a major trading hub and the export-zone initiatives in Canton in the 1970s, led the development of electronics industries, while the city of Shanghai (and the Yangtze River Delta) initially suffered from the need to reorganize state-owned enterprises, heavy industries and coal mines. The establishment of the Shanghai Baoshan Ironworks with the introduction of foreign (Japanese) technology and management was a turning point in China's commitment to the seafront development model. By the 1990s, the Yangtze River Delta had re-established itself as the main industrial complex with large imports of resources from abroad.[32]

In China the linkage between 'new' electronics-related industries and resource-intensive industries took a different form. Three 'megapolises', a chain of connected metropolitan areas, located in Pearl River and Yangtze River deltas and the national capital region (Beijing-Tianjin-Hebei), respectively, grew into a centre of progressively larger urban networks. While heavy and chemical industries, especially the steel and petrochemical sectors, were concentrated on the seafront to maximize the benefits from economies of scale and access to imports, electronics and machinery industries were located across a variety of cities and the countryside, so that the region could create intra-industry linkages and links to a large consumer market.[33] This was a more embracing model for combining the strength of natural and human resources than the earlier experiments in Japan and elsewhere, with accompanying, often more serious, problems such as air pollution. It also had equally powerful political and social consequences for the inequality and uneven resource allocation with other parts of China.

Local Resources under Pressure

Figure 13.5 shows a marked shift in the economic gravity from Japan and NIEs back to China, although much of this comes from the growth of coastal areas within China (and to a lesser extent India) in the period 1980–2016. It is clear by now that Asian growth began to include the 'hinterland', as well as smaller countries in the Eurasian continent. By making a vast rural population closer to trade-led industrialization, the policy changes in China and India had a major impact on the rise of emerging economies in particular and global economic development in general.

In these countries the rising export capacity made it possible to import raw materials and fossil fuels. But, while food and fossil fuels could be imported relatively easily, the resulting growth could put less tradeable factors of production under unprecedented pressure. Such resources include water for agricultural use and local biomass energy. Seasonal and annual variability of water supply could be crucial for the stability of agriculture. Nearby forests or the 'waste land' from which timber, twigs or crop residues had been obtained could disappear as a result of population increase and expansion of arable land, and this could make it difficult for the peasant household to secure biomass energy for cooking, lighting and heating, and for the local economy to secure biomass resources for fuels and building materials.[34] In other words, there was a great deal of environmental diversity, which had collectively worked for sustaining a large population. As industrialization occurred and tradeable resources were brought in, however, some areas such as the Pacific coast or port cities prospered, while hinterlands, semi-arid regions and mountainous areas took longer to meet the increased demand for local resources.

In many parts of contemporary China, water became scarce and emerged as a focal point of local, national and regional politics. The most immediate problem was the supply

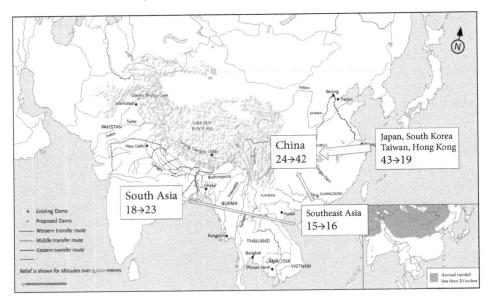

Figure 13.5 Change in the regional share in Asia's GDP, 1980–2016.
Notes and Sources: As per Figure 13.1. Figures for 2014 have been estimated, using *IMF, International Financial Statistics Yearbook.*

of water for agriculture as well as for industrial and domestic purposes. The problem was also aggravated by the need for dam construction for electricity generation. Figures 13.1, 13.3 and 13.5 outline the significance of a huge regional water and air circulation and the multi-scale character of issues involved in its governance. In contemporary India, a rapid progress in the use of tube wells largely solved the issue of self-sufficiency in food and raised agricultural productivity, but resulted in the lowering of water tables. Free electricity for tube well users also distorted resource allocation, for example, by making investments in the improvement of electricity supply more difficult than otherwise.[35] Where electricity is not always available, securing local biomass energy for cooking and heating purposes could still be a matter of life and death. Vast numbers of hours had been spent on water and fuelwood collection, mainly by women.[36]

Thus the growth of the resource nexus in the core parts of Asia has been accompanied by the intensification of local resource constraints in the less developed areas, increasingly derived from multi-scale causes. In many ways they have been two sides of the same coin.

Conclusion: Towards a Reinterpretation of Asian Industrialization in Global History

How would the path of global economic development look in the light of the Asian experiences described above? First, the fundamental difference between Asia and

Europe in the early modern period was the population holding capacity of the former. In monsoon Asia, intensive farming – based on rice cultivation under land scarcity – fed a very large population. Labour-intensive technology developed to increase land productivity and greater absorption of labour, including double-cropping, irrigation, the introduction of new seed varieties, and the use of human and animal waste. Micro-institutions such as the household and the village community helped reinforce labour absorption within the village by combining the main (farm) work with proto-industrial activities at home and during the off-peak seasons.

By contrast, in the European system of mixed farming (under the rotation system of grain and livestock production), land was less intensively used. Pasture implied a greater input of capital for the maintenance of cattle and its control, hence greater possibility for capital accumulation. Labour productivity, rather than land productivity, was pursued, both in large-scale capitalist agriculture and in peasant-based mixed farming. The result was that by 1820 the standard of living in the core regions of Western Europe was higher, while the size of the population in monsoon Asia was much larger. They could be interpreted as two different responses to the Malthusian problem of population exceeding beyond the capacity of food production.

Second, Europe offered another response to local resource constraints by developing overseas trade and capital markets and by exploiting fossil fuels, especially coal. This implied a progressive extension of its resource base to the biosphere of the New World and the tropics on the one hand and to the geosphere on the other (especially on energy). War, territorial acquisition overseas and mercantilist projects created the need for advancing scientific knowledge for navigation and military technologies. At the same time, new commodities were brought in from different parts of the world, which helped the development of consumer culture. The major urban centres acted as a 'nexus' for combining diverse resources and created the possibilities of innovation and capital accumulation. Artisans were gathered, food and raw materials for industrial products were brought from the countryside, luxuries were imported and capital was pooled and invested for the development of infrastructure and industry. Eventually the invention of steam engines and the use of coal made a decisive impact on the increase of labour productivity in production and transport. By the time of the Industrial Revolution, the region's resource base was transformed not only into an extra-territorial one (especially through the incorporation of land and forest-derived resources of North America but more generally by engaging in intercontinental trade), but also into an extra-organic type.[37] In these two respects, Europe laid the foundations of the modern interregional system of resource exchange.

Third, the two ways of responding to local resource constraints mentioned above were combined in post-war Asia. The foundations of Asia's industrialization had been laid earlier, but the scale of post-war industrialization was different. Resource-intensive industrialization first occurred in the Pacific industrial belt of Japan in the 1960s and 1970s, and then diffused across maritime monsoon Asia and beyond. For the first time in global history, a massive population of monsoon Asia was systematically connected to the international economy and global resources. The standard of living of its large population rose, and the worsening of global income inequality was arrested.[38] The region's factor endowment regime characterized by high land productivity, a high level of labour absorption, and the original environmental characteristics of monsoon Asia such as the availability and variability of water and biomass energy were now reorganized to create a resource nexus of global reach. The region sustained the ability to import resources, including minerals and fossil fuels, and combined them with local human and natural resources.

The key organizers of the nexus included the 'developmental state', as a substantial amount of capital and a strong leadership were needed for building large-scale infrastructure. The states were not always conscious of the environmental implications of these developments. Urban congestion and pollution and environmental degradation in the countryside also became a regional phenomenon. As the regional growth core shifted to the Chinese metropolis, the influence of the resource nexus increasingly included the Eurasian continent as well as maritime monsoon Asia.

Global environmental sustainability, including issues relating to global warming, biodiversity, deforestation, and health and ecosystem protection, now largely depends on Asia's response. The West has certainly been responsible for creating a technological and institutional path of resource exchange, but is not in a position to offer relevant historical experiences on a scale we see today.

Notes

1. A. Gerschenkron (1962), *Economic Backwardness in Historical Perspective: A Book of Essays*. Cambridge, MA: Belknap Press; A. Suehiro (2008), *Catch-up Industrialization: The Trajectory and Prospects of East Asian Economies*, trans. T. Gill. Singapore: NUS Press in association with Kyoto University Press; R. C. Allen (2011), *Global Economic History: A Very Short Introduction*. Oxford: Oxford University Press.

2. G. Austin (ed.) (2017), *Economic Development and Environmental History in the Anthropocene: Perspectives on Asia and Africa*. London: Bloomsbury Academic.

3. W. A. Lewis (1954), 'Economic development with unlimited supplies of labour', *Manchester School*, 22 (2), 139–91.

4. See K. Pomeranz (2000), *The Great Divergence: China, Europe, and the Making of the Modern World Economy*. Princeton, NJ: Princeton University Press.

5. For a brief description of the thinking of classical economy and its limits, see Y. Hayami and Y. Godo (2005), *Development Economics: From the Poverty to the Wealth of Nations*, 3rd edn. Oxford: Oxford University Press, 80–9.

6. In 1820, twelve countries in Western Europe had 115 million or 11 per cent of the world population. Data are from A. Maddison (2011), 'Statistics on world population, GDP and per capita GDP, 1–2008 AD', http://www.ggdc.net/maddison/ (last accessed 6 January 2018).

7. H. Oshima (1987), *Economic Development in Monsoon Asia: A Comparative Study*. Tokyo: University of Tokyo Press.

8. S. Ishikawa (1978), *Labour Absorption in Asian Agriculture: An 'Issues' Paper*. Geneva: Asian Employment Programme, ILO-ARTEP.

9. M. Elvin and Ts'ui-jung Liu (eds) (1998), *Sediments of Time: Environment and Society in Chinese History*. Cambridge: Cambridge University Press.

10. R. B. Wong (1997), *China Transformed: Historical Change and the Limits of European Experience*. Ithaca, NY: Cornell University Press.

11. K. Sugihara (2005), 'An introduction', in K. Sugihara (ed.), *Japan, China and the Growth of the Asian International Economy, 1850–1949*. Oxford: Oxford University Press, 4–8.

12. K. Sugihara (2013), 'Labour-intensive industrialization in global history: An interpretation of East Asian experiences', in G. Austin and K. Sugihara (eds), *Labour-intensive Industrialization in Global History*. London: Routledge, 30–8, and 43–55.

13. A. Reid (1993), *Expansion and Crisis: Southeast Asia in the Age of Commerce 1450–1680*. New Haven, CT: Yale University Press, 62–131.

14. For the Ayutthaya, see C. Baker and P. Phongpaichit (2017), *A History of Ayutthaya: Siam in the Early Modern World*. Cambridge: Cambridge University Press.

15. The territorial categories do not exactly match the ones I used for the population figures cited earlier, but the point basically stands.

16. See Pomeranz, *The Great Divergence*, 274–8.

17. Sugihara (2005), 'An introduction', 6–7.

18. The historical presence of intra-regional networks in these regions is well known, and it is possible to reconstruct trade statistics for at least some of them for the nineteenth and early twentieth centuries from British and other Western sources; however, they do not appear to have been as large as intra-Asian trade. See K. Sugihara (2015), 'Asia in the growth of world trade: A re-interpretation of the "long nineteenth century"', in U. Bosma and A. Webster (eds), *Commodities, Ports and Asian Maritime Trade c.1750–1950*. Basingstoke: Palgrave Macmillan, 41–51. Trade statistics assembled by the League of Nations and the United Nations for the more recent period do not show high figures either. For example, the share of intra-regional export trade in Sub-Saharan Africa was 12 per cent in 2004, after which it steadily rose to 19 per cent in 2015, reflecting the progress of regional integration. Data are from IMF, *Direction of Trade Statistics Yearbook*. Asia's post-war figures, shown in Figure 13.4, essentially come from the same source.

19. An estimate suggests that a PPP (purchasing power parity)-adjusted per capita income of Japan in the mid-1930s (at current prices) was 32 per cent of the US level, which means that the gap between the two countries was greater than the Maddison estimate suggested. Since Japan's level was far higher than other Asian countries', there was no sense of 'catching up' with the West in this respect. See K. Fukao, Debin Ma and Tangjun Yuan (2007), 'Real gap in pre-war East Asia: A 1934–36 benchmark purchasing power parity comparison with the US', *Review of Income and Wealth*, 53 (3), 503–37.

20. K. Sugihara (2010), 'Formation of an industrialization-oriented monetary order in East Asia', in Shigeru Akita and Nicholas J. White (eds), *The International Order of Asia in the 1930s and 1950s*. Farnham: Ashgate, 61–102.

21. J. S. Arpan, M. Barry and T. Van Tho (1984), 'The textile complex in the Asia-Pacific region: The patterns and textures of competition and the shape of things to come', *Research in International Business and Finance*, 4 (B), 112–7, 136–49, and 159.

22. Post-war Japan is not normally classified as 'export-oriented', as the high-speed growth was driven mainly by the domestic market. On the other hand, as we shall see below, the need to earn foreign exchange through exports to import crucial resources was so great that the strategy she developed for industrialization arguably provided a proto-type of 'export-oriented industrialization'.

23. Sugihara (2013), 'Labour-intensive industrialization in global history', 50–1.

24. R. Amjad (1981) 'The development of labour intensive industries in ASEAN countries: An overview', in R. Amjad (ed.), *The Development of Labour Intensive Industries in ASEAN Countries*. Geneva: ILO, 1–28; Amjad (1987), 'Human resource development: The Asian experience in employment and manpower planning: An overview', in R. Amjad (ed.), *Human Resource Planning: The Asian Experience*. Geneva: ILO, 1–37.

25. Many developing countries in Asia overspent on tertiary education, while spending too little on primary education at the early stage of industrialization. See P. H. Lindert (2003), 'Voice and growth: Was Churchill right?', *Journal of Economic History*, 63 (2), 315–50; ibid. (2004), *Growing Public: Social Spending and Economic Growth*, vol. 1: *The Story*. Cambridge: Cambridge University Press.

26. A. Singh (1979), 'The "Basic Needs" approach to development vs the new international economic order: The significance of third world industrialization', *World Development*, 7 (6), 585–606; E. Lee (1979), 'Egalitarian peasant farming and rural development: The case of South Korea', *World Development*, 7 (4–5), 493–517.

27. Sugihara (2015), 'Asia in the growth of world trade', 34–8.

28. S. Kobori (2010), *Nihon no Enerugi Kakumei: Shigen Shokoku no Kingendai* [The energy revolution in Japan: The modern and contemporary history of a resource-poor country]. Nagoya: Nagoya Daigaku Shuppankai.

29. S. Kobori (2017), 'Rinkai Kaihatsu, Kogai Taisaku, Shizen Hogo: Kodo Seicho-ki Yokohama no Kankyoshi' [Seafront development, anti-pollution policy and nature conservation: An environmental history of Yokohama in the period of high-speed growth], in S. Shoji (ed.), *Sengo Nihon no Kaihatsu to Minshushugi: Chiiki ni Miru Sokoku* [Development and democracy in post-war Japan: Conflicts at local settings]. Kyoto: Showado, 71–104.

30. H. Hashiya (1995), 'Kankoku, Taiwan no Nizu-ka to Toshika' [Development of newly industrializing economies and urbanization in South Korea and Taiwan], in R. Kojima and N. Hataya (eds), *Hatten Tojokoku no Toshika to Hinkonso* [Urbanization and the poor in developing countries]. Tokyo: Ajia Keizai Kenkyusho, 43–6; N. Ishizaki (1996), 'Kankoku no Jukagaku Kogyo Seisaku: Kaishi no Naigai Joken to Jisshi Shutai' [South Korea's policy for heavy and chemical industries: Internal and external conditions for its establishment and actors for implementation], in T. Hattori and Y. Sato (eds), *Kankoku, Taiwan no Hatten Mekanizumu* [Patterns of development of South Korea and Taiwan]. Tokyo: Ajia Keizai Kenkyusho, 65–86.

31. R. Wade (1990), *Governing the Market: Economic Theory and the Role of Government in East Asian Industrialization*. Princeton, NJ: Princeton University Press, 86–112; Hashiya (1996), 'Kankoku, Taiwan no Nizu-ka to Toshika', 46–9; H. Sato (1996), 'Taiwan no Keizai Hatten ni okeru Seifu to Minkan Kigyo: Sangyo no Sentaku to Seika' [Government and private enterprises in the economic development of Taiwan: Choice of industries and their performance], in Hattori and Sato (eds), *Kankoku, Taiwan no Hatten Mekanizumu*, 96–101.

32. M. Zhou (2007), *Chugoku Keizairon: Kodo Seicho no Mekanizumu to Kadai* [Essays on the Chinese economy: The mechanism of high-speed growth and its problems]. Tokyo: Nihon Keizai Hyoronsha, 81–4, and 119–21.

33. Zhou (2007), *Chugoku Keizairon*, 72–128.

34. K. Sugihara (2012), '"Kaseki Shigen Sekai Keizai" no Koryu to Baiomasu Shakai no Saihen' [The rise of the fossil-fuel-driven world economy and reorganization of the biomass society], in K. Sugihara, K. Wakimura, K. Fujita and A. Tanabe (eds), *Rekishi no nakano Nettai Seizonken: Ontai Paradaimu wo Koete* [The tropical humanosphere in global history: Beyond the temperate zone paradigm]. Kyoto: Kyoto Daigaku Shuppankai, 164–79.

35. N. K. Dubash (2002), *Tubewell Capitalism: Groundwater Development and Agrarian Change in Gujarat*. New Delhi: Oxford University Press; T. Shah (2009), *Taming the Anarchy: Groundwater Governance in South Asia*. Washington, DC: Resource for the Future Press.

36. B. Agarwal (1986), *Cold Hearths and Barren Slopes: The Woodfuel Crisis in the Third World*. London: Zed Books.

37. See E. A. Wrigley (2016), *The Path to Sustained Growth: England's Transition from an Organic Economy to an Industrial Revolution*. Cambridge: Cambridge University Press; S. Pollard (1981), *Peaceful Conquest: The Industrialization of Europe, 1760–1970*. Oxford: Oxford University Press; and D. Theodoridis, P. Warde and A. Kander (2018), 'Trade and overcoming land constraints in British industrialization: An empirical assessment', *Journal of Global History*, 13, 328–51.

38. The GINI coefficient appears to have worsened since the diffusion of industrialization began in the nineteenth century, but stopped worsening around the middle of the twentieth century, largely as a result of the high economic growth of Asian countries. However, a further 'equalization' does not appear to have occurred over the last twenty years or so. Calculated from Maddison (2011), 'Statistics on world population'.

CHAPTER 14
GLOBAL COMMODITIES AND COMMODITY CHAINS

Bernd-Stefan Grewe

Since the 1940s, it has been customary for most married people in Europe and America to wear a golden ring, a symbol of eternal love. In India, a Hindu bride is also offered golden jewellery, not as a symbol of eternal love, but as a dowry. Usually such a dowry plunges a family into debt. On the other side of the Indian Ocean, in the Transkei in South Africa, a Mpondo groom has to pay a *lobola* to the bride's family. This bride-price is not paid with gold, but with cattle. Nonetheless, this marriage is as much linked to gold as the others, because the cattle for the *lobola* is mostly earned by young Mpondos employed as mineworkers in the Witwatersrand gold industry near Johannesburg.

In the Americas as in Europe, South Asia and Southern Africa, gold clearly plays a major role in weddings, but a different one in each case. The practices and meanings people attribute to this metal may also change over time, and such changes can have major repercussions on the demand for gold on international markets. For example in the first decade of the twenty-first century, each year about 10 million weddings took place in India alone at which jewellery – mostly gold and to a lesser extent diamonds of an estimated value of more than US$8 billion – was purchased. Yet in most economic history textbooks there is no indication of such large-scale demand and use, as gold is only mentioned in chapters on monetary history and especially in relation to the history of the gold standard.

Gold is a fascinating commodity and is here used to illustrate the potential and limits of approaches in global economic history based on the study of commodities. I focus on three approaches in particular: first on so-called *history of commodities*; second on *commodity-chain approaches*; and finally on *value-chain approaches*. I argue that commodity-based narratives provide unique insights into global economic processes but struggle to generalize or provide historians with suitable tools of analysis. In the past thirty years, economic historians have borrowed the concept of the commodity chain from sociology and political science. Here too one can see limitations both at a methodological and at an historical level. I therefore consider the concept of the global value chain and evaluate whether this might be a useful tool for economic historians.

Histories of Global Commodities

Histories of global commodities are not new. Several such histories were written many decades before the term 'globalization' was coined. Gold, for instance, is mined in specific areas of the world and over the centuries has been treasured and used by different world societies. It has been used not only for jewellery and precious objects but also, and in tandem, as a currency and as a form of treasure (either by rulers and merchants or as gold reserves held by central banks). Gold like silver has been essential for the development of global trade between America, Europe and Asia since the fifteenth century. The two precious metals were the material base for payment in far distant trade. Gold from Brazil and silver from Peru circulated around the globe and linked colonial Latin America with Europe and Asia in the early modern period. The form of labour exploitation changed over time – from slavery and forced labour to wage labour or free labour – but far too often people who worked in the mines had little choice but to work under harsh, unhealthy and dangerous conditions for little or no salary.

The case of gold alerts us to the fact that there are different ways to write about commodities: in particular we can distinguish three groups of commodity histories. First, commodity histories often describe the origins of a certain good, how it was discovered in ancient times, how different cultures and societies made use of it, how it was eventually reframed and remodelled during and after the Industrial Revolution, and how it was finally consumed. Early commodity histories and more recent coffee-table books contain information that can be of great value for historians today. A second group of commodity histories are of popular appeal and include titles such as Mark Kurlansky's *Cod* (1997), *Salt* (2002) or *Big Oyster* (2006), and Mark Pendergrast's *Uncommon Grounds* (1999) on coffee and *For God, Country and Coca-Cola* (1993). Finally, a third group of commodity histories is based on academic research and contributes to scholarly discussions.

One of the pioneering publications within this last group of academic commodity histories was *Sweetness and Power* (1985) by the anthropologist Sydney Mintz. His history of sugar starts with the cultural and social history of food in eighteenth- and nineteenth-century Britain, interlinking it with its production in the Caribbean. Mintz studied the anthropology of food in Europe and how sweetness slowly gained importance from the Middle Ages, its use rapidly developing from the nineteenth century onwards. Sugar changed its character from a former luxury good for the elite that was presented in silver or golden sugar bowls to a staple product and important food that even the working classes could afford to sweeten their tea or coffee. Sugar provided an increasing share of the calorie intake of common people in the nineteenth century. This change in relevance was closely linked to the plantation economy, of how sugarcane was cultivated, harvested and quickly processed into raw sugar. The increase in consumption provided an impetus for a capitalistic and intensified production process based on slave labour. The labour-intensive organization of the sugar plantations in the Caribbean attracted capital from Europe and further encouraged the development of capitalist economies.

More recent research on commodity history has evolved around the London-based network 'Commodities of Empire'.[1] Inspired by Mintz and already working on the economic history of colonialism in Latin America, Africa and South Asia, several researchers have started to investigate the commodity history of typical colonial products such as sugar, tobacco, palm oil, cotton, rubber, cocoa, coffee and tea. These studies have offered new insights into the functioning of the global economy and its various and often surprising effects on distant corners of the earth, like the example of coffee production in Kenya. Here, the overproduction of coffee in Brazil and Colombia endangered the colonial tax revenues derived from coffee sales. To preserve the coffee sector and the tax income from it, the colonial administration broke the former monopoly on coffee production of the white settlers and allowed African farmers to grow Arabica coffee. This case shows an active strategy of a colonial government to reorganize the commodity chain in order to raise production while maintaining quality but at lower costs.[2]

Other studies on commodity chains reveal new global connections with other chains that have often been ignored by traditional economic history. Since the publication of Mintz's *Sweetness and Power*, historians have acknowledged the role of sugar cultivated in the Caribbean plantations to the nutrition of British workers in the classic period of the Industrial Revolution. It is much more surprising to discover the extent to which North Atlantic salted cod was important for the feeding of slaves in the Caribbean and in Brazil. Taste and low price made it possible for salted cod to become a major staple in the West Indies and Brazil although ample supplies of fresh fish existed locally.[3] So cod fished by British fishermen off Newfoundland and Nova Scotia was salted and brought to the sugar plantations, which in turn produced sugar for British workers. Another overseen commodity chain linked Argentina with Europe through the export of skins and leather. Herds of cattle in the Argentine Pampa also delivered meat that was dried and salted in meat-salting plants, differentiated into standardized classes of quality, and then exported – like cod – to Cuba and Brazil to feed slaves on sugar plantations. The introduction of new technologies to produce corned beef and refrigerated ships to export frozen beef reshaped the commodity chain in the nineteenth century.[4]

Another recent variety of commodity history is Sven Beckert's *Empire of Cotton* (2014).[5] His book uses cotton as a lens through which to read the development of the modern economy. He reconstructs the rise of cotton from a locally cultivated crop that was hand-spun and woven into textiles for the same region where it was produced, to one of the most important commodities of the nineteenth century. The book shows the connection between cotton and the invention of new machinery and the development of industrialized production. Beckert distinguishes a phase of what he calls 'war capitalism', during which slavery and colonialism prepared the ground for a globalized cotton industry. This led to a phase of 'industrial capitalism' which involved the processing of fibres and the manufacturing of textiles. The author shows how both stages of industrialization rested on violence: on the militarization of the trade (with the East India companies), massive land expropriation in the Americas, genocide (of Native Americans) and the enslavement of millions of Africans. He also shows how 'industrial capitalism' depended on a strong, interventionist state 'capable of forging and protecting global markets, policing its borders, regulating industry, creating and then enforcing private property rights in land, enforcing contracts over large geographical distances, forging fiscal tools to tax populations, and building a social, economic and legal environment that made the mobilization of labor through wage payments possible'.[6] Like Beckert, many other approaches of commodity history are linked to a deeper understanding of capitalism and labour relation in particular.[7] A recent research network has emerged under the label of *Commodity Frontiers*, linking the history of capitalism with the expanding absorption of more land, labour and natural resources. Commodity frontiers study the social and environmental foundations and effects of capitalism in the global countryside.[8] This network has created a scientific journal (*Commodity Frontiers Journal*) and is currently preparing a *Lexicon of Commodity Frontiers*.

These types of commodity histories are based on many years of research. Mintz, for instance, started his archival research in Puerto Rico in the late 1940s, working on the lives of workers on sugar plantations.[9] Perhaps one criticism that can be made of commodity-based studies is that they rarely reflect on the methodological approach they adopt. Often, they rely on a synthesis of current historic knowledge, integrating different viewpoints and showing parallel developments in different parts of the world.

Commodity Chains

A commodity chain can be defined as the production of a tradeable good from the extraction of its raw materials through to its design and elaboration, followed by its transport and sale into the hands of the consumer. What would the commodity chain of gold look like? In the 1960s, this chain might have begun more than 2,000 metres underground in a South African gold mine in the Orange Free State from where the ore was hewn and brought to the surface. The ore was milled in large plants and then treated with cyanide to extract the gold, which was smelted into raw bars. These bars which still contained other metals were transported to the Rand Refinery at Germiston close to Johannesburg where the gold was refined out and melted into so-called London Good delivery bars of 995.0 per thousand purity. This bullion was shipped via plane to London, the leading international market for gold. Here the gold was bought either by one of the national reserve banks for its gold reserves or by a Swiss bullion dealer who resold and transported it to Dubai. The bars were then smuggled with dhows across the Indian Ocean to secret places on the Indian coast close to Mumbai. Only a few hours after its arrival, the gold was melted again, resold and distributed in small lots to local goldsmiths who worked and sold it to local consumers.

Gold is an example of the long-standing interest in commodity chains that goes back to times before the very label 'commodity chain' was invented. The work of Frank Taussig in the early years of the twentieth century reflected on the relationship between labour and production and investigated geographical divisions of labour.[10] John Davis and Ray Goldberg integrated different steps of production, distribution, transportation and marketing in a single analytical framework.[11] The interest in investigating commodity histories beyond national borders was further developed in the 1970s in the context of world-systems theory. Terence Hopkins and Immanuel Wallerstein were probably the first to use the expression 'commodity chains' and to think of them in a decidedly historical perspective.[12] Hopkins and Wallerstein proposed the analysis of commodity chains in order to overcome the distinction between different market levels ranging from national to international. Their concept was designed to dismiss the assumption that 'commodity chains developed first of all within the boundaries of the state and later began to cross state frontiers'.[13] Commodity chains cut across state boundaries and were thus of fundamental importance in the analysis of world systems and their core – periphery relations.[14] Wallerstein's concept of the world economy as being structured into core, semi-periphery and periphery could be substantiated through the study of commodity chains. Wallerstein showed that core activities commanded a large share of the surplus produced within a commodity chain while peripheral activities commanded only little or no surplus.[15]

The interest in commodity chains resurfaced in full in the 1990s when Gary Gereffi and Miquel Korzeniewicz published an edited volume entitled *Commodity Chains and Global Capitalism* (1994). Similar to Wallerstein's initial definition, their concept of a 'global commodity chain' (GCC) referred to the whole range of activities involved in the design, production and marketing of a product across national boundaries. Yet, their definition of commodity chain differed from that of world-system scholarship in several respects.[16] First, GCC is much more contemporarily oriented than Wallerstein's historical study which started in the long sixteenth century. GCC concentrates on the study of the contemporary apparel and automobile industries, as well as chains of production of foodstuffs such as bananas and tea or natural resources such as timber. Second, the GCC approaches are specifically interested in inter-firm networks and examine how global industries are organized. In opposition to the macro-focus of the world-system analyses that study the world capitalist order and how commodity chains structured and reproduced a stratified and hierarchical world system, GCC considers the macro–micro links between global, national and local units of analysis. Third, the GCC framework is a network-based and organizational approach. The GCC method helps to analyse processes of globalization in specific locations where production and related services occur and to understand how these locations and activities are connected to each other. GCC pays more attention to the specificity of locality and place than world-system approaches, and is therefore conducive to the study of local cultural or social aspects.[17]

Gereffi and his co-authors developed this approach primarily to analyse the power relations that are embedded in commodity chains and their governance. Overall, they defined four dimensions of the GCC framework: first, an input–output structure (a set of products and services linked together in sequence of value-adding economic activities); second, a territoriality (spatial dispersion or concentration of enterprises in production and distribution networks); third, the governance structure (authority and power relationships); and finally, the institutional context.[18]

GCC research starts from the assumption that a lead firm dominates the character of the chain. For the 1980s and 1990s, they identify in particular two types of governance structures for networked GCCs, which they call 'producer-driven' and 'buyer-driven' global commodity chains. The difference resides in the location of key barriers to entry. Producer-driven commodity chains are those in which large, transnational corporations play a key role in coordinating production networks. This type of GCC can typically be found in capital- and technology-intensive industries such the automobile, aircraft, computers and heavy machinery sectors where profit is generated by productive scale, volume and technological innovation. In buyer-driven GCCs, large retailers, marketers and branded manufacturers take the role of key agents and set up decentralized production networks in a variety of countries, typically located in the Global South. This is a typical pattern in relatively labour-intensive consumer goods such as garments, footwear, toys and housewares. The companies that develop and sell brand-named products exert control over how, when and where manufacturing takes place, and how much profit accrues at each stage of the chain. The dominant enterprises transfer economic competitive pressures to peripheral areas of the world economy.[19]

One of the most debatable aspects of the GCC research is that the control of commodity chains, and therefore the profit generated by the process, is considered to be in the hands of so-called key agents. Take for instance the case of gold in the late nineteenth and early twentieth centuries. Following the flows of gold, much of the gold from the late nineteenth-century rushes in California, Australia and South Africa was channelled to London from where it was sold and distributed to the rest of the world. Before the First World War, the City of London and the Bank of England had a hegemonic position in world finance and much gold was shipped to London in order to pay for credit and for hoarding. London attracted more than a third of all the gold mined in this period, thus acting as the 'key agent' in this commodity chain. But did the bankers and bullion dealers exert any control of the global flows of gold? The key agents in the City of London comprised not only the Bank of England and large merchant banks such as Rothschild's but also a group of five bullion brokers who later became members of the London Gold Market Fixing (Mocatta, Rothschild, Sharps Pixley & Co., Johnson Matthey and Samuel Montagu). Although the Californian and the other gold rushes in America did not take place within the British Empire, the American need for credit brought much of its gold to London. For the Australian and South African gold, the most important factor was not that both territories were part of the British Empire but the fact that the big mining companies that ran the mines were financed by the City of London. Not only the gold but also most of the profits from gold mining flew to London, which was distributed as a dividend to stockholders.

One disadvantage of the GCC approach as exemplified through gold is that much research has a strong European or American orientation.[20] Few studies examine in detail the agency and interests of stakeholders in other world locations. Hence in the case of gold, the role of Indian, South African and Australian actors is rarely given as much prominence as that of Western reserve banks.[21] A closer inspection of the GCC of gold in the 1920s, for instance, reveals that the control of the different segments of the chain was far from the prerogative of a single 'key agent' (such as the Bank of England or

Rothschild's), and chains could be organized without any major driver. This does not mean that these chains are necessarily organized in a more equal way without major players or imbalances of power, but it is not necessary to assume the presence of either a visible hand to manage and control the whole of a chain or the invisible hand of markets. Power and control are surely not absent from markets and in commodity chains, but they are not necessarily concentrated in one key agent.

A second problem with a GCC approach is that it often implies that initiatives for change in the chain originate mainly from the industrialized countries in the North (or as Wallerstein calls it, the core). In this perspective, the role of actors from the Global South (Wallerstein's periphery) is seen as passive. This may be due to the fact that most commodity-chain studies concentrate on commodities that are consumed in the developed countries of the northern hemisphere, ignoring the fact that many chains find final consumers in the so-called 'developing countries' (or colonized areas). Populations in former colonies and in the Global South are often considered as producers, leaving researchers with little knowledge of their consumption patterns. For gold, two observations from the 1920s illustrate this issue. Once the gold mining houses in Johannesburg had erected their own refinery – the Rand Refinery in Germiston – they became technically independent from the London refiners and market. As they could guarantee the purity of the gold themselves, they sold it directly to the United States and to the Indian subcontinent, thus circumventing the London market. The London network of bankers, bullion dealers and insurance brokers continued to manipulate prices, shipment tariffs and insurance rates; yet in the second half of the 1920s, South Africa started to export its gold directly from Durban to Bombay. But shortly afterwards, in 1931, it was forced again to sell its gold in London when Indian demand collapsed due to bad harvests and falling agricultural prices. The flow of gold was therefore determined not by key agents in London, but by other economic factors in South Asia.[22]

A third critical aspect of the GCC approach is the assumed imbalance of power within the chain. Indeed, many studies have shown the power of leading firms and how these so-called drivers reaped the largest share of profits in the chain. However, a group of Latin American historians – including Steven Topik, Carlos Marichal and Zephyr Frank – have rejected the claim that profits invariably accrued in the more developed countries. Instead they have shown that the arrangement of production and the distribution of profit were dependent on the endowment of the different actors in the commodity chain. They have showed, for instance, how Brazilian coffee producers have been able to get a high share of profit.[23]

Notwithstanding these caveats, GCC provides an alternative method for the economic analysis of global economic processes that link industrialized and developing countries both at a macro and at a micro level. GCC methods of analysis have continued to develop theoretically and empirically over the past quarter of a century. By the early 2000s, however, researchers became interested in a subfield that has come to be known as the 'global value chain'.

Global Value Chains

A new interdisciplinary and international initiative to examine different approaches of global production networks started in 2000. Its main objective was to create a new theory of governance to help policymakers explain and predict governance patterns in cross-border production networks. Global value chain research was designed to study the different ways in which global production and distribution systems are integrated in the global economy. The intention was to explore the possibilities for firms in developing countries to enhance their position in global markets. Thus the authors hoped that the theory of global value chain governance would be useful for the crafting of effective policy tools related to industrial upgrading, economic development, employment creation and poverty alleviation.[24] Therefore it was claimed that this new model of analysis should be robust, relevant and easily applicable to real-world situations.[25]

The shift from 'commodity chains' to 'value chains' is not simply a terminological one as some critics first suggested.[26] Many empirical studies observed that an increasing number of producer-driven chains were changing as lead firms started to outsource large parts of their global production to external manufacturing firms. Some chains became more buyer-like. The distinction between the two types of producer- and buyer-driven chains was no longer sufficient and other network types were needed. The GCC typology was based on a rather static view of technology and barriers to entry, but technological change and firm- and industry-level learning stimulate change and make chains rather dynamic. Many industries showed a clear shift away from vertically integrated producer-driven chains, while buyer-driven chains could not encompass all the different networks observed in the field. The decision to replace the term 'commodity' with 'value' was taken because commodities are too often identified with undifferentiated products, mainly primary products (i.e. crude oil) or agricultural products (such as coffee, cocoa, wheat or jute).[27] Another reason to choose 'value' is that the term captures the notion of 'value added' and thus the application of human effort to generate profit on invested capital.

The building of a new global value chain (GVC) theory rests on the centrality of 'nodes' considered to be 'the pivot points in transformation sequences: extraction and supply of raw materials, the stages of industrial processing, exports, and final marketing'.[28] GVC addresses in particular three questions related to nodes: first, what kind of activities are bundled up in one node of the chain or split among various nodes? Second, how are knowledge, information and materials passed from one node to the next? And finally, where are these nodes located? Based on a comparison between case studies, a GVC working group was able to identify five ways in which firms governed or coordinated the linkages between value chain activities:

1. *Market linkages* that are governed by price, and in which the costs of switching to new partners are low for both parties.
2. *Modular linkages* in which suppliers make products to a customer's specifications. Complex information regarding the transaction is codified and digitized before it is passed to highly competent suppliers.

3. *Relational linkages* in which complex interactions between buyers and sellers take place, creating mutual dependence and high levels of asset specificity. Trust and relationship are often built over time and might work in spatial proximity as well as in spatially dispersed networks. Tacit information is exchanged between buyers and highly competent suppliers.

4. *Captive linkages* in which less competent suppliers are provided with detailed instructions and are dependent on much larger buyers. Suppliers have to face significant switching costs and are therefore 'captive'. These linkages are often characterized by a high degree of monitoring and control by lead firms. [29]

5. *Hierarchical linkages*, which are a governance form characterized by vertical integration and managerial control, flowing down from headquarters to subsidiaries and affiliates.[30]

This typology is the first step towards an operational theory of global value chain governance and helps us to study under which conditions market, modular, relational, captive or vertically integrated chain governance arises. GVC identifies three key determinants of governance patterns: complexity of information and knowledge transfer that are required to sustain a particular transaction, particularly with respect to product and process specifications; the extent to which information and knowledge can be codified and efficiently transmitted; and the capabilities of suppliers in relation to the requirements of the buyers.[31]

What makes GVCs attractive for economic historians is that the evolution of governance structures over time is integral to their study. By considering several sectors, GVC observes a trajectory from one type of governance to another and identifies causal factors in the hope of being able to anticipate future change in GVC. The evolution of the bicycle industry serves as an example of how hierarchies and vertical integration in the early years of the industry (in the 1890s) evolved towards inter-firm governance and reliance on market mechanisms. In this GVC, specialist firms such as Sachs, Shimano or later SRAM, producing just one component of a bicycle, became more competitive than vertically integrated producers of complete bicycles. Another example is provided by the apparel industry whose governance changed from captive to relational value chains. The suppliers in many East Asian countries moved in a few decades from simply assembling imported inputs to full-scale supply as they learned how to make internationally competitive consumer goods. This, however, requires the capacity to interpret designs, to produce samples, to source all needed inputs, to control product quality, not to exceed the buyer's price, and to guarantee on-time delivery.

Other value chains changed in a different direction, as in the case of fresh vegetables. As a primary product, the GVC of fresh vegetables in Kenya had for a long time been the typical example of a market-based form of governance. But this changed in the 1980s when large UK supermarket chains (Tesco, Asda and Sainsbury's) wished to attract new customers by offering year-round supply and guarantee them high quality. At the same time, they had to meet stronger standards of food safety, especially concerning pesticide residues. The supermarkets' strategy was to increase their control over the chain and to explicitly coordinate their supply. They therefore signed renewable annual contracts with their suppliers and monitored the entire chain.

The differentiation of the GVC model between five different governance types (market, modular, relational, captive and hierarchical) is useful in the analysis of global economic connections. The example of the commodity chain of gold in the 1960s illustrates this: at the production end of the chain in South Africa, most of the mines were directed by a handful of large 'mining houses' (who also controlled about three-quarters of all the joint-stock companies listed in the Johannesburg stock exchange – an enormous concentration of economic power). Most of the mines were organized as stock companies and run by these so-called mining houses. These holdings took care of the transactions of their shares at stock exchanges in Europe and the United States and to a smaller extent in Johannesburg. They had the know-how to run a mine and therefore appointed the directors and mining engineers. This was obviously a hierarchical linkage. However, most of the profits from these mines that left South Africa as dividends were paid to the shareholders located overseas. The mining houses were able to govern their business with as little as 30 per cent of the shares as most international investors did not attend shareholders' meetings in Johannesburg.

Often GVC studies focus on the vertical direction of a network, paying little attention to the horizontal dimension of such linkages. Although the control of the individual mines by the holdings was hierarchical, at the same time the different mines and mining houses did not compete on a market for gold. In an atmosphere of mutual trust, they shared technical information and mining innovation. This was greatly facilitated by the fact that the mines did not have to compete for a lower price of gold when their product did not differ in quality and when the market absorbed any amount of gold for a guaranteed price (under the gold standard, the central banks of the gold pool countries guaranteed the price of the gold). Cooperation allowed firms to save on costs and even to coordinate their sales. The gold derived from the ores that lay many thousands of feet underground, which the miners brought to the surface, was milled, treated with chemicals and refined at the Rand Refinery. This refinery was run by the Chamber of Mines of South Africa and was deemed to embody the cooperation of the mining houses in Johannesburg. The bars were then shipped via Durban to Southampton and London. The gold was then either sold for a fixed price to the Bank of England or on the gold market. It is highly questionable whether the London gold market was governed by market linkages as the volatility of the gold price was limited within a small range of fixed prices. Under the Bretton Woods system, the reserve banks of the gold pool countries stabilized the gold price and thus the value of their currencies by selling gold to the market or buying it whenever it was necessary to stabilize its price.

As stated above, the biggest demand for gold for private purposes came from India. But after the military conflict with China in 1962, the Indian government completely banned the import of gold in an attempt to shift the capital spent on jewellery towards investment for the development of Indian industry. However, what came to be known as the 1963 Gold Control Act did not affect the demand for gold in India at all. The uncurbed demand stimulated a black market and the smuggling of gold via the Indian Ocean, with Dubai as a major connecting port. As the price of gold was 75 per cent higher in India than on international markets, smuggling was extremely lucrative.[32] It is estimated that between 107 and 217 tonnes of gold were smuggled into India annually between 1968 and 1972.[33] The sophisticated smuggling business was not run by individuals, but by professional cartels operated from Dubai. Thus, the little sheikdom of Dubai that in the 1960s had less than 60,000 inhabitants became the single largest gold buyer at the London gold market. As this cursory analysis of gold reveals, the GVC model proved to be a useful analytical tool to better understand global interconnections.[34]

Critiques

However, for historians wishing to adopt a commodity-chain or value-chain approach, there are several methodological problems and challenges to overcome: first, most studies present the commodity and value chains in a linear form. Several authors have stressed the problem of the linearity of commodity chain studies.[35] They question how chains are presented and argue that the competitive position of various actors at specific nodes of the chain is excluded.[36]

Second, a possible solution to the problem of linearity could be to scrutinize the construction of chains and question the decision-making processes in the identification of chains. Most chains are presented as linking different nodal points at which new actors enter the chain and participate in different ways. Historians, who often tend to make their decision depending on the availability of sources, should openly discuss the ways in which the haphazardness of recordings has effects on the results they produce.

Third, historians have favoured certain commodity chains, especially luxury goods, exotic commodities, or strategic resources like rubber and oil. When they have considered agrarian products, most historians preferred the products of the plantation complex (sugar, coffee, tea, cocoa, cotton and rubber) but for a long time ignored the contribution of the small farmers to the same commodity chain. This raises fundamental questions, not only in which direction to orientate the research at the nodal points, but also which commodities we should study: the study of rice, maize and potatoes, silicon, cobalt, copper, aluminium and uranium might be of greater relevance for global history than the study of luxury goods or even gold.[37]

Fourth, entire segments of commodity chains are organized in ways that defy formal control on the part of states or of any other formal institutions. This informal part of the economy does not just exist in countries of the economic periphery where the power of the state is supposed to be weaker than in the industrialized countries. Informal relations are the domain of cities not only in developing countries such as Bangladesh, Pakistan, Vietnam or Indonesia, but can be found also in Western metropolises, as for example within sweatshops that produce haute-couture textiles in Paris and New York.

Finally, GCC and GVC approaches and sometimes historic studies making use of these methods ignore the cultural dimension of economic interaction.[38] The action is often conceived in a way as if the origin of the actors involved, their language, their conceptions of work and leisure, their ideas of dignity and honour, their estimations of goods and services, and many other cultural aspects are of no importance to the functioning of commodity chains. GCC and GVC overlook the relevance of cultural patterns because they seem to have little bearing on the distribution of power and wealth.

Conclusion

The study of global commodities and of value chains has slowly gained acceptance among historians and is now shaping a new research field at the intersection between economic and global history.[39] Commodity-chain and value-chain approaches offer many new insights on global economic processes that link industrialized and developing countries. Furthermore, they help us to overcome the traditional opposition between micro versus macro approaches to economic history as they consider processes and decision-making practices at different levels. The somewhat naïve assumption of the early commodity-chain approach (GCC) that such chains were managed by key agents has been refuted both theoretically and empirically. Yet, the legacy of GCC is still important as it investigates systematically the different ways in which global commodity and value chains were governed at different levels and under a variety of conditions. Historical studies of commodities and their chains have shown their potential for gaining a better understanding of the basic characteristics of global economic interconnections. The metaphor of chain helps us to develop a comprehensive narrative that is never simplistic.

Notes

1. Commodities of Empire. A British Academy Research Project, https://commoditiesofempire. org.uk/. See also the special issue of the *Journal of Global History* (4) published in 2009.

2. David Hyde (2008), 'Global coffee and decolonisation in Kenya: Overproduction, quotas and rural restructuring', *Commodities of Empire Working Paper* No. 8, https:// commoditiesofempire.org.uk/publications/working-papers/working-paper-8/.

3. M. W. Herold (2015), 'Nineteenth-century Bahia's passion for British salted cod: From the seas of Newfoundland to the Portuguese shops of Salvador's Cidade Baixa, 1822–1914', *Commodities of Empire Working Paper* No. 23, https://commoditiesofempire.org.uk/ publications/working-papers/working-paper-23/.

4. A. Sluyter (2010), 'The Hispanic Atlantic's Tasajo trail', *Latin American Research Review*, 45 (1), 98–120; A. Sluyter (2012), *Black Ranching Frontiers: African Cattle Herders of the Atlantic World, 1500–1900*. New Haven, CT and London: Yale University Press, 169–210.

5. Sven Beckert (2014), *Empire of Cotton: A Global History*. New York: Alfred A. Knopf.

6. A. Komlosy and G. Musić (eds) (2021), *Global Commodity Chains and Labor Relations*, Leiden: Brill.

7. S. Beckert, U. Bosma, M. Schneider and E. Vanhaute (2021), 'Commodity frontier and the transformation of the global countryside: A research agenda', *Journal of Global History*, 16 (3), 435–50, https://commodityfrontiers.com/ (accessed 7 March 2023); *Commodity Frontier*

Journal, https://library.wur.nl/ojs/index.php/commodity-frontiers/issue/archive (accessed 7 March 2023); E. Landsteiner and E. Langthaler (eds), (2020) 'Global commodities/Globale Waren', *Österreichische Zeitschrift für Geschichtswissenschaften* 30 (3), https://journals.univie.ac.at/index.php/oezg/issue/view/305 (accessed 7 March 2023).

8. Beckert (2014), *Empire of Cotton*, 76; A very different commodity history dominated by actors from the Global South, in P. Machado, S. Mullins and J. Christensen (eds) (2019), *Pearls, People and Power: Pearling and Indian Ocean Worlds*. Athens, OH: Ohio University Press.

9. S. Mintz (1960), *Worker in the Cane: A Puerto Rican Life History*. New Haven, CT: Yale University Press.

10. F. W. Taussig (1911), *Principles of Economics*, Vol. 1. New York: Macmillan, 15 and 30–48. See also M. van der Linden (2007), 'Labour history: The old, the new and the global', *African Studies*, 66 (2–3), 169–80.

11. John H. Davis and Ray A. Goldberg (1957), *A Concept of Agribusiness*. Boston, MA: Harvard University Press, vii, 1–2, thank explicitly the Russian economist Wassily Leontief who had designed a related approach in the 1920s. There is an (shortened) English reprint of his article (German original in *Archiv für Sozialwissenschaft und Sozialpolitik*, 60 (1928), 577–623); W. Leontief (1991), 'The economy as a circular flow', *Structural Change and Economic Dynamics*, 2 (1), 181–212, 182: 'At this point the concept of a circular flow comes into play as a tool which enables us to identify those causal relationships that are specific to the economic sphere. Circular flow analysis only takes into account those relationships which allow us to return to the initial starting point.'

12. T. K. Hopkins and I. Wallerstein (1977), 'Patterns of development of the modern world-system', *Review: Fernand Braudel Center*, 1 (2), 128.

13. Hopkins and Wallerstein, 'Patterns of development', 128–9.

14. I. Wallerstein (1974–2011), *The Modern World-System*, 4 vols. New York: Academic Press (vols. 1–3, 1974–89); Berkeley, CA: University of California Press (vol. 4, 2011).

15. G. Arrighi and J. Drangel (1986), 'The stratification of the world-economy: An exploration of the semiperipheral zone', *Review: Fernand Braudel Center*, 10 (1), 11–12.

16. An excellent comparison between these concepts can be found in J. Bair (2005), 'Global capitalism and commodity chains: Looking back, going forwards', *Competition & Change*, 9 (2), 153–80.

17. Bair, 'Global capitalism', 159.

18. The last dimension was added later and is still the less developed, as the governance structure is by far dominant in GCC research. G. Gereffi, M. Korzeniewicz and R. P. Korzeniewicz (1994), 'Introduction: Global commodity chains', in G. Gereffi and M. Korzeniewicz (eds), *Commodity Chains and Global Capitalism*. Westport, CT: Praeger, 7; G. Gereffi (1995), 'Global production system and Third World development', in B. Stallings (ed.), *Global Change, Regional Response*. Cambridge: Cambridge University Press, 100–42.

19. Gereffi underlines the similarities with Michael Porter's value-chain approach. See M. Porter (1985), *Competitive Advantage: Creating and Sustaining Superior Performance*. New York: Free Press. This value-chain approach is also recommended in Michael Porter's 'Competitive advantage and business history', *Business and Economic History*, 21 (2), 228–36. P. Scranton and P. Fridenson (2013), *Reimagining Business History*. Baltimore, MD: Johns Hopkins University Press; R. Kaplinsky (2004), *Competitions Policy and the Global Coffee and Cocoa Value Chains*. Brighton: Institute of Development Studies.

20. For gold, see the excellent study by B. Eichengreen (1992), *Golden Fetters: The Gold Standard and the Great Depression, 1919–1939*. New York: Oxford University Press.

21. J. McGuire, P. Bertola and P. Reeves (eds) (2001), *Evolution of the World Economy, Precious Metals and India*. New Delhi: Oxford University Press.

22. B.-S. Grewe (2013), 'The London gold market, 1910–1935', in C. Dejung and N. P. Peterson (eds), *Power, Institutions and Global Markets: Actors, Mechanisms and Foundations of World-Wide Economic Integration, 1850–1930*. Cambridge: Cambridge University Press, 112–32.

23. S. Topik, C. Marichal and Z. Frank (eds) (2006), *From Silver to Cocaine: Latin American Commodity Chains and the Building of the World Economy, 1500–2000*. Durham, NC and London: Duke University Press.

24. G. Gereffi, J. Humphrey and T. Sturgeon (2005), 'The governance of global value chains', *Review of International Political Economy*, 21 (1), 79.

25. A very concise presentation of the GVC theory and the scientific context from which it was derived can be found in T. J. Sturgeon (2009), 'From commodity chains to value chains: Interdisciplinary theory building in an age of globalization', in J. Bair (ed.), *Frontiers of Commodity Chain Research*. Stanford, CA: Stanford University Press, 110–34; S. Ponte, G. Gereffi and G. Raj-Reichert (eds) (2019), *Handbook on Global Value Chains*. Cheltenham: Edward Elgar.

26. B. Daviron and S. Ponte (2005), *The Coffee Paradox: Global Markets, Commodity Trade and the Elusive Promise of Development*. London: Zed Books, 27.

27. For this type of commodity chain, John Talbot proposed the term 'tropical commodity chain'. J. M. Talbot (2002), 'Tropical commodity chains, forward integration strategies and international inequality: Coffee, cocoa and tea', *Review of International Political Economy*, 9 (4), 701–34.

28. Bair, 'Global commodity chains', 66.

29. D. Nathan, M. Tewari and S. Sarkar (eds) (2016), *Labour in Global Value Chains in Asia*. Cambridge: Cambridge University Press.

30. Sturgeon, 'From commodity chain to value chain', 119.

31. Out of the eight possible combinations of the three variables, there are only five value chain types that the group can actually find. It is unlikely to find a combination of low complexity of transactions and low ability to codify which excludes two combinations. If the complexity of the transaction is low and the ability to codify is high, then low capacity suppliers would be excluded from the chain.

32. See T. Green (1981), *The New World of Gold*. Johannesburg: Jonathan Ball, 172–5.

33. A. Sarma et al. (1982), 'Gold mobilisation as an instrument of external adjustment: A discussion paper', Bombay: Reserve Bank of India, 29. According to estimates of Consolidated Gold Fields Ltd, the total illegal gold imports amounted to an estimated 4,770 tonnes of gold between 1958 and 1990. For comparison: at the end of 1991 the largest gold reserves in a central bank amounted to 8,146 tonnes (the United States), and the second largest 2,960 tons (Germany). See G. O'Callaghan (1983), 'The structure and operation of the world gold market', *IMF Occasional Paper*, no. 105, 11.

34. I. Suwandi (2019), *Value Chains: The New Economic Imperialism*. New York: Monthly Review Press.

35. J. Henderson, P. Dicken, M. Hess, N. Coe and H. Wai-Chung Yeung (2002), 'Global production networks and the analysis of economic development', *Review of International*

Political Economy, 9 (3), 442; Bair, 'Global commodity chains', 16; Sturgeon, 'From commodity chains to value chains', 126.

36. Bair, 'Global commodity chains', 15. In addition, one could also criticize that the environmental dimension of commodity chains is not sufficiently considered: J. Bouchard (2021), 'Making the leap: Commodity chains and the potential for global environmental histories of capitalism', *Esboços: Historias em Contextos Globias* 28 (49), 698–715.

37. B.-S. Grewe (2016), 'Raum und Macht – Eine Stoffgeschichte des Goldes im frühen 20. Jahrhundert', *Jahrbuch für Wirtschaftsgeschichte*, 57 (1), 59–89; I. Prodöhl (2013), 'Versatile and cheap: A global history of soy in the first half of the twentieth century', *Journal of Global History* 8 (3), 461–82; T. D. DuBois (2019), 'Many roads form pasture to plate: A commodity chain approach to China's beef trade, 1732–1931', *Journal of Global History*, 14 (1), 22–43; A. Steffen (2020), 'A fierce competition! Silesian linens and Indian cottons on the West African coast in the late seventeenth and early eighteenth centuries', in J. Wimmler and K. Weber (eds), *Globalized peripheries: Central Europe and the Atlantic world, 1680–1860*, 37–56; J. E. Robins (2022), *Oil Palm: A Global History*. Chapel Hill, NC: University of North Carolina Press.

38. M. Granovetter (2005), 'The impact of social structure on economic outcomes', *Journal of Economic Perspectives*, 19 (1), 33–50.

39. See the calls for papers of the IISH Amsterdam 'Commodity Frontiers' (Amsterdam, July 2015), ITH conference 'Commodity Chains and Labour Relations' (Linz, September 2016), and 'Global Commodity Frontiers in Comparative Historical Context' (London, December 2016).

CHAPTER 15
THE RISE OF GLOBAL FINANCE, 1850–2000
Youssef Cassis

What is global finance? At its roots lie international capital flows – the export of capital from some countries and the import of capital from others. However, global finance is more than that. It should be considered as the plant rather than simply the roots. It could be described as the complex web of financial institutions, markets and agents involved in moving capital across nations and regions, each fulfilling a set of functions in the nations and regions connected by these multiple transactions. Within these nations and regions, global financial transactions have concentrated in specific places, usually cities, where the various financial services required by these transactions have gathered, primarily in order to achieve external economies of scale. International financial centres thus form the fabric of global finance.

This chapter takes the third quarter of the nineteenth century as its point of departure, because of the extent – both quantitative and qualitative – of finance in the age of industrial capitalism. International capital flows started their long upswing wave, which would continue until 1914 (perhaps even 1931) when new financial institutions and markets emerged in all advanced economies, in particular with the rise of the big banks and the development of the securities markets. However, the rise of global finance has not continued unabated from the mid-nineteenth century to the early twenty-first century. World wars, financial crises and economic nationalism have led to periods of domestic (or imperial) withdrawals or the exclusion of nations or regions from international financial exchanges – especially during the decades from the early 1930s to the late 1970s. And the resumption of global finance from the 1980s has taken new forms as a result of technological and financial innovations as well as the transformation of the world economy.

The chapter follows a chronological order and is divided in three parts: the first deals with the first era of modern globalization, from the 1850s to 1914; the second with the era of wars, depression and regulation, from 1914 to 1973; and the third with the wave of deregulations and innovations that marked the second globalization, from 1973 to 2000 and includes a brief epilogue discussing the effects of the financial debacle of 2008 and the rise of new economic powers, above all China, in global finance. It is structured around the development of financial centres in both the core industrial countries and the periphery, paying particular attention to their differences and similarities as well as the interactions between them.

The First Modern Globalization, 1850–1914

Foreign investment began to grow substantially from the mid-1850s, the capital stock invested outside its country of origin going from just under $1 billion in 1855 (it was at the same level thirty years earlier) to $7.7 billion in 1870. It then rose to $23.8 billion in 1900 and to $38.7 billion in 1914.[1] Throughout these years, Britain was the largest exporter of capital, followed by France, and, later in the nineteenth century, Germany. Small European countries (the Netherlands, Belgium and Switzerland) exported substantial amounts of capital, especially when measured as a proportion of their GDP. The United States became a capital exporting country by the turn of the twentieth century, even though it remained a net debtor until the end of the First World War.

While Britain maintained its lead during the long nineteenth century, it was seriously challenged by France during the 1850s and 1860s. The two countries exported similar amounts of capital ($75–$100 million per year in the 1850s and $150–$175 million in the 1860s), with a slight advantage for France, though Britain still held a larger stock of foreign investments.[2] Following its defeat by Prussia in 1871, France was no longer able to challenge Britain but retained its second place. The volume of capital exports increased markedly from the beginning of the twentieth century, having fallen in the 1890s in the wake of the Baring Crisis. Between 1880 and 1913, capital exports amounted to 40 per cent of available savings for Britain and between 20 and 25 per cent for France.

Figures are less reliable for the destination of capital exports, especially before 1900. The United States was definitely the largest recipient, with 16 per cent of the world's total in 1913 (40 per cent of which came from Britain), followed by Canada and Russia (each with 8 per cent), Argentina (7 per cent), and Brazil, Mexico, India, Australia, China, South Africa, Spain and the Austro-Hungarian Empire (with 4–6 per cent).

International capital flows were part of a broader globalization of the world economy, in particular free movements of people, transport facilities, speed of communication and expanding trade, which required huge transfers of capital and/or facilitated international financial transactions. From 1850 international migration increased on an unprecedented scale: 36 million Europeans left the Old Continent between 1870 and 1915, most of them, some 70 per cent, heading for the United States and almost all the others for Argentina, Australia, Canada and Brazil – in other words mainly to temperate regions where European immigration was still recent. Advances in transport and communication made the world smaller and brought countries and continents closer together. The building of railway lines, starting in the 1830s, continued on a much larger scale, world mileage increasing from 205,000 kilometres in 1870 to 925,000 kilometres in 1906. Maritime transport also made considerable progress with the development of oceanic steamships, which really got under way in the 1890s, when steam tonnage finally overtook that of sailing ships. Telecommunications sped up to the point of becoming instantaneous, first with the telegraph (a cable linked Britain to the European continent as early as 1851, and the first transatlantic cable between London and New York was laid in 1866), then with the telephone (Paris and London were connected in 1891, transatlantic links having to wait until the 1920s), and finally with wireless telegraphy (messages were transmitted across the Atlantic from 1901).[3] Foreign trade grew dramatically in the nineteenth century. In the case of Europe, the proportion of exports, measured as a percentage of GDP, went from 9 per cent in 1860 to 14 per cent in 1913.[4]

The global financial order was organized around a dominant economy: Great Britain – even though it was challenged and then overtaken by the United States (in industrial output in the 1880s and GDP by 1900) and Germany (in industrial output in around 1905). Britain's position rested on the leadership it retained in foreign trade (still 14 per cent of world trade in 1913, down from 20 per cent in the mid-nineteenth century) and services and finance (as the largest capital exporter and the largest provider of trade finance), as well as its key position in the system of multilateral trade, on account of its deficit with the major industrial countries and its surplus with its colonial empire.[5] Britain's weight in the world economy was thus primarily due to the role of the pound sterling – the main international trading and reserve currency and the cornerstone of the international monetary system in force at that time, the gold standard.

Britain's financial pre-eminence was embodied in the global role played by the City of London, the world's leading financial centre.[6] The City offered an unrivalled range of financial services, which made it the principal engine of financial globalization. First, the bulk of world trade was financed through the medium of bills of exchange drawn on London. And second, with nearly 50 per cent of foreign capital stocks held by British investors, London was the main centre for the issue of foreign loans. These two essential functions were carried out by a group of private banks, known as merchant banks.[7] The issuing business, the most prestigious activity in international finance, was the preserve of the most select houses (Rothschilds, Barings, Morgan Grenfell, Hambros, Schroders and a few others, including Kleinworts, the leading accepting house). The accepting business (in other words guaranteeing the payment of a bill exchange when it came to maturity) was the bread and butter of a growing number of firms, possibly as many as 105 in 1914, several of them from abroad. In the heart of the world's financial capital, the wheels of global finance were thus activated by old-established family-owned private banks rather than by the new joint-stock banks that had emerged in the mid-nineteenth century. The latter (Lloyds Bank, Midland Bank, London County and Westminster, and National Provincial Bank, to name but the four largest in 1913), known as the clearing banks, confined themselves to deposit banking activities within the domestic economy, but they provided the cash credit required by the merchant banks' operations.

Another group of newly formed joint-stock banks, known as overseas banks (London and River Plate Bank; Hong Kong and Shanghai Banking Corporation; Chartered Bank of India, Australia and China; Standard Bank of South Africa; and others) were directly involved in international finance. They usually had their head office in London (one exception was the Hong Kong and Shanghai Banking Corporation), but operated a network of branches in the formal and informal empire. Their goal was to provide facilities, especially foreign exchange, to merchants in the regions in which they were established. They also offered financial services in regions often lacking in banking infrastructure, thus winning a clientele from among well-off members of the local community. While the number of overseas banks doubled between 1860 and 1913 (from fifteen to about thirty), the number of branches increased more than tenfold (from 132 to 1,387).[8] But there was also a movement in the opposite direction. As a result of its financial predominance, the City attracted large foreign banks that came there to seek profitable business opportunities. Thirty of them – more than in any other centre – had opened an office by 1913, belonging to twelve different countries, and included the major French and German banks.

The City of London's other major activity as an international financial centre was the London Stock Exchange – a secondary market where the securities issued on the primary market could be negotiated. The nominal value of the securities listed there went from £2.3 billion in 1873 to £11.3 billion in 1913, more than the New York Stock Exchange and the Paris *Bourse* combined.[9] As evidence of its highly cosmopolitan character, foreign stocks, which represented between 35 and 40 per cent of the total in 1873, exceeded 50 per cent from 1893 onwards. By 1914 one-third of all securities in the world were quoted on the London Stock Exchange. The City hosted major commodity markets, such as the London Metal Exchange and the Baltic Exchange; and it provided specialized professional services, especially legal and accounting, whose leading firms soon expanded abroad to follow their clientele or to build up a new one. Price Waterhouse, for example, opened a branch in New York in 1890 and another in Chicago in 1892, where its business took off very quickly. Finally, in the centre of global finance, the Bank of England was, to use Keynes's words, the 'conductor' of the international monetary system, whose leadership the other central banks were prepared to follow in order to maintain monetary stability.[10]

No other centre had the same global range of services as London. Paris has been accurately described by Alain Plessis as a 'brilliant second'.[11] Its strength lay above all with its long-term capital market, especially for foreign securities, which was second only to London. Until the negotiation of the war indemnity loans in 1871–2, the issuing business had remained in the hands of the *Haute Banque* (Rothschilds, Fould, Mallet, Hottinguer, Seillière and a few others), a group of private banks akin to the London merchant banks. From then on, it was taken over by the new joint-stock banks – the investment banks (Paribas) as well as the big commercial banks (Crédit Lyonnais, Société Générale and Comptoir National D'escompte de Paris) which, unlike their English counterparts, were involved in international finance, especially the placing of foreign loans. They also established a network of foreign branches in 1913: the Crédit Lyonnais owned twenty, compared with eight in 1878, and the Comptoir d'Escompte owned twenty-eight. Overseas banks were far less prominent than in the City of London, owing partly to competition from the commercial banks but mainly to France's weaker presence in the world. However, the most important among them (Banque Impériale Ottomane and Banque de l'Indochine) were forces to be reckoned with in international finance. Paris also attracted foreign banks, though less than London (around fifteen in 1913). And the Banque de France, with its large gold reserves, played a key role in the international monetary system alongside the Bank of England, maintaining regulation and stability by allowing its gold to flow to London when the need arose.

The rise of global finance coincided with the rise of new financial powers. Frankfurt, Hamburg and Cologne had been European financial centres of some significance since the seventeenth century, but it was only after German unification in 1871 and rapid industrialization in the following decades that Germany and its new political and financial capital, Berlin, rose to financial prominence. More than anywhere else, business was dominated by the big banks (Deutsche Bank, Dresdner Bank, Disconto-Gesellschaft and Darmstädter Bank). They were universal banks, engaged in both commercial and investment banking, and controlled most international financial transactions. In addition to a number of foreign branches, they also established subsidiaries to conduct business in less developed countries. The Deutsche Bank, for example, created the Deutsche Überseeische Bank (active in Latin America) and the Deutsch-Asiatische Bank, the latter in conjunction with the Disconto-Gesellschaft and Bleichröder, a private bank.[12] However, Berlin was not in a position to rival London or even Paris seriously, if only because Germany invested far less capital abroad than Britain and France did. Moreover, the Berlin Börse was strictly regulated in order to curb speculation and combat fraud – the law of 1896 considerably limited forward transactions, and actually prohibited them on the securities of mining and manufacturing companies. As a result, speculative transactions, which represented the bulk of stock market business, moved out of Germany, towards Amsterdam and London in particular.

Specialized services were offered by lesser European financial centres – a broad and diverse secondary market in Amsterdam; finance companies in Brussels and Switzerland (Zurich, Geneva and Basel) that contributed to the development of the power industry worldwide by transferring funds provided by the big German banks to electrical engineering companies.[13] All in all, the bulk of international financial business was conducted in the financial centres of the leading capital exporting countries.

New York's position was somewhat peculiar. Its arrival among the leading financial centres was more as an entry point for foreign funds than as a point of departure for capital exports – though the situation had changed by 1900. New York's importance became increasingly decisive because of the massive amount of foreign investment in the United States, the dynamism of the American economy (foreign investment only made a small contribution to the huge domestic accumulation of capital) and the city's position as the country's financial centre. Like the City merchant banks, the Wall Street investment banks (J. P. Morgan, Kidder Peabody, Lee Higginson, Kuhn Loeb, Seligman, and Speyer), also family-owned private banks, formed the cornerstone of New York's financial centre.[14] Revealingly, they had close links to foreign financial centres, above all the City of London. Unlike in London, the largest national banks were themselves involved in investment banking, with the National City Bank in the lead.[15] Nevertheless, New York's international influence was still limited and it was dependent on London for the financing of American foreign trade, but the institutional foundations of its future predominance were laid during the pre-war years.

International financial centres developed in other borrowing countries, but with different characteristics from the providers of global finance. Centres such as

Hong Kong, Shanghai and Peking, Bombay and Calcutta, Cairo and Alexandria, Sydney and Melbourne, Yokohama, Buenos Aires, Rio de Janeiro, Constantinople and St Petersburg all hosted between six (St Petersburg) and twelve (Shanghai) 'transnational' banks.[16]

By comparison London had sixty-two, Paris thirty-one and New York twenty. Other centres in advanced economies were well behind: Brussels and Hamburg had ten, Berlin nine and Amsterdam eight. Other European centres, such as Vienna, Milan, Madrid, Stockholm and Zurich, hardly featured at all. Emerging centres, including New York, tended to attract foreign banks rather than host the head office of multinational banks. In China, India, the Middle East, Latin America and Australasia, virtually all 'transnational' banks were branches of foreign banks that primarily financed foreign trade. With the exception of London, which combined the two, capital exports were the dominant feature of established financial centres, and trade finance that of emerging ones, especially in Asia.

The position of financial centres in less developed countries points to an important feature of global finance before 1914 – the fact that opening up the world went hand in hand with the establishment of colonial empires and the imperialist powers' direct or indirect domination over most of the world on an unprecedented scale. In 1914, the British Empire stretched over 30 million square kilometres and included 450 million inhabitants, while the French colonial empire stretched over 10 million square kilometres with 50 million inhabitants. On top of this, they informally held sway over regions as vast as China, the Ottoman Empire and Latin America.

The costs and benefits of global finance must be considered in this context. There is no doubt that capital transfers played a positive role in the economic development of capital-importing countries – though with major differences between countries and regions. Government loans were certainly not always put to productive use, whether in connection with military expenditure or, more often, with servicing an already contracted debt. Yet significant achievements were made, especially in infrastructure: railways, roads, docks, ports, power stations and urban development. These achievements enabled natural resources to be developed and exported, thus stimulating economic growth; and only foreign capital could ensure their success. Recent research has emphasized, from a strictly financial perspective, the links between the cost of a loan and the risks associated to it.[17] Favourable conditions included the borrowing country's adherence to the gold standard, which was seen as a guarantee of good financial order, or membership of the British Empire, which provided additional assurance.[18] Borrowing on the international capital market was more expensive for Turkey than for Argentina or Russia, and even more expensive than for Australia or Japan. Indebtedness could, however, have another cost, and, even allowing for the complexities of the relationships between political and financial interests, it did contribute to the partial or total loss of political independence – from the occupation of Egypt and the foreign interference in the Ottoman Empire's finances to the division of China into 'spheres of influences'.

Wars, Depression and Regulation, 1914–73

The First World War did not put an end to capital exports. Between 1914 and 1918, debts totalling nearly $20 billion – in other words an amount equivalent to the stock of British foreign assets on the eve of the war – were incurred among the Allies. The two main creditor countries were the United States ($9.2 billion) and the United Kingdom ($8.5 billion), with France ($1.7 billion) trailing far behind – although Britain also had to borrow from the United States ($4.2 billion) and the French from both the United States ($2.7 billion) and the United Kingdom ($2.5 billion), while the other Allies (Italy and Russia) were only borrowers.[19] However, despite these vast amounts of capital transfers, one cannot talk of a global market. These loans were essentially contracted between governments and did not activate the mechanisms usually associated with credit transfers between international financial centres. France, for example, borrowed $2.9 billion from the American government compared with only $336 million from banks, and $2.1 billion from the British government, compared with $625 million from banks, including the Bank of England. Only a few intermediaries and privileged partners were involved in these operations, most of which were managed from New York and London, from where they continued to offer their expertise and their network of relationships. In this respect, the First World War marked the end of the Rothschilds' supremacy in government loans and the advent of the House of Morgan, which was responsible for issuing the first Anglo-French loan for $500 million in October 1915, followed by four more loans amounting to a total of $950 million on behalf of Britain in 1916 and 1917, and was to dominate global finance in the 1920s.

Global financial transactions, both capital exports and trade finance, resumed after the war. Some $10 billion flowed from creditor to borrowing nations during the second half of the 1920s. One major difference with the pre-war years was the proportion of short-term capital – about half the total in the case of European borrowers, not least Germany.[20] Another difference was the respective position of the financial powers. The great victor was the United States, which in a few years changed from a debtor country to a creditor country (having net private liabilities in excess of $3 billion in 1913 to net assets of $4.5 billion in 1919). Europe was no longer the world's banker. Germany lost nearly all its foreign assets; France most of it, probably three-quarters of its assets in Europe, mainly in Russia; and Britain some 20 per cent, essentially the $3 billion worth of American stock that it was obliged to sell. The situation was complicated by the questions of war debts ($19.4 billion in total, mainly due to the United States and Great Britain) and reparations (132 billion gold German marks – three times Germany's GDP). There was thus no return to pre-war stability. The gold standard was finally restored between 1924 and 1926, but its functioning was beset with difficulties and unable to achieve its objective, namely, to permit balance-of-payments adjustments. This was caused by the overvaluation of the pound and the undervaluation of the French franc, the uneasy cooperation between central banks, and insufficient expansionary policy in the surplus countries (France and the United States).

Nevertheless, London remained the world's leading financial centre in the 1920s, having soon regained its predominance in most activities, despite the success of acceptances drawn on New York, thanks to the establishment of the Federal Reserve in 1913, which allowed national banks to accept bills of exchange. However, London had to cede first place to New York in foreign issues. Britain remained the largest holder of foreign investment in terms of stocks, but no longer the largest capital exporter in terms of annual flows, because of the constraints weighing down its balance of payments. This role was now devolved to the United States. During the second half of the 1920s, foreign issues placed in New York generally exceeded those offered in London by 50 per cent (respectively, $969 and $592 million in 1924, $1,337 and $676 million in 1927, and $671 and $457 million in 1929). Overall, New York ranked number two, but it should not be forgotten that in spite of its new world role, it remained as much an American as an international financial centre. Foreign issues played a secondary role to domestic issues and accounted for only 15 per cent of the total amount of new issues in the 1920s. In addition, foreign capital continued to be invested in the United States, both long term and short term, especially with the bullish trend that marked the decade. This interaction between national and international business was one of the main characteristics of New York when compared to London.[21]

Paris was weakened by the war and dropped from second to third place. France was crippled by the weakness of the franc, capital flight and reconstruction requirements. However, the stabilization of the franc by Raymond Poincaré in December 1926 marked a turning point: Paris recovered part of its pre-war vitality, rekindling ambitions to compete with London and New York. Berlin paid the price of defeat and hyperinflation in 1923. Germany became the world's largest capital importing country in the 1920s, and it is mainly in this capacity that the German capital remained a significant international financial centre. Amsterdam, on the other hand, was commonly described as Germany's effective financial centre during the years of inflation and hyperinflation. All the major banks set up there after the end of the war were active on the foreign exchange market and later in the acceptance market, and Amsterdam enjoyed spectacular growth during the 1920s and established itself as the foremost centre in continental Europe. Zurich and the other Swiss centres (Geneva and Basel) played a lesser though not insignificant role in attracting foreign capital and redirecting it abroad – mainly to Germany.

Financial institutions played fundamentally the same role as before the war. Foreign issues continued to be handled by the merchant banks in the City, with limited competition from the clearing banks; and by the investment banks in Wall Street, with increasing competition from the securities affiliates of the big banks, with National City Bank in the lead. As before the war, both merchant and investment banks were in family hands, some organized as partnerships, others as limited companies but still controlled by their owners. With the exception of J. P. Morgan which towered above the rest, they were small or medium-sized companies. Their global transactions were conducted from New York or London, without a significant presence abroad – some had a branch or a subsidiary in another centre (J. P. Morgan, for example, held a majority stake in

Morgan Grenfell in London and Morgan Harjes in Paris), but most worked through correspondents.

The big banks somewhat retreated on the global financial front. The emergence of the 'Big Five' in England in 1918, which became the world's largest banks, did not fundamentally alter their functions. The French banks were weakened by the depreciation of the franc, the loss or closure of several foreign branches (in Russia, the Middle East, and Latin America), and the slow resumption of foreign investment. The German banks were stripped of their foreign assets (foreign branches and subsidiary companies). The American banks made only a short-lived attempt at expanding abroad in the early 1920s: their total number of foreign branches soared to 181 in 1920 though it had decreased to 107 by 1925. In the end, British overseas banks were the only ones to expand: their network of branches increased by nearly a thousand to reach 2,353 in 1928, almost exclusively in their areas of specialization.

The Great Depression was a watershed in the history of global finance. It consisted of four interrelated shock waves: the Wall Street Crash of October 1929, a series of banking crises occurring over a period of five years, the collapse of the world monetary order, and an economic slump of dramatic proportions. Long-term capital investments almost completely stopped in the 1930s. New York saw its role as an international financial centre shrivel: foreign loans, which had been its speciality, fell to less than $300 million in 1931 – less than the issues offered in London – and to less than $100 million in 1932 and 1933. But the domestic capital market was also shaken, issues on behalf of companies going from $8 billion in 1929 to $160 million in 1933. In London, foreign loans outside the British Empire ceased almost completely after September 1931, adding up to a mere £28.5 million between 1932 and 1938 – that is to say less than 3 per cent of the total amount of issues in London, as against 17 per cent for imperial issues (£186.7 million), which continued throughout the decade.[22] The number of foreign issues as a whole, including in the empire, thus dropped considerably in the 1930s. However, Britain's imperial retreat, strengthened by the formation of the sterling area, made it possible to conduct international financial transactions from London. Overseas banks, for example, added another thousand branches to their worldwide, mainly imperial, network.

From the perspective of global finance, the Second World War was different from the First if only because global financial activities had started to decline several years earlier. Moreover, the state's hold over the economy was stronger than it had been during the Great War, leaving hardly any opportunity at all for bankers and financiers to take charge of the large financial transactions required by the war effort. Capital transfers mainly took place within each of the two camps and consisted of state-to-state transactions, or exactions – the American lend–lease programme on the Allied side and the extensive use of resources from the occupied territories made by the Reich on the Axis side.[23]

Global finance did not rise from the ashes after the Second World War. The regulations inherited from the 1930s and those established in the immediate post-war years, including exchange controls, contributed to financial stability but hampered the re-emergence of a globalized financial world. Until the 1960s, or in some cases the 1970s, the international financial centres' business remained mostly confined within national borders: the golden age of economic growth, between 1950 and 1973 when annual GDP growth averaged 5 per cent in Europe and 8 per cent in Japan, was not accompanied by intense international movements of private capital. The largest capital transfers were not left to the private sector, but were undertaken by governments, state bodies and, to a lesser extent, multilateral agencies like the International Monetary Fund or the World Bank. Between 1955 and 1962, foreign issues floated in New York barely reached $4.2 billion – a feeble sum compared with the $126.5 billion for domestic issues, or the $98 billion in economic and military aid granted by the United States to foreign countries between 1945 and 1952.[24]

New York emerged as the world's financial capital and its position remained unchallenged until the 1960s. However, New York's pre-eminence corresponded to a period in which international capital flows were far smaller than before 1931 or after 1980. London's position was considerably weakened after the war, but it refocused on the Commonwealth and, particularly, on the sterling area, which enabled it to resume, in a more limited way, the role it had played on the world stage prior to 1914.[25] Paris's international position after 1945 was a mere shadow of what it had been only some thirty years earlier. Even more than in Britain, the state's grip ended up stifling the Parisian capital market, with foreign issues practically nil during this period.[26] In Germany, Frankfurt took over from Berlin as the country's financial centre but remained a centre of national rather than international significance until the late 1970s.[27] Zurich was one of the rare financial markets, along with New York, to strengthen its international position, probably ranking third (together with Geneva, Basel and, to a lesser extent, Lugano) behind New York and London in the 1960s as the Swiss markets quickly developed their role for accommodating and investing foreign capital, through international issues and wealth management.[28]

In a climate of state intervention and regulation, global business and finance resurfaced in the late 1950s with the advent of the Euromarkets. The Euromarkets are markets for transactions in dollars taking place outside the United States, free of American regulations. For various reasons, dollars started to accumulate in Europe, especially in London, in the 1950s – the Cold War and the Soviet Union's fears of having its dollar deposits frozen in the United States; the overseas investment and growing payment deficit of the United States; banking regulations, especially Regulation Q, which put a ceiling on the rate of interests which US banks paid on domestic bank deposits. The Eurodollar market, a short-term money market, was the first to develop, when London banks began to use dollars rather pounds to finance third-party trade, after the British government had banned the use of sterling instruments for such purposes following the sterling crisis of 1957.[29] With the European currencies' return to external convertibility in December 1958 and, from the early 1960s, the gradual relaxing of controls on capital flows, the Eurodollar market expanded rapidly. It was supplied mainly by American multinationals and by European central banks and provided credit on a worldwide scale and in hitherto unprecedented proportions, mainly to finance international trade and other short-term loans. From approximately $1.5 billion when it started in 1958, this market reached $25 billion ten years later and $130 billion in 1973.[30]

The Eurodollar market quickly gave birth to the Eurobond market, a long-term capital market using Eurodollars not only for bank loans but also for issuing dollar-denominated bonds, in London rather than in New York. The first Eurobond was issued in London in July 1963 by Siegmund Warburg, on behalf of Autostrada Italiana, a subsidiary of the state holding company IRI.[31] Eurobonds quickly proved very popular, especially as they were issued to bearer, which means that they were anonymous and exempt from withholding tax. The Eurobond market grew from about $250 million in 1963 to a yearly average of over $4 billion ten years later.

A third form of Euro credit – medium term this time, lasting from three to ten years – developed in the mid-1960s, between short-term, mainly interbank, Eurodollar deposits, and long-term Eurobonds. These were international bank loans wholly financed by resources in Eurodollars and generally granted on the basis of floating interest rates. In view of the growing demand for these loans and the size of the amounts required, they took the form of syndicated loans bringing several banks together. Despite the risks associated with interest rate fluctuations, the borrower found this a more flexible source of funding than a bond issue. From barely $2 billion in 1968, Euro credits quickly swelled to exceed $20 billion in 1973 – or more than four times the amount of Eurobonds.

The Euromarkets reshaped the world of international finance. They marked the start of the huge multinational expansion of American banks. They went from having 131 branches abroad in 1950 to having 899 in 1986, in addition to their 860 foreign subsidiaries. Europe was the preferred destination: by 1975 the eight largest American banks had set up 113 branches and 29 representative offices there, London alone having 58 of them.[32] Competition from American banks was particularly strong. While London bankers were the founders of the Euromarkets, American banks soon dominated it. The rise of the Euromarkets also signalled the rebirth of the City of London, which quickly became their natural home. London was certainly well equipped for hosting these new financial activities – because of the age-old experience of its bankers, their expertise in international finance, and the diversity and complementarity of its institutions and markets. The positive attitude of the British monetary authorities, in contrast to that of their European counterparts, also made a difference. The first sign of the rebirth of the City was the attraction that it held for banks throughout the world: the number of foreign banks represented in London went from 59 in 1955 to 159 in 1970 and 243 in 1975 – that is to say, nearly twice the corresponding number in New York.[33]

The City merchant banks and the Wall Street investment managed to retain a share of the Eurobond market – the issuing business was one of their historical specialities – but they faced strong competition from both American and European and, later, Japanese big banks in an increasingly global market. While twelve of them (including Kuhn Loeb, SG Warburg, Hambros, Morgan and NM Rothschild) featured among the top twenty co-lead managers of Eurobond issues in the market's first five years, between 1963 and 1967, their number had fallen ten years later to six, between 1973 and 1977. In both periods, the ranking was headed by Deutsche Bank.[34] Investment banks and merchant banks were still dominant in corporate finance, especially mergers and acquisitions, an activity that took off in the 1960s but was not to become global for another twenty years.

However, they were starting to lose their private bank character as most of them not only converted into public companies (some had done so earlier) but opened ownership and control to outside interests.

Innovations and Deregulations, 1973–2000

The end of the Bretton Woods system in 1971–73 opened a new era of international capital flows. According to recent estimates, in 2000 foreign assets ($28,984 billion) represented 92 per cent of world GDP, up from 25 per cent (with $2,800 billion) in 1980 and barely 6 per cent ($147.7 billion) in 1960.[35] At the turn of the twenty-first century, the United States was – as indeed it had been since the end of the Second World War – the largest holder of capital outside its territory, ahead of Britain, Japan, Germany and France – the same countries, in a different order, as before 1914, with the addition of a newcomer, Japan. The destination of foreign investment, on the other hand, had changed. At the beginning of the twentieth century, it was the colonies and new countries that received the bulk of these transfers. A century later, it was the rich countries of Europe and North America that, with Japan, absorbed more than 80 per cent of foreign investment.

The upsurge in capital exports started with the demise of the Bretton Woods system in 1971–73. With the end of fixed exchange rates, free movements of capital became compatible with an independent monetary policy – in line with the Mundell-Fleming's trilemma, according to which only two of these three policy options can be pursued together. Their continued expansion took place within a new climate marked, in particular, by financial deregulations and innovations.

The deregulation movement started in the United States, with the liberalization of the New York Stock Exchange (abolition of fixed commissions) in May 1975, making competition keener and leading to a consolidation in investment banking. The City of London followed in October 1986 with 'Big Bang', also a reform of the stock exchange (abolition of fixed commission and of the separation, unique to the London Stock Exchange, between the functions of brokers, who acted on behalf of clients, and jobbers, who were market-makers); it was also decided to open the London Stock Exchange, and by extension the City, to the outside world by permitting banks, both domestic and foreign, to buy member firms, hitherto banned. In Paris, the stockbrokers' monopoly was abolished in 1992. In Germany, the Bundesbank authorized floating-rate issues in 1984–5, despite its distrust of financial innovation, and allowed foreign banks to act as lead banks for foreign issues in Deutsche marks.[36] The wave of deregulation culminated in 1999 when the Glass-Steagall Act of 1933 was repealed by the Financial Modernization Act. Commercial banking and investment banking could again be brought together on the grounds that new financial instruments justified greater concentration among the various intermediaries in the world of finance.

Financial innovation became, as never before, an integral part of global finance. Three main factors account for this development. One was the incredible progress made in computing, which enabled the new financial products to reach an otherwise impossible degree of sophistication. Another was the application to the market of theoretical advances made in the field of financial economics (Markowitz and Sharpe's modern portfolio theory, Fama's efficient market hypothesis, Black and Scholes options pricing model, and others), opening the way for the design of ever more complex financial products. And a third was the liberalization of the financial markets, whose aim was to improve their efficiency by encouraging financial innovations – which remained very lightly, if at all, regulated.

The end of Bretton Woods offered an incentive. Modern derivatives, which were at the heart of the financial revolution of the late twentieth century, came into being in Chicago in 1972 with the creation of the International Monetary Market, where currency contracts were traded – a facility for hedging against foreign exchange fluctuations. The Chicago Board Options Exchange, where options were traded on shares, was founded a year later. Europe followed with LIFFE (London International Financial Future Exchange) in 1982, MATIF (Marché à Terme des Instruments Financiers) in Paris in 1986, and DTB (Deutsche Termin Börse) in Frankfurt in the early 1990s.

Derivatives were also combined with a new investment medium: alternative management funds, better known as hedge funds, which appeared in the 1980s.[37] They were usually domiciled in an offshore centre, were highly leveraged, and took short positions, through derivatives or forward operations. Their managers, who often made the headlines in the financial press, earned high bonuses – generally reaching 20 per cent of profits above a certain threshold plus 1.5 to 2 per cent management fees – and, as a rule, invested their own funds alongside those of their clients. Their growth was phenomenal during the 1990s, from a few hundreds to nearly 3,000 by 2006, with nearly $1,000 billion of funds managed. And if they enjoyed spectacular successes (with George Soros allegedly making £1 billion in 1993), they also suffered severe setbacks, most spectacularly with the failure of LTCM (Long-Term Capital Management) in 1998, which had a debt-to-equity ratio of 25 to 1 and two economics Nobel Prize winners (Robert Merton and Myron Scholes) on its board of directors.

Banking and financial practices have been deeply transformed by what has become known as securitization – the conversion of various types of debt, especially loans, into marketable securities. Its novelty resided in the type of assets converted into securities and the type of 'financial products' emerging from this conversion. Typically, they were derivatives. Mortgages were the first debts to be securitized, in the form of mortgage-backed securities; other assets, in particular consumer debt (insurance policies, car loans, credit card loans, student loans and so on), were in turn securitized, bearing the generic name of assets-backed securities; credit derivatives were also developed, in the first place Credit Default Swaps, which offered protection against the risk of default on a debt through a contract between two parties, the seller as it were insuring the buyer in return for the payment of a regular fee.

The securitization process was mainly undertaken by investment banks in New York and London, thus enhancing the position of these two centres in the age of global finance. By the turn of the twenty-first century, New York was still in the first place, by far the largest capital market, even if London had the edge in direct international financial activities, ranking first for international banking, asset management and foreign exchange, and attracting the highest number of foreign banks (481 as against 287 in New York). These two centres were well ahead of the pack. New York clearly set the tone in international banking and financial business, if only because of the might of the American banks, mostly based in New York, and on which a great deal of London's international influence depended. London's policy of opening up to the world had been kept up relentlessly and had borne fruit, at the cost, however, of a certain eclipse of British financial institutions and the City's dependence on foreign banks – what has sometimes been called the 'Wimbledon effect'.[38]

The major newcomer of the post-war era was Tokyo. As a result of Japan's rise to the rank of economic superpower, Tokyo established itself as a major international centre during the 1970s, going in twenty years from being a regional financial centre to a centre of world dimensions. And the possibility that Tokyo might overtake New York and become the world's leading financial centre did not seem entirely fanciful at the end of the 1980s, though such judgements proved too hasty. The American economy, far from declining, enjoyed spectacular growth in the 1990s, whereas the Japanese economy went into a long slump after the burst of the stock exchange and property bubbles in 1990, which had severe repercussions for Tokyo's international position.

Frankfurt only overtook Zurich and Paris to become continental Europe's leading financial centre in the late 1980s. The decision in 1992 to establish the headquarters of the new European central bank in Frankfurt gave it a further boost, raising hopes that it might eventually overtake London, but this appeared highly unlikely a decade later. Paris regained some ground from the 1980s, without, however, really finding its role. Paris did not dominate any of the main fields of international financial activity, but held some aces, especially in asset management as well as in the bond market and derivatives. Zurich and Geneva continued to figure among the leading centres, increasingly specializing in wealth management, with 35 per cent of the world's private offshore wealth in the early 2000s, as against 21 per cent for Britain and 12 per cent for the United States.

The number of emerging, or rather aspiring, international financial centres increased significantly in the last two decades of the twentieth century. Several cities, especially in emerging economies, were actively promoted with the aim of their gaining the status of regional or even global international financial centre. Two centres were particularly successful in managing this transition: Singapore and Hong Kong, both with solid banking institutions, inherited from the British overseas banks, advantageous geographical location and stable political regimes, despite the uncertainties related to Hong Kong's return to its big neighbour in 1997 – all essential requirements for the rise of an international financial centre, which were rarely met in most emerging economies.

Singapore's development was nonetheless the result of a systematic effort made on the part of the authorities, immediately upon the country's independence in 1965, to turn it into an international financial centre by hosting the nascent Asian dollar market (the counterpart of the Eurodollar market in London) and encouraging the emergence of a bond market. Singapore's financial markets really took off in the 1980s, and the foreign exchange market grew in its wake to reach fourth position in 1998, behind London, New York and Tokyo; derivatives started being traded in 1984 with the foundation of SIMEX; and, as a result, an increasing number of foreign banks set up there, reaching 260 in 1995.[39] In Hong Kong, by contrast, the authorities adopted a non-interventionist stance, at the same time creating conditions conducive to developing financial activities, notably a favourable tax system and modern infrastructure, in addition to the absence of exchange control, a robust legal system, the existence of the rule of law, and its position as the door for a China that began to open up to the world at the end of the 1970s.[40] Syndicated Euro credits found a home here, with operations on behalf of enterprises and governments in the region's main economies – Japan, Taiwan, South Korea, Australia and New Zealand, later joined by Thailand, the Philippines and, above all, China. In the space of about ten years, Hong Kong established itself as the world's third centre for Euro credits, behind London and New York. Its international status was mirrored in the presence of foreign banks, numbering 357 in 1995, that is to say more than any financial centre except for London.[41]

New York, London, Hong Kong and Singapore stood at the apex of a hierarchy of financial centres. The Global Financial Centres Index listed forty-six centres when it was first published in 2007, with London ranked first (in terms of competitiveness) and Athens forty-sixth. The number had nearly doubled nine years later. Multinational banks expanded considerably in the second age of global finance, with a much stronger presence in the financial centres of both advanced and emerging economies – from about 20 per cent, in terms of number, in 1995, to 34 per cent in 2009, with some countries, especially in Eastern Europe, having more than 50 per cent of assets controlled by foreign banks.

These developments were at once the cause and the consequence of the emergence of a new type of multinational banks, that some have called 'transnational banks', in a different meaning from the one used earlier in this chapter, to underline both the quantitative and qualitative differences with their predecessors – in terms of size, internal organization, geographical spread and range of activities.[42] The specialized British overseas banks, which had dominated multinational banking since the mid-nineteenth century, had lost their competitive advantage by the 1960s. By the turn of the twenty-first century, global finance was dominated by the world's leading universal banks (Citigroup, J. P. Morgan Chase, Bank of America, HSBC, RBS, Barclays, Deutsche Bank, BNP Paribas, UBS, Credit Suisse and a few others). The largest, Citigroup, had offices in over 100 countries and employed nearly 370,000 people in 2007, before the crisis. It was engaged in all types of banking and financial activities, including retail banking, investment banking, trading, wealth management and alternative investments such as hedge funds and private equity. Even more significantly, the bank had internalized its international activities, and was able to draw resources from one place and exploit them in another. All universal banks had more or less adopted this model.

Conclusion

This chapter, like the rest of the book, ends around 2000, in other words before the financial crisis of 2008. However, it is impossible to end this overview of the rise of global finance since the mid-nineteenth century without briefly considering the effects of the most severe *financial* crisis in modern history – the result of global imbalances and low interest rates, highly complex and not always well-understood financial instruments, and irresponsible risk-taking reflected in exceptionally high leverage ratios hidden in off-balance-sheet operations. From the perspective of global finance, two points are noteworthy:

First, the financial crisis slowed down the tremendous rise of finance – as an economic, social, political and cultural phenomenon, sometimes called 'financialization'. However, despite the regulatory measures taken at both national and international levels, the financial sector, in other words global finance, as the two had been inextricably linked since the end of the twentieth century, continued to grow – in contrast with what happened during the half-century that followed the Great Depression. There are several reasons for this: the costs of cutting the financial sector down to size, if only because of its share of national income and employment; the political climate in the advanced economies most affected by the crisis, which has been able to accommodate protest against financial abuses; and the international context, where old and new tensions have not threatened the globalization of the world economy.

Second, the financial crisis did not fundamentally alter the balance of power in global finance. New York and London have remained the two leading international financial centres and were not toppled by Hong Kong, Singapore, Shanghai or Dubai. Changes of this magnitude have occurred very rarely in history – only three cities (Amsterdam, London and New York) have in turn been the world's leading financial centre in the last 300 years – and were very slow processes – as witnessed for example by the replacement of London by New York as the nerve centre of world finance. Emerging markets will have to meet several conditions, not least in terms of wealth, depth of skill and openness, before claiming the mantle. The relative weakening of London and Hong Kong in the early 2020s was due to other reasons, respectively Brexit and the national security law.

The financial debacle of 2008 may have undermined global finance, but it did not kill it. One question is whether the crisis was severe enough and will be remembered long enough to serve as a warning and ensure that the global financial system rests on more solid grounds. A retreat from global finance has never been a natural swing of the pendulum. It has always been the result of a devastating financial crisis. And the upheavals of the world's financial order have tended to take place in the midst of military cataclysms.

Notes

1. M. Obstfeld and A. Taylor (2004), *Global Capital Markets: Integration, Crisis and Growth.* Cambridge: Cambridge University Press, 52.

2. Estimations based on A. Imlah (1952), 'British balance of payments and the export of capital, 1816–1913', *Economic History Review*, 2 (2), 235–6; and M. Lévy-Leboyer (1977), 'La balance des paiements et l'exportation des capitaux français', in M. Lévy-Leboyer (ed.), *La*

position internationale de la France: Aspects économiques et sociaux XIXe–XXe siècles. Paris: Éditions de l'École des Hautes Études en Sciences Sociales, 119–20.

3. P. Bairoch (1997), *Victoires et Déboires: Histoire Economique et Sociale du Monde du XVIe Siècle à Nos Jours*, 3 vols. Paris: Gallimard, vol. 2, 123, 127, 175–9.

4. P. Bairoch (1976), *Commerce Extérieur et Développement Economique de l'Europe au XIXe Siècle.* Paris: La Haye Mouton.

5. See S. B. Saul (1960), *Studies in British Overseas Trade, 1870–1914.* Liverpool: Liverpool University Press; and F. Crouzet (1964), 'Commerce extérieur et empire: l'expérience britannique du libre-échange à la Première Guerre mondiale', *Annales: E.S.C.*, 19 (2), 281–310.

6. See D. Kynaston (1994), *The City of London*, vol. 1: *A World of Its Own 1815–1890.* London: Chatto & Windus; ibid. (1995), *The City of London*, vol. 2: *Golden Years, 1890–1914.* London: Chatto & Windus; R. Michie (1992), *The City of London: Continuity and Change, 1850–1990.* Basingstoke and London: Macmillan; Y. Cassis (2006), *Capitals of Capital: A History of International Financial Centres 1780–2005.* Cambridge: Cambridge University Press.

7. See S. D. Chapman (1984), *The Rise of Merchant Banking.* London: Allen & Unwin.

8. G. Jones (1993), *British Multinational Banking 1830–1990.* Oxford: Clarendon Press.

9. R. Michie (1999), *The London Stock Exchange: A History.* Oxford: Oxford University Press, 88.

10. B. Eichengreen (1996), *Globalizing Capital: A History of the International Monetary System.* Princeton, NJ: Princeton University Press.

11. A. Plessis (2005), 'When Paris dreamt of competing with the City', in Y. Cassis and E. Bussière (eds), *London and Paris as International Financial Centres in the Twentieth Century.* Oxford: Oxford University Press, 42–54.

12. P. Hertner (1990), 'German banks abroad before 1914', in G. Jones (ed.), *Banks as Multinationals.* London: Routledge, 99–119.

13. W. J. Hausman et al. (2008), *Global Electrification: Multinational Enterprise and International Finance in the History of Light and Power, 1878–2007.* New York: Cambridge University Press.

14. V. Carosso (1970), *Investment Banking in America: A History.* Cambridge, MA: Harvard University Press.

15. H. van B. Cleveland and T. H. Huertas (1985), *Citibank 1812–1970.* Cambridge, MA: Harvard University Press.

16. For the purpose of this study, 'transnational banks' has been defined as comprising both the multinational banks headquartered in a financial centre and the branches/subsidiaries of foreign banks established in that centre. See Y. Cassis (2016), 'International financial centres', in Y. Cassis, R. Grossman and C. Schenk (eds), *The Oxford Handbook of Banking and Financial History.* Oxford: Oxford University Press, 302–3.

17. M. Flandreau and D. Zumer (2004), *The Making of Global Finance 1880–1913.* Paris: OECD.

18. M. Bordo and H. Rockoff (1996), 'The Gold Standard as a "Good Housekeeping Seal of Approval"', *Journal of Economic History*, 56 (2), 389–428; N. Ferguson (2005), 'The City of London and British imperialism: New light on an old question', in Cassis and Bussière (eds), *London and Paris*, 57–77.

19. D. Artaud (1978), *La Question des Dettes Interalliées et la Reconstruction de l'Europe (1917–1929).* Paris: Champion.

20. C. H. Feinstein and K. Watson (1995), 'Private international capital flows in Europe in the inter-war period', in C. H. Feinstein (ed.), *Banking, Currency and Finance in Europe between the Wars*. Oxford: Oxford University Press, 94–130.

21. M. Wilkins (1999), 'Cosmopolitan finance in the 1920s: New York's emergence as an international financial centre', in R. Sylla, R. Tilly and G. Tortella (eds), *The State, the Financial System and Economic Modernization*. Cambridge: Cambridge University Press, 271–91.

22. T. Balogh (1947), *Studies in Financial Organization*. Cambridge: Cambridge University Press, 250.

23. A. S. Milward (1977), *War, Economy and Society, 1939–1945*. London: Allen & Unwin.

24. M. Nadler, S. Heller and S. Shipman (1955), *The Money Market and Its Institutions*. New York: Ronald Press, 290–1; R. Orsingher (1964), *Les Banques dans le Monde*. Paris: Payot, 140–1.

25. Michie, *The City of London*; D. Kynaston (2001), *The City of London*, vol. 6: *A Club No More 1945–2000*. London: Chatto & Windus.

26. L. Quennouëlle-Corre (2015), *La Place Financière de Paris au XXe Siècle: Des Ambitions Contrariées*. Paris: Comité pour l'Histoire Economique et Financière de la France.

27. C.-L. Holtfrerich (1999), *Frankfurt as a Financial Centre: From Medieval Trade Fair to European Banking Centre*. Munich: C. H. Beck.

28. M. Iklé (1970), *Die Schweiz als Internationaler Bank- und Finanzplatz*. Zurich: Orell Füssli.

29. C. Schenk (1998), 'The origins of the Eurodollar market in London, 1955–1963', *Explorations in Economic History*, 35 (2), 221–38; S. Battilossi (2002), 'Introduction: International banking and the American challenge in historical perspective', in S. Battilossi and Y. Cassis (eds), *European Banks and the American Challenge Competition and Cooperation in International Banking Under Bretton Woods*. Oxford: Oxford University Press, 1–35.

30. (1996), *International Capital Markets Statistics, 1950–1995*. Paris: OECD.

31. I. M. Kerr (1984), *A History of the Eurobond Market: The First 21 Years*, London: Euromoney Publications; N. Ferguson (2010), *High Financier: The Lives and Time of Siegmund Warburg*, London: Allen Lane.

32. T. F. Huertas (1990), 'U.S. multinational banking: History and prospects', in Jones, *Banks as Multinationals*, 253.

33. M. Baker and M. Collins (2005), 'London as an international banking centre, 1950–1980', in Cassis and Bussière (eds), *London and Paris*, 248–53.

34. Kerr, *A History of the Eurobond Market*, 29 and 53.

35. Obstfeld and Taylor, *Global Capital Markets*, 53.

36. G. Franke (1999), 'The Bundesbank and financial markets', in Deutsche Bundesbank (ed.), *Fifty Years of the Deutsche Mark*. Oxford: Oxford University Press, 246–53.

37. S. Mallaby (2010), *More Money than God: Hedge Funds and the Making of the New Elite*. London: Bloomsbury.

38. R. Roberts and D. Kynaston (2001), *City State. How the Markets Came to Rule Our World*. London: Profile Books.

39. R. C. Bryant (1989), 'The evolution of Singapore as a financial centre', in K. S. Sandhu and P. Wheatley (eds), *Management of Success: The Moulding of Modern Singapore*. Singapore: Institute of Southeast Asian Studies, 337–72; D. R. Lessard (1994), 'Singapore as an

international financial centre', in R. Roberts (ed.), *Offshore Financial Centres*. Aldershot: Edward Elgar, 200–35.

40. Y. C. Jao (1983), 'Hong Kong as an international financial centre: Evolution and prospects', in R. Roberts (ed.), *International Financial Centres of Europe, North America and Asia*. Aldershot: Edward Elgar, 491–534; C. Schenk (2001), *Hong Kong as an International Financial Centre: Emergence and Development, 1945–1965*. London: Routledge.

41. R. Roberts (1998), *Inside International Finance*. London: Orion.

42. C. Kobrak (2016), 'From multinational to transnational banking', in Cassis, Grossman and Schenk, *The Oxford Handbook of Banking*, 163–90.

PART III
REGIONAL PERSPECTIVES TO GLOBAL ECONOMIC CHANGE

CHAPTER 16
AFRICA: ECONOMIC CHANGE SOUTH OF THE SAHARA SINCE c.1500
Gareth Austin

This chapter tries to identify the major sources of economic change in Sub-Saharan Africa from the external slave trades onwards, to highlight the implications for the global debates about the evolution of inequality between different world regions, and assess the respective importance of resources and institutions as engines of economic change.[1] It will be argued that, while external influences have often facilitated and triggered economic change in Africa, internal influences have been crucial to the extent and shape of those changes. It will also be suggested that it is neither resource endowments nor institutions as such that have usually been decisive, but rather the interaction between them: with institutions generally not only responding to the resources available but also gradually changing them.[2]

The main discussion is organized in four sections. As a preface, the first problematizes the traditional Eurocentric periodization of Africa's economic past. The second section focuses on the internal variables by summarizing the main features of Africa's changing resource ('factor') endowment from the sixteenth to the early twentieth century, and tracing a cluster of institutions with which that resource complex was associated. The third section considers the impact on African economies of the combination of external changes in technology and patterns of demand. The fourth section discusses what otherwise contrasting literatures consider to be the most important set of institutional changes: those in property and labour regimes associated with capitalism (arrangements which in Africa are traditionally seen as imported innovations and whose implementation and evolution have, however, been strongly shaped by the land–labour ratio within the region) and its transformation over the last century. The conclusion draws the threads together, emphasizing their entanglement, and reflects on their implications for the global issues.

Period and Agency in African History

Over the last sixty years, specialists in African history have challenged the traditional perception that economic change in the Sub-Saharan subcontinent was largely absent or essentially exogenous. In this view, a long-term stagnation was initially modified by North African, Asian and especially European commercial contact, most notoriously the external slave trades; with major economic and demographic change starting under colonial rule and continuing since independence – still in the context of continued dependence on external relationships, with disappointing welfare results often accompanied by political instability and violence. In contrast, the historical research conducted in recent decades generally emphasizes the importance of African agency (Africans making, or actively participating in making, their own histories) and change and variation within African economies. Yet to a certain extent, the old view, in various forms, continues to frame the ways in which most scholars in various disciplines view African history. This is partly because the revisionist research has tended to be relatively local in focus, whereas the older views have been restated at a general level, in the categories of successive theories (dependency and world systems[3] and some forms of rational-choice institutionalism[4]) that have themselves functioned to re-dress (rather than redress) the narrative of European (or North Atlantic) exceptionalism against which Sub-Saharan Africa continues to be used as a convenient 'other'.

The continued priority of external sources of change in contemporary understandings of African economic history is expressed most strongly in the persistence of the traditional tripartite political periodization: pre-colonial, colonial and post-colonial. For economic history, this has been questioned, but the most influential challenges tend to be at sub-regional level. For South Africa, it is widely accepted that a critical watershed was the mineral revolution of the 1860s–80s, without which the subsequent growth of manufacturing would have been greatly attenuated.[5] Again, A. G. Hopkins made an influential proposal that 'the modern economic history of West Africa' should be dated not from colonization in the late nineteenth century but from the early nineteenth-century transition in the Atlantic trade, from the export of slaves to that of agricultural produce. This was a defining watershed in that it involved the entry of small-scale producers into intercontinental trade for the first time on a wide scale.[6] But the only commonly accepted challenge to the traditional periodization for the region as a whole is the view that the independence of most of tropical Africa, around 1960, was a lesser turning point than the growth of state intervention in African economies, dating from the Second World War and its immediate aftermath, or indeed from the 1930s.[7]

Let us consider the respective roles of external and domestic influences on the turning points of African economic history in more detail, taking as an example the post-independence era. Within this, it makes sense to identify the 1980s as a policy watershed: when state-led development policies gave way, via 'Structural Adjustment', to the liberal economic regimes that have characterized the region ever since. Regarding economic growth, three periods can be distinguished at the level of the region as a whole: relatively slow growth of output (in real GDP per capita), averaging little more than 1 per cent per year c.1960 to 1975; stagnation over the following two decades, with some years of actual decline; and a general expansion over the twenty-plus years from c.1995, at about 2 per cent per capita. The external influence on this regional growth record is palpable: the first OPEC oil price shock, in 1973, was a brake on economic growth in most Sub-Saharan countries, few of whom were yet oil exporters. Conversely, the recent general economic expansion – spread more widely across the region than earlier booms – was at least initially stimulated by the rise in world commodity prices led by China's industrialization. Yet, at least until that boom, shifts in interregional terms of trade correlate rather weakly with the records of individual national economies. Most African economies did relatively well in part of their post-independence history, but almost all of them also had at least one period of stagnation or even decline.[8] Côte d'Ivoire and Ghana, cocoa-growing neighbours with similar factor endowments, followed almost opposite trajectories for half a century: a contrast which cannot be explained primarily by external influences, but rather owes much to very different policy choices in the early decades of independence.[9]

The general policy shift that was Structural Adjustment is often casually attributed entirely to external pressure, from the International Monetary Fund (IMF) and the World Bank. They provided loans in return for which national governments accepted packages of economic liberalization, shifting the mechanism of allocation of resources and goods from administration to markets. Certainly, the Washington-based institutions were crucial to the process, but it is important not to overlook the domestic pressures, which in many countries led governments to embark on Adjustment. In contrast to Latin America, at the beginning of the 1980s, few African governments had big debts to foreign banks, because the banks would not lend to them. Indeed in Africa huge sovereign debt-to-export ratios were usually a consequence of Adjustment rather than a cause. Between 1980 and 1995, for Sub-Saharan Africa, the ratio of external debt to exports jumped from 90 per cent to 241 per cent, whereas for Latin America and the Caribbean the rise was from 206 per cent to 212 per cent.[10] A bigger problem for many African countries at the start of the 1980s was profound shortages of government revenue and import-purchasing power as a result of having increasingly overvalued more or less non-convertible currencies that acted effectively as instruments of penal taxation on their exporters (this did not apply to nearly the same extent, nor in the same way, to the franc zone countries, for whom Adjustment was less radical because their currency was already fully convertible). Faced with official prices that made it unprofitable to produce or sell, including for domestic markets, farmers and traders in countries from Guinea to Tanzania to the then (Congo) Zaire bypassed official markets.[11] This unorganized economic resistance from below did much to end the era of state-led development policy. It does much to explain why the governments concerned reluctantly decided to accept the IMF and World Bank's offer of credit to assist them to shift from state to market-based development policies. Thus, for both policy and performance, the major trends and turning points of post-independence economic history have been very much the outcome of interactions between external and internal variables.

Resources, Techniques and Institutions within Africa, 1500–c.1918

Most of Sub-Saharan Africa, most of the time, was characterized by a relative abundance of cultivable land in relation to labour, often until far into the twentieth century, and in some areas, even until today. That is to say, over any period longer than it took to clear the bush, the expansion of agricultural output was unconstrained by the physical availability of land. Because most of the capital goods used in arable agriculture, handicraft production and small-scale mining were created by simple tool-aided labour, output was mainly a function of labour inputs. In much of tropical Africa, labour scarcity was relieved by an extremely uneven seasonal distribution of rainfall: for much of the dry season, there was (as of 1500 and, in most areas, even 1850) little that could be done in agriculture, freeing labour variously for hunting, mining and handicraft production. Meanwhile, sleeping sickness made the use of large animals unsustainable, whether for transport or ploughing, wherever the parasite's host, the tsetse fly, was endemic: the forest zones and shifting zones within the savannas.[12] In this forbidding context, it is almost superfluous to add that, of two geographical features particularly favourable to early industrialization, Africa was short on one, navigable rivers, and completely lacking in the other, large supplies of coal and iron ore in close proximity to each other. The physical abundance of land at least reduced certain sources of risk to food security. The downside was that the fertility of the soils, derived from one of the oldest bedrocks on the planet, was often low; and where it was high, it tended to be easily exposed to degradation from severe rain or sun.[13]

While agricultural techniques varied across Africa, it is difficult not to see their prevailing features as specific responses to these physical conditions: a preference for land-extensive methods in the prevalence of itinerant pastoralism in herding areas, and various forms of hoe-based land rotation in arable ones, with the largest trees often being left to stand in cultivated fields. Conversely, the low opportunity cost of dry season labour facilitated labour-intensive production off the farm, notably a preference (especially in West Africa) for cloth woven on the narrow loom.[14]

Despite the prevalence of land-extensive techniques in agriculture, intensification (defined as raising the ratio of capital and/or labour inputs per unit of land) in such forms as terracing and irrigation was ancient in parts of eastern, southern and even western Africa. It used to be thought that, nevertheless, there was no cumulative trend towards intensification, because irrigation or terracing came and went in particular sites, albeit in some cases lasting centuries before their demise. Recent research suggests, however, that there was a net expansion of intensive agriculture during the sixteenth to nineteenth centuries,[15] though the extensive methods mentioned above remained predominant until land became scarce, which it did it in many countries in the twentieth century.

Alongside the general (though not universal) preference for land extensiveness in agriculture was a cluster of very widespread institutional features, notably strong social approval for mothers (and fathers) who had many children;[16] broadly defined kinship groups and diverging inheritance;[17] relatively open access to land, in the sense of readiness to grant use rights in land even to strangers providing they acknowledged the ultimate ownership of the existing owners, who were often a lineage or chieftaincy;[18] widespread property in people, including children, wives, subjects, and also slaves and pawns;[19] and the persistence of 'stateless' (segmentary lineage) societies and small states alongside large kingdoms and empires, through to the European partition of Africa from 1879.[20] These institutional patterns, like the characteristic choices of technique, can be understood as reflecting the combination of land abundance and constraints upon intensification: settings in which the production of large grain surpluses was unnecessary (given low population density and widespread self-sufficiency in basic staples) and/or difficult (where soils did not readily support short fallowing cycles). In such contexts, there was usually no market in land rights (any payments were token or customary) but people – not only children and adults, kin, but also immigrants – especially people who were in some sense dependents, were valued as current or future producers and reproducers, and possessing them raised the owners' prestige. Inheritance systems were organized not to transmit capital to narrowly specified heirs, but rather to spread what property there was widely, the better to reinforce alliances and thereby share and reduce risks, whether to nutritional or physical security. State formation was inhibited (though not prevented) by the difficulty in concentrating the means to support political and military specialists. Meanwhile, long-distance trade, spanning polities (large or small) and cultures, could be facilitated by the construction of ethnic and religious trading diasporas, which created internal moral communities, offering gains from (otherwise much more limited) trade to producers and consumers at the cost of some monopoly profit for the intermediaries.[21]

The argument for seeing these institutional patterns as responses to the characteristic complex of resource conditions described above is borne out by what happened where resources were different, or when they changed. The most enduring exception to the difficulty of political centralization was the kingdom of Abyssinia in what is now northern Ethiopia. This was indeed an 'exception that proves the rule' as its fiscal and logistical base was grain surpluses paid as tribute by a peasantry in an environment supportive of at least semi-intensive agriculture, with a long history of plough use.[22] Where land rights became locally scarce, land markets could emerge, as in Akwapim district in southern Ghana in the pre-colonial and early-colonial nineteenth century,[23] and access to land could be newly restricted to close kin, as on the 'Kikuyu reserve' in central Kenya in the 1940s, when young, unmarried adults who had been 'squatting' on land reserved for European settlers returned home to find that cash crops and population growth had made previously cheap and abundant land economically valuable.[24]

Conflicts of interests, in some cases violent, were not limited to when the older institutions broke down or were transformed. High social valuation of children was one of the motives for polygamy, which tended to promote the concentration of wives among older, wealthier men.[25] In certain circumstances the value of labour was converted into slavery and debt bondage, especially when the demand for labour for commodity production rose, as in both West and East Africa during much of the nineteenth century.[26] The widespread survival of stateless societies and small states owed much to the determination of some small-scale societies to resist incorporation,[27] combined with the failure of state-builders to establish or extend their boundaries as far as they wished: reflecting the widespread difficulty of extracting regular grain surpluses sufficient to support a substantial class of military specialists.

The propensity to use land-extensive methods of production, noted above, is best seen not as a static residual but as a path of development. Specifically, for most of sub-

Saharan Africa, the pattern of endogenous change from the fifteenth century to the late nineteenth or twentieth century can be described as following an overarching land-extensive path of economic development within which, however, there were intensive elements.[28] The land-extensive path may be defined as 'a general, long-term revealed preference for methods which used additional land where that would raise returns on labour or capital, or conserve the latter'.[29] To enlarge on a point introduced above, this preference could be seen most widely and importantly in arable farming, notably with the predominance of the hoe over the plough, the avoidance of clear felling and the preference for polyculture (planting more than one crop in the same field) over monoculture. In pastoralism it was found, albeit to a large extent of necessity, in the widespread practice of transhumance, motivated especially by the need to keep the cattle away from the tsetse flies when the latter advanced during the rainy season. Even slave-raiding can be viewed as a form of land extensiveness, albeit with extremely high costs to the region as a whole.

A land-extensive *path* of development, as distinct from a land-extensive strategy at a given moment, actually entails phases of intensification: when it was necessary to increase the ratio of labour and/or capital per hectare in order to take a step forward in total factor productivity. This is not to be confused with labour intensity by default, as in the reliance on headloading in the tsetse-fly zones, where pack animals were unavailable. It is also not to be confused with the labour intensity in dry-season occupations, such as mining and handicrafts, made possible by the low opportunity cost of labour during the agricultural off season. Rather, the most general example of a phase of intensification within an overarching path of land extensiveness was the transition from hunting and gathering, or even from itinerant pastoralism, to settled agriculture, though the former transition had mostly occurred before our period. The most important example in the early colonial period was the adoption of tree crops in certain colonies, notably cocoa beans in Ghana and Nigeria. This entailed a new production function and much fixed capital formation.[30] Even so, West African farmers chose to farm cocoa in as land-extensive a fashion as possible, planting trees close together to minimize weeding at the cost of lower output per hectare, and temporarily abandoning capsid-infested farms so that the cocoa trees became overshadowed by the returning bush, leading to the disappearance of the pests. The farm could then be literally cut out of the bush and restored to production; this practice is distinct from the intense application of sprays and labour time to direct but unsuccessful action against the infestation. The efficiency of this approach, under tropical African conditions, was demonstrated by the comprehensive victory of Ghanaian cocoa farmers, large and small scale, in competition with European planters during the early colonial period.[31]

Given the relative scarcity of labour, there were three major ways of raising the rate of return for principals, whether they were individual farmers, household heads or rulers.[32] The first was raising labour productivity in agriculture. African farmers did this, above all, through trial and error with crops and crop varieties, resulting in the selective adoption and adaptation of a range of exotic cultigens, on which more in the next section. Agricultural productivity was also raised in some contexts by the adoption of the plough, where soils were thick enough and demand high enough, as in the Cape and Natal in the mid-nineteenth century. The second approach to increasing the rate of return was to raise the productivity of labour outside the traditional agricultural year. There are a range of examples of how this was done before colonization, including double-cropping where new crops made that possible. In the twentieth century, the most important contribution was the mechanization of transport. The third strategy was to reduce the supply price of labour by coercion. The Nieboer-Domar hypothesis, that coercion of labour paid under conditions of land abundance in the absence of sizable capital formation or economic advantages of scale, applied strongly to tropical Africa before colonization and again into the early twentieth century.[33] From the fifteenth to the end of the nineteenth century, in arable and mixed farming areas, increases in demand for commodities tended to be met by the acquisition of slaves, usually by purchase from the original captors, often via more than one set of intermediaries. The nineteenth century saw a major increase in the scale of slavery in West Africa and parts of East Africa, such as the kingdom of Buganda.[34] The same logic was operative under colonial rule, where, if slavery was forbidden, other forms of coercion could be applied to the same end, as will be highlighted below.

The overall effect of the non-coercive human responses to relative scarcity of labour in relation to land, limited soil fertility and the other features of the physical environment of fifteenth- to early twentieth-century Africa was to loosen – and ultimately to transform – the resource constraints: extending the effective agricultural year, raising productivity in and outside agriculture and, after 1918, beginning to move the overall factor ratio from land abundance to land scarcity. High social approval of large families contributed to the demographic expansion that improving public health made possible over subsequent decades.[35] In the twentieth century as a whole, the population of Sub-Saharan Africa rose perhaps sixfold. In much of this, however, interaction with external influences was critical.

External Influences: Technology and Demand from 1500 to the Present

Let us turn to the interaction of African economies with external markets and, relatedly, external technological changes. While Sub-Saharan Africa had an endogenous trajectory of land-extensive economic growth, however intermittent and long-term, the growth that was achieved, and the costs involved, owed greatly to its involvement in trade between different regions of what became the world economy. Three features stand out.

First, and most positively, as Paul Richards has phrased it, the present crop repertoire of African agriculture reflects selective adoptions and adaptations, via local trial and error – natural and cultural selection – over many centuries.[36] Sub-Saharan Africa was an integral part of the Old World, and the initial borrowings were from Asia: notably the banana-plantain family, which was eventually adopted throughout the tropical latitudes of the continent, and beyond. In the Bugandan environment, for example, it made possible an exceptionally high productivity food culture, covering nutritional requirements with labour inputs that were unusually small by African standards.[37] After the Portuguese connected Africa and the New World, effectively from the sixteenth century, a series of crop imports from the Americas began, including maize and cassava (manioc), groundnuts (peanuts), different varieties of cotton and in the nineteenth century, cocoa beans, while some rice varieties moved in the opposite direction. For the productivity of both labour and (less important at the time) land in African agriculture, maize in particular was 'revolutionary', according to major sub-regional histories.[38] Cassava was adopted more selectively and gradually, and incorporated into local diets in differing ways. Crucially, its drought resistance improved food security, and its tolerance of relatively poor or depleted soils prompted a further round of adoption in the mid-twentieth century, in export-crop-growing areas in which fertile land was becoming scarce.[39] This long-standing readiness to experiment with, and selectively adopt, exotic cultigens is a reason for optimism about the prospects for raising agricultural productivity in contemporary Africa.

The second feature of Sub-Saharan Africa's external trade is notorious: the longevity and geographical breadth of slave exports. The Atlantic trade alone accounted for about 13 million captives forcibly embarked, from its beginning in 1441 to the last voyage in 1866. The trades across the Sahara, through the Nile Valley, and from the Indian Ocean and Red Sea coasts were both older and longer lasting, though less intense. A combination of estimates for the Atlantic trade, and guesstimates for the other trades, puts the grand total of slaves shipped or walked out of Sub-Saharan Africa between 1500 and 1900 at nearly 18 million.[40] The available figures for pre-colonial populations are almost entirely dependent on backward projection from colonial censuses.[41] Thus we have only a rough sense of the size of the populations from which these people were taken – and of the collateral losses, in deaths in raids and slave-trade-inspired wars, plus deaths en route to the coast or to the starting points for the Saharan crossing, and while awaiting the final journey. The margin of error is such that it is impossible to be sure of the scale of actual depopulation.[42] The latter may have been specific to particular areas, given that the biggest slave-exporting parts of West Africa were among the more densely populated in the early twentieth century. Even so, the removal of many millions of people from a labour-scarce region, which probably had only about 100 million people by 1900,[43] can only have been damaging for its long-term economic development; much more so, given the violence and insecurity that resulted from the slave trades, causing casualties, and requiring communities and traders to give priority to defence. A particular politically decentralized society based near Rufisque in Senegal cultivated a reputation for killing strangers on sight.[44] While rational as a defence mechanism this was hardly conducive to 'Smithian' growth, that is, the trade-based pattern of economic growth and specialization often seen as crucial in the early modern world. It seems, as Joseph Inikori argues, that the intensification of the Atlantic slave trade from the 1680s put a stop to what was otherwise a general tendency for production and exchange to expand in West Africa, a stop that was itself ended only by the abolition of the trade, a gradual and uneven process which effectively began in 1807.[45] The external slave trades had major repercussions for social structure and institutions. The nature of the activity meant that it was virtually monopolized by large traders and rulers, and thereby was a force for inequality, over hundreds of years.[46] It also rewarded militarism; conversely, when the Atlantic slave market was closed to the kingdoms of Asante and Dahomey, 'peace parties' emerged in both, advocating a reorientation away from wars and slave exports to peaceful trade.[47]

In a sense, it was paradoxical that the external slave trades were profitable even to the sellers and buyers themselves, given labour scarcity within the region and the existence of an intra-regional market for slaves, which competed with the overseas and cross-desert demand. Part of the demand from the Ottoman Empire was for girls and eunuchs for harems, but otherwise African slaves were wanted mainly for agriculture, on New World plantations and North Africa, and for specialized roles such as (in the case of Somali boys) pearl diving in the Gulf of Arabia. One motive for selling captives to ship or camel-borne merchants was to obtain state-of-the-art military tools, especially firearms from Europe and horses from North Africa. But the majority of imports comprised the kinds of commodities that were also produced widely in Sub-Saharan Africa, such as textiles. This makes it hard to avoid the conclusion that, over several centuries and much of the continent, the productivity of (even enslaved) African labour was lower within Sub-Saharan Africa than in the areas to which African slaves were taken.[48] Part of this may have been a function of effective proximity to markets, raising the unit price of the commodities produced by Africans in the unfree diaspora compared to the prices obtainable at home. But the productivity gap was also partly a function of relatively low physical productivity of labour in Africa, because of environmental constraints in agriculture and transport, as well as the low labour productivity of labour-intensive, dry-season handicraft production.[49] Thus the geographical breadth and chronological length of the slave trades across ocean and desert was made possible – made privately profitable – by supply-side elements. These trades were external but by no means entirely exogenous.

The last comment applies also to the political conditions that permitted and sustained the sale of captives outside the region. In Sub-Saharan Africa, as usual in the world history of slavery, the vast majority of enslaved people were outsiders, foreigners to the society that originally enslaved them, and in the society (which was very often a different one, in the intra-regional as well as interregional trades) where they were eventually set to work. A crucial difference was that, by 1500 in Europe, the Middle East and North Africa, intra-regional slave procurement had been greatly reduced or eliminated where the emergence of huge empires and 'world' religions obliged would-be slave owners to obtain slaves from much greater distances: the foreigners and unbelievers were much further away than before.[50] This externalized the collateral casualties of slaving, in that the initial violence took place far away. In contrast, the multitude of polities in Sub-Saharan Africa meant that enslavable people – 'aliens' – were often relatively near in physical terms, bringing the mayhem and insecurity of slaving close to home.[51] The problem was compounded by military competition between African polities, small and large alike. To refuse to sell people to the Europeans would reduce a ruler's access to firearms and gunpowder.

Besides the selective importation of exotic cultigens, and the external markets for slaves, there has been a third major feature of Africa's long-term incorporation in the world economy: a succession of technological innovations overseas altered the content and scale of external markets for African products, in ways that contributed to the progress of African economies along the land-extensive path of economic development. It was the first industrial revolution that created or greatly enlarged the markets for groundnuts and palm oil in Europe, commodities that could be grown profitably by land-extensive methods in West African soils. Likewise, the inventions of the Second Industrial Revolution, notably milk chocolate, the bicycle and the internal combustion engine, created a new and vast market for rubber, and greatly enlarged the demand for cocoa beans. Tyres made wild rubber valuable: eliciting responses not only by Leopold's armed adventurers in the Congo but also by small-scale African migrant tappers in West Africa.[52] The emergence of a mass market for chocolate made it profitable for African entrepreneurs to initiate a major innovation in Ghana and Nigeria, adopting an exotic crop, and a tree crop at that, changing the factor ratios in forest zone agriculture, while finding methods of production which adapted the product to the kinds of soils available.[53] This pattern has continued to the present, from the advances in the technology of extracting and transporting petroleum that made Africa's oil deposits commercially valuable, to the invention of the mobile phone, which made coltan a mineral to kill for in Congo-Kinshasa in the later 1990s and 2000s. Economically, the most important category of imports paid for by these primary product exports was surely the tools of mechanized transport: loosening, and ultimately releasing, the vice in which the constraints on the use of animals had held the majority of Africa. A range of other imports have helped make African economies more efficient, among which the most recent major example is again the mobile phone, the widespread adoption of which has greatly improved information flows in local markets.

The Emergence of Capitalist Institutions during and since Colonial Rule

The otherwise often contrasting Marxist, dependency and rational-choice institutionalist schools of thought on economic development south of the Sahara implicitly agree on one thing: that such development has depended and continues to depend on the extent of the establishment within the region of a particular complex of institutions often associated with capitalism: individual ownership of land, labour that is free of coercion but 'unencumbered' by the possession of land rights, and a system of government and law that upholds private property.[54] These institutions have traditionally been seen as essentially exotic to Africa. Historians have increasingly qualified this: labour markets and, though only rarely, wage labour preceded colonial rule; land tenure was often individual at the point of agricultural use and, as we have seen, land markets might emerge where land became scarce; and pre-colonial states defended certain forms of private property, including in people.[55] But it remains true that widespread individual title in land and the near-ubiquity of free labour, where they have emerged in Sub-Saharan Africa, did so during or after colonial rule. To be sure, capitalism was compatible with slavery and other forms of labour coercion, as was indeed shown again in the early colonial period; but by then free labour was at least considered as part of the ideology of capitalism, or of self-consciously 'modern' societies, as colonial administrations were frequently reminded by the international abolitionist movement and the International Labour Organization.

Before going further, it is necessary to highlight the lateness and brevity of colonial rule in most of Sub-Saharan Africa: sixty or seventy years in many countries, roughly half a millennium after the beginning of European overseas colonialism. When it finally arrived, European rule in Africa proved to be colonialism on the cheap. Governors were expected to balance their budgets, rather than ask for money from the metropole. In a chicken-and-egg fashion, under-resourced administrations then imposed relatively limited tax demands on their populations. For the largest empire, Ewout Frankema has calculated that the tax demand on an unskilled wage earner in the interwar period amounted to only a few days a year in some of the British colonies in Africa. While that burden could be painful at the margin, the fiscal ambitions of the colonial administrations were strikingly low compared to the white dominions, such as Australia.[56] In part, this was a response to the weakness of colonial coercive power on the spot: troops could be shipped in to suppress a rebellion, but the ratio of European officials, police and soldiers to the population over which they presided was tiny: in the 1930s, 1:19,900 in British tropical Africa and 1:27,000 in French West Africa.[57] In this context, it is not surprising that, in the non-settler colonies, early imperial ambitions to transform African societies quickly gave way to a pragmatic gradualism.

Individual land ownership was a key part of what A. G. Hopkins has called 'Britain's first development plan for Africa', a mid-Victorian enthusiasm for private property rights as the key to economic advance anywhere in the world.[58] The British imposition of a protectorate on Lagos in 1851, and the annexation of that city state a decade later, was indeed motivated in part by calls from British and some African traders for the British to impose private ownership in land and real estate, in order to animate the credit market by providing good security for loans. By the time Britain came to annex the rest of Nigeria, during the general European partition of the continent, officials had abandoned such ambitions. Only in settler colonies did the British introduce compulsory registration of title before 1945, and then only on land reserved for Europeans.[59] Elsewhere, the British invoked 'customary' law, which they generally interpreted as forbidding land sales or mortgages. The result in some cash-cropping areas was to freeze the existing land tenure systems at a moment when some of them had been evolving to permit land alienation, as in the Akwapim case noted above. Part of the British reticence was economic: in southern Ghana and southwest Nigeria, the rapid expansion of African investment in tree crop agriculture proved that the existing systems were capable of providing reassurance to investors that their property rights were secure (in Akan land tenure in southern Ghana, for instance, the farmer who planted a crop was secure in possession of the crop, even if the land on which it grew was litigated over by rival chiefs). Thus it was a case of 'if it ain't bust, don't fix it'.[60] But there was also a powerful social and political reason to discourage land sales among Africans, a consideration which applied both to the so-called peasant colonies, where Africans retained virtually all the land under their ownership and control, and to the 'reserves' into which Africans were crowded in settler colonies. This was the fear that a land market would result in the poorer farmers selling up and moving to the towns, creating dangerous problems of social control. In practice, though less so in law, the story was similar in the French colonies. There were partial exceptions in the late-colonial period, notably in central Kenya, where the British reacted to the Mau Mau revolt by adopting a rather Stolypin-like land reform, designed to reward and strengthen the wealthier cash-cropping peasants, as opposed to the landless former squatters who provided a disproportionately large number of recruits for the guerrillas.[61] The case for colonial promotion of individual land ownership was made strongly and repeatedly within colonial administrations, but the reality of African enterprise on the ground, and the fear that the population might get out of control, ensured that it was not much acted upon.

Indeed, colonial officials, of all nationalities, were not keen to see the mass of the population lose their land rights completely and move to the towns. But the imperial governments had justified their annexations in Africa partly by the promise to implement in their new colonies the abolition of slave trading and slave holding that they had already applied in their existing colonies. They had to contend with the fact that colonization had not abolished the Nieboer-Domar problem: at the beginning of the twentieth century labour coercion remained profitable to employers. In much of tropical Africa, colonial administrations responded with a policy that can be described as gradualist: banning the slave trade, in some cases (e.g. Northern Nigeria), announcing that no one could be born a slave, but taking a decade or two (sometimes more) before making slaveholding illegal. In French West Africa, emancipation was proclaimed only in 1905, perhaps precipitated by mass walkouts of slaves, leaving their masters, in parts of what is now Mali.[62] The problem for masters (and in French West Africa about 30 per cent of the population were estimated to be slaves at the beginning of the colonial period) was real: how could they afford to become employers instead? The answer depended on whether they were able to enter export agriculture and, if so, on the profitability of the crop concerned. In the cocoa belt of southern Ghana and south-western Nigeria, the transition to hired labour was relatively smooth, with the workers migrating seasonally from areas where the soils and/or transport costs made export agriculture unaffordable. In some other cases, including south-east Nigeria, former slave owners were reduced to reliance on family labour.[63] On the desert edge in what is now the Republic of Niger, lack of fertile soil and lack of cheap transport combined to encourage states and, later, also a foreign development agency to demand unpaid labour from the population.[64] Overall, the transition to free labour in West Africa, and parts of East Africa, was thus the result of the interaction of government policy and the geographically uneven spread of export agriculture, spearheaded by African enterprise. In British West Africa, especially, freedom proved no euphemism: workers in these non-settler colonies were able to obtain wages that were relatively high by comparison with labour-abundant parts of Asia.[65] In the cocoa-growing areas, they went on in subsequent decades to negotiate successively more favourable contracts, crucially including – at their insistence – a switch from annual wage contracts to a form of sharecrop labouring. Thus, at the initiative of the workers, West Africa reversed the conventional model of labour market development, from sharecropping to wage labour.[66]

Besides going slow on abolishing slavery, colonial governments all over Sub-Saharan Africa resorted to various forms of forced labour. This was least so – though it still happened[67] – in the more prosperous export-crop zones, where it was both least necessary and hardest to enforce, because the opportunity cost was higher. The International Labour Organization adopted a Forced Labour Convention in 1930, which turned up the international and metropolitan pressure on the supposedly more liberal colonial regimes to match their own rhetoric of liberty. But it was only in 1945 that the post-liberation assembly in Paris passed a law, moved by the young Felix Houphoet-Boigny, future president of Ivory Coast, abolishing forced labour throughout the French Empire.[68]

In the settler colonies (among which South Africa became politically independent in 1910, and Southern Rhodesia partly autonomous in 1923, both under white minority rule), the solution had been found as far back as the seventeenth century, in the Cape: a policy of denying Africans access to land in order to force them to sell their labour. The classic embodiment of the policy, implemented also in Rhodesia and Kenya in particular, was the 1913 Natives Lands Act, which extended to the whole of South Africa the two prongs of the policy: 93 per cent of land was reserved for whites, and Africans were not allowed to work on white-owned land except as wage labourers. Though by no means fully implemented (the abolition of black sharecropping tenancy threatened the economic survival of many poor white farmers, who depended on their tenants for capital as well as labour),[69] it was sufficiently enforced to be the cutting edge of an ambition to drive Africans out of the market for agricultural produce and into the labour market. They were not supposed, however, to form a proletariat. Hence, under the policies of segregation and later of apartheid, in principle blacks were prohibited from living permanently in towns. Even in the 'peasant' colonies, where there was no such law, it was not until the 1940s that colonial officials began to abandon the conviction that Africans were essentially rural folk.[70]

Thus, as far as land and labour relations were concerned, colonial governments in Africa hardly fulfilled the orthodox Marxist expectation that the imperialism of capitalist powers would comprehensively destroy pre-capitalist social relations and establish the most modern of capitalist ones. Their legacy as state-builders was no more convincing from a market perspective. On paper, they brought to an end the long history of stateless societies and micro-states. But the purpose of the Berlin conference of 1884–5, which formally partitioned Africa, was to prevent European powers fighting each other in Africa and – with exceptions during the world wars, especially Tanganyika – that aim was largely fulfilled. As Jeffrey Herbst pointed out, the guarantee that they would respect each other's borders, even when the details were yet to be fixed on the ground, reduced the incentive to colonial powers to establish firm state control right up to their frontiers. At a lower level of centralization, the reliance of colonial powers on governing through African intermediaries such as chiefs and emirs ('indirect rule' applied to a greater degree in the British case but to some extent in all the empires), combined with the preservation or ossification of customary land law, prevented the emergence of national land markets and ensured that collective identities would be, in future, more rather than less strongly 'ethnic', and only weakly national.[71]

During the first twenty years after colonial rule, any spread of land titling was rather sporadic, and actively rejected by left-leaning governments. With Structural Adjustment in the 1980s, the World Bank managed to engineer a liberal land reform in the republic of Guinea,[72] but a general, Africa-wide shift towards intensified buying and selling of land, with or without formal title, seems to have waited for the post-1995 boom. The subsequent 'land rush' has been propelled partly by a renewed external demand for African lands, for growing food and fuel crops for overseas markets, which 'structurally adjusted' governments have tended to try to satisfy. But it has also been driven by the growth of commercial agriculture supplying the rapidly urbanizing populations of African countries.[73] The poor in Africa used to be people mainly with insufficient labour power at their free disposal to use the land which they were entitled to use. Now they are, in effect, increasingly landless, and looking to the cities for their subsistence.[74] The resource ratio hindered the growth of wage labour in the early colonial period, when land was still overwhelmingly abundant except where settler regimes made it artificially scarce. But by the twenty-first century, the growth of population, as well as export agriculture and especially the cities, favoured the free labour market: on the supply side at least.

Conclusion

This chapter has emphasized the interaction of African and external agency in African economic history, arguing that the endogenous propensities towards a land-extensive path of development were energized at various points by exchange with other world regions, with results more negative than positive (during the slave trades) or the other way around (during the export-crop revolution of the early colonial period in non-settler colonies, and in the recent general African boom). Africa was 'developing' before the Great Divergence, increasing food security and agricultural productivity, and with a resilient handicraft manufacturing sector, especially in West Africa. The Atlantic slave trade, and the intensification of the other slave trades during the nineteenth century, surely hindered the economic progress of the region as a whole. But the very fact that the export of slaves was so widespread, and lasted so long, suggests that labour productivity in the region tended to be lower than in the solely slave-importing parts of the world, even if the gap was aggravated by the slave trades themselves. Thus, it is argued here that Africa was on a development path, of a specific kind – land-extensive – but it is not suggested that even West Africa, the strongest candidate to be an economic 'core' in the Pomeranz sense, was on course for an indigenous industrial revolution before the intensification of the Atlantic slave trade in the late seventeenth century.

Following the beginning of industrialization in Europe, interactions with technologies of overseas origin, and relatedly with overseas markets, encouraged Africans to specialize in agricultural exports, especially in West Africa, even before colonial governments arrived to invest further in the transport infrastructure of the import–export economy. There were some successes in the nineteenth century and since. Africa has experienced intermittent episodes of economic growth per capita,[75] though they were mostly specific to particular sub-regions (such as West Africa in the decades between the beginning of the end of the Atlantic slave trade and the outbreak of the First World War, and South Africa following the mineral revolution) until the post-1995 boom. It should also be noted that the mere fact of having increased per capita income at all during the twentieth century, when child-friendly social values combined with public health advances to produce perhaps a sextupling of population, is an impressive case of what Kuznets called 'extensive growth'.

It is possible to view African economic history as, to a large extent, a story of resource rents, and African political economy as the struggle over them.[76] But raising productivity has also been part of the story, though mostly in very particular contexts. As land has become scarcer, and as urbanization has proceeded, over the last century, poverty has increasingly ceased to be associated with lack of access to labour. Historical comparisons, especially with Southeast Asia, suggest that the prospects for a general breakthrough to much higher living standards in a region that is well advanced in transition from labour scarcity to (an increasingly educated) labour surplus depend greatly on whether at least some African economies can industrialize.[77]

Notes

1. In thematic emphasis, and also in being more discursive and less formally quantitative and chronologically organized, this chapter complements G. Austin (2016), 'Sub-Saharan Africa', in J. Baten (ed.), *A History of the Global Economy from 1500 to the Present*. Cambridge: Cambridge University Press, 316–50.

2. 'Institutions' is used here in the sense of the formal and informal rules surrounding economic activity. D. North (1990), *Institutions, Institutional Change and Economic Performance*. Cambridge: Cambridge University Press, 3–4.

3. W. Rodney (1972), *How Europe Underdeveloped Africa*: London: Bogle L'Ouverture Books; I. Wallerstein (1976), 'The three stages of African involvement in the world economy', in P. Gutkind and I. Wallerstein (eds), *The Political Economy of Contemporary Africa*. Beverly Hills, CA: Sage, 30–57.

4. D. Acemoglu, S. Johnson and J. A. Robinson (2001), 'The colonial origins of comparative development: An empirical investigation', *American Economic Review*, 91 (5), 1369–401. For a critique of this and related work, see G. Austin (2008), 'The "reversal of fortune" thesis and the compression of history: Perspectives from African and comparative economic history', *Journal of International Development*, 20 (8), 996–1027. For a distinctly different rational-choice institutionalist perspective on African political economy in the twentieth century and before, see R. H. Bates (1983), *Essays on the Political Economy of Rural Africa*. Cambridge: Cambridge University Press; and Bates (2008), *When Things Fell Apart: State Failure in Late-Century Africa*. New York: Cambridge University Press. Bates focuses on internal sources of political–economic change.

5. C. H. Feinstein (2005), *An Economic History of South Africa: Conquest, Discrimination and Development*. Cambridge: Cambridge University Press.

6. A. G. Hopkins (1973), *An Economic History of West Africa*. London: Longman, 124–35. See also R. Law (ed.) (1995), *From Slave Trade to 'Legitimate' Commerce: The Commercial Transition in Nineteenth-Century West Africa*. Cambridge: Cambridge University Press.

7. This sense of period is represented in a history of contemporary Africa which sets economic change in a broader context. F. Cooper (2002), *Africa since 1940: The Past of the Present*. Cambridge: Cambridge University Press.

8. J. C. Bertélemy and L. Söderling (2001), 'The role of capital accumulation, adjustment and structural change for economic take-off: Empirical evidence from African growth episodes', *World Development*, 29 (2), 323–43. See, further, M. Jerven (2014), *Economic Growth and Measurement Reconsidered in Botswana, Kenya, Tanzania, and Zambia, 1965–1995*. Oxford: Oxford University Press.

9. J. C. W. Ahiakpor (1985), 'The success and failure of dependency theory: The experience of Ghana', *International Organization*, 39 (3), 535–52; M. Eberhardt and F. Teal (2010), 'Ghana and Côte d'Ivoire: Changing places', *International Development Policy*, 1 (1), 33–49.

10. N. van de Walle (2001), *African Economies and the Politics of Permanent Crisis, 1979–1999*. Cambridge: Cambridge University Press,

11. V. Azarya and N. Chazan (1987), 'Disengagement from the state in Africa: Reflections on the experience of Ghana and Guinea', *Comparative Studies in Society and History*, 29 (1), 106–31; J. MacGaffey (1987), *Entrepreneurs and Parasites: The Struggle for Indigenous Capitalism in Zaire*. Cambridge: Cambridge University Press.

12. G. Austin (2008), 'Resources, techniques, and strategies south of the Sahara: Revising the factor endowments perspective on African economic development, 1500–2000', *Economic History Review*, 61 (3), 587–624.

13. Austin, 'Resources, techniques, and strategies'. The soil quality issue is discussed further in Austin (2017), 'Africa and the Anthropocene', in G. Austin (ed.), *Economic Development and Environmental History in the Anthropocene: Perspectives on Asia and Africa*. London: Bloomsbury, 95–118. My friend Joseph Inikori claims that soil scientists take a much more optimistic view: J. E. Inikori (2014), 'Reversal of fortune and socioeconomic development in the Atlantic world: A comparative examination of West Africa and the Americas, 1400–1850', in E. Akyeampong, R. H. Bates, N. Nunn and J. A. Robinson (eds), *Africa's Development in Historical Perspective*. New York: Cambridge University Press, 79–80. But this is contrary to the soil science studies cited in my own earlier work, and indeed to the volume on which he relies: B. Vanlauwe, J. Djiels, N. Sanginga and R. Merckx (eds) (2002), *Integrated Plant Nutrient Management in Sub-Saharan Africa: From Concept to Practice*. Wallingford, UK: CABI Publishing and the International Institute of Tropical Agriculture. For example, the chapter by U. Mokwunye and A. Bationo (2002), 'Meeting the phosphorus needs of the soils and crops of West Africa: The role of indigenous phosphate rocks', provides a quantitative survey of the characteristics of West African soils, concluding 'Across all agroecological zones, the soils are poor in organic matter content, base exchange capacity and available phosphorus' (p. 209).

14. Austin, 'Resources, techniques, and strategies'.

15. M. Widren (2017), 'Agricultural intensification in Sub-Saharan Africa, 1500 to 1800', in G. Austin (ed.), *Economic Development and Environmental History in the Anthropocene: Perspectives on Asia and Africa*. London: Bloomsbury, 51–67.

16. J. Iliffe (1989), 'The origins of African population growth', *Journal of African History*, 30 (1), 165–9.

17. J. Goody (1976), *Production and Reproduction: A Comparative Study of the Domestic Domain*. Cambridge: Cambridge University Press.

18. C. H. Perrot (ed.) (2012), *Lignages et territoires en Afrique aux XVIIIe et XIXe siècles: Stratégies, compétition, intégration*. Paris: Karthala; G. Austin (2004), 'Sub-Saharan Africa: Land rights and ethno-national consciousness in historically land-abundant economies', in S. L. Engerman and J. Metzer (eds), *Land Rights, Ethno-Nationality, and Sovereignty in History*. London: Routledge, 276–93.

19. G. Austin (2017), 'Slavery in Africa', in D. Eltis, S. L. Engerman and D. Richardson (eds), *The Cambridge World History of Slavery*, vol. 4: *Slavery since 1804*. Cambridge: Cambridge University Press, 174–96.

20. J. Herbst (2014), *States and Power in Africa*. Princeton, NJ: Princeton University Press, 2nd edn.

21. P. D. Curtin (1984), *Cross-Cultural Trade in World History*. Cambridge: Cambridge University Press, 38–57; G. Austin (2002), 'African business in nineteenth-century West Africa', in A. Jalloh and T. Falola (eds), *Black Business and Economic Power*. Rochester, NY: University of Rochester Press, 114–44.

22. D. Crummey (1980), 'Abyssinian feudalism', *Past & Present*, 89, 115–38.

23. G. Austin (2007), 'Labour and land in Ghana, 1879–1939: A shifting ratio and an institutional revolution', *Australian Economic History Review*, 47 (1), 95–120.

24. R. H. Bates (1990), 'Capital, kinship, and conflict: The structuring influence of capital in kinship societies', *Canadian Journal of African Studies*, 24 (1), 145–64.

25. A neat abstract analysis is C. Meillassoux (1972), 'From reproduction to production: A Marxist approach to economic anthropology', *Economy and Society*, 1 (1), 93–105.

26. Austin, 'Slavery in Africa'.

27. See, for instance, J. F. Searing (2002), '"No kings, no lords, no slaves": Ethnicity and religion among the Sereer-Safèn of Western Bawol, 1700–1914', *Journal of African History*, 43 (3), 407–30.

28. This argument is developed, successively, in Austin, 'Resources, techniques and strategies'; G. Austin (2013), 'Labour-intensity and manufacturing in West Africa, c.1450–c.2000', in G. Austin and K. Sugihara (eds), *Labour-Intensive Industrialization in Global History*. London: Routledge, 201–30; and Austin, 'Africa and the Anthropocene'.

29. Austin, 'Africa and the Anthropocene', 102.

30. G. Austin (2014), 'Vent for surplus or productivity breakthrough? The Ghanaian cocoa take-off, c.1890–1936', *Economic History Review*, 67 (4), 1035–64.

31. G. Austin (1996), 'Mode of production or mode of cultivation: Explaining the failure of European cocoa planters in competition with African cocoa farmers in colonial Ghana', in W. G. Clarence-Smith (ed.), *Cocoa Pioneer Fronts: The Role of Smallholders, Planters and Merchants*. Basingstoke: Macmillan, 154–75.

32. The first part of this paragraph is based on Austin, 'Resources, techniques, and strategies'.

33. For an exposition of the concept and a case study, see G. Austin (2005), *Labour, Land and Capital in Ghana: From Slavery to Free Labour in Asante, 1807–1956*. Rochester, NY: University of Rochester Press, 155–70, 236–49, 495–8, 512–15.

34. Austin, 'Slavery in Africa'; P. E. Lovejoy (2012), *Transformations in Slavery: A History of Slavery in Africa*, 3rd edn. Cambridge: Cambridge University Press, 160–243, 327–44. For Buganda, see R. Reid (2002), *Political Power in Pre-Colonial Buganda: Economy, Society and Warfare in the Nineteenth Century*. Oxford: James Currey.

35. Iliffe, 'The origins of African population growth'.

36. That was an oral observation in a presentation at the West Africa Seminar in the Anthropology Department of University College London in 2010. See further, Richards, 'A Green Revolution from Below? Science and Technology for Global Food Security and Poverty Alleviation', retirement address, Wageningen University, 18 November 2010, published online at http://edepot.wur.nl/165231.

37. D. L. Schoenbrun (1998), *A Green Place, a Good Place: Agrarian Change, Gender, and Social Identity in the Great Lakes Region in the 15th Century*. Portsmouth, NH: Heinemann, 79–83.

38. For an overview, see J. C. McCann (2005), *Maize and Grace: Africa's Encounter with a New World Crop, 1500-2000*. Cambridge MA: Harvard University Press.

39. For example, in the Ghanaian cocoa belt: Austin, *Labour, Land and Capital*, 66, and 474.

40. See Lovejoy, *Transformations in Slavery*, 19, 46, 138. For the Atlantic slave trade, see further *Voyages: The Trans-Atlantic Slave Trade Database*, http://www.slavevoyages.org, launched in 2008 by a team led by David Eltis.

41. For the state of the debate about how to interpret colonial censuses, see P. Manning (2014), 'African population, 1650–2000: Comparisons and implications of new estimates', in E. Akyeampong, R. H. Bates, N. Nunn and J. A. Robinson (eds), *Africa's Development in Historical Perspective*. New York: Cambridge University Press, 131–50; E. Frankema and M. Jerven (2014), 'Writing history backwards and sideways: Towards a consensus on African population, 1850–2010', *Economic History Review*, 67 (4), 907–31.

42. D. Henige (1986), 'Measuring the immeasurable: The Atlantic slave trade, West African population and the Pyrrhonian critic', *Journal of African History*, 27 (2), 295–313.

43. Austin, 'Resources, techniques, and strategies', 590–1; and references in n. 41 above.

44. Searing, '"No kings, no lords, no slaves"'.

45. J. E. Inikori (2007), 'Africa and the globalization process: Western Africa, 1450–1850', *Journal of Global History*, 2 (1), 63–86; Inikori (2009), 'The economic impact of the 1807 British abolition of the transatlantic slave trade', in T. Falola and M. D. Childs (eds), *The Changing Worlds of Atlantic Africa: Essays in Honor of Robin Law*. Durham, NC: Carolina Academic Press, 163–82.

46. Hopkins, *Economic History of West Africa*, 125; E. Evans and D. Richardson (1995), 'Hunting for rents: The economics of slaving in pre-colonial Africa', *Economic History Review*, 48 (4), 665–86.

47. I. Wilks (1975), *Asante in the Nineteenth Century*. Cambridge: Cambridge University Press; R. Law (1997), 'The politics of commercial transition: Factional conflict in Dahomey in the context of the ending of the Atlantic slave trade', *Journal of African History*, 28 (2), 213–33.

48. S. Fenoaltea (1999), 'Europe in the African mirror: The slave trade and the rise of feudalism', *Rivista di Storia Economica*, 15 (2), 123–65.

49. Austin, 'Resources, techniques, and strategies'.

50. J.-F. Paul (2009), 'Empire, monotheism and slavery in the Greater Mediterranean region from antiquity to the early modern era', *Past & Present*, 205, 3–40.

51. J. I. Inikori (2003), 'The struggle against the transatlantic slave trade: The role of the state', in S. A. Diouf (ed.), *Fighting the Slave Trade: West African Strategies*. Athens, OH: Ohio University Press, 170–98.

52. Leopold's regime needs no introduction; on African enterprise in the wild rubber boom in West Africa, see K. Arhin (1980), 'The economic and social significance of rubber production and exchange on the Gold and Ivory Coasts, 1880–1900', *Cahiers d'études*

africaines, 20 (77–78), 49–62; E. Osborn (2004), '"Rubber fever", commerce and French colonial rule in Upper Guinée, 1890–1913', *Journal of African History*, 45 (3), 445–65.

53. A. G. Hopkins (1978), 'Innovation in a colonial context: African origins of the Nigerian cocoa-farming industry, 1880–1920', in A. G. Hopkins and C. Dewey (eds), *The Imperial Impact*. London: Athlone, 83–96, 341–2; P. Hill (1997), *The Migrant Cocoa-Farmers of Southern Ghana: A Study in Rural Capitalism*. Hamburg: LIT; first published Cambridge 1963.

54. J. Sender and S. Smith (1986), *The Development of Capitalism in Africa*. London: Methuen; S. Amin (1976), *Unequal Development: An Essay on the Social Formations of Peripheral Capitalism*. Hassocks, UK: Harvester; Acemoglu, Johnson and Robinson, 'Colonial origins'.

55. S. J. Rockel (2006), *Carriers of Culture: Labor on the Road in Nineteenth-Century East Africa*. Portsmouth, NH: Heinemann; G. Austin (2009), 'Factor markets in Nieboer conditions: Pre-colonial West Africa, *c*.1500–*c*.1900', *Continuity and Change*, 24 (1), 23–53.

56. E. Frankema (2010), 'Raising revenue in the British empire: How "extractive" were colonial taxes?', *Journal of Global History*, 5 (3), 447–77. See also L. A. Gardner (2012), *Taxing Colonial Africa: The Political Economy of British Imperialism*. Oxford: Oxford University Press.

57. A. H. M. Kirk-Greene (1980), 'The thin white line: The size of the British colonial service in Africa', *African Affairs*, 79 (314), 25–41.

58. A. G. Hopkins (1995), 'Britain's first development plan for Africa', in Robin Law (ed.), *The Commercial Transition in West Africa*. Cambridge: Cambridge University Press. See also A. G. Hopkins (1980), 'Property rights and empire building: Britain's annexation of Lagos, 1861', *Journal of Economic History*, 40 (4), 777–98.

59. Though African land purchases were permitted in certain contexts. See, for instance, A. K. Shutt (2002), 'Squatters, land sales and intensification in Marirangwe Purchase Area, colonial Zimbabwe, 1931–65', *Journal of African History*, 43 (3), 473–98.

60. Austin, *Labour, Land and Capital*, 339–48, 531–3.

61. D. Branch (2009), *Defeating Mau Mau, Creating Kenya: Counterinsurgency, Civil War, and Decolonization*. Cambridge: Cambridge University Press, 120–5.

62. M. A. Klein (1998), *Slavery and Colonial Rule in French West Africa*. Cambridge: Cambridge University Press.

63. D. C. Ohadike (1999), '"When the slaves left, the owners wept": Entrepreneurs and emancipation among the Igbo people', in S. Miers and M. A. Klein (eds), *Slavery and Colonial Rule in Africa*. London: Frank Cass, 189–207; generally, G. Austin (2009), 'Cash crops and freedom: Export agriculture and the decline of slavery in colonial West Africa', *International Review of Social History*, 54 (1), 1–37.

64. B. Rossi (2015), *From Slavery to Aid: Politics, Labour, and Ecology in the Nigerien Sahel, 1800–2000*. Cambridge: Cambridge University Press.

65. E. Frankema and M. van Waijenburg (2012), 'Structural impediments to African growth? New evidence from real wages in British Africa, 1880–1965', *Journal of Economic History*, 72 (4), 895–926.

66. Austin, *Labour, Land and Capital*, 315–24, 401–30, 442–3, 452–4, 527–9, 540–6.

67. For example, K. O. Akurang-Parry (2000), 'Colonial forced labor policies for road-building in southern Ghana and international anti-forced labor pressures, 1900–1940', *African Economic History*, 28 (1), 1–25.

68. F. Cooper (1996), *Decolonization and African Society: The Labor Question in French and British Africa*. New York: Cambridge University Press.

69. A marvellously thought-provoking case study is C. van Onselen (1990), 'Race and class in the South African countryside: Cultural osmosis and social relations in the sharecropping economy of Transvaal', *American Historical Review*, 95 (1), 99–123.

70. M. Lipton (1985), *Capitalism and Apartheid*. Aldershot: Gower; Cooper, *Decolonization*.

71. M. Mamdani (1996), *Citizen and Subject: Contemporary Africa and the Legacy of Late Colonialism*. Princeton, NJ: Princeton University Press. For a highly perceptive recent analysis see C. Boone (2014), *Property and Political Order in Africa: Land Rights and the Structure of Politics*. New York: Cambridge University Press.

72. J. Clapp (1997), *Adjustment and Agriculture in Africa: Farmers, the State and the World Bank in Guinea*. London: Macmillan.

73. C. Oya (2013), 'The land rush and classic agrarian questions of capital and labour: A systematic scoping review of the socioeconomic impact of land grabs in Africa', *Third World Quarterly*, 34 (9), 1532–57.

74. Compare J. Iliffe (1987), *The African Poor: A History*. Cambridge: Cambridge University Press.

75. Austin, 'Resources, techniques, and strategies', 610–14; further, M. Jerven (2010), 'African growth recurring: An economic history perspective on African growth episodes, 1690–2010', *Economic History of Developing Regions*, 25 (2), 127–54.

76. I owe this thought to William Gervase Clarence-Smith, in a conversation many years ago.

77. Austin, 'Labour-intensity and manufacturing'; G. Austin (2016), 'Is Africa too late for "late development"? Gerschenkron south of the Sahara', in M. Andersson and T. Axelsson (eds), *Diverse Development Paths and Structural Transformation in the Escape from Poverty*. Oxford: Oxford University Press, 206–35; G. Austin, E. Frankema and M. Jerven (2017), 'Patterns of manufacturing growth in Sub-Saharan Africa: From colonization to the present', in K. O'Rourke and J. G. Williamson (eds), *The Spread of Modern Industry to the Poor Periphery since 1870*. Oxford: Oxford University Press, 345–73.

CHAPTER 17
TRADE AND DEVELOPMENT IN THE MIDDLE EAST, 1500–1914
Laura Panza

This chapter aims to provide an overview of the economic development of the Middle East and its commercial interactions with the global economy from 1500 to 1914. During this historical period, most of the Middle East shared the same political and institutional environment, being unified under the authority of the Ottoman Empire. The rise of the Ottomans as a major sea power in the Mediterranean in the fifteenth century was followed by their imperial expansion to the Arab lands of the Levant, extending from Syria to Palestine, and of North Africa, extending from Egypt to Algeria.[1] Further military campaigns led to the conquest of much of the Gulf: Yemen was annexed in 1517, and Iraq (the regions of Baghdad and Basra) recognized Ottoman sovereignty from 1534 to 1538. The vast Ottoman territory was organized in provinces (*eyalets* or *beylerbeylik*) and their administration was under the responsibility of a governor-general (*beglerbegi*); they enjoyed a degree of relative autonomy, including in terms of fiscal organization.[2] While many of the trends described in this chapter apply to the whole Middle East, most of the narrative focuses on its largest economic regions: Turkey, Egypt, the Levant (Iraq and Greater Syria) and the Arab peninsula.[3]

There is extensive evidence that thanks to its strategic location at the intersection of three continents – Europe, Asia and Africa – the Ottoman Empire played a key role in world trade, both as a major importer and exporter of goods and as the main intermediary in commercial exchange between Asia and Europe, at least since the fifteenth century. Its position as a vital international trade hub strengthened in the sixteenth century.[4] Recent empirical research on market integration illustrates that, despite some fluctuations, trade between Europe and the Ottoman Middle East was active and heterogeneous from 1500 to 1914, reflecting increasing levels of commercialization in both regions.[5] However, the Middle East's role as a strategic international trade hub deteriorated with the rise of the Atlantic economy: while overall trade volume and value continued to grow in the region in the seventeenth and eighteenth centuries, the contribution of Middle Eastern trade to the world economy declined. The shift in economic dominance from the Mediterranean to the Atlantic, together with a series of permanent territorial losses incurred by the Empire, were once considered to be clear signs of the decline of the Empire, often labelled 'the sick man of Europe'.[6] As explained in this chapter, this once prevalent idea, particularly within the Orientalist tradition, has now been thoroughly questioned and is no longer accepted: the period from 1700 to the outbreak of the First

World War is seen as an era of renovation in which the Empire strived to find a synthesis between the centrifugal forces within its own territory and the changing international system.[7] Indeed, despite the undergoing process of change and the relatively weakened political and economic position played in the international arena, at the height of the nineteenth century the Ottoman Empire represented both a leading Islamic state and a world empire of vast influence at the crossroads of intercontinental trade.

The nineteenth century brought a further structural break to the region, which participated in the first wave of globalization, an era of growth and unprecedented transformations for the global economy, moulded by new patterns of production, division of labour and balance of power among nations. The Middle East, which took part in these sweeping global changes as a member of the periphery, underwent a process of agricultural commercialization and specialization, while becoming increasingly dependent on the import of European manufactures. The region shifted from being an agrarian economy where cultivation was centred on subsistence crops to the production of cash crops for the external market. Complementary to this development was the decline in manufacturing activities, owing to competition from cheaper imported finished products.[8]

Despite the considerable expansion in trade volume and value during the nineteenth century, the extent to which the Ottoman economy came to be connected with the world market differed from area to area: in some regions the first signals of these changes became manifest in the early years of the nineteenth century (and in some cases even in the last decades of the eighteenth century) particularly in port cities such as Aleppo, Alexandria and Izmir. The expansion of cash crops grown for export, like cotton in Egypt and silk in Lebanon, brought millions of cultivators into contact with the global market, while other commodities such as tobacco in Syria, dates in Iraq and coffee in Yemen followed a slower path in the process of market expansion. On the other extreme of the spectrum, in Arabia and in parts of Sudan, the vast majority of the population continued living in a subsistence economy.

How did the engagement of the Middle East in the global economy relate to its own economic development? A reliable proxy of economic performance in the premodern era, where GDP estimates are not available, is the rate of urbanization, which reflects the ability of economies to produce an agricultural surplus to provide resources needed to sustain cities.[9]

Figure 17.1 provides a snapshot of average urbanization rates by country in the Middle East in the period between 1500 and 1800, defined as total urban population divided by total country population (times 100). A few conclusions can be seen: Yemen and Saudi Arabia were the least urbanized areas of the region throughout the period; urbanization levels remained stable in Palestine, Saudi Arabia and Yemen; they deteriorated in Iraq in the sixteenth century, but improved thereafter. Furthermore, Egypt became more urbanized throughout the period of analysis, while Syria and Turkey experienced a decrease in urbanization in the eighteenth century. The Middle East as a region had higher urbanization rates than Europe until at least 1700.[10]

To better understand the Middle East's engagement with the world market from 1500 to 1914, it is important to mention one of the principles that guided the Ottoman Empire's management of the economy throughout its existence: *provisionism*, that is the

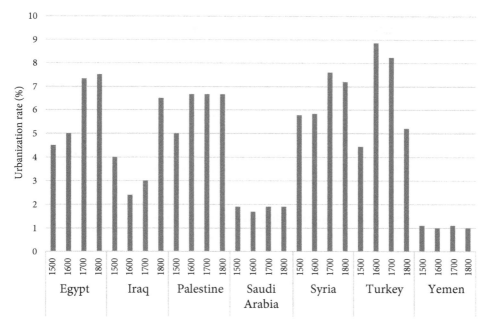

Figure 17.1 Urbanization rate in the Middle East, 1500–1800.

Notes and sources: M. Bosker, E. Buringh and J. L. Van Zanden (2013), 'From Baghdad to London: Unraveling urban development in Europe, the Middle East, and North Africa, 800–1800', *Review of Economics and Statistics*, 95 (4), 1418–37. Urbanization rate is defined as total urban population divided by total country population (times 100). The following cities were used to construct urbanisation rates; Palestine: Acre and Jerusalem; Yemen: Sana'a; Saudi Arabia: Mecca; Iraq: Basra, Baghdad; Syria: Damascus, Aleppo; Turkey: Istanbul; Egypt: Cairo.

maintenance of a steady supply of goods and services to avoid shortages in the domestic market.[11] With respect to foreign trade, this translated to discouraging exports and encouraging imports. Hence, unlike Europe, the Ottoman Empire's approach to trade was not shaped by mercantilist concerns: imports were considered beneficial to the economy, given that they increased the amount and range of available goods in the market; on the other hand, the export of necessities, such as grains and raw materials, was sometimes prohibited, with the aim of preventing shortages. Overall, the management of the economy was more consumer- than producer-oriented and the protection of domestic labour and industries were not of primary concern for the government: in fact, state provisionism was not tied to import-substitution policies.

The First World War led to the collapse of the Ottoman Empire, thus ending centuries of political and institutional unity in the Middle East: its former unification under a single imperial authority was substituted by nine separate states with their own custom regulations and currencies: Egypt, Syria, Lebanon, Transjordan, Iraq, Palestine, Turkey, Saudi Arabia and Yemen. Only the latter three exercised full sovereignty. The League of Nations granted Britain the right to administer Transjordan, Palestine and Iraq, and France the right to administer Lebanon and Syria.[12]

The rest of the chapter will provide a detailed discussion of the trends in international trade and economic development experienced by the Middle East between the sixteenth century and the First World War. The last section will cover the role played by trade in services in the region. Overall, this chapter highlights how an economic history of the Middle East and North Africa could improve the understanding of the history of Europe, given that the economic development of these two regions was deeply entwined. In so doing, it complements the existing accounts of Middle Eastern and European history, which identify economic exchange as an important area of interaction between the two cultures, characterized by a high level of interdependence – notwithstanding their political rivalries and recurrent military confrontations.[13]

Growth and Stability in the Sixteenth Century

The sixteenth century is considered a period of economic stability and growth for the Ottoman Middle East: the state was strong, centralized, able to ensure law enforcement, to invest in infrastructure (transportation and irrigation) and to guarantee safety along trade routes.[14] The whole region had strong economic connections with Europe and Asia and constituted an important node of exchange between East and West. During this period, global commercial transactions involved predominantly trade in high value-added goods, with Asia being the main exporter of spices and manufactures, predominantly cotton and silk textiles, to Europe.

Trade between the Middle East and Europe was regulated by a system of capitulations, bilateral treaties akin to today's most favoured nation status agreements, which allowed non-Muslim foreigners to travel and trade freely in the Ottoman Empire.[15] In the first century of the early modern era, Ottoman–European trade patterns were shaped by Ottoman exports of silk cloth, cotton goods and mohair in exchange for tin, lead and steel, gunpowder and chemicals, and to a smaller extent luxury goods such as fine woollen cloths, jewellery and watches.

While in the fifteenth century most trade with Europe took place via Venice and Genoa, from the mid-sixteenth century the English (and from the seventeenth century the Dutch) started engaging in Middle Eastern markets, replacing the mercantile and industrial cities of Italy.[16] English traders, who used Izmir as their main centre for trade with the Levant and Iran, exported woollen cloth (kerseys and shortcloth), tin and lead in exchange for raw silk, spices and currants, see Table 17.1. While the balance of trade with the Levant was unfavourable for England (imports dominated exports), the Middle East was a primary export destination for the products of its expanding woollen industry: the Ottomans were both direct importers and re-exporters of English woollens to Iran and other Asian countries.[17] The establishment of strong commercial connection between Izmir and Europe contributed considerably to its economic development, as demonstrated by its almost tenfold increase in urbanization rate (from 0.16 per cent to 1.4 per cent): in comparison, during the fifteenth century its urbanization rate was the lowest among the cities listed in Figure 17.2.

Table 17.1 Main English imports from and exports to the Levant, in 1588 and 1589

Levantine exports to Britain (1588): total value £55,261

Currants	613,300 lb
Raisins	10,850 lb
Oil	6 barrels
Nutmeg	49,705 lb
Indigo	54,120 lb
Gall nuts[1]	104,500 lb
Black pepper	8,380 lb
Aniseed	10,000 lb
Cinnamon	12,296 lb
Other spices	10,826 lb
Mastic	600 lb
Raw silk	9,133 lb
Cotton	66,500 lb
Cotton yarn	15,840 lb
Flax	700 lb
Cotton cloth	11,590 lb
Turkish carpets	13 pieces lb

Levantine imports from Britain (1598): total value £4,278

Shortcloth[2]	750 pieces
Kersey[3]	18,126 pieces
Tin	2,125 cwt
Iron wire	42 cwt
Rabbit skin	26,600 pieces
Sarsaparilla	34 cwt
Brazil-wood	4 cwt
Long-wood	15 cwt

Source: T. S. Willan (1955), 'Some aspects of English trade with the Levant in the sixteenth century', *English Historical Review*, 70 (276), 399–410.
Notes:
[1] Gall nuts were used as a dye and medicinal purposes. Aleppo galls have the highest concentrations of tannin among the galls (50–65%), providing a strong astringent and a treatment for fevers, burns, mouth ulcers and toothache.
[2] Shortcloth (or broadcloth) is a plain, woven cloth made of short-staple wool.
[3] Kersey is a type of coarse woollen cloth. Cwt stands for hundredweight, equivalent to 112 lb (50.80 kg).

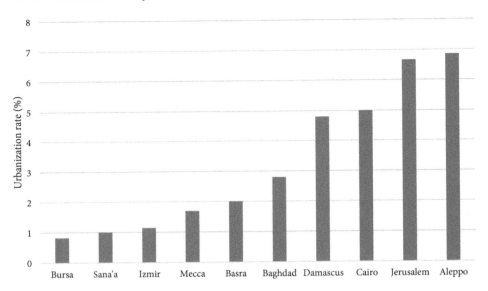

Figure 17.2 Urbanization rates in Middle Eastern cities in the sixteenth century.
Notes and source: M. Bosker, E. Buringh and J. L. Van Zanden (2013), 'From Baghdad to London: Unraveling urban development in Europe, the Middle East, and North Africa, 800–1800', *Review of Economics and Statistics*, 95 (4), 1418–37. Urbanization rate is defined as total urban population divided by total country population (times 100).

During the sixteenth century spice trade remained the most lucrative branch of international trade and the most important branch of long-distance trade between East and West. European imports of spices included indigenous products of the Middle East, such as alum (a dye fixer) as well as re-exports from Asia, particularly from India. Therefore, ensuring control over Middle Eastern trade with India was of paramount importance as a revenue-generating activity for the Ottoman Empire. Trade with India took place via two routes: the Red Sea and the Gulf. The former went through Yemen, who exported madder (a red dye root), an essential raw material for the dying industry of Gujarat, and imported spices, indigo and fine cotton textiles.[18] As a result, Yemen received an exceptionally high percentage of revenue from custom dues coming from the Indian transit trade, and had positive spillover effects also for Egypt, with Suez being an entrepôt for trade with Yemen, Arabia, India and the Far East. From the early sixteenth century Indian goods were exchanged also via caravan roads, especially via the Basra-Aleppo route. The growing importance of the Persian Gulf–Aleppo caravan route was at the basis of Aleppo's unprecedented commercial expansion during the second half of the sixteenth century: as illustrated in Figure 17.2, it became the second most urbanized city in the Middle East, after Istanbul.[19] Furthermore, the city of Basra flourished thanks to its direct connection with the Arabian Peninsula and Iran.[20]

Economic exchange with Iran played a dominant role for the Ottoman Middle East too: Persian raw silk represented an indispensable import for the silk industries of both the Empire, particularly in Amasya, Bursa, Istanbul, Mardin and Diyarbakir, and of

Europe. Basra, Bursa and Aleppo became the most important silk exporting markets in the Middle East: like with spices, during the first half of the sixteenth century, raw silk reached Europe via Venetian and Genoese merchants; they were later replaced by the British and the Dutch, who re-exported their surplus imports to the rest of Europe.[21]

Crisis and Recovery in the Seventeenth Century

The role played by the Ottoman Middle East in world trade changed dramatically at the turn of the sixteenth century, with the rise of the Atlantic economy. Atlantic trade impacted the region in several aspects: first, trade in colonial goods (sugar, cotton, tobacco, coffee) overshadowed that of spice and silk, the key Ottoman exports to Europe, in terms of both value and volume. This had direct consequences for the pattern of Indian–Levantine trade, which underwent a major change and re-oriented itself to focus on the export of Indian cottons. During the seventeenth century the production and export of Indian cotton fabrics to the Middle East and Europe reached unprecedented levels, thanks to their competitive prices driven by low wages.[22] The arrival of cheap Indian textiles pushed Ottoman weavers to produce imitations of Indian fabrics in industrial centres such as Bursa and Aleppo. Another industry that was negatively affected by commerce in colonial goods was sugar processing production, as cheaper production in the Canaries and Brazil led to a decline in Ottoman sugar refineries, particularly in Egypt and Cyprus.[23]

Second, not only did cotton textiles trade eclipse spice trade, but the latter de facto stopped being traded via the Levant after 1625, when the Dutch and English established their domination in the Indian Ocean by ensuring state-sponsored monopoly rights via their respective East India companies (the Dutch VOC and the English EIC). Third, as a result of the large monetary inflows from the New World, a wave of inflation was transmitted from Europe to the Ottoman territories, which led to considerably higher prices for basic commodities in the Empire.[24]

Despite these dramatic changes, a growing literature has emphasized that the Ottoman Middle East did not simply undergo a process of decline from the seventeenth century, but that it was rather adapting to a changing global economic and political environment.[25] From the perspective of international trade, the decline in Levantine transit trade in spices was replaced by a rise in imports of coffee from the Atlantic to supply domestic markets. Cairo continued to be an important trade hub, shifting its focus from spices to coffee, dyestuffs and Indian textiles.[26] As illustrated in Figure 17.3, its urbanization rates rose from 5 to 7.3 per cent between the sixteenth and seventeenth century. Tunisia developed close commercial ties with Marseilles and Livorno, exporting grains and olive oil.[27]

The Iranian raw silk export market shifted from Bursa to Izmir, driven by the stronger connections with British traders. It was during the seventeenth century that Izmir developed from a port of local importance to a major centre engaged in Ottoman–European trade.[28] The change in relative importance between the two cities is illustrated

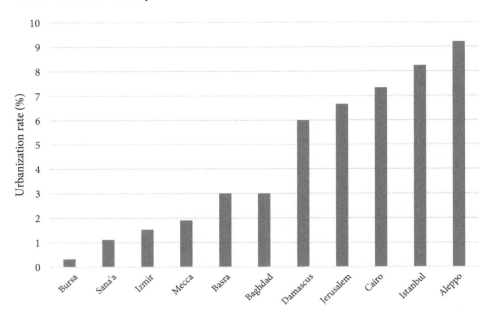

Figure 17.3 Urbanization rates in Middle Eastern cities in the seventeenth century.
Notes and source: M. Bosker, E. Buringh and J. L. Van Zanden (2013), 'From Baghdad to London: Unraveling urban development in Europe, the Middle East, and North Africa, 800–1800', *Review of Economics and Statistics*, 95 (4), 1418–37. Urbanization rate is defined as total urban population divided by total country population (times 100).

in the change of their urbanization ranking (see Figures 17.2 and 17.3): while Izmir's position advanced (its urbanization rate grew from 1.1 to 1.5 per cent), Bursa's regressed (its urbanization rate dropped from 0.8 to 0.3 per cent). Alongside Izmir, Aleppo continued to be the other major hub to export raw silk to Europe.[29] Commerce along the caravan routes of the Eastern Mediterranean revived, too: Aleppo's position as a major player in local, regional and interregional trade continued in the seventeenth century, its hinterland expanding to supply not only agricultural produce but also industrial goods, overtaking Istanbul in terms of urbanization rate.[30] Also, the city of Basra continued engaging in international trade and flourished as an important commercial and cultural centre: its urbanization rate grew from 2 to 3 per cent between the sixteenth and seventeenth century (see Figures 17.2 and 17.3).

The seventeenth century was not only a period of change in the Empire's involvement in the world economy but also one of political transformation. The central government's power started to decline, as its capacity to secure law and order and protect domestic trade routes weakened.[31] Thus, the Ottoman Empire transitioned from a strong centralized state to a more decentralized one: this process culminated with the rise of the *ayans* (local notables) as a class of powerful and well-connected individuals, who might be merchants, moneylenders, military officers or landholders.[32] They eventually secured the right to collect taxes on behalf of the state and increased their wealth by keeping profits after sending a portion of revenues to the central government.[33] Involvement in tax collection was more lucrative than investing in agriculture, trade or manufacturing; nevertheless, adapting to the new socio-economic reality of expanding commercial systems in the Atlantic, the Indian Ocean and the Mediterranean fostered a process of commercialization of agriculture and, to a lesser extent, of manufacturing, thus enriching Ottoman provincial elites.[34] By the end of the century, high-ranking officials, *ayans*, members of the religious judiciary, and the army emerged politically and economically stronger: despite this decentralization process, the central bureaucracy was able to retain its leading position in Ottoman society and politics until the end of the empire.[35]

Peace and Stability in the Eighteenth Century

Following this phase of transition, characterized by a structural transformation of the socio-economic and political reality in the Middle East and a partial recovery from the 'crisis' brought about by the new international environment, the eighteenth century was a period of relative peace and economic expansion until the 1770s. Many regions of the Ottoman realm experienced a phase of prosperity and GDP per capita is estimated to have increased from about US$640 in 1700 to $720 in 1820, measured in 1990 international prices.[36] The economic linkages within the empire, such as those between the main commercial centres in Anatolia, Syria and Egypt, strengthened, as demonstrated by the increase in agricultural and industrial economic activity. However, while the Middle East's engagement with the international economy grew (for instance, overall trade with Western Europe more than doubled), it remained small relative to intra-Ottoman trade. Moreover, the degree of openness of Middle Eastern economies (measured as a ratio of trade to GDP) continued to remain relatively small, around 2–3 per cent throughout the eighteenth century.[37]

Ottoman external trade in the eighteenth century was characterized by three main shifts: in the composition of exports, in the geographic distribution of trade, and in the ranking of its trade partners.[38] The composition of imports with Europe remained similar to those established in the previous century, being dominated by woollen textiles and, to a lesser extent, colonial goods (sugar, coffee, tobacco). However, the composition of exports saw an increase in the share of agricultural goods, despite continuing to include some textiles.[39] Particularly, there was an intensification of the export of raw materials previously dedicated to internal consumption and industry.[40] Furthermore, the decline in European interests in Persian silk caused a decline in its re-export, substituted by locally grown raw cotton and cotton yarn, imported predominantly by France and Germany.[41]

In terms of trade partners, France emerged as major player, while trade with Britain stagnated.[42] French traders used Marseille as their main trade hub with the Ottomans and established commercial connections in most of the Middle East, particularly in Izmir, Istanbul, Aleppo, Sidon, Alexandria and Cairo, Tunis and Algiers.[43] The general trend in commodity of French–Middle Eastern trade is characterized by a constant growth throughout the eighteenth century from an average of 20 million livres in the 1720s to

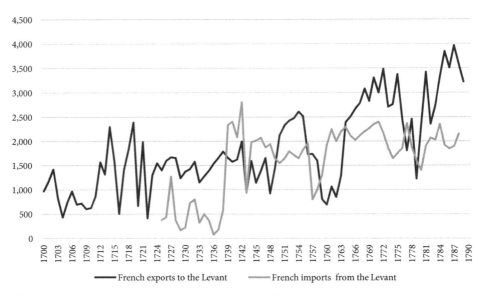

Figure 17.4 French Trade in the Levant, in thousand *livres tournois*.
Source: E. Eldem (1999), *French Trade in Istanbul in the Eighteenth Century*. Leiden: Brill, 14.

over 50 million at the end of the century (Figure 17.4). French imports included hides, olive oil, cotton and cotton yarn while exports were predominantly made of colonial goods, such as sugar, cochineal, coffee and indigo.

Like in the seventeenth century, trade with India continued to flourish and had a similar composition: imports consisted of Indian cotton goods, and to a smaller extent drugs, dyestuffs and spices, while exports included animals, raw materials and dyestuffs.[44] Imported Indian textiles, which were cheaper and of better quality, continued to face competition from local producers in the Middle East.[45]

The eighteenth century saw the establishment of a new fiscal institution, the life-term tax farming system (*malikâne*), which allowed tax collection for life (rather than for a single year), with the aim of providing incentives to increase long-term investments. This system had some positive economic impact, as new contractors helped improve productivity in the *malikâne* they bought.[46] However, while the rates of return on various *malikâne* investments reached 35–40 per cent, this did not translate into a considerable increase in fiscal capacity: tax revenues in the hands of the central treasury remained low, around 3 per cent of GDP.[47] Moreover, many *malikâne* owners turned into rentier bureaucrats, and started subcontracting their tax-collecting rights to second and third parties, thus transferring resources from productive to unproductive hands.[48]

The period of stability involving Middle Eastern economies for most of the eighteenth century came to an end in the 1770s and was replaced by decades of war (with Russia and the Habsburg), fiscal difficulty, inflation and heightened power struggle between the provincial elites and the central government. These developments impacted negatively domestic production in agriculture and manufacturing as well as trade, both long-distance and intra-Ottoman. The central government financed heightened war expenditures with additional borrowing and frequent currency debasements, which led to a dramatic depreciation of the Ottoman lira, and to rising inflation.[49]

Commercialization and Integration with the World Economy in the Nineteenth Century

It is well documented by a large literature that the nineteenth century was a period of swift and unprecedented transformations for the Ottoman Empire, which undermined the survival of its territorial unity and deeply modified its economic structure.[50] This last century of the life of the empire was characterized by a continuous striving by the central authorities to find a synthesis between the centrifugal forces within its own territory and an international system that was progressively becoming more globalized. This resulted in the deterioration of the absolute rule of the sultan and the incapability of the central state to control its own territories, which led to permanent territorial losses both in Europe and North Africa: Algeria and Tunisia fell into French hands in 1830 and 1881, respectively; Egypt increased its level of autonomy during the late eighteenth century in both the administrative and financial spheres under a revived Mamluk order; in 1882 it was occupied by Great Britain.[51]

The response to the combination of these external and internal pressures was the implementation of a set of military and fiscal reforms, known as *Tanzimat* (reorganization), aimed at increasing the power of the central government and modernizing the economy. The other important reform was the signing of a series of international free trade agreements, starting with the 1838 Anglo-Turkish Convention, followed by similar agreements with most European countries.[52] These agreements signalled the government's formal commitment to abolish industrial, commercial and agricultural monopolies. These two reforms have been considered as the engines of a process of market integration between the Middle East and the world economy.

Following an experience common to many other developing countries, the most visible signs of the region's rising participation in the world market were the commercialization of agriculture and the rise in manufactured goods imports from Europe. Hence, the Middle East shifted from being an agrarian region where cultivation was centred on subsistence crops to the production of cash crops for the international market. Complementary to this development was the decline in manufacturing activities owing to competition from cheaper imported finished products. The commercialization of agriculture took the extreme form of monoculture-specialization in Egypt, where cotton became the country's major export commodity, covering more than 85 per cent of total exports and contributing considerably to GDP growth.[53] Other Middle Eastern regions switched production from subsistence to cash crops and became net food importers: for example, Lebanon specialized in raw silk and Palestine in orange production for export. In the rest of the Ottoman Middle East, exports were more diversified, and no single commodity exceeded 15 per cent of total exports.[54] Imports were dominated by textiles, especially cotton cloth and yarn.

International trade kept on growing during the nineteenth century and in 1914 it represented a larger proportion of total trade than in 1800: the considerable intensification of the linkages between the empire and the world market was visible through a substantial expansion of trade volume and value (Figure 17.5 and appendix Table 17.A1). Total exports from the empire increased 6.5 times, from Egypt 22 times, from Syria 13.2 times and from Iraq 3 times. The rate of increase was not uniform throughout this period: for instance, during the Napoleonic wars trade declined sharply, but the period 1825–1833 was one of rapid expansion, caused by the surge in world trade and partly by the establishment of British rule in Egypt, which stimulated trade across the region.[55] The low figures for the early 1860s reflect the decline in British cotton exports during the so-called 'cotton famine' generated by the American Civil War. From the late 1870s the upward trend in trade accelerated and remained strong until the outbreak of

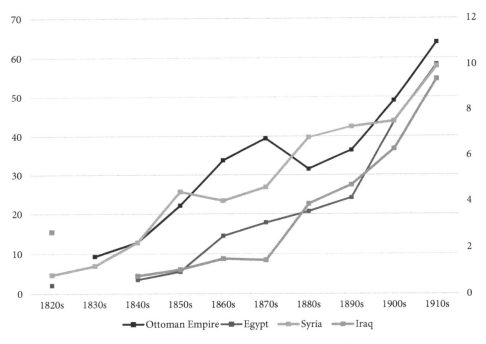

Figure 17.5 Annual average trade value in million GBP in the Middle East, 1820–1913.

Notes and Sources: Author's calculations based on: for Egypt: C. Issawi (1966), *The Economic History of the Middle East 1800–1914*. Chicago, IL: Chicago University Press, 373; R. Owen (1969), *Cotton and the Egyptian Economy, 1820–1914: A Study in Trade and Development*. Oxford: Clarendon Press, 168, 306 for Egypt. For the Ottoman Empire: Ş. Pamuk (1987), *The Ottoman Empire and European capitalism: 1820–1913. Trade, Investment and Production*. Cambridge: Cambridge University Press, 149. For Syria and Iraq: C. Issawi (1988), *The Fertile Crescent, 1800–1914: A Documentary Economic History*. Oxford: Oxford University Press, 129–30, 173–5. See Appendix Table A1 for a breakdown between imports and exports. Syria and Iraq's trade values are reported on the left axis. Syria's trade includes imports and exports from Acre, Alexandretta, Beirut, Haifa, Jaffa, Latakia, Saida, Tripoli and Tyre. Iraq's trade includes imports and exports from Basra, Baghdad and Mosul.

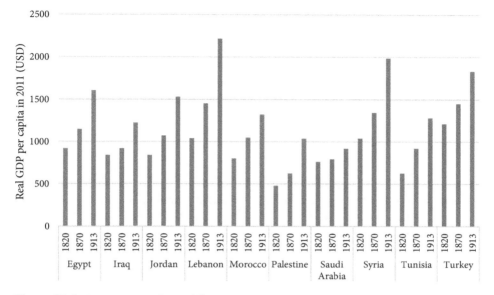

Figure 17.6 GDP estimates for Middle Eastern countries, 1820–1914.

Source: The Maddison Project: https://www.rug.nl/ggdc/historicaldevelopment/maddison/releases/
maddison-project-database-2020. Estimates based on Ş. Pamuk (2006), 'Estimating economic growth in the
Middle East since 1820', *Journal of Economic History*, 66 (3), 809–28.

the First World War. Iraq's trade followed similar patterns, and it was particularly its commercial relationship with India that flourished. Furthermore, the opening of the Suez Canal in 1869 provided a great stimulus to trade in the Gulf.

Growing commercialization in agriculture and increased integration with global markets were accompanied by slow increases in per capita income, by about 0.5 per cent per year between 1820 and 1870.[56] This is confirmed by revised Maddison's GDP estimates illustrated in Figure 17.6.

The remarkable improvements in the transport sector during the nineteenth century acted as a catalyst in linking markets worldwide, including Middle Eastern ones. The intensification of the connection with the international market had a double effect on Middle Eastern economies: on the one hand new market opportunities arose, both around the port areas served by shipping and in the regions served by railroads, while on the other hand exposure to foreign competition increased dramatically.

Specialization in primary commodity was coupled by a decline in manufacturing output. From Anatolia to Greater Syria, from Iraq to Egypt, a process of de-industrialization took place across the Middle Eastern region. However, this initial process of de-industrialization did not always proceed in a monotonic manner and slowed down in many areas of the so-called periphery, including the Middle East, between the end of the nineteenth and the beginning of the twentieth century.[57] In some cases, like that of cotton textiles production in Western Anatolia, de-industrialization was reversed, supplanted by a new stage of re-industrialization.

The process of increased integration with the world market was disrupted by the outbreak of the First World War, which led to the political and economic dismantlement of the Ottoman Empire, marking the end of its large free trade area and the beginning of significant economic divisions within the region. These dynamics were reinforced by the worldwide spread of protectionist practices, which contributed to lowering international trade flows and led to the disintegration of the global market.[58]

Trade in Services

While commodity exchange is the type of trade most documented by the literature, transactions in services represented another important economic activity in the Middle East. As science and learning flourished particularly in the early centuries of the Ottoman Empire, trade in intra-Ottoman useful knowledge and skills was most active in the fifteenth and sixteenth centuries, when the most significant advances in technology took place: from the early fifteenth century, Arabic and Persian texts produced in medieval Islam by mathematicians, astronomers and physicians of the Golden Age of Islam were translated into Turkish and circulated into Ottoman lands among the empire's communities.[59] Students from all over the Muslim world travelled to study to the main cultural centres of the empire, Istanbul, Cairo and Baghdad, where research in arithmetic, astronomy, philosophy and faith (known as the religious sciences) was carried out.[60]

The Ottoman education system, based on the madrasa, considered 'useful sciences' those that involved the study of religious subjects. As precise timekeeping was required to perform religious obligations, a big part of advances and knowledge diffusion throughout the empire were in the field of astronomy. From the thirteenth to the early twentieth century about 400 manuscripts were compiled on astronomical measuring instruments and the manufacture of timekeeping instruments, like quadrants and clocks, and circulated throughout the empire.[61] Notable indigenous innovations of this time include the construction of the Constantinople Observatory by Taqi al-Din in 1577;[62] the creation of astronomical instruments such as mechanical astronomical clocks; and the development of astronomical calculations measuring minutes and seconds by Muhammad al-Qunawi.

While the notion of linking useful knowledge to religion did not completely stifle innovation, it contributed to slowing it down in the long run.[63] It is further argued that the omission of certain natural sciences from the list of useful sciences and the narrow scholastic madrasa curriculum impeded the production of useful and practical Western knowledge which eventually promoted labour productivity in Europe.[64]

The seventeenth century saw a petering off of indigenous knowledge creation, a process that continued in the following centuries. As relations with Europe intensified, the Ottomans borrowed new knowledge, weaponry, maps, instruments and medical concepts from Europe, thus becoming importers of technology rather than innovators. This was facilitated by a broadening of the notion of 'useful knowledge', which gradually transformed and started including administrative, martial and medical fields.[65] The influx of new knowledge from Europe to the Ottoman Empire intensified during the reign of Selim III (1789–1807) and Mahmud II (1808–39) whose military, administrative and educational modernization reforms led to the secularization and Westernization of both the state apparatus and the military order. They also gave rise to a class of enlightened bureaucrats eager to import 'useful knowledge' from Europe.[66]

Islam's quintessential journey, the hajj – the pilgrimage to Mecca and Medina – represented one of the most important trades in services during the period under analysis, attracting tens of thousands of pilgrims every year. Travel was enabled by the Ottoman state's considerable investments in both the physical and textual infrastructure of pilgrimage: significant expenditures were devoted to maintain caravan routes and to the military, deployed to ensure the security of the caravans from Bedouin attacks.[67] Other cities of religious importance benefited from the large network of caravan routes connecting the Middle East to the holy cities of Mecca and Medina, as the hajj also became an extended pilgrimage to visit other sites of veneration (*ziyaret*), such the Sufi lodges, tombs, mosques, madrasas and mausoleums of Syria, Palestine, Egypt and Iraq. While until the eighteenth century the hajj was predominantly undertaken by wealthy merchants and secular and religious elites, the beginning of the steamship era and the opening of the Suez Canal in 1869 revolutionized Muslim mobility: the contraction of space and time via faster and cheaper rail and steam connections gave new travel opportunities for nearly all classes of pilgrims.[68] The new physical infrastructure by the Ottoman dynasty was matched by a concomitant investment in books explaining the hajj and translating them into high and low Ottoman idiom.[69]

On the other hand, trade in artisanal skills was predominantly local in nature, as craftsmen did not travel much across the Ottoman Empire: they did not relocate to different cities to gain experience or respond to labour market demand needs. On the contrary, once they obtained a licence to practice their profession independently (*gedik*), they would remain in their master's workshop. Overall, the Ottoman artisan world was characterized by immobility, perpetuated by the *gedik* system, which was often inherited and passed from father to son.[70]

Appendix

Table 17.A1 Annual average trade value in million British £ in the Middle East, 1820–1913

Period	Ottoman Empire		Egypt		Syria		Iraq	
	Exports	Imports	Exports	Imports	Exports	Imports	Exports	Imports
1820s			1.45	0.66	0.5	0.3	1.26	1.40
1830s	4.20	5.10			0.74	0.45		
1840s	6	6.90	1.75	1.73	1.35	0.85	0.21	0.56
1850s	9.80	12.3	3.30	2.21	2.20	2.20	0.52	0.52
1860s	15.4	18.3	10.17	4.36	2.40	1.60	0.84	0.66
1870s	18.6	20.8	12.36	5.47	2.80	1.80	0.78	0.66
1880s	15.5	16	12.97	7.66	4.60	2.20	1.75	2.12
1890s	17.7	18.6	14.57	9.56	4.20	3.07	1.91	2.79
1900s	23	26	23.59	20.05	4.90	2.60	2.68	3.60
1910–3	27.3	36.6	32.19	26.14	6.60	3.32	3.66	5.71

Sources: Author's calculations based for Egypt on C. Issawi (1966), *The Economic History of the Middle East 1800–1914*. Chicago, IL: Chicago University Press, 373; and R. Owen (1969), *Cotton and the Egyptian Economy, 1820–1914: A Study in Trade and Development*. Oxford: Clarendon Press, 168, 306. For Turkey: Ş. Pamuk (1987), *The Ottoman Empire and European capitalism: 1820–1913. Trade, Investment and Production*. Cambridge: Cambridge University Press, 149. For Syria and Iraq: C. Issawi (1988), *Fertile Crescent, 1800–1914: A Documentary Economic History*. Oxford: Oxford University Press, 129–30, 173–5.

Notes: Syria and Iraq's trade values are reported on the left axis. Syria's trade includes imports and exports from Acre, Alexandretta, Beirut, Haifa, Jaffa, Latakia, Saida, Tripoli and Tyre. Iraq's trade includes imports and exports from Basra, Baghdad and Mosul.

Notes

1. Sultan Selim I's victories ended Mamluk's rule in Syria and Egypt and the Hejaz in 1516–17, which gave the Ottomans the title of protectors of Mecca and Medina.

2. Some provinces had more autonomy than others: for instance, Egypt was responsible also for affairs in Yemen and northern Abyssinia; the governor of Baghdad for Basra, the Gulf, and part of the Arab peninsula; the governor of the Aegean islands for Tunis, Algeria and Tripolitania. H. Inalcik and D. Quataert (1994), *An Economic and Social History of the Ottoman Empire, 1300–1914*. Cambridge: Cambridge University Press.

3. Greater Syria (*ash-Shām*) comprises modern-day Syria, Lebanon and Palestine/Israel.

4. Both the East–West trade routes across the Mediterranean, connecting the Middle East to Europe via Venice and Genoa, and the North–South route linking the two regions via Damascus–Bursa–Akkerman–Lwow, were instrumental in supplying the West with so-called oriental goods: spices, silks and cotton. Inalcik and Quataert, *An Economic and Social History of the Ottoman Empire*, i:4.

5. On market integration between the Ottoman Empire and Europe, see Z. Li, L. Panza and Y. Song (2019), 'The evolution of Ottoman–European market linkages, 1469–1914: Evidence from dynamic factor models', *Explorations in Economic History*, 71 (1), 112–34 for the 1500–1800 period; and L. Panza (2013), 'Globalization and the Near East: A study of cotton market integration in Egypt and Western Anatolia', *Journal of Economic History*, 73 (3), 847–72 for the nineteenth century.

6. Most of Hungary was ceded to the Habsburgs (1699), Russia obtained the northern shores of the Black Sea (1700), Romania and Crimea (1774); in Africa, Algiers and Tunis had fallen away in the eighteenth century and then formally in the nineteenth century. These were followed by further territorial losses in the nineteenth century: nationalist uprisings in the Balkans led to the independence of Serbia (1830), Greece (1832), Moldavia and Wallachia (1856), Bulgaria, Montenegro, Bosnia, Herzegovina and other areas of the Caucasus (1878); Cyprus fell into British hands in 1878.

7. For a discussion of the role of orientalism in shaping Ottoman historiography, see H. I. Inan (1987), *The Ottoman Empire and the World-Economy*. Cambridge: Cambridge University Press.

8. L. Panza (2012), 'Globalisation and the Ottoman Empire: A study of integration between Ottoman and world cotton markets', unpublished PhD dissertation, La Trobe University.

9. J. de Vries (1984), *European Urbanization, 1500–1800*. London: Methuen.

10. Urbanization is defined as total urban population divided by total population in each region. In 800 CE the urbanization rate in the Middle East and North Africa was around 6 per cent, almost three times higher than in Europe. Over the next centuries, Europe's urbanization rate rose much faster than in the Middle East, and in 1800, Europe had also overtaken it. See M. Bosker, E. Buringh and J. L. Van Zanden (2013), 'From Baghdad to London: Unraveling urban development in Europe, the Middle East, and North Africa, 800–1800', *Review of Economics and Statistics*, 95 (4), 1418–37, especially Figure 3 and discussion on p. 1424.

11. M. Genç (1994), 'Ottoman industry in the eighteenth century: General framework, characteristics, and main trends', in D. Quataert (ed.), *Manufacturing in the Ottoman Empire and Turkey, 1500–1950*. Albany, NY: SUNY Press, 59–86.

12. See L. Panza (2020), 'From a common empire to colonial rule: Commodity market disintegration in the Near East', CEPR DP 17349, on the effect of the disruption of the Ottoman Empire on market integration in the Near East.

13. See, among others, F. Braudel (1995 [orig. French 1949]). *The Mediterranean and the Mediterranean world in the Age of Philip II.* London: University of California Press; Inalcik and Quataert, *An Economic and Social History of the Ottoman Empire*; Ş. Pamuk (1987), *The Ottoman Empire and European Capitalism 1820–1913.* Cambridge: Cambridge University Press.

14. Ş. Pamuk (2021), 'The Ottoman Empire, 1700–1870', in S. Broadberry and K. Fukao (eds), *The Cambridge Economic History of the Modern World,* vol. 1: *1700 to 1870.* Cambridge: Cambridge University Press, 173.

15. The first capitulations were granted to the Genoese in 1453; France received them in 1535, Britain in 1580, the Dutch in 1612.

16. R. Davis (1961), 'England and the Mediterranean, 1570–1670', in F. J. Fisher (ed.), *Essays in the Economic and Social History of Tudor and Stuart England.* Cambridge: Cambridge University Press, 118.

17. Davis, 'England and the Mediterranean'.

18. Inalcik and Quataert, *An Economic and Social History of the Ottoman Empire.*

19. After reaching Egypt and Syria, Indian spices were exported to Western markets via Venice which supplied a vast area of Europe including Italy, Germany and Central Europe. D. Sella (1968), 'The rise and fall of the Venetian woolen industry', in B. Pullan (ed.), *Crisis and Change in the Venetian Economy in the 16th and 17th Centuries.* London: Methuen & Company, 106–26. On the other hand, the spices reaching Bursa and Istanbul were exported overland to the Balkans, Eastern Europe and Lwow via caravan routes. Inalcik and Quataert, *An Economic and Social History of the Ottoman Empire.*

20. The Arabian Peninsula covered an important share of Basra's international and regional trade via the export of horses, fabrics and cloaks of camel wool, Syrian soap and Yemen's madder.

21. R. Davis (1970), 'English imports from the Middle East, 1580–1780', in M. A. Cook (ed.), *Studies in the Economic History of the Middle East.* London: Routledge, 195.

22. K. N. Chaudhuri (1978), *The Trading World of Asia and the English East India Company, 1660–1760.* Cambridge: Cambridge University Press; S. Broadberry and B. Gupta (2009), 'Lancashire, India, and shifting competitive advantage in cotton textiles, 1700–1850: The neglected role of factor prices', *Economic History Review,* 62 (2), 279–305.

23. B. McGowan (1981), *Economic life in Ottoman Europe: Taxation, trade and the struggle for land, 1600–1800.* Cambridge: Cambridge University Press.

24. Ö. Lufti Barkan (1975), 'The price revolution of the sixteenth century: A turning point in the economic history of the Near East', *International Journal of Middle East Studies,* 6 (1), 3–28.

25. Özmucur and Pamuk (2002).

26. A. Raymond (1973-4), *Artisans et commerçants au Caire au XVIIIe siècle,* 2 vols. Damascus: Presses de l'Ifpo.

27. Inalcik and Quataert, *An Economic and Social History of the Ottoman Empire.*

28. Ibid.

29. An estimated 198 tons of raw silk passed through the Ottoman Empire to reach Europe every year in the seventeenth century. Ibid.

30. Particularly important were olive oil and soap production in Tripoli and cotton weaving in Idlib.

31. Pamuk, 'Ottoman Empire, 1700–1870'.

32. B. McGowan (1994), 'The age of the Ayans, 1699–1812', in H. Inalcik and D. Quataert (eds), *An Economic and Social History of the Ottoman Empire, 1300–1914.* Cambridge: Cambridge University Press, 662.

33. G. Piterberg (1990), 'The formation of an Ottoman Egyptian elite in the 18th century', *International Journal of Middle East Studies*, 22 (3), 275–89. While tax collectors and *ayans* were at first separate groups with distinct functions, a single class emerged with time. There were two types of *ayan*: notables whose families had ties to the local elites; and centrally appointed officials. A. Yaycioglu (2016), *Partners of the Empire: The Crisis of the Ottoman Order in the Age of Revolutions*. Stanford, CA: Stanford University Press.

34. A. Salzmann (1993), 'An ancien régime revisited: "Privatization" and political economy in the eighteenth-century Ottoman Empire', *Politics & Society*, 21 (4), 393–423.

35. Ş. Pamuk (2004), 'Institutional change and the longevity of the Ottoman Empire, 1500–1800', *Journal of Interdisciplinary History*, 25 (2), 225–47.

36. M. Genç (1995), 'L'économie ottomane et la guerre au XVIIIe siècle', *Turcica*, 27, 177–96; Pamuk, 'Ottoman Empire, 1700–1870'.

37. Pamuk, 'Ottoman Empire, 1700–1870'. The relative insulation of most Middle Eastern markets from European competition in manufactures, particularly in the interior before the nineteenth century, allowed the expansion of a range of manufacturing activities, especially textiles. S. Faroqhi (2011), 'Ottoman cotton textiles: The story of a success that did not last, 1500–1800', in G. Riello and P. Parthasarathi (eds), *The Spinning World: A Global History of Cotton Textiles 1200–1850*. Oxford: Oxford University Press, 2009, 89–103.

38. McGowan, 'Age of the Ayans', 727.

39. Pamuk, 'Ottoman Empire, 1700–1870'.

40. Li, Panza and Song, 'Evolution of Ottoman–European market linkages'.

41. McGowan, 'Age of the Ayans'.

42. E. Eldem (1999), *French Trade in Istanbul in the Eighteenth Century*. Leiden: Brill.

43. France was Egypt's main foreign trade partner throughout the eighteenth century, with the re-export of Yemeni coffee dominating their bilateral trade until the 1740s. Other exports included rice, wool, cotton thread, flax, linen, pelts and saffron, while Egypt imported colonial goods, dyestuffs and luxuries. France also dominated the foreign trade of Tunisia and Algeria. McGowan, 'Age of the Ayans', 732.

44. The balance of trade was unfavourable to the Ottomans, as imports into the Ottoman Empire far exceeded exports to India. Pamuk, 'Ottoman Empire, 1700–1870'.

45. Faroqhi, 'Ottoman cotton textiles'.

46. Genç, 'Ottoman industry', 61.

47. Salzmann, 'An ancien régime revisited', 406; Pamuk, 'Ottoman Empire, 1700–1870', 174.

48. Genç, 'Ottoman industry'.

49. Ş. Pamuk (2000), *A Monetary History of the Ottoman Empire*. Cambridge: Cambridge University Press; N. Hanna (2011), *Artisan Entrepreneurs in Cairo and Early Modern Capitalism (1600–1800)*. Ithaca, NY: Syracuse University Press. The silver content of the Ottoman lira declined by more than 90 per cent as a response to increase war expenditures and borrowing; price levels increased more than twelvefold from 1770 to 1840. Pamuk, *A Monetary History*.

50. R. Kasaba (1988), *The Ottoman Empire and the World Economy: The Nineteenth Century*. Albany, NY: State University of New York; R. Owen (1993), *The Middle East in the World Economy*. London: Methuen; Ş. Pamuk (1987), *The Ottoman Empire and European capitalism: 1820–1913. Trade, Investment and Production*. Cambridge: Cambridge University Press; Panza, 'Globalisation and the Ottoman Empire'.

51. Muhammad Ali, recognized by Istanbul as the Ottoman governor of Egypt in 1805, transformed the country from a subordinated province to a military and politically

autonomous power. L. Panza, and J. G. Williamson (2015), 'Did Muhammad Ali foster industrialization in early nineteenth-century Egypt?', *Economic History Review*, 68 (1), 79–100.

52. The Anglo-Turkish convention fixed duties at 5 per cent for imports, 3 per cent for transit commodities and 12 per cent for exports. In 1861–2 import duties rose to 8 per cent and export duties reduced to 8 per cent, with a further reduction of 1 per cent a year until they reached 1 per cent. Export duties rose to 11 per cent in 1907 and again to 15 per cent in 1914. C. Issawi (1988), *The Fertile Crescent, 1800–1914: A Documentary Economic History*. Oxford: Oxford University Press, 127–8.

53. U. Karakoç, Ş. Pamuk and L. Panza (2017), 'Industrialization in Egypt and Turkey, 1870–2010', in K. H. O'Rourke and J. G. Williamson (eds), *The Spread of Modern Industry to the Periphery since 1871*. Oxford: Oxford University Press, 142–65.

54. Inalcik and Quataert, *An Economic and Social History of the Ottoman Empire*, 833.

55. Issawi, *The Fertile Crescent*, 131.

56. Ş. Pamuk (2006), 'Estimating economic growth in the Middle East since 1820', *Journal of Economic History*, 66 (3), 809–28. Using real wages of unskilled construction workers in the Ottoman Empire to measure changes in living standards, S. Özmucur and Ş. Pamuk (2002), 'Real wages and standards of living in the Ottoman Empire, 1489–1914', *Journal of Economic History*, 62 (2), 293–321 find that they increased by about 30 per cent between mid-eighteenth and mid-nineteenth century, and by another 40 per cent during the late nineteenth and early twentieth centuries.

57. L. Panza (2014), 'De-industrialization and re-industrialization in the Middle East: Reflections on the cotton industry in Egypt and in the Izmir region', *Economic History Review*, 67 (1), 146–69.

58. W. Hynes, D. S. Jacks and K. H. O'Rourke (2012), 'Commodity market disintegration in the interwar period', *European Review of Economic History*, 16 (2), 119–43.

59. G. Saliba (1995), *A History of Arabic Astronomy: Planetary Theories during the Golden Age of Islam*. New York: New York University Press, vol. 2.

60. E. İhsanoğlu (2002), *History of the Ottoman State, Society & Civilisation*. Istanbul: IRCICA.

61. F. Günergun (2021), 'Timekeepers and Sufi mystics: Technical knowledge bearers of the Ottoman Empire', *Technology and Culture*, 62 (2), 348–72.

62. Taqi al-Din (1526–85) is excellent evidence of sixteenth century knowledge exchange: he was a madrasa-educated scholar, born in Damascus who studied in both Damascus and Cairo Islamic jurisprudence, exegesis, mathematics and astronomy; he authored a book on mechanical clock construction and moved to Istanbul to teach at the Edirnekapı Madrasa.

63. İhsanoğlu, *History of the Ottoman State*.

64. T. Kuran (2011), *The Long Divergence: How Islamic Law Held Back the Middle East*. Princeton, NJ: Princeton University Press.

65. Günergun, 'Timekeepers and Sufi mystics'.

66. M. A. Yalçınkaya (2015), *Learned Patriots: Debating Science, State, and Society in the Nineteenth-Century Ottoman Empire*. Chicago, IL: University of Chicago Press.

67. N. Shafir (2020), 'In an Ottoman Holy land: The Hajj and the road from Damascus, 1500–1800', *History of Religions*, 60 (1), 1–36.

68. M. C. Low (2020), *Imperial Mecca: Ottoman Arabia and the Indian Ocean Hajj*. New York: Columbia University Press.

69. Shafir, 'In an Ottoman Holy land'.

70. S. Faroqhi (2014), *Travel and Artisans in the Ottoman Empire: Employment and Mobility in the Early Modern Era*. London: I.B. Tauris.

CHAPTER 18
THE NEW WORLD SILVER AND THE MAKING
OF A GLOBAL ECONOMY
Alejandra Irigoin

After the publication of *The Great Divergence* more than twenty years ago (2000), the knowledge of the divergent economic trajectories within Eurasia has leapt forwards, fostering a substantial shift in the focus of economic history scholarship from Europe and the Americas to Asia. In that journey, the New World has remained marginal to such reciprocal comparison.[1] According to Adam Smith, the discovery of the Americas and of a passage to the East Indies by the Cape of Good Hope had been the 'two greatest and most important events recorded in the history of mankind'.[2] Economic historians of the pre-modern period have emphasized one or the other of these two events leading alternatively to what we might call a Euro-Atlantic centrism (as for instance in the concept of a triangular trade proposed by Eric Williams) or to a Sino-Asian one (for instance in the Great Divergence debate). Yet, these narratives have provided little help in understanding why Adam Smith's East and West Indies were so crucial to the European economy, and arguably the development of a global economy.

With a few exceptions, the incorporation of the New World into the pre-modern international economy has been a subject of secondary order in recent studies in global economic history. Jonathan Hersh and Joachim Voth underline the contribution of the New World in terms of ghost acreage for the production of food and fibres for differential European consumption and living standards. More recently, Nuno Palma has estimated the macroeconomic impact of the windfall that Europeans derived from importing and re-exporting precious metals.[3] A vast literature on the Columbian Exchange has revealed the New World contribution to the stock of biodiversity, and – more prosaically – of foodstuff and raw materials to the rest of the world derived from her natural resource abundance. The result is unclear, and not always seen as a blessing. Some economists have considered it a 'curse' for the region's subsequent development.[4] Others attributed to the institutions at the root of an extractive path dependent development explaining the relative lower living standards alleged in recent global comparisons.[5] Factor endowments, and a particular European political economy have created a narrative that associates Spanish or Iberian colonialism with the exploitation of New World riches and peoples.[6] Finally, the trade – and domestic reproduction – of enslaved people and commodities is also central to the economic narratives of the Atlantic New World, although most economic historians of Europe are yet to fully account for the economic, financial and fiscal returns of slave trade and of slave labour in the macroeconomic history of Europe.[7] Interpretations based on growth models focus on the endogenous sources of development. Such a perspective obscures the role of long-distance trade in fostering the Smithian economic growth of the pre-modern period.

Trade matters and arguably trade with the Americas is intimately associated with the making of the global economy after 1500.[8] Of the basket of American goods, silver was the most conspicuous, and silver production, manufacturing and trade became fundamental for the development of a global economy. This chapter highlights the significance of the New World in global economic history by concentrating on the role of Spanish American silver. It reassesses the factors that drove the expansion of trade, and the integration of markets to an unprecedented level in the three centuries after 1500. In so doing, it also revisits available narratives of the development of the early global economy, away from views centred in either Asia or Europe, as it revises current interpretations of the region's own economic history.

Silver was 'indispensable' for the European trade with Asia with decisive consequences for the elasticity of demand and of supply in the Old World economies; it had no substitute and was available in extraordinarily large quantities in Spanish America. This is a truism in economic history; however, the global impact of silver and the consequences for the New World remain a work in progress. Historians have mostly focused on partial aspects of the production – i.e. labour mainly, and mostly on a regional or local scale – a bias from an excessive 'national' focus. Mining is thus analysed separately from commerce, often relying on fiscal sources and merchants accounts, and from minting, overlooking the technological and financial implications of money manufacturing at the scale Spanish America did it. There is a fair volume of quantitative information on output and coinage – less so on exchanges – but there is still little understanding of the transformation of silver into money. Increasingly since the 1680s, American silver was manufactured, traded and used mostly in a monetary form until the collapse of mining following Independence from Spain.[9] For the world economy, quantity, however, was much less important than its quality; after all, rising China demand for silver at its peak was just a fraction of the extraordinary volume produced in Spanish America. It was the quality – on top of such abundance – that made of the coins the preeminent means of payment of the international economy, i.e. a currency standard for settlement of long distance trade for more than two centuries before a Gold Standard came to define the classic economic globalization of the late nineteenth and twentieth centuries. This chapter considers the Americas' contribution to the world economy through the role of silver.

Silver, Trade and the Early Modern World Economy

Monetary historians explain the stream of silver flowing towards Asia as the result of a difference in gold-to-silver ratios within Eurasia.[10] For reasons not yet explored, unlike Europeans, Asians preferred silver as money to gold in their means of exchange and payment. Given the size of these economies and populations, the demand for silver had major consequences.[11] The New World produced large quantities of silver – and to a lesser extent gold in the early eighteenth century – that soon dwarfed the supply by Central European mines estimated at 50 tons per year at its peak in the 1540s.[12] By the early sixteenth century, Japan had adopted the Korean technology of cupellation (the process of separating precious metals from ore); production boomed and Japan became the source of silver for China, the world's largest economy of the time. The Japanese output peaked in the 1620s at 130–160 tons per annum.[13] Although production continued into the eighteenth century, the level of exports declined so dramatically that Japanese silver was already all but absent from China in the 1680s. The 'Japanese silver century' (1580–1680) paled, however, in comparison with the quantities and, more importantly, the higher quality of Spanish American silver arriving in Asia through the Portuguese.[14] In those years, the New World aggregate output was already 280–300 tons a year and it doubled in the following century. It is estimated that all Spanish American mining combined might have consistently produced 75 to 80 per cent of world supply at the time.[15]

The global impact was enormous: between 1500 and 1820, aggregate global trade grew at an average rate of 1 per cent per annum and European intercontinental trade in the eighteenth century grew at 1.26 per cent.[16] The aggregate production of Spanish American silver grew at 1.09 per cent a year in the same period. European tonnage to Asia grew at 1.16 per cent and Mexican silver production – the major but not the single producer of silver in Spanish America – grew at 1.35 per cent over the eighteenth century.[17] Whereas there are a number of theories that might explain the relation between the growth trends of world trade and the expansion of European commerce, the co-evolution between the development in the extraction and trade of silver and the growth of world trade in this long run is not fully appraised.[18]

Global monetary historians point to arbitrage – that is buying cheap in one market for sale in another where the goods are expensive – that Europeans carried out in their silver commerce with Asia and especially with China.[19] The relative abundance or scarcity of specific metal can explain the different bimetallic rates in the Americas, Europe and Asia. However, the gold/silver ratio also reveals a lack of relation between the price of silver and its relative availability in world markets. For instance, in China the ratio equalized to that of Europe by 1750, though silver imports not only continued but also expanded further with significant increases in the latter part of the century.[20] As argued elsewhere, by 1800 it was apparent that what China, and perhaps Asia at large, demanded was not silver bullion per se, but specie, a widely acceptable means of payment that China lacked.[21] Without its own coinage of silver, China became reliant on foreign money and the currency standard that the Spanish American coin provided. British market prices of silver on the other hand, do not seem to match any trend in the observed gold/silver ratio in the eighteenth century (Figure 18.1). Britain had a Mint and a standard certified by the Trial of the Pyx (annual testing of coinage) against which an official par value (base) for all foreign silver and gold was established.[22]

It remains true, however, that the arbitrage between rich and poor silver markets produced a windfall for Europe. Macroeconomic historians have estimated the 'substantial and persistent' material impact on real economic activity that the monetary

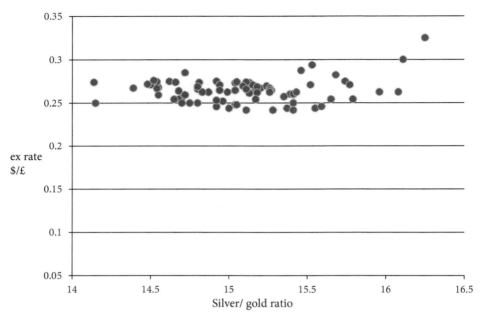

Figure 18.1 The Market Price of Silver Peso in Sterling, in London 1717–1818.

Sources: Silver/Gold Ratio from L. H. Officer (2016), *Between the Dollar-Sterling Gold Points: Exchange Rates, Parity, and Market Behavior.* Cambridge: Cambridge University Press; Exchange rate from E. M. Kelly (1976), *Spanish Dollar and Silver Tokens, An Account of the Issues of the Bank of England, 1797–1816.* London: Spink & Son.

expansion in early modern Europe caused by the injection of American precious metals.[23] To Europe, American silver was a means to trade in Asia. Silver accounted for 93 per cent of the European cargo values to China and 79 per cent of the India-bound cargo.[24] With American silver, the European companies in Asia bought spices, tea, cotton and silk textiles for European consumers, for re-export to Africa to purchase slaves and gold, and to the Americas to purchase silver and 'luxury' foodstuff mostly produced with African labour.[25] In the Americas, African slaves cultivated commercial crops such as sugar and coffee for the growing consumer markets in Europe, thus establishing a truly global multilateral trade in people, goods and money.[26] Later, American foodstuff, dyes and cotton found a market in Europe, but silver and gold were the main returns of the Spanish New World until well into the late eighteenth century.

Acting as intermediaries, European traders linked different parts of the early modern world economy. Economic historians have argued, however, for a 'peripheral' role for the New World in the economic development of Europe since allegedly three quarters of the commodity exports in Europe had another European port as destination.[27] They did not, however, consider the actual composition of such intra-European trade: American, African and Asian commodities such as textiles, tea, sugar, slaves and silver were key to European trade as they were re-exported within, and indeed beyond, Europe. Along the way, European states taxed their imports and consumption, thus creating much needed revenue for the rising European nation states.[28] The old mercantilist idea that precious metals were to be stocked, misunderstood the profits derived in their intermediation; of all these goods only coined silver had no surrogate. A more modern understanding of mercantilism now explains how specialization and trade contributed to European economic growth. Thus, without silver, the scale of European commerce would have been much smaller and any resulting Smithian growth improbable.[29]

The Production of Silver in Latin America

How was silver obtained from the New World? Mining in Spanish America was a wholly private enterprise, which enjoyed royal subsidies for taxes paid to the king on the volume of metal produced. Spanish colonialism imposed the royal ownership of land and the subsoil. Thus, the king granted the right to mine the precious metals to individuals – even to indigenous communities – for a direct tax share on the production. Thus, mining, smelting and refining were private affairs. Even minting was in private hands, by design until the 1680s, or by default as mints offices in America were purchased. Owing to the collapse of the indigenous population, coerced labour was the exception rather than the norm, despite the emphasis by both neo-institutionalist and Marxist economic historians on the exploitative nature of Spanish colonialism.[30] African slaves made up only a small part of the Potosí workforce and Huancavelica's quicksilver mines and they mostly worked in the foundries of the mints.[31] Hugely concentrated in one highly productive mine in today's Bolivia, other forms of unfree labour existed: the *Mita* (quechua for 'shift' or 'turn') was an adaptation of the pre-Hispanic tributary system that persisted under Spanish rule. Labour was regularly drafted from neighbouring peasant communities for periodical shifts at the mines as part of their tribute to the Spanish king. At the expense of the indigenous communities, owning collectively their land, mining withdrew adult male labour for mostly unskilled jobs. *Mita* workers coexisted with a larger number of free and occasionally self-employed labourers, whose numbers paradoxically grew with the decline of the Potosí mine productivity.[32] This form of unfree labour performed more as a 'rent' to miners than a core input to mining. Mining was geographically more dispersed in Mexico, so competition for scarce labour favoured other forms of labour organization. Large and smaller mines there employed overwhelmingly free wage labour – a very sizable workforce of around 50,000 men in the eighteenth century.[33]

The largest mining site in the northern periphery of the Spanish settlement, Zacatecas, developed from the mid-sixteenth century in an area without a sizable native population. Indigenous and increasingly mixed-race people made a, spatially, very mobile labour force in mining. African labour, by contrast, was not best suited for mining at more than 2,500 metres altitude as in Zacatecas, or at 4,200 metres altitude in the Potosí mine, though slaves and wandering labourers worked the gold mines of Colombia and Brazil. Indigenous people and increasingly mestizos provided the bulk of the labour force in silver mining. Spaniards were relatively more numerous among refiners, smelters and renters of mines, and definitively controlled the exchange of ore and bars for coin as they ran the financing of mining and controlled the mint offices.

The persistence of communal property rights to land by the indigenous communities was a by-product of the collapse of the native population that followed the encounter with Europeans. It warranted the subsistence of peasants when the population shrank but increased the opportunity cost of wage labour even in the most populated regions of the New World when the population recovered. Throughout, nominal wages were high and 'sticky' over time. This explains the extraordinarily high (and steady) nominal wage of compulsory labourers in Potosí; they received about 12.5 grams of fine silver a day, a rate comparable to skilled labour in late eighteenth-century London.[34] Indeed, earnings were raised and adjusted via sizable non-monetary compensation that followed the demographic trends. Their reduction from the 1780s followed population recovery and the growing impoverishment of indigenous villages so other coerced forms appeared (as debt peonage) in the nineteenth century. This dynamic makes Malthusian varieties of comparative living standards models unsuitable and inadequate for the colonial New World.[35] The combination of indigenous property rights, regulated prices of urban food supplies and the peculiarity of a silver-abundant economy shaped a very different labour market and higher standards of living in Spanish America than recent studies posit.

So, mining was widespread both geographically and socially. The location and size of mines varied more in Mexico than in Spanish Peru, where the population and silver were more concentrated and compulsory forms of labour persisted longer. Potosí production peaked in the early seventeenth century, to then start a slow but protracted decline into the nineteenth century. With more numerous and dispersed silver deposits of comparable size, and a faster population recovery, Mexico became the dominant world supplier of silver in the eighteenth century, producing an estimated 45 to 55 per cent of the total world silver.[36] Potosí continued producing silver in the nineteenth century, though with marginal decreasing profits. Other mining sites, such as Pasco and Oruro, operated throughout the period.[37]

Europeans had originally relied on indigenous technology for the extraction, smelting and casting of silver in wind-blown furnaces.[38] The incorporation of amalgamation (the blending of pulverized ore with mercury) and the availability of mercury in nearby Huancavelica in the Andes, or from Almaden in Spain, fostered a steady growth in the production from the late sixteenth century. To some Andean historians, the new technology was also prejudicial to indigenous miners, subjecting them to a wage labour relation in lieu of former sharing systems. This, together with the commutation of tribute in kind for cash payments established a mix of compulsory and market relations for production factors and goods very early in the Spanish New World.

Yet, the volumes produced are extraordinary. Throughout the period, the combined output of Mexican and Peruvian mines added 300 tons a year to a stock that largely exceeded the contemporary Asian demand. At its peak in the 1780s to 1800s, registered silver output in Spanish America totalled 600 tons a year. Even at the peak of gold production in Brazil in the 1730s and 1740s silver never represented less than 60 per cent of precious metals total output. Gold and silver accounted for around 60–70 per cent of the value of the whole of New World exports throughout the 1740s. This share diminished only with the growth of exports from the British colonies in the mainland and record production in West Indian sugar by the 1760s. Yet by 1800 silver still constituted one-third of total New World exports, and at least two-thirds of Iberian America's. War in Europe between the 1790s and 1810s made the trade more direct, raised the purchasing power of silver and thus lowered the price of imports, giving an additional boost to the production of non-precious metal commodities in Spanish America. Silver production collapsed only with the implosion of Spanish rule in the1820s creating serious problems for the succeeding republics.[39]

So, if silver was 'indispensable' for European trade in Asia, trade with Spanish America was a 'necessity'. Silver was obtained only by means of trade – not from colonial extraction. Historians like Hamilton for the seventeenth century, and Morineau and Garcia Baquero for the eighteenth century, showed that, until the late 1770s, at least 70 per cent of the 'treasure imports' to Spain was made of privately owned silver. Moreover, at around 20 million pesos annual average, private remittances reached up to 90 per cent of total silver sent to Europe in the 1790s when exports boomed.[40] With such an extraordinary volume of private silver shipped out of the New World, the levels of private consumption attained in the New World ought to be of equivalent significance.[41] With a population of 12 million estimated for Spanish America and another 2–2.5 million for the whole population of Brazil – total population of Iberian America by 1800 amounted to about 15 million inhabitants;[42] this was about one and a half times that of Spain or Britain and 1:20-24 of China's. It should not be surprising then that the greatest risk for commerce in the Atlantic and the Pacific were glutted markets.[43] However, comparative studies of living standards seem to underestimate this potential for consumption.

The Spanish Silver Trade

Over the period 1580s to 1730s, export values increased ten times, from around a million pesos a year in the 1580s to 10 million (250 tons of pure silver) in the 1730s. These volumes doubled after the 1750s and increased by another half to nearly 30 million (750 tons) annual average in the 1770s. Thus, European re-export of silver to China, estimated at an annual average of 114 tons of silver between 1719 and 1833, was less important than we may think. By and large, the first destination of silver was Spain, through a trade that was carried out via the few authorized ports – Seville first and Cadiz since 1700 – from where silver was re-exported into Europe and beyond. Figure 18.2 shows the relation between output and coinage of silver in America and shipments to Europe throughout the eighteenth century.

For most of the eighteenth century, when data are available, the relation between the pace of mining and minting, and the shipment of silver to Europe was weak, suggesting some time lag in the process.[44] The export of precious metals to Europe was not immediate or automatic as often assumed. Instead, most of the silver remained in circulation in the domestic economy before it was traded for goods and services

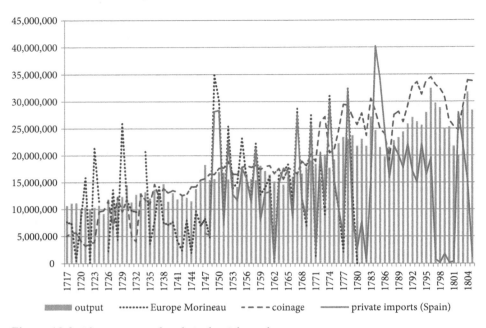

Figure 18.2 Silver output and trade in the eighteenth century.
Sources: For silver output, J. TePaske, and K. Brown (2010), *A New World of Gold and Silver*, Leiden, Brill.
For silver trade at Cadiz: A. Garcia Baquero (1996), 'Las remesas de metales preciosos americanos en el siglo
XVIII: Una aritmética controvertida', *Hispania*, Appendix. For silver arrivals in Europe, M. Morineau (1986),
*Incroyables gazettes et fabuleux métaux: Les retours des trésors américains d'après les gazettes hollandaises,
16e-18e siècles*. Paris: Editions de la MSH. For coinage, author's elaboration from G. Cespedes (1996), *Las
Cecas Indianas en 1536–1825*. Madrid: Fabrica de Moneda y Timbre.

overseas. Although agriculture accounted for the largest share of the colonial economy,
mining was its engine. Provisioning, labour and services such as transport disseminated
silver domestically throughout the empire. Internal and external commerce was the
main source of revenue for the Spanish administration as trade and consumption
taxes became the fiscal backbone of the empire in the eighteenth century.[45] Thus, the
growth of population and of mining, together with the expansion of the Europeanized
economy over the territory suggests that some Smithian growth was ongoing. Living
standards estimates indicate a declining trend in these decades when the population
was replenished, without a clear explanation. Concerned with the supply-side aspects
of silver mining, economic historians have misread the importance of consumption and
the expansion of the domestic economy in the New World.

Surely the markup price of goods exported to Spanish America was huge considering
the various costs incurred: transportation costs within and outside Europe, trading costs
and taxes, as most of these goods were re-exports from Asia and other European countries,
plus the intermediation costs charged by the Spanish privileged participants in the
American trade. Economic historians have assumed the New World need for imports as
driving the direction of these flows. However, the Spanish settlements in the mainland and

in the Caribbean islands were self-sufficient in food with plenty of high-quality foodstuffs like sugar and meat – thus the consumption levels assumed by studies of comparative living standard seem clearly underestimated. There is also an idea that the Spanish commercial system was organized for the profit of the Spanish king and metropolitan merchants, to the prejudice of economic development in the region. However, the structure of this trade is poorly known. Indeed, as in Africa, European exporters over the Pacific and the Atlantic were price takers when trading for silver in Spanish America.[46]

Despite the bad reputation of their monopolistic practices, metropolitan merchants enabling other European exchanges in Seville or Cadiz had a limited effective control on the commerce with overseas possessions. A maritime empire with an undeveloped merchant navy seems an oxymoron. Yet, Spain's shipping capacity did not match the geographical and maritime extension of its empire. Remarkably, trade to the Spanish East Indies, the so-called Manila Galleon, was 'rationed' to one or two ships a year only.[47] The size of the two fleets crossing the Atlantic in the 1720s and 1730s averaged barely 10–12,000 tons on a dozen vessels per journey. On arrival, the fleet and galleons traded their goods for silver in timed fairs in Jalapa/Veracruz and Portobello/Cartagena as in Acapulco, where similarly privileged cartels of local merchants controlled the supply of silver and the sale of imports further inland. From the 1740s, fleets started to be spaced out and were discontinued in the 1760s; occasional individual vessels doubled in number, increasing the risks of glutted markets and prejudicing the rents of those intermediaries. After the 1760s more ports were licensed in the metropolis and colonies to trade, legalizing de facto an existing large irregular trade.[48] This 'liberalization' eroded the rents of cartels that controlled each step of the trade. More frequent shipping brought in increasing competition; the domestic purchasing power of silver, so artificially maintained, necessarily reduced giving an opportunity to other investments, as for instance in land purchase, and to export other commodities. When Spain allowed US shipping to carry colonial commerce as 'Neutrals' after 1797, they were already regulars: more than 200 foreign ships a year stopped in Havana in the 1800s.[49] The Napoleonic Wars threw the Spanish American trade open to the United States' vessels in the 1790s and to the British after Trafalgar in 1805. This explains why US merchants became dominant in the silver trade to Asia after the 1780s. They supplied 80 per cent of the estimated 3,800 tons of silver that China imported after 1790 and were large exporters to India too into the nineteenth century.

Formally, until 1778, Andalusian ports enjoyed the privilege of organizing the trade with America. The subsequent 'greater trade opening' did not change Cadiz's primacy among Spanish ports as the city continued receiving 75–80 per cent of all American imports in the last two decades of the eighteenth century. In reality, foreigners had always dominated the Spanish colonial commerce. The *Catastro de Ensenada*, a census of the 640 traders in Cadiz compiled in 1762, reveal that around 80 per cent of the commerce was in foreign hands, 42 per cent controlled by French mercantile houses, 15 per cent by English/Irish and Dutch/Flemish merchants respectively, and 10 per cent by Italians.[50] Spaniards were numerous among the smallest freighters or acted as figureheads for foreign houses.[51] Indeed, the Cadiz merchant guilds (Consulado) were constantly at odds with similar corporations in the New World or in Asia as they competed for the control of silver returns for foreign goods.[52] The influence of the powerful Consulados of Mexico and Lima started to wane and in the 1790s when similar corporations appeared in Caracas, Guatemala, Guadalajara in Mexico, and Buenos Aires, Cartagena, Veracruz, Havana, Santiago de Chile and Manila with royal charters for their own mercantile jurisdiction. More direct trade meant that more silver was imported with lower trade costs – at better prices as arbitrage was reduced – into Europe. Neither the composition nor the origin of goods changed, but terms of trade improved for New World producers, and gave a boost to non-precious metals commodities. Access to direct shipping opened a cleavage between new commercial interests and the established merchant networks that controlled inland commerce. The carry trade by the US and Britain catalysed competition among colonial elites and led to the civil conflict that followed the collapse of the Spanish government in the 1810s.

Elsewhere, silver improved the barter terms of trade for Europeans. Silver eased trade in the Baltic, and with the Ottoman Empire, in Central Asia, and certainly with maritime Asia.[53] For example, in the 1620s the President of the English East India Company (EEIC) in Surat wrote to the Company in London: 'Should the Company determine to revive that trade, it would be advisable, instead of sending *rials* thither direct, to forward them, in the first instance, to Surat, where they might be invested in goods that would produce 100 per cent profit at Bantam.'[54] Still in the 1800s, US merchants trading outside the Chinese Hong reckoned that deals including silver would improve by 20 per cent the price they ought to pay for tea in Canton. Allegedly tea, silks and nankeens were often not procurable on credit or by bartering with other goods, as they were 'cash goods'.[55] And the cash was overwhelmingly Spanish American reals or dollars (pesos) after the 1730s, so silver continued flowing into Asia beyond the equalization of the bimetallic ratios within Asia.

Thus, the 'silverization' of the world economy ought to have an equivalent impact on levels of private consumption of the relatively smaller population, roughly one twenty-fifth that of China, in the silver-rich New World, inequality notwithstanding. The local production of manufactures there oscillated between the 'protection' of geography, high transport costs (both overseas and overland) and the costs of intermediation of several rent-seekers, but also from the underlying Dutch Disease effects from the growing world demand of silver.

The quantity of silver exported was probably less important than, and of secondary importance to the purchasing power of silver in Asia and the profits Europeans made in its global re-export. These were not 'super-profits' derived from the exploitation of extra-European people and riches. They were the rents that all mercantilist states in Europe competed for in order to obtain a less costly and more direct access to silver. Thus, silver as driver of global trade was also the driver of institutional and production changes in European economies to secure cheaper goods and more profitable trade. That meant the increasing substitution of imports and lower domestic financial costs of war making. Ultimately, it was the marginal acquisition of silver which allowed the continuation of trade; and trade was the means to increase the elasticity of supply and demand in the European economy. Mercantilism might have been a zero-sum game within Europe, but the process of Smithian growth worldwide since 1500 owed a great deal to the intermediation of silver and the trade it fostered.

Silver in Europe and Asia

It is unclear whether silver was imported into Europe and Asia as a commodity or money. In any case, the overwhelming proportion of it was coined with very consistent pure silver content, size and weight.[56] It was taken by count and considered legal tender in most parts of the world – England being an exception. Historians use the term silver to indicate bullion or specie. However, private agents, bankers and states beyond the Spanish American world had a more informed view. For example, in the mid-seventeenth century, the Genoese financed the Spanish king through *Asientos* and traded a great deal of silver so obtained into Europe in the mid-seventeenth century; they valued the piece of eight over its intrinsic content of pure silver, thus overvaluing their local currency. In the 1640s, the price for the Spanish coin oscillated between 103.35 and 108.11 soldi which was their money of account. Their own silver coin, the scudo, had 36.7929 grams of pure silver and quoted between 117.75 and 122.33 soldi, while the exchange rate with the peso hovered between 1.12 and 1.14 per scudo.[57] Given that the piece of eight (the Spanish coin)[58] had 25.560 grams of pure silver, the exchange rate at silver parity was 1.4394 soldi, indicating that the piece of eight as specie enjoyed 20 per cent premium in Genoa.

Seafarers on English ships in the mid-seventeenth century demanded pieces of eight for their wages; lawsuits records at the High Admiralty Court show the variation in the exchange rate with sterling, depending on the distance from Cadiz where it was exchanged at 48 pence, to 57–67 pence in Smyrna and 78 in Mozambique.[59] The exchange rate in sterling that Britons fetched at Malaga in the same years was 54 pence and in Genoa it fluctuated according to local market conditions.[60] It is unlikely that these rates reflected the gold price of silver in each place; they reflect the different demand for the coins. It should not be surprising that sailors demanded pieces of eight for wages in international shipping; they also hoarded pieces of eight – or pesos after 1732 – for savings, as the Old Baily records attest.[61] In turn, Chinese seamen engaged in the junk trade to Batavia preferred the Spanish American coin to send remittances home; and in the mid-nineteenth century, 'fearing the eventual collapse of the Qing regime' during the Taiping rebellion, people hedged against inflation and turmoil, transferring 'their savings into silver, mostly in the form of the Spanish Dollar (peso)'.[62]

Individuals were not the only ones who invested in pieces of eight or Spanish pesos. Most Europeans had trouble keeping their monies of account on a sound footing with the irregular silver flows in and out of their money markets – especially those who aimed at trade in the East Indies. The Dutch fixed the exchange rate for foreign coins and the English set a parity for silver and gold coins' weight and fineness against their sterling standard. After the massive monetary turmoil in seventeenth-century Spain, the metropolis and colonies performed with money of the same name but different value. Silver coined in America after 1686 had a 25–30 per cent premium in the Spanish exchange markets.

European sovereigns had different ways to take part in the intermediation of specie. The Spanish monarchy had no means of controlling the rates at which her American specie was to be transacted in Cadiz or in the colonies. Exchange was a private open business, subject to royal privileges or tax-exempting licences (*indultos*) granted to export silver out of Spanish America. Eventually, the market came to be controlled by different sets of foreigners who obtained one privilege (*asientos*) or another to import goods and slaves or to provision the Spanish 'contractor state'. Amsterdam, by contrast, was a free market for precious metals with fixed exchange rates for foreign coins slightly above the mint price; France in turn struggled during the *ancien régime* to stabilize the silver price of her currency. Napoleon took pains to move the French monetary system to a silver-based currency in the first decade of the nineteenth century, leading to the establishment of the modern Banque de France. Even then, *piastres* imported from Spain continued to Amsterdam and beyond.[63] Some European countries smelted the imported silver and cut their own specie, but debasements and recoinages were frequent.

In the seventeenth century, South Asia operated with multiple metallic currencies, but used the piece of eight (real) to fix different exchange rates as reported by the English East India Company's factors. One of them, Charles Lockyer, in 1711 indicated that the 'pillar dollars (since 1686) are the most esteemed and therefore bear the highest price (at Fort St George)'. In Madras 'silver in any form passes currant by weight instead of money, reckoning from a take decimally to the smaller matter imaginable, in payments made with tankards, dishes, bowls, plates, spoons and silver porringers'. According to Lockyer, the Chinese, however, were well acquainted with the English goldsmith mark, therefore, 'old plate is the most profitable silver you can carry with you, *when dollars are dear*'.[64] Following the booming silver production and new technology of coinage of Mexico after 1730 – and in 1750s Lima and 1770s Potosí – the Spanish dollar (or peso of 8 reals) became dominant worldwide. Most Southeast Asian rulers assigned the Spanish dollar as legal tender or made them money of account, even if coins were seldom seen in their markets, as late as in 1820s Penang or Singapore, or 1850s Hong Kong.[65] This was not a new feature: already in later seventeenth century when silver flows reached Surat through European trade, the Spanish real was the preferred silver coin 'from Mokha to Canton'. The real or peso, i.e. Spanish dollar, circulated widely in the intra-Asian trade and enjoyed a growing premium over its intrinsic value in Asian cities throughout the eighteenth century. For example, whereas in 1789 the dollar was priced at 54d (in English currency) in London, it was worth 62d at Basra, 63½d at Bombay, 50d at Batavia, 57d in Malacca and 64½d in Surat.[66]

Some economies involved in the silver exchange were exceptional in their own way. In Qing China, from the 1780s at least, silver specie circulated as money in southern regions, adding another layer of complexity to the peculiar monetary system of an empire that did not coin silver but relied on imported specie.[67] In England, silver coinage was drastically reduced after 1696. Thereafter gold and small change in copper formed the nation's currency. Goldsmiths continued producing silver plate in sizable quantities through the eighteenth century and the English East India Company exported silver to record levels.[68] In the 1740s the exchange business with bullion and specie shifted from goldsmiths to the Bank of England, which became the market place aligning the private rates with the Mint's official rate for the silver peso along with the exchange rate for gold and silver bullion.[69] Notably, England practically did not coin silver in the eighteenth century, although remained a main exporter to the rest of Europe and Asia; the banking services of former goldsmith bankers were declined in favour of discount banks and the Bank of England.

Distinctly, Asian imports of coins from Europeans increased throughout the eighteenth century. In the 1720s the Dutch exported a maximum value of 63 tons, 80 per cent of which were made of pesos and rupees;[70] 72 per cent of France's exports to Asia between 1725 and the 1780s were composed of silver, of which 78 per cent were Spanish coins (*piasters*).[71] Up to 1719, silver accounted for 80 per cent of British exports, half of which were Spanish American reals; 75 per cent of the trade was with China between 1710 and 1759 (Figure 18.3).[72] Between 1788 and 1809, the English East India Company and private traders together exported an average 70 tons of silver a year, 92 per cent of which were foreign – overwhelmingly Spanish American – coins.[73] Similarly, foreign coins made about 65 per cent of the US total exports to China up to 1825.[74]

It is worth exploring further the role of the Bank in steering the market for specie and the business with the English East India Company. A particular cooperation between three major institutions (The East India Company, the Bank of England and Parliament) at the time allowed the English to have an incomparable arrangement for the market of specie. Remarkably, the English East India Company replicated the mechanism in India;

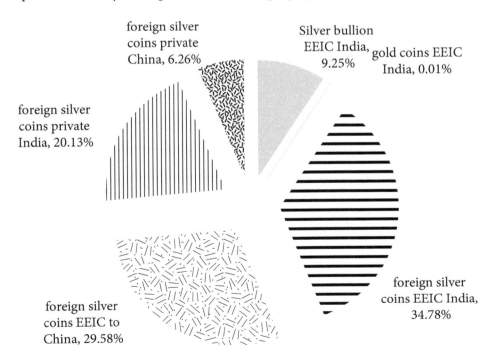

Figure 18.3 Composition of Britain' precious metals exports to Asia, 1788–1809.

Source: Own data from Parliamentary Papers, HC, *The Bullion Report* (1810).

it fixed the price of the silver peso/Spanish dollar as their invoice price, which added the trade costs to the prime price of the coins: the par mint price. It used it for their accounts in transactions, which involved silver bullion and a variety of species. It was the rate against which discounted bills in London, and priced goods in India, suggesting that the Company dealt with Treasure exports in a comparable fashion to the Bank of England, which ran the market for exchange in London.[75]

The Napoleonic Wars in Europe, which led to both the Restriction period and the implosion of the Spanish rule in America, resulted in a definitive cleavage in monetary matters too. The Gold Standard of the British pound eventually replaced the currency standard that the silver peso had created in the mid-seventeenth century. In England, the Mint, the Bank of England and the East India Company concurred to stabilize and develop a market for bullion and species while expanding the silver commerce with Asia; at the same time, a particular monetary regime and banking practices were established, foreshadowing a new international currency standard.

More than twenty years ago, Michel Morineau thought that 'the incorporation of precious metals in the general circulating medium of European economies, their effective role in the development of the economy and of the armed forces, the concurrence with other cashless means of payment, and the transition to the different modern monetary regimes of the nineteenth century' remained to be explained.[76] His research on silver import to Europe was crucial to debunk Hamilton's ideas about the Price Revolution and the crisis of the seventeenth century, which persisted in the economic historiography for a long while. Nevertheless, the trade conduits and the monetary mechanism are still to be properly investigated.

Conclusion

For Adam Smith, New World commodities were 'new values, new equivalents' in the global economy to be exchanged for the surplus of each intervening country, even in those which 'never sent any commodities to America, (and) never received any from it.'[77] Among those, silver, in his words was 'one of the principal commodities by which the commerce between the two extremities of the Old [World] is carried on, and by means of it, in a great measure, that those distant parts of the world are connected with one another'.[78] Moreover, Smith pointed out that what has been said of the East India trade might possibly be true of the French – that though the greater part of the East India goods were bought with gold and silver, the re-exportation of a part of them to other countries brought back more gold and silver to that which carried on the trade than the prime cost of the whole amounted to, revealing the crucial importance of the carry trade among European nations and of silver as a factor in the contemporary process of Smithian growth in Europe.[79]

Therefore the 'general advantage which Europe, considered as one great country', derived from the discovery of America and of the Passage to the East Indies, 'consisted first, in the increase of its enjoyments, and secondly, in the augmentation of its industry'. Despite the largesse of its production and exports to the world, Spanish American silver did not have persistent inflationary effects on prices worldwide. On the contrary, it led to 'the gradual enlargement of the market for the produce of silver mines in America'. The market became ever 'more extensive' and marginally better integrated both in America – and with Asia – and the 'greater part of Europe has been much improved, England, Holland, France and Germany, even Sweden and Denmark and Russia have all advanced considerably both in agriculture and in manufactures'.[80]

For Adam Smith, these improvements 'must necessarily have required a gradual increase in the quantity of silver coin to circulate it'.[81] He flagged that 'America is itself a new market for the produce of its silver mines; and its advances in agriculture, industry and population are much more rapid that those of the most thriving countries in Europe; its demand must increase much more rapidly'.[82] However, scholars within and outside the region have overlooked this relationship between silver and the development of the global economy because of an inaccurate understanding of the colonial economy in Spanish America. Thus, the role of the global silver trade is still insufficiently understood. The incorporation and circulation of silver and specie in the European economy, and further re-exported to Asia, and the importance of private consumption in the Spanish New World are yet to be mined by global economic historians.

Notes

1. K. Pomeranz (2000), *The Great Divergence: China, Europe and the Making of the Modern World Economy*. Princeton, NJ: Princeton University Press.

2. A. Smith (1979 [1776]), *An Inquiry into the Nature and Causes of the Wealth of Nations*. London: The Electric Book Company: http://www.myilibrary.com?ID=124076 Book IV, part III, ch. 7: 829.

3. J. Hersh and H. Voth (2009), 'Sweet diversity: Colonial goods and the rise of European living standards after 1492', *Discussion Paper CEPR* 7386; N. Palma (2020), 'American Precious Metals and their consequences for Early Modern Europe' in S. Battilossi, Y. Cassis and K. Yago (eds), *Handbook of the History of Money and Currency*. Singapore: Springer, 14.

4. J. D. Sachs and A. M. Warner (2001), 'The curse of natural resources', *European Economic Review*, 45 (4), 827–38.

5. R. C. Allen et al. (2011), 'Wages, prices, and living standards in China, 1738–1925: In comparison with Europe, Japan, and India', *Economic History Review*, 64 (Supplement 1), 8–38. R. C. Allen et al. (2012), 'The colonial origins of the divergence in the Americas: A labor market approach', *Journal of Economic History*, 72 (4), 863–94; L. A. Abad and et al. (2012), 'Between conquest and independence: Real wages and demographic change in Spanish America, 1530–1820', *Explorations in Economic History*, 49 (2), 149–66; L. A. Abad and J. L. van Zanden (2016), 'Growth under extractive institutions? Latin American per capita GDP in colonial times', *Journal of Economic History*, 76 (4), 1182–215.

6. K. Sokoloff and S. Engerman (2000), 'Institutions, factor endowments and paths of development in the New World', *Journal of Economic Perspectives*, 14 (3), 217–32; S. Engerman and K. Sokoloff (1997), 'Factor endowments, institutions and differential paths of growth. A view from economic historians from the United States', in S. Haber (ed.), *How*

Latin America Fell Behind: Essays on the Economic Histories of Brazil and Mexico. Stanford, CA: Stanford University Press.

7. K. Ronnbäck (2014), 'Sweet business: Quantifying the value added in the British colonial sugar trade in the eighteenth century', *Revista de Historia Económica / Journal of Iberian and Latin American Economic History*, 32 (2), 223–45; E. David and L. E. Stanley (2000), 'The importance of slavery and the slave trade to Industrializing Britain', *Journal of Economic History*, 60 (1), 123–44.

8. As De Zwart and Van Zanden show, their book starts the narrative of globalization origins precisely in Latin America 'the part of the world most transformed by the process'. Following Adam Smith, this region is seen as transformative of the world economy. P. de Zwart and J. L. van Zanden (2018), *The Origins of Globalization: World Trade in the Making of the Global Economy, 1500–1800*. Cambridge: Cambridge University Press. See also Irigoin's review of the title in the *International Review of Social History*, (2019) 64 (3), 533–6.

9. A. Irigoin (2020), 'The rise and demise of the global silver standard', in S. Battilossi, Y. Cassis and K. Yago (eds), *Handbook of the History of Money and Currency*. Singapore: Springer, ch. 13.

10. D. O. Flynn and A. Giráldez (1996), *World Silver and Monetary History in the 16th and 17th Centuries*. Aldershot: Variorum; ibid. (1997), *Metals and Monies in an Emerging Global Economy. Expanding World*. Brookfield: Variorum.

11. I. Habib (1982). 'Monetary system and prices', in T. Raychaudhuri and I. Habib (eds), *The Cambridge Economic History of India*. Cambridge: Cambridge University Press; R. Von Glahn (1996), *Fountain of Fortune: Money and Monetary Policy in China, 1000–1700*. Berkeley, CA: University of California Press. Copper, tin or brass also circulated as small change in different Asian states. R. Von Glahn (2014), 'Chinese coin and changes in monetary preferences in maritime East Asia in the fifteenth-seventeenth centuries', *Journal of the Economic and Social History of the Orient*, 57 (5), 629–68.

12. Soetbeer (1886), cited by J. Nef (1941), 'Silver production in Central Europe, 1450–1618', *Journal of Political Economy*, 49 (4), 589.

13. I. Seiichi (1976), 'Japanese trade in the 16th and 17th centuries', *Acta Asiatica*, 30, 1–18 who estimated this volume equivalent to the 30–40 per cent of the world production at the time.

14. R. Innes (1980), 'The door ajar: Japan's foreign trade in the seventeenth century', unpublished PhD thesis, University of Michigan, Ann Arbor, 379, and 582.

15. J. TePaske and K. Brown (2010), *A New World of Gold and Silver*. Leiden: Brill, Table 3.20.

16. A. Maddison (2007), *Contours of the World Economy, 1–2030AD: Essays in Macro-economic History*. Oxford: Oxford University Press; K. O'Rourke and J. Williamson (2002), 'After Columbus: Explaining Europe's overseas trade boom, 1500–1800', *Journal of Economic History*, 62 (2), Table 1 at p. 421.

17. J. De Vries (2003), 'Connecting Europe and Asia: A quantitative analysis of the Cape Route trade, 1497–1975', in D. O. Flynn, A. Giráldez and R. Von Glahn (eds), *Global Connections and Monetary History 1470–1800*. Aldershot: Ashgate.

18. Williamson and O'Rourke did not examine precious metals because of their monetary role and did not consider relevant their 'impact of intercontinental silver flows on aggregate price levels'. O'Rourke and Williamson (2002), 'After Columbus', fn. 4. See D. O. Flynn and A. Giráldez (2004), 'Path dependence, time lags and the birth of globalization: A critique of O'Rourke and Williamson', *European Review of Economic History*, 8 (1), 81–108.

19. A. Gunder Frank (1998). *ReOrient: Global Economy in the Asian Age*. Berkeley, CA: University of California Press; and Flynn and Giráldez (various years).

20. In India the ratio equalized by 1670 at 15/16:1 but reverted to 13:1 and even 11.5:1 in the early eighteenth century, it remained below the European ratio for reminder of the century. Habib, 'Monetary system', Table 9.

21. A. Irigoin (2013). 'A trojan horse in Daoguang China? Explaining the flows of silver in and out of China', *LSE Economic History Working Papers*, 173/13.

22. N. Biggs (2019), 'Thomas Harriot on the coinage of England', *Archive for History of Exact Sciences*, 73, 361–83.

23. 'An exogenous 10 per cent increase in the production of precious metals in America measure relative to the European stocks leads to a front-loaded response of output, and to a lesser extent inflation (with) a positive hump-shaped real GDP response, with a cumulative increase up to 0.9 per cent six to nine years later.' N. Palma (2022), 'The real effects of monetary expansions: Evidence from a large-scale historical experiment', *Review of Economic Studies*, 89, 1593–627. A comparable argument about the importance of liquidity in Europe and Asia can be found in R. Findlay and K. O'Rourke (2009), *Power and Plenty: Trade, War and the World Economic in the Second Millennium*. Princeton, NJ: Princeton University Press, 201 and 206.

24. L. Dermigny (1964). *La Chine et l'Occident; le commerce à Canton au XVIIIe siècle, 1719–1833*. Paris, S.E.V.P.E.N. II, 686.

25. H. Klein (1990), 'Economic aspects of the eighteenth-century Atlantic slave trade', in J. Tracy (ed.), *The Rise of Merchant Empires Long Distance Trade in the Early Modern World 1350–1750*. Cambridge: Cambridge University Press, 287–310; K. Weber (2002), 'German rural industry and Trade in the Atlantic, 1680–1840', *Itinerario*, 26 (2), 99–119.

26. US cotton became a prime export commodity after 1815 but, strictly speaking, it was cultivated with home-grown slave labour of African descent, which makes this crop distinct from the traditional West Indies exports.

27. P. K. O'Brien (1982), 'European economic development: The contribution of the periphery', *Economic History Review*, 35 (1), 4.

28. P. K. O'Brien (1998), 'Inseparable connections: Trade, economy, fiscal state and the expansion of empire', in P. J. Marshall and A. Low (eds), *The Oxford History of the British Empire*, vol. 2: *The Eighteenth Century*. Oxford: Oxford University Press, 53–78; O'Brien (2014), 'The formation of states and transitions to modern economic, England, Europa and Asia compared', in L. Neal and J. Williamson (eds), *The Cambridge History of Capitalism*, vol. 1: *The Rise of Capitalism*. Cambridge: Cambridge University Press, 357–64.

29. Findlay and O'Rourke, *Power and Plenty*, 210.

30. M. Dell (2010). 'The persistent effects of Peru's mining mita', *Econometrica*, 78 (6), 1863–903; M. Van der Linden (2011), *Workers of the World: Essays toward a Global Labor History*. Leiden: Brill.

31. E. Tandeter (1981), 'Free and forced labour in late Colonial Potosí', *Past & Present*, 93, Table 2; P. Bakewell (1984), *Miners of the Red Mountain: Indian Labour in Potosí*. Albuquerque, NM: University of New Mexico Press.

32. R. Barragán (2017), 'Working silver for the world: Mining labour and popular economy in colonial Potosí', *Hispanic American Historical Review*, 97 (2), 193–222.

33. C. Marichal (2006), 'The Spanish American silver peso: Export commodity and global money of the ancien regime (16th–18th centuries)', in S. Topik, C. Marichal and Z. Frank (eds), *Latin American Commodity Chains and the Building of Global Economy*. Durham, NC: Duke University Press, 30.

34. E. Tandeter (1993), *Coercion and Market: Silver Mining in Colonial Potosí, 1692–1826*. Albuquerque, NM: University of New Mexico Press; R. C. Allen (2001), 'The Great Divergence in European wages and prices from the Middle Ages to the First World War', *Explorations in Economic History*, 38 (4), 411–47.

35. See fn 5 and also R. Dobado and G. Montero (2014), 'Neither so low nor so short: Wages and heights in Bourbon Spanish America from an international comparative perspective', *Journal of Latin American Studies*, 46 (2), 291–321; and A. Challu and A. Gomez (2015), 'Mexico's real wages in the age of the Great Divergence, 1730–1930', *Revista de Historia Económica / Journal of Iberian Latin American Economic History*, 33 (1), 83–122 for a different view.

36. TePaske and Brown, *A New World*, 140.

37. A. Irigoin (2019), 'The New World and the Global Silver Economy, 1500–1800', in T. Roy and G. Riello (eds), *Global Economic History*. London: Bloomsbury, 275 fig. 15.1.

38. C. S. Assadourian (1982), *El Sistema de la economía colonial. El mercado interior. Regiones y espacio económico*. Mexico: Nueva Imagen, 22.

39. A. Irigoin (2009) 'Gresham on horseback: The monetary roots of Spanish America political fragmentation in the nineteenth century', *Economic History Review*, 62 (3), 551–75.

40. J. Cuenca (2008), 'Statistics of Spain's colonial trade, 1747–1820: New estimates and comparisons with Great Britain', *Revista de Historia Económica / Journal of Iberian and Latin American Economic History*, 26 (3), 323–54.

41. Significantly, these data do not include Brazilian gold exports or the silver smuggled by European interlopers or traded in the Pacific commerce. Gold was also produced in Peru, Colombia, Chile and Mexico.

42. For Spanish American figures, see J. Lockhart and S. B. Schwartz (1983), *Early Latin America*. Cambridge: Cambridge University Press, 338, Table 4; for Brazil, D. Alden (1963), 'The population of Brazil in the late eighteenth century: A preliminary study', *Hispanic American Historical Review*, 43 (2), 173–205.

43. F. Tronchin, 'Colonies angloises, Commerce des Indes espagnoles, Commerce de Russie, Douane de Londres', Bibliothèque de Genève – Manuscrits et archives privées, Arch. Tronchin 372, undated, second half of the eighteenth century (around the Austrian Succession War); J. Baskes (2005), 'Risky ventures: Reconsidering Mexico's colonial trade system', *Colonial Latin American Review*, 14 (1), 27–54.

44. The r² is .30, whereas the correlation between output and coinage is .94. Without similar data for the seventeenth century, as imports to Spain ceased to be registered, the impression of falling silver trade linked to the 'general crisis' in Europe seems a result of under-registration and of the expansion of the domestic economy in the colonies.

45. R. Grafe and A. Irigoin (2006), 'The Spanish Empire and its legacy: Fiscal redistribution and political conflict in colonial and post-colonial Spanish America', *Journal of Global History*, 1 (2), 241–67. Taxing commerce a 'developmentalist' state enlarged its fiscal base along the way. Grafe and Irigoin (2012), 'A stakeholder empire: The political economy of Spanish imperial rule in America', *Economic History Review*, 65 (2), 609–51.

46. Baskes, 'Risky ventures'; D. Brading (1971), *Miners and Merchants in Bourbon Mexico, 1763–1810*. Cambridge: Cambridge University Press, 97.

47. Findlay and O'Rourke attribute this restraint to a compromise between 'a permit to trade, but to restrict it to a prescribed level permitting the survival of the import competing silk industry' (in Mexico and Spain). Findlay and O'Rourke, *Power and Plenty*, 168.

48. Numbers compared with the English East India Company in the East Indies and China.

49. L. Salvucci (2005), 'Atlantic intersections: Early American commerce and the rise of the Spanish West Indies (Cuba)', *Business History Review*, 74 (9), 781–809.

50. D. Ozanam (1968), *La colonie française de Cadiz au XVIII siècle*. Madrid: Mélanges de la Casa de Velázquez.

51. M. Bernal (1992), *La financiación de la Carrera de Indias (1492–1824). Dinero y crédito en el comercio colonial español con América*. Cadiz: Fundacion El Monte.

52. Litigations before the court between the different Consulados in Seville, Mexico, Lima and Manila were constant. Probably the dispute around the introduction of Asian silks and textiles to the New World over 150 years recapitulated by A. Alvarez de Abreu (1977 [1736]), *Extracto historial del comercio entre China, Filipinas y Nueva España*. Mexico: Instituto Mexicano de Comercio Exterior, is the best example.

53. M. Malowist (1958), 'Poland, Russia and western trade in the 15th and 16th century', *Past & Present*, 13, 26–41; S. Pamuk (1994), 'Money in the Ottoman Empire, 1326–1914', in H. Inalcik and D. Quataert (eds), *History of the Ottoman Empire, 1300–1914*. Cambridge: Cambridge University Press, 947–85.

54. President Wylde and Council at Surat to the Company, 31 December 1628, in W. Foster (1909), *The English Factories in India, 1618–1669*, vol. 3: *1624–1629*. Oxford: Clarendon, 307.

55. 'The Young Hyson, Gunpowder and Hyson teas – because they are "cash articles"'. The correspondent suggests loading ships only with dollars: 'I had rather have and do the business of a ship with dollars for nothing, than meddle with skin ships'. S. Dorr and H. Corning (1945), 'The letters of Sullivan Dorr', *Proceedings of the Massachusetts Historical Society*, 67, 212, 224, 234, 266, 281, 312, 324, 332 and 342 (citation p. 224). On the 'premium on cash' in Canton, p. 299.

56. Mintage in America was done locally and overwhelmingly made of one peso coin. R. Romano (1998), *Moneda, Seudomoneda y Circulación Monetaria en la Economía de México*. Mexico: Fondo de Cultura Económica.

57. Thanks to Claudio Marsilio for sharing the exchange rates information.

58. The coin had a fractional equivalent to 8 reals. It was called *peso de a ocho* after 1732 when started to be milled. Henceforth it was known as Spanish dollar in English and *piastre* in French.

59. R. Blakemore (2017) 'Pieces of eight, pieces of eight: Seamen's earning and the venture economy of early modern seafaring', *Economic History Review*, 70 (4), 1153–84.

60. C. Marsilio (2012) 'The Genoese and Portuguese financial operators' control of the Spanish silver market (1627–1657)', *Journal of European Economic History*, 41 (3), 67–89.

61. A. Dolan (2015) 'The fabric of life: Linen and life cycle in England, 1678–1810', unpublished PhD thesis, University of Hertfordshire.

62. L. Blussé (2011) 'Junks to Java: Chinese shipping to the Nanyang in the second half of the eighteenth century', in E. Tagliacozzo and W. Chang (eds), *Chinese Circulation: Capital Commodities and Networks in South East Asia*. Durham, NC: Duke University Press, 285; J. Ch'en (1958), 'The Hsien-Feng Inflation', *Bulletin of the School of Oriental and African Studies*, 21 (3), 580.

63. M. Zylberberg (1993), *Une si douce domination. Lex milieux d'affaires françaises et l'Espagne vers 1780–1808*. Paris: Comité pour l'histoire économique et financière de la France.

64. C. Lockyer (1711), *An Account of the Trade in India*. London: Samuel Crouch, 136 and 140.

65. L. Wong (1960), 'The trade of Singapore, 1819–69', *Journal of the Malayan Branch of the Royal Asiatic Society*, 33 (4), 4–135; A. Reid and F. Radin (1996), 'Shipping on Melaka and Singapore as an index of growth, 1760–1840', *Journal of South Asian Studies*, 19 (1), 59–84.

66. *An Account of the Monies, Weights and Measure in General Use in Persia, Arabia, East India and China* … (1789). British Library

67. Irigoin, 'A Trojan horse'; R. Von Glahn (2013) 'Cycles of silver in Chinese monetary history', in B. K. L. So (ed.), *The Economy of Lower Yangzi Delta in Late Imperial China*. London: Routledge, 17–71.

68. N. Mayhew (2012), 'Silver in England, 1600–1800: Coinage outputs and bullion exports from the records of the London Tower Mint and the London Company of Goldsmiths', in J. Munro (ed.), *Money in Pre-Industrial World: Bullion, Debasements and Coin Substitutes*. London: Pickering & Chatto, 97–108.

69. J. H. Clapham (1941), 'The private business of the Bank of England, 1744–1800', *Economic History Review*, 11 (1), 77–89; A. Hotson and T. C. Mills (2015), 'London's market for bullion and specie in the eighteenth century: The roles of the London Mint and the Bank of England in the stabilization of prices', in M. Allen and D. Coffman (eds), *Money, Prices and Wages: Essays in Honour of Prof. Nicholas Mayhew*. Basingstoke: Palgrave, 217–27.

70. H. Van der Wee (2012), 'The Amsterdam Wisselbank's innovations in the monetary sphere: The role of "Bank Money"', in J. H. Munro (ed.), *Money in Pre-Industrial World Bullion, Debasements and Coin Substitutes*. London: Pickering & Chatto, 95.

71. L. Dermigny (1959/60), *Cargaisons indiennes Solier et Cie, 1781–1793*. Paris: S.E.V.P.E.N., i: 122,124 and 138.

72. K. N. Chaudhuri (1968), 'Treasure and trade balance: The East India Company's export trade, 1660–1720', *Economic History Review*, 21 (3), Table 1; H. B. Morse (1922), 'The provision of funds for the East India Company's trade at Canton during the eighteenth century', *Journal of the Royal Asiatic Society*, 54 (2), 228.

73. Parliamentary Papers (UK), House of Commons, 'The Bullion Report' (1810).

74. Irigoin (2009) 'Gresham on horseback'. Between 1802 and 1808 the US exported £1.7 million worth of silver ('treasure'), making two-thirds of the total British exports. A. Seybert (1818). *Statistical Annals Embracing Views of the Population, Commerce, Navigation … of the United States of America*. Philadelphia, PA: T. Dobson & Son, 56.

75. Chaudhuri, 'Treasure and trade balance'.

76. Morineau cited in A. García-Baquero González (1996), 'Las remesas de metales preciosos americanos en el siglo XVIII: Una aritmética controvertida', *Hispania: Revista Española de Historia*, 56 (192), 266.

77. Smith, *Wealth of Nations*, Book IV, ch. 7: 782.

78. Ibid., Book I, ch. 11: 287.

79. Ibid., Book IV, ch. 3: 629, 621–5.

80. Ibid., Book IV, ch. 7: 780

81. Ibid., Book III, ch. 11: 282–3.

82. Ibid.

CHAPTER 19
BUSINESS, TECHNOLOGY AND THE AMERICAN ECONOMY, c.1800–2000
Regina Lee Blaszczyk

In 1872, John Gast, a Brooklyn-based painter and lithographer, created an allegorical painting for George A. Crofutt, a local publisher, to put in his popular guidebooks on the American West (Figure 19.1). Crofutt reproduced the picture, *Westward the Course of Destiny*, or *American Progress*, in his handbooks and, in 1873, he gave subscribers a free chromolithograph of the image suitable for wall decoration. The picture is widely used today by United States history teachers because it portrays the technological hubris that undergirded the American economy in 1872 and still holds sway in the digital age.[1] *American Progress* opens the doors onto our discussion of the North America economy over the past two centuries, a period of technical dynamism and cultural, social and ideological upheavals.

American Progress is striking for its enduring economic relevance. Gast imagined the North American landscape as a vast open plain from the eastern seaboard to the western territories. In the distance to the northeast, the viewer glimpses the heavily populated port of New York. We can see outline of lower Manhattan with sailing ships and steamboats coming and going, and the Brooklyn Bridge, built from 1869 to 1883, spanning the East River. In the centre, people, animals and machines march westward across a green space suggestive of the Great Plains. The main motif is the allegorical figure of America, the embodiment of European civilization or whiteness. *American Progress* depicts a world defined by technical achievement, enormous distances, natural abundance, prescribed gender roles and racial differences.

Two generations ago, the historian Thomas P. Hughes, writing in *American Genesis*, argued that an unbridled enthusiasm for technology and technological systems differentiated the United States among industrial nations in the century between 1870 and 1970.[2] System builders like Thomas Edison and Henry Ford loomed large in Hughes's sweeping synthesis on American technology. Recent studies of US history have turned away from the achievements of white men, making the case for race as the defining element of American history and offering a vision that puts slavery and the legacy of enslavement at the centre of the American experience.[3] But as Gast's artwork shows, technological enthusiasm was a popular nineteenth-century trope that coexisted with racialized and gendered hierarchies. Hughes, writing before the Web and the iPhone, believed he had witnessed the end of an era, lamenting the rise and fall of technological enthusiasm. In retrospect, it seems that Hughes wrote at low tide. Today, the reliance on

Figure 19.1 America depicted as the pure white virgin. John Gast's *American Progress* portrayed the technological enthusiasm, circumscribed gender roles and racialized hierarchies that shaped the North American economy in the Gilded Age.
Source: Library of Congress, Prints and Photographs Division, Washington, DC.

and fetishization of digitalization, the most modern of systems, shows that technological enthusiasm endures, making the relationships among technology, enterprise and culture a fitting lens for our examination of the North American economy.

Capitalism and Cotton

By twenty-first-century standards, James Henry Hammond (1807–1864) was a repulsive human being. This prominent South Carolina planter operated two plantations, inherited from his wife's family, that produced cotton, corn and meat using slave labour. An early devotee of efficiency, Hammond took pride in running his estates at peak performance, adopting the latest crop-management techniques. To diversify his assets, he bought railroad stocks and invested in cotton textile mills. He entered politics in 1835 and served as a United States Congressman, the South Carolina governor and a United States Senator.[4] In 1858, as tensions grew between North and South, Hammond delivered his infamous 'Cotton Is King' speech in the Senate chamber of the United States Capitol.

Hammond's passionate articulation of the pro-slavery position embodied the ideas of many elite white men in the Southern planter class. He justified slavery on the grounds that blacks were 'of another and inferior race', famously claiming they were 'the very mud-sill of society', a people of 'low order of intellect and but little skill'. In his view, Southern patriarchs, as superior human beings, had the responsibility to feed and care for them in perpetuity. Hammond pointed to the hypocrisy of the North. No white factory worker there, he said, was guaranteed a job for life. Free labour could be thrown out of work at the drop of a hat, forced to beg in the crowded streets of New York. Which labour system was better, he posited, free or unfree?[5] Hammond embodied the complexities, contradictions and cruelties of antebellum America.[6] On the one hand, he was a shrewd businessman who understood how to manage his investments and watch his costs, foreshadowing better-known entrepreneurs like Andrew Carnegie, the Gilded Age steel magnate. We could say that Hammond was, in matters of plantation management, somewhat of a systems enthusiast. On the other hand, his worldview was rooted in racism, sexism and deceit, guided by the impulse to judge everyone by their value and utility in relation to the white male gentry.

For generations, the institution of slavery was studied as a subset of American history, a specialty among students of the labour system, but more recently, researchers concerned to blend economic and social history have put slavery at the centre of the early American past. In the late twentieth century, scholars began to explore everyday experiences within the slave system, be it the cotton plantations of the Carolinas, the auction blocks in New Orleans, or the iron forges of the Shenandoah Valley.[7] In 1994, the historian Ronald Bailey emphasized the need to probe the relationships among antebellum Southern slavery and New England textile manufacturing to develop a fulsome analysis of American industrialization.[8] In recent years, a project to identify slavery as the foundational institution of American capitalism has become the *raison d'être* for a new group of progressive historians.[9] This 'New History of Capitalism', with its roots in social justice, is not without its academic critics.[10] For our purposes, suffice to say that nineteenth-century Southern cotton, grown on slave plantations, was channelled into the spinning and weaving mills of New England, the site of the American Industrial Revolution. Thus, as Bailey and others explained long ago, the two parts of the antebellum economy were engaged in a fateful dance: South and North, pro-slavery and abolitionist, unfree and free labour, and plantation agriculture and industrial technology.[11]

Among the sites of Northern industrialization, the city of Lowell, Massachusetts, was the most famous cotton manufacturing centre, often called the 'Manchester of America'. Sited on the Merrimack River some 25 miles northwest of Boston, this planned industrial community, built in the 1820s, was named after Francis Cabot Lowell (1775–1817), a merchant who made a fortune in the China trade, visited the textile mills of England and Scotland, and dreamt of recreating Manchester's factories with better working conditions. After erecting America's first fully integrated textile mill in Waltham just outside Boston, Lowell died before he could fulfil his ambition for a factory utopia based on the ideals of Robert Owen. Fellow merchant Nathan Appleton, together with other businessmen collectively known as 'the Boston Associates', executed his vision for a planned factory city, first in Lowell, next down river in Lawrence, and to one degree or another, elsewhere in New England.[12] Initially, the Lowell mills only hired single farm women from the countryside to operate the spinning machines and power looms. Starting in 1834, the Yankee mill girls asserted themselves by striking against wage cuts, and from the 1840s, they were gradually replaced by cheaper labourers: men, women and children from famine-ravaged Ireland. Other immigrant groups flooded into Lowell to become the backbone of the mills for generations to come.[13] Many of the facilities funded by these Boston investors were used by the textile industry into the twentieth century, with some of the factories and boarding houses still standing. They were among the largest, most heavily capitalized firms in New England, with each textile city specializing in a different type of cloth.[14] Lowell was known for calicoes, for example, while Lawrence built its reputation in worsteds (Figure 19.2).

On the eve of the Civil War (1861–65), the North controlled 70 per cent of the country's wealth, 80 per cent of its banking assets. By the 1850s, just three Northern states – Massachusetts, New York and Pennsylvania – accounted for more than half of the nation's manufacturing capital and output. While the North invested in human capital and a range of new technologies, from power canals to mechanical reapers, sewing machines and telegraphy, the South mainly relied on slave labour.[15] In December of 1860, William Tecumseh Sherman, a former military man who would in due course serve the Union army with distinction, penned a letter to a friend in

Mills on the Merrimac River, Lawrence, Mass.

Figure 19.2 The factory as a symbol of progress. By the early twentieth century, giant factories dominated the riverscapes of many New England mill cities, reminding everyone of the centrality of industry to the North American economy.
Source: Postcard, author's collection.

the South, highlighting the technological superiority of the industrial North. 'The North can make a steam engine, locomotive or railway car; hardly a yard of cloth, or a pair of shoes can you make', Sherman wrote. 'You are rushing into war with one of the most powerful, ingeniously mechanical and determined people on earth – right at your doors. You are bound to fail'.[16] The prospect of a Confederate loss did not please James Henry Hammond. On his deathbed, Hammond told his son, if the South is 'subjugated, run a plow over my grave'.[17] While the 13th Amendment to the US Constitution ploughed over the institution of slavery, it did not eradicate racism or eliminate the South's dependency on agriculture. In an effort to maintain social control and compete in global markets against cotton producers in Egypt and India, postbellum Southern planters adopted sharecropping, a peonage system using poor whites and poor blacks to toil in the fields, which cemented the region's backwardness vis-à-vis the North.[18]

The Civil War energized Northern industry, particularly after the federal government repeatedly imposed higher duties on imports as part of a broader tax scheme to raise funds for defence.[19] The textile trades, for one, increased production of ready-made clothing by using the latest technology. Introduced in the antebellum era, the sewing machine, operated by hand and foot, was marketed by I. M. Singer & Co. (and successors) and made its way into homes and businesses, first in the United States and then around the world.[20] On the forefront of innovation, the federal government showed what could be done by blending technics and planning. The tremendous need for tents and uniforms led the United States Quatermaster's Department, the procurement wing of the Union army, to set up its own clothing halls in Cincinnati, Ohio, where women and girls sewed up the goods, cutting out the subcontractors.[21] In the private sector, various Northern industries, be it the makers of iron, guns and boots for the military or the weavers of silk fabrics for luxury consumption, benefited from wartime conditions.[22] While not without its critics, the tariff shielded domestic manufacturing against competitive imports and launched an era of protectionism that would help to fuel the Second Industrial Revolution.

Technology, the Visible Hand and the National Market

Great Britain is a cosy country, roughly the size of the Northeastern United States. The island nation would roughly fit into the ten-state area running north–south between southern Maine and Washington, DC, and east–west from New York City to Pittsburgh, Pennsylvania. The British engineers who developed the first steam locomotives probably did not make this comparison; they were concerned to develop machines to conquer time and space, a steam-powered transportation system to supersede the canals. The vast distances of North America, represented in *American Progress*, created the imperative for a railway system on steroids. The transcontinental train network drew sustenance from early industrialization and westward expansion, while furthering the development of manufacturing, mining, agriculture and mass consumption.

While some statistically minded economic historians used quantitative methods to assess the Iron Horse's impact on national growth, one major scholar who embraced narrative evidence to argue for the importance of the railway system was Alfred D. Chandler Jr (1918–2007).[23] A professor at the Harvard Business School for most of his career, Chandler launched the modern discipline of business history and lorded over the field from the 1960s through the 1990s.[24] His publications focused on the rise and dominance of 'big business' as a distinctive feature of the North American economy in the late nineteenth and early twentieth centuries, a research topic in part influenced by his grandfather's editorial career at the *American Railway Journal* and his father's association with a major locomotive builder.[25] A naval officer turned historian, his life's work was to dig deep into the American past to identify and analyse the factors that allowed for the 'miracle of industrial mobilization' during the Second World War and the later widespread emulation of the America business model around the world.[26] Chandler and his followers held that American economic superiority was rooted in a distinctive business system, born during the Second Industrial Revolution, that harnessed cutting-edge technologies, first to penetrate domestic opportunities and later to exploit global markets.[27]

Chandler was a technological enthusiast whose theories intersect with the object lessons of *American Progress*. In his view, the most important economic institutions of the nineteenth-century United States were the firms that capitalized on technology and expertise to turn the sprawling wilderness into a national market. 'New technology made possible an unprecedented output and movement of goods', he wrote. 'Enlarged markets were essential to absorb such output'.[28] In turn, first modern business enterprises were institutional innovators who from mid-century onwards replaced the 'invisible hand' of the market, a metaphor first used by the Scottish philosopher and political economist Adam Smith, with the 'visible hand' of management.[29] The railroads set the stage, taking advantage of a slew of novel materials, inventions, processes and know-how: communication by telegraphy, coal-fired steam engines, steel produced by modern methods, mechanical signalling systems, gas lighting, standard time, and university-educated engineers to get it all organized. Chandlerian business bureaucracies were ultra-masculine institutions led by a new group of all-male executives and middle managers – men who thought strategically and introduced the multi-divisional organizational structure, all with the aim of gaining control over new markets ushered in by technological change.

One big business at the centre of the North American economy was the Pennsylvania Railroad Company (nicknamed the Pennsy), which by the 1850s ran trains from Philadelphia, a port on the Atlantic seaboard, to Pittsburgh, a manufacturing hub at the headwaters of the Ohio River, with connections to Chicago, St. Louis and other western cities.[30] The fate of the railroads was entwined with that of steel. Thomas A. Scott, superintendent of the Pennsy's western division in Pittsburgh, was a forward-looking manager, and his protégé was a Scottish boy named Andrew Carnegie. Young Andy worked as his telegraph operator and private secretary, learning the railway's secrets.[31] He ventured into the stock market, invested in Pullman sleeping cars, and took special note of a Pennsy experiment to replace wooden bridges with iron. Realizing the future lay in high-technology metalworking, Carnegie (after leaving the Pennsy) established a bridge company, which built the impressive steel span, designed by James B. Eads, across the Mississippi River at St Louis.[32] In the last three decades of the century, his energies focused on squeezing every dollar out of his steelmaking plants near Pittsburgh, including the Homestead Steel Works, the site of a major labour dispute over wages and working conditions in 1892.[33] In 1901, following a shake-up with his business partner, Carnegie sold his firm to the New York financier J. P. Morgan, who merged it with other assets to control 60 per cent of the nation's steel output under the United States Steel Corporation, the world's first billion-dollar corporation.[34] As Thomas J. Misa argued, steel was a great modernizing technology, giving backbone to the North American infrastructure. The transcontinental railroad, the gunships of the American navy, and the skyscrapers of Chicago and New York would not have been possible without steel.[35]

The railroads and the steelmakers did not stand alone at the centre of the American industrial economy. Chandler explored other extractive, manufacturing, processing and distributive businesses that came to dominate their sectors by exploiting technology, integrating mass production with mass distribution and merging with related firms to achieve scale economies. Chicago meatpacker Gustavus F. Swift adopted the moving disassembly line and the refrigerated railway car to build a national market for packaged meats.[36] The flour millers of the upper Midwest streamlined grain processing and cereal production.[37] Businesses like the Duke tobacco interests in North Carolina, the Heinz pickle empire of Pittsburgh, and other agricultural processors turned to new production techniques, improved their assembly lines, invested in the nascent field of marketing and hired more managers to plan, strategize and organize.[38] Some firms at the centre of the North American economy remained family firms, among them, E. I. du Pont de Nemours and Company, a chemical manufacturer, and the Ford Motor Company, a carmaker. But as the Gilded Age faded into memory, ever more large corporations turned to men in the new professional management class, tasking them with the job of exerting a 'visible hand' over the opportunities made possible by new technologies.

The Great Industrial Heartland

By the turn of the century, an impressive manufacturing belt stretched from the Eastern seaboard across the Appalachian Mountains to the Mississippi River, bordered by the Great Lakes to the North and the Ohio River to the south. Some of the firms in this industrial district were the big businesses studied by Chandler, but most were not. From New York to Cincinnati and St Louis, factories and workshops sprouted up to produce goods for the North American consumer culture. The Ohio River valley specialized in making tableware from pottery and glass. Grand Rapids built furniture in every imaginable style: Eastlake, Mission, Colonial Revival and more. The New England and Mid-Atlantic textile industries made fabrics of cotton, wool and silk, generating endless designs for upholsterers, interior decorators, home sewers, tailors and ready-to-wear factories. During the British Industrial Revolution, entrepreneurial firms – Birmingham metalworkers, Lancashire calico printers and Staffordshire potters – catered to the gentrified taste for glittery shoe buckles, colourful cloth and tea-drinking accoutrements. A century later, small and mid-sized American manufacturers capitalized on the culture of respectability, offering an expanded portfolio of consumer goods to a much larger, more geographically dispersed and ethnically diverse market.

The industrial heartland was built on the backs of entrepreneurs, factory owners, engineers, designers and production workers – but it also owed a good deal to federal trade policies. During the early days of the republic, Alexander Hamilton, the founding father most concerned with economic matters, had advocated for a central financial institution comparable to the Bank of England, a strong manufacturing base, a single internal market, and federal tariffs to raise revenues and protect the country's infant industries.[39] The customs rate hikes of the Civil War acclimated the United States to protectionism, and in the words of tariff expert Frank W. Taussig, the 'restraint of trade with foreign countries by means of import duties ... came to be advocated as a good thing in itself'.[40] As Midwestern industrialization ramped up during the Gilded Age and Progressive Era, Congress repeatedly voted to retain protective tariffs on certain types of imports, including many of the style goods produced in Europe.[41] From the Civil War through the 1913 passage of the Underwood Tariff (a free-trade initiative supported by the Democratic Party in the agricultural South), American factories sprung up to manufacture the durable consumer goods that otherwise might have been imported.[42] The tariff wall kept out most foreign manufactures except at the upper end of the market where high retail prices did not matter.

Benefiting from protectionism, the Second Industrial Revolution witnessed a flowering of small-scale manufacturing geared toward consumer culture, a story that is absent from the Chandler thesis. In the late nineteenth century, the sphere of the 'mechanical arts', a term used to describe the artisanal workshops of the craft economy, morphed into a larger space called the 'industrial arts'. Factories working in the industrial arts tradition often employed highly skilled European immigrant artisans or 'practical men' to oversee matters of design, production and aesthetics, alongside the lesser-skilled labourers who ran the machinery and garnished the goods. Industrial art schools emerged in the larger cities to train people for these jobs.[43] The most proficient of these artisans were, in the words of Taussig, 'alert, intelligent, and what is popularly called high-priced'.[44] The North American industrial arts complex produced what might be dubbed 'everyday luxuries' for personal embellishment and household adornment: fabrics, ready-to-wear, millinery, shoes, costume jewellery, household linen, silverware, furniture, picture frames, bric-à-brac, crockery, glassware, parlour organs and chromo prints like *American Progress*. Women were the principal purchasers of these items because they had oversight of the home and family, but men indulged in personalized shaving mugs, cut-glass liquor decanters and finely tailored suits. By creating an economic space for the 'style industries', protectionism thus encouraged the growth of mass consumption.

The creative economy that generated the much-coveted style goods was dominated by small family firms and, unlike the powerful Chandlerian corporations, those businesses did not have a direct lifeline to the market. A large steel mill could negotiate directly with a few major customers whose orders kept the blast furnaces going, but a costume-jewellery factory produced items that were retailed by thousands of different shops all around the country. These manufacturers needed help getting in touch with the customers, and for market reconnaissance, they relied on merchants. Factories in the industrial heartland created the style goods, and the merchants put the accoutrements of respectability in front of strivers who yearned for middle-class status.[45]

The symbiotic manufacturer–merchant relationship was a commonality that linked the First to the Second Industrial Revolution. In the earlier period, the Staffordshire potter Josiah Wedgwood famously complimented his business partner, the merchant Thomas Bentley, by writing, 'You have taste'. A seasoned salesman with social connections in Liverpool, Manchester and London, the classically educated Bentley brought a knowledge of tradition, social customs and fashion to the pottery partnership. Bentley turned the Wedgwood brand into a must-have collectable by opening lavish showrooms in trendy areas of London and Bath, where men and women of fashion could browse and handle creamware teapots, basalt vases and jasper cameos of politicians, philosophers and actors. While the showrooms pushed high-end products to the 'Great People', the factory sold spin-off products in great quantities to 'the middling People'.[46] A century later during the Second Industrial Revolution, North American companies in the style industries similarly engaged with merchants, notably tapping into their unrivalled knowledge of consumer habits and social emulation. Along these lines, the Homer Laughlin China Company of East Liverpool, Ohio, and Newell, West Virginia, became the largest pottery in the world by forging partnerships with the new retailers that emerged after the Civil War and dominated the North American commercial scene for the next hundred years.[47]

The Retailing Revolution

Merchants performed the indispensable task of linking manufacturers to consumers and, in their role as 'fashion intermediaries', they helped to usher in the age of mass consumption.[48] In the immediate postbellum era, manufactured goods found their way into consumers' hands only after passing through multiple layers of distributors.[49] Factories in Trenton, New Jersey, sold their teapots and dinner plates to large wholesalers who in turn sold the dishes to regional crockery jobbers who paid travelling salesmen to market them to small chinaware shops in towns and cities around the country. Each party added a markup, increasing the cost.[50] Many style goods remained out of reach to the average consumer because of the high retail price. This began to change in the closing decades of the nineteenth century with the deflationary economy and the appearance of mail-order catalogues, department stores and chain stores. These new merchants bypassed the jobbers, sourced goods from the manufacturers, and sold them directly to consumers.[51] They often collaborated with factories in the industrial heartland to 'imagine the consumer' and design style goods that suited the tastes of discrete market segments.[52]

As a major city in the industrial heartland, Chicago played an important role in the rise of modern mass distribution. In the 1860s, this boom town on Lake Michigan, was populated by small businesses that collected raw materials from the hinterlands and processed them for local and regional distribution. After the Great Chicago Fire of 1871, the city reinvented itself to become a major national distribution centre for raw materials, producer goods and consumer products by capitalizing on geography and the railroad boom. An intricate railway network snaked across middle America, transporting Texas cattle, Iowa corn and Ohio glassware to the shores of Lake Michigan for processing, packaging and redistribution to small cities and towns from Appalachia to the Rockies.[53] A distinctive type of business – the mail-order house – emerged to distribute these goods to remote parts of the country. Established in 1872, the first major mail-order company was Montgomery Ward & Company, which encountered major competition with the rise of Sears, Roebuck and Company in the 1880s. Besides these leaders, countless other Chicago mail-order houses sold furniture, farm equipment, seeds, appliances and clothing. Rural Free Delivery and Parcel Post, two initiatives by the United States Post Office dating to 1896 and 1913, respectively, gave a big boost to the mail-order business.[54]

In 1893, Chicago celebrated its commercial success by hosting the World's Columbian Exposition, a fair commemorating the arrival of Christopher Columbus in the western hemisphere some 400 years before. The lakefront fairground, filled with alabaster buildings suggestive of Renaissance grandeur, was nicknamed the 'White City' because the neoclassical architecture was brightly illuminated after dark with the new electric lightbulbs.[55] After visiting the White City, tourists could go to the downtown shopping district at The Loop, where they saw other marvels of the new technological age: elevated railways, skyscrapers ornamented with colourful terra cotta, and a proliferation of stores. A major State Street attraction was Marshall Field & Company, one of the city's biggest department stores, recently expanded with an annex by Daniel H. Burnham, the distinguished skyscraper architect.[56]

American merchants did not invent the department store. They borrowed the idea of a large, fashionable emporium offering a range of goods from the French and adapted it to suit a much larger, more complex market. A pioneer department store appeared in mid-nineteenth-century Paris when the Bon Marché, a haberdashery on the Left Bank, diversified from selling fabrics, thread, buttons and other sewing supplies into early ready-made clothing and household products. Emile Zola's historical novel *Au Bonheur des Dames*, first published as a serial in 1882–83, popularized the idea of the Parisian department store as the great tantalizer whose seductive displays stimulated desire and opened wallets.[57] But even before Zola's book, American merchants who visited Europe on buying trips studied the new Parisian merchandising methods. Back home, they started to diversify their merchandise and experiment with the departmentalized format. In New York in 1874, R. H. Macy and Company added a chinaware section at the suggestion of crockery importer Nathan Straus.[58] In Philadelphia in 1876, the clothier

John Wanamaker opened his spacious Grand Depot in an old Pennsy freight station, offering tempting merchandise to tourists in town for the Centennial Exposition, a world's fair celebrating America's hundredth birthday.[59] By 1907, Marshall Field had a Renaissance Revival skyscraper store designed by Burnham, and in 1911, John Wanamaker got one too. Field and Wanamaker engaged in a long-distance rivalry, each claiming that his department store was the best one ever.

By the early twentieth century, nearly every Main Street in the United States had one or more family-owned department stores that stocked a variety of fabrics, ready-made clothing and home goods suited to local tastes.[60] Larger cities had a handful, each catering to a different market segment. The big stores competed for customers by making themselves into technological marvels. They accessorized with the latest high-tech equipment: enormous plate-glass show windows, revolving doors, elevators, escalators, cash registers, pneumatic tube systems for circulating orders, marble staircases, wood panelling, spacious display areas, central heating and brilliant electric lighting. In Philadelphia, Wanamaker targeted wealthy shoppers while stores like Gimbel Brothers and the now-forgotten Frank & Seder stocked goods for the throngs of clerks, domestic servants, factory workers and small business owners who wanted to buy their way to respectability (Figure 19.3).

The growing market generated the need for smaller, reliable shops that sold odds-and-ends for the household. In rural areas, consumers could buy these necessities at the old-fashioned general store or by mail through a catalogue. At mid-century, the streets of

GRANBY STREET BY NIGHT, NORFOLK, VA.

Figure 19.3 One hallmark of technological modernity was the downtown shopping district with large retail stores having plate-glass show windows and electric illumination.
Source: Postcard, author's collection.

larger cities witnessed the appearance of specialized chain retailers selling tea, coffee, sugar and drinking vessels, foremost among them the Great Atlantic and Pacific Tea Company, or the A&P. In 1879, the entrepreneur Frank W. Woolworth emulated this model to open his first 'five-and-ten', a small bazaar jam-packed with household essentials, and was soon operating a string of these dime stores. In the 1890s, Woolworth studied census reports about the expanding manufacturing cities of the Northeast and concentrated on opening stores in places with large working-class and immigrant populations, people with aspirations and a tad of spending money. By 1913, Woolworth's had expanded internationally, having nearly 700 stores in the United States, Canada and England.[61]

Historians have focused on the department store as a transformative space, as the great urban consumption palace whose alluring displays whet women's appetites for the latest designs, thereby helping to democratize consumption.[62] However, for much of this period, department stores were mainly stand-alone, one-of-a-kind institutions that buttressed the status quo and maintained the social hierarchy. The John Wanamaker store in downtown Philadelphia exuded such an air of exclusivity that working-class girls dared not pass through the impressive brass-and-glass doors. In Houston, Foley's remained off-limits to black shoppers until after the Civil Rights Movement took off in the 1960s.[63] In contrast, the Chicago mail-order houses reached out to rural America with style goods that suited country tastes. Chain stores were also remarkably astute marketers. The branch system meant that they had many different types of stores, operating in different neighbourhoods to reach people of various classes, races and ethnicities. Showy illuminated department-store windows may have ignited consumer desire, but old-fashioned shops, mail-order houses and chain stores also did their part to advance the consumer economy, delivering style goods to a broad swathe of the North American population.

The American Dream and Mass Consumption

In 1931, James Truslow Adams, a popular writer and historian, coined the term 'American Dream' in his book, *The Epic of America*. Adams offered the first detailed analysis of an abstraction that had been circulating for generations, the aspiration without a name.[64] By no coincidence did the phrase American Dream enter the popular lexicon in the wake of the Jazz Age and the Stock Market Crash, two moments that encapsulated, respectively, the glittery façade and the dark underbelly of unfettered American capitalism.

The Second Industrial Revolution had established the United States and Germany as economic rivals to Great Britain. During the First World War, the proliferation of high-paying manufacturing jobs in war plants encouraged a population shift akin to the westward swoosh in *American Progress*. The Great Migration of rural blacks out of the South – where Jim Crow policies carried on the Confederate legacy of Hammond and his ilk – ultimately reconfigured the racial make-up of large northern industrial cities. On the one hand, the migration planted the seeds for African American entrepreneurship in businesses like beauty products, and on the other, introduced

Jim Crow to the North, segregating new arrivals into less-desirable neighbourhoods. The post-war recession yielded to an economic boom that celebrated capitalism while hiding its major weaknesses. A renewed commitment to protectionism and restrictive immigration laws went into effect at mid-decade, revealing more dark undercurrents. Technologically driven firms put a new spin on consumer culture by promoting high-tech goods: cameras, phonographs, records, radios, electrical gadgets, plastic boudoir sets and rayon dresses. The industrial arts complex, mass retailing and the creative industries benefited the heightened technological enthusiasm. On the East Coast, New York cemented its position as the national style centre, its major industry being ready-to-wear, while on the West Coast, Hollywood exerted a powerful sway over mass entertainment and celebrity culture.

It was in this context that Adams posited that every American could strive to achieve something better. He encouraged his readers to abandon hedonism for introspection. Adams critiqued the rising culture of personality and the seductive allure of modernity for the simpler times of his imagination. But modern advertising, retailing, movies and celebrity fandom exerted a powerful influence over strivers as the pull of church and community diminished. As modernity came to be associated with technological sophistication, ever more consumers looked to project an image of who they wanted to be through the things they owned. Despite Adams's noble ambitions, the American Dream came to be defined by leisure, lifestyle and the acquisition of stylish, high-tech goods.

The motor car emerged as the ultimate symbol of the American Dream, as rooted in technological progress and consumer culture (Figure 19.4). As with the department store, the Americans did not invent the gasoline-powered vehicle, but they figured out how to make cars accessible to a broad swathe of the population. Chandler justified his laser focus on firms like the Pennsylvania Railroad, the DuPont Company and the General Motors Corporation (GM) because they pioneered modern management practices. The modernization of consumer society and the role of Detroit automakers in this process was beyond his remit. In 1920, the Ford Motor Company, a family firm headed by tinkerer–founder Henry Ford, dominated the American car industry due to the popularity of the reliable, no-frills Model T. Ford built his reputation, maintained control over his workforce and offered affordable cars through a series of innovations that collectively defined Fordism: interchangeable parts made on special-purpose machine tools, the moving assembly line operated by workers earning the high wage of $5 per day, and functional vehicles sold at low prices. Ford customers – farmers, small businessmen and factory workers – liked his cars because they were plain and you could fix them yourself. Fordism, it turned out, was not well suited to consumer culture of the 1920s. By mid-decade, Ford grappled with the challenge of a lifetime as his firm locked horns with GM for control of the North American automobile market.[65]

Among the Detroit automakers, GM was the firm that most directly engaged with the rising consumer culture and most thoroughly understood the relationships among technology and taste. GM's visionary president, Alfred P. Sloan Jr (1875–1966), was the quintessential organizational man who, over the course of four decades,

Figure 19.4 The personal automobile became part of the consumer identity kit in the 1920s. Here we see fashionably dressed New Yorkers waiting to board a steamship, a sedan in the background.
Source: Cover of mail-order fashion catalogue, author's collection.

turned a struggling car company into an international giant. He not only introduced the multi-divisional structure that made it easier to manage a big business, but also capitalized on the growing cultural interest in aesthetics and style. GM adopted some of Ford's manufacturing practices and augmented them with marketing innovations. Under Sloan, GM introduced comfortable closed sedans, created the General Motors Acceptance Corporation to push the instalment plan, targeted women by advertising the car as a fashion accessory, and introduced the concept of trading up, among other things.[66] Further, GM stood out among big business by making design an integral part of corporate strategy. Sloan foregrounded aesthetics by establishing an Art and Colour

Section charged with transforming functional vehicles into desirable consumer products. The division was headed by the designer Harley J. Earl, who had built customized luxury vehicles for Hollywood royalty, and was guided over the rainbow by H. Ledyard Towle, formerly a wartime camoufleur, adman and colourist for DuPont lacquers.[67] Over time, GM introduced a family of cars for every purse and purpose and made the annual model change into the hallmark of the Detroit auto industry. Trained as an engineer, Sloan was himself a dapper dresser, always perfectly turned out in a starched white collar, a flamboyant silk cravat, an exquisitely tailored suit and ultra-shiny shoes.[68] The Chandler school never seems to have noticed Sloan's fashionable demeanour or connected his personal interest in style to his corporate investment in aesthetics.

GM introduced style to the durable goods revolution of the 1920s, which included big-ticket items such as kitchen stoves, refrigerators and bathroom fixtures. Everything including the kitchen sink received a fashion makeover, be it changes to the shape or the application of brilliant colour. While creative professionals were new to Detroit, the commercialization of style was the modus operandi in many other manufacturing sectors. The Ohio potteries were masters of the annual model change and segmented markets. Often touted as innovative, GM's investment in design and production thus echoed some of the long-established practices of the style industries, rather than vice versa.

The Walmarting of America

In the popular imagination, the two decades after the Second World War are often romanticized as the golden age of the North American economy, the era of new suburban development, TV shows like *Leave It to Beaver*, and upward mobility for blue-collar factory workers. The Pittsburgh steel mills, Cleveland oil refineries and Detroit automakers earned record profits. Their male employees achieved some access to the American Dream, benefiting from high union wages and, if veterans, mortgage guarantees provided by the GI Bill of Rights. The modern house outfitted with shiny new appliances became part of the consumer identity kit, new potent symbols of the American Dream alongside a Detroit dream machine.[69] This rosy picture, while not as fantastical as a romp through Disneyland, was little more than a veneer, the camouflage that covered up the hairline cracks in the North American economy.

The American Dream was a cultural promise and a character-building exercise, a carrot dangled before strivers. It was not inclusive. In the interwar years, the American Dream skirted most blacks, unskilled workers, shop girls, clerks, farmers and mountain dwellers, many of whom had probably never heard of it. In the post-war years, African American veterans eligible for mortgage guarantees through the GI Bill encountered discrimination in the government's administration of loans and in restrictive zoning ordinances implemented in the new suburbs. Prohibited from buying new homes in developments like Levittown, New Jersey, they were often relegated into older, segregated urban neighbourhoods.[70] Within a few short years, the white working class also saw their version of the American Dream fracture. The Midwest, heavily dependent on the auto industry, was hit early and hard by de-industrialization. Since 1965, the United States and Canada had enjoyed a single auto market, with Detroit's 'Big Three' – Ford, GM and the Chrysler Corporation – operating plants in both countries and moving parts and new vehicles freely across the border.[71] As inexpensive Datsuns and Toyotas from a revitalized Japan gained a toehold in the North American market, particularly during the oil crises of the seventies, Detroit reassessed its commitment to the industrial heartland. In 1989, hometown boy Michael Moore filmed *Roger & Me*, a documentary about the economic decline of Flint, Michigan, in response to the mid-decade decision of Roger B. Smith, the chairman of General Motors, to close several GM plants, most in Flint, and move production to Mexico.[72]

The auto industry was not unique. Low-wage economies in Asia, Europe and Latin America updated their manufacturing sectors with an eye to exploiting international markets. From the 1960s onward, trade policies set by the multilateral General Agreement on Tariffs and Trade (GATT) eroded the competitiveness of many North American industries vis-à-vis the overseas competition. The old manufacturing firms who had trusted mass retailers to absorb their output were left high and dry when those customers looked abroad. The Woolworth's pottery buyer in New York who had sourced crockery in West Virginia during the Great Depression and the Second World War could, by the sixties, brag that he was a member of the jet set, justifying expensive international flights on the grounds that cheaper, more appealing goods could be found in Italy or Japan.[73] Elsewhere, large firms in the technology sector, such as RCA, a radio and television manufacturer, continued their quest for ever-cheaper labour, first by moving plants from the Northeast and Midwest to the South and then from the United States to Mexico.[74] The United States was net exporter of manufactured goods until 1983, when a trade deficit appeared. Imports continued to climb. In 1970, manufactured goods accounted for 68 per cent of total imports; thirty years later in 2000, they accounted for 83 per cent.[75] In the closing decades of the twentieth century, the great manufacturing district that once stretched from Lowell to St Louis entered a period of long decline. Addressing Cleveland steelworkers during his 1984 presidential campaign, Walter F. Mondale, a Democrat, blamed the supply-side economic policies of the Republican incumbent, President Ronald Reagan, for 'turning our industrial Midwest into a rust bowl', a term that journalists evolved into the better-known pejorative, 'the Rust Belt'.[76]

Other regions of the United States were shaped by new technologies, industries and government policies. The Cold War and the expansion of the military–industrial complex dramatically reshaped the South, the Southwest, northern California and the Pacific Northwest. In the South, massive government spending was channelled into high-technology research facilities and defence plants. Federal dollars attempted to pull the eleven ex-Confederate states and their geographic neighbours into modern times, turning a backwards region – a region called 'the Nation's No. 1 economic problem' by President Franklin Delano Roosevelt – into the 'Sunbelt' by the 1970s. Many white citizens benefited, while blacks were often left behind, echoing the injustices perpetuated long ago by Hammond and later buttressed by the Jim Crow laws.[77] The West Coast, home to Hollywood, took on a new persona around high-technology industries. In the interwar era, the counties south of San Francisco nurtured an electronics cluster, and in the post-war years, scientists and engineers were lured away from the East Coast for promising careers in high-tech industries. Inventions like the new audio oscillator, developed by William R. Hewlett and David Packard in 1938, and the integrated circuit, which emerged from Fairchild Semiconductor Corporation in 1960, laid the foundation for the region that became known as Silicon Valley in 1971.[78] Subsequent generations of Silicon Valley entrepreneurs, Steve Jobs foremost among them, made digital experiences an integral part of the American Dream with video games, personal computers and smartphones.

These economic and geographic upheavals reshaped mass consumption, foregrounded 'technology' in the consumer's mind and eroded the old social habit of striving. By the 1950s, downtown department stores like John Wanamaker and Marshall Field faced declining profits as young families turned to the new strip malls and shopping centres in the suburbs. At the low end of the trade, the new 'soft goods supermarket', a super-sized dime-store, provided free parking, lunch counters and rock-bottom prices. Among those 1,500 stores in 1962 were the brand-new K-mart, Walmart and Target, destined to become the dominant players in discount retailing.[79] The race to sell more goods at ever-cheaper prices began in the interwar years when national grocery chains invaded Main Street and lured customers away from traditional stores. In 1975, President Gerald R. Ford, a Republican, signed the Consumer Goods Pricing Act, which repealed the New Deal fair-trade laws.[80] Breaking away from the concept of shopping as an urban luxury experience, the no-frills discount stores offered piles of inexpensive goods for the whole family, everything from Barbie dolls to Kodak cameras and RCA televisions. Over the course of the late twentieth century, the discounters went from being regional chains to serving the national market. While the luxurious surroundings at Marshall Field encouraged aspiration, the warehouse atmosphere of the discount stores signalled to shoppers that it was okay to show up in flip flops.

A brief look at Walmart sheds light on how this sea change affected the consumer economy. Established in 1962 in Arkansas, Walmart by 2023 was a multinational corporation with retail stores in twenty countries. North American operations included 5,317 units in the United States, 2,852 in Mexico and 401 in Canada.[81] For a brief period in the mid to late 1980s coincident with de-industrialization, Walmart advertised 'Made in the USA' merchandise in a feeble assertion of red-state, Evangelical Christian, Buy American patriotism. In the early 1990s, Walmart, still an upstart, looked beyond the Sunbelt to establish a national footprint. Eyeing the wallets of rural and small-town America, it sought ways to cut prices, and in doing so, turned to foreign merchandise. The container revolution that reduced shipping costs starting in the 1960s encouraged Walmart and other discounters to scour low-wage sweatshop economies that could make goods at rock-bottom prices.[82] Walmart became a master of supply-chain management and logistics, exerting greater control over US suppliers like Procter & Gamble, a giant in personal and home-care products, as well as factories on the other side of the world.

The retailers' shift to imported goods coincided with a series of free-trade initiatives launched in the Reagan–Bush era. These included, but were not limited to, the Canada–United States Free Trade Agreement of 1989; its successor, the North American Free Trade Agreement of 1994; and the World Trade Organization that replaced the GATT in 1995.[83] Seeking to avoid the tariff wars that deepened the Great Depression, these free-trade agreements aimed to build a new global order around international commerce. China joined the WTO in December of 2001, and on 1 January 2005, the WTO removed the last bilateral quotas on apparel and textiles.[84] By 2023, those bargain blue jeans from Walmart, once sewn in a unionized clothing factory in the industrial heartland, were most likely made by sweatshop labour somewhere in Asia.

At the turn of the century, other retailers emulated the Walmart model and remade themselves into big-box discount stores. Notable examples were Home Depot and Lowe's in hardware; Best Buy in electronics; Bed, Bath & Beyond in soft home goods; Christmas Tree Shops in holiday decorations; and Staples in office supplies, among others. By the New Millennium, no-frills big-box stores were the major players in North American retailing and the dominant feature of the suburban commercial landscape. Their rise killed off the regional discount chains and brick-and-mortar operations of the old Chicago mail-order houses and eroded the profitability of the last department stores.[85] In recent years, online shopping has invaded the big-box space, necessitating an investment in digital merchandising and home delivery.

Conclusion: American Progress Redux

John Gast's vision of technology as a driver of economic change is worth revisiting as we close this chapter. In 1872, *American Progress* showed transport and communications enabled by the telegraph, the steamship and the railroad. Nobody in Gast's world uttered the word 'technology', referring instead to 'the machine' when talking about the latest inventions. In the early twentieth century, the moderns let go of the idea of 'the machine' as a mark of progress and began to think about how 'technology' might overcome the conventional use of time and space. Modern consumers were the first to live with cars, electricity and electronics. Post-war consumers saw further innovations: the interstate highway system, jet travel, televisions, transistor radios, analogue mainframe computers and the new digital calculators and minicomputers.[86] The march of technology continues in our own time, the digital age.

When Steve Jobs announced the Apple iPhone in 2007, few imagined it would launch an electronics revolution that would make 'information snacking' commonplace and shatter consumption habits that had been evolving since the First Industrial Revolution. By the time Jobs held up the first smartphone, consumers were no strangers to personal computing and portable telephony.[87] Many adults in the United States were accustomed to cruising the Web, with three-quarters owning a desktop computer. By 2023, the percentage of mobile-phone ownership had grown to 97 per cent of American adults, and of those, 90 per cent owned a smartphone that could provide access to the Web.[88] Consumers now invest more time and energy in digital devices, services and programmes than in the legacy products of the Second Industrial Revolution, the durable goods that defined the American Dream for earlier generations. Today, 'technology' is synonymous with consumer electronics, testifying to the persuasiveness of Silicon Valley in marketing as well its prowess in engineering. If John Gast's allegorical America came to life in the Metaverse, she might be nonplussed by the shift away from respectable striving but would smile knowingly at the smartphone and our other electronic gadgets, nodding to the American enthusiasm for 'the machine' in its newest form.

Notes

1. See, for example, Martha A. Sandweiss, 'John Gast, American Progress, 1872', in American Social History Project, Center for Media and Learning, The Graduate Center, City University of New York, *Picturing United States History*, at picturinghistory.gc.cuny.edu (accessed 9 February 2023).

2. T. P. Hughes (1990), *American Genesis: A Century of Invention and Technological Enthusiasm, 1870–1970*. New York: Penguin Books, 1–12.

3. One example is 'The 1619 Project', *The New York Times Magazine*, 14 August 2019, at www.nytimes.com (accessed 9 February 2023).

4. D. Gilpin Faust (1982), *James Henry Hammond and the Old South: A Design for Mastery*. Baton Rouge, LA: Louisiana State University Press.

5. James Henry Hammond, Speech on the Kansas-Lecompton Constitution, U.S. Senate, 4 March 1858. In *Congressional Globe*, 35th Cong., 1st session, Appendix, 70–71.

6. Recent research has uncovered Hammond's sexual abuse of his nieces and female slaves. See R. Brown (1989), 'Monster of all he surveyed', *The New York Times*, 29 January 1989.

7. Examples include Faust, *James Henry Hammond*; W. Johnson (1999), *Soul by Soul: Life inside the Antebellum Slave Mark*et. Cambridge, MA: Harvard University Press; and C. B. Dew (1994), *Bond of Iron: Master and Slave at Buffalo Forge*. New York: W. W. Norton & Company.

8. R. Bailey (1994), 'The other side of slavery: Black labor, cotton, and textile industrialization in Great Britain and the United States', *Agricultural History*, 68 (1), 35–50.

9. S. Beckert (2015), *Empire of Cotton: A New History of Global Capitalism*. London: Penguin Books; and Beckert (2017), 'Cotton and the global origins of capitalism', *Journal of World History*, 28 (1), 107–20.

10. T. Burnard and G. Riello (2020), 'Slavery and the new history of capitalism', *Journal of Global History*, 15 (2), 225–44.

11. Bailey, 'The other side of slavery'.

12. R. F. Dalzell (1987), *Enterprising Elite: The Boston Associates and the World They Made*. Cambridge, MA: Harvard University Press; L. F. Gross (1993), *The Course of Industrial Decline: The Boott Cotton Mills of Lowell, Massachusetts, 1835–1955*. Baltimore, MD: Johns Hopkins University Press, 3–6.

13. National Park Service, Lowell National Historical Park, 'Women's Activism in Lowell' and 'The Acre', at nps.gov (accessed 25 February 2024).

14. J. Greenlees (2019), *When the Air Became Important: A Social History of the New England and Lancashire Textile Industries*. New Brunswick, NJ: Rutgers University Press, 17–18.

15. A. Greenspan and A. Wooldridge (2018), *Capitalism in America: A History*. London: Allen Lane, 80.

16. Sherman cited by Greenspan and Wooldridge, *Capitalism in America*, 80.

17. Brown, 'Monster of all he surveyed'.

18. Greenspan and Wooldridge, *Capitalism in America*, 86–87.

19. F. W. Taussig (1910), *The Tariff History of the United States*, 5th edn, New York: G. P. Putnam's Sons, 155–70.

20. D. A. Hounshell (1984), *From the American System to Mass Production, 1800–1932: The Development of Manufacturing Technology in the United States*. Baltimore, MD: Johns Hopkins University Press, 67–123; A. Godley (2006), 'Selling the sewing machine around the world: Singer's international marketing strategies, 1850–1920', *Enterprise and Society*, 7 (2), 266–314.

21. M. R. Wilson (2006), 'The politics of procurement: Military origins of bureaucratic autonomy', *Journal of Policy History*, 54–5.

22. S. Beckert (2003), *The Monied Metropolis: New York City and the Consolidation of the American Bourgeoisie, 1850–1896*. New York: Cambridge University Press, 120, 135–6; F. Allen (1876), *American Silk Industry, Chronologically Arranged, 1793–1876*. New York: Silk Association of America, 30.

23. Robert W. Fogel led the pack. See D. Costa et al. (2013), 'In memorium: Robert W. Fogel', *Journal of Economic History*, 73, 1164–7.

24. On the enduring influence of Chandler's work, see S. W. Usselman (2006), 'Still visible: Alfred D. Chandler's The Visible Hand', *Technology and Culture*, 47, 584–96. For a more critical assessment, see M. H. Rose (2008), 'Alfred DuPont Chandler, Jr., 1918–2007: An introduction', *Enterprise & Society*, 9, 405–10.

25. T. K. McCraw (2008), 'Alfred Chandler: His vision and achievement', *Business History Review*, 82, 216, 219–20.

26. McCraw, 'Alfred Chandler', 217. Major works that focus on the United States include A. D. Chandler Jr (1959), 'The beginnings of "big business" in American industry', *Business History Review*, 33, 1–31; A. D. Chandler Jr (1962), *Strategy and Structure: Chapters in the History of the Industrial Enterprise*. Cambridge, MA: The MIT Press; and A. D. Chandler Jr (1977), *The Visible Hand: The Managerial Revolution in American Business*. Cambridge, MA: The Belknap Press of Harvard University Press.

27. On the American model abroad, see A. D. Chandler Jr and T. Hikino (1990), *Scale and Scope: The Dynamics of Industrial Capitalism*. Cambridge, MA: The Belknap Press of Harvard University Press.

28. Chandler, *Visible Hand*, 8 ('New').

29. F. E. Heath, 'Invisible Hand', *Encyclopaedia Britannica* at Britannica.com (accessed 19 February 2023).

30. Pennsylvania Rail Road Company, 'Great Central Penna. Rail Road Route for the West', February 1855, flyer, Westmoreland Coal Company Collection, acc. 1933.233, Group 1, Album, p. 27, Audiovisual Collections and Digital Initiatives Dept., Hagley Museum and Library, Wilmington, DE, USA [hereafter cited HML-AVD], at digital.hagley.org (accessed 23 February 2023).

31. J. F. Wall (1989), *Andrew Carnegie*. New York: University of Pittsburgh Press, ch. 6.

32. Wall, *Andrew Carnegie*, chs 8–9.

33. Ibid., ch. 11, 15–16.

34. Ibid., ch. 20; Chandler, *Visible Hand*, 361.

35. T. J. Misa (1995), *A Nation of Steel: The Making of Modern America, 1865–1925*. Baltimore, MD: Johns Hopkins University Press.

36. Chandler, *Visible Hand*, 299–301.

37. Ibid., 293–5.

38. Ibid., 290–2, 295–6.

39. Greenspan and Wooldridge, *Capitalism in America*, 61–5.

40. Taussig, *Tariff History*, 174 ('restraint').

41. Ibid., Part II.

42. On the importance of European consumer goods in North America, see K. Hoganson (2002), 'Cosmopolitan domesticity: Importing the American Dream, 1865–1920', *American Historical Review* 107, 55–83.

43. This discussion draws on the author's research on the industrial arts tradition, most fully articulated in two monographs: R. L. Blaszczyk (2000), *Imagining Consumers: Design and Innovation from Wedgwood to Corning*. Baltimore, MD: Johns Hopkins University Press; and R. L. Blaszczyk (2012), *The Color Revolution*. Cambridge, MA: The MIT Press. See also P. B. Scranton (1991), 'Diversity in diversity: Flexible production and American industrialization, 1880–1930', *Business History Review*, 65, 27–90; E. Shales (2010), *Made in Newark: Cultivating Industrial Arts and Civil Identity in the Progressive Era*. New Brunswick, NJ: Rutgers University Press; and F. Carnevali (2011), 'Fashioning luxury for factory girls: American jewelry, 1860–1940', *Business History Review*, 85, 295–317.

44. F. W. Taussig (1905), 'The present position of the doctrine of free trade', *Publications of the American Economic Association*, 3rd series, 6, 29–65 (37, 'alert').

45. On aspiration and consumption, see J. Wills (2003), 'Respectable mediocrity: The everyday life of an ordinary American striver, 1876–1890', *Journal of Social History*, 37, 323–49.

46. Blaszczyk, *Imagining Consumers*, 6–9.

47. Ibid., chs 3, 4 and 7.

48. See, for example, Blaszczyk, *Imagining Consumers*, 12–13, and chs 3–4.

49. Chandler, *The Visible Hand*, ch. 7.

50. Blaszczyk, *Imagining Consumers*, ch. 2–3.

51. R. L. Blaszczyk (2009), *American Consumer Society, 1865–2005: From Hearth to HDTV*. Hoboken, NJ: Wiley.

52. The importance of merchant–manufacturer relationships to product design is explored in Blaszczyk, *Imagining Consumers*, chs 3–4.

53. For an overview of Chicago as a commercial centre, see W. Cronin (1991), *Nature's Metropolis: Chicago and the Great West*. New York: Norton.

54. Blaszczyk, *American Consumer Society*, 84–90.

55. Bureau International des Expositions (2017), 'Illuminating the White City: Tesla vs. Edison at Expo 1893 Chicago', at bie-paris.org (accessed 24 February 2023).

56. National Register of Historic Places (1977), Inventory–Nomination Form, 'Marshall Field & Company Store', in Record Group 79: Records of the National Park Service, National Archives and Records Service, Washington, DC, at catalog.archives.gov/id/28891548 (accessed 24 February 2023).

57. M. B. Miller (1981), *The Bon Marché: Bourgeois Culture and the Department Store, 1869–1920*. Princeton, NJ: Princeton University Press.

58. Blaszczyk, *Imagining Consumers*, 66.

59. *The Golden Book of the Wanamaker Stores: Jubilee Year, 1861–1911* (1911). Philadelphia, PA: John Wanamaker, 43–8.

60. V. Howard (2015), *From Main Street to Mall: The Rise and Fall of the American Department Store*. Philadelphia, PA: University of Pennsylvania Press.

61. Blaszczyk, *American Consumer Society*, 79–82.

62. W. Leach (1994), *Land of Desire: Merchants, Power, and the Rise of a New American Culture*. New York: Vintage Books.

63. T. Tomkins-Walsh (2014), 'Remembering Foley's', *Houston History Magazine*, 11, 31–35.

64. J. T. Adams (1933), *The Epic of America*, new edn. Boston, MA: Little, Brown & Company; J. Cullen (2003), *The American Dream: A Short History of an Idea that Shaped a Nation*. New York: Oxford University Press; and L. R. Samuel (2012), *The American Dream: A Cultural History*. Syracuse, NY: Syracuse University Press.

65. R. S. Tedlow (1996), *New and Improved: The Story of Mass Marketing in America*. Boston, MA: Harvard Business School Press, ch. 3.

66. Ibid.

67. Blaszczyk, *The Color Revolution*, ch. 5.

68. Photographs of Sloan testify to his taste in fine clothes. See, for example, 'Launching party for the yacht, Rene', 19 September 1929, Pusey and Jones Corporation Photograph Collection, acc. 1972.350, HML-AVD, at digital.hagley.org (accessed 26 February 2023).

69. Blaszczyk, *American Consumer Society*, Part 3.

70. J. M. Stahura (1986), 'Suburban development, black suburbanization and the Civil Rights Movement since World War II', *American Sociological Review*, 51, 131–44.

71. M. Levinson (2016), *An Extraordinary Time: The End of the Postwar Boom and the Return of the Ordinary Economy*. New York: Basic Books, 128.

72. Dog Eat Dog Films (1989), *Roger & Me*, produced by Michael Moore, Warner Brothers.

73. Joseph M. Wells III, interview by Regina Lee Blaszczyk at the Homer Laughlin China Company, Newell, WV, August 1993.

74. J. Cowie (1999), *Capital Moves: RCA's Seventy-Year Quest for Cheap Labor*. New York: The New Press, 1–2.

75. E. Bonacich with K. Hardie, 'Wal-Mart and the logistics revolution', in N. Lichtenstein (ed.) (2006), *Wal-Mart: The Face of Twenty-First Century Capitalism*. New York: The New Press, 164–5.

76. J. Wallenfeldt, 'Rust Belt', *Encyclopaedia Britannica*, at Britannica.com (accessed 19 February 2023).

77. B. J. Schulman (1994), *From Cotton Belt to Sunbelt: Federal Policy, Economic Development, and the Transformation of the South, 1938–1980*. Durham, NC: Duke University Press, xi–xv, 3.

78. M. Kenney (ed.) (2000), *Understanding Silicon Valley: The Anatomy of an Entrepreneurial Region*. Stanford, CA: Stanford University Press; C. Lécuyer (2007), *Making Silicon Valley: Innovation and the Growth of High Tech, 1930–1970*. Cambridge, MA: The MIT Press.

79. Blaszczyk, *American Consumer Society*, 208–9.

80. Ibid., 212.

81. Walmart Inc., 'About', at corporate.walmart.com (accessed 26 February 2023).

82. N. Lichtenstein, 'Wal-Mart: A template for twenty-first century capitalism', 3–30, in Lichtenstein (ed.), *Wal-Mart*.

83. R. L. Blaszczyk (2017), *Fashionability: Abraham Moon and the Creation of British Goods for the Global Market*. Manchester: Manchester University Press, 232, 250, 260.

84. Ibid., 260.

85. Blaszczyk, *American Consumer Society*, ch. 7.

86. Ibid., 268–9.

87. Ibid., ch. 9.

88. Pew Research Center (2024) 'Mobile fact sheet', 31 January, at pewresearch.org (accessed 25 February 2024).

CHAPTER 20
ECONOMIC CHANGE IN EAST ASIA FROM THE SEVENTEENTH TO THE TWENTIETH CENTURY
Debin Ma

What Is East Asia?

Although defying precise demarcation, East Asia can be defined in geographic, political and cultural terms. Situated largely at the eastern end of the Asian continent, East Asia is more closely associated with today's nation states or regions of China, Japan, North and South Korea, and Northern Vietnam but could, for cultural reasons, include the far-flung city state of Singapore. Three interrelated historical identities are shared in varying degrees across East Asia. First is the use of classical Chinese characters among the educated elites and the corresponding adoption of the teachings of Confucius as the ruling ideology. This is coupled with a hierarchical civil bureaucracy inculcated in the teachings of Confucian classics and superimposed upon a predominantly agrarian economic structure. And finally, East Asia is an international order based on what is called a 'tributary system'.

As a reflection of a Neo-Confucian cosmology, the political order of the tributary system consisted of radiating concentric rings, with political power emanating from the imperial seat of the Chinese emperor out towards administrative provinces, tributary or vassal states, and mutual trade zones. The tributary states system created a political framework in which neighbouring small states maintained a status of near protectorate and within which cross-national trade, although restricted, was conducted. This China-centred hierarchical worldview was internalized by periphery states such as Korea, Northern Vietnam and, to a certain extent, Japan, who, in turn, imposed a 'satellite tributary system' upon other smaller states.[1] East Asian states prevailed within the tributary system until aggressive Western imperialism reached China's shore by the mid-nineteenth century.

East Asia in the Seventeenth to the Nineteenth Centuries

The seventeenth century saw the onset of new political regimes in Qing China (1644–1911), Tokugawa Japan (1603–1868), and the consolidation of the Choson dynasty in Korea (1392–1897). Despite being a minority tribe hailed from China's north-eastern border, the Manchu rulers turned Qing China into a mature, highly centralized, unitary political regime governed by an absolutist emperor at the top of the power pyramid, aided by a formal bureaucracy recruited through a highly structured national civil service examination based on Confucian classics. The formal imperial regime coexisted alongside the emperor's personal rule, his personal entourage of eunuchs, consort and other inner court staffs.[2] While Korea more faithfully reproduced the Chinese system of governance with variation and adaptations, the Japanese system of governance remained far more fractured and decentralized under the Tokugawa regime when the emperor was sidelined in Kyoto as a symbolic figure. The real power resided instead in the hands of a military general-bureaucrat (the Shogun) in Tokyo. But even the Shogunate's rule only directly controlled part of the Japanese territory and coexisted with 300 autonomous daimyos.[3]

Both cohesion and diversity characterized East Asia as an integrated cultural zone or sphere. Firstly, despite the dominance of Chinese classics across the entire area, the diversity of ethnic and national identities remained important. Indeed, the Qing Empire was ruled by a non-Han minority group from Manchuria (in north-eastern China) who had had a long-standing engagement with the Han Chinese over the centuries. In fact, the ascendancy of Manchu rule over the vast Han Chinese population through the founding of Qing in 1644 sparked a prolonged legitimacy crisis as both Japan and Korea did feel the once lowly Manchus were far from qualified to be legitimate heir to the great Confucian ideology once held by the Ming dynasty. The interaction between Han Chinese or Confucian cultures and other cultures in the region should be viewed as a bi-directional flow rather than that of Han Chinese dominance.[4] Secondly, connected with political and ideological exchange was the trade in goods and perhaps more importantly in technology – both formally and informally – under the tributary system. Despite the relative isolation, exchange led to the diffusion of technology that allowed regions and states of East Asia to catch up economically and technologically through import substitution during the early modern period. Among the outcomes was the creation of a well-articulated intra-Asian trading network somewhat independent of the Western trade systems that made serious inroads into East Asia only after the mid-nineteenth century.[5] Trade between East Asia and the world beyond remained limited though of critical importance. The export of Chinese silks and tea fuelled a passion for Chinoiserie in the West that eventually led to imitation and import substitution of Chinese products in Europe and India. In the opposite direction, the inflow of Latin American silver ingots and coins lubricated the engine of Chinese commerce and supported the monetization of public finance from the sixteenth century onwards. The introduction of New World crops such as maize, peanuts and potatoes sustained the population, which tripled during the Qing Empire.

The beginning of the nineteenth century may have seen the turn of the tide that had once favoured the fortune of Qing China. Population growth sustained by rising agricultural land productivity and the introduction of new crops may have finally stretched the limits of the constraints on resources. Beginning with the White Lotus

(1796–1804), a series of domestic rebellions culminating in the vast Taiping uprising (1851–64), one can observe an erosion of the Qing regime. Externally, following the collapse of East India Company's monopoly in 1833, British imperialism driven by private commercial interest intensified to the detriment of Chinese trade. The rise of the trade in Indian opium to China reversed China's long-standing trade surplus, draining silver specie out of the empire. The increasing scarcity of silver specie caused havoc across the economy, diminished the government's capacity to collect taxes and decreased the morale of the military.[6] This occurred because during the sixteenth and seventeenth centuries, mid-Ming reforms had led to the silverization of tax revenue and the use of silver as one of the mediums of exchange in the economy. Prompted by an urge to act, but armed with little understanding of the might of the rising Western imperialism, the Qing's military confrontation with England in the now famous Opium War of 1842 turned out to be a humiliating defeat. It also marked the fall of the world's largest and most remote empire into the orbit of Western imperialism. British arms forced the Qing to accept the Treaty of Nanking (1842), which ceded Hong Kong to the British, imposed a regime of virtual free trade and initiated the 'treaty port' system by opening five Chinese ports to British and other Western merchants. This agreement, which set the tone of China's international economic relations during the century prior to the Pacific War (1941–5), subsequently expanded to include dozens of treaty ports where foreign residents were protected by extraterritoriality at the expense of Chinese sovereignty.

In the eighteenth and nineteenth centuries, Tokugawa Japan shared commonalities as well as differences with Qing China. In contrast to the eighteenth-century population growth of Qing China, Japan's population remained stable. This led an early generation of historians to interpret this as a form of early modern Japanese exceptionalism vis-à-vis other Asian countries, creating a unique 'social structure' that allowed a precocious demographic transition for Japan. However, population stagnation can similarly be interpreted as the result of Japanese population being trapped by its land territory, which – unlike Qing China which saw a doubling of its territory – was circumscribed by its coastal borderlines.[7] However, there is little dispute that Japan diverged from China at the beginning of the nineteenth century as the country remained relatively peaceful, and sheltered from the dual crisis of opium and silver outflows that had gripped China. But this divergence should not be overstated as the onslaught of Western imperialism exerted equal if not more pressure on isolationist Tokugawa Japan. Indeed, after the opening up of East Asia to free trade under Western imperialism in the mid-nineteenth century, during their early attempts to expand business overseas, the Japanese suddenly found themselves under the pressure of a remarkable resurgence of China-based mercantile dominance across regions of East and Southeast Asia. In particular, Shanghai, as a newly opened treaty port, rapidly emerged as an important node in a vast trading network that enveloped, among others, the Japanese treaty ports of Yokohama and Kobe. The dominance and cohesion of Chinese merchant networks throughout Asia posed a challenge to the young Meiji government as formidable as the agenda of catching up with the West.[8]

Recent attempts at constructing new long-term Chinese GDP series seem to confirm earlier estimates by Maddison.[9] The claim that China was the world's leading economy in the seventeenth and eighteenth centuries was somewhat misleading based on a conflation of aggregate and per capita figures. Based largely on guesstimates, Maddison put China's annual per capita income at about $500–600 (international $ in 1990 prices), a level that was about 80 per cent (in 1500) and 35 per cent (in 1700) of the world's leading but much smaller economies of Britain and the Netherlands, respectively. But Maddison was right in trumpeting the aggregate size of the Chinese economy.[10] With a doubling of its territory and a tripling of its population between the fifteenth and the eighteenth centuries, no other early modern political entity achieved such size in both territory and population under a single political regime. But it will be a far cry to claim that any of this gave the Chinese economy the leading position that it may have held in the early centuries of the second millennium under the Song dynasty (960–1279 CE). The commercial, financial, political, technological and scientific revolutions that characterized a fragmented and quarrelsome Europe largely sidestepped the centralized but rigid Qing state, only to haunt it by the mid-nineteenth century. We can get a more comprehensive profile of the evolution of Chinese living standards and human capital in the nineteenth and twentieth centuries based on integrated estimates of real wage and anthropometric evidence. They confirm a general decline in living standards and human

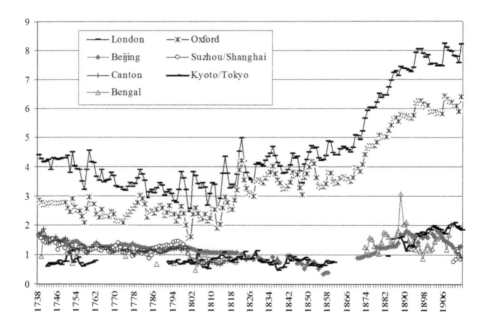

Figure 20.1 Real wages in Asia and England, 1738–1914.

Source: R. Allen, J.-P. Bassino, D. Ma, C. Moll-Murata and J. L. van Zanden (2011), 'Wages, prices, and living standards in China, Japan, and Europe, 1738–1925', *Economic History Review*, 64 (S1), 8–38.

capital after the mid-nineteenth century followed by a recovery only at the turn of the twentieth century (Figure 20.1). The real wage data also reveal that in the eighteenth and nineteenth centuries Chinese living standards were probably closer to the relatively underdeveloped parts of Europe but lower than Northwestern Europe. They confirm that a divergence in living standards and per capita income between Europe and China already existed before the Industrial Revolution and only widened from the nineteenth century onwards.[11] However, in contrast to the findings based on real wages and heights, the basic numeracy index reveals a relatively high level of Chinese human capital, which in the eighteenth and nineteenth centuries was closer to that of Northwestern Europe than countries with a comparable low level of living standards such as India or Turkey.[12]

Economic Change in Modern East Asia

Western imperialism represented an external threat drastically different from China's traditional nemesis on its Northern frontier and was therefore a watershed in Chinese history. The challenge was economic, political, institutional and ideological. The new era saw China start off disastrously with the outbreak of the devastating Taiping Rebellion (1850–62). It must be said that the Qing under the so-called Tongzhi Restoration (1861–75) engineered a remarkable economic recovery through the revitalization of traditional institutions: the reinstatement of Confucian orthodoxy, the restoration of the national civil service examination (largely interrupted during the Taiping Rebellion), and the initial exemption from land taxes to lure cultivators back to war-torn agricultural regions.

The Qing did not remain entirely passive to Western incursions. As a natural extension to the Tongzhi Restoration, powerful regional bureaucrats such as Li Hongzhang and Zhang Zhidong sponsored the Self-Strengthening Movement (1860–94), a programme that aimed to expand Chinese military strength by developing a small number of Western-style, capital-intensive enterprises financed by the state and directed by eminent officials who possessed the highest credentials awarded under the Confucian academic system. Although these enterprises – which included arsenals, factories and shipyards – were fraught with inefficiency and corruption, they did manage to record modest achievements. Nonetheless, the overall ideological orientation during this period remained conservative. In contrast to the concurrent Meiji reforms in Japan, no Chinese reform touched the fundamentals of the traditional regime: there was no introduction of modern constitution or commercial law; no reform in the currency system; modern banks or modern infrastructures such as railroads were expressly prohibited; and steamships were limited to major riverways such as the Yangzi River.

The direct impact of the treaty port system according to which Chinese trade tariffs were restricted to a modest 3–5 per cent was the expansion of China's international trade. China's maritime customs data show how real imports more than doubled in the quarter of a century prior to 1895, with exports increasing by half of that. Trade statistics suggest that after 1895 trade grew at a slower pace, around 2–3 per cent per annum. Despite its modest scale, trade gradually integrated major domestic commodity markets into the international exchange system of the Pacific Basin.

The treaty system accelerated the arrival of new technologies, initially to the treaty ports themselves, which became staging points for the diffusion of technologies into the domestic economy. However, industrialization continued to lag behind the opportunities opened up by trade and the inflow of new technology, partly due to powerful obstacles to innovation that existed within China's domestic economy. These barriers, which negatively affected the expansion of infrastructure such as modern railroads and inland steam shipping, are most clearly visible in the history of private efforts to introduce new technologies and new business arrangements in the processing of agricultural commodities like soybeans and silk larvae.[13]

In sharp contrast to Qing China, the Samurai clans that overthrew the old Tokugawa regime and came to power with the 1868 Meiji Restoration made no pretence to 'restore' Japan to her old days, but instead proclaimed to seek knowledge throughout the world. They embarked on a reform programme to forge a modern nation state modelled after the West. Japan's decisiveness in turning outwards in facing the Western imperial challenge stood in stark contrast to the contemporaneous Qing's determination to reinstate an orthodox Neo-Confucian ruling ideology to an empire that had been brought to the brink of collapse. In contrast to the Self-Strengthening Movement (1860–94) that pursued the modernization of the Chinese military through a series of either government-financed or government-controlled Western-style industrial enterprises, Meiji Japan threw its full support behind the private sector, which – with the sell-off of the limited number of government enterprises in the 1880s – was designated as the mainstay for Japan's industrialization. The self-strengtheners in China displayed either indifference or hostility towards private enterprise in modern sectors, supplied few critical modern public goods, and in most cases even opposed private efforts to build public infrastructure such as railroads and inland steam shipping. By contrast, the Meiji leaders engaged in the build-up of crucial social and physical infrastructures such as a modern legal system, public education, research and technological diffusion, a modern monetary and banking system, and modern transportation and communications. While there was little overhauling of its traditional political, legal, monetary and education system in nineteenth-century Qing China, the 1890s saw the birth of a newly transformed modern constitutional monarchy in Japan.[14]

Available macroeconomic statistics give an annual growth rate of Japanese per capita GDP at 2.25 per cent between 1887 and 1897. By 1910 the Japanese economy was 50 per cent larger than it had been in 1887. Japan's share of manufacturing and mining in total GDP rose from 8.7 per cent in 1887 to 11 per cent in 1897, and to 16 per cent in 1910.[15] Although rigorous quantitative comparison with Qing China are impossible due to the lack of reliable macroeconomic statistics for the late nineteenth century, it is clear that in China there was little industrial expansion except for government-sponsored enterprises which, however, created little spillover effect across the economy. As for agriculture, technological progress and productivity gains were largely absent while the effects and degrees of commercialization during this period were mixed.[16]

The absence of macroeconomic statistics hinders any attempts to pinpoint the critical historical moment when Japan overtook China in economic terms. However, China's humiliating naval defeat by Japan in 1894–5 serves as the litmus test of the merits of almost three decades of contrasting political and economic policies. This ignominious military defeat by a nation long regarded as China's minor tributary neighbour inflicted a profound mental shock on Chinese elites and the public at large. An immediate economic impact followed the 1895 signing of the Treaty of Shimonoseki, which granted foreigners the right to establish factories in the treaty ports. Eliminating the prohibition against foreign factories in treaty ports sparked a rapid expansion of foreign direct investment in China. This new arrangement indirectly legitimized Chinese modern enterprises. Despite some setbacks from the repression of the Hundred Days' reform centred in the southern province of Hunan in 1898, followed by the subsequent debacle surrounding the Boxer Rebellion in 1900, the Qing constitutional movement of 1903–11 was a far more comprehensive and ambitious initiative. It aimed at steering China towards a constitutional monarchy by drafting a formal modern constitution with national, provincial and local level parliaments. Military modernization was high on the reform agenda. Administrative reform sought to modernize public finance and adopt a national budget, as well as the setting up of new ministries of education, trade and agriculture, and encouraged the founding of local chambers of commerce.[17]

From the very end of the nineteenth century, Chinese activity in mining and manufacturing accelerated sharply from its small initial base. Overall industrial output showed double-digit real annual growth during the period 1912–36, a phenomenal result for that period, especially in view of China's turbulent political scene and the impact of the Great Depression. Factory production, initially focused on textiles, food processing, and other consumer products, concentrated in two regions: the Lower Yangzi area, where both foreign and Chinese entrepreneurs pursued factory expansion in and around Shanghai; and China's northeast or Manchurian region, where Japanese initiatives predominated. By 1935, Chinese factories, including some owned by British and Japanese firms, produced 8 per cent of the world's cotton yarn (more than Germany, France or Italy) and 2.8 per cent of global cotton piece goods production. Despite the importance of foreign investment in Shanghai and especially in Manchuria, Chinese-owned companies produced 73 per cent of China's 1933 factory output. The growing production of light consumer and industrial goods, combined with the accumulation of experience in operating and repairing modern machinery, generated backward linkages that spurred new private initiatives in machinery, chemicals, cement, mining, electricity and metallurgy. Official efforts (including semi-official Japanese activity in Manchuria) also promoted the growth of mining, metallurgy and arms manufacture.[18]

China's economic prospects acted as a magnet for trade and investment during the pre-Second-World-War decades. China's foreign trade rose to a peak of more than 2 per cent of global trade flows in the late 1920s, a level that was not regained until the 1990s. Between 1902 and 1931, inflows of foreign direct investment grew at annual rates of 8.3 per cent for Shanghai, 5 per cent for Manchuria and 4.3 per cent for the rest of China. By 1938, China's stock of inward foreign investment amounted to US$2.6

billion – more than any other underdeveloped region except for the Indian subcontinent and Argentina. Although estimates of pre-war capital flows often blur the distinction between direct and portfolio holdings, it is evident that China played a substantial role in global capital flows. The above- mentioned 1938 figure of US$2.6 billion for China's stock of foreign investments amounts to 8.4 per cent of worldwide stocks of outward foreign investment and 17.5 per cent of outward foreign direct investment in that year. By contrast, China's 2001 share of worldwide inward foreign direct investment was only 2.1 per cent. Domestic investment also showed substantial growth. 'Modern-oriented' fixed investment (calculated from consumption of cement, steel and machinery) grew at an average annual rate of 8.1 per cent between 1903 and 1936, outpacing Japanese gross domestic fixed capital formation in mining, manufacturing, construction and facilitating industry, which advanced at an annual rate of 5 per cent. Despite the effects of the Great Depression and political tumult, economy-wide gross fixed investment exceeded 10 per cent of aggregate output during 1931–6.[19]

Transport development contributed substantially to economic expansion. China's railway track length grew from 364 kilometres in 1894 to over 21,000 by 1937, and newly constructed north–south lines slashed economic distances across a landscape dominated by rivers flowing from west to east. The completion of railway and telegraph connections linking Peking (now Beijing) and the central China river port of Wuhan in 1906 reduced the time needed to ship commodities between these cities. In a remarkable triumph of a free-banking version of the silver standard, privately owned Chinese banks, often cooperating with foreign financial institutions and traditional moneylenders, transformed the financial face of China by persuading households and businesses to transact with paper banknotes that were convertible into silver on demand. This monetary transformation reduced transaction costs. The expansion of branch networks allowed major domestic banks to attract deposits from all regions and recycle them to the areas of greatest demand, contributing to the emergence of an embryonic national market for funds. All in all, these developments in industry, transport and finance precipitated an episode of modern economic growth at the national level during the early decades of the twentieth century.

Table 20.1 **Annual real growth rates of modern industry output in China and Japan, 1880–1936**

	China (%)	Shanghai (%)	Japan (%)
1880–1895			10.0
1895–1912		9.4	5.7
1912–1925	10.0	12	8.6
1925–1936	5.4	6.5	9.5

Source: D. Ma (2008), 'Economic growth in the Lower Yangzi region of China in 1911–1937: A quantitative and historical perspective', *Journal of Economic History*, 68 (2), 385–92, and sources cited therein.

Table 20.2 GDP structure in East Asian countries

		China (percentage of total)	Japan (percentage of total)	Taiwan (percentage of total)	Korea (percentage of total)
1914–18	Agriculture	71	29	48	66
	Industry	8	20	29	7
	Services	21	51	23	24
1931–36	Agriculture	65	19	44	53
	Industry	10	28	27	13
	Services	25	53	29	34
Annual per capita NDP growth rate in 1914–18 and 1931–36		0.53	1.4	1.5	1.1

Source: D. Ma (2008), 'Economic growth in the lower Yangzi region of China in 1911–1937: A Quantitative and Historical Perspective', *Journal of Economic History*, 68 (2), 385–92, and sources cited therein.

Table 20.3 East Asian per capita GDPs in 1934–6 (in 1934–6 US dollars) and relative to the United States

	United States	Japan	Taiwan	Korea	China
Per capita GDP (exchange rate conversion) As percentage of US GDP	574.7	77.1	49.2	29.1	20.1
	100.0	13.4	8.6	5.1	3.5
Per capita GDP (purchasing power parity conversion) As percentage of US GDP	574.7	180.8	129.6	70.9	63.6
	100.0	31.5	22.6	12.3	11.1

Source: K. Fukao, D. Ma and T. Yuan (2007), 'Real GDP in pre-war East Asia: A 1934–36 benchmark purchasing power parity comparison with the U.S', *Review of Income and Wealth*, 53 (3), Table 8.

These forces resulted in increased per capita output and structural changes of the sort associated with Simon Kuznets' concept of 'modern economic growth'. This was the case in two major regions: the Lower Yangzi, where private domestic and foreign investment in and around Shanghai served as a key driver, and the northeast (Manchuria), where Japanese investment and eventual takeover provided momentum for economic development. Table 20.1 details the comparative growth pattern in modern industries in Japan and China. It shows that growth rates in China (including Shanghai) were comparable for the 1895–1911 and 1912–36 periods, and were possibly matched only by those of Korea in the period 1912–36.[20] Tables 20.2 and 20.3 show the changing economic structure and per capita GDP levels of China, Japan, Taiwan and Korea during the 1930s at the national level. Clearly, sectoral structural change came much faster in the smaller economies of Taiwan and Korea than that of China.[21] Overall, Japanese economic development preceded that of China by nearly two decades and emerged as three times that of China in the 1930s in purchasing power parity terms after controlling for domestic price differences.

East Asia in the Shadow of the Japanese Empire

The rapid modernization of Japan is one of the most significant events in world history. Accompanying this modernization was its immediate impact across East Asia, particularly across areas of shared cultural heritage. Japan's emergence on the international scene was initially seen as a challenge to the China-dominated tributary order. Being subject to a similar treaty port system, Meiji Japan manoeuvred itself from a semi-colonial status onto a relatively independent sovereign state, which, like all other 'civilizing European states', developed its own forms of imperialism in the region. Japanese imperialism in East Asia developed within the context of the unequal treaty port system (under the cloak of free trade) imposed by European imperialism. Slowly, however, Japanese imperialism became increasingly formal with the acquisition of Taiwan and Korea following the Sino- Japanese War of 1894–5 and the Russo-Japan War of 1904–05, respectively. It was in these two territories on the Chinese peripheries that Japan began a massive transfer of the Meiji modernization programme. Such a programme included the full-scale transplant of Japanese monetary and banking institutions, public infrastructural investment, and the transfer of industrial and agricultural technologies. It was later extended to include the education system. Both Korea and Taiwan were developed into major agricultural and raw material producers for the benefit of Japan.[22]

In the end, Japan's relationship with China was qualitatively different from that imposed on China by the Western powers through the treaty port system. The two countries shared a common culture and linguistic similarities and both had been the objects of Western gunboat diplomacy. Indeed, following Japan's victory over China in the 1890s, there emerged the notion that the Japanese, in repayment of their cultural debt to China, should help pull China up in the path of 'civilization'. Many Japanese felt empowered or even obliged by their successful modernization to help the Chinese climb the path to national wealth. But these yearnings for solidarity with China were often confounded by a sense of Japanese superiority, which partly laid an ideological basis for Japanese imperialism in China.

Equally important to the rise of Japanese imperialist sentiment is the country's changing economic structure. In 1902, Japanese investment in China was a mere 0.1 per cent of total foreign investment, but by 1931 it formed more than 50 per cent of total foreign investment in China. The total number of Japanese residents in China dwarfed the Western residents in China. In 1910, the total volume of Japanese commodity trade with China was about five times that of Korea and Taiwan combined. While that disparity declined over time as Japanese colonies developed important food crops, China remained an important exporter of key raw materials and a consumer market for Japanese manufactured goods.[23] The Japanese production and trade structure were maturing: while Japanese exports to Western Europe and North America remained confined to labour-intensive products, Japan became a major and highly competitive exporter of (capital and skill-intensive) manufactured goods to other parts of Asia.[24]

Japan's increasing penetration of the China market came at a time when Western powers were beginning to retreat and compromise with Chinese nationalism after the fall of Qing in 1911. More importantly, while British investment in China was only about 7 per cent of its overall foreign direct investment in 1929, Japanese investment in China reached about 90 per cent of the country's foreign direct investment in the 1930s. According to Peter Duus, this may have prompted Japanese imperialism to turn from informal (maintained jointly within China by all the powers) to direct control (and a later full-scale invasion). In an almost act of cynicism, Japan's direct control started with the full annexation of Manchuria and with the re-instalment of the once-deposed last child emperor of the Qing as puppet ruler of the so-called Manchuguo in 1931. The Japanese aggression, however, coincided with a global downturn. Beginning in 1929, China's economy faced a succession of shocks caused by the Great Depression and falling export demand, the severance of Manchuria in 1932 by the Japanese, and rapidly rising silver prices triggered by Britain's decision to exit the gold standard and the US Silver Purchase Act of 1934.

Considerable debate remains over how well the Chinese economy weathered the storm and the severity of the combined impact of these events on aggregate economic activity. But there is no dispute about what happened afterwards: the disastrous full-scale invasion of mainland China in 1937 degenerated into a protracted and brutal eight-year war, which spelled the end of nearly three decades of economic growth in East Asia. It is also ironic that the Sino-Japanese War marked the direct confrontation of Japanese imperialism against the newly risen Chinese nationalism, itself inspired by Japan's modernization success.

Conclusion

An integrated global history is critical to our understanding of the past, present and future of East Asia. In the absence of a single unified religion, East Asia was forged by shared culture and writing scripts which defined some important economic and social features. These in turn directed the long-term economic trajectory of this region. A shared identity served to enhance the diffusion of modernization and industrialization but also led to conflicts and warfare. In the aftermath of the Second World War, East Asia witnessed economic miracles in Japan and two of her former colonies, South Korea and Taiwan. The last three decades have also seen China's miraculous emergence as the world's second largest economy. These miracles would have been impossible without the positive cooperation and competition among East Asian countries. But changing political and economic imbalances could also lead to renewed tension or conflict. It is hoped that the shared heritage and identities will become the source of future cooperation rather than conflict in East Asia.

Notes

1. E. Rawski (2015), *Early Modern China and Northeast Asia: Cross Border Perspectives*. Cambridge: Cambridge University Press.
2. D. Ma (2012), 'Political institution and long-run economic trajectory: Some lessons from two millennia of Chinese civilization', in M. Aoki, T. Kuran and G. Roland (eds), *Institutions and Comparative Economic Development*. Basingstoke: Palgrave Macmillan, 78–98.
3. Rawski, *Early Modern China*.

4. Ibid. For problems of Qing legitimacy and its coping strategy, see Mark C. Elliot (2001), *The Manchu Way: The Banners and Ethnic Identity in Late Imperial China*. Stanford, CA: Stanford University Press.

5. T. Hamashita and H. Kawakatsu (1991), *Ajia Koekiken to Nihong Kogyoukyoka* [Asian trading networks and Japanese industrialization 1500–1900]. Tokyo: Libro.

6. Man-houng Lin (2006), *China Upside Down: Currency, Society, and Ideologies, 1808–1856*. Cambridge, MA: Harvard University Asia Center: distributed by Harvard University Press.

7. For a reinterpretation of the comparison between China and Japan based on a regional perspective, see D. Ma (2008), 'Economic growth in the Lower Yangzi region of China in 1911–1937: A quantitative and historical perspective', *Journal of Economic History*, 68 (2), 385–92.

8. T. Hamashita and H. Kawakatsu (1991), *Ajia Koekiken to Nihong Kogyoukyoka*. [Asian Trading Networks and Japanese Industrialization 1500–1900]. Tokyo: Libro.

9. J. Bolt and J. L. van Zanden (2014), 'The Maddison Project: Collaborative research on historical national accounts', *Economic History Review*, 67 (3), 627–51. Among the series of new works on Chinese GDP estimate is S. Broadberry, H. GuanH. Guan and D. D. Li (2018), 'China, Europe and the Great Divergence: A study in historical national accounting', *Journal of Economic History*, 78 (4), 955–1000.

10. A. Maddison (2007), *Chinese Economic Performance in the Long Run*, 2nd edn. Paris: Development Centre of the Organisation for Economic Co-operation and Development.

11. R. Allen, J-P. Bassino, D. Ma, C. Moll-Murata and J. L. van Zanden (2011), 'Wages, prices, and living standards in China, Japan, and Europe, 1738–1925', *Economic History Review*, 64 (Supplement 1), 8–38.

12. It should be said that in comparison to the high level of Japanese numeracy, Chinese numeracy displayed great volatility during the nineteenth century. J. Baten, D. Ma, S. Morgan and Q. Wang (2010), 'Evolution of living standards and human capital in China in 18th–20th century', *Explorations in Economic History,* 47 (3), 347–59.

13. See L. Brandt, D. Ma and T. Rawski (2014), 'From divergence to convergence: Re-evaluating the history behind China's economic boom', *Journal of Economic Literature*, 52 (1), 45–123, for details.

14. Ma, 'Economic growth in the Lower Yanzi'.

15. Ibid.

16. Ibid.

17. For the role of ideology in political change, see D. Ma (2022), 'Ideology and the contours of economic change in modern China, 1850–1950', in D. Ma and R. Von Glahn (eds), *The Cambridge Economic History of China*. Cambridge: Cambridge University Press, ii: 15–47.

18. Brandt, Ma and Rawski, 'From divergence to convergence'.

19. Ibid.

20. For industrial growth in Taiwan and Korea during this period, see T. Mizoguchi and M. Umemura (eds) (1988), *Basic Economic Statistics of Former Japanese Colonies, 1895–1938*. Tokyo: Toyo Keizai Shinposha, 273 and 276, respectively. Note that as the growth spurt of modern industry in Japan started well before 1895, Japanese industrial expansion in twentieth century expanded from a larger base than Shanghai.

21. For the importance of Japanese imperial investment in social overhead capital and education in Korea and Taiwan in the facilitation of this rapid sectoral transformation

and growth in GDP, see Anne Booth (2007), 'Did it really help to be a Japanese colony? East Asian economic performance in historical perspective', *Asia-Pacific Journal*, 5 (5), 1–26.

22. Mizoguchi and Umemura (eds), *Basic Economic Statistics*. Clearly in the long-run investment in education and infrastructure also provided a basis to support the rapid independent economic development of both regions after 1960. See Booth, 'Did it really help?'.

23. P. Duus (1989), 'Japan's informal empire in China, 1895–1937: An overview', in P. Duus, R. Myers and M. Peattie (eds), *The Japanese Informal Empire in China, 1895–1937*. Princeton, NJ: Princeton University Press, xiii.

24. Duus, 'Japan's informal empire', 3.

CHAPTER 21
EUROPE IN THE WORLD, 1500–2000
Peer Vries

A Diverse Continent

Europe's history of the last half millennium is one of almost uninterrupted warfare, culminating in the twentieth century in two disastrous world wars.[1] These violent conflicts were the main cause of the marked reduction in number of the continent's polities. At the end of the Middle Ages, Europe counted several hundred of them; immediately after the Second World War, only some thirty. At the very end of the period under discussion we see two trends: an increase in the number of polities because of the disintegration of the Soviet Union, Yugoslavia and Czechoslovakia and a further reduction in the number of fully sovereign states as Europe's economic and political integration became deeper and wider. This increasing integration, however, did not create a homogeneous economic entity, as will be pointed out on several occasions in this text. Differences in wealth, development and growth between countries have continued to be substantial and in several cases even increased.

The units of analysis and comparison in this chapter will almost exclusively be states, as we currently know them. There are disadvantages to such a focus. It can easily become anachronistic and even in relatively tiny states in Europe regional differences were and often are substantial. The decision to nevertheless focus on states has been made for pragmatic reasons – the number of pages available, intelligibility and comparability, and the available data.

Until the sixteenth century the centre of gravity of Europe's civilization and economy had primarily been the Mediterranean area. In that century, the slow and protracted process started in which the region lost its primacy.[2] It became less 'integrated' because of the rise of the Ottoman Empire just when with the increasing importance of the Atlantic world the centre of the European economy shifted northwest. The Mediterranean economies, moreover, had few direct exchanges with the emerging Atlantic economy, and their overseas connections to East and Southeast Asia were less tight than those of the Dutch, the British or the French. Southeastern Europe became part of the Ottoman Empire, which most scholars regard as retarding for its economy. That empire never directly engaged in the upcoming Atlantic economy. Its exchange with the Far East never became intense. The parts of Southeastern Europe that came under its rule were also only weakly integrated in the European economy as a whole, even in the nineteenth century, not least because of geographical reasons (see Table 21.1). Much of the rather low amount of their international trade, moreover, was in foreign hands. The region became

Table 21.1 The position of the region 'Europe'* in the world (Europe as a percentage of the world)

Year	Land surface	Population	GDP**
1500	< 4	16	20
1820	< 4	16	27
1913	< 4	19	38
2003	< 4	8	21

* Here as in the entire chapter, without Russia, the Russian Empire, or the Soviet Union.
** The figures for GDP are, of course, for the period until 1913 estimates.
Source: A. Maddison (2007), *Contours of the World-Economy, 1–2030 AD. Essays in Macro-Economic History.*
Oxford: Oxford University Press, 378 and 381, for population and GDP.

one of the poorest of Europe, which it still is.[3] Other parts of the Mediterranean world also saw their position change: the economy of Italy was probably already stagnating at the beginning of the early modern era. A widening gap emerged between a North that continued to be relatively speaking quite wealthy and a relatively poor South. Spain and Portugal became the centres of huge, primarily Atlantic, empires but nevertheless their economies faltered. Incomes per capita tended to stagnate or even decrease. Compared to Northwestern Europe they began to look poor and backward.[4] At the end of the twentieth century, notwithstanding sometimes quite impressive efforts at catching up, their income was still below the average of the Euro area.

Overall from the end of the sixteenth century onwards we see a retreat of the Mediterranean and a rise of the Atlantic. Northwestern Europe, which had been fairly marginal until the later Middle Ages – in particular in the case of the later Dutch Republic and the British Isles – became Europe's wealthiest and most dynamic region. Because of the British and Dutch role in European economic development they will receive considerable attention in the rest of this text, so I confine myself to this brief comment here.

Overall Central Europe – here for convenience defined as the lands of the Holy Roman and Habsburg empires – became more peripheral during the early modern era, although with important regional differences. Trade connections with Northern Italy, Castile and Aragon, and the Southern Low Countries became less intense. Its importance as producer of silver and iron declined. The German, non-Habsburg, regions of the Holy Roman Empire lost leverage, politically and economically. Their economies were severely damaged during the Thirty Years' War (1618–48). In the eighteenth century, Prussia started to fill the political void, but it was only after 1870 that a unified Germany with a dynamic and strong economy emerged. From then onwards, Germany almost without interruption had the strongest single economy of Europe. The Habsburg Empire had great power status but apart from some regions – all in its Western half – like Bohemia, Silesia and parts of present-day Austria, it continued to be relatively poor.[5] Yet, at the end of the twentieth century Austria had become one of the wealthiest countries in Europe. This is also the case for Switzerland that deserves separate mention here as a central

European country that enjoyed autonomy for seven centuries and industrialized quite early.[6]

The economies of most of East, Central and Southeastern Europe overall developed differently from those of North and Northwestern Europe. From the early sixteenth century, if not earlier, the region became more 'peripheral' and 'fell behind'. Previously existing states lost their independent statehood and became part of more 'coercion-intensive' polities like the Habsburg, Russian or Ottoman empires, just when in Western Europe polities emerged with more potential for development that started reaping benefits of overseas expansion. However, there also existed internal reasons. First and probably foremost is the re-institution or strengthening of 'feudal' structures. In particular, east of the Elbe, unfree labour became the rule in agriculture, where many scholars speak of a 'second serfdom' and in several other sectors of the economy. In towns, a more restrictive guild system began to prevail. Levels of urbanization were low and there was no strong modernizing bourgeoisie. The region participated in international trade, but it did so as a periphery. Intercontinental trade was all but absent.[7] After the Second World War, there was a major – but ultimately unsuccessful – effort to 'catch up' behind an Iron Curtain in a communist setting of planned development. When the curtain fell, most of the region returned to a peripheral position. Several countries even saw a sharp decrease in their GDP per capita.

The history of Northern Europe here defined as Scandinavia, including Finland and Iceland, has its ups and downs. It has never been economically or politically a powerful European 'core' region, although Sweden in the seventeenth century came close to it. Things have fundamentally changed here, in particular during the twentieth century. Over the last decades it has even become one of the richest and most developed parts of Europe.[8]

Differences in wealth in Europe in the period discussed here have always been substantial, as Tables 21.2 and 21.3 show. In the case of Table 21.2 they provide no more than very rough estimates, which, moreover, in several instances are not completely identical to those of Table 21.3 for the years 1820 and 1870. For many countries we still lack sufficient good statistical information. Differences in patterns of development and levels of wealth are striking.[9] Eastern and Southeastern Europe, of which only the Polish case is presented in Tables 21.2 and 21.3, have not caught up with Western Europe since the beginning of the nineteenth century, while Southwestern Europe and certainly Northern Europe have managed to diminish or even close the gap.

The concept of Europe is not only problematic because of the substantial and shifting cleavages within the geographical entity that bears that name, but also because Europeans, over almost the entire period discussed here, held sovereignty over large regions outside their continent. By 1800 Western states – European states and their overseas settler colonies' offshoots – controlled some 35 per cent of the world's land surface. By 1914 they had increased that total to almost 85 per cent. In 1500 it had only been 7 per cent.

For many people all around the world globalization took the form of being colonized by Europeans (Table 21.4).[10] But when it comes to importance and size of their empires we again see big differences between different parts of Europe.

Table 21.2 Comparative levels of GDP per capita in Europe, in real terms (United Kingdom in 1820 = 100)

	c. 1500	c. 1700	c. 1750	1820	1870
United Kingdom	57	73	87	100	187
The Netherlands	67	109	109	107	162
France	n.a.	n.a.	n.a.	72	110
Italy	83	71	76	65	88
Spain	63	61	58	62	71
Sweden	64	66	67	70	97
Poland	50–54	38–42	34–37	41	55

Source: S. Broadberry and K. O'Rourke (2010), 'Introduction to Volume 1', in S. Broadberry and K. O'Rourke (eds), *The Cambridge Economic History of Modern Europe*, vol. 1: *1700–1870*. Cambridge: Cambridge University Press, p. 2.

Table 21.3 GDP per capita in several European countries, 1820–2000, in real terms (Great Britain in 1960 = 100)

	1820	1870	1910	1960	2000
Great Britain	23	37	53	100	243
The Netherlands	21	36	43	96	256
France	13	22	34	86	235
Italy	17	18	25	63	217
Spain		14	22	36	182
Sweden	10	16	29	100	241
Poland		11		37	84

Source: Calculated on the basis of J. L. van Zanden et al. (eds) (2014), *How Was Life? Global Well-Being since 1820*. Paris: OECD, 67.

The economic consequences of being absorbed into a European empire differed too. The so-called Western offshoots (the settler colonies in the United States, Canada, Australia and New Zealand) in the end all became rich. The United States became independent already in the 1770s. The other three countries were integrated into the British Empire quite differently from 'normal' colonies. As a rule, colonies, British and otherwise, did *not* develop into wealthy countries.[11]

Discussing Europe in a global context over the period of half a millennium requires making clear choices. This text sets out to discuss developments that occurred in Europe's economic history over the last 500 years that are of worldwide relevance. I single out

Table 21.4 Size and population of the overseas empires of the main colonial powers of Europe

In 1760					
	Spain	Portugal	United Kingdom	The Netherlands	France
Area	12.3	8.5	3.2	0.2	0.065
Population	18.8	1.6	2.8	3.3	0.6

In 1938					
	United Kingdom	France	Italy	Belgium	The Netherlands
Area	33.6	12.2	3.4	2.4	2.1
Population	496.8	70.6	12.9	14.3	68.4

Data in million of square kilometres and million inhabitants.
Source: B. Etemad (2007), *Possessing the World: Taking the Measurements of Colonisation from the Eighteenth to the Twentieth Century.* New York: Berghahn Books, 135–6, 167, 171, 174 and 178.

three: first, Europe's dominant role in creating a global economy; second, the fact that Europe became the first region in the world characterized by modern economic growth; and finally, Europe's political economy, in terms of how it actually worked and in terms of the prevailing ideas about it.

Europe and Globalization

Let us begin with economic globalization, that is, the increase in intensity, extent, speed and impact of intercontinental economic contacts. Some caveats are in order. Firstly, the fact that focusing on Europe's intercontinental exchanges with the rest of the world can easily be misleading. Those exchanges were important but must be put into perspective. Trading bulk goods over a long distance, even over water, continued to be expensive and laborious until at least the second half of the nineteenth century. Even in Europe with its many waterways and its long coasts, regions in the interior were often hardly integrated in intercontinental networks of exchange.[12] Even at the very end of the twentieth century the bulk of trade by Europeans still was with other Europeans. For most of the period discussed, long-distance and certainly intercontinental trade was only a small fraction of total trade. Secondly, the focus in this text will be on European particularities and on European agency. That is because this is a text about Europe, not because Europe would be exceptional in all respects or because the rest of the world would be without any agency.

Economic globalization was not a unilinear process. From Columbus and Vasco Da Gama onwards, it intensified. During the seventeenth century there was a setback, after which it got a new impulse in the next century. In the nineteenth century a major intensification of intercontinental exchanges set in that was only interrupted during the period between the two world wars. From the 1970s onwards, it became very intense.

The so-called Columbian Exchange of flora, fauna and diseases between the Old and the New Worlds was probably the most consequential form of pre-industrial intercontinental exchange.[13] There was also an intercontinental transfer of people, first and foremost the transatlantic slave trade that brought enslaved people from Africa to the Americas. Europeans were heavily involved in it as slave traders and as consumers and sellers of the goods made through the use of slave labour. Between 1519 and 1867, some 11 million enslaved Africans were shipped from Africa to the Americas, almost half of them by Portuguese and Brazilians, some 28 per cent by British traders and some 13 per cent by French carriers, and the rest by people from the Dutch Republic, Spain or the United States.[14] Europeans not only brought slaves to the Americas, they also traded slaves in Asia.[15] On top of that, over the entire early modern period, they imported in total some 600,000 enslaved people to Italy and some 375,000 enslaved Africans to the Iberian Peninsula. Less well known is the fact that Europeans could be enslaved by others: more than 1 million white Christian Europeans were enslaved by traders from North Africa, whereas some 3 million East Europeans were sold on slave markets in the Middle East.[16]

The number of people who left Europe for other continents over the entire pre-industrial period was rather small: for the Americas before 1820 only an estimated 3 million, and for Asia before 1800 only some 2 million, and for Africa certainly not more than 100,000 (Figure 21.1).

In discussing the main routes of pre-modern commodity trade, one must differentiate between the triangular trade between Europe, Africa and the Americas, and the trade between Europe and Asia along the Cape.[17] In quantitative terms, the Atlantic world was more important as a trading zone for Europe than Asia. The goods exchanged between these zones were different too. From South and Central America, Europe imported bullion, sugar and cotton. Together with tobacco, cotton also came from the southern states of what is now the United States. From the 1820s onwards, coffee was imported from Brazil. Europeans brought slaves and manufactured goods in return. From the northern half of the American continent came fish, furs and wood. In return that region imported primarily manufactured goods from Europe. Africa provided mainly slaves and at times gold and ivory. It received mainly textiles, weapons and also alcoholic drinks.

Asia provided 'Oriental' luxuries. It all began with spices coming from what are now Indonesia and India. Over time cotton textiles became India's most important export product to Europe. In return Europeans mainly sent bullion. China's main exports to Europe consisted of porcelain, silk, raw as well as in the form of textiles, and from the last decades of the eighteenth century onwards almost exclusively tea. In return it received mainly American silver, directly from Mexico or indirectly via Europe. Japan for some time was an important exporter of silver. Later copper became its main export. Imports from Europe via the Dutch were confined to a variety of specific manufactured 'luxury' products. Closer to home the Ottoman Empire increasingly provided Europe

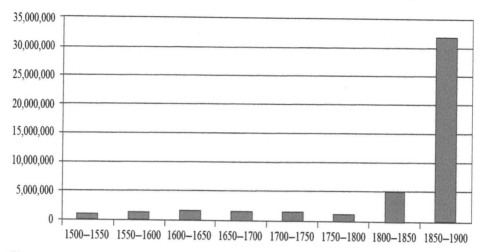

Figure 21.1 European migration to other continents, 1500–1900.
Source: J. Lucassen and L. Lucassen (2009), 'The mobility transition revisited, 1500–1900: What the European case can offer to global history', *Journal of Global History*, 4 (3), 356.

with raw materials, over the eighteenth century in particular cotton. It imported mainly manufactured goods and colonial re-exports from Europe. The impact of Asian trade on Europe's economy as a whole continued to be quite confined till the end of the eighteenth century. The lubricating oil of this intercontinental trade consisted of bullion from Latin America. The drain of it to Asia certainly was substantial, but the bulk of the gold and more than half of the silver that Europe got from the Americas stayed in Europe.

Europe's trade tended to be organized differently depending on its trade partners. Spain's (or rather Castile's) and Portugal's governments as colonial rulers tried to regulate or in any case skim the trade between mother country and colonies. Full control was impossible especially in the Americas. Barriers to entry were low and smuggling, privateering and piracy too attractive. Governments of other European countries faced the same problems. Overall, trade with 'the West' was less regulated and restricted than trade along the Cape. Chartered companies, for example, were less prominent in it. True enough, England's Hudson Bay Company continued to exist till the 1860s, but it was as much a territorial ruler – over a huge territory in what now is Canada – as an enterprise. In European trade with the East, the role of such companies – the type of company-states that combined private enterprise and sovereign rights like the right to conclude treaties, have armies and navies, wage war or coin money – was more substantial and lasted longer. The biggest among them, the English and Dutch East India companies, in the end, just like the Hudson Bay Company, acted more like territorial rulers than traders.[18] The Dutch and in particular the British became major territorial powers in parts of Asia. The French were less successful: they did not manage to keep strong footholds in India, nor for that matter in the Americas. Portugal was active in Asia too, in India in principle via the *Estado da India*. In practice, however, private initiative, improvization and corruption prevailed. Spain in Asia only ruled over the Philippines but for lack of resources this never became a successful colonial project.

In the Americas, where European settlement had a major impact, the main conflicts of interest actually arose between the motherland and the settler elites – with the hold of the motherland often being rather weak and decreasing – but less so with any 'indigenous' groups. The economic effects of the independence of all major colonies between the 1770s and the 1820s differed widely, especially between the north and the rest of the continent. In Africa, until well into the nineteenth century, European direct political leverage was marginal. European settlements were tiny. The Dutch settlement in South Africa with some 60,000 settlers of European descent was the only relative exception. In the big empires in Asia, for a long time Europeans were only on sufferance. Imperial China did trade with them but allowed them hardly any freedom of movement and manoeuvre on its territory. That would only change with the Opium Wars of the 1840s and 1850s. In Japan, between 1633 and 1639, the Tokugawa Shogunate enacted what has become known as the *sakoku* or 'locked country policy'. That stayed in effect until 1853. Except to some extent for the Dutch, the country became forbidden territory, at least for Europeans. Korea was even more closed to the outside world. The Mughal rulers initially considered the Europeans at best useful suppliers of goods and services and at worst a nuisance, but certainly not a serious threat. In particular in the case of the English, that proved to be a mistake. In the Ottoman Empire economic power relations changed too. At the start, with the Ottoman Empire at its height, the so-called capitulations, grants by successive sultans to Christian nations conferring rights and privileges in favour of their subjects resident or trading in Ottoman dominions, were voluntary gifts. Over time, however, they became signs of European penetration and encroachment.

If possible Europeans tried to manipulate exchange. In particular, overseas trade and politics were mixed up. Distinctions between the private and the public, including those between private and public violence, were blurred. Only a thin line separated trade, privateering and piracy. Trade and empire building often went hand in hand. In particular European overseas imperialism had a peculiar twist. It combined exploration, control and utilization[19] and involved sustained efforts to create a division of labour in which a European motherland functioned as 'core' and its overseas trade partners as peripheries.[20]

Until the second half of the eighteenth century, these peripheries were located first and foremost in the Americas, in small parts of Asia, in the slave-exporting regions of Africa whose 'slave-production' became an integral part of the emerging Western world system, and in those parts of Europe that had become peripheral to Northwestern Europe. Examples here are the Baltic region that provided the Dutch Republic with rye and materials needed for its fleet; Russia that exported flax, hemp, rye and wood to Great Britain; Hungary that provided Northwestern Europe with cattle, or Ireland that until well into the nineteenth century functioned as a semi-colony of Britain.

In the European core the import of 'exotic' commodities like cocoa, coffee, spices, sugar, tea, tobacco, textiles and porcelain led to changing patterns of consumption. Several scholars even speak of a 'consumer revolution'.[21] In the wealthier parts of

Northwestern Europe the wish to consume Asian 'novelties' often acted as a driving force behind another revolution, the so-called industrious revolution: a substantial increase of the total supply of labour on the labour market as more people began to work longer and harder in order to earn more monetary income. Such industriousness often was accompanied by specialization, increasing market integration, and growth.[22] A third effect of imports from overseas consisted in the efforts undertaken to produce substitutes and sometimes export previously imported commodities as for example silk and cotton textiles and porcelain. When it was not possible to transfer production to the mother country, European merchants often transferred it to extra-European regions they controlled. Examples here would be the Dutch who began to grow coffee on Java or the British who started growing tea in India.

Between 1750 and 1850, that is, still before Western Europe could be called 'industrial', the global economic position of Europe or more generally 'the West' underwent major strengthening. In the Americas, the United States became politically independent but intensified its economic ties with its former colonizer Great Britain. Most of the Spanish colonies – but also Brazil – became part of the 'informal empire' of the United States and the United Kingdom. In Asia, too, Europeans increased their leverage. The Battle of Plassey in 1757 has become the symbol of Great Britain's rise in India, that actually had already begun earlier. With increasing political power, the British changed their trade relations with the country and also got some grip on production there.[23] The Ottoman Empire was 'opened' in 1838 by the Treaty of Balta Limani – with the United Kingdom – that stated that the empire would abolish all monopolies, allow British merchants and their collaborators full access to all Ottoman markets, and tax them equally to local merchants. Silver had already started leaving China as payment for opium from the first decades of the nineteenth century, but the turning point here was the First Opium War (1839–42). Following that war, the Qing Empire retained its formal independence, but lost much of its sovereignty. Japan was 'opened' from the 1850s onwards. It, too, signed unequal treaties but it never became a real periphery. In Southeast Asia, Great Britain, France and the Netherlands further expanded their empires into what is today Malaysia, Cambodia, Laos, Vietnam and Indonesia.

From the end of the eighteenth century and even more so after 1850 when industrialization deepened, the gap in wealth and power between 'the West' and 'the Rest' became so big that Western countries could start a new round of empire building. The clearest victim was Africa. The fact that parts of Europe industrialized would already have sufficed to create a worldwide 'Great Divergence'.[24] But its effect became even bigger because the industrializing countries in Europe also dominated global trade, transport, communication and finance at a time when economic globalization switched into a higher gear. Global trade, to confine us to that aspect, not only increased but also changed character. Before, a very substantial part of what Europeans exported to other continents had not been produced by themselves. Now for about a century global trade became characterized by the 'Great Specialization', a global division of labour in which developed, 'industrialized' countries produced and exported manufactured goods while non-developed countries produced and exported primary commodities.

In order to facilitate their imports from their peripheries, European core countries invested enormous sums of money to create the relevant infrastructure there. Moreover, in the century between 1815 and 1914, more than 40 million migrants left Europe for other continents, in particular the Americas, and so provided extra labour for producing export commodities. The effects varied according to the region, but overall the outcome of this 'division of labour' was not positive for the non-developed countries. With the exception of Japan, countries outside the West not only 'failed' to industrialize, their manufacturing sector was also severely damaged by Western competition.[25]

The exact impact on the economies of European core countries of this global division of labour – that for 'old' peripheries had already originated before industrialization and the heydays of European imperialism – continues to be subject of acrimonious debate. The focus has long been on the extent to which 'unequal exchange' – and sheer coercion and extraction – enabled Western accumulation of capital.[26] With the increasing awareness that the motor of modern growth is innovation rather than accumulation, research has now broadened and takes on board all potential positive and negative effects of specializing in the production of certain goods.[27]

In global economic history, understandably, the focus is on the Great Divergence and the Great Specialization on a global scale. But economic development over roughly the last two centuries was not an even process in Europe itself either. There have also been shifts within the core of the 'Western' world itself. Until the First World War, Europe's industrial nations held economic global primacy. After 1918, the United States took over and became not only the world's largest but also increasingly its leading economy. The period of the Great Depression of the 1930s was an era of de-globalization in which intercontinental trade, investment and migration decreased and the economies of European countries tended to become more closed.[28] The boom of the economies of Western Europe in the period 1945–73, after the backlash of the Great Depression and the Second World War, in a context of increasing trade between developed countries was primarily a matter of successfully catching up with the United States.

Several of the previous comments already took us to the last decades of the twentieth century. In the second half of that century, three major changes in Europe's global position occurred. Firstly, in a few decades, the decolonization of Europe's overseas empires unfolded. One of the effects was that, between 1945 and the beginning of the 1990s, some 5–7 million Europeans and non-Europeans alone left the (former) European colonies for Europe. They were joined by labour migrants from North Africa and Turkey. Secondly, the Great Specialization came to an end. Non-Western countries increasingly began to massively produce and export manufactured goods, whereas the most advanced parts of Europe 'de-industrialized'. And finally, the increasing integration of European economies into a common market allowed the continent to become a big global player. In 2000, the GDP of the countries of the European Union was about a quarter of global GDP, their exports some 40 per cent of global exports. But as indicated earlier on, integration did not mean convergence.

Modern Economic Growth

Europe became the cradle of modern economic growth, that is, a sustained and substantial increase of GDP per capita in real terms. Before industrialization, the available natural resources set fairly strict limits to its economic growth and development. It experienced periods of 'efflorescence', but growth in such periods was fragile and as a rule short-lived.[29] The direct and overwhelming dependency on nature made the economy vulnerable and 'volatile' in the short run, and fairly stagnant in the long run. Even in its most advanced economies, Great Britain and the Dutch Republic, increasing population easily led to economic problems or stagnation.[30]

Modern economic growth has taken different shapes but the same fundamental changes underlie all its varieties.[31] One is a major change in sources and use of energy away from the traditional energy sources such as muscle power, water, wind and wood. Industrializing Europe increasingly began to rely on fossil fuels like coal, later oil and natural gas, and later still nuclear power as its main sources of energy, producing heat *and* power.[32] A second major change was in the materials used: Europe's modern economies began to thrive on iron, steel, concrete and (mineral-based) synthetic materials instead of organic materials. The third major change was the fact that innovation became the most important motor of growth.

When industrialization began in Great Britain, water power was still important, but from the first decades of the nineteenth century, steam power became omnipresent in mechanized production and transport as for instance the railways. Steel, heavy engineering, electricity and chemical industry were central in what is often called the 'Second Industrial Revolution' from roughly 1870 to 1914. After the First World War, oil, automobiles and motorization held centre stage. After the Second World War, developed economies entered the age of mass production for mass consumption. With the digital revolution, yet another new leading sector came to the fore.[33]

The emergence of modern growth is normally identified with industrialization. Clearly, industry as such was very important, but innovation and the use of new sources of energy and new technologies can also lead to ever-increasing productivity in agriculture and services. The shift from the primary to the secondary and then tertiary sector that is considered characteristic for modernizing economies did indeed occur in all of Europe but with major differences in timing and intensity. Only rarely did industry employ over 50 per cent of the total labour force. The service sector eventually became by far the biggest sector in all advanced European economies. The growth of employment in the government sector, at least when it comes to civilian employment, needs separate mention. In several European countries, it employed up to 20 per cent of the labour force at the end of the twentieth century.[34]

There has never been one model of European industrialization. Ivan Berend distinguishes three varieties.[35] The first one is a fairly close and relatively early imitation of the British example characterized by the use of coal and the mechanized production of textiles and iron, using British technology. This route was taken in Great Britain, France, Switzerland and to some extent in Austria and Bohemia after 1880. The second one, a route usually described as the 'the Second Industrial Revolution' with an emphasis on chemical industry, electricity and automobiles, was best exemplified in Western parts of Germany but, in the later phases of their industrialization, France, Switzerland and Northern Italy also followed it, just like Great Britain and Belgium, and Scandinavia after 1870. The third one is characterized by industrialization based on agricultural products and food processing. Classic examples would here be Denmark and the Netherlands, and to a lesser extent Switzerland and Austria/Bohemia, in particular in the period 1840–80.

Differences in wealth, growth, development and economic 'modernity' did not disappear with industrialization (Table 21.5). Over the long nineteenth century (1780s–1914) attempts at economic modernization in Europe were successful in Western Europe including Switzerland, Austria, Bohemia and Silesia, and with some retardation in Scandinavia. The industrial trajectory of Ireland, Eastern parts of Germany and Southern Italy was much less successful. Medium income levels as compared to Western Europe and a certain level of industrialization were reached in most of Central Europe, the Baltic region, Finland and Ireland. Then there was a third group of countries with some islands of modernity but where, overall, modernization failed. That group would include Russia, the Iberian Peninsula and Southern Italy. A lack of industrialization, only a semblance of economic modernization and the lowest income levels of Europe could be found in the Balkans and the easternmost and southernmost borderlands of the Habsburg Empire. With some exceptions, a listing of regions in 'order of development' at the end of the twentieth century would be fairly similar. Levels of industrialization and development *inside* countries as a rule were also quite different, as the process of development often undergoes virtuous and vicious circles.

Table 21.5 Levels of industrialization in Europe, 1750–1900 (United Kingdom in 1900 = 100)

	1750	1800	1830	1860	1880	1900
Europe as a whole	8	8	11	16	24	35
United Kingdom	10	16	25	64	87	100
Habsburg Empire	7	7	8	11	15	23
France	9	9	12	20	28	39
German States/ Germany	8	8	9	15	25	52
Italian States/Italy	8	8	8	10	12	17

Source: P. Bairoch (1982), 'International industrialization levels from 1750 to 1980', *Journal of European Economic History*, 11 (1/2), 269–333.

Europe's Political Economy

Scholars claiming that Europe's economy was exceptional in its institutional set-up, almost without exception, refer to the fact that it was the continent where 'capitalism' first came to full maturity. As long as capitalism is not simply equated with a market economy based on private property and private enterprise with 'free' and, as mainstream economics defines it, 'fair' competition, that indeed seems correct. Market economies, especially for consumer goods, have been fairly normal throughout global history. In the variety of capitalism that was unique to certain parts of Europe, markets, private property and private enterprise were indeed prominent. But those markets often did *not* function according to the logic of 'perfect' competition. They existed in combination, in particular in certain sectors, with state intervention going far beyond just enabling the market to work. The driving forces of modern capitalist development – large-scale capital accumulation and major technological innovations – do not easily flourish in a setting characterized by completely open and fair competition. Most scholars would now agree that competition was important in pushing innovation and creating growth in Europe. The wealthiest parts of Europe were regions with high levels of market integration.[36] Although the market mechanism was often tampered with, apart from some specific instances, it was not eliminated in Western Europe. But one should not underestimate the importance of forms of market manipulation and regulation like monopolies, oligopolies and cartels, and of protectionism and government regulation.

One must differentiate according to time and place and realize that there were different kinds of markets. Scholars like Marx and Weber claiming that Europe was 'the cradle of capitalism' have always emphasized the fundamental importance of a labour market with free labour. Yet, even in Europe such free wage labour was far from normal. Simplifying to the extreme, one can distinguish three labour regimes in agriculture, the main sector of production, until well into the nineteenth century: a regime with chiefly unfree, manorial subordination; one in which peasants and their families constituted the main labour force; and one with chiefly wage labour.[37] The first regime was predominant in Central and Eastern Europe, but certainly not unknown elsewhere in Europe. In Prussia serfdom was only formally abolished in 1806 and in Austria–Hungary only in 1848. The second regime became predominant in England and the western and northern parts of what is now the Netherlands, but also on large *latifundia* in, for example, Southern Spain, Portugal or Italy. A peasant, household mode of production could be found all over Europe but was predominant in most of France, present-day Germany and Scandinavia.[38] City air did not always make you free in every respect. Until 1810 only members of a guild could practise a certain trade in Prussia. That rule was only abolished in the rest of Germany in 1869, and even then not entirely. In Austria it existed till 1859. Free wage labour, that 'even' in Europe for very long coexisted with all sorts of unfree labour, certainly was not uniquely European but it was probably more common there than elsewhere in the world and the number of wage labourers increased over the eighteenth and nineteenth centuries. In Great Britain, the first industrial nation, it was already common before industrialization.

In practice, occupations – and economic sectors – were not neatly distinguishable. Manufacturing and later industry tend to be associated with towns and factories, but for very long they continued to be found in the countryside, with towns specializing in processes that required skilled labour and advanced implements. Many people, in particular in the countryside, operated in an 'economy of makeshifts', switching between activities like taking care of their own tiny farms (if they still had land) and selling some of their produce or their labour. By far the majority of them worked in a system called 'putting out', in which they got raw materials from merchants, processed them and returned the processed materials to those same merchants, who then paid them a piece rate. Less common was the so-called *Kaufsystem* in which the actual producers themselves acquired the raw materials, processed, and sold them. Although in particular the first form of domestic manufacturing has been described as 'proto-industry', it was often not a preparatory stage of industrialization at all.[39] Next to markets for labour, there also emerged markets for land and money. Overall, land markets continued to be subject to restrictions for very long – in several countries till far into the nineteenth century – as land owned by the church or aristocrats was often all but inalienable. Money markets apparently worked quite well. Interest rates in any case, overall, first and foremost in northwest Europe, were relatively low.

A second claim that is often made with regard to European capitalism is that it was characterized by exceptionally well-described and protected property rights.[40] That claim exaggerates 'European exceptionalism' and assumes that securing property rights suffices to create modern growth, which is incorrect. That some sort of protection of property is indispensable for sustained growth is not disputed.

This emphasis on protection highlights the role of the modern state as a guarantor of those property rights and creator of institutional arrangements without which economic growth cannot be sustained. The fact that Europe over the past two centuries has had so many functioning states is already fairly exceptional: the world is full of 'failed' states. In such states, the chances of having modern economic growth are nil. But what is striking is that, in those parts of Europe that first knew modern economic growth, the state was actually very present and active in the economy. In most European countries, rulers have always tried to influence and change the economy. Innumerable examples exist of government initiatives and policies that failed completely. But the wealthiest European countries all had states that at one time or another wanted to be and effectively *were* 'developmental'. The modern state as we now define it was a European invention that slowly took shape and only really 'matured' after the French Revolution.[41] Its actual policies and power differed substantially according to time and place. Most European polities *before* the first decades of the nineteenth century are described as 'fiscal–military states' and their policies as 'mercantilist'. The expression 'fiscal–military state' speaks for itself. Such states – or maybe better 'proto-states' – had levels of government revenue (and expenditure and indebtedness) that were higher than in any of the major world empires, and spent the bulk of their revenues on war.[42] Obviously, high taxes and high spending on the military are not necessarily good for the economy, even though high deficit spending may have had 'Keynesian' effects. But in several European states, first and foremost those with some form of political representation for those who provided the state with substantial amounts of taxes and especially loans, the permanent bargaining over claims and counterclaims between rulers and the ruled embedded the state in society, which often led to institutional innovations, strengthening of the economy and higher revenues.[43]

Most of the fiscal–military states pursued mercantilist policies. There has never been an elaborate system of thought called 'mercantilism', but there is a set of core notions that are referred to time and again. They have to be understood against the background of fierce competition between states in which increased production and trade counted primarily as means to strengthen the state. Domestically, mercantilist rulers strove to eliminate hindrances to production and trade and to create efficient markets. That, as such, could already help strengthen the state. The most effective way to do that, so it was claimed, was to stimulate, protect *and* tax the production and export of high value-added goods and confine imports to raw materials. As far as possible, domestic products should substitute for expensive imports. In their view, competitiveness of the national economy and the military strength of their states could further be enhanced if subjects worked hard and at low wages. Labour, therefore, had to be disciplined. Creating monopolies, such as the chartered companies, was also supposed to make the country more competitive. Besides, it made revenue collection easier for government.[44] Mercantilists were permanently 'benchmarking' and comparing their state and economy with that of others, something which European rulers and ruled have continued to do ever since.[45] Often the effects of mercantilist policies on the economy were negative, and many of the positive 'developmental' effects actually unintended and indirect. Such policies, moreover, were not, as often suggested, typical only for seventeenth- and eighteenth-century Europe. Even in Great Britain, the home country of Adam Smith, mercantilist measures, for example, very high tariffs, remained in force well into the nineteenth century. But often mercantilism 'worked'.

After the Napoleonic Wars, the nature of the state and of state spending began to change. The fiscal–military state seemed to have reached its limits. No longer were the bulk of expenditures for the military. Civil spending on material (transport and communication) and immaterial infrastructure (first and foremost education) became much more important. In the period from c.1820 to 1870, states tended to become somewhat leaner and less interventionist, especially when it came to international trade. From the 1870s onwards, however, many countries in Europe – though not the United Kingdom – again became more protectionist, in particular because of pressure by agricultural interests that felt threatened by imports from the New World and Russia. The growth in the volume of international trade slackened. Domestically, governments could no longer ignore the 'social question' and had to care more about the welfare of their citizens. Ideologies and scholarly disciplines emerged that claimed to know how 'the economy' worked.

With the First World War, state intervention reached an unprecedented level of intensity as war more than ever depended on total mobilization of resources. In particular, in Germany the war economy came close to what would later be called a 'planned economy'. During what turned out to be the interwar period, the Great Depression in particular hit Western Europe, but the ensuing problems led to a Europe-wide new wave of large-scale state intervention. In the few European countries that continued to be parliamentary democracies, governments attempted to combat unemployment and protect their economies. In some cases they cautiously experimented with 'Keynesian' policies. In countries that had authoritarian, fascist/national–socialist and communist rule, dictatorial intervention in or even control of the economy became normal to make the country strong and catch up with potential enemy countries. The Second World War, of course, again meant massive state planning and control.

The post-war period saw the gradual emergence of the welfare state in Western Europe.[46] Thinking in terms of laissez-faire had lost most of its attraction during the Great Depression. Recovering from the massive destruction of the Second World War required massive state intervention. Citizens in now democratic states increasingly regarded the state as guarantor of basic welfare and promoter of growth. Advanced economies also required a quickly expanding infrastructure in the form of transport, communication and education. Government expenditure and the presence of the government in the economy increased accordingly. Whatever the political colour of government and whatever its plans or claims, the state in terms of taxes, expenditures, debts or employment continued to grow almost without interruption (Table 21.6).

In the 1980s, there was increasing talk of liberalizing the economy; in the sphere of banking and finance that certainly occurred, though for the rest of the economy it proved very hard to tame the Leviathan.

Modern economic growth in Europe never was simply the result of a rise of the market and laissez-faire. It required a state that did not confine itself to being night

Table 21.6 Government spending* as a percentage of GDP, 1870–2009

	1870	1913	1920	1937	1960	1980	1990	2000	2005	2009
Austria	10.5	17.0	14.7	20.6	35.7	48.1	38.6	52.1	50.2	52.3
Belgium	n.a.	13.8	22.1	21.8	30.3	58.6	54.8	49.1	52.0	54.0
Britain	9.4	12.7	26.2	30.0	32.2	43.0	39.9	36.6	40.6	47.2
France	12.6	17.0	27.6	29.0	34.6	46.1	49.8	51.6	53.4	56.0
Germany	10.0	14.8	25.0	34.1	32.4	47.9	45.1	45.1	46.8	47.6
Italy	13.7	17.1	30.1	31.1	30.1	42.1	53.4	46.2	48.2	51.9
The Netherlands	9.1	9.0	13.5	19.0	33.7	55.8	54.1	44.2	44.8	50.0
Spain	n.a.	11.0	8.3	13.2	18.8	32.2	42.0	39.1	38.4	45.8
Sweden	5.7	10.4	10.9	16.5	31.0	60.1	59.1	52.7	51.8	52.7
Switzerland	16.5	14.0	17.0	24.1	17.2	32.8	33.5	33.7	37.3	36.7

*1870–1937 central government; 1960–2009 general government.

Source: 'Taming Leviathan: A Special Report on the Future of the State', The Economist, 19 March 2011, p. 4.

watchman. State intervention played a role in *all* successful and unsuccessful processes of industrialization and economic modernization. The connection between power and profit moreover was never severed. Countries that wanted to catch up realized that it would require a strong, modern and active state. This suggests that Europe's impact on the world economy was not confined to the realm of the economic and the material. The global impact of its thinking about 'the economy', the way it should be organized, and its economic policies were just as pervasive. From the French Revolution till at least the Second World War, Europe was by far the major producer and exporter of economic doctrines and practices. Economists like to focus on materialist factors but actually the global impact of European economic ideas like mercantilism, laissez-faire liberalism, socialism and communism, and Keynesianism can hardly be overestimated.

Conclusion

At the beginning of the twenty-first century the relative decline of 'Europe' on the global scene is undeniable. Its military and political power has dwindled and it certainly no longer rules the waves. It is still an economy of major global importance but even if it actually were an economic unity, it can no longer be called 'dominant'. Modern economic growth is no longer a Western monopoly. Other parts of the world show more impressive growth figures and more dynamism than Europe. Europe's states and economies and mainstream European ideas about the economy are no longer a source of inspiration.

Notes

1. My definition of Europe is strictly geographical. It encompasses the western most part of Eurasia without Russia/the Russian Empire/the Soviet Union. For debates on the question *what* and *where* Europe is, see K. Wilson and J. van der Dussen (eds) (1993), *What Is Europe?* Milton Keynes: The Open University.

2. F. Tabak (2008), *The Waning of the Mediterranean, 1550–1870: A Geohistorical Approach.* Baltimore, MD: Johns Hopkins University Press.

3. For the economic history of the Ottoman Empire, see H. Inalcik and D. Quataert (eds) (1994), *An Economic and Social History of the Ottoman Empire*, 2 vols. Cambridge: Cambridge University Press. For the situation since 1800, see M. Morys (ed.) (2021), *Economic History of Central, East and Southeast Europe, 1800 to the Present Day.* London: Routledge.

4. See C.-A. Nogal and L. Prados de la Escosura (2012), 'The rise and fall of Spain 1270–1850', *Economic History Review*, 66 (1), 1–37; N. Palma and J. Reis, *Portuguese Demography and Economic Growth, 1500–1850*, http://studylib.net/doc/12315291/portuguese-demography-and-economic-growth-1500-1850-1; P. Malanima (2011), 'The long decline of a leading economy: GDP in Central and Northern Italy, 1300–1913', *European Review of Economic History*, 15 (3), 169–219.

5. For the economic history of 'Germany', see M. North (2005), *Deutsche Wirtschaftsgeschichte. Ein Jahrtausend im Überblick*, 2nd rev. edn. Munich: C.H. Beck. For the economic history of the Habsburg Empire, I refer to general histories of this empire.

6. For Austria, see for example, R. Sandgruber (1995), *Ökonomie und Politik. Österreichische Wirtschaftsgeschichte vom Mittelalter bis zur Gegenwart*. Vienna: Ueberreuter. For Switzerland, see for example, J.-F. Bergier (1983), *Wirtschaftsgeschichte der Schweiz: Von den Anfängen bis zur Gegenwart*. Cologne and Zurich: Benzinger.

7. I. Berend (2003), *History Derailed: Central and Eastern Europe in the Long Nineteenth Century*. Berkeley, Los Angeles, CA and London: University of California Press; M. Cerman (2012), *Villagers and Lords in Eastern Europe, 1300–1800*. Basingstoke: Palgrave Macmillan; D. Chirot (ed.) (1989), *The Origins of Backwardness in Eastern Europe: Economics and Politics from the Middle Ages until the Early Twentieth Century*. Berkeley, Los Angeles, CA and London: University of California Press. For the situation during communist times, see I. Berend (2006), *An Economic History of Twentieth-Century Europe: Economic Regimes from Laissez-Faire to Globalization*. Cambridge: Cambridge University Press.

8. See the references to Scandinavia in Berend, *Economic History of Twentieth-Century Europe*.

9. See Berend, *Economic History of Twentieth-Century Europe*, chs 4–6, and G. Therborn, (1995), *European Modernity and Beyond: The Trajectory of European Societies, 1945–2000*. London, Thousand Oaks, CA and New Delhi: Sage Publications.

10. D. Abernethy (2000), *The Dynamics of Global Dominance. European Overseas Empires 1415–1980*. New Haven, CT and London: Yale University Press.

11. See G. Bertocchi and F. Canova (2002), 'Did colonization matter for growth? An empirical exploration into the historical causes of Africa's underdevelopment', *European Economic Review*, 46 (10), 1851–71, and G. Gozzini (2010), *Un'idea di giustizia. Globalizzazione e ineguaglianza dalla rivoluzione industriale a oggi*. Turin: Bollati Boringhieri, ch. 4.

12. See R. Studer (2015), *The Great Divergence Reconsidered: Europe, India, and the Rise to Global Economic Power*, Cambridge: Cambridge University Press, ch. 4, and V. Bateman (2012), *Markets and Growth in Early Modern Europe*. London: Pickering & Chatto.

13. N. Nunn and N. Qian (2010), 'The Columbian Exchange: A history of disease, food and ideas', *Journal of Economic Perspectives*, 24 (2), 163–88. See also J. R. McNeill's chapter in this volume.

14. R. Findlay and K. O'Rourke (2007), *Power and Plenty: Trade, War, and the World Economy in the Second Millennium*. Princeton, NJ and Oxford: Princeton University Press, 228.

15. For European slave trade in the Indian Ocean region, see R. Allen (2015), *European Slave Trading in the Indian Ocean, 1500–1850*. Athens, OH: Ohio University Press.

16. L. Lucassen (2016), 'Connecting the world: Migration and globalization in the second millennium', in C. Antunes and K. Fatah-Black (eds), *Explorations in History and Globalization*. London and New York: Routledge, 19–46, 29–30.

17. I focus on Europe's role in intercontinental trade. For intercontinental trade in a more global perspective, see the chapter by Giorgio Riello and Tirthankar Roy in this volume.

18. See P. J. Stern (2011), *The Company-State: Corporate Sovereignty and the Early Modern Foundations of the British Empire in India*. New York: Oxford University Press.

19. Abernethy, *Dynamics of Global Dominance*.

20. I. Wallerstein (1974, 1980, 1989 and 2011), *The Modern World-System*. The volumes have been published in different places and not all by the same publisher.

21. F. Trentmann (2016), *Empire of Things: How We Became a World of Consumers, from the Fifteenth Century to the Twenty-First*. London: Allen Lane. See further the contribution by Maxine Berg to this volume.

22. J. de Vries (2008), *The Industrious Revolution: Consumer Behavior and the Household Economy, 1650 to the Present*. Cambridge and New York: Cambridge University Press.

23. See the chapter by Giorgio Riello and Tirthankar Roy in this volume.

24. See the chapter by Prasannan Parthasarathi and Kenneth Pomeranz in this volume.

25. Findlay and O'Rourke, *Power and Plenty*, ch. 7; J. G. Williamson (2011), *Trade and Poverty: When the Third World Fell Behind*. Cambridge, MA and London: MIT Press.

26. P. Emmer, O. Pétré-Grenouilleau and J. Roitman (eds) (2006), *A Deus ex Machina Revisited: Atlantic Colonial Trade and European Economic Development*. Leiden: Brill; P. O'Brien and L. Prados de la Escosura (eds) (1998), *The Costs and Benefits of European Imperialism from the Conquest of Ceuta, 1415, to the Treaty of Lusaka, 1974. Proceedings of the Twelfth Economic History Congress*. Madrid: Published as Revista de Historia Económica, 16, first issue of 1998.

27. E. Reinert (2007), *How Rich Countries Got Rich ... and Why Poor Countries Stay Poor*. New York: Caroll & Graf, chs 4, 5 and 8; and Williamson, *Trade and Poverty*.

28. Findlay and O'Rourke, *Power and Plenty*, ch. 8.

29. See the contribution by Jack Goldstone in this volume.

30. For the logic of pre-industrial (advanced) organic economies, see E. A. Wrigley (2016), *The Path to Sustained Growth: England's Transition from an Organic Economy to an Industrial Revolution*. Cambridge: Cambridge University Press.

31. For the concept 'modern economic growth', see P. Vries (2013), *Escaping Poverty: The Origins of Modern Economic Growth*. Vienna and Göttingen: Vienna University Press and Vandenhoeck & Ruprecht.

32. A. Kander, P. Malanima and P. Warde (2013), *Power to the People: Energy in Europe over the Last Five Centuries*. Princeton, NJ and Oxford: Princeton University Press.

33. C. Freeman and F. Louçã (2001), *As Time Goes By: From the Industrial Revolutions to the Information Revolution*. Oxford and New York: Oxford University Press.

34. For changes in sectorial employment, see A. Carreras (2003), 'El siglo XX, entre rupturas y prosperidad (1914–2000)' in A. di Vittorio (ed.), *Historia Económica de Europa*. Barcelona: Critica, 303–435, 324 and 327, and Therborn, *European Modernity and Beyond*, ch. 4.

35. I. Berend (2013), *An Economic History of Nineteenth-Century Europe: Diversity and Industrialization*. Cambridge: Cambridge University Press, ch. 5.

36. V. Bateman (2012), *Markets and Growth in Early Modern Europe*. London: Pickering & Chatto.

37. See the chapter by Alessandro Stanziani in this volume.

38. For the situation in Central and Eastern Europe, see note 7. For the emergence of capitalist agriculture in Great Britain and the Netherlands, see M. Overton (1996), *Agricultural Revolution in England: The Transformation of the Agrarian Economy 1500–1860*. Cambridge: Cambridge University Press; and J. de Vries (1974), *The Dutch Rural Economy in the Golden Age, 1500–1700*. New Haven, CT: Yale University Press. Very informative and detailed is T. Scott (ed.) (1998), *The Peasantries of Europe: From the Fourteenth to the Eighteenth Centuries*. London and New York: Longman.

39. M. Cerman and S. Ogilvie (eds) (1996), *European Proto-Industrialization: An Introductory Handbook*. Cambridge: Cambridge University Press.

40. See for example D. Acemoglu and J. Robinson (2012), *Why Nations Fail: The Origins of Power, Prosperity and Poverty*. London: Profile.

41. P. Vries (2016), 'States: A subject in global history', in C. Antunes and K. Fatah-Black (eds), *Explorations in History and Globalization*. London and New York: Routledge, 155–76.

42. P. Vries (2015), *State, Economy and the Great Divergence: Great Britain and China, 1680–1850s*. London: Bloomsbury Academic, under 'fiscal-military state'.

43. M. Dincecco (2011), *Political Transformations and Public Finances: Europe, 1650–1913*. Cambridge: Cambridge University Press; D. Stasavage (2011), *States of Credit: Size, Power and the Development of European Polities*. Princeton, NJ and Oxford: Princeton University Press.

44. P. Roessner (ed.) (2016), *Economic Growth and the Origins of Modern Political Economy: Economic Reasons of State, 1500–2000*. London and New York: Routledge.

45. S. Reinert (2011), *Translating Empire: Emulation and the Origins of Political Economy*. Cambridge, MA and London: Harvard University Press.

46. For a short introduction, see D. Garland (2016) *The Welfare State: A Very Short Introduction*. Oxford: Oxford University Press. A quantitative analysis is provided by P. Lindert (2004), *Growing Public: Social Spending and Economic Growth since the Eighteenth Century*. Cambridge: Cambridge University Press.

CHAPTER 22
SOUTH ASIA IN THE WORLD ECONOMY, 1600–1950
Bishnupriya Gupta and Tirthankar Roy

Defining South Asia

The South Asian Association for Regional Cooperation demarcates South Asia as a world region consisting of six large countries – Afghanistan, India, Pakistan, Bangladesh, Nepal and Sri Lanka, and two smaller ones, Bhutan and Maldives. Together these countries contain about a fifth of the world's population today. Most historical debates on economic change and globalization in this territory, however, relate to the area now included in India, Pakistan and Bangladesh. This is so because the rule of two long-lasting powerful empires, the Mughal (1526–c.1720) and the British empires (c. 1765–1947), extended over a large part of the combined territory of the three countries, imparting a certain consistency in the political and economic history of these countries. The imperial connection extended to Afghanistan in an uneven fashion. The history of lower Burma (Myanmar), which was ruled by the British, also overlaps with the history of mainland South Asia in important ways. Yet these two countries were also distinct from the mainland on many points. Sri Lanka or Ceylon was ruled by a different entity from that of British India. Nepal, Bhutan and Maldives were not colonized. The historical scholarship centred on these countries, therefore, does not speak directly to the scholarship that has developed on mainland South Asia. This chapter, therefore, will define South Asia as the combined territory of India, Pakistan and Bangladesh. The term 'India' will be used interchangeably with South Asia to refer to the Indian subcontinent under the two empires of the Mughal and British.

Even this region demonstrates diversity in geographical and political terms, and it will be useful to examine this briefly before discussing the major debates and controversies about the region's economic history. Geographically, the region can be divided into four zones – the Himalayas, the Indo-Gangetic Basin (the floodplains of the Ganges and the Indus), the arid or semi-arid areas including the Deccan Plateau, and the littoral. Much of South Asia has a tropical climate, with a hot season that lasts half the year, broken by the southwest and northeast monsoon rains. The monsoon, the rivers that flow through the Indo-Gangetic Basin, and good soil conditions in the floodplains make agriculture possible, but extreme aridity also makes it seasonal and often dependent on expensive irrigation systems. Yet although agricultural conditions are uneven, South Asia's position in the middle of the Indian Ocean sustained a great maritime trade with

West and East Asia along the coastal zone. The integration of markets away from the coast depended on navigable rivers in the north and land routes used by pack bullocks before the advent of the railways from the middle of the nineteenth century. South Asia saw large variations in prices across regions as well as frequent famines, driven by the weather and political conflicts.

Politically, the region can be divided into two types. The Indo-Gangetic Basin forms one type. The flat terrain and good agriculture supported a lot of overland trade, as well as wheeled and river traffic, urbanization, and thus strong states for centuries. The empires sustained themselves by means of agricultural taxation. Not all of the 700,000 square kilometres of the basin was integrated; the Bengal Delta in particular was intermittently part of imperial states that formed in north India. But a great deal of this zone was politically integrated. These conditions occurred in the Deccan Plateau to a more limited extent. In the arid areas, the uplands and near the coasts, states tended to be smaller in extent and less powerful. Political and military power was more contested. Agriculture was more precarious, and overland trade dependent on the expensive and inefficient system of bullock caravans.

This brief overview of geography and politics should give us a sufficient backdrop for introducing the key historiographical debates around South Asia's encounter with the world economy from the seventeenth century. Two sets of historiographical debates will frame this chapter: one relating to the eighteenth-century passage of empires and the other on the impact of colonialism on development. The context for both the debates is set within the European expansion in the Asian commercial world.

Europeans in South Asian Trade

South Asia had been a trading zone for millennia. The Mughal Empire traded a great deal with West and Central Asia by road and by sea. The coastal areas, as we have seen, traded with maritime Asia on both sides of the Indian Ocean.

The *bazaars* symbolized a well-developed commercial system. Local communities of traders engaged in internal trade in grain and industrial goods. Some artisans worked directly for the nobility or the government; others sold to the merchants involved in long-distance trade. There was widespread use of 'hundis' or bills of exchange reflecting the well-developed network of banking and commerce. Indian merchant ships carried goods to Alexandria, Basra and Baghdad to the west and to Sumatra in the east, but were not sturdy enough to sail the China seas. Commodities traded included not only raw silk but also manufactured goods such as textiles. Both China and India imported bullion from outside, spices from Southeast Asia, horses from West Asia and ivory from East Africa.

This booming trade in the Indian Ocean and South China Sea was comparable to the European trade. One key difference in the institutional setting between India and Europe was that customary community laws and the long-term relationship between members of the same social network governed the system of trade and commerce in India rather than a formal system of universal law as in Europe. The contract enforcement mechanism of the Indian trading communities was similar to the private order institution highlighted by the work of Avner Greif.[1] Caste- and community-based networks of Hindus, Muslims, Jains, Parsis and Baghdadi Jews specialized in different trading operations at different locations.[2] Their commercial exchange depended on maintaining trust and reputation of members who belonged to the community, and exercised the primary means of contract enforcement.

From the 1600s, a new element was added to this picture: European merchants, some of whom operated as employees of highly organized companies. The arrival of the European trading companies disrupted the existing trading pattern, though only gradually. Indian cotton textiles were previously traded all over the Indian Ocean region. Increasingly in the early eighteenth century, Indian textile exports were directed to European markets.[3] This trade was in the hands of the European trading companies from the seventeenth century through monopoly trading rights granted by European governments. Like many other merchant communities in the area, the European companies negotiated with the local rulers the right to conduct trade and sign treaties. The treaties allowed trading posts to be established along the Indian littoral. The two main organizations were the Dutch and the English East India companies. They imported silver from Europe to purchase cloth, silk and spices. The textile weavers entered into contracts with the companies to supply specified types of cloth over a period of time. In return the companies provided them with advances to buy raw material and cover their living costs. Indian calicoes and muslins became items of fashion and were sold in European, African and American markets as well as in East Asia. Trade in textiles began to rapidly increase, and rising exports from India created a picture of prosperity in the urban centres.

European expansion and Indian Ocean trade joined in the early seventeenth century along the South Asian coast. Intense rivalry among Europeans and the British East India Company's need to protect a trade monopoly also drew the Europeans into politics from time to time. The political engagement involved mainly the Mughals or their vassals until the early eighteenth century. From about 1720, the Mughal Empire started breaking apart into a number of 'successor' states, and the field of political engagement shifted to these states. Anglo-French conflict in Europe spilled over into India, and complicated these processes. In the 1760s, the British East India Company had established areas of strong influence, even indirect rule, in Bengal and in the state near Madras known as Carnatic. By 1800, the British Empire was more or less an accomplished fact.

Two major historical debates about South Asia address the causes and consequences of these eighteenth-century shifts. One questions whether the eighteenth century was a period of decline or a period of growth, the other why Indo-European trade led to a new empire. In other words, why did British merchants take over state power?

The Eighteenth-century Transition

The context of the former question lies in the nineteenth-century account of how the British came to acquire state power, emphasizing that anarchy and warfare among successor states made a third-party intervention likely. A state of anarchy points at a dark age in economic history, followed by a new era of flourishing enterprise after the takeover of power by the British. However, was the eighteenth century really a time of decline? This 'imperialist' narrative of how India came to be ruled by the British stayed more or less intact until the 1970s. Some historians of imperialism used Karl Marx's notion of a 'primitive accumulation' to suggest that officers of the company were driven by a desire, not to save India from anarchy, but to plunder its wealth. However, they did not challenge the orthodox view of the eighteenth century as a dark age.

That idea was questioned in the 1980s, through new accounts of the eighteenth century offered by historians at Cambridge, notably C. A. Bayly and David Washbrook.[4] Their work revealed the significant extent of capital accumulation by Indian merchants and bankers in the eighteenth century. Some of the successor states ruled over rich territories with lots of trade. Warfare and revenue farming improved the political clout of bankers. European enterprise needed the association with, and partnership of, Indian merchants. Almost the entire credit of the East India Company (hereafter Company), until the Indian Mutiny in 1857, came from Indian bankers. These historians, in other words, described a world in which overseas merchants and capitalists in the interior zones developed compatible interests, and both seemed to do better, not worse, in the eighteenth century.[5]

A deeper view of the emergence of an empire from trade began to form out of this reinterpretation, giving birth to the second of the two main debates on the eighteenth century, questioning why trade led to an empire, or why European merchants took over state power. Older views of the Company's successes on the battlefield during the imperialist wars focused on the imbalance of military strength or the disunity among the Indian rivals. Newer perspectives helped change the existing discourse in at least three ways.

First, to a significant extent, warfare in eighteenth-century India was a reflection of warfare in contemporary Europe. The two huge processes of state formation were more interdependent than it might seem from the Indian-bound explanations of the Company's rise. The eighteenth-century political process in South Asia was a chapter in what Bayly calls *The Birth of the Modern World*, in which Europe's own state-making and commercial expansion into Asia was a part.[6] Second, whereas historians previously saw conflict, in the new interpretations, they now saw consensus in the form of alliances. The Company's acquisition of state power between the 1740s and the 1770s did not happen through outright conquest. And therefore, the idea of alliance is an attractive one. It works particularly well in the context of Bengal, where a palace intrigue involved a section of the Company officers. This idea also has possibilities as a broader paradigm for understanding Indo-European relationships at this time.

Some of these revisionist writings suggest a broad continuity between Indian history before and after the collapse of the Mughal Empire. The Company could be seen as just another Indian type of state. As will be discussed more below, other contributors to these debates emphasize discontinuity and the European origin of the new state to explain its success.

Third, whereas the older views of Company's ascendance focused on military capability alone, new works interpreted the Company's comparative advantage in the battlefields differently. We should add that the theme of military capability has also received an emphasis in Phil Hoffman's recent work, which connects European history and global economic history in a new fashion.[7] On the other hand, research using South Asian data points at two ways the Company represented a distinctively European state in the South Asian setting. The oversight the British Parliament exercised over its operations in India made the Company a more credible ally among contending powers in the late eighteenth-century South Asia.[8] Military conquest came with the right to revenue collection, and changed the nature of trade between Britain and India. The East India Company, as a trading agent, exchanged bullion for textiles. Now the textiles could be bought by tax revenues paid to the Company as the ruler.

The Company marked itself out as a distinctively European power in the way it undertook institutional reforms to the land ownership structure in Bengal. This process had begun between 1772 and 1793, when the rulers of the Indian territories acquired by the British East India Company set up a centralized land tax collection system replacing the old feudal system that relied on warlords and intermediaries to do the job for the ruler. The transition owed not only to the capacity of the Company to coerce and threaten the intermediaries, known as the zamindars, but also to an understanding reached with them. In Bengal, the understanding took the form of the Permanent Settlement, where the zamindars received ownership rights over the land they once collected taxes from, but ceased to enjoy sovereign and military power over them. The move had complex origins, including, as Ranajit Guha had shown, the influence of physiocrat doctrines that privileged private land ownership.[9] However, fiscal and military motives also played roles, and evidently paid off when there was a sharp rise in tax collection in the early nineteenth century. The Company used the fiscal capacity to create a standing army, ending dependence on allies and mercenaries, who still ruled in other states. According to this second approach, a superior ability to raise resources was the reason why the British succeeded in establishing a stable rule, which lasted for so long in South Asia, and why it prevailed over its rivals and imposed its command on the princely states.[10]

British Empire and the Economy of South Asia

The British Empire in South Asia, which rose to power between the mid-eighteenth and mid-nineteenth centuries, achieved a degree of political, bureaucratic and military centralization that the region had not seen before. Britain by this time had abolished Corn Laws and, with that, protective tariffs. As the first country to embrace the doctrine of free trade, it imposed it on India. As South Asia integrated into the world economy, trade, investment and migration rose to far higher levels than before. The trade to GDP ratio increased dramatically, from 2–3 per cent in the mid-1800s to 20 per cent on the eve of the First World War. Though only a small proportion of British capital went to land scarce colonies,[11] South Asia received a large share of this investment. British capital went mainly into the railways to develop a modern transport network.

Nationalist historians have argued that the railways connected the agricultural hinterland to the ports and paved the way for the rising volume of trade in agricultural goods that met the demand for food and raw material in industrial Britain.[12] India also provided the much-needed outlet for industrial goods, in particular textiles. Millions of Indians emigrated to work in the plantation colonies of the British Empire in the far away tropical lands of Fiji and the West Indies as well as closer to home in Malaya and Ceylon. Consequently, the Indian economy de-industrialized and became more agricultural. There is a counter-narrative, however, one that points out that the scale of the de-industrialization cannot be precisely measured and that there was a reversal in the fortunes of traditional industry including textiles from around 1900, thanks to product differentiation. Only some product groups competed with machine-made alternatives.[13]

Measures of Globalization: Volume and Composition of Trade

The first phase of globalization began in 1870 with the introduction of new technology in intercontinental telegraph, shipping, the opening up of the Suez Canal and thousands of miles of railway networks built in different parts of the world with British capital. Sailing ships were replaced by steam, bringing down transport costs together with the shortening of the trade route from Europe to Asia. Conditions to bring about a fast increase in trade were all there. The British Empire also removed another barrier to trade: tariffs and trading rules. The creation of an international market under the hegemony of Britain brought with it an international division of labour defined by comparative advantage.

The decline of Indian textile exports, faced with cheaper textiles of the modern cotton industry, and the integration of the Indian economy into the empire created new sectors of export. South Asia's comparative advantage was in the production of agricultural commodities, while British advantage lay in manufacturing. As the British economy became more industrial, it relied on imported food and raw materials from the rest of the world. South Asia became an important supplier. This was reflected in the changes in the composition of Indian trade. Figures 22.1a and 22.1b show the rise in the merchandise trade from 1840 to 1914. Both imports and exports rose, but the share of trade with Britain did not rise comparably. India's exports were more diversified by country than Indian imports. Total imports and imports from Britain rose in line until the end of the nineteenth century. Thereafter, India began to import more from the rest of the world. For exports, Britain was less important in the Indian merchandise trade after the end of the American Civil War, during which most of the raw cotton used in the British cotton textile industry was supplied by India.

India's net exports were positive all through this period and rising as shown in Figure 22.1c. However, the net exports with the United Kingdom turned negative from the 1870s. India's reliance on British imports was larger than Indian exports to Britain, suggesting that imperial connections in trade may have been more advantageous to

Britain. India imported mainly industrial goods. The import of machinery from Britain rose with the rise of modern industry in India. The Indian railway infrastructure was set up through British investment and also relied on the import of rolling stock and other equipment from Britain.

Table 22.1 shows that the composition of exports underwent significant changes. Cotton piece goods accounted for the largest share in exported merchandise in 1811, yet by 1850 this was insignificant. Raw cotton, indigo and opium constituted 80 per cent of total exports. In half a century, the composition of India's export trade had changed dramatically. By 1935, tea had emerged as the second largest export after raw cotton. New products emerged such as raw jute and manufactured jute goods. Indigo, opium and sugar declined as exportables. The rise in exports of cotton goods from the late nineteenth century reflected the growing importance of the domestic modern industry and its competitive advantage in markets in Asia. Agricultural exports increased at 4 per cent per year between 1876 and 1913.

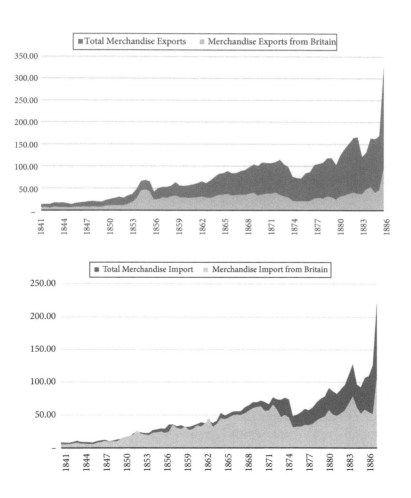

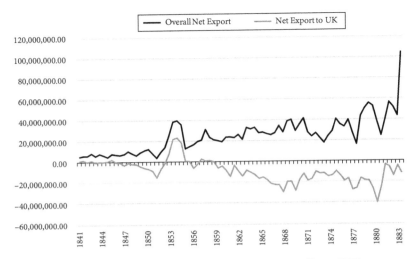

Figure 22.1 A. Merchandise exports from India, 1840–1920 (in millions GBP);
B. Merchandise imports to India, 1840–1920 (in millions GBP);
C. Indian net exports, 1840–1920 (in millions GBP).
Source: Constructed from Statistical Abstracts of British India.

The Impact of Globalization on the Economy of South Asia

What effect did this have on production and productivity?

The effect of trade on growth and the implications of trade in agricultural goods as opposed to trade in manufactured goods are debated topics. The literature on trade and growth suggests that specialization by comparative advantage increases welfare. What matters is factor endowment-based specialization. Countries with abundant land relative to labour gain by specializing in agricultural products, while labour abundance provides comparative advantage in industrial products. Both countries can gain by specializing and trading. The Prebisch-Singer thesis cautioned us against this by showing empirically that terms of trade of agricultural products relative to industrial products declined from the middle of the nineteenth century to the middle of the twentieth century.[14] Therefore specialization in agricultural production can adversely affect economic development. Since then, Frankel and Romer have showed, using cross-country data from the second half of the twentieth century, that trade has a causal positive effect on economic growth. Output per capita depends on the volume of trade. Evidence from the nineteenth century is much more mixed.[15] Mitchener and Weidenmier show that being a colony increased the volume of trade.[16] Pascali uses cross-country data to show that for the colonies trade had a negative effect on indicators of economic development.[17]

From within Indian economic history, a few other dimensions of the globalization process have generated a great deal of controversy. Three such debates are especially important. First, if free trade destroyed a part of the indigenous textile industry, how large and how bad was the impact? Second, if average levels of living standards in India

Table 22.1 Changing composition of Indian trade, 1811–1935

	Raw cotton	Cotton goods	Indigo	Raw silk	Food grains	Raw jute	Jute goods	Opium	Sugar	Tea
1811	4.9	33.0	18.5	8.3				23.8	1.5	
1828	15.0	11.0	27.0	10.0				17.0	4.0	
1850	19.1	3.7	10.9	3.8	4.1	1.1	0.9	30.1	10.0	0.2
1870	33.2	2.5	5.8		8.1	4.7	0.6			2.1
1890	16.5	9.5	3.1		19.5	7.6	2.5			5.3
1910	17.2	6.0	0.2		18.4	7.4	8.1			5.9
1935	21.0	1.3			13.5*	8.5	14.5			12.3

Source: K. N. Chaudhuri (1983), 'Foreign trade and balance of payments', in Dharma Kumar and Meghnad Desai (eds), *The Cambridge Economic History of India*, vol. 2. Cambridge: Cambridge University Press, Tables 10.10 and 10.11.

rapidly fell behind Western European levels from the 1800s, was this 'divergence' due to globalization? Did colonization contribute to the divergence? Third, although a great deal of the exports came from agriculture, why did peasants not seem to gain from the process? Let us consider these three aspects separately.

De-industrialization

In the first half of the nineteenth century, there was a fall in industrial employment, at first driven by the decline of textile exports and then by the rising market share of British industrial goods. The penetration of British textiles in the Indian market followed a slightly different chronology. Several authors show that the decline in the share of Indian textiles in the domestic market occurred mainly between 1850 and 1880.[18] In 1850 imports were roughly 10 per cent of domestic consumption, but by 1880 imports supplied 60 per cent of domestic consumption. Thereafter Indian cotton mills began to take over a share in the Indian market. The textile market expanded not only in response to population growth but also due to a rise in per capita cloth consumption as the relative price of textiles declined.

The decline of traditional industries and the loss of industrial employment is known as de-industrialization. There have been several notable attempts to measure the extent of the decline; the majority of these deal with eastern India.[19] Bagchi showed that the proportion of the working population engaged in industry was higher in 1800 at around 15–18 per cent, compared to 9–10 per cent in 1900. The most recent of these estimates by Ray shows that de-industrialization affected 4 per cent of the workforce over several decades in the nineteenth century. This was a significant figure, but not a catastrophe. Another recent paper by Clingingsmith and Williamson reaches the same conclusion, calling the early nineteenth century a period of 'weak de-industrialization' that shows a relative, rather than an absolute, decline of industry.[20]

The corresponding loss of income is harder to measure because the large hand-spinning industry mainly employed part-time domestic workers. The opportunity cost of shifting out of this activity was low. The income loss, therefore, should be smaller than the employment loss. The effect of de-industrialization on social welfare is also difficult to measure. There was a rise in unemployment. At the same time the massive fall in yarn and cloth prices arising from the higher productivity of the British industries enabled more consumption of cloth. Handloom weavers started to use imported yarn, which increased the profitability of cloth production. Per capita consumption of cloth rose from 11 yards in 1880 to 15 in 1913 and to 17 in 1930. The net effect is therefore ambiguous.

New research by Broadberry and Gupta sheds light on the chronology of changing comparative advantage of British textiles in India.[21] The textile industry in Britain saw total factor productivity growth with the introduction of new technology, while textile technology in Indian industry changed little. British products became competitive in the home market between 1770 and 1790. British products became competitive in third markets between 1790 and 1820. Consequently, India's exports began to decline. It was only after 1830 that British goods saw a high enough productivity increase to displace Indian goods in the Indian market. British total factor productivity was twice as high as that of Indian products and increased to three and a half times between 1680 and 1790. The price of British goods was twice as high in 1680, but only 35 per cent as that of Indian textiles goods in 1820 (Table 22.2).

The free trade policy imposed by the colonial state on India encouraged the growth of the cloth trade but did not protect domestic industry as in many other countries, including Germany and the United States. Might the Indian textile industry have survived with a protectionist policy? The magnitude of the price difference between British and Indian textiles was so large that it is difficult to conceptualize a high enough rate of tariff that could have protected the hand-spinning sector. What if tariff rates of 20–40 per cent, as adopted by many European countries and the United States, had been imposed? This might have prolonged the demise of some sectors of the handloom industry. Tariffs, however, might have had a positive impact on the nascent modern textile mills, which developed from the 1860s despite the absence of any kind of state support.

This discussion leaves two big questions unanswered. First, why did any Indian artisan producer of textiles survive at all? Artisans supplied nearly a quarter or more of the cotton cloth market as late as 1942, and employed well over 2 million full-time workers. Studies on artisanal weaving point at the diversity of consumption norms in India, and the fact that, in certain types of clothing, Indian consumers continued to buy handmade goods even when machine-made alternatives were available.[22] Second, why did a mill industry develop in India that competed directly with Manchester? The Indian merchants involved in the raw cotton trade had made large profits during the American Civil War. When these profits collapsed at the end of the war, they invested in modern cotton textile firms and began to produce yarn and cloth for local markets. The textile machinery producers in Britain were only too willing to sell to Indian entrepreneurs. Indian entry into modern industry was facilitated by profits made in the cotton trade, domestic availability of raw cotton, low wages and the easy terms on which Indians could buy machines and hire foremen abroad.[23] Indian machine-made goods made inroads into the domestic market for textiles at the cost of both imports and traditional products.

Table 22.2 Productivity and price advantage of British textile goods over Indian goods (India = 100)

Year	Total factor inputs	FOB price	Total factor productivity
1680	206	200	206
1770	270	200	270
1790	357	147	357
1820	150	35	150

Source: S. Broadberry and B. Gupta (2009), 'Lancashire, India, and shifting competitive advantage in cotton textiles, 1700–1850: The neglected role of factor prices', *Economic History Review*, 62 (2), Table 9.

Imports per capita had risen from 1 yard in 1840 to 7 yards in 1880, but the increase slowed down and by 1930 the number had declined to 5 yards.

Divergence

The conventional narrative has been that something special happened with the Industrial Revolution in Britain. The economy of Britain moved from a Malthusian equilibrium to modern economic growth, while most other countries fell behind. India was another example of retaining extensive growth until the middle of the twentieth century.

The timing of the Great Divergence has generated a large literature. The California School and the world historians, however, propose a different view. They claim that colonization was a primary determinant of the Great Divergence. This literature sees 1800 as the starting point of the divergence between Europe and Asia. In the eighteenth century, living standards in the rest of the world were on a par with the developed parts of Europe, such as Britain (Pomeranz on China, and Parthasarathi on India; see the contribution by Pomeranz and Parthasarathi in this volume).[24] Others argue that the divergence began before colonization and may be explained in terms of a large high productivity urban sector in northwest Europe.[25] New research shows that Britain was the first country to move out of the Malthusian trap, and much earlier than the advent of the Industrial Revolution.[26] High mortality due to war and disease in the expanding urban sectors shifted the economy to a low population growth regime and allowed per capita income to rise in England.[27] Per capita GDP declined or stagnated in most other parts of the world, making way for the Great Divergence.

Systematic quantitative evidence of wages and incomes puts this date in the middle of the seventeenth century for India. Broadberry and Gupta (2006) use a large data set on silver and grain wages from different parts of India.[28] While the silver wage was one-fifth of the British level in 1600, the grain wage was over 80 per cent due to the low price of food grains in India, suggesting that the difference in living standards was not large. However, this difference widened over time, driven partly by a decline in wages in India and by a rise in Britain. Allen et al.'s (2011) estimates using welfare ratios of consumption baskets confirm this picture. While most countries were at a basic subsistence level, London wages bought much more than a barebones consumption basket.

Estimates of per capita GDP put that of India at 62 per cent of the British level in 1600 and show a decline all the way up to the middle of the nineteenth century.[29] The average Indian was worse off in 1750 compared to 1600 (Table 22.3). This evidence suggests that the Great Divergence began well before the Industrial Revolution. The widening of the divergence after 1800 was mainly driven by a rapid increase in British GDP per capita, while Indian GDP per capita stagnated. The evidence suggests that Indian per capita income declined slowly but steadily during the golden age of the textile trade. As the textile trade declined and India turned into an exporter of agricultural commodities, the per capita GDP grew a little in the first phase of globalization but stagnated mostly in the nineteenth century and after 1914 (Table 22.4).

Table 22.3 Measuring the Great Divergence

Year	Indian grain wage as percentage of British wage	Indian GDP per capita as percentage of British GDP per capita
1600	21	62
1650	27	59
1700	25	40
1750	21	34
1800	14	28
1850	12	19

Note: Grain wage is nominal wage divided by the price of the local grain.
Sources: S. Broadberry and B. Gupta (2006), 'The early modern Great Divergence: Wages, prices and economic development in Europe and Asia, 1500–1800', *Economic History Review*, 59 (1), 2–31; and S. Broadberry et al. (2015), 'India and the Great Divergence: An Anglo-Indian comparison of GDP per capita, 1600–1871', *Explorations in Economic History*, 55 (1), 58–75.

Table 22.4 Economic growth in the long run

	Per capita income (percentage per year)
1860–1885	0.5
1885–1900	0.8
1900–1947	0.1

Source: B. Gupta (2019), 'Falling behind and catching up: India's transition from a colonial economy', *Economic History Review* 72 (3), 803–27.

The timing of the decline is important in order to find explanations. There are two different explanations with very different implications for the role of colonization and globalization on economic development. First, if the decline in living standards occurred after 1800, we can think of colonization and integration into a global economy in a system of 'unequal exchange' as a possible explanation. Colonization of India began in the mid-eighteenth century. The world economy became increasingly integrated in the nineteenth century through colonization and technological changes in transportation. The Industrial Revolution in Britain created demand for raw material for industry. The textile industry was at the centre of the Industrial Revolution and British textile products competed with Indian textiles in the world market. In this scenario, the decline in the Indian textile trade and the consequent decline of industrial activity in India may be an important factor in explaining the decline in per capita GDP and living standards. However, if the decline began closer to 1700, then the decline must be explained in terms of a failure to raise productivity in the largest sector, agriculture.

The first explanation in the literature uses very little quantitative evidence. Parthasarathi's work on the living standards of Indian weavers is an exception. Instead, this literature points to the thriving trade in textiles and other commodities from the Indian subcontinent in the seventeenth and the eighteenth centuries as indicative of a prosperous economy. Although the Indian economy did not fit the picture of a backward, self-sufficient village economy, the presence of a vibrant trading sector does not tell us much about the size of this urban economy. The Indian urbanization rate was at its highest at 15 per cent in 1600 and declined slowly until the nineteenth century, when the decline accelerated. In 1871, India's urban population stood at 9 per cent. Indian living standards declined during the years of a prosperous trade in textiles.[30] There is no doubt that the decline of the textile trade had some effect, but its magnitude was not large enough to explain the stagnation of per capita GDP.

How large was the textile trade? Reliable estimates relate to European trade with Asia. However, it is difficult to gain such estimates of the Indian Ocean trade carried out by Indian merchants. Om Prakash calculates the employment arising from the export trade from Bengal in the eighteenth century at less than 11 per cent. If trade by Asian traders was included, this number would be higher, but unlikely to be more than 15 per cent for India as the whole. Bengal was one of most globalized and industrialized regions with 15–18 per cent employment in industry in 1801. The share of industry for India overall was lower. In Britain, on the eve of the Industrial Revolution, the share of industrial employment in total male labour force was 24 per cent, rising to over 47 per cent in 1840 with a similar proportion of the population living in urban areas. The pre-colonial Indian economy, though a major exporter of industrial goods in the world, was not an industrial economy.

Figure 22.2 shows that the trend in per capita GDP tracks per capita agricultural output, but bears no relationship to per capita industrial output. Agricultural exports increased in the nineteenth century, when GDP per capita shows a slight positive trend or stagnation. Therefore, it is difficult to argue that the decline in textile exports had serious consequences for the economy overall. Certainly, there were regional effects, but the aggregate rise in agricultural exports stabilized incomes. The agricultural sector employed two-thirds of the labour force and therefore it had a more significant effect on the economy.

Agricultural Stagnation

Even as agricultural trade grew, peasant incomes on average did not. There was, however, considerable regional variation to this picture. The regions growing wheat did better than those cultivating rice. Western India did better than eastern India. The colonial government embarked on a policy of infrastructure building, and the construction of the railway network integrated markets, while the creation of the irrigation network was on a much smaller scale and had strong regional bias. Expenditure on irrigation was small compared to that for the railways. The share of capital formation in GDP remained less than a quarter than was achieved after 1947. Within this limited investment, agriculture had a small share which declined over time.[31]

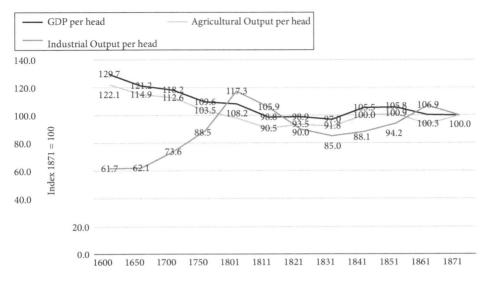

Figure 22.2 Trends in GDP, agricultural output and industrial output per head (1871 = 100).
Source: B. Gupta (2019), 'Falling behind and catching up: India's transition from a colonial economy', *Economic History Review* 72 (3), 803–27.

Although the share of spending on irrigation was low, the colonial government built one of the largest irrigation networks in the world. Large areas were covered in some regions, but only 20 per cent of the total cultivated land was irrigated. Agricultural output increased at the extensive margin as expansion of land under cultivation came through increasing provision of water and irrigation. Overall, there was a difference in productivity growth between food and non-food agricultural products, which may suggest that rising agricultural productivity in cash crops fitted well with the objectives of colonial trade (Table 22.5).

However, most irrigation was directed to non-food cash crops, which were the main exportable, at the expense of food grains. Yield per acre in wheat increased on irrigated land. Wheat exports rose too. Falling productivity in food grains was driven by falling agricultural productivity in rice. The failure to raise agricultural productivity led to stagnation under colonial rule. This is not due to increasing share of agricultural exports, but rather the failure to invest in an appropriate infrastructure and technological change that led to stagnation as the extensive margin dried up.

Conclusion

This chapter has traced the transformation of the South Asian economy from the 1600s to the end of British colonial rule. It traces the rise and fall of the textile export trade and its political implications. India lost its status as an exporter of industrial goods after 1800

Table 22.5 Change in agricultural production and productivity, 1891–1946

	Output	Acreage	Yield/acre	Growth in yield per acre		
				1891–1916	1916–21	1921–46
All crops	0.37	0.40	0.01	0.47	−0.36	−0.02
Food grains	0.11	0.31	−0.18	0.29	−0.63	−0.44
Non-food grains	1.31	0.42	0.67	0.81	0.34	1.16

Source: T. Roy (2006), *The Economic History of India, 1857–1947*. New Delhi: Oxford University Press, Table 4.2.

and became an exporter of food and raw materials to the industrial economy of Britain. This transformation had little to do with India's colonial status and subordination to British trade policy. The main reason for the shift in Indian advantage in the cotton textile market came from the superior and more productive technology of the Industrial Revolution.

In the long run, average levels of living were depressed in India. As India began to export increasing quantities of primary products, per capita GDP did not decline further. Instead it rose at a very slow rate in the nineteenth century and then stagnated in the twentieth century. The neglect of agricultural investment by the colonial government and the consequent failure to raise agricultural productivity account for the lack of intensive growth in the Indian economy. India's integration into the global economy from the nineteenth century had few consequences for actual economic growth.

Notes

1. A. Greif (2006), *Institutions and the Path to the Modern Economy: Lessons from Medieval trade*. Cambridge: Cambridge University Press.

2. U. Dasgupta (2001), *The World of the Indian Ocean Merchant, 1500–1800*. New Delhi: Oxford University Press.

3. K. N. Chaudhuri (1978), *The Trading World of Asia and the English East India Company, 1660–1760*. Cambridge. Cambridge University Press; S. Chaudhury (1995), *From Prosperity to Decline: Eighteenth Century Bengal*. New Delhi: Manohar.

4. C. A. Bayly (1983), *Rulers, Townsmen and Bazaars: North Indian Society in the Age of British Expansion, 1770–1870*. Cambridge: Cambridge University Press; D. Washbrook (2007), 'India in the early modern world economy: Modes of production, reproduction and exchange', *Journal of Global History*, 2 (1), 87–111.

5. L. Subramanian (1987), 'Banias and the British: The role of indigenous credit in the process of imperial expansion in western India in the second half of the eighteenth century', *Modern Asian Studies*, 21 (3), 473–510; T. Roy (2013), 'Rethinking the origins of British India: State formation and military-fiscal undertakings in an eighteenth-century world region', *Modern Asian Studies*, 47 (4), 1125–56; C. Markovits (2017), 'The Indian economy and the British

Empire in the Company period: Some additional reflections around an essay by David Washbrook', *Modern Asian Studies*, 51 (2), 375–98.

6. C. A. Bayly (2003), *The Birth of the Modern World, 1780-1914*. London: Wiley-Blackwell.

7. P. T. Hoffman (2015), *Why Did Europe Conquer the World?*. Princeton, NJ: Princeton University Press.

8. M. Oak and A. V. Swamy (2012), 'Myopia or strategic behavior? Indian regimes and the East India Company in late eighteenth century India', *Explorations in Economic History*, 49 (3), 352–66.

9. R. Guha (1982), *A Rule of Property for Bengal: An Essay on the Idea of Permanent Settlement*. New Delhi: Orient Longman.

10. T. Roy (2013), *An Economic History of Early Modern India*. London: Routledge.

11. Most of British investment was in the land-abundant colonies of North America and Australia.

12. For a discussion, see Dan Bogart and Latika Chaudhary (2016), 'Railways in colonial India: An economic achievement?', in Latika Chaudhary, Bishnupriya Gupta, Tirthankar Roy and Anand V. Swamy (eds), *A New Economic History of Colonial India*. Abingdon and London: Routledge, 140–60.

13. See T. Roy (1999), *Traditional Industry in the Economy of Colonial India*. Cambridge: Cambridge University Press.

14. H. W. Singer (1989), 'Terms of trade and economic development', in *Economic Development*. London: Palgrave Macmillan, 323–8.

15. J. A. Frankel and D. Romer (1999), 'Does trade cause growth?', *American Economic Review*, 91 (5), 379–99.

16. K. J. Mitchener and M. Weidenmier (2008), 'Trade and empire', *Economic Journal*, 118 (533), 1805–34.

17. L. Pascali (2017), 'The wind of change: Maritime technology, trade and economic development', *American Economic Review*, 107 (9), 2821–54.

18. M. J. Twomey (1983), 'Employment in nineteenth century Indian textiles', *Explorations in Economic History*, 20 (1), 37–57.

19. A. K. Bagchi (1976), 'De-industrialization in India in the nineteenth century: Some theoretical implications', *Journal of Development Studies*, 12 (2), 135–64. I. Ray (2011), *Bengal Industries and the British Industrial Revolution*. London and New York: Routledge.

20. D. Clingingsmith and J. G. Williamson (2008), 'Deindustrialization in 18th and 19th century India: Mughal decline, climate shocks and British industrial ascent', *Explorations in Economic History*, 45 (3), 209–34.

21. S. Broadberry and B. Gupta (2009), 'Lancashire, India, and shifting competitive advantage in cotton textiles, 1700–1850: The neglected role of factor prices', *Economic History Review*, 62 (2), 279–305.

22. Roy (1999), *Traditional Industry*; D. E. Haynes (2012), *Small Town Capitalism in Western India: Artisans, Merchants and the Making of the Informal Economy, 1870–1960*. Cambridge: Cambridge University Press.

23. For more detailed discussion, see B. Gupta (2015), 'The rise of modern industry in colonial India', in L. Chaudhary, B. Gupta, T. Roy and A. V. Swamy (eds), *A New Economic History of Colonial India*. London: Routledge.

24. K. Pomeranz (2000), *The Great Divergence: China, Europe, and the Making of the Modern World Economy*. Princeton, NJ: Princeton University Press; Parthasarathi, 'Rethinking wages and competitiveness in the eighteenth century', 158, 79–109.

25. S. Broadberry and B. Gupta (2006), 'The early modern Great Divergence: Wages, prices and economic development in Europe and Asia, 1500–1800', *Economic History Review*, 59 (1), 2–31; R. C. Allen, J. P. Bassino, D. Ma, C. Moll-Murata and J. L. Van Zanden (2011), 'Wages, prices, and living standards in China, 1738–1925: In comparison with Europe, Japan, and India', *Economic History Review*, 64 (supplement 1), 8–38.

26. S. Broadberry, B. M. Campbell, A. Klein, M. Overton and B. Van Leeuwen (2015), *British Economic Growth, 1270–1870*. Cambridge: Cambridge University Press.

27. N. Voigtländer and H. J. Voth (2012), 'The three horsemen of riches: Plague, war, and urbanization in early modern Europe', *Review of Economic Studies*, 80 (2), 774–811.

28. S. Broadberry and B. Gupta (2006), 'The early modern Great Divergence: Wages, prices and economic development in Europe and Asia, 1500–1800', Economic History Review, 59 (1), pp. 2–31; R. C. Allen et al. (2011), 'Wages, prices, and Living Standards in China, 1738–1925', In Comparison with Europe, Japan, and India', Economic History Review, 64 (supplement 1), 8–38.

29. Broadberry et al. (2015), 'India and the great divergence: An Anglo-Indian comparison of GDP per capita, 1600-1871', *Explorations in Economic History*, 55 (1), 58–75.

30. Broadberry and Gupta (2006), 'The early modern Great Divergence'; and Broadberry et al. (2015), 'India and the Great Divergence'.

31. B. Roy (1996), *An analysis of Long-Term Growth of National Income and Capital Formation in India (1850–51 to 1950–51)*. Calcutta: Firma KLM Pvt.

CHAPTER 23
CHANGING DESTINIES IN THE ECONOMY OF SOUTHEAST ASIA

J. Thomas Lindblad

Southeast Asia is an important player in today's world economy. The region, embracing the ten member states of the ASEAN (Association of South East Asian Nations), counts 625 million inhabitants, 8.3 per cent of the world total. Total GDP nears US$2.5 trillion or 3.3 per cent of world GDP. Per capita GDP varies enormously across the member states, presently averaging about US$4,000 at nominal prices, which corresponds to more than US$10,000 if measured at purchasing power parity.[1] Yet, for centuries this region remained spectacularly underpopulated, and when colonial rule came to an end, virtually all the newly independent nation states faced grave problems of economic development. A true metamorphosis has taken place within living memory. Was this anticipated or delayed by earlier changes in the region's economic destiny? Or, to put it differently, could the economic success in much, but not all, of the region have been predicted by observers in the colonial period, let alone in pre-colonial times? The time frame of my exploration stretches from the sixteenth century up to the mid-twentieth century.

Three key variables need to be surveyed to adequately assess the region's long-run economic development. The first one is economic growth, whether or not associated with per capita gain, whereas the second one refers to the underlying economic structure. Both have been prominently at play during the dramatic changes in the post-war era. Sustained high growth rates qualified four ASEAN member states (Singapore, Malaysia, Thailand and Indonesia) to be included among the prestigious HPAEs (highly performing Asian economies) as designated by the World Bank in 1993. A decisive shift from agriculture to manufacturing occurred in five of the large economies (Indonesia, Thailand, Malaysia, the Philippines and Vietnam) between the late 1960s and early 1990s.

The third key variable concerns the openness to world markets. The region is literally located at major crossroads in the world economy. Four major economies exhibit an exceptionally high ratio of foreign trade to GDP – Singapore, Malaysia, Thailand and Vietnam – while others, notably Indonesia and the Philippines, remain more strongly oriented towards their own domestic markets. In earlier centuries, the main external influences came from either India or China. Then the radius was widened to include the Middle East and Europe, and eventually the Americas. The strong external impetus had far- reaching repercussions for both economic growth and economic structure. Did openness generate sustained growth and encourage an economic structure conducive to such growth?

In his authoritative account of the *longue durée* in Southeast Asian history, Anthony Reid identifies a succession of distinct phases of development.[2] The 'Age of Commerce', applying the label Reid himself coined in an earlier seminal study to identify the period in Southeast Asian history from 1480 to 1630, came to fruition in an aggregation of societies that more often than not succeeded in evading state formation. This is all the more remarkable as it goes contrary to expectation from experience elsewhere, where the formation of strong states preceded economic expansion or even formed a prerequisite for such a change of economic fortune. Was Southeast Asia with its 'Age of Commerce' of one and a half-century the exception that proves the rule?

The subsequent Western colonialism put an indelible mark on the entire region except for Thailand (Siam until 1930). The outcome was a process of formation of states, but not nations. To what extent did colonial rule during the nineteenth and early twentieth centuries prepare the region for the challenges of economic development after independence? Addressing this issue acknowledges the need to study post-colonial economic development in relationship to the colonial legacy. In a path-breaking study, Anne Booth adopts a comparative perspective, arguing that Japanese colonialism in East Asia laid stronger foundations for rapid development after independence than did Western colonial rule in Southeast Asia.[3]

As said, this contribution focuses on the first two phases of Reid's classification, only touching on the third phase, the current post-war situation, in passing. Most attention is given to economic matters, on occasion in juxtaposition with political trends, and for reasons of space leaving aside social change and related issues.

Society without State

Southeast Asia covers a land area of 4.5 million square kilometres. Still, by the beginning of the seventeenth century, the entire region counted less than 25 million inhabitants and even by 1800 total population was estimated to be no more than 34 million. Reid ascribes this peculiar feature of historical demography to a climate and geography that encouraged collection of forest produce and maritime trading rather than labour-intensive agricultural production.[4] With the possible exception of Central and East Java and Luzon, population concentrations were simply too low to support centres of power and authority.

The half millennium or so preceding the 'Age of Commerce' (1480–1630) saw an extreme fragmentation of polities based on charters between rulers and the surrounding population. By the mid-fourteenth century, there were twenty-three kingdoms in the broad mainland belt from Burma to Vietnam, and numerous more or less autonomous units in the 'empty' area of the Malay Peninsula and the western part of the Indonesian archipelago. Of the region's three famous ancient 'empires', Srivijaya with its centre in South Sumatra had practically collapsed already, whereas Mataram and Majapahit in Java effectively covered territories of ever diminishing size.[5] Although some recentralization took place on the mainland between the mid-fourteenth and the mid- sixteenth centuries, the 'state-light' domain, an expression borrowed again from Reid, remained characteristic of the region with its bewildering array of amorphous 'states and non-states, large and small', often with unclear and porous borders.[6]

The long sixteenth century, the period from 1480 to 1630, was one of a dramatic expansion of foreign trade and shipping. The products in highest demand were spices from Maluku (Moluccas), supplemented by a wide range of forest products such as woods and resins, even ivory, rhinoceros horns and birds' nests. Towards the end of this period of expansion, the range of tradeable goods had come to include also cane sugar and cotton. The traders included Chinese, Indians, Arabs and a variegation of indigenous peoples from all parts of the region. The Europeans were the last to be added to the long list of participants in the region's booming trade.

A web of shipping connections evolved with nodal points. Melaka, dating from around 1400, profited from its strategic location at the main road of access by sea to the region and effectively shouldered the legacy of the defunct Srivijaya 'empire'. Similarly, Demak and other ports along the Pasisir, Java's north coast, rose to prominence in the vacuum left by the fading Majapahit 'empire'. Other thriving ports in the expanding Muslim Malay sphere included Brunei in north-western Borneo while Hoi An in the Chinese sphere of influence on Borneo played a crucial part in maintaining shipping links with East Asia. Cities of impressive size arose. At the peak of the commercial expansion in 1630, Reid identified ten cities with an estimated population in excess of 100,000 people, five on the mainland (Pegu, Ayutthaya, Hanoi, Hue and Melaka) and five in the Indonesian archipelago (Aceh, Banten, Batavia, Mataram and Makassar).[7]

Trading in Southeast Asia during the 'Age of Commerce' was initially largely conducted within the region itself, even if the traders often originated from other regions. The global or interregional dimension, as opposed to the intra-regional one, was gradually strengthened. Spices from Maluku had entered Europe through Middle Eastern intermediaries already since late medieval times, and this branch of trade received a powerful boost when the Portuguese established direct shipping links with Europe around 1500. Imports of Indian textiles played an increasing part in the trade with South Asia, rising threefold in value between the early sixteenth and the first half of the seventeenth centuries. During the concluding decades of the sixteenth century, the important bullion trade was added to exchanges with other parts of the world. The influx of American silver from Acapulco through the region's eastward gateway at Manila rose fourfold between the 1580s and the 1620s.[8]

Pepper became the most spectacular of success stories. The total volume of exports of pepper from Southeast Asia doubled between the 1530s and 1560s, from 1,300 tonnes to 2,700 tonnes on average per year, climbing to a peak at 3,800 tonnes in the 1620s that was sustained into the 1640s. An increasing proportion of total exports was destined for the European market, where the Southeast Asian product soon surpassed Indian pepper in popularity. The share of Europe in total Southeast Asian pepper exports rose from one-quarter in the 1530s to about one-half in the 1560s and oscillated around 40 per cent in the 1590s and the 1620s (Figure 23.1). Meanwhile the total annual value – based on prices in Southeast Asian ports – rose fourfold from less than 80,000 Spanish dollars (real) in the 1530s to 340,000 in the 1590s, eventually reaching a peak level of 600,000 Spanish dollars in the 1640s. The latter figure was twice as high as the total value of exports of the region's second-ranking spice product, cloves from Maluku in particular. It is worth noting that the pepper exports were far more voluminous than the exports of cloves, which reflects a lower price for pepper, 0.15 Spanish dollars per kilogram in the 1620s against 0.80 Spanish dollars for cloves.[9]

The pepper trade was exceptionally profitable. This is best illustrated by trends in pepper exports during the aftermath of the 'Age of Commerce'. There was a huge divergence in the value of the shipments of pepper, depending on where they were priced. The total value of imports of Southeast Asian pepper, measured at the international market in Amsterdam in the 1630s, was 4.3 times as high as the value of exports measured at the point of departure. This 'multiplier' (markup) in the transfer from one market to the next even climbed to 6.4 in the 1660s and still averaged at 4.7 times in the final decade of the seventeenth century (Figure 23.2). The discrepancy between Southeast Asian and European value was even more pronounced in the case of cloves, where the European value from the 1650s to the 1690s represented a multiple of ten or more compared to the value in Southeast Asia.[10] The key to high profits in European trade with Southeast

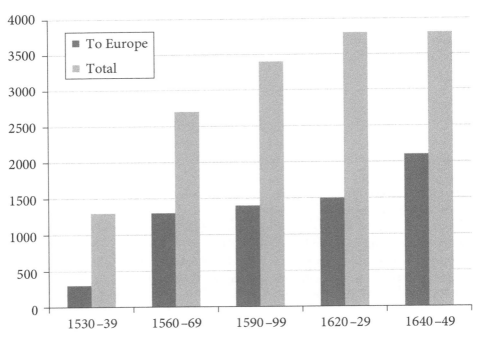

Figure 23.1 Average annual volume of pepper exports from Southeast Asia, 1530–1649 (metric tons).

Source: A. Reid (2015), *A History of Southeast Asia: Critical Crossroads*. Chichester: Wiley-Blackwell, 78.

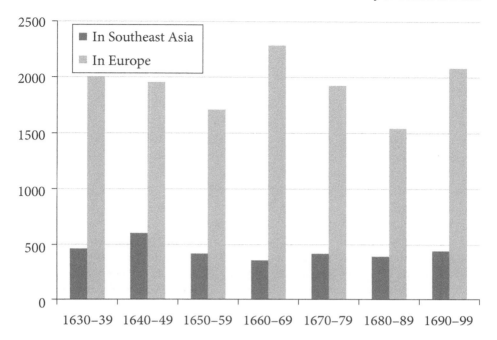

Figure 23.2 Average annual value of pepper exports in Southeast Asia and in Europe, 1630–99 (in thousand Spanish dollars).
Source: A. Reid (2015), *A History of Southeast Asia: Critical Crossroads*. Chichester: Wiley-Blackwell, 147.

Asia lay in imperfect information about market conditions. Exporters in Southeast Asia did not have the slightest idea of how much their spices were worth in Amsterdam.

Three events stand out as landmarks in the history of European participation in the expansion of Southeast Asia in this period. The first is the conquest of Melaka by the Portuguese in 1511, which opened up the direct spice trade between Southeast Asia and Europe. The second is the foundation of Manila by the Spaniards in 1571 that exposed Southeast Asia to the bullion trade. The third is the establishment of the Dutch East India Company, VOC (Vereenigde Oost-Indische Compagnie) in 1602, arguably the world's first multinational. European involvement in Southeast Asian trade began in the 'Age of Commerce' and part of it survived beyond the peak in the region's expansion. The Dutch took over from the Portuguese, whereas the Spaniards remained largely confined to the Philippines.

There has been a lively discussion among historians about the role of European traders during the 'Age of Commerce' and its aftermath. Were they merely aloof observers from the sideline or did they outrank their Asian rivals? The debate has been moving back and forth between these two positions for some time, but current scholarship seems to favour the externalist view above the autonomous one. The European traders had an impact disproportionate to their numbers because of their control of long-distance trading, naval supremacy and ready access to bullion.[11] Commercial success was secured through competition and cooperative ventures with both migrant Asian and indigenous competitors.

State-light Power

The eclipse of the 'Age of Commerce' was signalled by several seemingly unrelated events: exports of silver from Japan were banned in 1635, the fall of the Ming dynasty in China in 1644 severely disrupted Chinese shipping, and the conquest of Melaka by the VOC in 1641 secured the Dutch monopoly in the spice trade. Just as Southeast Asia had benefited more than others from the booming 'long sixteenth century', the region was especially hard hit by the seventeenth-century depression in the world economy. Economic setbacks were aggravated by military conflict and adverse physical circumstances, such as earthquakes, possibly also tsunamis, and disturbances in the climate somehow occasioned by the 'Little Ice Age' in Europe and the northern part of Asia.[12]

Although the spice trade remained potentially highly profitable, Southeast Asia was losing its comparative advantage due the rigidly enforced Dutch monopoly as well as declining demand among consumers in Europe. The overall downward trend in the economic tide is well borne out by estimates of the value of cargo entered in the port of Manila. The high annual average at nearly 600,000 Spanish dollars prevailing for

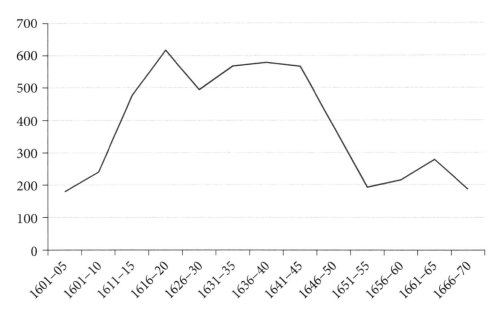

Figure 23.3 Average annual value of cargo entering Manila, 1601–70 (in thousand Spanish dollars).

Source: A. Reid (1993), *Southeast Asia in the Age of Commerce, 1450–1680*, vol. 2: *Expansion and Crisis*. New Haven, CT: Yale University Press, 289.

the period 1610–50 declined to one-third of its former level in the 1650s and 1660s (Figure 23.3).

The VOC emerged as the winner from the competitive strife in regional trading during the seventeenth century. By 1660 the Dutch-owned business enterprise with its diverse international labour force stood above competition in leading branches of trade. The success can be ascribed to the synergy between selective trading monopolies, the exercise of territorial power, and access to a global network. Among its rivals, the VOC was unique in combining commercial advantage with political and military operations resembling those of an autonomous state. From about 1680 onwards, the VOC's suzerainty over the decaying Mataram 'empire' was undisputed. The VOC came to function as one participant among many in the fragmented multi-state system of the archipelago, albeit one with military superiority.[13]

In the eighteenth century, the trade of the VOC grew increasingly oriented towards intra-Asian trade as opposed to trade with Europe. Total annual turnover in trading in Asia exceeded 30 million guilders in the early 1710s and reached a peak at nearly 39 million in the mid-eighteenth century. The Indonesian archipelago usually accounted for more than one-half of the total, but almost all of the other half accrued from possessions outside Southeast Asia. By the early 1770s, a decline had set in with a total turnover around 20 million guilders, two-thirds of which originated from the archipelago (Figure 23.4). The final downfall in the late eighteenth century was conditioned by heavy losses during the Fourth Anglo-Dutch War (1780–4), revolution and political upheaval in Europe during the 1790s, widespread corruption and private trading by employees, and possibly also systematic errors in accounting practices.[14]

The VOC interfered in an unprecedented way in the regional economy of Southeast Asia, in particular in the island world. The company reinforced or opened up profitable avenues of exploiting the region's natural resources and comparative advantages, primarily to its own gain, although local elites also shared in the spoils. In the process, the VOC became an active participant in the slave trade of the Indian Ocean and the eastern Indonesian islands. Through the juxtaposition of its commercial and political or military operations, the company had a deforming impact on the development of indigenous statecraft, especially in Java. Differently from merchant communities of other ethnic origin, however, the Dutch bequeathed a state under construction to the region. The powerful alien state in Java was based on territorialization through taxation, applying devices inherited from the company's Portuguese predecessors.[15] The VOC reaped the benefits from local fragmentation of authority. A trend in the opposite direction became visible in the mainland, where a consolidation occurred of three integrated territories under new dynasties: Kon-baung in Burma from 1752, Chakri in Thailand from 1782 and Nguyen in Vietnam from 1802. This reinforced an existing cleavage between the mainland and the archipelago, the latter here also including the Malay Peninsula. The island world was more susceptible to external influences, especially Western colonialism, and this was to become all the more important during the next phase of development.

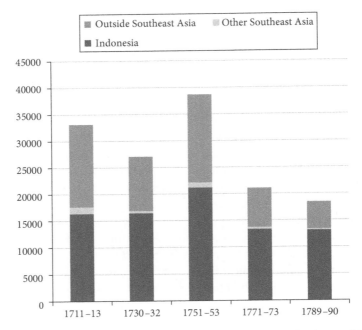

Figure 23.4 Average annual turnover of VOC trade in Asia, 1711–90 (in thousand Dutch dollars).
Source: E. M. Jacobs (2006), *Merchant in Asia: The Trade of the Dutch East India Company during the Eighteenth Century*. Leiden: CNWS Publications, 306.

State without Nation

Towards the end of the eighteenth century, colonialism in Southeast Asia was virtually confined to the old and highly indigenized Spanish possession of the Philippines and the tiny Portuguese enclave in East Timor, not counting the quasi-state functions performed by the VOC in Java. Scarcely more than one century later, the entire region except Thailand had been subjugated to effective colonial rule. From being one of the least colonized regions of the world, Southeast Asia became a region where colonial power had profound repercussions for the development of society. The discontinuity with the pre-colonial past was especially strong in the archipelago and on the peninsula. Our concern here is with the economic impact of colonialism, leaving it to political historians to address such intriguing issues as the continuity between colonial constructions and post-colonial nation states.

The region became host to several Western colonial powers. The Dutch claim to the entire Indonesian archipelago found its legal basis in the inheritance from the dissolved VOC, but actual colonial state formation remained confined to Java for the better part of the nineteenth century. The British started out from the three strategically located ports of the Straits Settlements (Penang, Melaka and Singapore), only to extend their authority over the nine Malay sultanates of the peninsula several decades later. The conquest of Burma and what then became French Indochina took place at about the same time and in a similar gradual fashion during the latter part of the nineteenth century. Spain was replaced by the United States in the Philippines in 1898, whereas the Portuguese continued to control East Timor. The metropolitan powers erected a range of colonial states, each with characteristics of their own and only sharing the common feature (with the exception of Thailand) that they were not founded on the conception of a nation.[16]

The Dutch historiography has repeatedly struggled with the issue whether the extension of Dutch colonial power to all corners of the Indonesian archipelago in the late nineteenth and early twentieth centuries fitted into or differed from prevailing patterns of modern imperialism. A consensus has emerged that the only exception from the standard pattern was the belated switch in Dutch imperialism from reluctant to aggressive expansion following the conquest of Lombok in 1894.[17] The international historiography has been more concerned with differences in colonial administration and the resulting endowment with regard to post-colonial development. The British were known for indirect colonial rule, notably through the Malay sultans on the peninsula. This contrasted with both the highly centralized control of French Indochina and the Dutch tendency to far-reaching intervention, often in conjunction with local elites. The American administrators of the Philippines were the only colonial rulers in the region bent on preparing their subjects for independence. Differences in the style of colonial rule were reflected in budgetary and welfare policies with important consequences for standards of living, a matter to which we shall return later.[18]

From the early nineteenth century, the region's population began to grow more rapidly. Total population rose almost threefold during the nineteenth century and more than doubled between 1900 and 1950 (Figure 23.5). The proportion of the total population accounted by colonial Indonesia rose to a stable level of some 45 per cent, whereas second-ranking French Indochina lagged behind neighbours with its share in the total falling from 27 per cent in 1800 to 16 per cent in 1930. Meanwhile, Burma was surpassed by the Philippines in the third position. The demographic transition finally caught up with Southeast Asia, but it is hazardous to make inferences from the acceleration in population growth to the development of standards of living over time; some of the increase may even be ascribed to better statistics.[19]

Colonialism radically altered economic relations with other parts of the world. Seeking to revitalize the commercial supremacy of the VOC, the Dutch colonial authorities in Java embarked on a state-run exploitation of the island's fertile soils, dispatching export crops to the staple market in Amsterdam. In effect, this was a reversal of the preceding trend of the VOC to emphasize intra-Asian trade at the expense of trade with Europe. The cultivation system in Java in the period 1830–70, with coffee, sugar and indigo as its foremost products, proved extraordinarily profitable. At least 6 per cent of Java's GDP was siphoned off on occasion, contributing as much as 4 per cent of total Dutch GDP and one-third of the public budget.[20] The cultivation system was abandoned eventually,

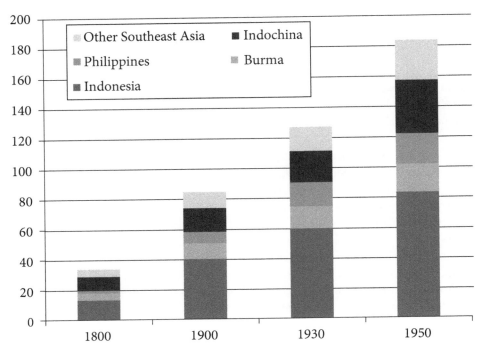

Figure 23.5 Population of Southeast Asia, 1800–1950 (millions).
Sources: R. E. Elson (1997), *The End of the Peasantry in Southeast Asia: A Social and Economic History of Peasant Livelihood, 1800–1990s*. Basingstoke: Macmillan, 76–7; H. Gooszen (2000), *A Demographic History of the Indonesian Archipelago*. Singapore: Institute of Southeast Asian Studies, 43; J. Touwen (2001), *Extremes in the Archipelago: Trade and Economic Development in the Outer Islands of Indonesia, 1900–1942*. Leiden: KITLV Press, 330; A. Reid (2015), *A History of Southeast Asia: Critical Crossroads*. Chichester: Wiley-Blackwell, 263.

because the state-run estates in Java had been an anomaly in the pervasive movement towards exploitation of natural resources by private capital in Southeast Asia.

The local economy provided land and labour wherever population densities were high enough to permit a release of cheap, unskilled workers from food production, which was notably the situation in Java and Luzon, but scarcely elsewhere. Private firms supplied investment capital, technology and management and relied when necessary on coolies shipped in from poor regions far away, such as South India, South China and Central Java. A twin system of labour mobilization emerged in the region, one operating in symbiosis with the local economy, the other consisting of enclave economies with little interaction with the surrounding society. Both systems found large-scale application in colonial Indonesia, the former one in Java and the latter one in the Outer Islands.[21] In British Malaya, however, preference was given to coolie labour relying on Indian immigrants.

The plantation belt of Deli on Sumatra's east coast (now North Sumatra) grew famous for its highly profitable cultivation of tobacco and rubber, but also notorious for scandals about abuse of labour. The system of coolie labour was devised and first tried out under the auspices of the ill-reputed penal sanction that rendered excessive powers to employers against employees. The total number of coolies doubled between 1910 and 1920, and increased by another 40 per cent during the 1920s. By the peak in 1929, the total approached 550,000 individuals, mostly men in productive ages, a number corresponding to 8 per cent of the entire population of British Malaya, including women and dependents. Although North Sumatra continued to have the majority of the coolies in colonial Indonesia, it is worth noting that other regions among the Outer Islands accounted for 30–40 per cent of the total (Figure 23.6). The system's decline in the 1930s was prompted by the abolition of the penal sanction due to international pressure and accelerated by reductions of output during the worldwide depression.

Foreign direct investment (FDI) by private firms was relatively slow in entering the region around the turn of the twentieth century, although some important fresh investments did take place in the Javanese sugar industry in the shadow and aftermath of the cultivation system.[22] One plausible explanation could stem from real or perceived uncertainties associated with investing large sums of capital on remote production sites, where protection by the colonial administration had not yet been secured. The extension of effective colonial rule over large territories in the Indonesian Outer Islands, and also in Malaya and Indochina, combined with booming markets for Southeast Asian exports to trigger massive new investment. By 1914, total FDI in the region amounted to US$1,100 million, of which US$675 million (60 per cent) was invested in Indonesia alone. The estimated total for the late 1930s was two and a half times that level and might even have been slightly higher in 1930 before the effects of economic depression were felt. The distribution across the colonies was largely unchanged with Dutch Indonesia up front accounting for more than one-half of the regional total, followed by British Malaya, the Philippines and French Indochina, in that order (Figure 23.7). The sole non-colony, Thailand, ranked last on both counts, which lends support to the idea that colonial rule and FDI were intimately connected.

Liberalism with respect to investment and trade was vigorously celebrated by the Dutch, the British and the Americans, less so by the French. Nevertheless, there was a strong bias in FDI patterns in favour of investors from the colonial mother country. Dutch firms accounted for 70 per cent of FDI in colonial Indonesia, British investors held similar stakes in Malaya, and American firms were good for more than one-half of the total in the Philippines, whereas Indochina appeared as the most extreme case, with a virtual monopoly enjoyed by French companies.[23] Familiarity with legal regulations, language and culture obviously hid behind preferences among investors for colonial targets, but direct contacts with colonial administrations were most probably important as well. Colonialism in Southeast Asia implied at least a partial reorientation in economic relations towards the outside world away from Asia and in favour of the Western metropolitan countries.

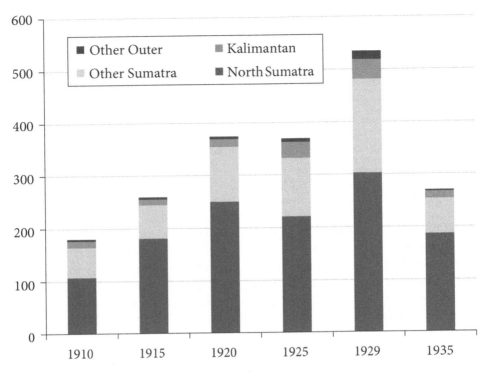

Figure 23.6 Coolie labour in colonial Indonesia, 1910–35 (thousands of workers).
Sources: J. T. Lindblad (1999), 'Coolies in Deli: Labour Conditions in Western Enterprises in East Sumatra, 1910–1938', in V. J. H. Houben, J. T. Lindblad et al. (eds), *Coolie Labour in Colonial Indonesia: A Study of Labour Relations in the Outer Islands, c.1900–1940.* Wiesbaden: Harrassowitz, 72–3; ibid. (1999), 'New destinations: Conditions of coolie labour outside East Sumatra, 1910–1938', in ibid., 101–7.

The colonial relationship also surfaced in foreign trade. The trend of the VOC in the eighteenth century to trade more in Asia, and less with Europe, was reversed by the Dutch cultivation system in Java. When foreign trade, just as foreign investment, was liberalized in the Dutch colony after the cultivation system ended, nearly one-half of imports entering the colony came from the colony, whereas the share of the Dutch in the opposite flow of trade was as high as 60 per cent. Thirty years later, the Dutch proportion in the trade of colonial Indonesia was down at one-third. Another three decades later, by the late 1930s, only one-fifth of Indonesia's foreign trade was with the Netherlands. The delinking of mutual trade between colony and metropolitan mother country proceeded even further in the British colonies of Malaya and Burma, where the share of the United Kingdom in total trade scarcely exceeded 15 per cent. In Indochina, by contrast, one-half of the foreign trade was conducted with France. The strongest trading relationship with the mother country in the late 1930s was found in the Philippines, with the United States buying more than 80 per cent of exports and supplying 70 per cent of imports.[24]

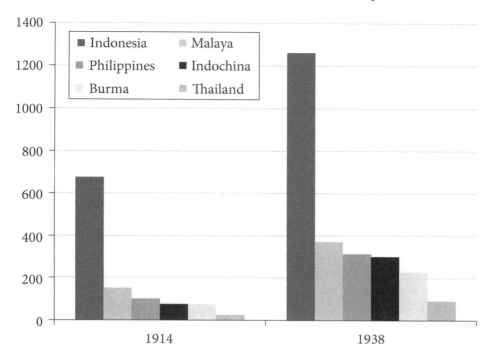

Figure 23.7 Foreign direct investment in Southeast Asia in 1914 and 1938 (in million USD).
Source: J. T. Lindblad (1998), *Foreign Investment in Southeast Asia in the Twentieth Century*. Basingstoke: Macmillan, 14.

Total exports from Southeast Asia started to increase dramatically from about 1905 onwards, and the expansion continued unabatedly up to the very eve of the economic depression of the 1930s. By the late 1930s, total exports from the entire region were estimated at US$1.6 billion, of which two-thirds originated in colonial Indonesia and British Malaya alone.[25] The expansion of exports was only in part accompanied by an increase in imports, since per capita incomes were lagging behind and failed to make a larger contribution to aggregate demand in the domestic economy. The result was a very substantial surplus in the balance of trade in all the region's colonies as well as in independent Thailand.[26] In colonial Indonesia, to cite but one example, 38 per cent of export earnings on average in the period 1900–38 were not spent on imports, a figure that also reflected the growing disparity between Java, where the surplus percentage was 25 per cent, and the Outer Islands, where it exceeded 50 per cent.[27]

Some time ago, C. P. Kindleberger aptly explained the region's trade-induced expansion as follows: 'demand was right abroad and supply was right at home.'[28] In the early twentieth century, Southeast Asia could offer a wide range of exportable products, which at that time were in high and rapidly rising demand in the world market. Java became one of the largest suppliers of cane sugar in the world, together with Taiwan and Cuba. The Outer Islands of Indonesia and the Malay Peninsula emerged as two of the world's leading exporters of tin and natural rubber, later supplemented by palm oil. Together with Burma, colonial Indonesia became the region's main oil producer. Tobacco, coffee, tea and copra all occupied prominent positions in the wide range of exports from the archipelago; colonial Indonesia even enjoyed a virtual world monopoly in the small-scale but literally vital trade in cinchona, at the time crucial in combatting malaria. By 1929, exports per capita ranged from US$4–13 in Indochina and the Philippines to as much as US$126 in British Malaya. This statistic amounted to only US$10 in the Indonesian archipelago due to the colony's very large population.[29]

The key to success in international trade was, as British Malaya and colonial Indonesia demonstrate, not just a question of having a favourable resource endowment that enabled goods in high demand to be offered on the world market. It was also a matter of building up a capacity to raise output targets in response to market signals. In the event, export volumes were rapidly enlarged in colonial Indonesia and British Malaya during the long boom in prices of primary products from about 1905 to the mid-1920s, but also by way of compensation for the general fall in prices in the second half of the 1920s and during the 1930s. Only at the nadir of the worldwide depression, when prices for primary products had reached rock-bottom levels, did export producers in Southeast Asia revert to curtailing output, notably in rubber, tin and sugar.[30]

Export production was organized in one of two ways. There was the Western colonial model, based on FDI, imported or locally mobilized labour and the overt or tacit support by colonial governments. In addition, an Asian model of export expansion took shape involving Chinese intermediaries in finance and trade and indigenous smallholder producers in cash crop agriculture. Indigenous entrepreneurship was particularly important in the rubber industry of Sumatra and Kalimantan and the Malay Peninsula, and in the copra trade of Sulawesi. By the late 1930s, smallholders supplied about one-half of the total exports of rubber and almost all exports of copra from colonial Indonesia and British Malaya.[31] The parallel modes of export expansion in Southeast Asia in the late-colonial era testify to the region's dynamic potential, decidedly in anticipation of what was to come to fruition after independence.

The pre-war export expansion was rooted in a highly traditional economic structure that above all emphasized the primary sector, including mining, at the expense of manufacturing and services. About two-thirds of the labour force in colonial Indonesia, the Philippines and Burma were still engaged in agriculture around 1930. Even in British Malaya with its substantial trading sector, three out of five worked on the land, and in Thailand the share of agriculture in employment exceeded 80 per cent. Only an embryonic industrialization, attracting about 10 per cent of labour, was taking place in these colonies but, significantly, not in Thailand.[32] The traditional economic structure in almost the entire region on the eve of independence was without doubt a factor that forestalled the switch to modern, sustained economic growth.

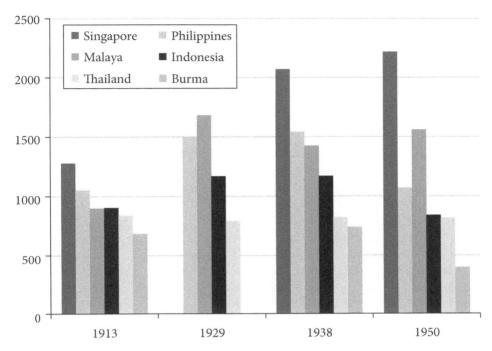

Figure 23.8 Per capita GDP in Southeast Asia, 1913–50 (in 1990 USD).

Sources: A. Booth (2007), *Colonial Legacies: Economic and Social Development in East and Southeast Asia.* Honolulu: University of Hawai'i Press, 22; ibid. (2015), 'A century of growth, crisis, war and recovery, 1870–1970', in I. Coxhead (ed), *Routledge Handbook of Southeast Asian Economics.* London and New York: Routledge, 43–59, Table 3.4; A. Reid (2015), *A History of Southeast Asia: Critical Crossroads.* Chichester: Wiley-Blackwell, 321.

Note: Per capita GDP expressed in 1990 Geary-Khamis dollars.

Global connections intensified and foreign trade grew but actual income gains for the region's colonies remained unimpressive. The richest colonies, Singapore and the Malayan Peninsula, registered a growth rate of GDP per capita of only about 2.4 per cent on average per year between 1913 and 1938. British Malaya was more or less on par with the Philippines, but the long-term growth rate in the latter colony was lower still. Despite having witnessed a spectacular trade expansion, colonial Indonesia figured in the ranking between Malaya and Thailand, with a growth rate of scarcely more than 1 per cent per year. Burma appears to have been the least fortunate in terms of reaping benefit from Western colonialism (Figure 23.8).[33]

The Japanese occupation in the 1940s, revolution, and upheaval of Dutch decolonization severely depressed per capita incomes in all colonies except Malaya (including Singapore) to below the level of the late 1930s. Yet, even discounting the devastating effects on society and economy in the 1940s, it remains a fact that the rewards for the region from a protracted expansion of foreign trade were deeply disappointing.

Colonialism offered stability, especially for foreign investors, and also ample commercial opportunities, but it did not encourage structural change necessary for future growth. Interestingly, however, the situation was no better in the only Southeast Asian country escaping colonial rule: Thailand.

Conclusion: Change and Continuity

Income disparities in Southeast Asia today are probably larger than in any other major region of the world. In terms of GDP per capita, adjusted for differences in purchasing power, Singapore ranks on par with Luxemburg, Thailand with Brazil, and Indonesia with Egypt, while Cambodia lags behind at the level of Uzbekistan.[34] Nevertheless, economic development since about 1950 has been truly astounding in the region at large, considering also that lags in development have more often than not been caused by prolonged warfare and political strife. The financial crisis that struck in part, yet not all, of the region in the late 1990s turned out to be a relatively short-term dip, which even equipped the region to better withstand the adverse effects of the more recent Great Recession.[35] With the benefit of hindsight, could any observer of the situation in earlier centuries have foreseen the dramatic change in the region's economic destiny since the mid-twentieth century?

The most conspicuous historical discontinuity is found in the vein of state formation. Full-fledged nation states, loosely bound together in the ASEAN context, where first largely stateless societies and then colonial states lacking national identity prevailed. Recent state formation by definition rested on political decolonization, accompanied by a full or partial economic decolonization, and was reinforced by surging population growth. The ASEAN now has a population 20 per cent above that of the European Union.

A further important discontinuity is in economic structure. The excessive focus on trading, coupled with some cash crop cultivation prior to colonialism, gave way to an almost exclusive concentration on food agriculture and deliveries of unprocessed primary products to the world market. Neither was particularly conducive to modern economic growth based on high value-added production, at first in manufacturing, and later in services. At the moment, Singapore is the sole ASEAN member state to have joined the world's rank of post-industrial economies.

A third discontinuity worth noting concerns the process of economic growth itself. The pace of increase in GDP and standards of living has quickened beyond recognition, although one must not forget that much still needs to be done with respect to unequal income distributions. The acceleration in growth began at different points in time: in the 1950s for Singapore, Malaysia and Thailand; in the late 1960s for Indonesia; in the 1990s for Vietnam and the Philippines, the last at independence ahead of all its neighbours in the region except Singapore and Malaysia. Time will tell whether this process is repeated also in Laos, Cambodia and Myanmar.[36]

There are also continuities discernible over time that strike the eye. Openness to the world economy to varying degrees has been a constant factor for centuries in the region's economic life, owing to its strategic geographical location of resource endowments as well as a strong receptiveness to influences from the outside. The strength of the market forces in trading, both intra-regional and interregional, more than compensated for the lack of support by strong states in triggering the 'Age of Commerce'. Colonialism altered the trading relations, enhancing the exclusiveness of mutual trade with the metropole at the expense of the wider global connections. Yet, this tendency was reversed during the late-colonial period. Post-colonial developments have seen a revitalization of genuinely global trade in most, but not all, countries in the region.

A second important continuity may be observed in the spirit of entrepreneurship, both indigenous and in conjunction with foreign participants, traders and investors alike. The most obvious manifestation was again the 'Age of Commerce', when the European trading companies jumped on the bandwagon towards the end of the boom. It is likely that Western intrusion in the region's economy had a stultifying impact on the region's economic development both in the eighteenth century and under the conditions of colonial rule in the nineteenth and twentieth centuries.

The discontinuities and continuities in the economic past of Southeast Asia cannot fail but to underscore the essentially dynamic potential of this region, even if circumstances have not always been conducive for a full realization of the possibilities. This appears to be the main lesson to be learned from surveying the changing destinies of an exciting region.

Notes

1. Statistics for 2014 or 2015 from the website of the World Trade Organization (www.wto.org). For a critical discussion of the concept of purchasing power parity, see A. Deaton and A. Heston (2010), 'Understanding PPPs and PPP-based National Account', *American Economic Journal: Macroeconomics*, 2 (4), 1–35. I was alerted to this reference by Patrick O'Brien.

2. A. Reid (2015), *A History of Southeast Asia: Critical Crossroads*. Chichester: Wiley-Blackwell, 16, 214, 390.

3. A. Booth (2007), *Colonial Legacies: Economic and Social Development in East and Southeast Asia*. Honolulu: University of Hawai'i Press, 196.

4. Reid, *A History of Southeast Asia*, 6–8. The population figure for 1800 is based on R. E. Elson (1997), *The End of the Peasantry in Southeast Asia: A Social and Economic History of Peasant Livelihood, 1800-1990s*. Basingstoke: Macmillan, 76–7; and A. Reid (1988), *Southeast Asia in the Age of Commerce 1450-1680*, vol. 1: *The Lands below the Winds*. New Haven, CT: Yale University Press, 13–14.

5. V. Lieberman (2003), *Strange Parallels: Southeast Asia in Global Context, c.800–1830*, vol. 1: *Integration on the Mainland*. Cambridge: Cambridge University Press, 21–66; ibid. (2009), *Strange Parallels: Southeast Asia in Global Context, c.800–1830*, vol. 2: *Mainland Mirrors: Europe, Japan, China, South Asia and the Islands*. Cambridge: Cambridge University Press, 58–60, 768. The ancient kingdoms were not empires in the common sense of turning into cohesive systems with a centralized authority.

6. Reid, *A History of Southeast Asia*, 27–9.

7. A. Reid (1993), *Southeast Asia in the Age of Commerce, 1450–1680*, vol. 2: *Expansion and Crisis*. New Haven, CT: Yale University Press, 13–24, 60, 76; ibid., *A History of Southeast Asia*, 62–3.

8. Reid, *Southeast Asia in the Age of Commerce*, vol. 2, 27, 30.

9. Reid, *A History of Southeast Asia*, 78.

10. Ibid., 147.

11. Lieberman, *Strange Parallels*, vol. 1, 6–15; ibid., *Strange Parallels*, vol. 2, 823–4. The modern debate about the significance of European trading in Asia was sparked off in 1955 with the English translation of J. C. van Leur's PhD dissertation in Dutch from 1934. J. C. van Leur (1955), *Indonesian Trade and Society: Essays in Asian Social and Economic History*. The Hague: Van Hoeve.

12. Reid, *Southeast Asia in the Age of Commerce*, vol. 2, 286–98; ibid., *A History of Southeast Asia*, 143–51. It is tempting, yet hazardous, to link the decline in Southeast Asia in the seventeenth century to the 'Great Divergence' debate.

13. Lieberman, *Strange Parallels*, vol. 2, 841–4.

14. E. M. Jacobs (2006), *Merchant in Asia: The Trade of the Dutch East India Company during the Eighteenth Century*. Leiden: CNWS Publications, 290–4. See also J. P. de Korte (2000), *The Annual Accounting in the Dutch East India Company (VOC)*. Amsterdam: NEHA.

15. Lieberman, *Strange Parallels*, vol. 2, 862–3. See also M. van Rossum (2015), *Kleurrijke tragiek: De geschiedenis van slavernij in Azië onder de VOC* [Colourful tragedy: The history of slavery in Asia under the VOC]. Hilversum: Verloren. The continuity between Portuguese and VOC taxation procedures was pointed out to me by Catia Antunes.

16. This section deals only in passing with Burma (administered as it was from India and at the time not recognized to be part of Southeast Asia), and Thailand (that was not subjected to colonial control).

17. E. B. Locher-Scholten (1994), 'Dutch expansion in the Indonesian archipelago around 1900 and the imperialism debate', *Journal of Southeast Asian Studies*, 25 (1), 91–111. Reports on the debates in the Dutch-language journal *BMGN*, 86 (1971) and the *BMGN Low Countries Historical Review*, 128 (2010).

18. J. Gommans (2015), 'Conclusion: Globalizing empire: The Dutch case', in C. Antunes and J. Gommans (eds), *Exploring the Dutch Empire: Agents, Networks and Institutions, 1600–2000*. London: Bloomsbury, 270–2; Booth, *Colonial Legacies*, 67–87.

19. Population statistics from before 1900 are proverbially weak. The figure for 1800 is based on approximations for Thailand and British Malaya, and almost certainly too low. In the case of colonial Indonesia, improvement of statistics may explain a more than fivefold increase for Java between 1800 and 1900 and a threefold increase for the Outer Islands between 1900 and 1950.

20. J. L. van Zanden and D. Marks (2012), *An Economic History of Indonesia, 1800–2010*. London and New York: Routledge, 50–1.

21. On the late-colonial mode of production in the Outer Islands, see J. Touwen (2001), *Extremes in the Archipelago: Trade and Economic Development in the Outer Islands of Indonesia, 1900–1942*. Leiden: KITLV Press, 101–61.

22. G. R. Knight (2013), *Commodities and Colonialism: The Story of Big Sugar in Indonesia, 1880–1942*. Leiden and Boston, MA: Brill, 97–135.

23. J. T. Lindblad (1998), *Foreign Investment in Southeast Asia in the Twentieth Century*. Basingstoke: Macmillan, 18–19.

24. H. Dick et al. (2002), *The Emergence of a National Economy: An Economic History of Indonesia, 1800–2000*. Crows Nest, NSW: Allen & Unwin, 128–9; Booth, *Colonial Legacies*, 91, 177.

25. Lindblad, *Foreign Investment*, 17.

26. Booth, *Colonial Legacies*, 105–7.

27. Dick et al., *The Emergence of a National Economy*, 130.

28. C. P. Kindleberger (1962), *Foreign Trade and the National Economy*. New Haven, CT: Yale University Press, 211.

29. Booth, *Colonial Legacies*, 90.

30. Dick et al., *The Emergence of a National Economy*, 124–7, 155; van Zanden and Marks, *An Economic History of Indonesia*, 96–100.

31. Touwen, *Extremes in the Archipelago*, 163–223; A. Booth (2014), 'Trade and growth in the colonial and post-colonial periods', in A. Schrikker and J. Touwen (eds), *Promises and Predicaments: Trade and Entrepreneurship in Colonial and Independent Indonesia in the 19th and 20th Centuries*. Singapore: NUS Press, 24–7. On Chinese capital in the economy of late-colonial Indonesia, see A. Claver (2014), *Dutch Commerce and Chinese Merchants in Java: Colonial Relationships in Trade and Finance, 1800–1942*. Leiden and Boston, MA: Brill.

32. Booth, *Colonial Legacies*, 30. The distinction between agriculture and other pursuits is not always clear-cut since many rural dwellers did some non-agricultural work on the side.

33. Per capita GDP in dollars at 1990 price levels according to adjustment by the Geary-Khamis procedure. Original data in A. Maddison (2003), *The World Economy: Historical Statistics*. Paris: OECD, 180–1, as corrected or supplemented by Booth and Reid in the sources cited. Regrettably, their figures do not offer corresponding information for Indochina. For Singapore apart from British Malaya, see I. Sugimoto (2011), *Economic Growth of Singapore in the Twentieth Century*. Singapore: World Scientific Publishing, 185.

34. Based on most recent statistical data from databank.worldbank.org.

35. See further, H. Hill (2013), 'Southeast Asian macroeconomic management: Pragmatic orthodoxy?', *Masyarakat Indonesia*, 39 (2), 459–80.

36. My concern in this contribution is with general characteristics and trends in Southeast Asia at large. By implication, little attention can be given to the true outlier, Brunei, which on account of its huge oil reserves enjoys per capita incomes at the level of Norway and therefore is more comparable with the emirates in the Middle East. Issues of poverty alleviation and economic development are likely to play an all-important role in Timor Leste, scheduled to become the eleventh member state of the ASEAN.

GLOSSARY

compiled by Karolina Hutková

Abolitionism: Historical movement in Western Europe and America demanding the end of slavery.

Anthropocene: is a proposed current geological age, starting in the eighteenth century when human activities began to have an important influence and impact on the Earth's climate, environment and ecosystem.

Assets-Backed Securities (ABS): Also called securitized product or structured credit. ABS are securities backed by a pool of assets, such as leases, credit card debt, royalties or receivables. They are an alternative to investing in corporate debt.

Balance of Payments (BOP): statistical statement of net flows of all financial transaction between residents of a country and the world in a particular time period. These transactions consist of imports and exports of goods, services and capital, and transfer payments such as foreign aid and remittances.

Black Death: Pandemic of pneumonic plague that swept Eurasia. In Europe it peaked in 1347–51 and according to estimates killed 30 to 60 per cent of the European population.

Bill of Exchange: An instrument used primarily in foreign trade. It is a written order that binds one party to pay a fixed sum of money to another party at a fixed time or on demand.

Bretton Woods System: System for monetary and exchange rate management established in 1944 by the Bretton Woods Agreement. The Agreement was signed by forty-five, including the United States, Canada, Australia, Japan and several Western European countries. The Agreement established the US dollar as reserve currency, fixed the US dollar to gold and compelled signatories of the Agreement to peg their currencies to the US dollar. The Agreement also established the International Monetary Fund (IMF) and the World Bank (WB) group. The key role of the IMF was to bridge temporary imbalances of payment.

California School: The work and scholarly interventions of global historians such as Kenneth Pomeranz and Roy Bin Wong originally based at the University of California, Irvine and UCLA focusing on the Great Divergence between Western Europe and China.

Clearing Bank: A 'bank for banks', it uses a central clearing house to transfer credits and checks between banks. The role of a clearing house is to facilitate exchange.

Colbertism: Form of mercantilism pursued by Jean-Baptiste Colbert (1619–83), French Minister of Finance under Louis XIV. The core principle of Colbertism was state intervention into economy with the aim to accumulate gold. The goals of the economic policies were to achieve a positive balance of payments, impose protective tariffs, support to domestic industry, create systems of controls and inspection, and increase taxation.

Columbian Exchange: The process of transfer of plants, animals, diseases, populations and technologies between the Old World and the Americas in the fifteenth and sixteenth centuries.

Commodity Chain: Network of labour and production processes whose end result is a finished commodity.

Corn Laws: Tariffs and restrictions on imports and exports of food and grain in place in the United Kingdom and repealed in 1846.

Cosmology: System of beliefs about the nature of the universe internal to a certain culture or religion. Modern physical cosmology is a branch of physics that studies the origin and evolution of the universe.

Credit Default Swaps (CDS): Most widely used credit derivative, it is used to transfer risk associated with investing into a bond from one party to another without transferring this bond. CDS is a financial swap agreement that forms an insurance against default risk.

Crisis of the Seventeenth century: Term used to identify a period of widespread global economic, military and environmental instability from the early seventeenth to the early eighteenth century.

Developmental State: Type of state that takes an active role in development planning to facilitate the transformation from agrarian to modern manufacturing economies, typical for Asia after the Second World War. The legitimacy of the developmental state stems from achieving economic growth and improvement of living standard. The state is also committed to solving problems that arise as the outcome of social and economic restructuring.

(Nieboer-) Domar Model: Hypothesis explaining the causes of agricultural serfdom and slavery. It assumes that land and labour are the only factors of production, land is of uniform quality, location is ubiquitous, and marginal productivity of labour is constant. The hypothesis asserts that free land, free labour, and non-working landowners (i.e. large-scale agriculture) cannot all exist simultaneously. Only two can exist at one time and the combination depends on political factors.

Dutch Disease: Negative economic impacts associated with large inflows of foreign currency. Foreign currency inflows lead to the appreciation of domestic currency which makes domestic products less competitive on exports markets. Dutch disease is often connected to discovery of natural resources.

Dutch East India Company (VOC): Dutch chartered monopoly company founded in 1602. It is normally considered the first listed public company. The Dutch government granted the company the monopoly on trade between Cape of Good Hope and the Straits of Magellan. By the eighteenth century the VOC became an important colonial power controlling the Indonesian archipelagos. High level of debts and corruption led the Dutch government in 1799 to revoke the VOC's charter and to take over the VOC's debts and possessions.

Enclosure: Process of enclosing English open fields and common land to create units of privately owned land. Enclosure was legislated by the Enclosure Acts between 1604 and 1914.

English East India Company (EEIC): English Joint-stock monopoly company incorporated by royal charter in 1600. Initially it started as a trading body but became an agent of British imperialism. After defeating the Indian powers at the Battle of Plassey (1757) it took control over Bengal and gradually increased its territorial possessions in India. The EEIC's trading monopoly was removed by the 1833 Government of India Act; however, the Company continued to have administrative and political control of India until 1857.

Euromarkets: Markets for transactions in dollars taking place outside the United States, free of American regulations.

Export-led Industrialization: Also known as 'export-promotion industrialization', economic and trade policies focusing on promoting exports based on a country's comparative advantage. In general, export-led industrialization relies on the reduction of tariff barriers, floating exchange rates, and subsidies to exporters. This strategy was implemented in post-Second-World-War Japan, South Korea, Taiwan, Hong Kong and Singapore.

Factor Endowments: The amounts of land, labour, capital and level of entrepreneurship a country possesses.

Factor Prices: The price at which means of production – land, labour and capital – are sold.

Foreign Direct Investment (FDI): Investment made by an individual or company to acquire 10 per cent or more of shares or voting power in enterprises operating outside the economy of the investor.

Foreign Security: Security, that is, shares, stocks, bonds, debentures issued in a currency other than the home country of issuer.

Ghost Acres: Term popularized by Kenneth Pomeranz. It refers to the agricultural land of the Americas that enabled Europe to overcome the Malthusian trap of diminishing marginal returns to land. The Americas supplied Europe with commodities and foodstuffs such as sugar, timber and cotton used both as industrial inputs and final consumer products.

Global Value Chain (GVC): Series of activities performed by firms and workers in the production, distribution and sale of a product or service. Different stages of the processes of production, distribution and sale are normally located across several countries.

Glorious Revolution: English political change of 1688 in which the English Parliament overthrew King James II and offered the Crown to William III of Orange and his wife Mary II. The Revolution led to fundamental redesigning of governmental and fiscal institutions, constrained the power of the monarch and gave controlling powers to Parliament.

Gold Standard: Monetary system in which participating countries agree to fix the prices of their domestic currencies to a fixed quantity of gold.

Great Divergence: Term popularized by Kenneth Pomeranz, referring to the economic divergence between the West and the rest of the world that coincided with the Industrial Revolution.

Gross Domestic Product (GDP): GDP is used for measuring the size of a country's economy. It is the value of final goods and services produced within a country in a specific period of time, normally a year.

Guild: Professional body of artisans or merchants organizing and regulating the practice of a craft or trade. In early modern Europe guilds were common and often had political power.

Holocene: Current geological epoch, starting approximately 12,000 years ago.

Horizontal Integration: Process of acquisition or merger of companies operating at the same stage of production in the same or different industries.

Import-Substitution Industrialization: Economic and trade policy whose objective is to replace imports with domestically produced goods. It relies on a set of policies: active industrial policy with subsidies for strategic sectors; protective barriers to trade; overvalued currency to help manufacturers import capital goods; and restriction on foreign direct investment. This development strategy was pursued particularly in Latin America in the 1950s and 1960s as well as in several Asian and African countries.

Indentured Labour: Indentured servants or labourers are employed by a contract to work for a specified time for an employer. Indenture contracts were typically entered into in order to meet a legal obligation, such as debts bondage, or to pay for a service—this was a typical way for European workers to finance a passage to America.

Industrious Revolution: Concept first proposed by the Japanese demographic historian Akira Hayami and popularized by the Dutch/American economic historian Jan de Vries. It is a process of reallocation of household resources characterized by increased demand for market-supplied goods in the period 1600–1800. Since wages stagnated or even declined during this period, households needed to supply more labour to the market. This was usually female or child labour. Consequently also the supply of market goods increased.

Joint-Stock Company: A type of a business company that is owned by shareholders through stock. This type of business entity emerged in early modern Europe to support long-distance trade. Early modern joint-stock companies were given monopolies on trade with specific world regions. The best-known joint-stock companies were the English East India Company and the Dutch East India Company.

Laisser-Faire Policies: Policy of minimum government intervention. It is based on the assumption of 'natural' self-regulation of markets and faith that unregulated individual activity will achieve the best results for society as a whole.

Malthusian Theory: Theory of population proposed by the English cleric and scholar Thomas Robert Malthus (1766–1834). According to Malthus, human populations grow at an exponential rate while food production grows at an arithmetic rate. Population growth is limited by 'preventive' checks such as the postponement of marriage or celibacy, and by 'positive' checks such as war and famine.

Mercantilism: An early modern doctrine of political thought. Mercantilism never had clearly defined policies and therefore is interpreted in different ways. In the most popular sense, mercantilism was a state policy focused on achieving a positive balance of payments on trade. Mercantilism often advocated import-substitution policies.

Mortgage-Backed Securities (MBS): Type of asset-backed security secured by a mortgage or collection of mortgages.

Old Regime (Ancient Regime): Political and social order of Europe from the late Middle Ages to the French Revolution based on the power of absolute monarchy and on relatively fixed social hierarchies.

Open Access Social Orders: Social systems with open entry into social and political organizations. In such system, social order is sustained through political and social competition.

Political Economy: Discipline of the social sciences that studies both political and economic factors that shapes society, state and markets.

Poor Laws: Body of legislation governing poor relief in England and Wales. They were developed in the sixteenth century and reformed regularly over the following centuries. The Poor Laws provision was administered through parishes. From the seventeenth century workhouses, places offering employment and accommodation to the destitute, became an important part of the system.

Prebisch-Singer Thesis: Thesis that posits that over the long period the price of primary commodities declines relative to the price of manufactured goods. This is caused by the low elasticity of demand for primary commodities (demand for them does not increase with income). It implies that the terms of trade for countries specialized in exports of primary commodities deteriorate over time.

Price Elasticity of Demand: Percentage change in demand for a product after a change in the price of this product. If the quantity of demanded product considerably changes in response to its price change, the product is price elastic.

Price Revolution: An inflationary moment between the fifteenth and the early seventeenth century affecting Western Europe and most especially Spain.

Primary Commodities: Raw or unprocessed materials, according to OECD definition: food and live animals, beverages and tobacco, and crude materials.

Proto-industry: Pre-modern system of rural manufacturing widespread especially in European textile production. Primary production units were households, production was organized by merchants who provided raw materials and sold final goods on national and international markets.

Putting-out: System of production in which merchant–entrepreneurs provide ('put out') material to rural households to produce goods, taking advantage of low wages in rural areas. This system of subcontracting was particularly common in the pre-modern European textile industry.

Schumpeterian Growth: Economic growth driven by innovations which are the outcome of creative destruction. 'Creative destruction', a term coined by Joseph Schumpeter, is a process of industrial transformation. It identifies product and process innovation mechanisms by which new replaces old and outdated practices, products and so forth.

Serfdom: Legal and economic system in which tenant farmers are bound to land by their landlord, typical of medieval Europe.

Smithian Economic Growth: Growth that results from increasing density of markets.

South–South Divergence: The hypothesis according to which Southeast Asia's post-colonial economic growth was rooted in more profound regional trade, migration and investment than other parts of the world South.

Spillover Effect: When an event in a country, region or sector has a ripple effect on the economy of another region or sector.

Glossary

Stock: Type of security that is based on the fractional ownership of the corporation. Stocks are of two types: common and preferred. The holder of common stock is entitled to vote on corporate decisions. The holder of preferred stock does not have this right but is entitled to a certain level of dividend payments before any dividends can be issued to other shareholders.

Structural Adjustment (SAPs): Set of economic policies introduced as a condition to qualify for IMF and WB loans. The goal of SAPs was to reduce fiscal imbalances of borrowing countries and make their economies more market oriented. SAPs put emphasis on free-market policies of privatization, fiscal austerity, elimination of trade barriers, and deregulation.

Tacit Knowledge: The opposite to formal, codified or explicit knowledge. Tacit knowledge is knowledge embedded in a person and can be acquired only through personal experience and social contact.

Terms of Trade: The ratio between the index of export prices and the index of import prices. It is used as a measure of country's economic health. If a country's terms of trade are improving it means that it can buy more imports for every unit of exports.

Transaction Costs: Costs incurred in market exchange and in overcoming market imperfections. They are search and information costs, bargaining and decision costs, and policing and enforcement costs. High transaction costs can prevent market exchange.

Trial of the Pyx: An annual ceremony to ensure that newly minted coins produced by the Royal Mint of the United Kingdom conform to their required specifications.

Triangular Trade: Trading system operating between West Africa, the Caribbean and Europe exchanging slaves, primary commodities and manufactured goods.

Useful and Reliable Knowledge: Knowledge of natural phenomena linked to technology and technology advancement. It can be seen also as a pool of best-practice knowledge.

Vertical Integration: Process in which firm acquires further stages of the same production path, such as when a manufacturer acquires its supplier and/or distributor.

'Wimbledon Effect': British financial institutions and the City of London's dependence on foreign banks.

World-Systems Theory or **World-System Analysis:** is a macro-scale approach to the study of global and world history first developed by the sociologist Immanuel Wallerstein. It emphasizes the emergence of a world economic system and analyses the power structures and relations between different world areas.

INDEX

Index

Index

Index

Index

Index

CLASSIC GHOST

STORIES

FROM THE

LAND'S END

William Bottrell

TOR MARK PRESS • REDRUTH

THE TOR MARK SERIES

FOLKLORE

Classic Cornish ghost stories
Classic Devon ghost stories
Classic West Country ghost stories
Cornish fairies
Cornish folklore
Cornish legends
Customs and superstitions from
 Cornish folklore
Demons, ghosts and spectres in
 Cornish folklore
Devonshire customs and
 superstitions
Devonshire legends
Down 'long weth we
The pixy book
Strange tales of the Cornish coast

OTHER TITLES

Charlestown
China clay
Classic Cornish anecdotes
Cornish fishing industry
Cornish mining – at surface
Cornish mining – underground
Cornish mining industry
Cornish recipes
Cornish smuggling industry
Cornwall in camera
Cornwall's engine houses
Cornwall's railways
Devonshire jokes and stories
Do you know Cornwall?
Exploring Cornwall with your car
Fed fitty – recipes from a Cornish kitchen
Houses, castles and gardens
 in Cornwall
Introducing Cornwall
Jan Bedella's fiddle
King Arthur – man or myth?
Lost ports of Cornwall
Old Cornwall – in pictures
The pasty book
Shipwrecks around Land's End
Shipwrecks around the Lizard
Shipwrecks around Mounts Bay
Shipwrecks – Falmouth to Looe
Short Cornish dictionary
Strange tales of the Cornsih coast
The story of Cornwall
The story of the Cornish language
The story of St Ives
The story of Truro Cathedral
Tales of the Cornish fishermen
Tales of the Cornish miners
Tales of the Cornish smugglers
Tales of the Cornish wreckers
Twelve walks on the Lizard
What shall we do with the
 smuggled brandy?

The cover illustration is by Linda Garland

First published 1998 by Tor Mark Press,
United Downs Industrial Estate, St Day, Redruth, Cornwall, TR16 5HY
© Tor Mark Press 1998
ISBN 0-85025-365-9
Printed in Great Britain by Cornwall Lithographic Printers Ltd, Redruth

The Ghosts of Kenegie

Old folks of Gulval say that in their grandparents' time the ancient mansion of Kenegie and its grounds were constantly haunted by three 'sperats' and, on some nights, by many more.

The following stories were told by an aged tinner of Lelant, as they had often been related to him by his mother, who had lived for many years in service at Kenegie, previous to her marriage about 1790.

The first ghost of whom there is any remembrance, and the one which remained longest, was the spirit of a thrifty old Harris, who made great additions to the house and walled gardens, and was most unwilling to die and leave them. This spirit, however, gave but little trouble. He merely came on a certain night in every year – which was known to his descendants – to review the place in which he had taken so much delight; and only required that, on the night of his visit, the principal entrance door should be left open, as well as one opposite, opening into a paved court surrounded by offices.

It was believed that any negligence in leaving open these doors at the stated time would be a cause of misfortune to the Harris family, or a token of its decline. Consequently the custom was duly observed from farther back than there is any remembrance, until within a few years of the time when the last Harris of Kenegie disposed of his ancestral home. 'Tis said that when the spirit came and found the doors closed – through some mistake it is supposed – he made much unearthly wailing till cock-crowing, then went moaning away and never returned.

The next ghostly visitor, and a more troublesome one, had been housekeeper and a great favourite with a later Squire Harris, much to the prejudice of his son and heir. The very night after her funeral, disturbances began; the whole household were annoyed by this hussy of a ghost prancing along stone paved passages from one room to another – doors clashing and banging behind her – till she entered the kitchen, where she would next be heard winding up the great roasting jack – one of the old-fashioned noisy clockwork machines kept in motion by a heavy weight passing through the chamber floors, and attached to a rope or chain working over screeching pulleys fixed somewhere in the upper regions of the mansion.

After an interval of scolding, shrieking, and the other accessories of a row, she would beat the table or dresser with a rolling-pin, and make the pewter plates rattle, by way of announcing, as she was wont to do, that the roast was ready, and to summon the servants to dish it up.

Between the thumps she screamed, 'Quick, come quick!' and another voice replied, 'Anon, anon!' Then the parlour furniture would be shifted, as if preparations were in progress for entertaining a large company. At length the inmates were glad to hear her high-heeled shoes patting over stairs and along the gallery, until they stopped at her late master's bedroom chamber door, which was usually the conclusion of her noisy exploits for the night.

The shadowy figure of this old woman, in a long-bodied gown and kirtle, was frequently seen passing quickly through the court. Now and then it happened that a new servant, wishing to get ahead with her work – on washing days especially – and not hearing any disturbance, ventured downstairs in the small hours of the morning; but on entering the kitchen her light was almost always blown out, and she got a slap in the face from an invisible hand that 'made her see fire before her eyes'; and on turning to leave the room, received a kick behind which made her remember to stay abed till cock-crowing.

This housekeeper was 'put to rest' many years before the Harrises left their old house. There are no particulars known of the way in which this was done; it is only stated that some powerful exorcists – neighbouring clergymen, who were then supposed to possess power over ghostly visitants – succeeded, after much conjuration in quelling her, in some measure; but as she absolutely refused to leave the place, they compromised matters by confining her to a small room, on the eastern or northern side of the mansion; with her were placed a fleece of black wool, a pair of cards, a 'pole and kiggal' [distaff and spindle] and knitting needles. With these she was required to card the black fleece until it became white, and then to spin it and knit stockings of the yarn. Her closet door is walled up, so that few know exactly where it is situated, though old folks who served the Harris family say they have often heard the clinking of cards in some remote part of the buildings, and there was always a little hole, such as sparrows might nest in, through the wall. If filled up it was sure to be opened over-night, without being touched by mortal hands.

The last Ghost of Kenegie – at least of whom there is any trustworthy tradition – was that of a spendthrift heir, known as 'Wild Harris', who is best remembered because ordinary parsons' collective power was found insufficient to lay him. He extended his walks all over the grounds and far away in the 'bottom' towards the mill. He was also often seen on horseback, chasing with one hound, on Kenegie Downs and elsewhere.

The ghost mostly wore a steeple-crown and feather, hunting coat and riding boots, or a long black gown and flat cap, with lace and plume. He usually stood in an alcove just over the grand entrance. beside his family coat-of-arms, and glared down on the road with a look as immovable as that of the carved stone lions that guarded the gate. Sometimes, too, he was beheld seated beside the churchway stile a few yards further up the hill. Often on approaching this spot, people were made aware of the spirit being near, though invisible, by a sulphurous smell which pervaded the place.

At that time the grand entrance was approached by a straight, stately avenue, flanked by a bowling green, with a picturesque two-storied summer house or 'look-out' at its further end.

On winter nights, the Squire's ghost, with a dozen or more of his old comrades, would assemble in the summer house, where they might be seen and heard from the mansion even, talking, singing, swearing and shouting, in a state of uproarious mirth. Kenegie must have been a lively place at nights, with the old housekeeper reenacting scenes of her former rule within, and Wild Harris's nocturnal carouse in the 'look-out'. Few servants, however, lived there long; they didn't relish such ghostly merriment, in which they had no other share than to be kept awake and terrified all night.

The story of Wild Harris

He is said to have been an eager sportsman, with much wild-oats in his composition, who cared for little else but his hunter and hounds, except a young lady, a poor relation, dependent on his family, with whom she lived much like a fish out of water, being regarded as too low for the parlour on grand occasions; and at all times as too high for the kitchen, where she was treated as an intruder by the housekeeper and her creatures.

This unfortunate damsel passed much of her time in the pleasant upper room of the summer house with elderly maiden ladies of the family, who here wrought everlasting tapestry, fine lace or embroidery. Here too the ancient dames sipped choice cordials of their own distilling, enjoyed their tea and gossip, and from a balcony watched the gentlemen's sports on the bowling green.

When the poor gentlewoman was in her bloom, Wild Harris's father was a widower, in his dotage, and too much influenced by his housekeeper, who had been during his wife's lifetime, and was still, a special favourite of his. She ever disliked her young master, and detested the poor orphan lady, of whom she was jealous, fearing lest she might supplant her one day in governing the household. The dame was a malicious spy on the lovers, who frequently met in the summer house and for retired walks down the vale. The interviews were all the sweeter for being stolen; yet soon, alas, they resulted in sorrow to the young lady.

The old gentleman was much prejudiced against his poor cousin by being persuaded that, but for this unfortunate attachment, his son would have wedded a rich heiress whose lands lay near the Harrises' 'up-country' property. He declared that the day his son married his cousin, he would wed his housekeeper, so that she should still rule the roost. In spite of all opposition, the young man would have 'made an honest woman' of his betrothed, but was hindered by the malice of the old dame and his father until too late; for the poor damsel, distracted with grief, wandered away one night, she knew not whither, and next morning was found drowned in a mill-pond.

Shortly after this tragic event the old Squire died, and Wild Harris found himself master of Kenegie, but disinherited of much other property, bequeathed to his brothers in the army or navy. He had some satisfaction, however, in turning to doors the old mischief-making minion, but not much; she soon fretted herself to death, and was hardly laid in her grave ere she was back again, making such a din, out of mere spite, as hindered the inmates from getting a wink of sleep during the dead hours of the night.

The master of Kenegie became more restless than ever; his days were spent in hunting or holding games on the bowling green, and his nights were spent in revelry.

He kept open house, for rich or poor, who chose to partake of his hospitality. One and all were cordially welcomed. With all his faults, he had an open heart and hand; but in a few years he came to an untimely end, whilst still in his prime, by a fall from his horse when hunting on the Castle Downs. It is said that his horse was startled by a white hare that often followed him, and was said to be the poor lady's spirit.

He was borne to Gulval Church and laid in the vault at night, as was the fashion then with some of our old families. His burial was attended by many friends; and when some of them, who remained late at the funeral supper, came down the avenue to return home, they beheld him, as natural seemingly as life, standing by the summer house steps, arrayed in his hunting dress, and by his side a favourite old dog that had died when his master breathed his last.

Laying Wild Harris's ghost

Many ineffectual efforts were made to 'lay' Wild Harris's ghost, which only resulted in harm, by raising tempests which destroyed crops on land and life at sea. After these vain trials of parson power, the ghost became for a while more troublesome than he was before their interference with his walks.

Fortunately, however, Mr Polkinghorne of St Ives acquired the virtue whereby he became the most powerful exorcist and spirit-queller west of Hayle.

From the little that is known of this gentleman, one may infer that he wasn't, by any means, such as would now be styled a 'pious character'. He is said to have been the boldest fox-hunter of these parts, but he would never chase a hare; any attempt to kill one would make him swear like a trooper. He kept many of these innocent animals – the hares – running about his house like cats; foolish people said they were the parson's familiar spirits, or witches he found wandering in that shape. He was a capital hurler, and encouraged all sorts of manly games, as he said they encouraged a cordial 'one-and-all' sort of feeling between high and low. The parson was mostly accompanied by his horse and dog, which both followed him. When he stopped to chat, Hector his horse came up and rested his head on his master's shoulder, as if desirous of hearing the news too. If he called at a house, both his attendants waited at the door, his horse never needing to be held. He made long journeys with his steed walking alongside or behind him, the bridle rein passed round its neck and the stirrups thrown across the saddle. Wonderful stories are also told about the high hedges and rocky ground that the parson's horse would take him safely over, when after the hounds; and how the birds, which nestled undisturbed in his garden, and other dumb creatures, seemed to regard him as one of themselves.

On being requested to do his utmost that Wild Harris's ghost might rest in peace, or be kept away from Kenegie, the reverend gentleman replied that he hoped to succeed if it were in the power of man to effect it.

Other clergymen, hearing what was about to be attempted, expressed a wish to be present at the proceedings. Mr Polkinghorne replied that he neither required their assistance nor desired their presence, yet any of his reverend brethren might please themselves for what he cared. Moreover he charged them, if they came to Kenegie on the appointed night, not to intermeddle in any way whatever might happen.

A night in the latter end of harvest was appointed for this arduous undertaking. Several clergymen being anxious to see how the renowned spirit-queller would act with a ghost that had baffled so many of them, an hour before midnight four of them from westward of Penzance, together with a young curate of St Hellar [St Hilary] and another from some parish over that way, all arrived at Kenegie and waited a long while near the gate, expecting Mr Polkinghorne. At the turn of night a terrific storm came on, and the six parsons, drenched to their skins, took refuge in the summer house. Candles had been lit in the upper room of this building, as it was understood that the spirit-quelling operations would be performed there.

They waited long, but neither Polkinghorne nor Harris's ghost appeared; the curate of St Hellar, impatient of inaction, took from his breast a book and read from it some conjuring formulas, by way of practice or for mere pastime. As he read, a crashing thunderclap burst over the building, shook it to its foundations, and broke open the window. The parsons fell on the floor as if stunned, and on opening their eyes, after having been almost blinded by lightning, they beheld near the door a crowd of 'bukka-dhu' grinning at them, and then partially saw them disappear in a misty vapour, to be succeeded by others, who all made ugly faces and contemptuous or threatening gestures.

The reverend gentlemen crawled to the window and looked out, to avoid the sight of such ugly spectres and to get fresh air – that in the room smelt worse than the fumes of brimstone. Presently an icy shiver ran through them, and they felt as if something awful had entered the room. On glancing round, they beheld the apparition of a man standing with his back to the fireplace, and looking intently towards the opposite wall. His eyes never winked nor turned away, but seemed to gaze on something beyond the blank wall. He wore a long black gown or loose coat which reached the floor; his face appeared sad and wan, under a sable cap, garnished with a plume and lace. He seemed unconscious of either the black spirits or the parsons' presence. Over a while he turned slowly round, advanced towards the window with a frowning countenance, which showed the parsons that he regarded them as intruders; and they, poor men, trembling in every limb, with hair on end, pressed each other into the open window, intending to drop themselves to the ground and risk broken bones or an ugly qualk [concussion], for they were most of them fat and heavy.

Meanwhile scores of bukkas continued to hover behind the ghost, grimacing as if they enjoyed the parsons' distress. Every minute seemed an hour to the terrified gentlemen; but as some of them got their legs out through the casement, the tread of heavy boots was heard on the stone stairs, and Polkinghorne bounced into the room, when the ghost, turning quickly round, exclaimed, 'Now, Polkinghorne, that thou art come, I must be gone!' The conjurer quietly holding out his hand towards the ghost, said '*In nomine Domini*, I bid thee stay.' Then he turned to the black spirits, made a crack with his hunting whip, said 'Avaunt ye, bukka-dhu!' and off they went at his word, howling and shrieking louder than the tempest.

The ghost stood still. Polkinghorne uttered long words in an unknown tongue whilst he drew around the ghost with his whip-stick, on the sanded floor, a circle and magical signs, with a pentagram to 'lock the circle'. He continued speaking a long while without pausing, and his words sounded deep and full, as if at once near and far off, like the surging of billows on a long stretch of shore, or thunder echoing round the hills.

At length the spirit felt the able conjurer's power and crouched down at his feet holding out his hands as if praying him to desist.

Mr Polkinghorne, whilst still saying powerful words, unwound from around his waist a few yards of new hempen cord, leaving much more of it attached. Having made a loop at the end, he passed it over the ghost's head and under his arms; then, addressing him, said, '*In nomine Domini*, I bid thee stand up and come with me.' On saying this, he lifted from the floor, with his whip-stick, the spirit's skirts, and under them nothing was seen but flaming fire.

When Polkinghorne had the spirit standing beside him, with his eyes fixed and limbs motionless like one spellbound, he exclaimed, 'Thank the Powers it's all right so far.'

Casting a glance towards the other parsons, and seeing a book on the floor, he took it up, opened it, and speaking for the first time to his reverend brethren, said, 'You too may thank your lucky stars that I came in the nick of time to save ye from grievous harm.' Holding it towards the St Hellar curate, he continued, 'This belongs to you, my weak brother; strange such a book should be in your possession! The penmanship is beautiful; it must have cost a mint of money, yet it is worse than useless – nay, it is perilous to such as you. By good luck you read what merely brought hither silly bukkas; one can't properly call them demons, though no others were known here in old times; they now mostly keep to old ruined castles, crellas [Iron Age village sites] and fougoes [ancient underground passages], yet they are always abroad in such a night as this. But if you had chanced to pronounce a word, that you don't understand, on the next leaf, you would have called hither such malignant fiends, flying in the tempest this awful night, as would have torn ye limb from limb, or have carried ye away bodily. Perhaps, becoming tired, they might have fixed ye on St Hellar steeple. For my part, I wish ye were there, lest a greater evil befall ye this night.'

After a pause, in looking sadly at the ghost, who seemed to listen with attention, he continued addressing the gentleman of St Hellar, 'I suppose you have heard the old saying, "Women and fools can rise devils, but it takes wise men to lay them." Indeed tradition says that in ancient times fair young witches first obtained this dread knowledge from their demon lovers, to summon them whenever they desired; old hags soon pried into the secret – as they will into all kinds of deviltry – and quickly communicated from one to another, until witches became numerous in all Christian lands; thousands of them were burnt as a warning, but their burning didn't deter others from the same evil practices.

'The demons became disgusted of witches continually crying after them, to wreak their vengeance on innocent man and beast, and did their best to evade them. Much more may be said on this subject but time presses. I have still arduous work to perform, so only another word, my over-curious brother: burn this book of magic in the first convenient fire.'

Saying this, he cast down the book, spoke a few words which the others didn't understand, drew his foot over a mystic sign that locked the charmed circle, and turning to the spirit said, '*In nomine Domini*, come thou with me.' Wild Harris's ghost was led away quiet as a lamb.

Mr Polkinghorne, having reached the outer gate, took his horse, which he had left there. The poor beast trembled, though this ghost was not the first, by many, that had been near it. Having mounted, he gave the ghost more rope, and bade him keep further from Hector. A minute afterwards the four west-country parsons (but not the St Hellar curate and his friend) took downhill as fast as their horses could lay feet to ground.

In passing up Kenegie Lane, the parson's horse was very fractious. It jumped from side to side, tried to leap over hedges, and screeched like a child; yet it became pretty quiet at last when the spirit kept off to the end of his tether.

Few bleaker places are to be found than the old road to St Ives passing over Kenegie Downs. When they got there the wind seemed to beat on them from all directions at once. Rain and thunder never ceased; the Castle hill seemed all ablaze with lightning. At times, when a more violent blast than usual whirled around them, clouds of fiends hovered above like foul birds of prey. The sky was pitch black, and demons were only seen by the forked lightning that burst from their midst. The ghost, as if seeking protection, came nearer the parson; then his horse's terror became painful to witness, until a few magical words and a crack of his whip sent the devils howling away, and the ghost to the end of his rope.

At last they came within a stone's cast of a few dwellings called Castle-gate, and leaving the highway took a path on the left that wound up the hill to Castle-an-Dinas.

The foolish curate of St Hellar

One might think that the two parsons from eastward would have taken the nearest way home, over Market-Jew Green; but no, the St Hellar curate thought he would rather go many miles out of his way than miss seeing a spirit put to rest, and his friend was afraid to go home alone. So they both started after the ghost-layer, keeping sufficiently near to see him on horseback, leading the spirit as they ascended the hill. The lightning was almost continuous but otherwise the night was very dark. On reaching the open downs they found it impossible to keep their saddles, even by holding on with both hands to their horses' manes. Their hats were blown away and their cloaks flying from their necks like sails rent from the yards in a hurricane. They alighted and trudged along in single file, dragging their unwilling steeds behind them, for the horses wanted to take their accustomed road home and didn't like the ghostly company ahead.

When Mr Polkinghorne reached the hamlet called Castle-gate they were so far behind as not to see his departure from the high road; and on coming near the lonely cottages decided to stay there, if they could find shelter. But on a closer view the dwellings appeared to be deserted; the thatch was stripped from their roofs, leaving bare rafters on all but one of them.

On approaching that dwelling, they heard Mr Polkinghorne's Hector neigh from the downs. Their horses replied, and there was more whinnying from Hector, which showed the direction taken and set the St Hellar parson all agog to follow the ghost-layer. As they crossed the road and paused a moment, a whirlwind passed over the house where they thought of taking shelter, and took up a bundle of spars which a thatcher, who had been repairing the roof, had left there, pinned to the work with a broach, that he might find them to hand when he continued his thatching. The bundle being taken high up and whirled about, its bind broke and one of the devil-directed spars pierced the St Hellar curate's side just above his hip joint like an arrow shot from a bow. He fell on the ground as if killed and his companion, in drawing the spar out of his friend's side, had his hand burnt, just as if he had grasped red-hot iron.

Presently the black clouds rolled away westward and the wind lulled. Then the wounded man was raised by his companion, lifted on his horse and laid across the saddle like a sack of corn. They went slowly on and reached Nancledry about day-break. Having rested a few hours at the mill, it was found that the St Hellar curate was still unable to sit on horseback and he was taken home in a cart.

The reverend gentleman was, ever after, lame, and bore to his grave marks of his spar-shot wound.

Polkinghorne triumphant

At the time of this ghost-laying, there were around the Castle hill extensive tracts of open heath which are now enclosed, and where the highway is now skirted by hedges it was then open downs. The parson's Hector was well acquainted with the lie of the country all around, as he had often crossed it following the hounds; and after scrambling his way through the narrow lane, tried his utmost to take away over the moorland to a smith's shop in Halangove where he had often been shod. By a firm hand on the bridle rein, his master kept him uphill for a furlong or so, where they came to an old gurgie [ruined hedge] that once enclosed a fold. On one side there was a bowjey [cattle or sheep house]. Mr Polkinghorne alighted, turned his horse into the old shelter, and bade the ghost approach.

They walked on in silence until they came to the Castle's outer enclosure, which screened them from the blast. Then the reverend gentleman said, 'Now that we are alone, and not likely to suffer any more intrusion, tell me my unhappy brother what is it that disturbs thy rest? Be assured, my desire is to procure thee peace.'

The spirit replied that at the time of his decease he was much troubled because he owed several sums to work-people and others, fearing they would not be paid by his successor. Moreover, he had walked about for years, hoping some honest body would speak to him; how the longer he was left unspoken to, the more uneasy and troublesome he became; and when his relations brought the parsons to lay him, who were unqualified for that office, he was much exasperated and determined never to leave Kenegie.

'Be assured, my son,' replied the parson, 'that I will see all thy debts paid.'

'That will relieve me of much,' said the spirit, 'yet there are other subjects that trouble me; but you must promise me never to divulge them, ere I make a clean breast of them.'

'My profession obliges secrecy in such cases,' replied his adviser, 'therefore speak on without reserve.'

The poor ghost having unburthened himself, Mr Polkinghorne gave him words of comfort, then took the cord off, saying, 'This is no longer required to protect ye from evil spirits, for all of them have departed with the tempest they raised, and the sky is now serene.'

As they ascended the hill the moon shone bright on the old fort's inner enclosing wall, which was then almost intact. The upper enclosure is nearly oval in outline and they entered it at its south-eastern end. Stopping a minute on the hill-top, Mr Polkinghorne said to the ghost, 'There is no cure for a troubled spirit equal to constant employment and I shall allot you an easy task which, with time and patience, will procure you repose; but I must first make the whole of this enclosure secure against infernal spirits.'

Mr Polkinghorne then used a form of exorcism, which (as far as it could be understood from the old story-teller's account) was something like this: having placed the ghost on his right hand side he passed with him three times round the enclosed hill-top going with the sun and keeping close to the wall. At the first round, he merely counted the number of paces. At the next he uttered in some ancient eastern tongue such exorcisms and adjurations as serve to expel infernal spirits. At the last circuit he made, near the bounding wall, twelve mystic signs at equal distances. He then passed through the middle of the ground to its north-western end, cutting the air with his whip and tracing on the earth more magical figures. Being arrived at the end opposite the entrance, he drew a line with his whip stick from a large stone in the wall on one side to another opposite, and told the spirit to remember them as bound-stones.

'Now, my son,' said he, 'all within the Castle's upper walls is as safe for ye as consecrated ground; and here is your task, which is merely to count the blades of grass on this small space, bounded by the wall and a straight line from stone to stone. You must reckon them nine times to be sure that you have counted right; you needn't set about it till I leave; there's plenty of time before ye.'

The spirit looked disconcerted and said that he thought the assigned task a vain one, as it produced nothing of lasting use. He would rather be employed in repairing the Castle walls, or some such job.

'No, my dear son,' replied the parson. 'It would never do for ye to be employed on anything that would be visible to human eyes; the unusual occurrence would draw here such crowds of gazers as would greatly incommode ye. No more need ye trouble yourself on the score of its mere use, in your sense. If restless mortals employed themselves solely in such works of utility as you mean, the greater part of them would find nothing to do, and be more miserable than ghosts unlaid.'

The ghost seemed all down in the mouth, which the parson remarked and said, 'Don't ye be out of heart, brother, but have patience and you will find that, with constant work, years will pass away like a summer's day. Then you will wonder how your mortal crosses ever had the power to trouble ye. All remembrance of them will fade like a dream and you will rest in peace.

'When you have a mind to pause a while – say after each time of counting – you can go around the hill-top and enjoy the extensive prospect, as all within this rampart is a charmed circle for ye, which fiends dare not enter. There are other pleasant sights which you will often behold; for the small people still keep to the Castle hill, and hold their dances and fairs of summer nights within these ramparts. These are the spirits of old inhabitants who dwelt – it may be thousands of years ago – in the crellas at Chysauster.'

The poor ghost said not a word, so the parson went on, as if in his pulpit. At length, he stood up and said hastily, 'One might mention more of what will make your abode pleasant, but it's high time for you to become invisible and for me to leave ye. The cocks will soon be crowing.'

The parson, pointing to the eastern sky, told the spirit to put off his form. In a minute or so the apparition became indistinct and faded gradually away, like a thin wreath of smoke dissolving in air.

Mr Polkinghorne said farewell, and as he turned to leave the spirit to his task, he heard a hollow voice say, 'Good friend, do thou remember me and visit me again.'

As Mr Polkinghorne slowly wended his way homeward, he was grieved to see the wreck made by the preceding night's tempest. In Nancledry, low-lying as it is, dwellings were unroofed and trees, which had withstood the storms of centuries, were all uprooted. On higher ground, 'stones were blown out of the hedges', arish mows laid low and the corn whirled around fields.

About sunrise, St Ives folks standing at their doors were surprised to see their beloved parson coming down the Stenack, looking sad and weary, and surprised too that he didn't greet them with his accustomed cheerful tone and pleasant smile. Neither Mr Polkinghorne nor his steed were seen in the street for several days after this ghostly night's work.

The haunted lawyer

A little while ago, an aged native of Gulval spoke to me of another ghost that haunted Kenegie, but only for a short time. Whether it was the spirit of a Harris or an Arundel he couldn't say, but it was all in the same family; for a Harris, he believed, changed his name for that of Arundel; then, over a generation or two, the family resumed their former name. People round always called them Harrises, and this one was spoken of as the proud squire of Kenegie. He always rode a high horse. If he met people in the narrow lanes (and there were but few broad ones in his time) they had to get out of his way, by leaping hedges sometimes, else he'd ride over them.

Now when Harris the proud was on his deathbed he sent a man to Penzance for a lawyer, because he wanted to make an addition to his will. 'Take the fleetest horse in my stable,' said he to his servant, 'ride for thy life! for thy life! Stop not for anything in the road; if his own horse be unsaddled tell him to take thine and hasten away.'

On a chest near the squire's bed sat his son John, rocking himself to and fro and crying bitterly. 'What art thou crying for, my son?' asked his father. 'Oh, what shall I do, what shall I do?' And he went on crying more and more. 'Stop crying, my son, thou wilt do very well, for I am going to give thee Trengwainton; and Castle Horneck to look at. Don't cry any more my son, for I am very weak and want to sleep.'

The lawyer having arrived at the squire's bedside, and writing materials being ready, asked what must be added to the will. The squire, when propped up with pillows, gasped out, 'I wish, I wish,' several times, until he became exhausted and fell back in bed. After resting a while he made signs to be raised again, and then only repeated the same words, 'I wish, I wish,' until the lawyer told him to stop a moment and then say what he wanted to have written. 'That my son John shall have Trengwainton,' gasped the dying man.

The lawyer, who had also been the squire's steward for a long time, was quite confounded. In a minute or two he said, 'I don't know what you mean. How can your son have Trengwainton? The place doesn't belong to you, I can't understand 'e at all.' The little blood in Harris's body seemed to rush into his face and turn blue; then he became pale and cried as hard as he was able, 'Thou fool of a lawyer, not to know how, when – ' and unable to say any more he fell back in bed more exhausted than before.

Then he began twitching at the bedclothes, and kept on murmuring, 'I wish, I wish,' lower and lower, and slower and slower, until he breathed his last, with the words on his lips.

The lawyer returned homeward, very sad and much perplexed. He and the deceased had been constant friends from their boyhood. Of late years his connection with Harris was mainly as steward of his estate, and in that character we have to speak of him. The late squire had undertaken many improvements of his farm, as well as alterations in his premises, by his steward's advice; and the steward took just as much interest in his friend's family and estate as if they had been his own. He was also the only solicitor of note then in Penzance.

The unsatisfied dead man was laid in the family vault, when the customary time for keeping people of his quality above ground had expired. On the night of his funeral, towards the morning, doleful sounds were hear proceeding from the late squire's bedroom, with plaintive cries of 'I wish, I wish,' followed by agonising moans and groans.

Next day the steward came over to arrange some business that required his presence on the place; old greyhead servants of the family soon told him of the ghostly sounds heard in the ancient mansion, only a few hours past. The strong-minded man of law ridiculed them, and said it was only their fearful fancies, followed by disturbing dreams, which had caused all their dread of their old master's return. The old servants followed the lawyer to the outer gate, begging him to stay at the house over night. 'No, no, I've other fish to fry,' replied he. 'Go to rest before you're all tipsy, and let the squire come if he will or can.'

The steward proceeded slowly down the hill, thinking of his deceased friend. As he passed a churchway stile, a little below the principal entrance gate, a gentleman came over and walked close beside him, keeping pace with his horse. Neither spoke. The steward didn't even give the customary greeting of 'Good night,' so usual here when people meet in country lanes.

The strange gentleman's broad brimmed hat and drooping plume so shaded his face that his features could not be distinctly seen; but his tall figure was attired in a dress precisely like that which had been worn by Harris, and which was too grand a mode for anybody else in the immediate neighbourhood. The horse showed signs of great terror by rubbing his rider against the hedge, and by trying to run off at a gallop; yet however the steed altered his paces, the stranger kept alongside, with such an easy motion as if he floated in air, until, passing the stream which flows to Ponsandane, when this strange companion disappeared – there was no knowing whither.

Having crossed the water, and the road ascending for a little way, the rider let his steed take his course; then it went off at a furious rate, and only ceased its race when nearing the watering trough at the top of Market Jew Street, opposite the Star Inn. After slaking its thirst, it went down a lane, now built on and called New Street, which led to a yard, stable and garden at the back of the lawyer's house.

It is not known whether the lawyer surmised or not that the companion of his ride down Kenegie Hill was his late friend's ghost, which it was; for he, like most of his profession, could keep his own counsel, especially in doubtful cases. Next day, however, when he was expected by the family at Kenegie to settle such business as could only be arranged with his help, he begged for delay, on the plea of illness, and took to his bed, which he did not quit for some days.

Night was dreaded in the old mansion at Kenegie. The slamming of doors, rattling of furniture and other disturbances commenced earlier and continued later in the morning than they did at first; and the spirit's cries of 'I wish, I wish,' seemed to be uttered in anger rather than in grief.

During all the family's trouble the steward was unable, or unwilling, to come near them. Yet, almost daily, one or other of Harris's old servants came in to enquire after the lawyer's health, and told his family how their late master's ghost had been seen and heard before candle-lighting time in a court behind the house; and that it was intended, over a few nights, to try what 'spirit quellers' could do in order to give the troubled spirit rest.

The steward was still far from well, when one night about a week after his last visit to Kenegie, and just after he heard an eight-day clock on his stair landing strike two, he heard a loud knocking at his front door. Shortly afterwards his housekeeper came to his bedroom door and asked 'Are 'e a-waking, master? There's an old clergyman from over Hayle way below. I've seen him before. He must speak with you, he says. He has a message of the utmost importance to you.' The steward told her to strike a light and show the parson up at once, as he was an old acquaintance who didn't stand on ceremony with him.

The reverend gentleman, on entering the lawyer's bedroom, drew back the window curtains, and said, whilst shaking hands, 'I hope to be excused for calling at this unseasonable hour on account of the message I bring, the importance of which, to you, will be best understood when I tell ye of this night's occurrences.'

Now the lawyer was impatient to learn this urgent business, but it would seem as if the parson were in no hurry, for he went to the window and looked out, as if to recollect his thoughts. Returning to the lawyer's bedside, the reverend gentleman seated himself, and continued, 'I calculate, by the stars now rising, that it is now two hours and forty-five minutes since I, with four other clergymen, by a request of the deceased squire's family, assembled on the Bowling Green at Kenegie, in order to give rest to the unquiet spirit which quitted Proud Harris's mortal tenement a fortnight since.

'Having marked on the turf a circle, and placed on its circumference three lighted candles, to mark the points of an equilateral triangle within which a ghost is as safe as on consecrated ground – the devil and his hounds are always on the watch for vagrant spirits, roaming from churchyards – we formed ourselves in line, facing south and behind the lights, in order of precedence, my station being at the right hand of all. Then a reverend gentleman, who, like myself, has much knowledge of planetary influence and other occult sciences, as well as great ability in laying obdurate spirits, spoke a form of citation. Not a dozen words of this solemn summons were uttered when Proud Harris's ghost, in winding sheet and shroud came before us, and, with a frowning countenance and angry gestures, abruptly said, "Be gone about your own business, if you have any, for you have none here; and learn, vain mortals, that I will not leave this place for anything you can do or say until it pleaseth me to do so."

'On my commencing a powerful form of conjuration the spirit approached me and said, "Dear old friend of my youth, for the sake of those many happy days that we have passed together in the hunting field, do thou go from me, and at once, and tell that accursed lawyer and steward of mine, tell him that unless he comes here, and that shortly, to mind his business, I will go to him. Aye, you see that thin rim of the waning moon; if he be not here, attending to his duty to me and mine, ere that moon be renewed, I will appear before him when he least expects it, whether he be in his office, his bed-chamber, or elsewhere, alone." On my assenting to convey his message, the ghost vanished and I came hither with such speed as my three score and six years permit.'

The parson paused a moment, but the lawyer remaining silent he continued, 'I advise you as a friend, go as desired, before you are three days older, for by that time this moon's diminished horns will have recommenced their growth. As I have now faithfully delivered the spirit's message, I bid you adieu, hoping you will have grace to follow my advice.'

'I intend going to Kenegie,' replied the lawyer, 'before another night comes round. Stay and take breakfast. You must need rest after such trying work,'

'No, I must be gone,' said the parson, 'though I have neither eaten nor slept since my leaving Ruan yesterday morn.'

'Then, if you won't stop, I wish 'e well,' said the steward, 'hoping never more to see ye here with a message from the dead. Farewell.'

The steward lay awake and turned out of bed before his normal time of rising, with the intention of going to Kenegie without delay. Yet, from feeling very much out of order, when partly dressed he returned to bed and sent for a medical man. The doctor felt the lawyer's hot forehead and throbbing pulse, while the sick man told him he could neither sleep nor take his food with any appetite.

'My good friend,' replied the doctor, 'you are working yourself to death. You must not think of entering your office for a month at least. Go away to the country; your clients must have patience until you get well. If they won't, let them go to old Nick for advice. His counsel will please them better than the advice of an honest attorney.'

The patient then said, 'I am anxious first to go over and arrange some business in Kenegie which requires my presence there.'

'All right,' replied the doctor, 'you can do nothing better, when well enough, mind you, than ride over there daily; but don't stay long in the house, and say nothing of professional matters. After taking some light refreshment, ride away up to Castle-an-Dinas. When you are there you will breathe the sweet air of the hills, mingled with ocean's breezes, which will do you more good than any amount of drugs. You must, however, take a small dose at once, in order to procure tranquil sleep. Never mind your appetite, that will return when you are able to take daily rides over the hills, then you will eat like a horse.'

The doctor having sent for the medicine, and seen his patient take it, went downstairs and charged the household on no account to let their master be disturbed with business callers. 'If he should sleep for twenty-four hours, let him,' said the doctor. 'I'll call again shortly.'

The steward said nothing of having been accompanied by Harris's ghost on his ride down Kenegie Hill, nor of the spirit's message, knowing that his medical friend had no faith in supernatural appearances. The ailing man himself had but slight belief in such matters until the evidence of his own eyes, as well as the reverend gentleman's words, convinced him in spite of his reason.

The 'doctor's stuff' had its desired effect. The steward slept soundly through the night and until nearly noon next morning, when he took breakfast in bed, then more medicine, and slept again. About two o'clock the doctor called and asked the housekeeper how her master was. 'I suppose,' said she, 'that he's going on as well as can be expected, for he slept well, ate a good breakfast for a sick man, and is sleeping again. A few minutes ago, I went into his room and saw that his eyes were shut, and didn't speak to him as you told me not to, but I talked a little to myself, and he didn't ask me what I was grumbling about, as he mostly does if I speak a few words to myself.'

'A precious nurse you are,' said the doctor, 'can't you keep your tongue still while you're in your master's room?' The lawyer had the same tranquil rest on the following night, got up at his usual time, and soon after an early dinner took horse for Kenegie.

He arrived at the old mansion about three or four o'clock. Having stayed a few hours with the bereaved family, and said all he could to comfort them, he recollected that there were repairs going on down at the mill, which he ought to see. The lengthening shadows warned him that it was time for his departure, but he could see the mill on his way home. Having sent his horse down, by a servant, he took a path-way which made a short cut thither across some fields. This was always a favourite walk with him and the late squire, because it offered delightful views over land and sea.

On coming to a high-hedged and narrow lane near the mill, the steward went on slowly, with eyes cast down, musing on times past. Glancing upwards when his reverie ended, he saw at a distance of a dozen paces, the late squire, looking as formerly, slowly approaching him. The steward, though much terrified at first, noticed that the garb taken by the apparition was, from looped-up hat to silver spurs, exactly like that which Harris had usually worn when following his hounds. At a glance he saw the same bright and unsullied attire for which the late owner of Kenegie had been distinguished. Yet for all the bright-ness of dress, the ghostly face made his blood run cold. The eyes were like the unclosed eyes of the dead, and the other features were pale and motionless as those of a marble image lying upon a tomb. The lawyer had heard, like everybody else here, that one should never turn back from a ghost, but speak, if only a single word, as a spirit is pow-erless to impart its wishes till spoken to; and if long delayed, the per-son is in danger of receiving bodily harm, and will be haunted to death if he speak not before. The poor man forced himself to advance with his eyes cast down. When near, he could only murmur, 'What shall I do for 'e?'

'I am rejoiced that thou hast come to meet me here, and spoken in time, for on the morrow I should have gone to thee. Why shouldst thou fear me, frail mortal that thou art, when, ere long, thou wilt be as I am, and then seek me with a greater desire to meet me than thou hast now to shun my company? Besides, thou knowest I always liked thee for thy honesty, and thy regard to me and mine. Now, with regard to my son John,' continued the ghost, looking sorrowfully on his faithful steward, 'death as thou knowest cut short my efforts to explain my wishes touching Trengwainton. Thy eyes are cast on earth; dost thou attend to what I say?'

'I do my best to,' replied the poor steward, like one in a waking dream.

'Well, as thou knowest, there is much money owing to me on the place; no interest has ever been paid and more cash is wanted. Do thou supply more and more until the place is indebted to nearly its value. Our boy John is now about fourteen. Before he will be of age, foreclose the mortgage. If the estate be offered for sale, there will be no purchaser; everyone hereabouts has enough to do to keep the land he has. Yet if the place be worth anything more than its encumbrance, pay over the balance on putting my son in possession. The management of my family's property will be entirely on thy hands for many years, and thou wilt still be my trusty steward. Now understand me clearly, of a Harris it must never with truth be said that he got his lands unfairly.'

Before the lawyer could reply – if he had anything to say – Harris's ghost had vanished.

The servant who awaited the lawyer at the mill had become uneasy when it was almost night and the gentleman had not arrived. He rode slowly up the lane, and at last found the steward sitting on a bank beside the road, seeming all bewildered and stupid, like a person recovering from a trance or just come out of a fit. The servant roused him up, but the steward didn't speak, even when he mounted his horse and rode slowly homeward, with the servant following. We hear no more of the good lawyer, but hope he rode out no more until perfectly recovered.

Harris's ghost, satisfied with having told the lawyer how its wishes were to be carried out, has never more been seen or heard in Kenegie from that day to this.

The seaman's ghost

James Bottrell, one of the St Just family of that name, after having served many years aboard a privateer when he was a young man in Bonaparte's time, settled in Zennor about 1820. Shortly after he left sea, he was much troubled with a drowned shipmate's ghost.

Towards the morning part of a stormy winter's night, he was aroused by three loud raps on his chamber window; and on raising his head, he saw standing by his bedside the apparition of one John Jones, who had been his favourite comrade – looking pale and sad and, apparently, dripping wet. In a few minutes it disappeared, with the misty light which surrounded it.

Next day James tried to persuade himself that the vision might be merely a troubled dream, but the apparition continued to come on each succeeding night, stopping longer than at first. There was also much noise and disturbance in and around his dwelling, by day as well as by night.

Over a week or so the ghost, casting an angry look at the man, followed him about in broad daylight, so that James became weary of his life. His friends advised him to speak to the ghost and have confidence, as they had always been good friends; they told him that a spirit would never speak until spoken to; and they believed that his shipmate merely wanted him to do something that the ghost was unable to perform. Moreover they warned him that there was danger when a spirit was angered by delay in speaking to it.

At length James plucked up courage and one day, being at work in a field when his old mate's ghost stood by him – as usual looking sad and angry by turns – he spoke and said, 'Tell me John Jones, what shall I do to give thee rest?' The spirit replied, 'It is well thou hast spoken, for I should have been the death of thee if thou hadst much longer refused to speak! What grieved and vexed me most was to see that thou seemedst to fear thy old comrade, who always liked thee best of all his shipmates.'

'I no longer fear thee, Jack,' replied James, 'and wish I could grasp that hand of thine as in days gone by.' Indeed, he now felt no more dread of his seamate's ghost than if he were still a living man. The spirit, looking pleased, said, 'Now I see thee art like thyself again, staunch and true to thy comrade in life and death. Listen and learn why I am come to seek thy aid. The other stormy night, a few minutes before I appeared at thy bedside, I was on board a good ship in the Bay of Biscay, with a strong gale and a rolling sea. In clewing up a topsail, the ship gave a lurch: I lost my hold, fell overboard and was drowned before anybody noticed my mishap. When sinking, I thought of thee. Now much of my prize-money is in a chest, left in Plymouth at a public house well known to thee – the one we used most to frequent when everything was in common between us. My son, I want thee to go thither; take my chest to another house; pay what I owe to various people in Plymouth, and keep what remains for thyself. I'll meet thee there and direct thee how to act.'

Jim having promised to do all that was required, Jack's ghost looked happy, and a moment after said, 'I wish thee well, mate, till we meet again,' and disappeared.

Early next morning, James took a strong young horse and rode away to Plymouth. It was after candle-lighting of the second night when he arrived there, and put up at an inn – a short distance from the one where the chest was left.

Whilst he lay awake, thinking how he should proceed on the morrow, Jones appeared by his bedside and, as if knowing what passed in the man's mind, said, 'Don't 'e think, my son, that the landlady will make any difficulty about taking away the chest, for she don't know, d'ye see, that it contains valuables, nor that I shipped aboard an

Indiaman and got drowned a few weeks ago. But she remembers how – not long since – we wore each other's clothes and shared each other's rhino [slang, money], just as brothers should. Tell her I'm in town, and will see her before I leave. Tomorrow, bring here the chest and I'll direct 'e how to deal with my creditors; and now, good night mate,' Saying this he vanished.

The landlady was very glad to see James, and more so to have the sailor's chest taken out of her way; told him to give her love to Captain Jones (as she called him) and to say she hoped he wouldn't fail to call before he left port. The chest being opened, there was nothing to be seen in it but the seaman's best clothing; for all the money was concealed in secret drawers of the skibbet, and under a false bottom. The ghost accompanied James – though invisible to others – all the time until the business was settled. Then it left him – without saying goodbye, however.

James went over to Dock [now called Devonport]. Whilst he was there admiring the shipping, on turning around he saw Jones close beside him. If he had been visible to other people they would have taken him for an able seaman in his prime, for he appeared rigged out in bran new sailor's garb, and looked hale and hearty as when alive. 'I've just passed by the old inn,' said he, 'showed myself as I now appear, and kissed my hand to our old hostess, who was at her work near an open window; but before she could reach her door to welcome home the man she used to admire, lo! I'm here. So you see it's convenient to be a ghost!'

James didn't think so however; and they walked on in silence till they came to a fine ship ready to sail on a long voyage. Then the spirit stopped, and looking sorrowfully in the man's face said, 'My dear Jim, I will now bid thee farewell. I'm off to sea again, for, with an occasional trip to the Green, I know no way of passing the time that better suits me. Thou wilt never more see me whilst thou art alive, but if thou thinkest of me at the hour of thy death we shall meet, as soon as the breath leaves thy body.

'My poor clay lies deep in the Bay of Biscay, and when thine is laid in Zennor churchyard we will rove the seas together. A true-hearted tar has nothing to fear, and now my son, adieu.' A moment after, James saw him glide aboard the ship, and in the twinkling of an eye he vanished.

James returned to the inn feeling very wisht, and his sadness continued till he came in sight of Zennor Hills. Then he felt in pretty good heart; and well he might, for hadn't he brought home a bundle of capital clothes that he found in his comrade's chest, and many more pounds in his pocket than when he left Zennor? But the horse was never fit for anything again, from having been ridden to and from Plymouth in less than a week.

Sailors say that ships are often haunted with drowned seamen's ghosts, and they believe that such vessels are seldom wrecked, for the friendly spirits give warning of approaching tempests, and tokens of other dangers to their craft.

The Cornish sailors' Isle of Avalon

It is known to most persons who have mixed much with Cornish sailors that they often speak of 'the Green', which they frequently call Fiddler's Green amongst themselves. They describe this place as an 'Isle of the Blessed' in which honest tars, after the toils of this life, are to enjoy unmixed bliss with their old comrades and favourite fair ones. In orchards of fruit, ever ripe, they are to be entertained with music, dancing and everything else in which they delighted in their lifetime.

The old woman's ghost

Not long since, there lived at Trewey in Zennor a poor and aged woman, who much loved her neighbour's little girl and, when dying, bequeathed to her a shawl, which was all she had to leave of any value.

The departed woman's wish, however, was disregarded; and a few evenings after her funeral, the child would burst out in shrieks. On being asked what made her screech so, 'Oh, there's An Katty,' said she, 'with her face tied up in a white neckan and nothing on her but a sheet!' Thus the old woman's ghost continued to haunt her, until one evening a strong man, of great faith, took the child and carried her out of doors, when, over a while, the little girl exclaimed, 'Oh, there she is again.' Then the man saw the spirit too, and said to her, 'In the name of goodness, I command thee to tell me why thou art come back to trouble this cheeld?'

The spirit answered, 'Because the shawl isn't given to the cheeld, I cannot rest.' Then the man said he would see her wish complied with, bade her depart in peace, and told her that, if she hadn't been an old fool of a sperat, she would have scared the ones who kept the shawl and have left the cheeld alone! By that the ghost had vanished, without saying another word.

The same night the shawl was given to the child, and Trewey folks thought that all was then settled with the old woman; but in the course of two or three evenings, the little girl, being out in the town-place [farmyard] with her play-mates, was taken up over the furze-ricks by invisible means, and borne away out of sight in a minute. The other children ran home frightened.

She often stayed out in neighbours' houses for hours together, so her mother didn't miss her till bedtime. Then, as the woman was going to look for her, in she came, with only one shoe on.

Being questioned as to where she had been to lose her shoe, the child answered that she didn't know – only that she was taken up over the 'housen' and carried away as easy as if she had been rocked in a cradle to a Churchtown with lots of trees in it, and laid in the churchyard on a new grave; she heard nobody but heard like singing around her; somebody kissed her; then she shivered with cold, and was again carried up over the trees and back to her own town-place. She believed that her shoe was loosened as she skimmed the tree-tops, but where it dropped she couldn't tell.

From what the child said, all Trewey people thought she had been taken to Ludgvan, where the old woman was buried; and it was put beyond doubt the next day, when her missing shoe was found on the old woman's grave. There it was left, for the old woman 'might want something belonging to the child, to put her to rest,' and nobody would risk bringing her back again for the sake of a shoe.

And she has kept quiet from that day to this.

The reception party

The good people of Mousehole have a firm belief in the wandering spirits who are supposed to inhabit a mid-region (of which the name is now ignored, but the idea remains) and who are often permitted to occupy themselves with the same objects and pursuits as formerly constituted their business or their pleasure. The faith of the people respecting these visitors from the world of shadows is often confirmed by their favourite teachers from the pulpit.

A very intelligent woman of the place informed us that she heard a preacher, in the middle of his sermon on the invisible world, relate how, one Sunday night after the service at a country chapel, he went to visit a solitary cottage situated on a lonely moor. The footpath across the moor was scarcely visible in the darkening twilight; consequently he concentrated on the ground near him, best part of the way, so that he might keep on the path. A little before he reached the dwelling, looking towards it he saw three persons who appeared to be females, dressed in white, a few yards before him and proceeding towards the house.

The preacher quickened his pace as he wished to overtake them; yet whether he walked fast or slow, the white figures always kept the same distance ahead.

He noticed that they entered the small court before the cottage, but without the door being opened they disappeared, although there was no outlet from the cottage except the gate, which he was sure they did not re-pass. This surprised him and it was then impressed on his mind that the apparition was that of visitors from the other world. When he entered the cottage (which he did by lifting the latch without knocking) he saw an aged woman seated on the chimney-stool in the large fire-place, such as we find in the country, where the fuel is furze and turf.

After saluting the old woman, he enquired if any other persons had entered the cottage just before him. The old woman replied that they were the only living persons in the house, but that her daughter was lying dead on the bed in the next room. When the preacher related to her what he saw, the old lady said that she understood very well what the vision was which he beheld; it was that of the spirits of the rest of the family, who had last died, come down to take the soul of her daughter away with them. The reverend gentleman told his congregation that he felt that the aged mother was right – in fact he had not the least doubt about the correctness of what she felt sure of, from having known many similar instances of the kind himself.

Whether this story was that of a real apparition or mere fancy, the pleasing faith of the old lady was not less consoling. If the profane will say, it's all imagination, or apply the word 'superstition', yet it contains one of those amiable and instinctive feelings dear to the heart of the bereaved.

The haunted garret at Trove

In the manor house at Trove, high up in the gable, alongside an ivy-covered chimney stack, a little window might be discovered among the branching ivy, when one stood in the private garden at the time the sun was sunk so low as to glisten on the few diamond-shaped panes left in the casement.

Yet no one could ever find any room within to which this window belonged. The door of the room or closet was probably walled up, because that old part of the house was always disturbed at night with the humming of a turn [spinning wheel], rattling of cards, and other noises usually made when carding the wool or spinning the yarn.

It was said to be haunted by an ancient housekeeper of Trove, who had once been young and fair; that she had loved her young master but too well, all the better perhaps because he could not or would not make an honest woman of her, by making the beauteous lass his bride; however that may be, the favourite servant would never leave the place in life or in death, but always remained there in spite of all that the lady of the mansion and her lawfully begotten family could do to dislodge her.

Many generations had passed away before she was finally put to rest in a small upper room of the malt-house wing, by being bound by some learned priest to the task of carding a number of fleeces of black wool until it became white, and to spin as much from the same (without breaking the yarn) as would make her a shroud. Long after the spirit was put to rest, 'tis said that the maltsman, having to remain up late one October night to turn the malt, fill up the casks of fermenting ale, and for other work that requires to be attended to by night as well as by day in good careful malting and brewing, heard, when up in the chamber, a more than common racket with the turn and the clicking of cards in making the rolls of wool.

The maltsman was a jolly blade who cared but little for ghosts, and thought, by the sounds being so natural, that more than one person in real flesh and blood must be working overhead.

He did no better nor worse than make three taps on the planching overhead with the end of his shovel hilt. The roar of the turn and the click of the cards that instant stopped, and the three knocks were answered by three louder from above. Then he tapped the ceiling seven times with his knuckles. These were returned in the same gentle way. Now he was persuaded that some of the lasses who belonged to the house had found out a secret passage or stair in some adjacent garret or closet, by which they could reach the room over, and that they were then spinning for a wager; or perhaps some wool they had purloined for themselves was there being spun on the sly.

The man had no thought of fear, as he could still hear, late as it was, the boisterous mirth of the huntsmen and some of the hard-drinking guests who caroused in the distant hall; as soon as he had finished his work with the malt, he knocked again for the third time with the end of the hilt against the floor overhead. Again the spinning ceased and the same number of blows, like a signal, were returned. 'Stop a bit, and I am coming,' said he. A moment after, what seemed to be two hollow voices replied, 'Come, come, come.'

As the man descended the outside stone steps from the malt-chamber to the brewhouse, he saw the light shining bright and natural-like over against the yew hedge and on the plants in that part of the garden. Though he, and indeed all the rest of the servants, had often been cautioned never to meddle, to ask no questions, and check their curiosity about the haunted chamber, or ill luck would befall them, yet, finding when he came into the court a ladder left against the wall, like as if some evil spirit had put it there to tempt him to his doom, he fixed the ladder to rest on the roof of some low building which joined the towering gable, and contrived to place it so that the top of the long ladder nearly reached the wisht-looking little ivy-buried window. As he mounted the ladder he heard shrieks of laughter, which he thought might come from some of the servants' bedrooms at no great distance off; but when he reached the top and looked in through the window, all sounds had ceased – even the never-ending dismal night call of the owls was no longer heard, and the flitting bats had disappeared.

He could make out but little at first in the weak glimmering blue light within, which came neither from lamp nor candle that he could see; from the confused mass of things on the floor in the middle of the small room, he saw what he at last made out to be an elderly woman dressed in an ordinary bedgown. All her long skeleton body was closely wrapped and folded up in a sheet, except her long bony arms, that kept on wearily and ceaseless working a pair of cards, on a handful of black wool. He saw large heaps of black wool all around her, and piles of grey dust, or the tormented wool, that never lost all its colour, between him and what he took to be a chest, till the dust made him cough, and then the apparition raised its ghastly head, and the shroud fell off the face that looked as if it had long been in the grave. Deep in the holes of the skull, in the places where the eyes once shone, were lurid balls of fire, that shot out their light like the rays from a dark lantern, and left all else in gloom. When the glaring balls were turned on the man, he felt the marrow of his bones pierced as with darts of fire. He had neither the power to move nor to speak.

Then the ghastly corpse turned its fiery eyes around and rested them on the chest, but he saw then by their light that it was a white coffin. In the midst of the wool, a small treadle turn, like those old women use for spinning flax, stood beside the half-open coffin. From within it arose the figure of a younger and fairer corpse, but all covered with purple spots like poison marks. Pointing, and looking at the man as she arose, she said, 'Here is room enow for thee.' Then both the ghastly forms glided toward the window like things floating in the air, and shook the dust from their shrouds and winding sheets in the intruder's face. Lurid streams of fiery light from the eyes of the apparitions, choking dust from their shrouds, and the sickening smell of grave-clothes, made the man so dizzy, sick and faint that he fell from the ladder, broke his ribs by a fall on a grindstone, and crawled into the brew-house, where he was found senseless the next morning and could only be roused up long enough to tell how he came by his mishap; then he shook his head, groaned, kicked, sneezed and died.

The old women, who know all about such matters, put it down that the younger ghost, with the purple-spotted face, must have been another of the master's favourites – some fair maid of sixteen sent off by her jealous mistress with a cup of nightshade decoction or a bowl of hemlock broth. Long after the brew-house wing was a roofless ruin, these troublesome spirits, with others who joined them, might be heard couranting, raving, roaring or wailing all the night long.

The I'an ghosts

The story of the poor but genteel I'an family is told in another book in this series, *Folk tales from the Land's End*. The family's name was pronounced Jan. The ghosts would have included the spirits of Beaton (Beatrice) I'an, her brother John who lived by smuggling and was accidentally killed in a fog by his own crew, Beaton's lover Willy Taskes – accidentally killed by John just before Beaton and Willy could get married – and their daughter Mary, who pined away when her own young lover's family refused permission for him to marry an illegitimate (and impoverished) maiden.

Some few years ago, there might have been seen on rising ground, west of the road which passes through Treen, the remains of a very old dwelling, formerly known in that neighbourhood as the I'an's house. Though neglected and ruinous it still retained some signs of its former consequence, when it was regarded as a mansion.

Visitors to the Logan Rock often stopped to look at this forlorn looking old house, with great part of its mullioned windows and a doorway, that had once been a grand entrance, walled up. Its peculiar old style of masonry, the massiveness and irregularity of the rough granite blocks with which it was constructed, and its high-pitched thatched roof, made this old building an object of interest, though it was neither beautiful nor picturesque. And a few casements, still retaining their old lead-lights of small panes in various patterns, to which age had imparted purple or rather prismatic hues, glimmered and glanced with changing lights that gave to the habitation a very ghostly look.

What remained had long been divided into three or four dwellings; but one wing was mostly unoccupied, because few persons could be found so courageous or necessitous as to live in it and have their rest disturbed every night, and often by day, with the rumbling of a turn, varied by wild shrieks, unearthly laughter, and other frightful noises.

In this state the old house and appurtenances remained until destroyed by a fire about ten years since [1860s] and it always retained the name of the family that built it and resided there for generations, in the style of gentry, though never very rich or persons of much note beyond that locality.

Shortly after Beatrice I'an died – it would have been around King Charles's time – noises like the rumble of a spinning wheel and clicking of cards, with unnatural shrieks, were often heard in 'Beaton's chamber', which remained locked up, with its furniture just as it was at her death. Persons passing by the house at night, if they had courage to cast a glance at its windows, saw in that room and others a glimmer of light, and shadowy forms flitting to and fro. But almost everybody hurried by without casting an eye towards the house, or took a roundabout way rather than running a risk of having a fright, or having their rest disturbed by seeing those strange apparitions.

Over a while it seemed as if more spirits joined those that first arrived, till at length they made such a rattle-cum-stave throughout the whole house that it was left for years unoccupied – by mortal tenants at least. The turn continued its rumble upstairs, and what had formerly been a kitchen, hall and parlour seemed filled with a revel-rout all night long, and folks were often dismayed by unnatural appearances outside the house. Towards night, clouds of fog would roll in from over sea, settle around the I'ans premises and become denser and darker until the place seemed shrouded in thunder clouds; then lights would flash around the house, and such sounds be heard as if made by discharges of small fire-arms, with a roar of cannon now and then. One would also hear the surging and splashing of waves, flapping of sails, creaking of blocks and tackle, with other sounds usually heard on shipboard, till this apparition rose high above the houses, drifted away seaward, and disappeared.

Sometimes all the lights in the house would go out at the same instant, without any visible cause; this was such a common occurrence that the inmates would merely say, 'That's Beaton come again; but never mind, we shall soon hear her spinning, then we may light the candles again, and hope to be left in peace for a time.' When people would persist and occupy the house, it was often troubled by day, and all its mortal inmates, both man and beast, would be seized with fear, and run to doors, at times when nothing unusual was seen or heard. Often in the height of a clear summer's day, a blast of chilly air with a grave-like scent would pervade the dwelling. Then children would screech, dogs howl, cats, with their hair bristled up, run out of doors, or smash through windows if the doors were closed. The cats never returned, and died of fright if they could not escape the house.

A carpenter who was working about the place said he didn't believe all the I'ans' spirits would make him quit the house, or Beaton's chamber even. And he wagered a pint of brandy that he would see, that very night, what made the racket there, and hail the spirits if he saw any. That he might have a sight of them, without more ado he bored an auger hole in Beaton's chamber-door. Having primed himself with a drink, when night came and the usual noises began he fixed himself close to the door and peeped in. At first he only beheld a faint light glimmering above the bed, and what looked like a dead man stretched thereon, with shadowy figures moving about the room; then he saw more distinctly, and made out a woman dressed in grave clothes, sitting on a chair beside the bed.

Then the chamber became so dark that he could see nothing of the figures on the bed or in the chair but their eyes, that shone with purple light. The woman's eyes – he could see nothing else but her eyes glistening like coals of fire – arose from the bedside and approached the door, and still the carpenter could only see a pair of flaming orbs when they were within a few inches of his face; and he – terror stricken or spellbound – had neither power to move away nor withdraw his gaze. There he stood like one riveted to the spot for minutes that seemed hours, until a blast of cold air smote his face and something pierced his eye like a red hot nail. He fell on the floor, was found insensible when raised, and he ever remained blind in one eye.

The Captain's tomb

In the southern side of St Levan churchyard there is a low altar tomb on the grave of Captain Wetherel, whose ship sprung a leak and sank, and who was drowned near the Rundle Stone many years ago. This grave is regarded with fear and wonder by many persons of that neighbourhood; for ever since the Captain was laid there it has been believed that a ghostly bell strikes the hours, and half hours, in his grave, the same as on board ship.

'Tis said this sound beneath the sod may be heard the clearest by persons passing the churchyard at midnight, but also sometimes at mid-day. It was a few minutes before that hour when the Captain, finding his vessel sinking, made his crew take to the boat; but he himself refused to quit his ship and as she went down they heard him give eight loud and distinct strokes on the bell.

Many years since, several young people were assembled in the churchyard one Sunday forenoon, after service had commenced and the elders had gone into church. Time passed pleasantly with the young folks chatting about such occurrences in the St Levan world as interested them. In rambling among the graves, to look at the many garden flowers that bloomed on them, they approached Captain Wetherel's tomb, and a girl who stood by it reading the inscription started back on hearing a hollow sound beneath her feet. She, and others near her who saw her emotion, listened and lo! a ringing came up as of a bell at sea. All rushed into church in great fright.

There was much talk of the strange occurrence for a few weeks, and less loitering of the youngsters to gossip in the churchyard during service.

Shortly after, a young sailor belonging to St Levan who had been absent many years, came home for a few weeks.

Being in the 'Elder Tree' public house one forenoon with some of his former companions, their discourse led to the mention of the ship's bell sounding in Captain Wetherel's grave.

The young seaman said he believed the story was all nonsense, though things as strange or stranger happened in old vessels; but as it was then near upon twelve o'clock, for curiosity's sake he went out and stood near the Captain's tomb, while his companions remained by the church porch for a few minutes, watching the sun-dial. As it marked noon, the sailor rushed back to his companions, looking as pale as a corpse, and said with bated breath, 'True as I'm alive, I heard "eight bells" struck in the grave, and wouldn't go near the spot again for the world.'

The young seaman, on his next voyage, found his own grave in the deep.

I never heard of any other person who went purposely to hear the Captain's bell, for it is a general belief here that bad luck is sure to overtake those who endeavour to pry into ghostly doings that don't concern them.

s

Seddon Neudorfer

Wet Nose
Publishing Ltd

www.countrysidedogwalks.co.uk

First published in June 2013 by **Wet Nose Publishing Ltd**
Reprinted 2016 and March 2017

All enquiries regarding sales telephone: 01824 704398
email cdw@wetnosepublishing.co.uk
www.countrysidedogwalks.co.uk

ISBN 978-0-9573722-2-1

With a special thank you to: Charlotte Evans, Steve Peart, Graham and Lesley
Seddon, Lee Fildes, Norma Legat and Daisy Gibbs

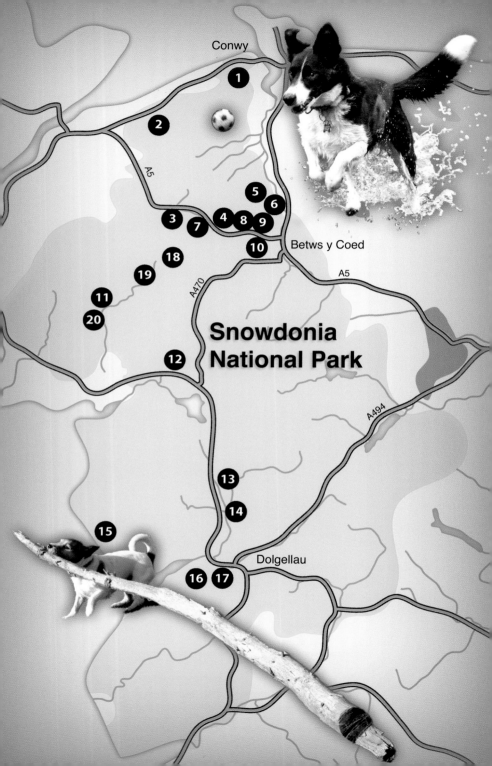

Contents

Introduction

Snowdonia National Park has a lot to offer in the way of dog walking, without mountainous climbs. The twenty walks included in this book are all designed so that you and your wet nosed friend have a really enjoyable time. There are a few specially designed stiles, which have lift gates for dogs. At a quick glance the information at the beginning of each walk will tell you what to expect and what you may need to take with you. The descriptive guides will also warn of any roads ahead or areas of livestock so that you can get your dog on the lead well in advance.

Dogs just love to explore new places. They really enjoy the new smells and carry themselves a little higher with the added excitement. Going to new places gets you and your dog out and about meeting new people and their dogs. It is important to socialise dogs, as they will be more likely to act in a friendly manner towards other dogs as they gain confidence.

The stunning pictures in this book are just a taster of what you can see along the way. A lot of the walks are crammed with fantastic views and you are never far from water or woodlands - the latter will provide shade in the summer and shelter on cold, wet days and your dog will love the freedom to run up and down in the woods.

The walks are graded Easy, Medium and Challenging and are mostly around one to three hours long, depending on your and your dog's pace. You may start with the easy ones and work up to the challenging walks depending on your and your dog's fitness. Different dog breeds and dog age must be taken into account when you decide which walks to do. If you are unsure of the distance that your dog can manage, why not try the linear walks first? You will be able to judge if your dog is getting tired and so you can choose to turn back at any time. This is always good for older dogs, as some days are better than others and the linear walks are often flat making it easier to manage.

Different breeds of dog have different levels of fitness. For example, bulldogs can only do short walks, whereas a border collie or a springer spaniel is extremely energetic and difficult to tire out. It is recommended that you research information on the breed of dog that you own to get to know what sort of exercise they require.

You may have a walk that you are happy doing with your dog every day, but this book will show you new areas to explore with a change of scenery and a chance to meet new people and their dogs. Dogs love new places to visit and you will see the change in them as they explore the new surroundings, taking in the new smells with delight. You will fulfil your life and your dog's just by trying different walks.

Llyn Parc, Coed y Brenin, Mynydd Penrhos and Llyn Elsi are mainly covered by trees where your dog can enjoy the freedom to run up and down without you having to worry about livestock. They are great for hot days, as many dogs don't cope well in the sun.

There is plenty of water for your dog to enjoy, whether it be lakes, rivers or streams, so your dog can get that needed slurp of water along the way. Some of the walks include bridleways, so you may encounter horses. It is important to have your dog under close control if you see horses approach. It is always helpful to say hello to the riders as they near so that the horse realises that you are not a threat.

Rivers

Some dogs love water and will think nothing of plunging into the river. With the extreme weather conditions over the last few years a river that may be safe for your dog to swim in can change in a matter of hours to become a swollen torrent that could wash your dog away. Please be careful when near rivers if there have been heavy periods of rain or if they look swollen or fast flowing. It is best to put your dog on the lead until you have assessed the situation.

Snowdonia National Park

The National Park was established in 1951, covering 827 square miles. Nearly 70% of the park is privately owned, with the Forestry Commission owning almost 16%, the National Trust 10% and the Countryside Council for Wales and the National Park Authority owning just 3% combined.

The Welsh name for Snowdon is Eryri which means 'Highlands'. Snowdonia is famous for its fantastic mountain ranges and has nine in all, Snowdon being the highest in Wales and England. It is not just about mountains however as there are fantastic valleys and beautiful ancient woodlands, bright green all year round because of the mosses, lichens and liverworts that blanket the ground and tree bark. There are waterfalls, rivers and gorges, lakes and streams, rocky outcrops and glacial boulders. There is even a coast line and estuary. The agricultural areas are nicely enclosed by fantastically crafted stone walls and beautiful ancient hedgerows.

There are some walks that are amongst the mountainous areas and a couple of mountain climbs, but because they have well-made paths, they are pretty much straight forward. However do take care, have respect for the environment you are in, and choose a clear day, checking local mountain weather forecasts and taking extra precautions in the winter months.

Ground Nesting Birds

During 1st March through to end of July there will be several species of birds that make their nest on the ground. Dogs can disturb or harm chicks if they roam amongst the heather and bracken. During this time it is essensial to keep your dog on the paths whilst walking amongst the heathland and grassland areas.

Birds in the United Kingdom are split into three categories of conservation importance - Red, Amber and Green. Red being the highest conservation priority, with species needing urgent action. Amber is the next most critical on the list followed by green. For more information on this please see the BTO or RSPB websites.

Birds that will be breeding on the Red data list include Sky lark, Twite and Hen harriers. Birds on the Amber list include Curlew, Snipe and Meadow pipits.

Livestock

All walks avoid areas that cattle and horses graze. This can change however, according to changes of farming with the individual landowner. If you find that

you need to cross a field with cattle and they seem interested in you or your dog it is recommended to let your dog off the lead. Never try to get between cattle and your dog. Your dog will get out of a situation a lot more easily with speed than you can. It is usually only cattle with young calves that can be a threat. Young heifers and bullocks also tend to get a little inquisitive. They will usually stop when they get close to you or your dog.

If you encounter horses and they seem to get aggressive towards your dog, let the dog off the lead. Most horses will come over for a fuss but a small percentage do have a problem with dogs and see them as a threat and will act to defend the herd. Horses that are out with a rider are completely different as they are not defending the herd and as long as you keep a safe distance there should not be a problem.

Sheep are not a danger to you, but your dog can be a danger to them. Where sheep are grazing it is vital that you have your dog on a lead or under very close control. You will know your dog, but if you are unsure it is better to play safe and keep your dog on a lead. It is important always to have your dog on a lead when around lambs. Lambs have a higher pitched bleat and are more cat size and your dog may act differently amongst them.

Forests

The forest walks in this book are a changing landscape, which makes them unique and interesting. Descriptions may change with time, for instance a path may be described as being in the shade of the forest, but as this is a worked forest a section could be clear felled at any time. Another change over the years could be where a view is described across a previously felled area. This could then be planted up and trees grown blocking the views. Paths may change but this is less likely. On rare occasions the Forestry Commission may temporarily close paths due to forest works but again this is even less likely on a weekend. Any changes to the path networks that may occur after the date of print will be updated on our website.

Ticks

If you have been walking in areas where sheep graze you should check your dog for ticks. They must be removed as soon as possible. It is best to use tick tweezers for this, which are specially designed to remove the head and leg parts of the tick. Ticks can carry diseases and the longer they remain latched on to your dog the greater the chance of spreading infections.

Dog Fouling

Please be a responsible dog owner and ensure that you pick up after your dog and place the dog bag in the bins provided. In the event that there are no bins please take the dog bag away with you to the nearest road-side bin. The Forestry Commission have a stick and flick policy so there is no need to pick it up, just flick it off the paths leaving it to degrade naturally. This is far better than leaving non-biodegradable bags on the ground, which looks unsightly and can stay there for months, maybe years.

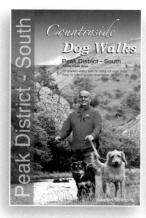

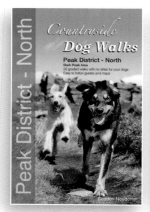

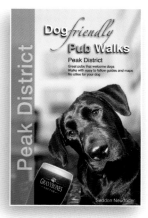

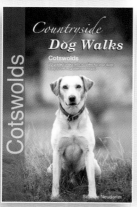

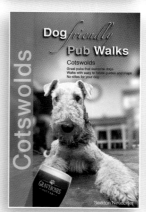

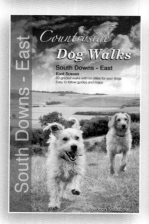

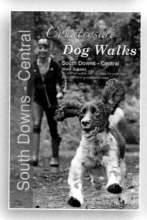

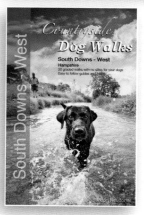

www.countrysidedogwalks.co.uk

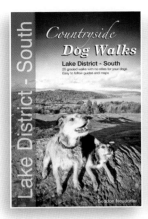

Countryside
Dog Walks
Lake District - South
20 graded walks with no stiles for your dogs
Easy to follow guides and maps

Lake District - South

Seddon Neudorfer

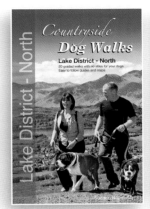

Countryside
Dog Walks
Lake District - North
20 graded walks with no stiles for your dogs
Easy to follow guides and maps

Lake District - North

Seddon Neudorfer

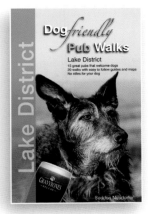

Dog*friendly*
Pub Walks
Lake District
15 great pubs that welcome dogs
20 walks with easy to follow guides and maps
No stiles for your dog

Lake District

Seddon Neudorfer

Dog*friendly*
Tea Room & Café
Walks
Lake District
15 tea rooms and cafés that welcome dogs
20 walks with easy to follow guides and maps
No stiles for your dog

Lake District

Seddon Neudorfer

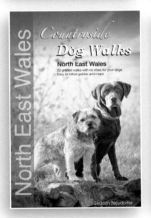

Countryside
Dog Walks
North East Wales
20 graded walks with no stiles for your dogs
Easy to follow guides and maps

North East Wales

Seddon Neudorfer

Countryside
Dog Walks
Greater Manchester
20 graded walks with no stiles for your dogs
Easy to follow guides and maps

Greater Manchester

Seddon Neudorfer

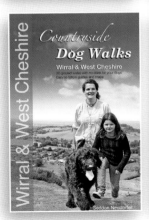

Countryside
Dog Walks
Wirral & West Cheshire
20 graded walks with no stiles for your dogs
Easy to follow guides and maps

Wirral & West Cheshire

Seddon Neudorfer

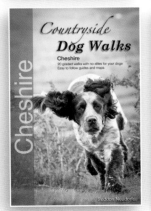

Countryside
Dog Walks
Cheshire
20 graded walks with no stiles for your dogs
Easy to follow guides and maps

Cheshire

Seddon Neudorfer

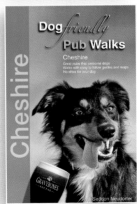

Dog*friendly*
Pub Walks
Cheshire
Great pubs that welcome dogs
Walks with easy to follow guides and maps
No stiles for your dog

Cheshire

Seddon Neudorfer

Follow us on Facebook for
progress reports on our latest
releases.

Search - Countryside Dog Walks

Wet Nose
Publishing Ltd

1. Conwy Mountain

Medium - 2.4 miles - 1hr

This is a stunning walk with both coastal and mountain views and a gentle climb to the highest point where you can see Conwy Castle. If you choose the summer months for this walk the heather hills look absolutely stunning. There are wild ponies on this walk and possibly goats so you will need to keep your dog under close control. Ground nesting birds are also vulnerable during April to the end of July. There are no roads on this walk.

How to get there –Take the Sychnant Pass road out of Conwy, passing a car park on the left, shortly after which there is a lay-by on the right hand side of the road.

Grid Reference – SH 749770

Parking – Free in the parking bay

Facilities – There are no facilities

You will need – Dog leads, dog bags

The Walk

❶ From the car park, facing away from the road take the path on the left, which descends beside the stunning rock face to your right. There are lovely views into the valley to the sea on your left.

After an ascent the path levels out, and you will have a stone wall to your right with small fields. Ignore a path to the left and soon you will see a way marker.

❷ Follow the way marker Llwybr Cyhoeddus taking the footpath on the right. Pass through a metal gate and continue straight ahead cutting through the middle of the hillside, which is a wash of glorious purple when the heather is in flower.

Once you reach another path, cross this to go straight on following the North Wales Path for a time. The path will widen out where you will have coastal views. When reaching another path turn right, walking amongst the hills and heather.

Once you reach a fork take the left path. Ignore a narrow path to the left a little further on and continue following the obvious worn path. Ignore a path to the right and as you climb you will see more views looking over the Conwy headland to the sea.

Once reaching another fork take the path to the right. You will see a mound of rocks here where the panoramic views are absolutely stunning. Ignoring paths to the right, ❸ continue on this path, which passes over a series of exposed

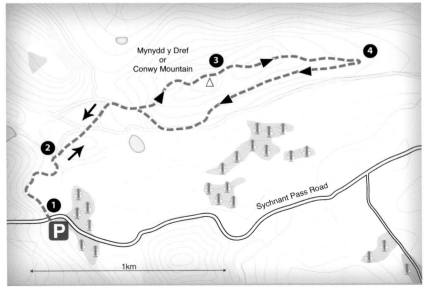

rocks, which are the remains of an Iron Age hill fort. The path will begin to descend.

You will soon be able to see Conwy Castle and harbour ahead of you. Continue on your descent, passing some rocky sections, following on the worn path amongst the heather.

4 Once the grassy path levels out, turn back on yourself and head for the path ahead of you on the left, returning in the direction that you came but on a lower path. Pass a lone tree on the right and then a stone boulder on the left. You will have stunning views to the left looking across the silver birch woodland, the neat stone walls and hedgerows that surround the fields and the hills beyond.

Continue on the grassy path where you will pass a section of exposed rock on the right. You will see a path that goes left and descends towards a stone wall. Take this path, turning right once reaching the track.

There are stunning rocky crags that are scattered amongst the heather and beautiful mountain views. Stay with the stone wall on your left for a while and then keep to the track where the wall reaches a corner, walking between the heather.

Just after passing a boggy flat area to your left take the familiar path on the left, which inclines slightly over the hill to descend again through the middle of the hillside and back through the gate. Once on the track turn left and continue back to your car.

2. Aber Falls

Easy - 2.5 miles - 1hr

This is a stunning linear walk, where you can experience the power in water as two rivers collide to become one. You will see beautiful scenery, woodlands, meadows, and a truly terrific waterfall, Rhaeadr Fawr. There may be sheep grazing in sections and the river is fast flowing, so avoid dogs entering the water; it is fenced off in places.

How to get there – From the A55 take the Abergwyngregyn turn off at junction 13. Follow the brown signs for Aber Falls/Rhaeadr Aber.

Grid Reference – SH 664719

Parking – Pay and display in the parking bay or Forestry Commission Car Park

Facilities – Toilets in the Forestry Commission Car Park

The Walk

1 From the parking bay proceed uphill with the river to your left. Do not go over the bridge but go through the kissing gate. Proceed down the steps and along the path following the river.

The path ascends with some stone steps into deciduous woodlands. There is a glorious sight ahead as two rivers collide to become one, racing between the rocky boulders.

2 Cross a bridge over the river passing traditional slate fencing to your left. Go through the gate then turn right onto the wider track. As livestock are grazing here please keep dogs on a lead.

Pass a nice barrel shaped gazebo on the left and go through a kissing gate. Dogs that insist on going in the river can get access here, so beware. Continue on this gravel track with grass verges on both sides. There is forest on the left and woodlands to your right.

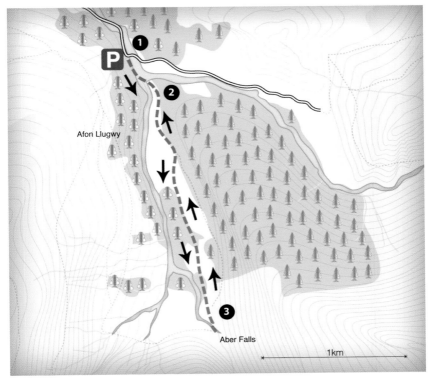

Afon Llugwy

Aber Falls

1km

As you ascend on this path the grass verges widen to become meadows with some scrub and hazel coppice in places. There are lovely views ahead of the hills and the waterfall. You will pass some mature oaks and alder to your left.

Stay on the main path and pass a visitor centre on your left and then a weather station. Pass through a couple of gates, staying on the track. The trees close in a little more here to become wood pasture.

❸ There are lots of mature ash trees here and old, gnarly hawthorns. Pass through another gate and as you near the waterfall be ready for a shower!

Now it is back the way you came, remembering to take the gate on your left after passing the gazebo. Go over the bridge and turn right until you reach the road once more to your car.

3. Devil's Kitchen

Easy - 2.7 miles - 1hr

This is a fabulous walk, which really gives you the feeling of being amongst the mountains without the hard work involved to get there. There are stunning mountain views and a lake, Llyn Idwal, which you and your dog can enjoy walking around. There are no roads but there may be sheep grazing the area.

How to get there – From Capel Curig take the A5 signed for Bethesda. When you reach the far end of Llyn Ogwen on your right you will see the car park on the left.

Grid Reference – SH 649603

Parking – Ogwen Cottage Car Park Pay and Display

Facilities – Toilets and refreshments at the car park

You will need – Dog leads and dog bags

The Walk

1 From the car park walk towards the toilet block and take the path to the left of the building. Go uphill and through the iron gate. You will cross a footbridge where your dog can enjoy the clear water from the mountains above.

Follow the path, which is made up of large stones. It has a gradual incline, with some steps. You can enjoy the mountainous scenes looking to the peaks of the Glyders straight ahead, with Y Garn to your right and Tryfan on your left. You will encounter lots of streams that pass under the paths where your dog can enjoy a drink.

2 Once you reach the lake, go across the footbridge on your right and through the iron gate. Walk along the grassy path keeping the lake to your left. Once the bank levels off you will be able to walk along the water's edge.

You will reach a stone wall where you go through an iron gate. Keep walking straight on along the path, which veers away from the lake. Ascend some stone steps as you incline a little way.

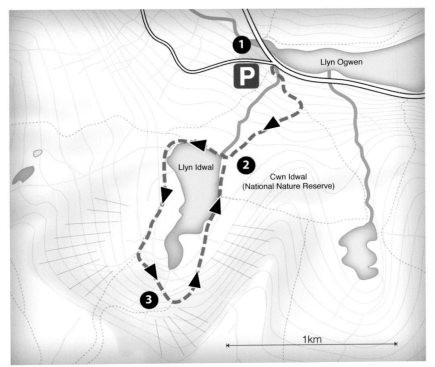

You will be walking now towards the stunning mountain face known as Devil's Kitchen. If you are lucky and the heather is in flower it will be a mass of purple. The path will meet with a stock fence to your left for a short while.

The path drops down a little and you will see a stone embankment with a hill to your right. Walk along this path and look out for a path that goes to your left just before you see the end of the lake. Once you pass two large rocks on the left between the path and the lake, you should see the path you need.

❸ Take this path left where you will cross a series of streams using the rocks as stepping stones. You will now be walking with the end of the lake on your left. The path will go uphill and you will meet another path where you can go left or right.

Turn left so that you will soon be walking along the other side of the lake. Keep on this stone path that has some steps down. You will pass through another iron gate at the stone wall.

You will recognise the stone bridge ahead; before reaching it, turn right and proceed back the way you came to the car park.

4. Swallow Falls

Medium - 2 miles - 1hr

This is a fantastic walk through woodlands and forest, descending to absolutely stunning views of a waterfall known as Swallow Falls. There are rock boulders and trees that are covered in mosses, lichens and ferns, with stunning rock faces and a view of the surrounding hills and mountains. The woodland floor has pockets of heather and bilberry. There is quite a long gradual ascent, then back to your car. There are no roads and no livestock. Your dog will find water in many places along the way. There are some cycle trails which cross the path in place, please keep your dog under close control.

How to get there – From the A5 out of Betws y Coed towards Capel Curig, pass the Swallow Falls hotel on your left and take the minor road on the right immediately before the Ugly House tea room.

Grid Reference – SH 765583

Parking – Free in the Ty'n Llwyn Forestry Commission car park

Facilities – There are no facilities

You will need – Dog leads, the Forestry Commission has a stick and flick policy

The Walk

❶ From the car park facing the road, turn left through a gap in the stone wall. Cross the picnic area and follow the yellow way markers along a path, passing through a gap in the fence.

There are views to the left across the valley to the hills beyond. Pass through an open wooded area with bracken and then, after passing through another gap in the fence, you will be in mixed woodland. The path will descend and you pass a path on the left.

Now in the forest amongst the conifers, the path will take a sharp left bend just as you pass some houses to the right. You will then enter under the canopy of mature oak trees with hazel understory.

❷ The path bends sharply to the right and then a little further along it will take another sharp bend, this time to the left, ascending once more.

There is another sharp bend to the right followed by a set of stone steps, then another sharp turn as you make your way down the hill. The path will narrow and then you will meet another wider track. Cross this path and continue to descend, a little more steeply now, into mixed woodlands.

Pass through a gap in the old stone wall, staying on the obvious worn path. At the bottom of the steps at the fork of another track, take the right track, descending still but only gradually. Continue on this path for some distance.

As you enter the beech woodland you will hear and then see the river on your right. Ignore the path to the right and then a little further along ignore a path to

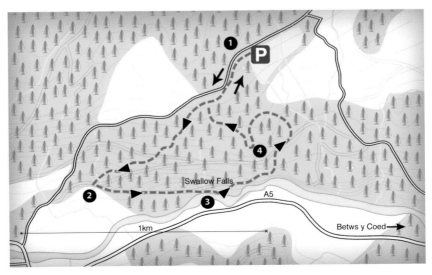

the left. Just afterwards you will see a narrow path to the right. If you take this path you can have close up views of the waterfall. Put your dog on a lead, as there is a chance he may get over the fence.

❸ This is a truly amazing scene as the wide waterfall races down over and around the rock boulders.

Back on the path, turn right to continue until you reach a set of steps on your right. If your dog is more adventurous, put him on the lead, then follow down the steps to a bench and a viewing area. Here you will see the full extent of the waterfall. It really is a wonderful sight to experience; your dog will get restless long before you are ready to leave.

Turn right back on the path, walking with stock fencing on your right and heading to the rock face ahead. You will pass the rock face to your left. There are views of the river with oak woods to both sides of the valley below.

Just after you pass between two wooden posts you will reach a fork. Take the left fork, where you begin your upward climb through the forest on a grassy track. You will meet with another track where you will see a stream ahead. Your dog can find water here.

Turn left on this track, where again the forest is replaced by woodland as you climb a little higher. The path has a series of switchbacks as you make your way up the hill. Once you reach another track turn right. As the path descends a little more steeply take the steps on the left, which lead back into the forest.

The path is a little steeper here, passing over rocks that are hidden with moss. Follow the yellow way markers for some distance as the path becomes unclear. ❹ You will reach a viewpoint just off the path. Put your dogs on a lead, as there is a bit of a drop and take a look.

Turn back on the path and turn left. You will pass through a gap in the stone wall, then follow the grassy path with a rock face to your right. On reaching another path turn right and continue through the trees back to your car.

5. Crafnant

Easy - 3.2 miles - 1hr 30min

This is a truly fantastic walk with stunning scenery, a reservoir, and lots of opportunity for dogs to drink from the many streams as you pass through delightful woodlands and forests. There is a short section that has sheep and wild ponies as you pass through open farmland and a quiet access road.

How to get there - Follow the signs for Trefriw on the B5105 form Conwy or Betws y Coed. Once reaching Trefriw follow the brown signs for Llyn Crafnant.

Grid Reference – SH 757618

Parking – Free in Forestry Commission Car Park

Facilities – Toilets in the car park and a café along the way

You will need – Dog leads, the Forestry Commission has a stick and flick policy

The Walk

❶ From the car park go back onto the quiet road and turn right, walking with the forest on both sides of the road and a river on your right. Just before you reach the reservoir turn right.

Your dogs will love the water here. The views of the mountains in the distance are absolutely stunning. Now go through the metal kissing gate and continue on the stoned path. You can let your dogs off the lead here.

Oaks on the right dominate the woodland and the lake is on your left. There is plenty of opportunity for dogs to drink here as water crosses under the path.

After some time you will reach a fork. Take the left path, which descends, keeping to the reservoir. The woodland is mixed here with deciduous and conifer trees and a clear felled area to your right.

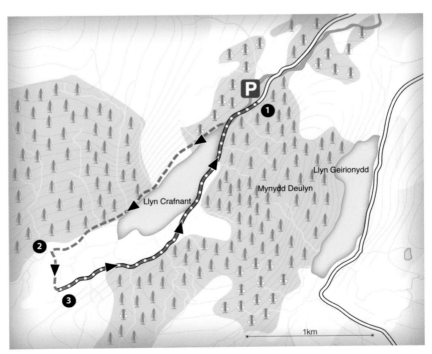

There is a lovely miniature waterfall to your right as a stream races down the hillside. There are splendid views of the mountains ahead of you. You will soon leave the reservoir behind as you continue on this path.

❷ Ignore an uphill track to your right and follow on the path, which winds around large boulders. You will reach a metal kissing gate; pass through this and then a little after, pass through another metal kissing gate. The path bends to the right, leaving the forest where you will reach a small wooden bridge.

Cross the wooden bridge over the stream and turn left. Once reaching a gate put your dogs on leads and then pass through, crossing a concrete bridge on the other side. There are sheep and wild ponies grazing here.

Continue straight ahead on this access track, passing a copse of oak trees. Pass the entrance to a house on the right. You will pass a rocky crag on your right and shortly afterwards another house on the right. The scenery here is really something, with the lake to the far left and the mountain peaks to the right and ahead.

❸ Go through a gate on your left onto a quiet road. There is water here for your dog before you go through the gate. The road is very quiet but there are blind bends so it is best to keep dogs on a lead.

Continue on this quiet sealed road all the way back to the car park. You will pass farmland on either side to begin with and then forest on your right and the reservoir on the left. You will pass some farm buildings and secluded houses and once passing a footpath on the right, you will soon reach a café where you can have a well earned break and enjoy the home made cake. Your dog will find water to drink and a dip in the reservoir near the end. Then turn back along the quiet road to the car park.

6. Llyn Geirionydd

Medium - 3.4 miles - 1hr 45min

This is a lovely walk through beautiful woodlands and forest, with glacial boulders draped in mosses and a lakeside walk along the length of Llyn Geirionydd. There is a steady climb as you pass through forest and you will finish with a walk part way along Llyn Crafnant. There is a small easy boulder section and stiles with dog gates. Part of the walk lies on a quiet access road and there are sheep for a short time. You will find plenty of water for dogs along the way.

How to get there – Take the B5106 from Conwy or Betws y Coed following signs for Trefriw. Once in the village of Trefriw follow the brown signs for Llyn Crafnant.

Grid Reference – SH 755615

Parking – Free in the Car Park

Facilities – Toilets in the Car Park and a Café with toilets along the way.

You will need – Leads, the Forestry Commission has a stick and flick policy

The Walk

❶ From the car park go back to the entrance and take the footpath on the opposite side of the road. Proceed uphill on this forest track. When you reach an exposed rock face, take the narrow path straight on, ignoring the forest track which bends sharply right.

Go over the stile, using the mesh lift gate to the left for your dog. This is an old quarry. When the heather is in flower it is a stunning sight. You will pass the remnants of an old quarry building on your right.

You will have lovely views across the hillside on your left and the rock face is on your right. When you reach a fork, take the right, which ascends up a rocky section. The landscape opens out with scattered trees and bracken. Stay on the obvious path.

You will meet another fork; take the path on the right. Keep to the path between the bracken on a rocky descent. You will see a stone wall to your left. When you reach the wall go through the gap and continue on the worn path through the trees, which are predominantly silver birch.

The area opens out again with scattered trees and bracken. There is stunning scenery all around here and rocky crags scattered across the landscape. Head towards another stone wall which has a ladder stile. Your dog will get through the wire mesh lift gate to the right at the end of the stone wall. Be sure to have your lead ready as there may be sheep grazing here.

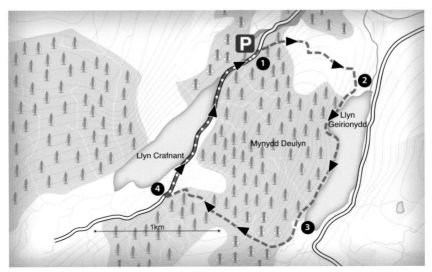

Continue on the obvious path through bracken and gorse. The path bends sharply to the right and ascends towards trees. When you reach the top of the hill keep the trees to your right. There is a stone wall to your left.

❷ There are stunning views ahead of the lake and the hills beyond. You will pass a monument on your left and a slate bench. Continue ahead toward the lake, veering right. When you meet the stone wall at the lake go through the gap, which brings you to the water's edge. Pass through another gap in the stone wall and then over a stile, using the lift gate on the left for your dog. You can now let your dogs off the leads. Continue on this path with the forest to the right and the lake on your left.

The path can get a little rocky in places. There are lots of glacial boulders and bilberry bushes here with some heather. You will need to leave the lake behind for a short while. The path has a little climb through the forest. Pick out your best route where the paths are worn. Follow the path keeping the water's edge in view. The last rocky section can get a little tricky on the descent.

Now you will head back to the water's edge on the path through the forest. You will reach another stile and lift gate (there may be sheep grazing on the other side) where you leave the forest behind, walking in the open grassland. Pass a house on the right and go over another stile. ❸ Go straight ahead, ascending on the forest track through the woods, which are predominantly sycamore to begin with. Ignore the gate and stile on the left and continue straight ahead.

Your dog can get water as a stream passes under the path. The gradient of the path becomes a little steeper here. You will take a left turn off the main track and into the forest, which is indicated by a blue way marker. Follow on this narrow ascending path. You will pass through a gap in the stone wall, continuing ahead on the obvious path through a forest glade. It is all downhill from here. Go through a gap in a fence where the path starts to descend out of the glade and into the dark forest.

Pass through a gap in the stone wall and pass under an oak tree, which is covered in moss. There is an ancient stone wall on the left, which is also green with moss. It is lighter here where the stone wall has allowed a gap in the forest. The path gets a little steeper. There is a stream on the left and below where your dog can get a drink. You will reach a ladder stile - don't go over it but turn left.

❹ There are stunning views on the right here across Llyn Crafnant. Cross the stream via rocks, where you need to put dogs on leads as there is a quiet road ahead. Go through a kissing gate and when reaching the quiet road go right.

You will soon pass a café where you can get a well earned cup of tea and homemade cake. This quiet road will eventually lead you back to the car park. After you pass a monument on your left you can get close to the water's edge and enjoy views over the lake and beyond to the Crimpiau and Creigiau mountains, before continuing on the road to your car.

Countryside Dog Walks - Snowdonia

7. Capel Curig
Medium- 3 miles -1.5hr

This is a beautiful walk with fantastic views of the mountain peaks. It passes through forests with lots of streams for dogs to quench their thirst. There is some fabulous Oak woodland, evergreen with mosses and ferns, glacial boulders and rocky crags. There are sheep in places and a small stretch on a busy road.

How to get there – Capel Curig village is located on the A5 and is sign posted from Betws y Coed and Bethesda. As you enter the village you will see signs for the car park, just to the side of the Pinnacle store.

Grid Reference – SH 721582
Nearest Postcode – LL24 0EN

Parking – Pay and Display car park

Facilities – There are toilets at the car park and a café in the Pinnacle store.

You will need – Dog leads, dog bags.

The Walk

❶ From the car park once on the road go right up the hill and through a gate to avoid the cattle grid. There may be sheep here so keep dogs under close control or on a lead. Take the path immediately left and pass the house on your left. Follow the stock fence on the left and pass the rocky hill on the right.

A stream goes under the path where your dog can get water. The path descends and there are lots of rushes on the right. Pass through another gate and continue to follow the fence line on your right.

Pass through another gate and proceed straight ahead across the middle of the field between the rushes. Your dog will find water as another stream passes under the path. You will see a gate ahead. Ensuring dogs are on leads, pass through the gate, cross the busy road and turn left walking in the lay-by.

❷ At the end of the lay-by take the path on the right through a gate. There are fantastic views across the lake and to Snowdon on your right. Continue

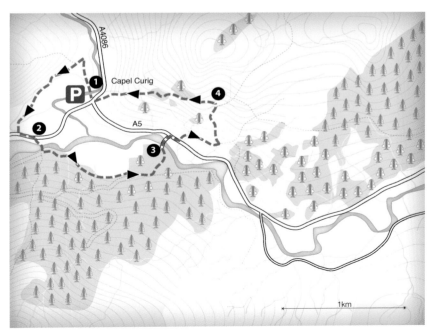

down the steps passing under the pine trees. Cross a bridge where the lake flows into the river. Pass through a gate and then across another bridge.

Where the path meets another path just before the forest, turn left. You will now be walking with the river to your left and the forest to your right. Go through the gate onto the stony path. You can let your dog off the lead here.

Soon you will have trees on both sides and the path starts to ascend as you near a house on the left. The forest is now woodland with some mature oaks that are cloaked in mosses and ferns. There are rocks and boulders all covered in moss and the woodland here is truly magnificent with mostly oaks and silver birch.

Your dog will find lots of water, because there are streams passing under the path in places. When you reach the house, pass through a gate and continue straight ahead. You will have views of Snowdon to the left in places where the trees allow.

Continue straight ahead ignoring the path that goes right and uphill as the paths merge. Now descend, staying on the main path as it bends sharply left. Pass through another gate at the brow of the hill. Dogs must be put on leads now as there is a road ahead.

❸ The track descends here. Cross a bridge and go through a gate to avoid the cattle grid. Cross the road and turn right. There is a dog friendly café here if you need a break.

Pass the café and car park then take the footpath on the left, which is an access road for a couple of houses. Go through a kissing gate on the right before reaching a house. Keep on this tarmac drive heading towards another house. Follow with the stock fence to your right and fields on a hillside to your left. Ascend the hill passing the house on your right.

The path bends sharply left. Pass through a gate and follow the hazel hedge left, where you will pass a wooden chalet to your right. A stream flows on the right of the path here where your dog can get water.

You will pass a silver birch copse of trees to your left followed by pine trees. Take the footpath through the gate on the left just as the path bends sharply to the right. Once through the gate, go right and follow the fence line on your right. Pass through another gate as you walk under the pine trees, then up some stone steps. Once at the top you will be met by water as it tumbles over some rocks.

Cross a couple of stone bridges over streams then follow the stone slab path for a short distance. Once the stone slabs end underfoot veer to the left, not

towards the bridge. Once crossing another stone slab you will see a path coming from the small bridge ahead. Turn left here. ❹

Pass through a gap in the stone wall and follow the path with the fence line to your left. Pass through open farmland with gorse scrub. Go through a gate and continue with the fence line to your left. You will have oak coppice on your right and views of Snowdon straight ahead. There are glacial boulders and bracken here.

Continue straight on, cutting across the hillside where you reach more mature oaks with the woodland floor covered in moss. Pass through another gap in the stone wall, ascending with some steps through the beautiful ancient woodlands.

Pass through a gate leaving the woodland behind, and again you will find yourself in open grassland with gorse scrub and rocky outcrops. Stay on the stone slab path through the field with stunning views of the mountains ahead. There is a lovely rocky crag on the left with oaks growing over it.

Pass through a gap in the stone wall and then keep to the right, following beside the stock fence for a short distance. Then head for the church ahead, descending the hill. Go through the gate. Once at the road turn right, and cross with care just after the bend in the road toward the shops on the opposite side. Take the road on the left of the shops to the car park.

8. Miners Bridge

Easy - 1.5 miles - 45min

This is a linear walk along the river Llugwy that passes through wonderful woodland, farmland and forest to reach an unusual bridge with a steep decline, taking you into a wonderful atmospheric rocky area where you stand next to the powerful river with a gentle waterfall that tumbles down from a height above you. There are no roads on this walk but there are sheep for a short section.

How to get there – Betws y Coed is reached from the A470 and the A5. Once in the village you need to cross the Pont y Pair Bridge and then left to find the car park.

Grid Reference – SH 795566
Nearest Postcode – LA24 0BB

Parking – Pay and Display at Pont y Pair Car Park

Facilities – Toilets in the car park and many places for refreshments in the village.

You will need – Dog leads, dog bags

The Walk

❶ From the car park turn right then almost immediately left onto the footpath, walking with the river to the left, between the trees. You can let your dog off the lead here. Pass over a wooden boardwalk through the mixed woodland.

Continue straight ahead after the boardwalk through the trees on the main path. Once reaching the picnic benches and rocky outcrop continue straight on, veering left towards the river passing the rocky outcrop on your right.

❷ Put your dog on the lead and then go through the kissing gate into farmland, crossing over the stone bridge across the river. Stay on this path following the river on your left. Cross another wooden bridge over the stream, passing under the lovely mature oak trees swathed with mosses and lichens. Pass through another kissing gate where you can let your dog off the lead once more.

Walk straight ahead over the small rocks and tree roots, following near to the river's edge. There are lots of boulders in the river, which look glorious as the river washes over them. There is a thick forest to your right and some deciduous trees on the edge of the river to your left, with boulders of rock that are dressed in moss. The path will start to ascend on the rocky outcrop.

❸ You will reach a sharply sloping bridge on your left that will take you across the river. This is the furthest point of the walk. You may cross the river if you wish, to stand on the rocky boulders below and watch as the river rushes past and the shower-like waterfall falls away from the rocks on the other side.

Now it's back the way that you came, remembering to put your dog back on the lead before going through the kissing gate to enter farmland. Follow the river back to where you have parked your car.

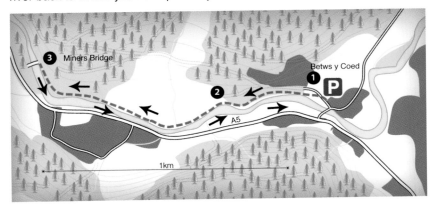

38

9. Llyn y Parc

Medium - 2.5 miles - 1.5hrs

This is a super walk through the forest following a stream with a beautiful waterfall. You will reach a lake, Llyn y Parc, where you can rest after an uphill climb. Then you will turn back along another path, passing through some woodland and following narrow paths through the middle of the forest, over some exposed bedrock. For small parts of the walk you may come across mountain bikes. There are no roads except a quiet one at the beginning and end and no livestock.

How to get there – Betws y Coed is reached from the A470 and the A5. Once in the village you need to cross the Pont y Pair Bridge and then left to find the car park.

Grid Reference – SH 795566
Nearest Postcode – LA24 0BB

Parking – Pay and Display at Pont y Pair Car Park

Facilities – Toilets in the car park and many places for refreshments in the village.

You will need – Dog leads, dog bags - once in the forest the Forestry Commission have a stick and flick policy.

The Walk

❶ From the car park turn right on the road and proceed uphill. Take the next road on the right and continue past the houses. As the road bends sharply left, ignore the first track on the right and take the next right, which is a wider track that ascends into the forest.

When you reach the brow of the hill take the narrow path on the left, which inclines and cuts across the hillside. Pass between moss covered boulders and then rock faces to your left. Your dog will find water where a stream goes under the path. Keep straight on here ignoring the paths left and right.

There are some oaks and holly here to the edge of the path, amongst the conifer trees. There is also heather and ferns amongst the mosses to the edges of the rock faces. Continue on the path, ignoring another path to the right.

Once the path levels out you will soon see the river as it flows down the hill. The path becomes a little steeper now and rocky underfoot. You will see mine workings to the left of the path and more streams flowing under the path where your dog can get water.

❷ You will see a retaining stone wall on your left and the waterfall on your right. You will now be walking close to the fast flowing stream on your right. Cross the bridge and continue on the forest path, passing a cottage to the left.

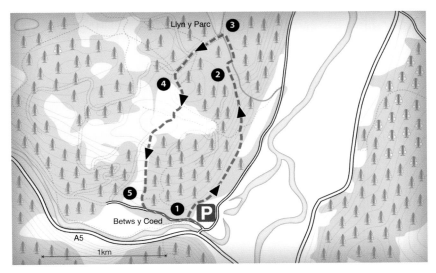

3 You will reach a lake where you can sit awhile and let your dog cool off. Once rested, standing by the bench with your back to the lake, take the track on the right. Stay on the wider track ignoring the path on the left and then a little further on ignore a footpath on the right. Turn left, once meeting another main forest track. When you reach a fork take the left turn. You will see some nice rock faces on the left and a stone wall to your right. There are some oaks here to the edge of the forest.

A little further on you will see a ruined house on the right, and just after, there is a small footpath to the right. This path descends into mixed woodlands with a stone wall to your right. **4** Turn left when meeting another track. You will be walking on a raised path through the woods, cutting across the hillside.

Continue straight ahead ignoring the path to the left. A little further take the path going right following blue way markers, passing fenced off old mine shafts. Ascend on a small rocky section where you will enter a forest clearing.

Follow the blue way markers here as you pass through gorse and heather. The path will descend and there is a left turn as you head back into the forest. Pass over another rocky section that is green with mosses, still descending quite steeply in places.

The path bends sharply to the right and meets a stream. Then it bends sharply left. Ignore a path to the left and continue straight ahead. You will meet up with a wider forest track; go left onto this path. This path merges with another path and you will pass houses on the left. Soon you will be on a familiar path where it bends sharply right. Stay on this road, turning left at the end onto another road, which descends back down to the car park.

10. Llyn Elsi

Medium - 2 miles - 1hr 30min

This is a super walk through forest and woodland with heathland and fantastic mountain views across the lake Llyn Elsi. Your dogs will enjoy running up and down the many paths through the forest. There are lots of streams where your dog can find water and no livestock. There are roads at the beginning and end of the walk with a steady incline at the start of the forest.

How to get there - Betws y Coed is reached from the A470 and the A5. Once in the village follow the signs for the train station and parking will be found on your left hand side of Station Approach road.

Grid reference – SH 794 567
Nearest postcode – LL24 0AE

Parking – Pay and display car park

Facilities – Toilets and shops next to car park

You will need – Dog leads, dog bags - once in the forest the Forestry Commission have a stick and flick policy.

Countryside Dog Walks - Snowdonia

The Walk

❶ From the car park go back onto the main road and turn left. Take the second road on the right, just before Cotswolds outdoor shop. Proceed uphill and after passing the garage on the right hand side take the public footpath before the Vagabond Hostel.

Go up the steps. The path will incline for a time, passing through some wonderful woodland with a field boundary to your right.

Turn sharp left at the rock face, then cross a footbridge over a stream. There is a sharp bend to the right when you reach a fence. Pass rocky crags and boulders that are draped in moss.

The trees become mixed broadleaved and coniferous. Stay on the path with the stone wall to your right. You will then pass the end of a stone wall on your left where you continue straight ahead. The stream will be on the right and below you.

You will cross the stream via another bridge and continue straight ahead. When you meet the wider forest track turn left and continue your ascent. Your dogs will find water to the right of the path.

Ignore a path on the right that goes over a bridge and continue straight ahead. You will have views on your left as you gain a little height. Ignore a couple of paths left and continue straight ahead, passing stone building ruins at ground level.

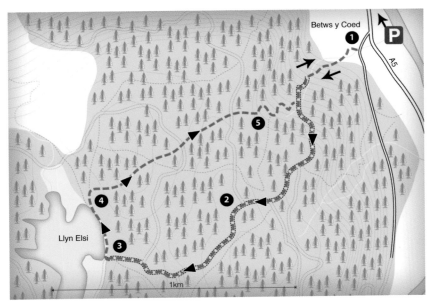

❷ As the incline levels out you will pass an old ruined building on the right. Your dog will find water on the left on this path. There are lots of mosses, ferns, bilberry and heather here on the forest floor. Continue on this path for some time.

When you reach another path turn right, then on meeting another path turn left. There are stunning views of the peaks ahead. Once near the lake you will see a path on the right between some standing stones. **❸** Take this narrow path where you pass some silver birch trees and gorse.

An incline brings you to the end of this path, where there is a bench and a monument. Stop and absorb the wonderful scenery over the quiet lake and beyond to the mountain peaks. The monument celebrates the opening of the water works in 1914. **❹** Standing with your back to the lake facing the monument, take the footpath to the right. Follow the well-worn path over some rocky sections. Pass through the heathland areas, where there has been clear felling in the forest. Walk between the gorse, bracken and heather.

On your descent you will pass rocky crags with some regenerating woodland. Cross a wider forest track and continue on a narrow path through the forest clearing towards a rocky crag and back into the forest. Follow the obvious path, which can get muddy. Again cross a wider forest track and continue on the narrow path descending through the trees. There are mixed woodlands here amongst the coniferous trees. Pass a stone wall on the left where the woodlands are again mostly deciduous.

❺ Follow the rocky descent on the narrow path, which has several sharp bends. Cross over a footbridge and turn left on the familiar wider forest track. Take the next footpath descending on the right. Cross the footbridge over the stream and then the path will turn sharply to the right and then left. Cross over another bridge and continue to follow the path, which descends back down to the road. Once at the road, turn left. When you reach the main road, turn left and continue back to Station Approach road where you have parked your car.

11. Gelert's Grave

Easy - 1.5 mile - 1hr

This is a lovely walk starting at the beautiful village of Beddgelert, passing the grave of the famous dog Gelert from which the village gets its name. You will pass alongside the river Afon Glaslyn and a short climb will bring you through some lovely woodland with many streams, where your dog can take a drink. The walk passes through farmland and some heathland. There are some roads and there may be sheep in parts.

How to get there – Beddgelert is situated between the A498 from Porthmadog/Betws-y-Coed and the A4085 from Caernarfon.

Grid Reference – SH 588481
Nearest Post Code – LL55 4YE

Parking– Pay and Display at the Dolfair Car Park

Facilities – Toilets and refreshments in the village

You will need – Dog leads, dog bags

The Walk

1 From the car park head back onto the road and take the second left. Pass the tourist information on your left and before reaching the road bridge turn right.

Pass the shop frontages to your right and the river on the left. You will pass the toilet block at the end of the shops. Do not cross the bridge at the end of the road, but go through the gate on the right just before it.
2 Walk on the concrete path with the river to your left.

Pass the church on the right and some mature trees that are covered in lichens. When you reach the stone wall turn right, following the sign to Gelert's grave. Go through a gate on your

GELERT'S GRAVE

In the 13th Century Llywelyn, Prince of North Wales had a palace at Beddgelert. One day he went hunting without Gelert "the faithful hound" who was unaccountably absent. On Llywelyn's return, the truant stained and smeared with blood joyfully sprang to meet his master. The Prince alarmed hastened to find his son and saw the infant's cot empty. The bed clothes and floor covered with blood. The frantic father plunged his sword into the hound's side thinking it had killed his heir. The dog's dying yell was answered by a child's cry. Llywelyn searched and discovered his boy unharmed but near by lay the body of a mighty wolf which Gelert had slain.
The Prince filled with remorse is said never to have smiled again, he buried Gelert here.
The spot is called

BEDDGELERT

left and follow the path to Gelert's grave. Continue on this path heading towards the ruined stone building. Be sure to look inside the building before passing it. **3** Pass the building and go through the gate crossing the middle of a field, heading for the gate on the opposite side.

Putting dogs on leads, pass through the gate and cross the road. Continue up a slope and through another gate taking care as you cross the railway. Continue uphill but take the gate on the right. Your dog will find water here as

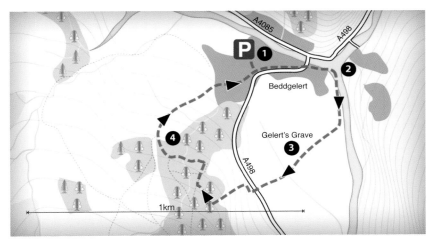

a stream passes under the path. Go immediately left up the grass bank. Pass a mature oak tree, which is covered in moss. Follow past the silver birch trees towards the rocky crag, which is green with moss. Keep the crag to your right, then walk with the moss covered stone wall to your left.

You will ascend some steps and again your dog will find water. Continue ascending on the obvious path to eventually cross a boardwalk over a stream. After the boardwalk go left. Go through a gate into beech dominated woods, with rocky outcrops. Walk between the rocky crags and head for the stone wall. You will see a gap in the stone wall towards the right.

Go through the gap and turn right at the way marker. Once you reach another way marker where the woods open out go right and descend with the stone wall on your right. Passing under the beech trees ignore the gate on the right and continue straight ahead, still descending. Pass the graveyard on your right and cross a stream via a footbridge. Continue along the edge of a stream on your right. You will reach a footbridge on your right, which crosses the stream. Do not cross this but follow the way marker towards the left following the worn path. You will reach another way marker, turn right, firstly crossing a stream. You will see a tall stone wall and a gate near the corner. ❹ Go through the gate and left towards the ladder stile but not over it or through the gate.

Follow along the stone wall on your left with stunning views of the mountain peaks ahead, walking along the edge of a field with lots of moss hillocks and soft rush. You will start to veer away from the stone wall, following the way marker. Pass a large boulder on your left and go through a gap in the stone wall, heading for the gable end of a house. Pass through a kissing gate and over the railway bridge. Pass the houses and head down the narrow lane straight ahead. Cross the quiet road following the road downhill passing more houses. You will reach a road where you turn left. Once reaching the main road turn left. Then take the next road left to the car park.

12. Llyn Mair

Medium - 2.5 miles - 1hr 30min

This is a fantastic walk with lakeside paths, following two quiet scenic lakes, Llyn Mair and later Llyn Hafod. You will pass through fantastic oak woodlands and quiet forests with glades, which have stunning mountain views, as well as the lovely Tan y Bwlch steam railway station where you can get refreshments. This really is a gem that both you and your dog will enjoy. There is a small section of road on this walk.

How to get there - From Porthmadog, take the A487 towards Blaenau Ffestiniog. At the Oakley Arms, turn left onto the B4410. When you see the lake Llyn Mair on the left look out for the car park on the right.

Grid Reference – SH 652413

Parking – Free in the car park

Facilities – There are no facilities in the car park but near the end of the walk there is a café and toilets at the railway station.

You will need – Dog leads, dog bags

The Walk

1 From the car park cross the road at the entrance and go through the wooden gate opposite. Your dogs can get water from a stream to your left as you walk towards the lake. Continue on the gravel path, passing through a gap beside a field gate. Passing through beautiful woodland, take a path that veers off to the left descending deeper into the woods towards the lake. Pass over a sleeper bridge to cross a stream. Go through the gap at the stone wall into Coed Hafod Llyn.

Walk beside the stone wall on the left, passing under the lovely mature oaks with lichens, ferns and mosses covering the bark. There are pockets of heather and bilberry where light enters the woodland floor. Cross over a couple of bridges to pass a pool, where a river flows through from the hillside, creating a small waterfall as it spills out into the river below. The path will get a little rocky as you walk over the exposed bedrock.

Staying with the side of the lake ignore the path on the right. Pass between the old gate posts as you reach a stone wall. Once reaching another path near to the end of the lake turn right. **2**

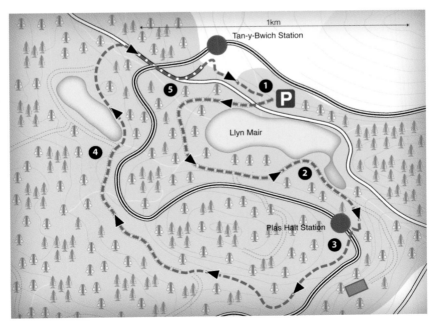

You will pass rocky crags to your left and a dammed section of the river below. Now take the next path on the right. Take another right turn, which has an upward slope. You will meet with another path, again turning right, staying on your ascent toward the railway line. The path has a number of switchbacks with lovely views as you climb through the trees. Ignore the paths to the right and left as you ascend. Taking care, with dogs on leads, pass through the gate to cross the railway. ❸ Turn left once through the second gate. The path will ascend across the edge of the hillside, entering into deciduous woodland. You will have views to the left where the trees allow.

The path will begin to descend, following the railway below for a short time passing rocky outcrops and patches of heather and bilberry. Where the path has a short ascent you will reach a rock outcrop to your left, where you will have amazing views across the valley to the hills and mountains beyond. Take care, as there is a drop here.

Continue along the path, where there are many oaks dominating the woodland. You will meet with another narrow path. Turn right here and pass between the old gate posts in the stone wall. Continue through the beautiful oak woodlands on the path, which ascends slightly passing exposed rock and boulders. Cross a small stream. Just after you will have forest on your left and oak woods on your right. A little further along, you will join another wider path turning left. Once reaching the forest track turn right. You will have wonderful mountain views to your right over the forest clearing.

On reaching another track turn left. You will pass a stream on the left that passes under the path where your dog can find water. Ignore a path that goes toward the railway crossing on your right. Continue straight ahead, passing a house to your left. Take the next path on the right that leads to the reservoir. This is a lovely place to stop at the picnic bench. ❹ Continue on this path passing the sluice gate and crossing a bridge into beautiful oak woodlands once more.

Keep to the gravel path, which follows the lake at first and then goes into the forest. After a while the path curves back around and you will meet briefly with the lake once more. Then, on meeting with a wider forest track, turn right, putting dogs on leads as there is a road ahead. Pass a parking bay and turn right at the road. Walking on the right hand side of the road you will pass under a railway bridge.

❺ Cross the road on reaching the entrance to Tan y Bwlch railway and proceed to the station where you can stop at the café to enjoy a well-earned cup of tea. Dogs are allowed in the outdoor seating area. Once rested continue towards the wooden railway bridge, but take the path on the right just before it. Descend the steps ignoring the path on the left. Continue on your downhill path and pass thorough a gap in the stone wall. When reaching a fork take the right-hand path, which takes you back into the lovely oak woodland. Keep to this path, which descends back to the car park.

Countryside Dog Walks - Snowdonia

13. Coed y Brenin

Medium - 4.5 miles - 2hrs

This is much more than your typical forest walk. It has beautiful deciduous woodland, two waterfalls which thunder down the rocks after rainfall, rivers, streams and delightful views. There are well marked guided routes through the forest, and this walk is the most challenging one. The walk is cleverly designed by the Forestry Commission to keep the tracks segregated from the popular mountain bike routes. There are some upward climbs but nothing too steep, with lots of level paths in between. There are other well-marked routes to choose from all starting from the visitor centre, but this one is a beauty. There are no roads and no livestock, but deer are in the area. There is lots of water along the way for dogs, but take care as the river can be fast flowing.

How to get there – From Betws y Coed follow signs for Blaenau Ffestiniog and then Dolgellau on the A470 where Coed y Brenin will be found before reaching Dolgellau on the left hand side of the road.

Grid reference – SH 725268
Postcode – LL40 2HY

Parking – Tyddyn Gwladys car park pay and display

Facilities – Café, visitor centre, toilets all from the car park

You will need – Dog leads, dog bags for car park area otherwise stick and flick

The Walk

❶ From the visitor centre, follow the path to the car park and turn right. Continue along the path; the visitor centre will be below and to your right. Follow on the slate gravel path passing the Britten pan display on your left and following the red way marked path.

You will be walking in the delightful mixed woodland, which are mostly broadleaved trees. There are wood sorrel, bluebells and ferns on the woodland floor and rocky boulders blanketed with moss, all giving a mix of colour. You will pass an old stone wall with thick moss covering the rocks on your left. The path inclines gradually, with switchbacks on the steeper sections making it easy to gain height. Once reaching a main forest track turn right following the red arrows all the way. You will meet with another forest track, cross this and take the narrow path straight ahead into the forest. **❷** This path ascends quite steeply at first then gradually. Follow the worn path with a stone wall on the right.

The path leads you back into mixed woodlands for a while, turning right once reaching a main forest track. A little further on turn left onto a narrow path, which gradually inclines for some distance. Once the path levels out there

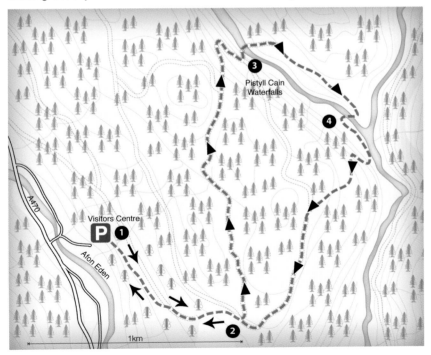

are rocky outcrops and pockets of heather and bilberry to the left. As you enter into the forest the path starts to decline with bright green mosses on the forest floor, adding colour where other plants can not grow. You will then pass through a forest clearing with natural regeneration taking place.

The path will incline again and you will come to a path junction. Beware of cyclists here as they cross the path ahead. Ignore the left and right paths and take the next right path immediately after and then turn left onto a wider forest track. Descend again until you reach the bottom and then turn right, looking down into the beautiful valley with mixed woodland dominated by silver birch. The path descends once more and at the bottom turn left and cross a stone bridge over the river. ❸

Continue straight ahead, now on a level path, and once reaching a sharp bend to the left take the path straight ahead and then turn onto a grassy path on your right almost immediately entering silver birch woodland. Take care ahead as mountain bikes cross the path. Cross the cycle path and continue straight ahead on an upward climb for a short section followed by a steep descent. Turn right when you reach another track and again you will cross a cycle path and continue to descend through the mature silver birch woodland. This path can get a little rocky and you will soon hear the waterfall.

❹ At the end of the path, before reaching a lovely bridge, turn right. The river is fast flowing here especially after rainfall so beware of dogs that love to get in the water. A little further along there is a path where you can access the river. Continue on the path now. Head towards the waterfall and just a little after reaching it you will see a path to the left; this is a detour to view the waterfall. It is best to have dogs on leads, as there are rock faces with drops into the river if they go off the path. You will see old mine buildings here, where gold panning took place.

Once viewing the waterfall go back to the path and turn left to continue where you will reach another waterfall. This is an awesome sight as the water powers down the rock face into the gorge below. Cross the bridge and view the gorge on both sides. It is truly tremendous, especially after rainfall when the rivers are swollen. Continue on with the river below, and just a little further

you can see where the two rivers meet to become one. You will pass an old mine building on the right and just after this take the narrow path on the right which inclines into the forest. The path cuts along the bilberry covered hillside.

Turn right when you meet a wider path to continue on an ascent. Soon after, just before reaching a bend, turn left onto another narrow path, which ascends quite steeply, with a number of switchbacks to lessen the gradient. You can stop every now and then and look behind at the views. When you reach the top of this path turn left onto a wider track, and you will be pleased to see a gradual descent. There is another cycle track ahead; ignore the left and right turn where mountain bikes cross the forest track. Continue straight ahead for some distance. Just as the track inclines, turn onto a path on the left where you retrace your steps descending with a stone wall on your left and farmland to the other side. Once reaching a wider track, cross it to continue straight ahead, taking the gravel path to the left of the track. Turn left onto a path once again through the deciduous woodland, with moss blanketing the trunks of the trees, following the path leading back to the visitor centre and car park.

14. Mynydd Penrhos

Chall.- 2.5 miles - 2hr

A walk in the forest, which begins beside a river that has a waterfall and white-water rapids. There is a quite a climb which brings panoramic views across the valley. There are sections of broad-leaved trees amongst the conifers. With mosses all year round on the forest floor adding a green glow. There is water along the way from the streams that flow beneath the paths. Your dog can run free as there are no livestock, although there may be deer.

How to get there - From Betws y Coed follow signs for Blaenau Ffestiniog and then Dolgellau on the A470, passing Coed y Brenin on your left. On passing the village Ganllwyd look for the brown signs for the forest park on the left, before reaching Dolgellau.

Grid reference – SH 716277
Nearest postcode – LL40 2HN

Parking - Free in the Tyn y Groes car park

Facilities – There are toilets, picnic tables and a BBQ

You will need – Dog leads

The Walk

❶ From the car park follow the green trail passing the toilet block on your left and cross the road to follow the path parallel with the river. Pass across the lawn area with picnic tables and a brick BBQ.

Take care with dogs as you near the river, because it is fast flowing. You will enter the forest with some mixed broadleaved trees to the edge, with wood sorrel, ferns and rhododendron on the forest floor.

Take the path on the right to view the waterfall as it enters the river. The path will then join back onto the original path turning right. The path inclines a little and you will pass a path on the right. Stay on the surfaced path, which veers away from the river.

❷ Put your dog on the lead, as there is a road ahead. Cross the road and follow the narrow path opposite which ascends the hillside. There are lots of spring violets on each side of the path. Take care here as a mountain bike trail crosses the path ahead.

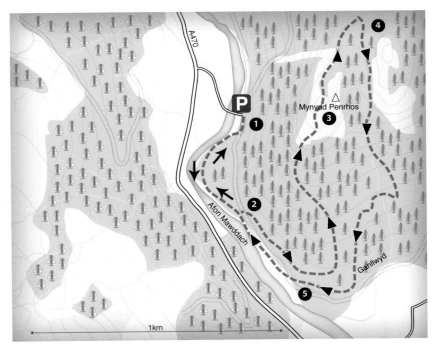

Take the path to the left above the cycle track, passing rock faces to the left and passing amongst the rhododendrons on each side of the path. Ascend the steps on the path as it cuts through the hillside.

You will walk beside the great root plates from the wind-blown trees. Bilberry and mosses cover the forest floor, with large tree roots crossing the path. Ignore a path on the right and continue on the ascent, which will get a little steeper.

The path widens and the forest opens out with some broadleaved trees. You will reach a turning circle for forest vehicles. Turn left here, passing through a wooden barrier. Continue on your ascent, where the path will get quite steep.

❸ You will reach a level, which brings panoramic views across the valley. Once you have got your breath back, continue on the path, which has a gradual slope, with heather, bilberry and gorse. There are some broadleaved trees here amongst the pines.

Pass a nicely carved bench, where you can get a well earned rest. There are views on both sides, wherever there are gaps in the trees. The path will start to descend. You will pass over an old stone wall at ground level and then again as you leave the walled enclosure.

❹ You will pass through another wooden barrier and then turn right onto a track, which has a little uphill section followed by a gradual descent. After passing through another barrier the path will descend more steeply.

Pass through another barrier and then, once you reach the path, turn right on another slight ascent. You will pass a stream here that goes under the path, where dogs can get a drink. Turn left now to descend, gradually into the forest.

When reaching a bend turn left on a steeper descent and when you reach another path turn right. You will pass over some exposed rock as the path levels out. When you reach a fork put your dog on the lead and take the left path, which parallels the road. **❺**

Once reaching the road cross over and turn right, where you will soon reach a path on the left, take this path back into the forest. You will pass another stream and then you will be on the path that parallels the river once more. The river has a stunning rapid white-water section, which races over rocks.

You will meet back on a familiar gravel path, following this back to the car park.

15. Tal-y-bont

Medium - 3.5 miles - 2hrs

This is an amazing walk that you and your dog will enjoy. Your dog will have plenty of opportunity to run free, as there are no livestock or roads in the beautiful oak woodland, where the trees are wrapped in green mosses and ferns - it really is delightful. You will see an ancient Iron Age burial chamber and mountain and sea views as you pass through farmland along a beautiful clear river with glacial boulders. Ferns and mosses dominate the woodland valley floor, making it all spectacular and plenty of water all the way for dogs. There is one quiet road and you will encounter sheep when walking through a section of farmland.

How to get there – Take the A496 from Barmouth heading to Harlech. Once in the village of Tal y bont cross over the road bridge and then turn right where you will find the car park. There is further parking if you need it: pass the car park, turn immediate right and go along the access road.

Grid Reference – SH 590217
Nearest postcode – LL43 2AN

Parking – Free in the car park

Facilities – There are toilets in the car park

You will need – Dog leads, dog bags

The Walk

❶ From the furthest car park go past the pub on your right and head for the stone building at the far end of the car park, passing the building by going to the right of it. As you pass the building you will be near the river.

Ignore the bridge on the right and pass through a gate into oak woodland. Ignore another bridge on the right and follow the path that parallels the river. Pass through a gap in the stone wall.

The path becomes a little rocky underfoot. Cross over a sleeper bridge where a lovely stream hurries down the hillside. The ground is blanketed in moss with pockets of heather adding lovely colours to the woodland floor.

Follow up the steps climbing high above the water, where there is lots of holly and ferns in the understory. Once reaching another path turn right to begin a descent back to the river.

Several tree species in this section of the woodland replace some of the oaks, becoming mixed deciduous woodland. As the path and river bend sharply to the left you will meet another path. **❷** Take the left turn, which ascends, leaving the river behind you and following near to a stone wall on your right.

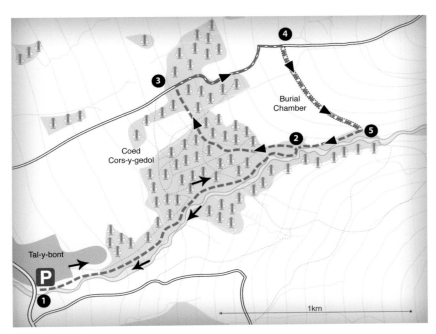

The river can be seen down below on your left. Ignore a path to the left and continue on the worn path through the woodland. Go through a gate to walk between two stone walls. You will now have sea views on your left.

❸ You will meet a gate onto a quiet road. Putting your dog on the lead pass through the gate and turn right onto the road. Head towards Cors y Gedol Hall and turn right on reaching the Hall entrance gate. Follow the quiet road passing Beudy Ronw farmhouse. You will have hill views ahead and to your right. Pass the farmyard on the left and Cors y Gedol farmhouse as the road bends sharply to the right.

Ignore the footpath on the left and continue on this road as it starts to ascend. Once reaching the end of the road, passing a parking area on your right which serves for walkers going to Moel Fre, you will see the hill straight ahead of you. **❹** Take the gate on the right hand side, not straight ahead. Sheep may be grazing here.

Continue on this tarmac path, with the stone wall to your right. You will have mountain views behind you, hills to your left and coastal views on your right. Passing between the gorse, which gives colour no matter what the month, you will soon see an ancient burial chamber on your left. The path will start to descend towards woodland. Ignore the footpath on the left immediately before a house and take the right path into the woods with the river below on your left. **❺**

Descend the path with some rocky sections through the beautiful mixed broadleaved woodland, passing huge rocky boulders in and around the river. Pass through a gate and continue along the path. Continue descending now close to the river, ignoring a path to your right. You are now back on a familiar path, which will eventually lead back to the car park. Remember to take the left lower path when the path splits into two.

16. Abergwynant Woods Med. - 4miles - 2hr

This is a super walk with fantastic mountain views across the estuary, where you can watch the wading birds on the marsh. Then there is a walk in beautiful woodlands beside a clear river, which your dog will love to explore and after a climb you can picnic on a bench with beautiful views. There are no roads but the Mawddach trail is popular with cyclists. Please avoid letting your dog go onto the marshes, as this is a wildlife reserve.

How to get there – From Dolgellau, take the A493 signed for Tywyn. Follow the signs for the Toll bridge and parking once reaching the village of Penmaenpool.

Grid Reference – SH 696185
Postcode – LL40 1YD

Parking – Free in the car park

Facilities – There are toilets in the car park and a pub

You will need – Dog leads, dog bags

Countryside Dog Walks - Snowdonia

The Walk

❶ Put you dog on a lead to begin with. From the car park pass the signal box and toilet block then cross the road beside the toll bridge. You will pass the old railway station with wonderful estuary views to your right. Continue on this path passing the hotel and car park and then several houses. Go through a gate, where the path narrows and is enclosed at first with trees on either side.

As the path opens out again you will have views once more of the estuary and mountain peaks beyond. Further ahead you will pass a picnic bench on your left and an interpretation panel on the right. Ignore the gate on your left and continue along the estuary. Looking down the estuary towards the sea you can almost see the hills on each side touching as they slope down into the water. You will pass woodlands to your left and lovely rock faces. **❷** Just before you reach a bridge across a river take the path on the left passing through a gate into the woodland. Ignore a path to the left and continue along the river. This is lovely and clear with a small beach area where your dog can enjoy the water. Continue now following the river for a while. You will meet with a stone wall on your right as the river veers away. Ignore the stile on your right. Pass a gateway to a farm where looking right you will have lovely mountain views.Pass a house, stone barn and a walled garden with another larger house to the right. The path now inclines quite steeply into the woods with some stone steps in places, passing lovely rock faces.

As the path levels out you will see a path on the right, where you can see more mountain views as you look across the valley and estuary. Take the path to the right, descending the steps. Take a narrow path on your right, which begins to incline. Ignore a path on the right and continue up the steps weaving through the trees. **❸** You will reach a picnic bench, where you can stop for a peaceful rest amongst the trees with stunning views across the estuary.

Turn back a little way until you descend two steps and then take the path left on a descent once again. You will descend through the delightful oak and holly woodland with patches of heather and glacial boulders hidden under mosses. There are steps made from split oak in the steeper sections. Pass through an oak hand-crafted gate and turn right on this familiar path back to your car.

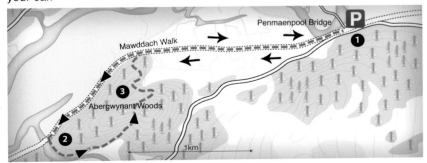

17. Dolgellau

Medium - 2 miles - 1hr 30min

This is a lovely walk, conveniently placed close to the town centre. It passes through fantastic native woodland with some forest and woodland pasture. There is a beautiful river and weir where you can sit and enjoy the tranquillity, and views over Dolgellau and the surrounding hills. There are gradual hills to climb with only one short steep section and a quiet wooded lane. There may be sheep for a short section of the walk and there are roads to and from the town. You will find water along the way for dogs.

How to get there – Take the A470 into Dolgellau and once in the main town centre follow signs for the car park.

Grid reference – SH 727179
Nearest postcode – LL40 1DL

Parking – Pay and display

Facilities – There are toilets in the town and various shops and cafes.

You will need – Dog leads, dog bags

The Walk

❶ From the car park facing the Yr Hen Efail tearoom take the passage to the right, passing the tearoom on your left. On reaching the road turn right and then turn left. You will reach a main road where you cross to the other side and turn right.

Pass a road on the right and then cross over to go up Pant yr Arran/Arran road. Pass over the road bridge to cross the river and then immediately right into the residential area. Once meeting with another road turn right and follow the road right to the end where you will see a way marker.

Ignore the footpath to the left at the way marker and take the path on the right. Ascend the sealed path, passing a house on the right. ❷ You will see an entrance for Coed Aberneint on your right. Go through the entrance and follow the grassy path descending the hillside. You will pass under some mature beech and oak trees. Once at the bottom you will see a weir to your right and a kissing gate on the left. Go through the kissing gate to cross the bridge over the river. Make sure your dog is under close control as there is a road ahead.

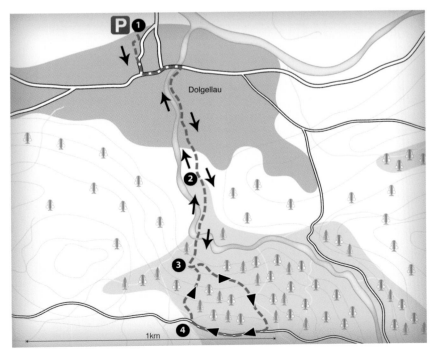

3 Cross the road and go through the entrance to the woods on the opposite side. Take the path on the right ascending into the woods. Ignore a narrow path on the left and a little further on pass another path on the right. Keep going on the ascent and on reaching a fork take the path on the right. There are lots of ferns on the woodland floor with wood sorrel and violets in the spring. The trees change to coniferous forest and the path will get quite steep. On reaching the top of the hill go through the gate where you will be in woodland once more. There may be sheep grazing here so keep your dog under close control or on a lead.

Keep to the worn path through the woods with only a slight ascent now. The woodlands are dominated by silver birch here and you will pass through woodland pasture. Continue following a stone track, passing through a kissing gate onto the road. Turn right and continue along this quiet road through wood pasture, with rocky boulders here and there.

There is a short incline and then the road descends gradually. Continue on until you reach a farm gate. **4** Turn right here to enter back into the woods. There is a stream to your left where your dog can get a drink. Follow the path through the woods, then ascend the steps passing through the gate and down steps again as you pass through the stone wall. Descend on the worn path through mixed woodland. You will meet with another path. Turn left here to descend, on a familiar path. Remember to call your dogs close, as there is a road ahead.

You will reach the road once more, crossing and taking the path opposite crossing the bridge again. You may wish to rest at the weir and enjoy the water, before ascending again through the hillside. Once nearing the top of the hill at the fork take the left path, where you will be met by stunning views over Dolgellau and the surrounding hills. Pass through the exit and turn left to retrace your steps. On reaching the road continue straight ahead, keeping the river on your left. You will pass once more over the bridge. At the main road in the town, turn left and follow the signs for the car park back to your car.

Mountains of Snowdonia

Our next three walks take you into the mountainous terrain of Snowdonia. On a fine summer day these three walks are a true pleasure and safe for reasonably fit dogs and dog walkers.

We do need to stress though that due care and caution are essential as the mountain weather can change within minutes. Please read the information in the Snowdon walk before venturing on these walks.

18. Snowdon

Challenging - 7.6 miles - 6hrs

A truly amazing experience: climbing the highest mountain in Wales and England. There are well made paths almost all the way to the top. There are no big drops to make you nervous; there are four or five small rocky sections to scramble but these are by no means difficult and you will only need to use your hands on the way down. Once reaching the top you will be rewarded with the most fabulous panoramic views, which are totally awe inspiring. The walk is linear and so you can choose to reduce the difficulty to medium by omitting the last section, making it a fantastic lake walk. The mountain lakes are very atmospheric, with beautiful, crystal clear water surrounded by mountain peaks. There is lots of water along the way for your dog until you reach the last section. Choose a clear day, but be careful on a hot one as there is no shelter and you will be out for over six hours. There are sheep grazing throughout but no roads once away from the car park.

MOUNTAIN SAFETY

Weather can be a serious concern. You need a clear day with good conditions, and unless you have mountain walking experience it is better to choose summer months with longer daylight hours

This is a big day out, and you and your dog will need to be fit and healthy

Leave plenty of time to do the walk, at least six hours of daylight time

Your dog will need to be kept under close control when not on a lead

The last section of the walk will take 1.5 hours to reach the top

When you are doing the last section of the descent it may be tricky with a dog that pulls on the lead

You will need to wear sturdy footwear

Keep to the surfaced paths at all times, except at the lakes

Check the specific mountain weather forecast at: www.metoffice.gov.uk for Snowdonia

How to get there – From Betws y Coed take the A5 signed for Capel Curig. Once reaching Capel Curig turn left on the A4086 and left at the next junction on the A498 parking in the pay and display lay-by just beyond the turning.

Grid reference – SH 659556
Nearest postcode – LL55 4NT

Parking – Pay and display in lay-by

Facilities – There are toilets and a café at Pen y Pass car park and at the top.

You will need – A clear day, dog leads and dog bags

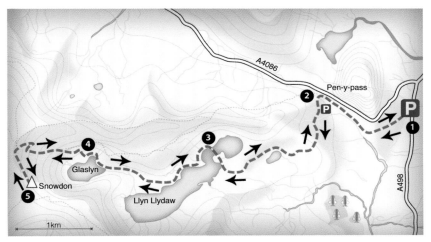

The Walk

❶ Put dogs on leads before leaving the car as there is a busy road to begin with. Cross to the opposite side of the ticket dispenser and turn left when you reach the path on the grass verge. On a slight descent you will reach a kissing gate. Pass through the gate and descend the stone steps to cross a bridge over a stream, where your dog can get a cooling drink. There are sheep grazing here so ensure that you keep your dog under close control or on a lead.

Ascend the steps and follow the stone slab path. There are beautiful valley views to your left, with Llyn Gwynant, the lake, taking centre stage. You will pass rocky boulders and outcrops along the way.

You will start to climb. The path has a switchback to avoid the rocky outcrop. When you reach a level on the path you will see a car park - this is where you are headed to begin with.

Ignore a footpath to the left and continue straight on, signed for Pen y Pass. You will reach a gate into the car park. Put your dog on the lead before going through the gate as there is a busy road.

❷ Pass through the kissing gate and once in the car park turn left. Following close to the stone wall on the left, continue, where you will reach a gate. Pass through the pedestrian gate and follow the surfaced path on a gentle upward slope.

You will have hills and mountains surrounding you, and rocky out crops along the way. As you climb a little higher and reach a bend to the right you will have your first view of Snowdon - it's the peak with the pointed top.

Pass a lake on the left and below, Llyn Teyrn, with a ruined building beside it. Don't go off the path to reach it as there is another ahead. You will lose sight of Snowdon for a while as the path winds in and out of view. Passing another bend you will see Snowdon once more. The path gets a little steeper ahead. Although the mountain will look daunting, as you get closer the path leading to it isn't too difficult and there are plenty of opportunities to stop and enjoy the stunning panoramic views.

❸ You will reach another lake, Llyn Llydaw, where your dog can enjoy a well-earned rest, cooling in the crystal clear water. This truly is a stunning spot to stop and take a break. Once rested turn back on the path and left, continuing on the well made path, which crosses over the lake.

The path will steepen on a stone slab path, with Snowdon directly ahead of you. You will pass another ruined building on your left as you head towards a waterfall.

❹ Reaching the waterfall as it spills out of another mountain lake at the foot of Snowdon, your dog can cool off once more. Have another rest here: you will need it, as the real climb lies ahead. This lake is called Glaslyn and the water is absolutely stunning in this mountainous setting.

Continue following the path with the lake to your left and just after passing more ruined buildings on the right, (almost at ground level) you will see a stone post; this marks the route up, where you begin ascending the steps. Keep your dog under close control, for his safety and the safety of other people.

There is a series of steps, rock climbs (but nothing serious, you won't need your hands on the upward climb) and some steep paths. You will lose the path a couple of times on the rock climbs, but don't worry; stop and look around and you will pick it out. The path doesn't ever go too near to an edge. If you are uncertain don't choose the scree (loose stone/gravel) on sloped areas - instead choose a rock on the inner side.

You will reach a level for a short section, then another ascent with steps. On reaching a stone post where another path merges, veer left. Continue on your ascent passing over a section of up turned rocks and then back on the path.

You will reach the last rocky section and then more steps. Up ahead you will see metal gabions - once reaching them you can have a sit down and admire the outstanding views, looking down on the path you have taken and way beyond.

The path has a couple of switchbacks now and when you reach a money post you will climb over one last rock. Then continue almost to the top. Turn left at another stone post and you will be amazed at the truly breath taking panoramic views. It really is worth the climb for such an awesome sight.

You are almost at the very top and it is best to put your dog on the lead now, to keep him and other people safe as there are some cliff edges. Continue now on a much gentler ascent. You will reach a path going left and one straight ahead. Turn left for the true summit, which means a little clamber onto the mound to reach your highest point. You may have to queue for this! Straight ahead brings you to the café and toilets.

5 Have a wander at your leisure, keeping to the well worn paths, but remember to give yourself plenty of time to get back down before dusk. (At least 2 hours).

Now it's back down, which is easier on the lungs, but just as tough on the legs! Following with the railway line over on your left, retrace your steps on the surfaced path remembering to turn right at the stone post.

Once turning at the post it is best to take your dog off the lead again if he is likely to pull you over, but only if you can keep him under close control. Follow the path back down, passing the money post once more after the first rocky section.

You will need to use your hands a little on some of the rocky sections now and take your time, as they are a bit trickier going down. Again remember to stay away from the scree and keep to the path, choosing the route you are most comfortable with at the rocky sections and keeping your eye on where the path is going.

Stop and look at the views every once in a while, as you will probably spend most of your time looking down at the path. When you reach another stone post turn right, and continue on the descent.

Once reaching level ground again at the lake, turn left and retrace your steps. Remember once reaching the car park to go to the end and just before the road turn right, passing through the gate and following the surfaced path. When you reach two paths ahead take the top left path. Continue back down to the road where you have parked your car.

19. Cwm Bychan

Challenging - 4 miles - 3hrs

This walk through the gorge of the Aberglaslyn Pass along the Fisherman's path is an absolutely stunning area of Snowdonia. There are rocky boulders and crags with beautiful woodlands and heathlands. You will see mountain scenes as you ascend the Cwm Bychan path for breath taking views of this beautiful landscape. Care should be taken beside rivers as they can be fast flowing, especially after heavy rain fall or snow melt. Watch the weather for mountainous conditions. There are plenty of opportunities for your dog to have a drink along the way. There are no roads but there may be sheep grazing in parts of the walk.

How to get there – From Betws y Coed take the A5 to Capel Curig. Once reaching Capel Curig take the A4086 signed for Beddgelert turning on the A498. Just before reaching Beddgelert park in the lay-by on the left as you reach the Sygun Copper Mines.

Grid Reference – SH 604490
Nearest Postcode – LL55 4NE

Parking – Free in the lay-by

Facilities – There are no facilities until you reach a car park part way around

You will need – Dog leads, dog bags

The Walk

1 From the car park take the path crossing the bridge, heading towards the Sygun Copper Mines. Ignore a footpath to the left and continue towards the mine entrance following the sealed road. Pass the Sygun car park and once reaching the mine entrance turn right, pass the water wheel, then, ignoring the footpath on the left continue straight ahead.

Continue on the quiet access road passing several streams where your dog can get a drink. Walking between the stone walls, pass a number of houses between rhododendron bushes and mixed woodland with rocky crags and boulders, with farmland to the right and mountain views.

As you pass two houses, up the hill a little to the left, it is best to have your dog on a lead as you will be approaching near to a busy main road. Go through a metal kissing gate on the left just before reaching the bridge.

Now you will be walking beside the stunning clear river with glacial rocks and boulders on a beautifully laid path, passing an old stone building on the left and surrounded by beautiful views. The masses of rhododendron bushes to

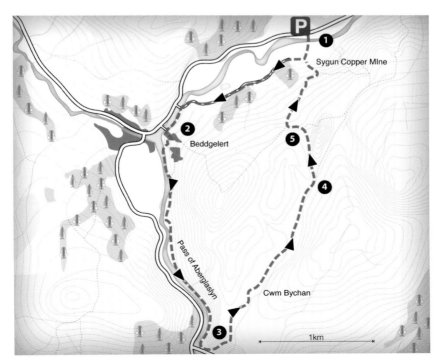

the left invade the hill looking more like a scene in the Himalayas than in Wales. These bushes are very invasive and overpower the native plants, some of which are rare alpine plants. The National Park is working hard to clear them but it is quite a stubborn plant to eradicate.

❷ Pass through a gate and onto a gravel path where you enter the lovely village of Beddgelert. Put your dog on a lead before going through another gate then walk along the path opposite, staying with the river. Pass the houses and head for the metal bridge ahead, but do not cross it (unless you need toilet facilities which are just after the bridge).

Take the path straight on, still with the river to your right. Go through a beautifully crafted gate into the National Trusts Aberglaslyn. Follow on the concrete path with boggy, marshy fields and craggy hills to your left.

Pass through a metal gate where you may now encounter sheep. There is some stunning scenery with hills, mountains and the river, with trees such as alder, silver birch and oak, heathland, and rocky boulders.

As you reach the railway turn left, with dogs on leads and pass with care through the kissing gate to cross the railway. Continue on the path between the river and the railway, passing amongst the stone boulders. Your dog will love exploring the rough grassland, searching out tracks of voles and mice in the thick tussocks.

The river picks up speed here and is a glorious sight, racing over boulders as it passes down through the gorge. You will pass a tunnel that goes under the railway on the left. Pass a large rock boulder on the left which is tinged with purple, then over a stone footbridge.

Cross over the rocky boulders, where in wet weather you can see traces of copper in the water. This part of the path is really awe-inspiring with the white water below and the stunning rock faces and woods that follow along the river.

The path becomes narrow at the edge of the rock as you pass around Craig y Fwtres. There are handles to hold on to if you feel a little nervous – they are a must if the rocks are wet and slippery or if your dog is the type to barge past you.

There is a bit of negotiating to do over the rocks, but the path is not close to the edge now. There is woodland to your left with heather and gorse. You will cross a couple of wooden bridges which have been neatly shaped to the edge of the rocks, with split wood rails. When you see a road ahead, take the path to the left that goes up a set of stone steps. Follow the worn path that ascends the oak woodlands with holly understory.

Pass through a gate, staying on the obvious worn path through the bracken. Ignore the path signed to the car park and continue to the fence line. Turn left and descend towards the tunnel. Pass under the railway into a lovely copse of trees passing through a picnic area. There are toilet facilities in the car park if you need them.

❸ The picnic area is a fantastic place to stop and rest before you begin your ascent up Cwm Bychan. Now continue on crossing the picnic area and up the steps ascending into the woods. You will soon follow an old stone wall on your right.

Pass over some rock steps and go through a gate near a small waterfall. Keep to the path with the stone wall to your right, walking alongside a river for a short while. Pass over another rocky section where you will have glorious panoramic views of Cnicht and the Moelwynion to your right and Traeth Bychan behind you. Follow beside mountain streams through the grassland with heather and gorse.

The path becomes sheltered as you pass into a valley. Cross a stream over rocks where you will meet with a stone wall on your right. When you reach a nicely crafted bench pass through the gap in the stone wall on the right and follow the path passing a couple of sheep folds. You will now see evidence of the old copper mines with the pylons dominating the valley.

There is gorse and heather here with some evidence of rhododendron as it fights its battle to stay on the mountain. Just ahead is the ruins of an old mining hut. The paths will split after the last mining pylon. Take the path on the left. ❹ At a fork turn right between the bracken and heather, ascending towards a larger hill buttress. Stay to the left of the small rocky crag, passing a shallow pond and when you reach another path on a steeper uphill section amongst a rocky area, turn left.

There is a rock face to your right. When you reach another rock face go left on the worn path. ❺ There are more stunning views across the valley as the path cuts through the hillside. Use caution here if your dog is on a lead as the hill is steep with scree.

As you make your way down a steep descent, the path will switchback and forth, getting a little rocky in places with loose gravel.

You will pass a view point to your left and a mining tunnel to your right. The path is much improved here, as it is part of the Sygun Copper Mine tourist attraction.

Following on the path you will pass first through a gate and then between thick rhododendrons, passing the side entrance to the copper mines where the path will become rough once more.

Turn on to a grassy path, which leads to a familiar road where you turn right and head back to your car.

20. Watkin Path

Medium - 3 miles - 2hrs

This is a fantastic linear walk with the option of making it circular. It passes through some beautiful oak woodland, green no matter what the season, with mosses and ferns covering the trees and woodland floor. Watkin path leads to the top of Mount Snowdon but there is a lot of scree so it is not recommended with dogs. Going part way up, following alongside a river and waterfall is a fantastic experience, passing old disused mining huts and some fantastic sheep folds with traditional slate fencing. The circular route veers off half way back down the path and is easy but for the stone footbridge across the river. You can choose to cross if you have the nerve, but if not, it is not far to re-join the path back down making the walk a linear one. There may be cattle on the circular section and sheep for a lot of the walk and there is a small section of road.

How to get there – Take the A498 from Beddgelert heading for Capel Curig and Betws y Coed. Stay on the A498 and turn into the car park on the right.

Grid reference – SH 628506

Parking – Pay and display car park

Facilities – There are toilets in the car park

You will need – Dog leads, dog bags

The Walk

❶ From the car park, facing the road, go to the pavement to the left of the car park. Cross the road and turn left. Take the footpath on the right up the steps on the Watkin path. Go through the gate, into the stunning oak woodlands with crags and boulders strewn in mosses. Water flows under the path in many places here for your dogs to quench their thirst. There are many ferns growing on the woodland floor.

Continue on this gravel path with some stone steps and pass over two bridges to cross the river. The water looks glorious as it races over the boulders on its fast descent. Go through the gate, where the woods change to mixed broadleaved and coniferous. Stay on the gravel path through the middle of the trees. Pass a ruined building on the left and rocky crags and on reaching a gate pass through it.

There are sheep grazing for the next section of the walk so be sure to put your dog on a lead. Go through another gate where there are views to the right. Follow the black estate fencing on the right on a gradual ascent and stunning rock faces to your left. There are lovely views ahead where you leave the fence behind and the path bends to the left. You can hear the water below as it races downstream. The landscape opens out to views of the hilltops, rocky crags with scattered trees and a beautiful waterfall ahead. A stream will pass under the path again, where your dog can get water.

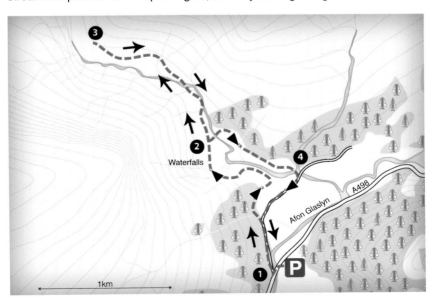

Follow the main path that will eventually skirt around the back of the waterfall, steadily ascending deeper into this stunning scenery. You will reach a gate and once passing through it you will be in a right to roam area. For nature conservation it is always best to stick to the main paths, as there are ground nesting birds and rare plants here that may be trampled upon. There are lovely wooded crags on the opposite side of the wall ahead and also on the opposite side of the waterfall.

❷ The path now leaves the waterfall behind and is made up of nice natural stone. Following the river you can see the wonderful colours of the stone on the riverbed and watch the river flow at its great pace over the boulders. You will pass a small trickling waterfall on the left as it flows down the hillside and under the path to join the river below and also some ruined mining buildings on the other side of the river.

Cross a sleeper bridge where there are beautiful rustic slate fencing sheep folds on your right. There are more ruined mining buildings a little further on.
❸ This is the furthest point of the walk. Head back the way that you came and enjoy the beauty of the water once more. Once you have passed through the gate and left the right to roam area behind, you can choose either option A (carry on the way you came making the walk linear) or option B (a circular walk). This may depend on whether you and your dog have the nerve to walk the stone bridge across the river. It is not far away so you can have a look before deciding.

A. Continue straight ahead, following the main path retracing your steps. Passing back through the two gates to enter back into the woodland. B. On passing through the gate, turn left and walk along the stone wall on your left, choosing the easiest path down the rocky section. Proceed towards the river. Go through the gate and cross the stone bridge with care. You should judge if it would be safer to have your dog on or off the lead here.

Once across the river follow the worn narrow path. Turn right and follow the direction of the river, just above the copse of trees that follow the edge of the river. You should see the worn path between the bracken. Walk with the river and stunning mature oak trees to your right. The bark of the oak trees is covered in mosses and lichens. You will pass another stream that flows under the path. You will soon see a stone wall on the left. There may be cattle on the next section of the walk. Pass through a gate and keep close to the stone wall on your left, until you see a stone wall ahead where you can pass through the gap. Keep to another stone wall on the left and head for the stone shelter.

❹ You will see a wooden bridge where you cross the river. Walk with the stone wall on your left, putting dogs on leads before passing houses on your right and over the farmyard. Continue on the access road passing buildings on your right. Go through the gate to avoid the cattle grid. Once at the road turn left and head back to the car park.